Agatha Christie

Agatha Christie

An English Mystery

Laura Thompson

headline
review

First published in 2007
by HEADLINE REVIEW

An imprint of Headline Publishing Group

1

Cataloguing in Publication Data is available from the British Library

Hardback 978 0 7553 1487 4
Trade paperback 978 0 7553 1534 5

Typeset in Galliard by Palimpsest Book Production Ltd,
Grangemouth, Stirlingshire
Text design by The Flying Fish Studio Ltd

Printed and bound in Great Britain by
Mackays of Chatham plc, Chatham, Kent

HEADLINE PUBLISHING GROUP
A division of Hachette Livre UK Ltd
338 Euston Road
London NW1 3BH

www.reviewbooks.co.uk
www.hodderheadline.com

To Vinny, my friend, O.F.D.
1992–2006

Contents

'The one thing people never forget is the unsolved. Nothing lasts like a mystery.'

from *The Ebony Tower*, by John Fowles

The Villa at Torquay

'Between the ages of 5 and 12 years old, I led a wonderfully happy life'
(from a letter written by Agatha Christie in 1973)

'I remembered another thing – Robert saying that there had been no bad fairies at
Rupert St Loo's christening. I had asked him afterwards what he meant and he had
replied, "Well, if there's not one bad fairy – where's your story?"
(from *The Rose and the Yew Tree*, by Agatha Christie writing as Mary Westmacott)

It is a steep climb up Barton Road in Torquay, and at the top there
is nothing to be seen. Here stood the house in which Agatha Christie
was born. Now only imagination can bring it back to life.

All her life Agatha was in love with her own childhood, and her
family home Ashfield was the arena of her childhood dreams. She
continued to dream about the house all her life. When it was demolished in the 1960s, twenty years after it had been sold – perhaps as
proof that she had finally grown up? – she cried like a child.

Walking up the road it is hard to grasp the past, because there
is so little of it left. Barton Road is out of the town proper, but
this has not protected it from modern England: gimcrack college
buildings, a wholesale and import warehouse, a school and a block
of council flats now line the hill that led to Ashfield. A couple of
bungalows stand on the approximate site of Agatha's house. A path
beside them leads to a secret triangle of earth, bounded by a rocky
wall; might it once have been an edge of her garden? It is possible.
Here, in the cool dark corner around a tree stump, may have been

the Dogs' Cemetery in which the family pets – including Tony the Yorkshire terrier, Agatha's first dog – were buried beneath little headstones.

So imagination works on this hidden piece of Torquay, and on the scratchy cry of seagulls, which would have been as familiar to Agatha as her own name, and on the unchanged shape of Barton Road, the sense of her walking up and down with the breeze in her hair and her ribs heaving joyfully. As a child, hand in hand with her nurse; later, laced tight into corsets and trailing a handsome skirt whose hem was thick with dirt. To climb that hill, in a corset! It was here that her first husband, Archie Christie, came chugging on his motorbike in search of the cool, slim girl he had fallen for at a dance near Exeter; he sat and took tea with Agatha's mother and waited for her to trip home from across the road. She had been playing badminton at Rooklands, one of the handful of houses that stood, like her own, within its own relaxed grounds. That was her world then. Those were the years of Edwardian serenity. Summer followed summer in a long haze: sloping lawns were shadowed with tea tables, with the arch of croquet hoops, with the soft droop of picture hats. The air smelled rose-sweet, and happiness was an easy business. Agatha Christie never lost the sense of those years; they always remained inside her.

From the top of Barton Road one looks down at Torquay, the rise and fall of its seven hills, the curved sweep of bay with the sea gleaming beyond. This is the view – part revealing, part hidden – that Agatha would have known and loved, so well that when she travelled the world with Archie, in the 1920s, she wrote back to her mother that South Africa was 'like all really beautiful places, just like Torquay!'.

That place no longer exists. The Torquay of Agatha's youth was configurative, complete; an elegant land of its own with its crescents and terraces, its huge pale villas shrouded amid trees and hills, its rituals and structures and distant wildness. It was a watering-place, gently restorative, the kind of town at which people arrived carrying letters of introduction. In summer the local newspaper published weekly lists of the names of holiday visitors, and it was said that these read like the *Almanack de Gotha*. The resident families were of Agatha's own class: middle, tending towards upper. This homogeneity was precious. Around her, all was protection and stasis. Within, therefore, her imagination could go free.

Could it have conjured the Torquay of the twenty-first century? In the years after the war Agatha had a respectful terror of social change and, in some ways, she was as much of a realist about life as her old lady detective, Miss Marple, who always expects the worst and is usually right to do so. But Agatha was also a woman of deep faith, in God and human nature. Could she, then, have foreseen the gleeful rupture within England that would rip the heart from her birthplace?

Torquay's handsome Fleet Walk splashed with lurid shop fronts; the proud Strand colonised by bare-chested inebriates; the 1851 town hall now a branch of Tesco; the old bank, with its pale gold stone façade, now Banx Café Bar; the elegant 1912 seafront Pavilion now a shopping mall; the palm trees shrivelling outside Mambo nightclub; the calm creamy villas advertising Vacancies and Cantonese food; the junkies and asylum-seekers lurching along Higher Union Street, where Agatha's father had bought china for Ashfield . . . modernity blurring every proud shape, the change in England writ large here because Torquay is a place of pleasure, and pleasure is what now defines us. Agatha believed in pleasure too: she loved ease and respite and idleness. But she would have doubted Miss Marple's other creed – that 'the new world was the same as the old', that 'human beings were the same as they had always been'[1] – when she saw the holidaymakers and their urgency for sensation, their burgers belched into the sun and their bottles swung like lances. She had begun to doubt the future in one of her last books, *Passenger to Frankfurt*, which she wrote in her late seventies:

What a world it was nowadays . . . Everything used the whole time to arouse emotion. Discipline? Restraint? None of these things counted for anything any more. Nothing mattered but to *feel*.

What sort of a world . . . could that make?

It made the England of today: bored, violent, decadent. It made a society with no sense of order, of cause and effect, of history. And

Agatha had foreseen this, although she had not entirely believed that it would come to pass: 'Can this be England? Is England *really* like this? One feels – no – not yet, *but it could be.*'[2] In fact *Passenger to Frankfurt* ends with an affirmation in 'hope', 'faith' and 'benevolence'. So Agatha would have been shocked and grieved by the twenty-first century. She would have mourned the town in which she had dreamed, loved, run up hills with Tony the dog, lost her virginity to Archie Christie, become a writer. Above all she would have been saddened by the new English joylessness, for life to her was a sacred gift.

In Torquay Agatha is everywhere – the shops, the museum – and yet she is nowhere. What she was, what made her, no longer exists. Only in flickering moments does one glimpse a girl in a white dress, skipping through shadowy sunlit streets, her head full of mysteries. No mystery greater than this one: that in an England apparently bent upon destroying everything she believed and embodied, Agatha Christie remains never more popular. The paradox would have intrigued her.

Then she would have contemplated her dinner and her garden, and retired to the world of her mind.

That was where she lived, throughout much of her childhood: in her imagination, within Ashfield. The two were indissoluble. Every corner, every shadow of her home was magical to her. She loved it with a child's directness; but also with an adult depth, seeming to intuit the sadness in love, the knowledge of impermanence that makes happiness so intense. She had an elegiac instinct. Unusually for a child, she had an overview. Even as she was steeped in their warm stillness, she sensed the ending of the eternal summers; and turned every moment of them into instant memory.

'There is no Joy like Joy in dreams . . .' wrote the adult Agatha Christie,[3] surely remembering how Ashfield had been hallowed by the visions that came to her in sleep:

> the dream fields at the bottom of the garden . . . the secret rooms inside her own home. Sometimes you got to them through the pantry – sometimes, in the most unexpected way, they led out

of Daddy's study. But there they were all the time – although you had forgotten them for so long. Each time you had a delighted thrill of recognition. And yet, really, each time they were quite different. But there was always that curious secret joy about finding them . . .

This is from *Unfinished Portrait*, published in 1934, one of the six novels she wrote under the name of Mary Westmacott. It is as close to her own story as the autobiography that was published posthumously. Many of the same childhood tales are told in both books, yet *Unfinished Portrait* feels closer to the truth of that time. It is written with a yearning quality, suffused with the love she felt for a past that had been wrenched from her eight years earlier; the wounds still weep on the page.

Agatha never lost the ability to experience the world through a child's eyes ('. . . in a great many years time, when you are still a child, as you always will be . . .' wrote her second husband, Max Mallowan, in a letter of 1930).[4] She retained both her memories and her direct sense of how these memories felt. Nothing was ever more alive to her. The first Westmacott, *Giant's Bread* (also 1930), has a boy, Vernon Deyre, as its protagonist, but much of his early life is a replication of Agatha's.

A new nursemaid came, a thin white girl with protruding eyes. Her name was Isabel, but she was called Susan as being More Suitable. This puzzled Vernon very much. He asked Nurse for an explanation.

. . . 'There are people who when they christen their children set themselves up to ape their betters.'

The word 'ape' had a distracting influence on Vernon. Apes were monkeys. Did people christen their children at the zoo?

As Agatha did, Vernon has waking dreams; like this one, which flourished in the infinity of the garden at Ashfield.

Mr Green was like God in that you couldn't see him, but to Vernon he was very real . . . The great thing about Mr Green was that he played – he loved playing. Whatever game Vernon thought of, that was just the game that Mr Green loved to play. There were other points about him. He had, for instance, a hundred children. And three others . . . They were called by the three most beautiful names that Vernon knew: Poodle, Squirrel and Tree.

Vernon was, perhaps, a lonely little boy, but he never knew it. Because, you see, he had Mr Green and Poodle, Squirrel, and Tree to play with.

Agatha never thought of herself as lonely. Such an idea would not have occurred to her. She treasured solitude and the space it gave her for other lives. She also treasured privacy; when she overheard her nurse discussing one of her earliest imaginary games with a house-maid ('Oh she plays that she's a kitten with some other kittens'), she was upset 'to the core'. She had cast a delicate spell over her home. Secrecy preserved the magic, and a photograph of Agatha as a child shows a face full of secrets: a stubborn little fairy girl, seated on a wicker chair in her enchanted garden.

'I was to know every tree in it, and attach a special meaning to each tree . . .'[5]

All her life she saw Ashfield through those child's eyes. Her detective novel *The Hollow* describes a house, Ainswick, that represents vanished happiness to the characters in the book and has a garden filled with Ashfield's trees.

There was a magnolia that almost covered one window and which filled the room with a golden green light in the afternoons. Through the other window you looked out on to the lawn and a tall Wellingtonia stood up like a sentinel. And to the right was a big copper beech.

Oh Ainswick – Ainswick . . .

What did Ashfield look like? A large villa, comfortable, not grand, with a fine lawn leading to a small wood. A family home. Photographs, pink-tinged and poignant, show it to have been a mass of harmonious accretions. Part two-storey, part three-, it had several chimneys, generous windows that reached down to the garden, and a porch shadowy with creeper. A conservatory, filled with palm trees, was a sultry hothouse in those days of heavy clothes. There was also a green-house – 'called, I don't know why, K.K.' – which housed a rocking-horse named Mathilde, and a small painted horse and cart named Truelove. Agatha wrote about these in her last book, *Postern of Fate*, in which she lets the conventions of detective fiction slip away and walks, free as a ghost, into her past. As with all her late writing the book was spoken into a Dictaphone;[6] her voice, in a brief recording, is cracked and vibrant with memory. Mathilde is described as 'looking forlorn and forsaken', with her mane fallen out and one ear broken, but when a character in the book jumps on her back she races back and forward in the same old way. 'Got action, hasn't it?' 'Yes, it's got action.'

A few years before she wrote *Postern of Fate*, Agatha received a letter from an old Torquay friend. 'Our gardens, yours and mine, were magical places . . . How sad that Barton Road is so changed, and that houses have been built over Ashfield.'[7] And yet, for all its charm, Ashfield did not compare with the home that Agatha would later make her own in Devon. The white Georgian perfection of Greenway, set like a pale jewel above the river Dart, was as magical in truth as the dream house that she had made of Ashfield. And for all that the child Agatha loved her home, she was always looking beyond its limits. 'I wanted', she wrote in her autobiography, 'above everything in the world, to be the Lady Agatha one day.' Within this lay a desire, not to do with snobbery, to inhabit the numinous place that hovered at the edges of her imagination. 'Something you want so much that you don't quite know what it is,' she wrote of the perfect house in one of her last novels, *Endless Night*. 'The thing that mattered most to me. Funny that a house could mean that.'

In *Giant's Bread* the young boy does not live at Ashfield: he is heir to a house called Abbots Puissant, which is of ineffable, ancient beauty. In another of the Westmacotts, *The Rose and the Yew Tree*, the heroine Isabella is as one with her home, St Loo Castle: 'medieval, severe and austere'. Agatha longed to walk through a world of that kind and call it her own. With Greenway she would do so, in a sense; but not the

Isabella sense. She was at once too middle-class and too much of a thinker. The very mind that could dream up a St Loo Castle would prevent her, always, from losing herself in its reality.

No doubt her inner life would have developed less freely had she been born into a different kind of family. Perhaps it would not have existed at all. But the Millers of Torquay were not as conventional as their appearance suggested, and the dynamic of the family left Agatha protected yet separate, which was ideal for the growth of her particular personality.

Agatha Mary Clarissa was the last of three children, born on 15 September 1890, eleven years after her sister Margaret (Madge) and ten after her brother Louis Montant (Monty). Her father, Frederick, was far too much the gentleman to interfere in his children's inner lives. Clarissa, her mother, whose inquisitiveness would have been far greater, had the instinctive wisdom of knowing just how much of this interest to show. Clara – as she was known – was like the nurse who attends Vernon in *Giant's Bread*, to whom 'he was able to speak of Poodle, Squirrel and Tree, and of Mr Green and the hundred children. And instead of saying "What a *funny* game!" Nurse Frances merely inquired whether the hundred children were girls or boys . . .'

Clara was, in fact, an original. Her influence upon Agatha – both by omission and involvement – was almost absolute. A distinguished-looking little person, with the near-black eyes of a clever bird, she was the centre of the Ashfield world, the person who made imagination both possible and safe. She was also, probably, the love of Agatha's life.

Written eight years after Clara's death, *Unfinished Portrait* is a testament to that love: a hymn of desperate loss. Agatha spares herself nothing in the book. 'Oh, Mummy – Mummy . . .' she writes, missing the mother who is on holiday abroad; and the pathos of eight-year-old Celia is also that of Agatha in her forties, longing still for Clara.

'In the evening, after Susan had given Celia [Agatha's fictional self] her bath, Mummy would come into the nursery to give Celia a "last tuck". "Mummy's tuck", Celia would call it, and she would try to lie very still so that "Mummy's tuck" should still be there in the morning.'

Clara's understanding of her daughter – the 'queer, luminous, searching look' that she would bend upon her – is almost total; certainly in Agatha's eyes. This is shown by a story, also told in the autobiography, of an episode in France in 1896, when Agatha was on an expedition with her father. A guide, thinking to please her, had pinned a live butterfly to her straw hat.

Celia was miserable. She could feel the wings of the butterfly fluttering against her hat. It was alive – alive. Skewered on a pin! She felt sick and miserable. Large tears gathered in her eyes and rolled down her cheeks.

At last her father noticed.

'What's the matter, poppet?'

Celia shook her head. Her sobs increased . . . how could she say what was the matter? It would hurt the guide's feelings terribly. He had meant to be kind. He had caught the butterfly specially for her. He had been so proud of his idea in pinning it to her hat. How could she say out loud that she didn't like it? And now nobody would ever, ever understand! The wind made the butterfly's wings flap more than ever . . .

Mummy would understand. But she couldn't tell Mummy. They were all looking at her – waiting for her to speak. A terrible agony welled up in her breast. She gazed dumbly, agonisingly, at her mother. 'Help me,' that gaze said. 'Oh, do help me.'

Miriam [Clara] gazed back at her.

'I believe she doesn't like that butterfly in her hat,' she said. 'Who pinned it there?'

Clara, too, had a wildly vital inner life. But hers, unlike Agatha's, was born of insecurity rather than protection.

She was born in 1854 to a glamorous army captain, Frederick Boehmer, who at the age of thirty-six had fallen for a beautiful girl of not quite seventeen, Mary Ann West. After twelve years of marriage and four children, Captain Boehmer, then stationed in Jersey, was

killed in a fall from his horse, leaving Mary Ann a young and impoverished widow. At almost exactly the same time, Mary Ann's older
sister Margaret made a less romantic, more lucrative marriage to an
American widower, much older than herself, named Nathaniel Frary
Miller. Mary Ann was in dire straits; Margaret immediately offered to
take one of the four children off her sister's hands. Clara – the only
girl, then aged nine – was handed over.

Agatha was fascinated by the story of these West sisters, orphan
girls who were taken in by relations, the Kelseys, in the early nineteenth century, and raised on their farm in Sussex. As a child she was
told lots of tales about her ancestry. She loved to hear about 'the
Kelseys at Primsted Farm' and the rich Crowder cousins, of whom
the Wests were jealous 'as they always had real lace on their drawers'.[8]
Particularly alive to her was the story of Mary Ann and Captain
Frederick. Perhaps because it had become for her a poignant ideal of
faithful romance, she wrote her own version of it to her second
husband, Max Mallowan, in a letter of 1944:

> [My grandmother] was married at 16 ('They say you're too
> young to marry me, Polly'. 'I'll run away with you tomorrow
> if they won't let me marry you') to a handsome Army officer
> twenty years older than she was . . .
>
>   She was exceptionally lovely – people stopped to stare after
> her in the street – she was left with hardly any money and had
> to do fine embroidery and sewing to support and educate her
> children. At least three of her husband's brother officers
> wanted to marry her – two of them well-off men. Economically
> it would have been desirable. But she refused everybody –
> certainly never had a lover – and up to the age of seventy
> steadfastly declared it was her wish her body should be taken to
> Jersey when she died and buried with her husband there . . .[9]

In fact her three sons – Harry, Ernest and Frederick – prevailed in
their wish for Mary Ann to be buried in England, so that they could
visit her grave. What her daughter thought on the subject is not
known. It is a modern freedom to criticise one's parents, and it would
not have occurred to Clara – in some ways very typical of her era –

to shun the mother who had given her away. She was a buttoned-up little girl, solitary like Agatha but lonely with it, wandering through her sickly uncle's house clasping a copy of her favourite book, *King of the Golden River*. She had suffered a good deal, being sent away. Yet her behaviour towards Mary Ann was always utterly correct. In her twenties she wrote a poem 'To Mother' full of irreproachable sentiment: 'Love is the angel who . . . guards the path to Heaven'. It could have been written to anybody, though. The poem for her aunt Margaret is a little more personal, and dutifully praises 'A character of worth, Beloved by all around . . .'

Agatha writes in her autobiography that Mary Ann could scarcely be blamed for what she did, that she probably gave Clara away because she thought a girl needed help in life while boys could make their own luck. Yet Clara always believed that her mother simply loved her less. She was too sensitive to withstand the rejection.

> I think the resentment she felt, the deep hurt at being unwanted, coloured her attitude to life. It made her distrustful of herself and suspicious of people's affection. Her aunt was a kindly woman, good-humoured and generous, but she was imperceptive of a child's feelings. My mother had all the so-called advantages of a comfortable home and a good education – what she lost and what nothing could replace was the carefree life with her brothers *in her own home* . . .

This is a recurring theme in Agatha's writing, the need for children to be brought up in their own surroundings, the damage that is done to them when they are given away (or, as in *Ordeal by Innocence*, sold for a hundred pounds: 'The humiliation – the pain – he'd never got over it'). It lies at the heart of *The Mirror Crack'd from Side to Side* and *The Mousetrap*; it is touched on elsewhere; and it is always treated with the same seriousness. It was Agatha's nature to feel Clara's emotions as if they were her own. Indeed, such was her love for her mother, she may have experienced greater agony than Clara herself ever did when, many years later, she wrote this speech for a female character in *Mrs. McGinty's Dead*:

'There was a woman writing in the paper the other day . . . A really stupid letter. Asking what was best to do – to let your child be adopted by someone who could give it every advantage . . . or whether to keep it when you couldn't give it advantages of any kind. I think that's stupid – really stupid. If you can just give a child enough to eat – that's all that matters.

'. . . *I* ought to know . . . My mother parted with me and I had every advantage, as they call it. And it's always hurt – always – always – to know that you weren't really wanted, that your mother could let you go . . . I wouldn't part with *my* children – not for all the advantages in the world!'

These are Agatha's thoughts, of course, and they would never have been voiced in this way by Clara. But there is no doubt that Clara's childhood experience affected her, in particular her relationship with her daughters.

It also played its part in her marriage. Margaret and her husband had no children of their own but Nathaniel, from his first marriage, had a son named Frederick. He was eight years Clara's senior and a real New Yorker, albeit with a Swiss education, a Frenchman's worldliness, an English sense of protocol and an *entrée* into the wildly select Union Club. He was an American straight out of *The Age of Innocence*, that is to say one who aspired to sacred Europeanism; but he was an American all the same and had something free within – an openness, a ribaldry, a refusal to take himself seriously – that was not of the Victorian world. Agatha was proud of her American blood and, as an old woman on a visit to New York, was adamant that she should visit the Brooklyn graves of her Miller relations, even though she had never met them. She, too, would prove to have a more open spirit than Torquay might have allowed: there was fresh air in her blood as well as her lungs.

The Miller fortune had been made in America but it had interests in Manchester. So after their marriage Nathaniel and Margaret settled in Cheshire, where Frederick – a fond son – would visit them, trailing a haze of cosmopolitanism and frankly dazzling the sad little Clara.

That she should have married him, in 1878, is a fairy story; a romance to rival that of Mary Ann Boehmer, except that there is a very faint air of patronage about the way in which Frederick abandoned his gay flirtations (with Winston Churchill's mother, among others) and proposed to his dear faithful cousin, whose soul he had set on fire years earlier with his careless praise for her 'lovely eyes'. Shades of Sonia in *Uncle Vanya*? 'When a girl is plain everybody says, you have lovely hair, you have lovely eyes . . .' Clara was *not* a beauty; indeed she turned down Frederick's first proposal because she felt herself to be 'dumpy'. But she had a remarkable character – far more powerful than that of her charming husband – and this, in the end, would redress the imbalances in their marriage.

During her engagement, though, she wrote poems to 'F.A.M.' (Frederick Alvah Miller), which show her brimful of passionate, anxious gratitude.

> God in Heaven listen to me, Listen to my whisper'd prayer
> Make me worthy, though so lowly, All his love and life to share.

There is also an odd, frequently struck note of fear: 'Keep him safe from every evil, And temptation's treacherous power.' Clearly she was aware of her husband's rakish past – 'He quickly loved o'er face and flower, With careless listless will' – and alert to the possibilities of repeat performances. Her poems, written in a conscientious hand in an 'Album' bought at Whiteleys, return continually to the apprehension of betrayal:

> Oh God! was it only a fancy
> That dream of my maiden life
> Is this the once wonderful hero
> Who won me for his wife?

In fact there is no reason to think that Frederick – who made occasional little changes to the poems, so knew perfectly well their serious substance – was anything but a faithful husband. But the loss of certainty as a child had prepared Clara to expect the worst; in this she was utterly unlike Agatha, the happiness of whose early life prepared her for nothing. 'Some people are wise – they never expect to be happy. I did,' she wrote later, in *The Hollow*.

A good deal of her childhood happiness came from Agatha's sense that her parents' marriage was serene and stable. Yet *Unfinished Portrait*, as always, understands more about the realities than she knew at the time. 'It isn't always wise – to care too much. It's a thorn in your side always,' says 'Miriam' to her daughter. And, later:

> 'Don't ever leave your husband too long alone, Celia. Remember, a man forgets . . .'
> 'Father would never have looked at anyone but you.'
> Her mother answered musingly.
> 'No, perhaps he wouldn't. But I was always on the look out. There was a parlour maid – a big handsome girl – the type I had often heard your father admire. She was handing him the hammer and some nails. As she did it she put her hand over his. I saw her. Your father hardly noticed – he just looked surprised . . . But I sent that girl away – at once.'

Frederick, meanwhile, had all the unassailable self-confidence of his class, which was subtly above that of Clara (the girl in *Mrs. McGinty's Dead* is also enabled, by her adoption, to marry a gentleman). He was no oil painting: photographs show him to have been a fat, bearded man looking years older than his real age, with the heavy, sleepy eyes inherited by Agatha. But he seems to have been liked by everybody who knew him. In her autobiography Agatha writes, of the happy atmosphere at Ashfield, that it was 'largely due to my father'.

He spent his life doing nothing. As a young man he was a socialite, in middle age a gentleman of leisure. 'He never was in business, having inherited a very comfortable fortune from his father,' read a testimonial sent from the Union Club to the American ambassador when Agatha was eighteen, about to come out in society. 'That I can vouch for him in the highest terms, is putting it mildly, and it would seem as if the daughter, Miss Agatha Miller, was in every way entitled to be presented.'

For all that she worshipped her quick, clever mother, Agatha had an irresistible admiration for Frederick's easy charm. His was the class to which she always felt herself to belong, although in adulthood she had neither his social manner nor his gift for indolence. But 'I cannot see what is morally *right* about working,' she pronounced in an interview in 1964.[10] 'My father was a gentleman of substance, and never did a hand's turn in his life, and he was a most agreeable man.'

He was also a fool, although not intellectually stupid by any means. He knew exactly the worth of the people around him, but it was not in his nature to present to them anything other than his 'agreeable' front. No doubt to show willing to his family he produced a couple of short stories; these had something of his daughter's instinctive insight into human nature. They also proved him a far better writer than Clara. Her bedtime tales danced with invention – Agatha was both frustrated and entranced by the way Clara would be unable to return to a story on the following night, so simply made up a new one – but her laboured writing drowned ever more deeply in Victorian convention ('So, I was dead! This then must be my spirit, which had consciousness . . .').[11]

Frederick's story entitled *Henry's Engagement* is a variation on his own courtship of Clara. Henry, a womanising dandy, is worshipped by Marian, who is 'religious and high-principled' and – like Clara – has absolutely no sense of humour. 'Henry was very much in love, but with characteristic indolence displayed no unseemly haste in putting the momentous question. After all, there was really no hurry.'

Frederick waited until he was thirty-two before he abandoned his gay-dog life and proposed. Henry never does marry Marian, instead telling her that he has fallen for another girl whose 'tiny hands excited Henry's admiration. Marian's were well-formed – but large.' Hearing this, Marian nobly renounces him. 'She had behaved splendidly, he would always think of her as one of the sweetest women he had ever met. The phrase pleased him . . .' Frederick was kind where Henry is cold, but the story hints at the same undercurrents that run through Clara's poetry.

Beneath her liveliness, there was always anxiety inside Clara. She burned with the passionate piety of a nun painted by Holman Hunt. Frederick took life lightly, merrily. Another story, *Why Jenkins Gave a Dinner*, is set in the kind of New York club that was his natural habitat: 'the toast – "The Ladies, God Bless them!" was drunk for the 27th time'. It has Frederick's own charm, and it also shows a certain self-knowledge.

> Jimmy spent every bit of his yearly income and a little over with a sublime disregard for the future. He was greatly liked by his club associates . . . It is true that one of his 'best girls' had said that it was a pity that he had more money than brains. When this was repeated to Jimmy by some kind friends, as of course it was, that youth remarked with great good humour that the lady was perfectly right and immediately went out and sent her a costly bunch of cut roses . . . Although hardly a heroic character, Jimmy was an affable and lovable one.

Like Jimmy, Frederick would squander his inheritance. He did so more through laziness than wilful profligacy. Perhaps if he had returned to America with Clara, as he had intended to do after their marriage, he would have had an eye on the mismanagement of his New York investments and properties. But that was not how things happened. Instead, after a long honeymoon in Switzerland, the newly-wed Millers came to stay at the fashionable resort of Torquay, where Madge was born in January 1879. Monty followed in June 1880 on a subsequent visit to New York, then Clara returned to England while Frederick 'attended' to business matters. When he rejoined her at Torquay – for a year or so, as he thought – he discovered that she had bought Ashfield with the £2,000 left her by her uncle Nathaniel. It was a better use of the Miller fortune than Frederick ever made. It was also a bold, independent action that turned Clara, at a stroke, from suppli-cant into equal partner.

Frederick had sown his wild oats in New York; in only his mid-thirties, he settled comfortably into middle age. In this he was much encouraged by Torquay. During the Victorian era it was an even more refined place than it would become in Agatha's youth: there was as yet no mixed bathing, no Princess Gardens in which to stroll, no Pavilion in which to hear concerts. It was a town full of the well-behaved rich and well-to-do invalids (Napoleon III had restored his health while staying at the Imperial Hotel; Elizabeth Barrett Browning had taken the waters at the Bath House on Victoria Parade). To some, it was overpoweringly genteel. 'Torquay is such a place as I do desire to upset by dancing through it with nothing on but my spectacles,' wrote Rudyard Kipling, not known for his Bohemianism. 'Villas, clipped hedges, fat old ladies with respirators and obese landaus . . .'

But all of this suited Frederick perfectly well. He had his family home and children, whom he adored in a frank, unVictorian manner: 'God bless you, my little Darling,' he wrote to Agatha from New York in 1896, 'I know you are a dear, good girl . . .' Beyond that his life consisted of large meals, walks to the Royal Torbay Yacht Club, and shopping: a thick sheaf of bills shows the ease with which he spent what he believed to be a limitless income. As one now knows that the money was draining away, the exquisitely written bills have a queasy look. One pictures Frederick, perfectly dressed and shaved, smiling his way along the streets every morning to the club, unable to resist the lure of Donoghue's or the Fine Art Repository on Victoria Parade. When in London he spent with similar abandon. There are many bills for the jewellery shops of W1, including one for £810. He also bought good furniture – five mahogany Chippendale chairs in Union Street – and rather less good paint-ings: clusters of oils jostled upon the walls at Ashfield, although the rooms themselves were airy and elegant. A local artist, N. J. H. Baird, was commissioned to paint Frederick, the three children, Monty's dog and Agatha's nurse; these pictures still hang at Greenway House. They have no great merit – 'All of you look as if you hadn't washed for *weeks*!' was Clara's judgement, but then of course her own portrait had not been painted – although the picture of 'Nursie', as she was called, has a soft Flemish warmth. 'A really lovely painting I think,' wrote Agatha in 1967, in reply to a woman who was cata-loguing Baird's pictures. 'My father always thought very highly of [Baird's] work.'[12]

So Frederick ambled through his life, leisurely and *largo*, a regal Torquay personage with his Saxe-Coburg appearance and unshake-able bonhomie. He and Clara entertained friends frequently to sump-tuous dinners. He was involved in charitable amateur-dramatic performances – had a 'most cordial reception', according to a local newspaper, in his role as Felix Fumer in *The Laughing Hyena* – and acted as official scorer for the cricket club, whose ground was beyond Ashfield on Barton Road. In 1943 Agatha received a letter that began:

> When ten years of age my parents lived near the Torquay
> Cricket Club Ground and to me there was, nor could be, any
> place on earth like it. I venerate its memory . . .
>   How well I remember Mr Miller! His likeness – at least I
> thought so, to King Edward! . . . In a feudal and impressive
> way he used to stroll on to the ground. I can see it all now as
> I lay on the slightly rising ground near the scoreboard with
> the fine red, white and black flag flying from its crest . . .[13]

Agatha would have remembered this too. She often accompanied Frederick to the cricket: 'I was extremely proud of being allowed to help my father with the scoring and took it very seriously.' She also learned mathematics with him, which she loved ('I think there's some-thing heavenly about numbers,' says a character in *The Moving Finger*), and these lessons were about as close as she came to formal educa-tion. Having sent Madge to the school in Brighton that would later become Roedean (Monty was at Harrow), Clara had the idea that Agatha should *not* go to school and should not learn to read until she was eight. So much for that: by the age of four Agatha had taught herself. 'I'm afraid Miss Agatha can *read*, ma'am,' Nursie explained apologetically to Clara.

There is no telling why Clara came up with this theory. Her deci-sions could seem arbitrary, although more often than not they were proved right, as when she bought Ashfield or when, in later years, she warned Agatha against marrying her first husband, Archie. She knew human nature, which made her wise. Yet she was also said to have the inexplicable instinct of a 'sensitive' (as a child she dreamed that Primsted Farm had burned down; soon afterwards it did) and this sometimes made her silly. It was an absurd whim to try to stop an intelligent child reading, particularly in a house like Ashfield, which was crammed with books. Among Frederick's bills are several for 'Andrew Iredale, Bookseller of Fleet Street', from whom he bought – among much else – forty-seven volumes of the *Cornhill*

Magazine for four pounds (still in the library at Greenway), the complete works of George Eliot for five pounds and 'French classics' at twelve shillings apiece. It was unthinkable that Agatha would remain shut out of that world. Such was her determination that she worked out the words of a children's book called *The Angel of Love* by Mrs L. T. Meade ('vulgar', according to Clara), which had been read to her so often that she could match sounds to pages. From then on she read anything and everything: Mrs Molesworth, Edith Nesbit,[14] Frances Hodgson Burnett, Old Testament stories, *Great Events of History*, her beloved Dickens and, later, the Balzacs and Zolas that served – in Clara's view – as wordly education (although the young Agatha was too innocent to see real life in literature; to her, books were their own reality). It has been said that Agatha never fully mastered spelling or grammar because of her unorthodox introduction to words, but this is an exaggeration. Letters do show her getting the odd word wrong – 'phenomenen', 'incomoded', 'meglamania' – but her detective fiction shows her as something of a stickler for good usage: '"It's me," said Miss Marple, for once ungrammatical.'[15]

In fact Agatha learned some grammar at a ladylike establishment in Torquay run by a Miss Guyer, which she attended two days a week from the age of about thirteen. The decision not to send her to full-time school was quite normal, although it was odd that she had no governess. Perhaps Clara, who knew full well the extent of Agatha's daughterly devotion, preferred to keep it all to herself. Perhaps her attempt to stop Agatha reading was a means of control. Or perhaps she simply wanted to try something different from what had been done with her elder daughter; it was unusual that Madge should have gone away to school and, when it was suggested that she was Girton material, Frederick put his gentlemanly foot down. ('She's got Girton written all over her' is an insult delivered in Mary Westmacott's *The Burden*.) Agatha, by contrast, received outside tuition only in music. Her father and Madge taught her to write and her mother flashed through the more interesting episodes in history. Aside from that, she was on her own.

It was probably the making of her. Agatha was one of those auto-didacts who go on learning and reading all their lives and whose minds, therefore, develop in the way most suitable to *them*. As an adult she had an avowed respect for 'academic' brains: her second husband, Max Mallowan, was an Oxford-educated archaeologist with a knowledge of the classics, and she admired him and his friends for that. Nevertheless she had an innate confidence in her own, less orthodox thought-paths. Her collection of short stories *The Labours of Hercules* recasts the twelve myths in what she would, smilingly, have called 'low-brow' form, as stories for her own 'Hercule' Poirot to solve: the Nemean Lion, for instance, is a kidnapped Pekinese lapdog. Meanwhile Poirot puts an irreverent, clear-eyed spin upon Greek mythology.

> 'Take this Hercules – this hero! Hero, indeed! What was he but a large muscular creature of low intelligence and criminal tendencies! . . . The whole classical pattern shocked him. These gods and goddesses – they seemed to have as many different aliases as a modern criminal. Indeed, they seemed to be definitely criminal types. Drink, debauchery, incest, rape, loot, homicide and chicanery – enough to keep a *juge d'instruction* constantly busy. No decent family life. No order, no method.

These were not the definitive opinions of Agatha herself, but she would have been happy to entertain them. Having never been 'taught', she had no hang-ups about learning.

So her mind ran free and, because it was a good mind, it began the process of creative absorption: the worlds of Ashfield; of Torquay; of family, servants, social ritual; of the mysteries that lay beyond, like the stealthy blue of the sea in the distance.

As a child she was protected by structure and certainty. She lived in what W. H. Auden described as the perfect ending place for detective fiction: 'the state of grace in which the aesthetic and the ethical are as one'.[16] Goodness was all around, in the love of her parents and of God, whom she took very seriously, so seriously that she feared for the soul of a father who played croquet in the garden on Sundays. And the running of her home was so efficient and seemly that it acquired a kind of morality. Servants, she was honest enough always to acknowledge, made a state of grace easier to attain.

Without Nursie, Jane the cook, and the various maids,[17] Ashfield could not have had its atmosphere of ordered leisure. Jane in particular was immutable and magnificent. She cooked for parties of eight or more on a regular basis, showing no sign of agitation except 'a slight flush'; Agatha would skip around her in the hope of a handful of raisins or a rock cake, crisp and steaming and straight from the oven: 'Never since have I tasted rock cakes like Jane's.' Food was the anchor that held daily life in place. A midday Sunday lunch for the family would consist of 'an enormous Sunday joint, usually cherry tart and cream, a vast piece of cheese, and finally dessert on the best Sunday dessert plates'. A menu of a dinner party for ten 'began with a choice of thick or clear soup, then boiled turbot, or fillets of sole. After that came a sorbet. Saddle of mutton followed. Then, rather unexpectedly, Lobster Mayonnaise. Pouding Diplomatique and Charlotte Russe were the sweets and then dessert. All of this was produced by Jane, single-handed.'[18] Agatha ate hugely, always, but remained very thin until her thirties.

The servants were the architects of Ashfield. They wove the stuff of daily life for Agatha and they were, she says in her autobiography, its 'most colourful part . . . One of the things I think I should miss most, if I were a child nowadays, would be the absence [sic] of servants.' The modern world cannot begin to comprehend her attitude towards them, which was free of all guilt and doubt. 'They "knew their place" as was said, but knowing their place meant not subservience but pride, the pride of the professional.'

A good servant was a person of real standing. 'I always wonder why people think it's so humiliating to go "into service" and that it's grand and independent to be in a shop. One puts up with far more insolence in a shop than . . . any decent domestic does,' says Midge, a character in *The Hollow*, who is obliged to earn her living selling clothes. Agatha thought that she herself would make a good parlourmaid (being tall was an asset); at one point she considered doing so, when she was travelling the world with her husband Archie and money was very short.

Bad servants, however, received no respect. When a parlourmaid could not do her job she was described as a mere mess of adenoids and dropped aitches. This *de haut en bas* attitude is one of the things that has caused Agatha Christie's reputation to suffer in recent years. 'Wonderful animal, the good servant,' says a character in *And Then There Were None* with a casual, admiring contempt, and our liberal hearts flutter like nervous old ladies.

But it was not quite that simple. For example the 'frightened rabbit' Gladys in *A Pocket Full of Rye* – apparently one of the worst examples of Agatha's lazy snobbery – is actually at the heart of the story, crucial to the plot and treated with real compassion. 'Life is cruel, I'm afraid,' says Miss Marple. 'One doesn't really know what to do with the Gladyses. They enjoy going to the pictures and all that, but they're always thinking of impossible things that can't possibly happen to them. Perhaps that's happiness of a kind. But they get disappointed . . .'

This is wise and true and yet, because of the stereotype that Agatha herself has created, we dismiss it as condescension and Gladys along with it. As she would often do, Agatha has used the familiarity of the stereotype to subvert our expectations. It was one of the cleverest tricks she would play. It was, in fact, more than a trick: by such sudden means she revealed her insight, her lightly worn understanding of human nature.

In *A Pocket Full of Rye* Miss Marple knows – it is stronger than a guess – the time of Gladys's death because, had she still been alive, 'she would certainly have taken the second [tea] tray into the drawing-room'. Thus an oblique tribute is paid to the importance of servants: to the structure they created in Agatha's life, and in her detective fiction.

All her life she was fascinated by the ordering of a home. In her 1957 book, *4.50 from Paddington*, she created a character called Lucy Eyelesbarrow, an Oxford graduate who becomes a rich woman by turning herself into the ideal servant. 'Lucy, with time on her hands, scrubbed the kitchen table which she had been longing to do . . . Then she cleaned the silver till it shone radiantly. She cooked lunch, cleared it away, washed it up . . . She had set out the tea things ready on a tray, with sandwiches and bread and butter covered with a damp napkin to keep them moist.' It is a litany, a hymn to crisp and shining ritual, a fantasy in which the familiar becomes sublime.

The loss of servants, post-war, changed the nature of Agatha's world. Her books became less regulated – not necessarily a criticism – and there is a continual plangent refrain of how different things are now that there are 'no servants . . . just a couple of women who come in'.[19] The modern reaction to this can be imagined (there are plenty of servants today, but few people as honest as Agatha in their attitudes towards them). Again, though, her views are a little more complex, at any rate when she wants them to be. For example, *The Hollow* has a character named David Angkatell, a young man full of left-wing disgust for his privileged family; in an entrancingly succinct scene he spouts politics at Midge, telling her that she would understand the class struggle better if she were a worker.

'I *am* a worker. That's just why being comfortable is so attractive. Box beds, down pillows – early morning tea softly deposited by the bed – a porcelain bath with lashings of hot water – and delicious bath salts. The kind of easy-chair you really sink into . . .'

Midge paused in her catalogue.

'The workers', said David, 'should have all these things.'

. . . 'I couldn't agree with you more,' said Midge heartily.

But the child Agatha was safe within order, and order delighted her. She loved the calm bustle of the kitchen and the starch in her muslin dresses almost as much as she loved to dream of the glistening river at the end of Ashfield's garden, towards which she would ride on a white palfrey. Later she loved Lucy Eyelesbarrow, mundane and magical, waving her scrubbing brush like a wand as she turned a house into a place of regulated beauty. For all the wanderings of her imagination Agatha was fascinated, always, by the power of the ordinary.

She grew up with ordinary female conversation in her ears and this, too, delighted her. She picked out phrases almost as if they were music, catching something of their meaning but loving far more the way they danced in her head. 'I haven't yet finished, Florence'; 'I beg your pardon, Mrs Rowe', was what she heard in the kitchen when a servant rose from the tea-table before Jane had finished her meal; she remembered the little interchange all her life. She liked to listen to the ladylike squabbles between Margaret Miller and Mary Ann Boehmer (whom she always described as her 'grandmothers', although Margaret was in fact her great-aunt). 'Nonsense, Margaret, I never heard such nonsense in my life!' 'Indeed, Mary, let me tell you . . .' She particularly liked the subtleties that bristled upon Margaret's comfortable pronouncements. 'Such a nice woman. Colonel L— is an old friend of her husband who asked him to look after her. There is, of course, nothing wrong about it. Everybody knows *that*.'[20] She stored these phrases away just as Margaret, in her home at Ealing, packed her cupboards with 'dates, preserved fruits, figs, French plums, cherries, angelica, packets of raisins and currants, pounds of butter and sacks of sugar, tea and flour', her bedroom trunks with rich velvets and silks.

When her parents went travelling together (Clara thought it her duty to be with Frederick), Agatha would visit the large house to which Margaret – 'Auntie-Grannie' – had moved, from Cheshire, as a prosperous and substantial widow. Mary Ann, or 'Granny B', lived in Bayswater. There was deep history between these two sisters. They were close companions in their old age, both stout, proud figures in their tight-wrapped black silk, but the difference in status was apparent. Margaret was the more assured, Mary Ann her foil. Margaret helped her sister with sums of money given 'in return' for errands carried out at the Army and Navy Stores in Victoria; back to Ealing Mary Ann would go with various buttons and ribbons and lengths of material, all of which would be rigorously judged and discussed and paid for out of Margaret's bulging purse, whose innards gleamed with gold. As Agatha wrote in her autobiography, the sisters regarded the Army and Navy Stores as 'the hub of the universe'. Occasionally she accompanied them there and, in *At Bertram's Hotel*, a book written in her own old age, she has Miss Marple recollect the scene:

Miss Marple cast her thoughts back to Aunt Helen seeking out her own special man in the grocery department, settling herself comfortably in a chair, wearing a bonnet and what she always called her 'black poplin' mantle. Then there would ensure a long hour with nobody in a hurry and Aunt Helen thinking of every conceivable grocery that could be purchased and stored up for future use . . . Having had a thoroughly pleasant morning, Aunt Helen would say in the playful manner of those times, 'And how would a little girl feel about some luncheon?' . . . After that, they bought half a pound of coffee creams and went to a matinée in a four-wheeler.

These performances, which to her is what they were, satisfied a desire in Agatha. They embodied a kind of robust feminine certainty: the human equivalent of the ordered home. She had had a version of this with Nursie ('After Nurse, there was God'),[21] although Nursie dealt with Agatha as a child and lacked, therefore, the worldly dimension. Clara, meanwhile, was too creative and mercurial to have, as Margaret Miller did, a wonderful womanly instinct that never doubted itself. 'Always think the worst about people'; 'Gentlemen need attention and three proper meals a day'; 'Never get into a train with a single man'; Waste not want not'; 'Gentlemen like a figure'; 'Every woman should have fifty pounds in five-pound notes in case of emergencies'; 'Gentlemen can be very agreeable, but you can't trust one of them'. Thus did Margaret express herself as she sat erect and dauntless among the heavy mahogany furniture at Ealing, whispering advice to Clara ('A husband should never be left alone too long'), dealing with a young man who has impregnated a servant ('Well, are you going to do the right thing by Harriet?'), chatting to her men friends among the tea things ('I hope your wife won't *object*! I shouldn't like to cause *trouble*!'). Her strong sane voice dealt in mysteries, rendering them murky and cosy; irresistible to Agatha.

These rhythmic phrases belonged to a world as different as could be from the palfrey and the gleaming river. But they had, nonetheless, their own beauty. She never repeated anything she heard, however interesting, and in this she was quite unlike 'the rest of my family, who were all extrovert talkers'.[22] Instead she listened to everything, absorbing it, not understanding it, perhaps never fully understanding it all, letting it form a pattern in her mind.

One day the Miss Marple who had sat with her Aunt Helen in the Army and Navy Stores would become a version of that aunt: wise, compassionate, unflinching from reality. This was not Agatha. She *did* flinch. Like most real writers, she was a stronger person in her books than in her life. But she had a constant urge to re-create the women of her childhood, the faith she had in their comforting omniscience. Miss Marple is the supreme example, and there are others, like Miss Percehouse in *The Sittaford Mystery* ('I hate a slobbering female'), or Miss Peabody in *Dumb Witness* ('Not the sort of young man I'd fancy if I were a young girl. Well, Theresa should know her mind. She's had her experiences, I'll be bound.') Also Dame Laura Whitstable in the Westmacott novel *A Daughter's a Daughter*, who is not so much a character as a magnificent mouthpiece. Her real reason for existing in the book is the pleasure that Agatha takes in her. 'I'm old-fashioned,' she says, puffing at a cigar. 'I would prefer that a man should have *knowledge* of himself and *belief* in God'; 'Nobody can really ruin another person's life. Don't be melodramatic and don't wallow'; 'Half the troubles in life come from pretending to oneself that one is a better and finer human being than one is'; 'The fewer people who love you the less you will have to suffer.' Nobody talks the way Dame Laura talks, yet she has artistic reality because to Agatha she is real. She is the authentic spirit of female certainty, speaking the thoughts of her creator, in a voice that Agatha always needed to hear.

Agatha grew up in a matriarchy. The strength was all on the female side: Clara, Margaret, clever sister Madge, Nursie, Jane the cook. Her father and brother never stood a chance. Frederick didn't mind a jot about this; Monty undoubtedly did.

Agatha was never a feminist but she knew perfectly well the value of women, which she considered feminism helped to devalue, as shown in an interview she gave to an Italian magazine in 1962. How, she was asked, had it happened that women now played a more active role in public life? Her answer is not what had been expected: 'Probably due to the foolishness of women in relinquishing their position of privilege attained after many centuries of civilisation. Primitive women toil incessantly. We seem determined to return to that state voluntarily – or by listening to persuasion, and therefore forfeiting the joys of leisure and creative thought, and the perfecting of home conditions.'[23]

Agatha believed that femaleness had its own power, entirely separate from the male: 'Surely, we are the privileged sex.' Yet as on most subjects her beliefs were fluid, complex, honestly uncertain. In her detective novel set in Ancient Egypt, *Death Comes as the End*, she wrote of

> the rich, varied noises of the kitchen, the high, shrill note of old Esa's voice, the strident tones of Satipy and, very faintly, the deeper, persistent contralto of Kait. A babel of women's voices – chattering, laughing, complaining, scolding, exclaiming . . . And suddenly Renisenb felt stifled, encircled by this persistent and clamorous femininity. Women – noisy, vociferous women! A houseful of women – never quiet, never peaceful – always talking, exclaiming, *saying* things – not *doing* them!
>
> And Khay – Khay silent and watchful in his boat, his whole mind bent on the fish he was going to spear . . .

Female life, in this book, is seen as something powerful – 'What are men anyway? They are necessary to breed children, that is all. But the strength of the race is in the women,' says Kait – but also limited and limiting. There is another, more difficult kind of happiness to be found, when a woman can grow up, and still touch her own childlike simplicity.

> Renisenb had got into the habit of going up to the tomb almost every day . . . She would sit in the shade of the rock chamber entrance with one knee raised and her hands clasped round it, and stare out over the green belt of cultivation to where the Nile showed a pale gleaming blue and beyond it to a distance of pale soft fawns and creams and pinks, all melting hazily into each other.

When Agatha travelled to the East, as she did with her second husband, she too would look out on transcendent landscapes and find this kind of demanding, almost troubling peace; a return, in a way, to what she had found years before, when she had seen other worlds in the garden at Ashfield. 'You are lucky, Renisenb,' says her wise old grandmother Esa. 'You have found the happiness that is inside everybody's own heart. To most women happiness means coming and going, busied over small affairs . . . It is made up of small things strung together like beads on a string.'

To Clara, the woman to whom Agatha was always closest, happiness was an elusive thing. She loved her home, although she was too restless to find absolute contentment in it. She sought artistic outlets for what were, in fact, indifferent artistic talents (even her embroidery was inept). Her spiritualism was both profound and unsettled, as if she felt its importance but did not quite know what to do with it. She cast around with different religions, seriously considering conversion to Roman Catholicism and flirting with Unitarianism, Christian Science and Zoroastrianism. She did find happiness in her family: the depths of her adoration were not always answered by Frederick's calm, gentlemanly, uxorious smiles, Monty was 'difficult', but Madge and Agatha were exceptional girls whose creativity gave an outlet to Clara's own. It was her youngest daughter, though, with whom Clara had her strongest bond. As Agatha was to write in *Unfinished Portrait*, she had inherited something from her mother: 'a dangerous intensity of affection'. For a time, Agatha and Clara would be the sole recipients of each other's devotion.

'Receipts for Agatha', it says, in Clara's rounded well-schooled handwriting, on the first page of an exercise book.

Poulard à la crème: Choose a good fat pullet . . . Eggs à la Monte Cristo . . . Mushrooms à la Henri IV . . . Grannie's Plum Pudding . . . Salad dressing: 2 yolks of hard boiled eggs made into a smooth paste add a teaspoonful of made mustard and also of salt a few grains of cayenne pepper. Then a teaspoonsful of vinegar. To this add 2 tablespoonsful of best oil, then after mixing put in 2 tablespoonsful of cream . . .

Friday night: Sole, Roast Pigeons, Fried potatoes and salad, Cherry tart, cream . . .

What dreams for Agatha lay within these painstakingly copied recipes; what visions of a perfect life, as ordered and kindly as childhood? One hundred years on, the exercise book in which they were written lay upstairs at Greenway House, in what had been Agatha's bedroom, in a tall and handsome chest of drawers. A green leather case embossed with the name 'Clarissa Miller' contained the book of recipes, with many other things. A wallet made of gold-coloured material, embroidered 'To Frederick from Clarissa', containing a dollar bill. A purse embroidered with the entwined initials F and C, and the line 'Set me as a seal upon thine heart, for love is strong as death'. An envelope containing a piece of Pears soap, used by Frederick, still faintly fragrant. Clara's album of poems. Pieces of edelweiss kept from her honeymoon in Switzerland, crumbling within the pages of a letter to 'F.A.M.'. Her marriage certificate. A green wallet containing letters. A programme for the 1894 Harrow School speech day. A picture of Agatha as a child, sitting on a wicker bench under a little palm tree. A picture of Frederick as a boy, looking like Agatha. A picture of Clara herself, wearing an embroidered robe at the dinner table at Ashfield. A letter to Agatha sent from Ealing: 'My darling wee Babsie, I am sure you must be very cold, with so much snow about Ashfield . . . Darling little girlie, Mother is longing to kiss and love her sweet pea again. Auntie-Grannie sends you much love . . . Tell Jane to please get a partridge to make you some potted meat for tea or breakfast.' A letter from Madge in London to Agatha: 'My dear little chicken, how are you getting on? I hope you are conducting yourself in a highly respectable way, and not forgetting me.' A letter from Frederick to Agatha in Ealing, dated 15 June 1894:

I am longing so much to see you and dear mother again. Ashfield is looking very lovely and I think you will find your room nice and pretty with new furniture and paper. Scot[24] looks very miserable when I talk about you and seems to say to me, 'Will my dear little mistress *never* come back! I do miss my walks with her and nurse so much.' I hear your Grannie is going to have your picture painted. I think it is a most lovely idea and I want you to put your little arms around Grannie's neck and give her a hug and kiss for me. You must always be good and gentle to her and I am pleased to think you are . . .

So many things kept, so many passions folded into papers, so strong the desire to hold memory within envelopes and miniature boxes and embossed cases. Every separate thing inside the case held, still, the breath of the instinct that had been moved to keep it.

There were other things, too, in the cupboards and drawers of Greenway. Christening gowns like heaps of soft snow. Birth certificates: Clara born in Belfast, Agatha born at Ashfield, Agatha's daughter Rosalind born at Ashfield. A framed menu of Clara and Frederick's 'Déjeuner du Mariage: Palace Gardens Terrace, 11 April 1878'. A bill dated 17 June 1940: 'Sale of Ashfield, Barton Road, Torquay – £2,400.00. Furniture and fittings – £21. 19. 6d.'

Box after box of photographs: Ashfield; Primsted Farm, the childhood home of Margaret and Mary Ann; Clara with Agatha's little dog Tony; Margaret Miller seated imperiously in a three-wheeler; Monty, dressed in coachman's regalia, sitting behind a harnessed goat in Truelove the toy cart; teenage Madge in her long skirt, her smile clever and confident; Agatha and a friend, aged around seven, peeping charmingly over the backs of the raffia chairs in the garden. A white fan, still in its long slim case, given by Frederick to Margaret. A scrapbook that belonged to Madge, in which she had stuck some of her dance-cards, and cut-outs of carriages full of flowers: 'Switzerland 1878. Souvenir of Mother's wedding journey'. Clara's copy of The Imitation of Christ by Thomas à Kempis, on whose flyleaf Agatha had written, 'Who shall separate us from the love of Christ?'

And, in another leather case, an 'Album of Confession', in which every member of the family wrote their replies to a list of questions: favourite virtue, favourite colour, heroes, heroines, present state of mind and so on. Imagination works easily upon this book. Its thin pages, scratched with slanted writing, conjure the Millers in the drawing-room at Ashfield: one sees them through the tall windows that stretched down to the garden, sitting within their magically enclosed world, fir-cones burning cleanly on the fire as they sipped cherry brandy and pondered their answers. The women of the family – sincere, high-minded – played the confession game very seriously.

In 1871 Margaret Miller wrote that her favourite virtue was 'self-denial', her chief characteristic was 'obstinacy', and to the question 'If not yourself, who would you be?', her reply was, 'A better individual.' Mary Ann Boehmer refused to be drawn on this question: 'I envy no-one.' She named her chief characteristic as 'want of caution' and her present state of mind as 'anxious'. Her idea of misery was 'to be in debt'. Her hero, she wrote carefully, was 'Nathaniel Frary Miller', the brother-in-law whose money had paid for Clara's upbringing.

Meanwhile Clara, then seventeen, described her present state of mind as 'wishing for a long dress', although she would have had no occasion to wear it, since despite her wealth Margaret had no plans to give her adopted daughter a social season. Perhaps Clara was aiming an oblique shaft at her aunt and mother when she wrote that her chief characteristic was 'a great love for children'. Her idea of happiness was 'always doing the thing that is right'. The fault for which she had most tolerance was 'reserve': her own lies heavy on the page.

What godly creatures these women were! And how Victorian their tastes: their love of Mendelssohn, Landseer, Prince Albert and 'Miss Nightingale', their dislike of 'deceit and affectation'. Naturally Frederick took the game far more lightly. In 1872 he wrote – perhaps with a cousinly wink at Clara – that his chief characteristic was 'doing nothing' and his pet aversion 'getting up in the morning'. Present state of mind? 'Extremely comfortable, thank you.'

Agatha first played the confessions game at the age of seven. Some of her answers were absolutely her own: her pet aversion was 'bedtime when you are wide awake'; if not herself she would be 'a fairy'. But her heavy eyes were in search of approval when she wrote that her idea of happiness was 'to be good', that her hero and heroine were 'Father' and 'Mother', her favourite painter the family portraitist 'Baird'.

She meant these things, of course. Nevertheless this was the public Agatha, who kept something of her real self withheld; a little girl who sought to please and draw loving nods from those around her. A 'serious little girl', as she wrote in *Unfinished Portrait*, who 'thought a good deal about God and being good and holy . . . alas! undoubtedly a prig'.

Agatha was being hard on herself, but perhaps she knew that her childish religiosity was not wholly real: it was essential to her dream world that she be clean in clothes and soul. She liked to see herself as a good girl, a character in a Victorian novel with her sashed waist and her hoop and her book of Bible stories by the bed. She liked to believe in duty. Such were the times in which she lived, the milieu in which she was raised. But it was also her nature.

Her imaginative wanderings were always in the land of virtue; morality, security and happiness were all bound up together. If Agatha was good she would be safe. If she was safe she would be happy. All of which she was; heartbreakingly so, because it could not last: the sweet structures of her life protected her too much. She was wrapped as carefully and precariously as Clara's edelweiss flowers. Somewhere inside herself she knew this, even at seven. Her happiness was complete; yet she wrote in her confession that her idea of misery was for 'someone I love to go away from me'. She had suffered, then, when her parents went on their little holidays to New York ('Home, with Mummy in it . . . Oh, Mummy – Mummy . . .'). And she dreamed, regularly, about evil.

In the 'Gun Man' nightmare, places that Agatha knew and loved – like the tea-table at Ashfield – were invaded by a spectre with a murderer's eyes and no hands. At first the Gun Man was a person in his own right. He wore a French uniform and had powdered hair in a queue. Then the dream changed.

It would be a happy dream – a picnic or a party [she wrote in *Unfinished Portrait*]. And suddenly, just when you were having lots of fun, a queer feeling crept over you. Something was wrong somewhere . . . What was it? Why, of course, the Gun Man was there. But he wasn't himself. One of the guests was the Gun Man . . .

And the awful part of it was, he might be anybody . . . It might be Mummy or Daddy or Nannie – someone you were just talking to. You looked up in Mummy's face – of course it was Mummy – and then you saw the light steely-blue eyes – and from the sleeve of Mummy's dress – oh, horror! – that horrible stump. It wasn't Mummy – it was the Gun Man . . .

*   *   *

Agatha was eleven when her father died, at his step-mother's house in Ealing. 'A hospital nurse came out and spoke to Grannie, who was coming up the stairs. "It's all over," she said.'

In the green wallet inside her leather case, Clara kept the letters sent and received in the year of her husband's death. 'Darling Daddy, I am so sorry you are still ill, we miss you very much,' Agatha had written to him at the start of 1901. 'I had a nice afternoon as Jane let me make cakes in the kitchen. I made some with sultanas, and some with ginger. I had Devonshire cream for tea!'

In May Clara went to Ealing with Agatha, who had not been well. Frederick himself was, by then, very ill indeed, but like the true gentleman he was he turned his thoughts outward. 'I was very much distressed to learn by your letter this morning that Agatha was not doing as well as you could wish ... Madge is having ten girls for Ping-Pong tomorrow; she is quite proud of this ... I still keep all right.'[25]

Meanwhile, throughout 1901, he was keeping a list of 'Heart Attacks'. He recorded thirty between June and September: 'Slight attack. Good night' was a typical entry. Clara may not have seen this list until after her husband's death, as he would not have wanted to worry her. In October he wrote from his club – the Windham in St James's Square – to tell her about a visit to a specialist in London: 'I saw Sansom this morning and he told me very much the same thing as last time. He insists that my trouble has more to do with the nerves of the heart than anything else ... I have felt wonderfully better the last two days ... I am now, please God, done with doctors.' Which was true, in a sense: a month later Frederick was dead. He was fifty-five and had been staying in Ealing to be close to London, where he had intended to look for a job.

Financial concerns, so long dismissed, had played their part in his early death. His heart and his fortunes weakened together, and he had not a clue what to do about it. 'I have had no letter from America since my return – which I try to think is good news,'[26] he wrote to Clara.

By that time there was nothing to do but endure the knowledge: of the New York properties that cost so much more to keep than they earned in rent, of the trustee who had gone into an asylum, of the other trustee who had shot himself, of the lurking suspicion of embezzlement.

Back in 1896, when the nature of the crisis first became apparent to him, Frederick had taken action of sorts. He had let Ashfield, with its servants, and moved with his wife and daughters to France for a year. This was a familiar economy made by the straitened gentry. Different things were cheap in those days: to stay in hotels on the continent cost less than it did to run a big house in England, and one could always take letters of introduction to ensure a social life. For the first six months the Millers stayed in Pau, considered healthful with its clear mountain air. They went on to Cauterets – also in the Pyrenees – then to Paris, and finally to Brittany. Agatha was too excited by the experience to miss Ashfield. Anyway she was always happy in the company of her mother. She did not, though, live an imaginative life in France: from the moment of her arrival she felt a certain disappointment that here was a world much like any other. Having longed to see mountains, she was hit by 'a disillusionment I have never forgotten. Where was that soaring height going up, up, up into the sky, far, above my head – something beyond contemplation or understanding?'[27]

So she lived contentedly in the realm of reality, for the first time in her seven years behaving like any other normal, lively little girl. She made friends easily and 'discovered . . . the joys of mischief', playing tricks on other hotel guests like hiding under the stairs with a peacock feather and tickling people's legs as they passed. She learned to swim: a lifelong pleasure. She watched the sexual blossoming of her sister Madge, had a crush on a saturnine lift boy and yearned for the day when she would fill out a 'striped blouse and collar and tie'. She grew fond of the young Marie Sijé, whom Clara had whisked from her job at a dressmakers' to become Agatha's companion and French conversationalist; like most of Clara's instinctive decisions, this was a success.

Agatha had no conscious sense of the reasons behind the family's removal to France. But *Unfinished Portrait* shows that she had understood more than she realised at the time. There is a scene in the book in which her parents meet friends from England, the Grants, at a hotel in Pau:

Celia overheard Mr Grant say to her mother: 'It gave me a shock to see old John [Frederick], but he tells me he is ever so much fitter since being here.'

THE VILLA AT TORQUAY

Celia said to her mother afterwards: 'Mummy, is Daddy ill?'

Her mother looked a little queer as she answered: 'No. No, of course not. He's perfectly well now. It was just the damp and rain in England.'

Celia was glad her father wasn't ill. Not, she thought, that he could be – he never went to bed or sneezed or had a bilious attack. He coughed sometimes, but that was because he smoked so much. Celia knew that, because her father told her so.

France was a help to Frederick; nevertheless the years of content were over for him. In the Album of Confession he had written that his idea of misery was 'consciousness of guilt', and he may therefore have suffered to know that he was leaving his beloved family with so little money, that he had let it all go through his gentlemanly negligence, that Clara would be forced to sell the Chippendales and Sheratons bought with such smiling abandon, that probably Ashfield itself would have to be sold. Yet he would have been comforted by the fact that there was no reproach in Clara's nature. She had viewed it as happiness beyond prize to be married to Frederick. In the confessions he, too, had described his idea of happiness, which was 'to be perfectly loved': many people might wish for this but for Frederick the wish had been granted, and he knew it. 'No man ever had a wife like you,' he wrote to Clara, shortly before the end.

More than a hundred years on this letter was still in her leather case, with the order of service from Frederick's funeral and leaves from trees in the cemetery at Ealing where he was buried. 'I see thee not, dear heart, and yet I see/As though mine eyes drew solace from thy face', Clara had written on the envelope containing the last piece of Pears soap her husband had used.

From then on, until Clara's death twenty-five years later, Agatha would be the heart of her mother's life. 'You've got to live for your children, remember, my dear,' said the nurse who had looked after Frederick at Ealing and who tended, afterwards, to Clara. 'Yes, I've got to live for my children. You needn't tell me that. I know it.' But it was really Agatha for whom she now lived. Madge was soon to be married, Monty was abroad with his regiment and anyway Agatha had always been special to Clara: her inexpressive depth of emotion, her secretive imagination, her heavy adoring eyes, her serene confidence in the love that, nonetheless, she constantly sought. Like Clara, she had understood the fear of loss, although she had never experienced it until Frederick's death; and so it was with Agatha that Clara made the bond she had never had with her own mother. The closeness between the two became as powerful as electricity. It was the light within Agatha and in later years it would sometimes blind her.

'My grandmother was a dangerous woman,' said Agatha's daughter Rosalind, many years later. 'Strong and dangerous. My mother never thought she was wrong.'[28]

The death of her father did not mean the end of Agatha's idyll. In *Unfinished Portrait* she is sent a letter by each of her parents, when they are abroad and she is staying with her grandmother at Ealing: 'Two lovely, lovely letters,' she writes; but it is her mother's that causes her agony. 'Home, she wanted to go home. Home, with Mummy in it . . .'

Although Agatha had loved her father dearly, so long as she was with Clara she could be happy without him. But until he died she had known only control and decorum. Suddenly, for a time, her life became unstable. 'I stepped out of my child's world . . . to enter the fringes of the world of reality.' She glimpsed raw and fearful things. Like a good Victorian girl she went to her mother's bedside to tell her that 'Father' was happy now in heaven. Clara wouldn't want him to have to leave Paradise, would she? 'Yes, I would. I would do anything in the world to have him back – anything, anything at all. I want him back *here*, now, in this world with *me*.' Clara was wild with grief, so much so that she too became ill. Her heart was weakened; she slept with *sal-volatile* beside her and, for a year or so, Agatha would stand outside her bedroom door at night, listening for her breathing, sometimes waiting for hours until she heard a sound.

In her kind but unimaginative way, Margaret Miller tried to share with Clara her own grief for her step-son. *Unfinished Portrait* shows her reading letters of condolence at the breakfast table:

'Mr Clark is a truly good man,' she would say, sniffing a little as she read. 'Miriam, you really should hear this. It would help you. He speaks so beautifully of how our dead are always with us.'

And suddenly roused from her quiescence Miriam would cry out: 'No, no!'

It was the last thing that Clara wanted. Frederick was hers and hers alone ('I could gladly die for thee,' she had written to him in 1877; how could Margaret understand that she had meant exactly that?). His removal from within the family had taken away its essential balance: the civilised, easy presence within that knot of complex women. All her life Clara had had to be grateful to Margaret. 'I am sure you are <u>very very</u> happy with dear Grannie,' she wrote to Agatha at Ealing in 1897. 'Dear little Agatha what a happy home you have with darling Grannie. You must be good to her and love her very much.' But Clara did not love Margaret, Margaret had never really loved Clara, and with Frederick gone the matriarchy was laid briefly, angrily bare. Clara's resentments slid out: towards both the mother who had given her away and the aunt who had offered to take her.

'Celia wondered whether Grannie really liked Mummy and whether Mummy really liked Grannie. She didn't quite know what put the idea into her head.' This was the real aftermath of death, a confused stir of emotions that were not necessarily to do with grief. Adult emotions, ambivalent and irrational.

No wonder Agatha retreated to the world of her imagination and created a new world for herself: The School, attended by The Girls.

First there was Ethelred Smith – who was tall and very dark and very, *very* clever . . . Then there was Annie Brown, Ethel's great friend . . . Isabella Sullivan, who had red hair and brown eyes and was beautiful. She was rich and proud and unpleasant. She always thought that she was going to beat Ethel at croquet, but Celia saw to it that she didn't, though she felt rather mean sometimes when she deliberately made Isabella miss balls . . .[29]

Among the seven girls there was one who refused to take on reality for Agatha: this was Sue de Verte, fair-haired with pale blue eyes, 'curiously colourless' in character. While the other girls chattered, engaged with each other, had definite pasts and futures – Elsie Green had grown up terribly poor, Sue's sister Vera de Verte was to become one of the world's great beauties – Sue remained the observer.

In old age Agatha still thought occasionally of The Girls. 'Even now, sometimes, as I put away a dress in a cupboard, I say to myself: "Yes, that would do well for Elsie, green was always her colour" . . . It makes me laugh when I do it, but there "the girls" are still, though, unlike me, they have not grown old.'[30]

The Young Miss Miller

'Pierrette dancing on the green, Merrily, so merrily!'
(from 'A Masque from Italy', written by Agatha Christie in around 1907)

'Where will one be next year or the year after? How wonderful it is that
ONE DOESN'T KNOW'
(from notes made by Agatha Christie in 1973)

After the death of her husband Clara faced the fact that Ashfield would have to be sold. Her children – Agatha in particular – were less realistic. They had not seen the letters from Frederick's executor in New York, Auguste Montant,[1] explaining that there was almost no money left: Clara had nothing except a tiny income from H. B. Chaflins, the firm at which Nathaniel Miller had been a partner. Running a big house like Ashfield would be a continual strain. 'To have kept it on was not a wise thing, I see that now,' wrote Agatha, in her autobiography. Nevertheless she begged for it, and Clara bowed to her daughter's wishes:

'Oh Mother, don't let's ever sell it . . .'

'Very well, darling. After all, it's a happy house.'

After losing her husband, a woman may find that the children who are supposed to help her through her loss do the opposite. They take away her rightful desire to think only of herself. Nobody could have cared more about Clara than Agatha did, yet with a child's innate selfishness she was determined to have her way and make her mother yield. To Agatha, staying at Ashfield meant that nothing had changed; but for Clara, everything had changed. The house was full of memories and bereft of so much else. Had she moved, as she briefly hoped to do, to a different life – she liked the idea of a cosy little house in Exeter – her relationship with her daughter might have been different too.

But perhaps she would not have wanted that. She, too, loved Ashfield with a passion – her own house, after all – and staying there was an expression of fidelity to Frederick. The oils he had bought still hung in clusters on the walls; the smell of his cigarettes still hovered, just within imagination, in the flower-scented air. Clara had become like her own mother, Mary Ann, who after the death of Captain Boehmer never thought to look at another man. But Clara was unlike Mary Ann, in that she would now make her daughter the centre of her life.

Ashfield was materially changed, of course. It became emptier and shabbier. The staff was reduced to 'two young, inexpensive maids', although Jane the cook refused to go. 'I have been here a very long time,' she said. When she eventually left, to keep house for her brother, she did so with two silent tears rolling down her cheeks. She was completely unable to get to grips with the loss of status that went with Clara's new poverty. It had been her great delight to telephone orders in her deep Devonshire voice – 'Six lobsters, *hen* lobsters' – and to create dishes for the gourmand Frederick, who would later step down to the kitchen with a word of graceful, private thanks. Now Jane, suffering intensely, found herself tipping avalanches of rock cakes into the bin and cooking macaroni cheese for two. She had to be reminded of the realities, but there was something magnificent in her refusal to admit them. She was like the servant Dorcas in Agatha's first detective novel, *The Mysterious Affair at Styles*, with her lament to Poirot for older, grander days:

'Five [gardeners] we had, before the war, when it was kept as a gentleman's place should be. I wish you could have seen it then, sir. A fair sight it was. But now there's only old Manning, and young William, and a new-fashioned woman gardener in breeches and suchlike. Ah, these are dreadful times!'

'The good times will come again, Dorcas. At least, we hope so . . .'

For Clara the good times were now held in her green leather case, repository of memories: of the young Frederick's smiling visits to the Miller household; of his miraculous proposal; of his arm through hers as they walked the New York streets; of his last letter to her. By the fire in the upstairs schoolroom, or while they were filling the house with 'great tall bouquets of white flowers' from the garden, Clara told Agatha all these stories of her life.

And so they found equilibrium again, mother and daughter at Ashfield.

At the end of Barton Road Agatha could wind her way downhill through the leafy lanes that led to All Saints' Torre, the grey Victorian church where she had been baptised, and say prayers for her father. She was a religious girl, 'firmly and strictly orthodox'. On the way to the church she passed Vansittart Road, whose name, many years later, she used for a character – Eleanor Vansittart – in her detective novel *Cat Among the Pigeons*. Elsa Dittisham, Colonel Luscombe, John Christow, Jean Instow and Mildred Strete bear other place names she remembered from her Devon childhood.

She began writing as a young girl. Her earliest surviving poem is carefully inscribed in an exercise book and dated April 1901.

> There was once a little cowslip,
> And a pretty flower too
> But yet she cried and petted,
> All for a robe of blue.

In the same book there is a poem about her cat, 'Ode to Christopher Columbus', written just after the death of her father.

> There was a little kittiwinks,
> Whose name (for short) was Cris.
> His fur stood out an inch all round,
> His tail: a dream of bliss.

She also had a poem published in an Ealing newspaper, whose first verse began:

> When first the electric trams did run,
> In all their scarlet glory . . .

This was Agatha Christie's first appearance in print.

Subsequent poems made it into the *Poetry Review* but it was Agatha's sister, Madge, who had more striking early success as a writer, and showed far more early ability. Before her marriage in 1902 she had had several stories – 'Vain Tales' – published in *Vanity Fair*. 'There is no doubt that Madge was the talented member of our family,' wrote Agatha in her autobiography. Both girls were encouraged to write, indeed to express their personalities in any way they chose. At the same time there was no thought that doing so would impugn their femininity. In that sense Clara was more enlightened than many women today, who would be quite capable of viewing Madge's *Vanity Fair* successes as offputting – 'threatening' – to potential husbands.

It is a quirk of parenting, more often than is realised, to treat one's children in the opposite way to which one was treated oneself. Clara had been ignored, had had her sensitive individuality swept aside by her upbringing. Now she shone a powerful searchlight on to her daughters' lives. She exerted herself to empathise with every aspect of them and believed there was nothing they could not do. She would probably have been a terrible mother for an ordinary girl. As it was, she had two bright sparks – effulgent, in Madge's case – and she kindled them to their utmost. The close influence of Clara, her highminded literary style, lies heavy upon the poems that Agatha wrote aged around thirteen.

> Have ye walked in the wood today?
> Have ye trodden the carpet of gold?
> Have ye heard the wind stirring the leaves at your feet?
> Have ye felt the mists rising tonight?
> Have ye wept for the world's disarray?
> Have ye counted the days that are told? . . .

Madge was freer, and always knew her own mind. She was as like Frederick as she was her mother, very much the half-American with her dry and limber wit, her lax disregard for convention. Unlike Agatha, she felt no need to behave like a 'good' girl, and nobody thought the worse of her for it. She was Bess Sedgwick in *At Bertram's Hotel* – impatient, adventurous, compelling – whereas Agatha was Bess's daughter Elvira: quiet, compliant, infinitely complex. Sent to Paris to be 'finished', Madge took a dare to leap from the balcony on to a table in a stately tea-room. Like her father she acted in amateur dramatics and loved to dress up, once meeting a visitor in the garb of a Greek priest: this may have given Agatha the idea, often used in her books, that being an actor makes a person an automatic master of disguise ('To assume the make-up and part of Pedro Morales was child's play to an actor . . .).[2] Late in life Madge came down to a family dinner in full cricket gear. Like her mother, she had something restless in her personality, but her abundance – excess? – of confidence meant that in her youth this turned to jokes and creativity.

She was magnetic, sexy, quick as a fox. Not beautiful, but that did not matter: she had personality. Agatha was dazzled by her and, as a young girl, she must have been a wonderful audience to whom Madge could show off her new dresses, flaunt her beaux and get laughs with her most throwaway remarks. 'Agatha is terribly *slow!*' Madge would say, but with affection: she was fond of her silent little sister. In 1903 Agatha made a second entry in the Album of Confessions, and named 'Mother and Madge' as her heroines.

As she grew older, however, she became jealous. 'I shall be furious if she arrives "on the film" before I do!'[3] wrote Agatha to her mother in 1922, by which time she herself was a published author but Madge, without warning and apparently without effort, had written a play for which she casually sought a West End producer.

She was also, at that point, a good deal richer than Agatha. Her marriage to James Watts – one of many suitors, who won her interest by appearing uninterested – was as lucrative as her namesake grand-mother's had been. James was heir to Abney Hall near Manchester, a vast Victorian mansion where Prince Albert had stayed and which Agatha used as the setting for several of her books. In *After the Funeral* the modern young cook calls the house a 'proper old mausoleum' and complains 'of the immense area of the kitchen, scullery and larder, saying that it was a "day's walk to get round them all"'. In *They Do*

It with Mirrors Abney – or 'Stonygates' – is mocked outright as a 'sort of Gothic monstrosity . . . Best Victorian Lavatory period.' In fact the house was hugely impressive, as Agatha was only too aware.

As a child she had loved to visit what was then the home of James Watts's parents ('And how is our dream-child?' Sir James would say to her). Abney had the dimension for which she yearned: it was a world of its own, with a life of its own, seemingly infinite with its 'quantities of rooms, passages, unexpected steps, back staircases, front staircases, alcoves, niches'.[4] Although Agatha loved sunlight and airiness she was compelled by Abney's Stygian quality, shrouded as it was from floor to ceiling in brocade curtains and tapestry hangings. Its rooms were shadowy, filled with richness and heaviness: green satin walls in the drawing-room, woodwork painted vermilion and ultramarine, oak furniture like miniature battleships. It had a magic made of depths, recesses, mysteries. Its very solidity seemed not quite real; in *They Do It with Mirrors* Stonygates is likened to a stage set, although 'the illusion is in the eye of the beholder, not in the set itself'.

After Madge's marriage, Agatha and Clara spent Christmas with the Watts family. Agatha later remembered the bursting stockings, presents heaped on chairs, a dining room that dimpled and glittered with lights, a meal beyond compass – oyster soup, roast turkey, boiled turkey, sirloin of beef, plum pudding, mince-pies, trifle, grapes, oranges, plums, preserved fruits. It was the world of the past made flesh. And the Abney image of Christmas was one that Agatha tried to re-create all her life: that plenitude, that Englishness, those Dickensian configurations of gleam and depth.

Madge became the chatelaine of Abney when James Watts took over the export business established by his grandfather. James, as Agatha's second husband Max put it, had a 'strange respect for money as a token of man's merit',[5] although when Agatha first met him in 1901 he was a shy young Oxford undergraduate with no plutocratic tendencies. 'I took a great fancy to him at once,' she wrote in her autobiography. 'He was kind to me, always treating me seriously, and not making silly jokes or talking to me as if I was a little girl.' Twenty-five years on he offered the idea (also claimed by Lord Mountbatten) for her most famous detective novel, *The Murder of Roger Ackroyd*.

James's reserve gave him an empathy with Agatha but made him an odd husband for the extrovert Madge. In later life she became frankly too much for him – he was unnerved by her penchant for disguise, for instance – and he was certainly not enough for her. 'They are an unhappy lot at Abney, I think,' Agatha would write in 1930.[6]

In her autobiography, Agatha wondered if her sister 'would have gone on writing if she had not married' (so it was probably a relief to Agatha that she *did* marry). Madge was the kind of woman who nowadays would have felt free to live alone, and that might have suited her best. It is certainly possible she would not have married James if Frederick, who never liked him, had still been alive. But Madge and Agatha had been left a hundred pounds each a year from the Miller estate. This was not negligible in the 1910s; still, the thought of Madge beneath the shelter of Abney must have been an irresistible relief to Clara, who was a realist about money. From her own upbringing she knew the damage that the lack of it could do. So she encouraged the couple not to wait, and – although Madge herself felt this was too soon – the wedding took place nine months after Frederick's death: 'Mother said, and truly I think, that it would be even more difficult to part with Madge as time went on and their companionship drew them closer.'[7]

In the period between Frederick's death and this marriage, Clara's relationship with Madge had an intimate intensity. They went to the South of France together for three weeks, leaving Agatha alone at Ashfield. She did not mind this; enjoyed ordering meals for herself from Jane ('technically, she was the mistress of the house!',)[8] and dimly understood that a grown woman was a better companion for a new widow than a pious girl bleating inadequately about Paradise. Had Madge not married so quickly, Agatha's relationship with Clara might have been rather different. As it was, from 1902 onwards she was first daughter.

Agatha put Madge into her story, 'The House of Beauty',[9] written around 1908 and the earliest of her works to find subsequent publication. Allegra Kerr mesmerises the hero, John. 'She was marvellously effective. Her effectiveness was, he thought, more studied than natural. But behind all that, there lay something else. Flickering fire, fitful, capricious, like the will-o'-the-wisps that of old lured men into the marshes.' She outdoes her young friend, Maisie – who is in love with John – with ease. 'You are hateful, Allegra,' Maisie tells her.

'But stimulating, darling.'

In *Unfinished Portrait* there is a version of Monty but no Madge character; Celia's sister, 'Joy', dies young. Agatha did not want Madge's dominant personality in the book, interfering with her own relationship with her mother, doing so many things better than she did: flirting, joking, telling stories, painting, acting, writing. When Madge's play *The Claimant* was taken up by a West End management – it went on at the Queen's Theatre, Shaftesbury Avenue, in 1924 – Agatha was obliged to be delighted for her. But the balance of their relationship, which for the past four years had been redressed by Agatha's literary successes, had tipped again. It is a rare writer who is not competitive, and an even rarer sister. Agatha had the sense that Madge, having touched her toe on the accelerator for one quick second, had leaped instant miles ahead of her.

She had believed Madge to be under control – thick of waist, mother to her grown-up son (Jack, born in 1903), locked away in her funereal mansion – while her terribly slow sister won plaudits from the outside world. She should have known better. When the eighteen-year-old Madge had played the confessions game she had written that her idea of happiness was 'to be successful'. It was an idea that she had not yet quite abandoned.

And with what blithe glee she rubbed it in, during rehearsals for *The Claimant*. The play was based on the true story of Sir Charles Tichborne – a Victorian Martin Guerre – who had laid claim to a baronetcy in the 1870s and gone on trial to establish his identity. Madge delighted in the fun of the story, although she treated its complexities with a lighter and more ragged touch than Agatha would have done: 'Inexperienced dramatists are apt to be over-lavish with their plots,' read the generally favourable review in *The Times*. It was a remarkable thing for an amateur to have pulled off – another triumph, in a sense, for Clara, who would have instilled in Madge the *certainty* that she could write a West End play – and Madge relished every moment of the experience. In the confessions game she had said that 'London' was the place she most wanted to live. Aged forty-five she was there at last, staying at the Garden Club in Mayfair, taking her vast reserves of assurance to the theatre every morning and bamboozling producer Basil Dean with them. Accustomed as he was to desperate actors and neurotic playwrights, the nonchalant grandeur of 'Mrs Watts' charmed him half to death. Or so she told her family.

> My Two Darling 1s [she wrote to her husband and son at Abney], it's going so well that Basil Dean says it might be produced earlier . . . I think the end of Act III is 'soft', always did think so. I want Fay Compton to have a speech – asked BD and he said 'Do exactly what you like; if you like you can make it terrific – anyway, anything you do I'm for. Very surprising? So – I'm typing again!
> . . . I went into Browns [Hotel] again. Said how I wanted rooms not for 16th but 11th. They were full but on my mentioning the play, she went quite mad, and said 'Of course, you shall have rooms no matter who is turned out!' Gives one a sheer sense of power. I hope I don't get very swelled headed . . .

Agatha was then living at Sunningdale – not far from London – so Madge spent some weekends with her: 'I went to Sunningdale yesterday – Sunday – but I was so tired I kept dropping off to sleep all the time!' It is possible that she was rather tiring herself at that time, especially to Agatha, who according to Madge was 'mad to see a rehearsal'; probably in order to reassure herself that *The Claimant* was no masterpiece. The tone of Madge's letters shows how irritating she must have been to her sister. 'Wrote and typed all night. BD came back in about five minutes seized me by the arm and said "My God! You can write – It's magnificent." So that's that. He now thinks me a sort of genius . . . They can't do without me'.

This was Madge's particular and provoking idiom: it could annoy to distraction but it could also charm. That she was the only woman in her family with her father's innate sense of humour is shown in this letter about the actress Lottie Venne, who had been cast in *The Claimant* for the natural barmaid qualities that – as she was playing an aristocrat – she felt at pains to suppress. 'I've an awful job this afternoon – I've got to tell Lottie Venne (orders from BD) that she is to be vulgar. She said "Of course, as a Duchess I can't do this or that" – <u>Frightfully</u> pleased at being one.'

Madge described the meeting thus:

> Dear Miss Venne, I'm so <u>charmed</u> to meet you! I'm dreadfully afraid everyone who's coming only to see <u>you</u>, will be so disappointed. They don't want to see <u>my</u> Duchess, they want to see <u>you</u>. They want their 'Lottie' . . .
>
> ME – I don't care about my lines. You <u>must</u> put yourself into the part. Let yourself go. Take it broadly.
>
> MISS V – But a duchess, y'know?'
>
> . . . Never have I found it so difficult to keep serious.

Agatha could not have written this; could not have been the woman who wrote it. She must have known, deep down, that such a direct expression of personality on the page is not the mark of a real writer. And she thought that she saw what lay beneath Madge's constantly rippling laughter. 'I've always suspected,' says a character in her late Westmacott *The Rose and the Yew Tree*, 'that a sense of humour is a kind of parlour trick we civilised folk have taught ourselves as an insurance against disillusionment. We make a conscious effort to see things as funny, simply because we suspect they are unsatisfactory.' Yet for all this Madge could always make Agatha feel 'curiously colourless', like her imaginary self Sue de Verte. 'My aunt was more entertaining than my mother,' said Agatha's daughter Rosalind.[10] 'She was great fun. Slightly buried in Manchester.'

After *The Claimant* came to the end of its short run, Madge returned to her vast, crypt-like house. She wrote a couple more plays but nothing else was produced. Instead it was Agatha who moved into the West End, where she achieved a remarkable dominance. It was as if a particular rivalry had to be settled in her favour; although there was a quality in both Madge and *The Claimant* – that sweet, airy essence of self – that would always elude her.

With a true lightness of touch, for example, the play portrays a character called Charles Cleghorne. 'Don't care about coppers, never did,' he says, tossing his small change on to the stage. Not that this was art, exactly, on Madge's part. It was a clever, elliptical and faithful reproduction of her brother Monty.

Monty never cared about small change, nor indeed about much else; or so he affected to pretend. He was a hopeless case. The matriarchy within which he grew up overwhelmed him. 'I mean, it makes you feel an awful ass!' says Eustace Leonides, the young boy in *Crooked House*, who lives in a family full of powerful women. This was the line that Monty took – his natural idiom was that of the Old Harrovian – but, as with Eustace, the sense of inadequacy went deeper. Eustace has suffered from infantile paralysis, and this is given as the explanation for his 'injured male pride' and possible murderousness: 'The more I think about it, the more it seems to me that Eustace might fit the bill . . . He's not normal.' With Monty there was no outward illness but there was, within, an odd paralysis of the spirit.

A normal man could have thrived, or survived, among all those women, since there was no lack of love for him in the family. Frederick adored him as the only boy: 'Monty, I think, was really his favourite,' wrote Agatha in her autobiography. But his closeness in age to the bright and brilliant Madge has started him off on the wrong foot. Thereafter he limped along, finding his way through life with a certain careless confidence and great dashes of luck. From Harrow – where he kept white mice ('Mr and Mrs Whiskers') and took no exams – it was hoped that he would go into banking, but this was beyond him and he was sent into a ship-building yard on the Dart. This too proved a failure. When the second Boer War broke out in 1899, he volunteered for the army and, having obtained a commission in the East Surreys, went to India. Army life suited him better than anything else would have done. But when he resigned his commission, in around 1910, it became clear that here was a quite extraordinary misfit.

Having come of age just after the death of his father, he ran at speed through the tiny amount left in the Miller estate. He acquired such desperate debts that he moved first to Kenya, then to Uganda, and sent begging letters to Madge asking for help in a scheme to run cargo boats on Lake Victoria. The *Batenga* was built with Watts money – 'My brother-in-law was livid,' Agatha later wrote – but by the time it was completed (with wildly luxurious ebony and ivory fittings) the

First World War had broken out. Monty sold the boat at a loss and joined the King's African Rifles. He narrowly avoided a court-martial when, against orders, he stopped his convoy of mules at a place he insisted was perfect for battle; while in the act of arguing with his commanding officer, a force of Germans arrived and was triumphantly beaten in what became known as 'Miller's Battle'.

Then Monty was wounded in the arm, the wound became infected, and he returned to Ashfield with his African servant, Shebani. He had come home supposedly to die. In fact his return 'nearly killed my mother', as Agatha wrote in her autobiography. Monty would eat dinner at four in the morning, if the whim took him, and shoot at people out of the window with his revolver. Calm, silent Barton Road had never known the like: 'Some silly old spinster going down the drive with her behind wobbling. Couldn't resist it . . .' There was a self-consciousness about his eccentricity that made it almost boring, as well as terrifying, and harder still to endure. Agatha and Madge were frantic for their mother, who had longed for her son's return and now longed for him to leave. In the early 1920s the sisters paid £800 for a cottage at Throwleigh on Dartmoor, where Monty lived with his sixty-five-year-old housekeeper, Mrs Taylor, a peroxide blonde with thirteen children. A few years later, Mrs Taylor died as she was moving with Monty to the South of France. Rooms had been taken for them there, again by Agatha and Madge; now Madge defied her husband's cold fury to travel to Marseille and do something for her brother, who pleaded that he was greatly weakened and lying alone in hospital. In fact the nurse who looked after him, Charlotte, had become the last to fall for his pitiable charm. Madge arrived to find him living in the nurse's flat. He was with Charlotte until he died in 1929, from a sudden stroke, while having a drink in a seafront café.

His death was probably a relief to his sisters. Nevertheless Agatha felt a kind of guilt about Monty; the chaos of his life haunted her, although he may have been less unhappy than she imagined. She sent occasional sums of money to ensure the upkeep of his grave in Marseille, and was anxious that flowers should be placed there on Armistice Day: 'You may rest assured it will be well looked after,' wrote one of Monty's fellow East Surreys in 1936.

Would Monty himself have cared? He grew up with love all around him, but the acceptance shown by his parents, the sense of responsibility felt by his sisters, made no difference in the end. None of it could fill the gaps. Perhaps that was why, when he filled in the Album of Confessions in 1897, he wrote that his favourite virtue was 'integrity': it was the quality he lacked above all others, although he *did* have others. He had all his father's charm – though less of his humour, and almost none of his moral sense – and he was not without self-knowledge. When asked whom he would be if not himself, his answer was 'a better man'.

His chief characteristics, he wrote, were 'skylarking and flirting, whittling, obstinacy, talking slang and getting into tempers'. His idea of misery was 'working and borrowing money'. His heroes were 'Fenians', his heroines Margaret Miller ('Gran') and Clara. His present state of mind was described as 'Oh my!?!' Pathetic answers, really; so unlike the sharp, crisp responses of his sister Madge. And the picture in which he sits behind a harnessed goat in the cart, Truelove, dressed in full coachman's regalia, is just the sort of joke that Madge might have conceived, but she would have pulled it off with an assured gleam in her eye. Monty looks merely silly. In another photograph he is in uniform: sitting on a bamboo bench at Ashfield, his legs hooked over those of two young men at either side of him, his eyes full of a confused zest for life. The last picture shows him outside his cottage on Dartmoor. He is leaning on a stick, wearing a dressing-gown, cravat and mangled hat, a cigarette dropping from his mouth. He looks dissolute beyond measure; a Lord Lucan discovered in sick old age; but a certain ashen charm survives.

Agatha was acutely aware of this charm, and having been under its spell she came to understand its nature. As a child, when Monty had dismissed her scathingly as 'the scrawny chicken', she had found him hopelessly glamorous (he was the best-looking of the Millers). Adult life taught her that a man could be weak yet irresistible. Her last Westmacott novel, *The Burden*, has a young girl in love with just such a man.

She still found it delightful to be married to Henry, but she perceived that it had its disadvantages. Henry had by now had

four different jobs. It never seemed difficult for him to get a job
– he had a large circle of wealthy friends – but it seemed quite
impossible for him to keep a job. Either he got tired of it and
chucked it, or it chucked him. Also, Henry spent money like
water, and never seemed to have any difficulty in getting credit.
His idea of settling his affairs was by borrowing . . .

As a small boy, Monty would receive his pocket money for the week
and spend it all instantly. 'Later in the week he would suddenly push
my sister into a shop, quickly order three penn'orth of a favourite
sweet and then look at my sister, daring her not to pay. Madge, who
had a great respect for public opinion, always did. Naturally she was
furious about it . . . Monty would merely smile at her serenely and
offer her one of the sweets.'[11]

Twenty years later, when Monty took money from James Watts
with which to build a boat, he also used it to set himself up in style
at a Jermyn Street hotel, buying silk pyjamas and a bonsai tree for his
room. To placate Madge he spent large amounts of her husband's
money on giving her presents and lunch at the Berkeley. It was the
same trick he had pulled as a boy; and Agatha would later write of
the terrible sadness of 'a grown man with the mentality of a child . . .
One must put away childish things –'; 'Yes . . . A man who is a child
is the most frightening thing in the world.'[12]

Agatha learned a good deal from Monty. Her large, sombre eyes
took in the smiling anxiety of her father, the baffled frustration of her
mother, Madge's concerned contempt. Even when Monty was away
from home – the problem of him supposedly 'solved' – Agatha was
aware of the weak dark presence that trickled through her family. She
understood him, in so far as it was possible. He informed her views
on human nature; helped to make her the wise realist of her detective fiction.

'In wartime, a man like that is a hero. But in peace – well, in peace
such men usually end up in prison. They like excitement, they can't
run straight, and they don't give a damn for society – and finally
they've no regard for human life.' This is from *Taken at the Flood* and
does not quite describe Monty: he was not a criminal and he was
capable of affection. But he belonged to the type, often portrayed in

her books and sometimes a killer, of the man who could have made something of his life, were it not for a mysterious inner fallibility. 'A slightly different arrangement of genes,' wrote Agatha in her autobiography of Monty, 'and he might have been a great man.' David Hunter in *Taken at the Flood*; Philip Lombard in *And Then There Were None*; Mike Rogers in *Endless Night*; Charles Arundell in *Dumb Witness*; Michael Rafiel in *Nemesis*; Leonard Vole in *Witness for the Prosecution*; Jacko Argyle in *Ordeal by Innocence* – they all have something of Monty in them.

Jacko Argyle is of particular interest. He is one of the five children adopted by Rachel and Leo Argyle, each of whom is given an upbringing of perfect regularity, in the belief that they will become well-adjusted little Argyles and fuse as a family. Yet they remain disparate, dissimilar, true to their heredity and origins; Jacko, for all the love and attention lavished upon him, grows up seductive and conscienceless.

> . . . Jacko, the intrinsic human being. Was Jacko, in the words of the old Calvinistic doctrine, 'a vessel appointed to destruction'? He'd been given every chance in life, hadn't he? Dr MacMaster's opinion, at any rate, was that he was one of those who are born to go wrong. No environment could have helped him or saved him. Was that true? Leo Argyle had spoken of him with indulgence, with pity. How had he put it? 'One of Nature's misfits' . . .

That was how Agatha saw Monty: she believed in the essential man ('Where am I with God's mark upon my brow?') and she believed that her brother, like Jacko Argyle, was essentially unsalvageable. The modern view, that upbringing forges nature, was not one she shared. Of course she knew that circumstance could make a difference: she herself was the product of a particular set of variables that had pushed her character one way rather than another. 'Character, *mon cher*, does not stand still. It can gather strength. It can also deteriorate,' says Hercule Poirot in *Taken at the Flood*. But later in the book he says: 'The tragedy of life is that *people do not change*.' This is a mantra with Poirot. In *Cards on the Table* he refuses to accept a confession of murder that he knows to be false, saying, 'I am right. I must be right.

I am willing to believe that you killed Mr Shaitana – *but you cannot have killed him in the way you say you did*. No one can do a thing that is not *dans son caractère!*'

Poirot is voicing the ideas of his creator. Agatha had an absolute belief that each person had an immutable essence, usually unknown even to themselves. 'What a person really *is*, is only apparent when the test comes – that is, the moment when you stand or fall on your own feet'.[13]

Monty fell, and would always fall. Only his charm held him up. In *They Do It With Mirrors* Agatha addressed the post-war faith in the power of philanthropy to change lives; partly because of Monty, she found it wanting. The book is set in and around a school for young offenders, run by a man named Lewis Serrocold – 'another man with ideals!' – who attempts to rehabilitate social misfits through psychiatry and education. Lewis is 'bitten by that same bug of wanting to improve everybody's lives for them. And really, you know, nobody can do that but yourself.'

Miss Marple talks to him about his belief in social engineering. 'I think sometimes, you know, one can overdo things . . . I mean the young people with a good heredity, and brought up wisely in a good home – and with grit and pluck and the ability to get on in life – well, they are really, when one comes down to it – the sort of people a country *needs* . . . Not that I don't appreciate . . . real compassion – and one should have compassion—'

'It is born in a man to be happy and into others to be unhappy,' Monty himself wrote in 1924. After all, if every other member of his family could write, why shouldn't he? Why not create stories, as his clever sisters did? During the time he spent in the cottage on Dartmoor, he covered page after page of a notebook. 'To me is at last given understanding sufficient to carry through my project wait and you shall see. It's all going to be so simple you will wonder why read and learn learn and read . . .'

He started several poems, plays and stories in his notebook, usually writing no more than a few lines of each. One story, 'Black Ivory', begins with Monty lying wounded in Africa. His servant gives him 'two little brown tablets. What are they I asked? Opium . . . do you good.' It has been said that Monty was addicted to drugs[14] and, although there is no outside evidence for this, his own words suggest that he took them at some point. Not least because so much of what he wrote reads like hallucination:

> The Glorious Dream
> May happen to any
> But better by far to happen to me . . .
> Oh come oh come
> Oh come away to play I say I've dreamed
> A dream I say say say
> Today or tomorrow there will be no sorrow

Yet within these ramblings there is a desperate search for meaning and structure.

> It's a long time since I have felt so thoroughly dissatisfied with my own arrangements for living [he wrote on Dartmoor]. It seems to me we many just follow my leader, and not in any way one's inclinations, those poverty bound can't help themselves, but an individual there is a lot in this word how many of us are individuals. Surprisingly few . . .
>
> Tomorrow I begin, the search for freedom, true happiness, and true selfishness. Tomorrow.

Around the time of Monty's sudden death, Agatha published a collection of short stories, *The Mysterious Mr. Quin*. One of these, 'The Man From The Sea', contained a passage about 'a disreputable dog'. The dog, who has spent his life roaming the streets of southern Spain,

> was standing in the middle of the road, yawning and stretching himself in the sun. Having prolonged his stretch to the utmost limits of ecstasy, he . . . looked round for any other good things that life might have to offer.
>
> And then, without the least warning, a ramshackle car careered

wildly round the corner, caught him full square and passed on
unheeding.

The dog rose to his feet . . . a vague dumb reproach in his
eyes, then fell over.

What a long road Agatha had travelled – one on which she herself
had been caught 'full square' – from the charming young girl who
lived at Ashfield and wrote poems like this one, 'Ma Ville Chérie',
remembering her stay with her parents in France:

> Oh pays de mon coeur
> À toi seulement je pense
> Oh Pau ma ville chérie
> Vers toi mon coeur s'élance . . .

When she wrote this Agatha was still in her idyll; despite her father's
death, life had scarcely touched her. With her long slim body, her
rivers of hair, which gleamed almost transparent in the sun, like the
sea in the bay at Torquay, she belonged to the dream world of her
own creation. A childhood friend wrote to her in 1966,

> I remember your lovely long fair hair. I was so amused by you
> remembering the dancing class! Now I recall it too, and a big
> mirror on the wall, into which I gazed at my reflection on my
> sixth birthday . . . I remember you too – in a lovely accordion
> pleated silk dress, and longing rather hopelessly for such a
> dazzler too. You were like the sea nymph Thetis with your
> flowing golden hair.[15]

Agatha lived a far more social life in the years after Frederick's death,
although this made no difference to the fact that she was closer than
ever to her mother. She went to dance classes where she was 'one of
the elect' in her pleats, she attended Miss Guyer's school two days a
week, she made friends. James Watts's sister Nan, whom she had met
for the first time at Madge's wedding, remained close to her all her
life (and was briefly a crush of Monty's). Nearer to hand were the
five Huxley sisters – 'those Huxley girls' – who strode along the Strand

at Torquay with their arms swinging and heads thrown back with laughter and, 'cardinal sin against them, *they did not wear gloves*'; and the Lucys, who lived on the beautiful sweep of Hesketh Crescent[16] and 'had rather slurred lazy voices that I found very attractive'. Up and down the seven hills the girls would walk in their corsets, one hand on their hats, the clean sea air dancing around them. They were carefree. The Lucys in particular worried about nothing in the world, 'What does it matter, Aggie?' They ate whatever they wanted – sumptuous teas, Devonshire cream, nougat bought at seaside stalls – and worked it off with walking, tennis, roller-skating on the pier, swimming in the ladies' bathing cove. They went to Torquay Regatta, to the fair on the seafront with its coconut shy and firework display, to garden parties with their pistachio ices, muscat grapes and warm swelling nectarines. It seemed that the sun shone all the time upon these healthy young animals, 'kicking up their heels like fillies in a field'.[17] 'We were conscious of all the happiness that awaited us . . . we had belief and joy in life.'[18] It was an enchanted atmosphere, protected by structures as unyielding as the bathing-machine that took Agatha, in her black alpaca swimsuit, down to the sea, where she would swim out and be free.

'I remember you as Miss Miller,' read a letter written to Agatha in 1970 by a man who had known her when he was a small boy. 'Miss Beadon, of "Copthorne", I also remember, and I was thrilled one day to hear her say to you, "Come to tea," and my thinking how wonderful it was being able to invite anyone to tea like that, without asking your mother's permission first!'

Agatha loved it all – she had a gift for pleasure, 'anything she did, she enjoyed'[19] – and her mother encouraged it all. 'I wanted you to have a good time and pretty clothes and enjoy yourself in a young, natural way,' she says, in *Unfinished Portrait*. Clara delighted in Agatha's attractiveness, which had burst easily from the child's solemn little chrysalis. Nevertheless these were the thoughts that Agatha wrote for her mother, as Miriam, after Celia turns down a marriage proposal: 'And secretly, in spite of her disappointment and her fear for Celia's future, a little thread ran singing joyfully, "She will not leave me yet. She will not leave me yet . . ."'

After her husband's death Clara had little independent life. As a widow she found herself marginalised, although this was really more to do with lack of money. It made little difference to Agatha that she had to walk everywhere or paint her hats rather than buy new ones; that was how most of her friends lived anyway. None of the Torquay girls with whom she mixed was 'rich', they were merely 'comfortable', with all the attendant snobbery of the proudly non-vulgar (the Lucys are described in Agatha's autobiography as having a good laugh at the 'common legs' of the local dancing teacher).[20] But to a woman like Clara, money meant status. She was not importunate, as her mother had been, but neither did she have the powerful social assurance of Margaret Miller. Of course poverty is a relative thing. Clara lived in a big house with servants, she was helped from time to time by her son-in-law; she was not in actual need. Nevertheless she would seek to sell the Miller grave plot in the Greenwood Cemetery in New York, for which she had to pay just thirty dollars or so a year, saying that the family was 'never likely to be in America and [was] in extremely low financial circumstances'. Money was a continual worry to her, and the lack of it changed her life. She was unable to offer hospitality – the ingredients for a dinner party would have eaten deeply into her income – therefore could expect none in return. Her health had weakened to the point at which Torquay's unforgiving hills were beyond her, and she could not afford taxis. Although her mind bounced around as restlessly as ever, her world was inert; Agatha was at the centre of it and, in *Unfinished Portrait*, the force of the mother's personality lures her daughter into a soft, mesmerised submission.

> The evenings were some of the happiest times mother and daughter spent together. They had supper early, at seven, and afterward would go up to the schoolroom, and Celia would do fancy work, and her mother would read to her. Reading aloud would make Miriam sleepy. Her voice would go queer and blurry, her head would tilt forward . . .

Clara read Scott and Dickens to Agatha, missing out any bits she found boring ('All these descriptions,' she said of *Marmion*, 'one can have too many of them'). She took her off suddenly to see one of Sir Henry Irving's last performances, given in Exeter, in *Becket*. For all her physical diminishment she remained unchanged to Agatha: impulsive, magical, cleaving like a knife to the heart of life. 'Celia thought about her mother . . . her small eager face, her tiny hands and feet, her small delicate ears, her thin high-bridged nose. Her mother – oh, there was no one like her mother in the whole world.'

When Agatha was fifteen Clara let Ashfield for the winter and took her daughter off to Paris. They stayed at the Hôtel d'Iéna while Clara looked for a *pensionnat* at which Agatha might pursue her desultory education. 'To my mother trying a school was exactly like trying a new restaurant.' She was sent to 'Mademoiselle T's', where Madge had stayed before her, then to 'Miss Hogg's school' at Auteuil, then to 'Miss Dryden's' near the Arc de Triomphe. That was the kind of place girls like Agatha attended; if they failed to marry, it was the kind of place they ran.

Agatha stayed in Paris for almost two years, and was eventually very happy there, although when Clara had first returned to England she suffered terribly; as much for Clara as for herself, but then this amounted to the same thing. Sometimes it was as if she were the mother, Clara the child whom she yearned to protect. 'If she put on a blouse her mother had made for her, the tears would come into her eyes as she thought of her mother stitching at it.' Within her love there was a painful sense of her mother's vulnerability, of the pathos in her indomitable vitality. So sensitive was Agatha's imagination that she was able to *become* Clara, or so she believed: sitting alone at Ashfield, the spectacles slipping off her nose as she fell asleep over her copy of *Nicholas Nickleby*, the fire dying beside her in the schoolroom.

Yet the natural joy in Agatha would always, in youth, leap into life. The dusk and honey colours of Paris began to charm her eyes. She had her first adult clothes, among them a pale grey *crêpe de Chine* 'semi-evening dress', which had to be filled out with flounces due to her lack of chest. She saw Sarah Bernhardt and Réjane at the Comédie Française. She was taken to the opera by American friends of her grandfather, whose daughter was singing Marguerite in *Faust*. She took classes in painting, in *dictée* ('Vous, qui parlez si bien le français, vous avez fait vingt-cinq fautes!'), in dancing and deportment, ('Suppose, now, you were about to sit down by an elderly married lady. How would you sit?'). She ate cakes at Rumpelmayer's, 'those glorious cakes with cream and *marron* piping of a sickliness which was incomparable.' She fell for a hotel reception clerk, 'tall and thin, rather like a tapeworm', around whom she invented wild romantic fantasies. Later she met a young man, Rudy, half American and half French, with whom she skated at the Palais de Glace. 'From that moment forward I stepped out of the territory of hero worship . . . I did not fall in love with Rudy – perhaps I might have, if I had met him more often, but I did suddenly feel *different*.'[21]

It was delight, all of it; the life that any normal, healthy, attractive young girl would long to live. But it left something out. At the end of this passage in her autobiography Agatha wrote, almost matter-of-factly, 'One dream of mine faded before I left Paris.' She meant the dream of music. The truth was that during her time in France 'it was the music that really filled her life'. While the young Miss Miller was merrily engaged upon dress fittings and teenage crushes her pure, poetic soul was soaring inside her.

'Clearer and clearer, higher and higher – each wave rising above the last . . .' This is how she described music in one of her earliest stories, 'The Call of Wings'.[22] 'It was a strange tune – strictly speaking, it was not a tune at all, but a single phrase, not unlike the slow turn given out by the violins of *Rienzi*, repeated again and again, passing from key to key, from harmony to harmony, but always rising and attaining each time to a greater and more boundless freedom . . .'

Music, for Agatha, was the essence of the numinous. Its notes and sounds made the ineffable real, whole, graspable. For a brief time she believed she could inhabit its world. She was like a young girl who dreams of dancing in *Swan Lake*, entering the land of aquamarine and gauze; for such girls nothing, thereafter, is ever quite so strongly desired. At the age of sixty-three Agatha played the confessions game for the last time – in the drawing room at Greenway, with its beautiful Steinway in the corner – and, in reply to the question 'If not yourself, who would you be?', she wrote, 'an opera singer'. Writing, for her, was the thing that she did because she had failed at music.

She trained hard at the piano in Paris with a teacher named Charles Furster, practising for anything up to seven hours a day. But at an informal concert, towards the end of her stay, nerves overwhelmed her and she gave a catastrophic performance. 'To be an artist one must be able to shut out the world – if you feel it there listening to you, then you must feel it as a stimulus,' was how, in *Unfinished Portrait*, she recalled Furster's verdict upon her. 'But Mademoiselle Celia, she will give of her best to an audience of one – of two people – and she will play best of all to herself with the door closed.'

She learned singing with the prestigious Monsieur Boué. She had a fine, clear soprano voice which, mysteriously, flowered in public: when she sang, the outside world was a stimulus, and had been ever since she had triumphed as Colonel Fairfax in *Yeomen of the Guard* – 'one of the highlights of my existence' – which she had sung with the Huxley sisters at the Parish Rooms in Torquay.

After six months with Boué she was allowed to perform arias: 'Te Gelida Manina' from *La Bohème* and *Tosca*'s exquisite 'Vissi d'artè'. When she returned to England she continued to study, and sang to acclaim at parties and local concerts. Then, after a visit with Madge in 1909 to see *The Ring* at Covent Garden, the dream of singing – of becoming an Isolde – truly took flight. She could imagine nothing more magical than to pierce the heart of music, to sound the call of wings ('*I saw them* – the Wings! . . . the colour of them! *Wing colour* . . .'). Something in Agatha longed to step outside herself and her imaginative world, to burst clear of its solitude and perform.

Wagner she would love all her life: his music is at the heart of her very late novel, *Passenger to Frankfurt*. But when, in 1909, an American family friend with connections at the Metropolitan Opera House agreed to listen to her singing she was told, very kindly, that her voice was that of a concert singer only. Accomplished, charming, essentially weak.

'So I put wishful thinking aside,' she wrote in her autobiography. 'I pointed out to mother that she could now save the expense of music lessons. I could sing as much as I liked, but there was no point in going on studying singing. I had never really believed that my dream[23] could come true – but it is a good thing to have *had* a dream and to have enjoyed it, so long as you do not clutch too hard.'

Sane, wise, realistic Agatha: her idea of misery, in the confessions entry that she made in 1903, was 'to wish for the unattainable', and this was what she truly believed. But this, from her Westmacott novel

Giant's Bread, is what she truly felt. The character speaking is Jane Harding, whose beautiful soprano is too weak for opera but who sings it nonetheless. In doing so she wrecks her voice for ever.

'I pretend I don't mind – but I do . . . I do. I loved singing. I loved it, loved it, loved it . . . That lovely Whitsuntide music of Solveig. I shall never sing it again.'

Jane fails at the thing she most wants to do and, in the face of this, she is magnificent. 'It's been a gamble, you know, all along – my voice was never really strong enough. I gambled with it. So far I won – now, I've lost. Well, there it is! One must be a good gambler and not let the hands twitch . . .' This kind of courage, or personality, was not Agatha's, although she admired it more than almost anything. Yet there is something of the secret Agatha in Jane: Jane as Solveig in *Peer Gynt*, 'with her silver thread singing steadily upward and ever upward, higher and higher, till the last note was left to her – high and incredibly pure . . .' Then her voice was 'gone, my child. Gone for good.'

Jane is supremely generous: unselfish, and therefore unsuccessful, as both a woman and an artist. She gives up her voice for a man: Vernon Deyre, who as a small boy played with Poodle, Squirrel and Tree, and who has grown up to be a musician; he wants Jane to sing in his first opera and, because she loves him, she agrees. Yet Vernon falls for Nell Vereker, a drifting fair-haired beauty with the looks of a nymph and the soul of a *bourgeoise*. Nell has no talent, except for men, but even if she had she would have risked nothing for it. She is Agatha's lesser self. Her greater self is Vernon who, after a period of nervous breakdown, dedicates his life to art.

As a child Vernon had been frightened of the piano in his house – 'The Beast', as he thought of it, with its terrible white teeth – but that was because he was resisting his calling. As a young man he hears the words 'This night shall thy soul be required of thee', and knows that he must give his life to music:

I couldn't run away any longer . . . music's the most wonderful thing in the world . . .

There's so much to know – to learn. I don't want to play things – never that. But I want to know about every instrument there is. What it can do, what are its limitations, what are its possibilities. And the notes, too. There are notes they don't use – notes that they ought to use. I know there are . . .

Agatha began to write much more consistently in her late teens, although writing did not fill her mind as music had. It did not have the same capacity to stretch the world into its fourth dimension, which is what Vernon Deyre seeks to do and what interested Agatha so much in *Giant's Bread*. Music and infinity, music and mystery, music and art were as one to her: music left nothing out. Of Vernon Deyre she wrote:

He called it vision for it seemed more that than sound.[24] Seeing and hearing were one – curves and spirals of sounds, ascending, descending, returning.

. . . He snatched at paper, jotted down brief scrawled hieroglyphics, a kind of frantic shorthand. There were years of work ahead of him, but he knew that he should never again recapture this first freshness and clearness of vision.

It must be so – and so: a whole weight of metal – brass – all the brass in the world.

And those new glass sounds . . . ringing, clear.

He was happy.

And so 'The Call of Wings' was about the transubstantial power of sound; and Agatha's first full-length story, 'The House of Beauty', lived within the sphere of dreams, the places she had imagined as a child and to which music had taken her. 'He was at the door of the House. The exquisite stillness was unbroken. He put the key in the lock and turned it.

'Just for a moment he waited, to realise to the full the perfect, the ineffable, the all-satisfying completeness of joy . . .'

Clara had encouraged Agatha to produce stories, 'as Madge had done', and from the age of eighteen she banged them out on Madge's typewriter before signing them with various pseudonyms: Mack

Miller, Nathaniel Miller, Sydney West. Unlike Madge, however, she failed to get anything published. This must have driven her to distraction. She knew she was as good as Madge. Her autobiography insists upon her lack of ambition at this time, and indeed a good deal of her attention was taken up with dances and house-parties; but the creativity – and competitiveness – within Agatha would not be stilled. Her life was enchantingly ordinary. Her imagination was fierce and unstoppable.

> I pass
> Where'er I've a mind
> With a laugh as I dance,
> And a leap so high . . .
> And nobody ever sees Harlequin,
> Happy-go-lucky Harlequin,
> Go by.[25]

Photographs from this time tell the tale of Agatha's social life: the regatta at Torquay; a party of theatricals at nearby Cockington Court (Agatha dressed as a gypsy, 'Sister Anne'); a meet of the South Devon Foxhounds; a house-party at Thorp Arch Hall for the St Leger meeting at Doncaster; another at Littlegreen House[26] in Petersfield, for Goodwood. The captions are carefully inked next to the pictures, out of which Agatha smiles confidently. She was an extremely attractive girl. She was not brilliant but she had an air of charming self-assurance; partly because socially, at least, she was out of Madge's shadow. Despite her Roman nose and heavy grey eyes – her face was very much her father's – she oozed a delicate, firm femininity. Men liked her and she dealt with this easily, naturally.

'She took it for granted that she was pretty – and she *was* pretty – tall, slender, and graceful, with very fair flaxen hair and Scandinavian fairness and delicacy of colouring.'[27]

No doubt Clara told her how attractive she looked in her sweeping skirts, with her quantities of pale hair – so long that she could sit on it – piled on her head. But Agatha herself thought she was beautiful. 'I was a lovely girl.' She was Celia going to a fancy-dress ball as Marguerite from *Faust*, she was Nell Vereker in the moonlight with her 'princess's cascade of golden hair'. She was a pierrette in high-necked blouses, a Thetis in patent leather-buttoned boots, an Isolde with tonged curls. Despite the complex apparatus of Edwardian dressing, her images of herself were always of someone loose and free and ethereal. Memories of how she had once looked would haunt her in later life.

> The golden green light, the softness in the air – with them came a quickened pulse, a stirring of the blood, a sudden impatience.
> A girl came through the trees towards him – a girl with pale, gleaming hair and a rose flushed skin.
> He thought, 'How beautiful – how unutterably beautiful.'[28]

So the nymph danced through the worlds of her protected youth, gazing towards a blissful future. What would happen to her? It was obvious. She would meet a man – 'Her Fate' – and have a wonderful life with him, cooking or ordering the 'receipts' that her mother had copied into an exercise book, giving birth to his child and wrapping it in her own christening lace, creating a world like Ashfield.

> (Pierrot singing to the moon
> For love of me . . .
> Ages welling
> Find me dwelling,
> Ne'er rebelling,
> By his fire.)

This was the only future that Agatha consciously contemplated. It was with this end in sight that she danced, dressed herself prettily and sang after dinner (occasionally to a large teddy-bear: 'All I can offer in excuse is that all the girls did that sort of thing').[29] She was waiting to fulfil her female destiny; the one that women still dream of, on the whole.

'I wasn't sitting and writing,' she said much later,[30] 'I was going about meeting young men and embroidering great bunches of clematis on cushions . . . We did lots of creative things in those days; perhaps that's why we didn't feel the need for careers. When I was sixteen or seventeen only financial disability would have forced you out into the world. I think we had more fun then. Now girls have to worry about A levels . . . Flirtations to us meant a lot. You had lots succeeding each other, you went to all the dances and on your card you'd given three dances to one young man and only two to the other; it made you feel on top of the world. You were a young female, not bad looking, and they had to please you.'

(Columbine sits by my fire!
She is mine! She is mine!
Columbine!)

'People went to a lot of trouble arranging things. When you went to a house-party there were always three or four young men and nice-looking young girls so they could all have a good time . . . Even if you weren't allowed more than three dances with one young man, it was quite fun to get hold of him for that time.' More than three dances with the same man was considered 'fast' ('but one managed!').[31] The innocence of this world was absolute, and the men preferred it that way; they treasured the purity of the girls they might marry. 'Just to be a woman made one *precious* . . .'[32] Men had affairs with married women, or with 'little friends' in London. To Agatha, the idea that she would have sex with anyone but her future husband was as remote as catching the plague.

She and her friends were protected, necessarily she believed, against their own vulnerability. 'In the past there were safeguards,' as she wrote in her 1969 novel *Hallowe'en Party*. 'People were looking after them [girls]. Their mothers looked after them . . .' Yet Agatha was not ignorant. She had heard all her life the whisperings of her grandmothers. A girl she knew had gone to stay with a schoolfriend and, too innocent to know quite what was happening, had been made pregnant by the friend's *roué* father. A male friend was shocked to be invited by a young girl – apparently of the marriageable variety – to spend an hour with him at a hotel before they went on to a dance. 'I've often done it,' she said.

Agatha might not have been as shocked as the man had been: while she understood the importance of purity, she was no prude. She saw that purity derived its value from the concomitant value of sex. Later, she also saw that innocence need be nothing of the kind, and that conventional morality might have its own impurity. Jane Harding in *Giant's Bread* sleeps with Vernon, Nell marries him; there is no doubt whatever that Jane has the cleaner soul.

But Jane is of the *demi-monde*. The world of Agatha's youth did not admit to her kind of transgression. Its sins took place behind curtains that were shaken every morning by servants, within structures as rigid as corsets, while smiles were fixed and tea was poured. Agatha was starting to realise all this as she wrote her first novel, *Snow Upon the Desert*, in around 1909. Its subject matter is the arrangement of love lives: sex lives. It is as far removed as possible from the stories and poems that had flowered from dreams; it was born of observation rather than fantasy; and it shows her, for the first time, getting to grips with the realities of being a writer.

Poverty and ill-health had led Clara to give her daughter her first season in Cairo, rather than London. It was there that Agatha found the material for *Snow Upon the Desert*. The pretty but rather silent girl – 'You had better try to teach her to talk,' said a handsome captain to Clara, after a wordless turn with Agatha around the floor – was in fact noting everything, missing neither a trick nor a nuance of the sexual and social *ronde* taking place around her. Slowly, remorselessly, she was developing her grasp of human movements and motives, seeing and delighting in their predictability.

On holiday in Rhodes, watching the to-and-fro of hotel life, Agatha's detective Hercule Poirot comes to the same conclusion that she herself had done years earlier.

'Nature repeats herself more often than one would imagine. The sea', he added thoughtfully, 'has infinitely more variety.'

Sarah turned her head sideways and asked: 'You think that human beings tend to reproduce certain patterns? Stereotyped patterns?'

'*Précisement*.'[33]

Agatha loved her three months at the Gezirah Palace Hotel. At this time Cairo was a familiar – and cheap – destination for people of her class. She stuck into her albums many photographs from her stay, as usual carefully captioned: 'Polo'; 'Cairo races'; 'Picnic in desert'; 'Mrs Appleton, Duke of Connaught, Lord Feilding'. The exoticism of her surroundings, which would later set her imagination aflame, meant almost nothing to her. As far as she was concerned Cairo was Torquay with pyramids, Kensington-over-Sands. As one of the characters in *Snow Upon the Desert*, Lady Charminster, puts it: 'Egypt (social Egypt, not the tourists' Egypt, all mummies and tombs and pyramids, but our Egypt) . . .'.

During the winter there were five dances every week, and Agatha – coolly shimmering in a pale pink shot satin dress, made by a Levantine seamstress – met around thirty men. 'Cairo as Cairo meant nothing to me – girls between eighteen and twenty-one seldom thought of anything but young men, and very right and proper too!'[34] Considering how absorbed she professes to have been in enjoyment, it is remarkable how much she noticed. Agatha had been accustomed all her life to the conversation of women, the delicious phrases that could be picked out and stored. Like Miss Marple, 'who was very skilful in tones of voice', having 'done so much listening in her life'[35] – and, indeed, like the musician she was – Agatha had an immaculately tuned ear. The opening lines of *Snow Upon the Desert* showed her ease in re-creating what she had heard in Egypt:

> 'Rosamund', said Lady Charminster, 'is an amazing girl!' Then fearing that perhaps she had not done herself justice, she added, with a flash of inspiration: 'She can neither be ignored nor explained!'
>
> This was distinctly good. Lady Charminster felt that she had never done better. It was terse, it was apt, it was one of those concise sayings that have a certain backing of truth to their epigrammatic force . . .
>
> Of course, anywhere but in Cairo, Lady Charminster reflected, she would not have been sitting beside Connie Ansell, but Egypt, in its social sense, was distinctly limited.

Snow Upon the Desert is a comedy of manners, worldly in the extreme and, although its structure is hopelessly disordered – two ideas stitched determinedly into one – in terms of character portrayal it is the finished article. This was what Agatha could do, above all, as a writer: *understand people*. That was her true, her innate gift. As soon as she realised it, she was set free. The character of Rosamund Vaughan was her starting point, and she is almost worthy of a short story by Scott Fitzgerald: an ageing beauty, unmarried, with a slightly used quality that can perplex, repel and fascinate. 'Come what might, she would take her pleasure.'

Agatha had observed the original of this girl – 'hardly a girl in my eyes, because she must have been close on thirty'[35] – having supper at the Cairo dances, sitting between the same two men every night, keeping both in thrall. 'She will have to make up her mind between them some time,' was the phrase that Agatha overheard; it was the kind of thing Margaret Miller might have said, and it set her off: on Rosamund, on her novel, and on ideas that she would use all her life.

The way in which Rosamund plays off her two men recurs again and again in the detective novels. Here was one of the patterns that Agatha had begun to perceive, and in Rosamund there is something of – for instance – Arlena Marshall in *Evil Under the Sun*, or Valentine Chantry in *Triangle at Rhodes*. These women cannot exist without male admiration. For this reason the world sees them as dangerous. Agatha's instinct told her that they were in fact vulnerable: prey rather than predators. In Rosamund – who at the end of the novel is doomed, a *femme fatale* about to be killed – lie the origins of the belief that underpins Agatha's detective fiction, that it is a victim's character that determines his or her fate. It was this that always interested her: the distilled essence of human nature, contained within the act of murder.

She was later contemptuous of *Snow Upon the Desert*, which was rejected for publication. 'I made the heroine deaf,' was what she always said about the book, as if that in some way invalidated the whole enterprise. Encouraged by Clara, to whom Agatha's novel was both an excitement and an inevitability (what couldn't her daughters do, after all?), she sent the manuscript to a neighbour in Torquay, the writer Eden Philpotts. He responded with perceptive kindness – 'You have a great feeling for dialogue' – and sent Agatha an introduction to his own literary agent, Hughes Massie. This firm would later have the immeasurable good fortune to represent her. But Massie himself, whom Agatha went to see in London, told her that *Snow Upon the Desert* was best forgotten.

Better advice would have been to tell her to rewrite the book, as it is full of quality. Almost every character is given a phrase, an insight, that brings them to life: Agatha could see people almost as well as she could hear them and, above all, she could intuit. Bitchy little Hyacinth, for example, desperate for the attention of every man in Cairo, is 'clever, very clever, so clever that no man ever suspected the fact'. Told by one of her targets, Tony, that his fiancée is coming out to Egypt, she 'cogitated deeply. "Will she interfere with me?" was perhaps the burden of her maidenly meditation. After a moment's consideration of this knotty question, she turned to Farquhar with her sweetest and gentlest smile. 'Is not the sunset beautiful?' she murmured . . .' And the semi-deaf heroine, Melancy, engaged to Tony and meeting him again for the first time in months:

> It was all so different from what she had planned – but much nicer – oh, yes, much nicer! She impressed this latter fact on her mind, it was much more natural, much simpler – and jollier.
>
> 'This is just heavenly!' sighed Tony, gazing rapturously at his fiancée, with his mouth full of whitebait.
>
> 'I was so disappointed and lonely when you didn't come this morning,' murmured Melancy.
>
> 'Poor little girl!' said Tony, touched and distinctly approving. 'Very nice and right of Melancy,' so ran his thoughts . . .'

Then Melancy falls in love with another man, and Agatha's book moves tentatively towards the territory she would later explore in her Mary Westmacott novels: that of the human mysteries that cannot be solved.

> The breathing living personality of the man who had just left her replaced all else . . . Melancy looked around her. The beauty of the rose garden was as great as ever, but she saw it with different eyes. A world of warm living realities had taken the place of dreams . . .
>
> From Melancy's heart went forth a warm personal need of all this quivering, feeling world around her. In the distance, she

heard voices. They came to her with the human call of comrade-
ship. Her gladness was full and complete.

This was not yet Agatha's own experience: she did not fall in love in
Cairo, and would not do so for another three years. But she knew
what it would feel like, so she wrote it anyway.

She lifted a hanging rose, and laid it against her cheek. It was
not for its beauty, but because it was alive.

The Husband

'You think you admire moral qualities, but when you fall in love,
you revert to the primitive where the physical is all that counts'
(from *The Man in the Brown Suit* by Agatha Christie)

'She lifted up her eyes and loved him, with that love which was her doom'
(from *The Idylls of the King* by Alfred, Lord Tennyson)

Ugbrooke House, near Exeter, is one of the great Devon mansions,
a house of mythic beauty. By daylight its stone is rose-pink, at
night it is ethereal and shadowy. It was here, on 12 October
1912, that Agatha Miller first met Archie Christie, when he strode up
and asked for three dances on her card. After two of these he asked
for three more. Agatha's card was full but she gave in when Archie
told her to cut the other partners, showing what was, for her, an
unusual disregard for the conventions.

Archie was twenty-three, almost exactly a year older than Agatha.
He had a 'decided manner, an air of being able to get his own way
always'. He was long, lean, intense; and he had that mysterious
quality of romance before which women are helpless. He had fallen
too, though. He had no money with which to set up a home and
no short-term prospects, but he determined from the first to possess
Agatha.

At the time of their meeting he was a second lieutenant in the
Royal Field Artillery, ambitious for advancement. He had decided
upon the means: a career as a pilot. His clear brain, whose practi-

cality was so alien to Agatha that she found it romantically compelling, saw aeroplanes not as something magical but as an inevitable future in which he could play a part. He had therefore paid seventy-five pounds for flying lessons on Salisbury Plain and, three months before he met Agatha, became the 245th qualified aviator in Britain. All of this he wrote in the notebook that logged the important facts of his life. Archie liked to organise his memories in this way. '16th July: Got Royal Aero Club Certificate on a Bristol Box Kite after being at the school about a month on leave from Exeter. Applied to join the Royal Flying Corps and went back to Exeter.'

Archie was one of several members of the Exeter garrison invited to the dance at Ugbrooke by its owners, Lord and Lady Clifford of Chudleigh; Agatha had been asked by friends of the Cliffords. She had intended to meet there another soldier, Arthur Griffiths, with whom she had had a light flirtation at Thorp Arch Hall. He was unable to attend but wrote to her suggesting that she look out for his friend Christie, who was a good dancer and might amuse her.

'12th October: Went to dance at Lord Clifford of Chudleigh's,' wrote Archie in his notebook. And not long after his night amid the pink stone arches and moonlit balconies, he chugged up Barton Road on his motorbike. He took tea with Clara; he waited. Across the road at Rooklands, Agatha played badminton with the son of the house, also smitten with her. The last entirely carefree moments of her life were spent practising dance steps ('We were, I think, tangoing'); then her mother telephoned to summon her home. She was reluctant to come. 'One of your young men,' Clara had said, not having caught the name properly, and however much Agatha had dreamed of seeing Archie Christie again (but how, in those days?) she did not for a moment think it was he who might be waiting for her. Such an effort he had made to find her. He stood when she entered the drawing-room, and gave his embarrassed story about having been 'in the neighbourhood'. He stayed to supper.

The two saw each other several times afterwards in quick succession; exquisitely, increasingly frustrated by the customs of the time. Archie asked Agatha to a concert in Exeter followed by tea, Clara informed him that Agatha could not take tea in a hotel with a man, so he invited Clara to come too; she relented to the extent of allowing him to give tea to her daughter – alone – at Exeter railway station. Agatha asked Archie to the New Year Ball at the start of 1913, at which he was 'completely silent'. Two days later, on 4 January, Archie's log records that he 'went to Ashfield Torquay and concert at the Pavilion'. The music that night was Agatha's beloved Wagner. The Pavilion was then newly completed, a fresh white and green building on the seafront. She and Archie sat beside each other beneath its domed skylight, their sleeves touching, listening to the music. Afterwards they went upstairs to the schoolroom at home, as Agatha put it in her autobiography 'to play the piano'; then Archie turned to her with sudden fierceness and said, 'You've got to marry me, you've *got* to marry me.' She was surely not surprised, despite her superficial bemusement. He had known – he told her – from the night of the dance at Ugbrooke. He was leaving in two days' time to start his training at Salisbury Plain with the Royal Flying Corps, and he needed to be sure of Agatha first. She stalled, but the next day she spoke to Clara: 'I'm sorry Mother, I've got to tell you. Archie Christie has asked me to marry him and I want to, I want to dreadfully.' The wedding would not take place for almost two years, and its delays and cancellations – due to Clara's opposition, lack of money, the outbreak of war – look, in retrospect, like so many signs that it should never have happened. Yet the urge for it grew ever stronger in both parties. Every time one broke it off, the subsequent reunion was sweeter: so dependency grew, and the belief that here was love for ever.

At the time of the proposal Agatha was engaged to another man, an obstacle that Archie dismissed as a housemaid might swat a fly. She had received several offers of marriage from her late teens onwards. Her sweet, serene, assured femininity made her extremely attractive to men, both sexually and as wife material. 'You are very lovely (however ruffled your hair is) and have the most perfect nature I can imagine,' Archie wrote to Agatha in 1914, and this was how many saw her. Later she would tell her second husband that she had no gift for men – 'I shall never have the proper . . . Olympian attitude towards the male sex,' she wrote in 1930 – but as a girl, before her life changed so completely, hers was an entirely natural female instinct. Like Nell Vereker in *Giant's Bread*, she had a pleasure in herself that was both innocent and knowing. Agatha liked men very much – preferred them to women on the whole – and she showed this in a way that *they* liked.

Her first two proposals came from men she had met in Cairo. One made his approach through her mother: 'You know Captain Hibberd wanted to marry you, I suppose?' Clara told Agatha as they were sailing home. She had refused him on her daughter's behalf, a presumption to which even Agatha objected. 'I really do think, Mother, that you might let me have my own proposals.' Clara agreed; but she still hoped, to an extent, to control events.

There were three proposals before Archie that counted for something. The first was from a man she met in around 1911 while she was staying in Warwickshire with the Ralston-Patricks, 'great hunting people', who, most unusually for this time, owned a car (Agatha first became aware of cars at the end of the nineteenth century, when visiting Paris with her parents; 'Monty would *love* them,' Clara had said). She was sitting side-saddle on her mount when a man of about thirty-five, a colonel named Bolton Fletcher, was introduced to her. That evening she appeared at a fancy-dress party as Elaine, Tennyson's 'lily maid of Astolat', wearing a white dress and a pearl cap; it was a costume to suit her *princesse lointaine* allure and it certainly aroused the chivalric knight in Fletcher, who went straight into action. He pursued Agatha as hard as Archie did later, although with a good deal more money and experience at his command. He sent extravagant presents and wonderful love letters. 'Technically he knew a great deal about women,' was her judgement upon a similar type of man, in the Westmacott novel *A Daughter's a Daughter*.

Fletcher called Agatha the perfect Elaine, and this was the way she liked to see herself: sitting 'high in her chamber', as Tennyson wrote, combing her long pale hair, dreaming of Lancelot. She was flattered, she was enjoying herself, she wondered if perhaps this was love? In fact she went a fair way to being overwhelmed. When – in a distant echo of modern sexual mores – Fletcher proposed to her on their third meeting, she 'felt enveloped in a storm of emotion'; it had nothing really to do with the man himself, everything to do with his expertise. '"When you say you don't feel anything for me," he said softly, "you're a liar."'[1] Agatha was filled with an excitement she did not understand, and was confused and tempted. So too was Clara. Part of her liked the idea of an older husband for her daughter, a man of the world, who knew how to treat women and who, above all, was rich. 'I've been praying so that a good man would come along and give you a good home and make you happy . . . There's so little money,' she said in *Unfinished Portrait*. But she understood Agatha's bewildered resistance, and another part of her was relieved by it. She told Fletcher to wait six months. When, at the end of that time, he sent a telegram demanding a firm answer to his proposal, Agatha found herself writing, 'No,' then falling asleep like a tired little girl.

She never regretted turning down Bolton Fletcher, although later she played with the idea that the marriage might have worked. In her detective novel *Three Act Tragedy* she has the young 'Egg' Lytton-Gore in love with a much older man: 'Girls were always attracted to middle-aged men with interesting pasts.' The relationship is all about hero-worship on one side, youth-worship on the other, but this does not mean it would be more difficult to sustain than a marriage between apparent equals, or one that is apparently without illusions. 'Lady Mary, you wouldn't like your girl to marry a man twice her own age,' a character says to Egg's mother. 'Her answer surprised him. "It might be safer so . . . At that age a man's follies and sins are definitely behind him; they are not – still to come . . ."'

There was neither folly nor sin in Wilfred Pirie, with whom Agatha was next entangled. He was merely a terrible bore: 'young and intensely solemn about life', as she wrote of 'Jim', his fictional representation in *Unfinished Portrait*, and 'very strong on willpower. He had books about it which he lent to Celia. He was very fond of lending books. He was also interested in theosophy, bimetallism, economics, and Christian Science. He liked Celia because she listened so attentively. She read all the books and made intelligent comments on them.'

As a girl Agatha had sought to please, with her answers in the

Album of Confessions: her desire to be 'surrounded by babies', her dislike of 'affectation and vulgarity'. Now, in agreeing to marry Wilfred, she was doing the same thing. All her life she believed in duty ('She had a problem to solve, the problem of her own future conduct; and, perhaps strangely, it presented itself to her . . . as a question of duty.'[2]) It was a function of upbringing, of generation. But the complexity of Agatha's nature meant that pleasing other people was also, more perversely, a means to inner escape. If she did what was wanted, what was expected, who knew what mysterious thoughts she might hide beneath the facade?

She did not take Wilfred seriously as a man. Kissing him was deadly dull and her grandmother, the magnificent Margaret, despised his non-drinking, non-smoking, theosophical ways. ('He was very polite, very formal and, to her mind, intensely boring . . . The thought flashed across her brain, "Better stuff in our young days."'[3]) But he presented to her a future both safe and oddly liberating. His family, the Piries, were old friends of the Millers; his mother and Agatha had adored each other for years. Moreover, Wilfred was a sub-lieutenant in the Royal Navy, which meant that when he was away Agatha could live at Ashfield. In fact she need hardly leave home. Her relationship with Clara would be almost unchanged. 'A daughter's a daughter all your life', as Agatha wrote in her Mary Westmacott novel; this was what Clara wanted, for Agatha to move into the world of adulthood but to remain her child. And Agatha wanted it too: almost completely.

So Clara was desperate for the marriage to take place, and Agatha was desperate to make her happy, but the day came when she knew she could not do it. The real reason lay buried in her poetic ideas of love and fulfilment, the dark yearnings for 'the stranger knight' who would invade her life and take her beyond herself. The ostensible reason arose when Wilfred telephoned Agatha to say that he had been invited to join a party leaving for South America to look for treasure trove, and would she mind very much if he went? He was desperate to go, not least because the two mediums he visited regularly in Portsmouth had told him he should. 'They had said that undoubtedly he would come back having discovered a city that had not been known since the time of the Incas.'

Agatha might have been thought to take this kind of thing seriously. Her early stories were full of ghosts, phenomena, premonitions: 'The House of Beauty', with its vision of a wonderful house, in which 'dwelt the Shadow of an Unclean Thing'; 'The Call of Wings', in which music lifts the body 'free of its shackles'. But the supernatural was a means for Agatha to express her sense of the ineffable. It was never something believable in itself. Her mother took such things extremely seriously, which meant that Agatha tried to do so; she had also read Edgar Allan Poe and May Sinclair[4] and was, to an extent, influenced by them. Yet there was a robust side of Agatha – Margaret Miller's granddaughter, after all – that thought it utter nonsense. Unlike Clara, she was not mystical. The supernatural was entirely separate from the dreams and secrets that haunted her imagination. She saw its power, though, and used it in her writings; increasingly, against itself. As a young girl she had written what she called 'a grisly story about a séance'. Later she turned this into the detective novel *The Sittaford Mystery*, which is written with an apparent belief in ouija boards and table-turning but is, in fact, creating an atmospheric smokescreen. The séance has been engineered for the most base and practical of reasons, as an alibi for one of the people attending it; and more fool any reader who took it seriously.

The Agatha who could write this – or *The Pale Horse*, or *Dumb Witness*, or the short story 'Motive v. Opportunity',[5] all of which take the sceptic's view – would have found Wilfred Pirie irredeemably silly. The day he left for South America is described in *Unfinished Portrait*:

How beautiful an August morning can be . . .

Never, Celia thought, had she felt so happy. The old familiar 'pain' clutched at her. It was so lovely – so lovely – it hurt . . .

Oh, beautiful, beautiful world! . . .

'You look very happy, Celia.'

'I am happy. It's such a lovely day.'

Her mother said quietly: 'It's not only that . . . It's because Jim's gone away, isn't it?'

This, though, is more than just the blessed relief at no longer having to pretend an interest in theosophy. These are the emotions of a girl who loved freedom more intensely than most girls did; who perceived a life beyond the known limits, in which marriage did not bring the greatest happiness; whose most intense pleasures came not from fulfilment, completion or knowledge, but from the feelings that hover around the edge of these things. The moment of Archie standing to greet her in the drawing-room at Ashfield; the memory of Archie holding her dance-card and pointing carelessly at three names ('Cut this one . . . this one . . .'); the thought of Archie on his motorbike, climbing the hill she walked every day, looking intently for Ashfield: those were sweet in a way that no realisation could ever be.

'I don't really want to marry anyone yet.'

'Darling, how right you are! It's never quite the same afterwards, is it?'[6]

Yet Agatha *did* want marriage, nothing more, and so she accepted the proposal of Reggie Lucy. A major in the Gunners, he was elder brother to the girls with whom she had long been close if casual friends ('We've thought Reggie had his eye on you for some time, Aggie'), and he shared their easy engagement with life. If one missed a train, what did it matter? Another would come along. How pointless then to worry. If one was useless at golf, as Agatha was, despite Reggie's best efforts to improve her game on the course at Torquay, so what? She could still enjoy herself swinging a club. Agatha was mesmerised by this attitude, which was not her own, and she felt comfortable with Reggie in a way that did not entirely preclude sexual attraction. They would talk together, fall silent, talk again: 'the way I most like holding a conversation'. She liked his proposal too. 'You've got a lot of scalps, haven't you, Agatha? Well, you can put mine with them any time you like.' It was an idiom with which she was at home, and her mother sensed that here was the right man. 'I think this will be a happy marriage,' she said. Then: 'I wish he'd told you a little earlier, so you could have married straight away.'

As usual, Clara had gone to the heart of things. Reggie had proposed to Agatha during ten days' leave, after which he knew he would not return to Devon for some time; two years, as it happened. And he insisted that she should, throughout that time, consider herself free. It was an attitude with which, again, she was comfortable – so unlike the disturbing persistence of Bolton Fletcher – but which left her annoyed (should a man not be more assertive, more jealous?) and a little scared. It was as if she knew that somebody else would come along; that she would choose the unknown man over Reggie; and that this would be the wrong thing to do.

Hercule Poirot said softly:
'. . . Can you not accept *facts*? She loved Roderick Welman. What of it? With you, *she can be happy*.'[7]

In *Unfinished Portrait* Agatha thought a good deal about Reggie, or 'Peter' as she called him. She considered the results of his folly in not marrying her instantly, as she had begged him to do. Women often think about the men of their youth, wondering if they have let go the one with whom they would have been happiest; but Agatha did, in this case, have cause. Why did Reggie back off? Because of his nature: he had the Lucy trait of *laissez-aller* and, in his decent humility, he felt he did not have the right to keep Agatha from other offers. Hence the letter 'Peter' writes when Celia tells him she is going to marry 'Dermot', as Archie Christie is called ('It was exactly like Peter. So like Peter that Celia cried over it').

'Don't blame yourself, Celia. It was my fault entirely . . . The truth of it is you feel he's got more guts than I had. I ought to have taken you at your word when you wanted to marry me . . . He's a better man than I am – your Dermot . . .'

Agatha did not think that Archie was a better man than Reggie. In her early letters to her second husband, written not long before *Unfinished Portrait*, she thanked him over and over again for his 'kindness', the quality in which Reggie had been abundant and Archie was not. 'Not considerate,' Clara said of him; 'ruthless.' Nor did he have any money, which caused the one moment of bitterness in 'Peter's' letter. 'And now you've fallen in love with someone poorer than I am.'

Archie had eighty pounds a year, and no prospects of family inheritance. Agatha's hundred-pound annuity, meanwhile, was to be given up to Clara. Chaflins in New York, of which Frederick's father had been a partner, had finally collapsed in 1913, taking with it Clara's tiny income (Margaret Miller had moved her money out some time earlier). Mr Chaflin himself guaranteed Clara three hundred pounds a year from his personal fortune and, with help from Agatha and Madge, this would allow her to stay at Ashfield; by now Clara was determined to keep her home, which she saw as a magical protection against change.

Of course Agatha wanted to give her money in support of Ashfield. But she was in a difficult position: without her income, marriage to Archie seemed impossible. 'I told Archie that I could never marry him, that we should have to forget each other,' she wrote in her autobiography. 'Archie refused to listen to this. Somehow or other he was going to make money. We would get married, and he might even be able to help support my mother. He made me confident and hopeful. We got engaged again.'

On other occasions it would be Archie who said that marriage was impossible, and Agatha who talked him round. Clara, though, was consistently against the idea: there was not enough money, she said, and that was that. In fact her misgivings went deeper. But this was her best argument, the hardest for Archie to counter; although the two maintained a wary cordiality, Clara remained obdurate.

Leaving aside her more complex emotions, it must have frustrated her to see Agatha reject a procession of eligible men in favour of this penniless pilot. Marriage was the conventional route, but Archie was by no means a conventional choice. Madge, for all her 'daring', had played it infinitely safer when she accepted James Watts, and there would have been far less risk attached to rich Bolton Fletcher, stolid Wilfred Pirie or kindly Reggie Lucy. Life in the RFC, while it held prospects for promotion, was almost ludicrously precarious. There was also a more subtle point. The Piries and Lucys were family friends; Fletcher was a friend of friends; the Christies were not 'known' to the Millers, and had it not been for his soldiering career Archie would have been unlikely to come into Agatha's orbit. She was, in fact, of a slightly higher social class. Clara, who had similarly married above herself, may well have pondered the outcome of a meeting between her late husband, the refined Frederick, and Archie's Irish mother Ellen, known as 'Peg'.

Peg had made a good marriage, to a judge in the Indian Civil Service (Archie was born in Murree). But when her husband died after a fall from his horse she had settled in England, where life was not easy. At the turn of the century, while the Millers were living with their servants at Ashfield, Peg was lodging with Campbell, Archie's brother, in a house in Bristol;[8] Archie was at prep school in Godalming. She was good-looking – as were her sons – and later married a man named William Hemsley, who proved her saviour: he was kind, solid and – most usefully – a schoolmaster at Clifton College, where Archie later became head of school. But this was some distance from the world of the Union Club on New York's Fifth Avenue, in which Frederick had been so very much at home.

Of course Archie was wholly gentlemanly. There is no doubt, though, that Agatha was thrown by Peg's manner, a mixture of gush, dislike and jealousy. It was ironic that Campbell Christie should have warned Agatha that his mother was 'dangerous': an identical judgement to the one that her granddaughter later made about Clara. There were, indeed, similarities between the two women. Peg was as possessive a mother as Clara and equally, though not consistently, opposed to the marriage. The difference – which, in Agatha's eyes, was the fundamental difference between a lady and a non-lady, a distinction she never shied from making – was that Clara could hide her feelings. Peg hid nothing. This, for Agatha, was an entirely new experience. She had seen her mother lose control briefly after Frederick's death, but decorum had been restored as a matter of principle, and all her life Agatha would value the ability to maintain a façade. 'I remember my dear mother[9] telling me that a gentlewoman should always be able to control herself in public, however much she may give way in private', was how Miss Marple put it.[10]

Archie paid no attention whatever to his mother and her oddities. 'True to temperament,' wrote Agatha in her autobiography, '[he] was not particularly interested in what she thought of me or I of her. He had the happy attitude of going through life without the least interest in what anyone thought of him or his belongings: his mind was always entirely bent on what *he* wanted himself.'

Which, in 1913, was Agatha. This beautiful and mysterious man wanted her so badly that he demanded they marry instantly, without waiting and without seeking to please anybody but themselves.

To Agatha it was 'fate': her female destiny. Having been brought up to express herself in any way she chose, she expected only to marry. This was her upbringing, which she had no urge to question. Girls of her sort did not have careers. They had husbands. Her father had been horrified by the thought of his lovely, lively Madge among the earnest bluestockings of Girton, and his wife did not disagree with him: the care with which she had had to tread through her own early life had left her, in some ways, deeply conventional. She wanted happiness for her daughters, and to her that meant marriage. Agatha believed this too; or so she believed. In *Evil Under the Sun* Poirot discusses the question with the successful clothes designer, Rosamund Darnley.

> 'To marry and have children, that is the common lot of women. Only one woman in a hundred – more, in a thousand, can make for herself a name and a position as you have done.'
>
> Rosamund grinned at him.
>
> 'And yet, all the same, I'm nothing but a wretched old maid!'

The book ends with Rosamund blissfully abandoning her business for love. And Agatha, despite her extraordinary achievements, would always assert that a career was a man's job – 'Men have much better brains than women, don't you think?'[11] was a typical comment – and that the true value of a woman lay within the personal arena. 'It makes me feel that, after all, I have not been a failure in life – that I have succeeded as a wife,' she wrote to her second husband, Max, in 1943.

So as a girl she never chafed against the limits of her life: the conventions, the corsets, the need to speak low or to sing to a teddy-bear. Unlike her near-contemporary Dorothy L. Sayers – who, at the time

of Agatha's entry into the marriage market, was chewing the intellectual fat over cocoa at Somerville – she had no desire to break free.
She felt free anyway. Her imagination was infinite; her creative fires
burned within a brazier of contentment. There was nothing of the
Shavian 'new woman' in Agatha, striding towards a future of sexual
equality. For all that she loved the novels of May Sinclair, she shared
none of her feminist concerns. The frustrations of a girl like Vera
Brittain, then at Oxford with Sayers, whose *Testament of Youth* rages
against the male-dominated conventions of the time, would have been
utterly remote to her.

The truth is that she liked a man's world. She saw beyond it,
although not in a political sense; later she would live beyond it, with
her success and self-sufficiency; yet she loved being female, and never
felt circumscribed by her sex. She had grown up in a matriarchy, after
all. And she understood – as 'cleverer' girls, perhaps, do not – that
female strength could show itself in many different ways: that a
Margaret Miller, indomitable within her well-run ménage, had at least
as much power as a woman in the public sphere. She also knew that
women need not appear strong in order to be so. The fragile little
Mrs Franklin in *Curtain* is despised for her wiles by the grave young
scientist, Judith. 'She's a very stupid woman,' says Judith, but Poirot
wisely replies: 'She uses her grey cells in ways that you, my child,
know nothing about.' Agatha never despised femininity, even in its
most foolish form, although sometimes she pitied it. All her life she
valued what she had had – beauty, attraction, natural physical allure
– and then lost. 'What's the good of a woman like that?' asks a character in *Dead Man's Folly* of the gorgeous, empty-headed Lady Stubbs.
Again, Poirot defends her. 'One needs roots as well as flowers on a
plant . . .'

Agatha always defended the right to leisure – 'Without it, where
are you?' – and held that sensible women knew when they were well-
off, controlling the home with an authoritative finger and their men
with a compliant smile. But it was a profound contradiction in her,
that she put so high a value on doing nothing yet became so compulsively industrious. In fact she had a deep regard for working women.
Not the strident ones who waved the feminist flag, like the politician
Lady Westholme in *Appointment with Death*, proclaiming that 'If

anything is to be accomplished, mark my words, it is women who will do it.' No, Agatha admired the servants like Jane the cook, producing five-course dinners without turning a hair; the poor girls like Midge in *The Hollow*, battling through the days in her terrible dress shop; the impoverished ladies like Miss Carnaby, the paid companion in *The Labours of Hercules* ('I'm not a clever woman at all, and I've no training and I'm getting older – and I'm so terrified for the future . . .'); the women who pursued a vocation, teachers in particular. As Dorothy L. Sayers made clear in her Oxford novel, *Gaudy Night*, this tended to be a celibate life, which made it alien to Agatha. But she always portrayed it as worthy of absolute respect: 'Miss Williams' life had been interesting to her,' she wrote of the governess in *Five Little Pigs*. 'She had that enormous mental and moral advantage of a strict Victorian upbringing . . . she had done her duty in that station of life to which it had pleased God to call her, and that assurance encased her in an armour impregnable to the slings and darts of envy, discontent and regret.'

Later came the headmistress Miss Bulstrode in *Cat Among the Pigeons*, full of 'cosmopolitan aplomb' who, when murder comes to her school, sits 'cool and unmoved, with her lifework falling in ruins about her'. A version of this character appeared in *Third Girl*, *Hallowe'en Party* and, finally, as the doomed Miss Temple in *Nemesis*. 'A handsome woman, and a woman of personality. Yes, a thousand pities, Miss Marple thought, a thousand pities if the world was going to lose Elizabeth Temple.'

Agatha had not been taught by this kind of woman. But she had known one as a friend. Eileen Morris was a very different type from the charming, carefree Lucys. A natural and unresentful spinster, who lived in a big house overlooking the sea with her five maiden aunts, she was a few years older than Agatha but by around 1909, the age difference had ceased to matter and the two became close. At Greenway House there is a folded copy of one of Eileen's poems, 'Darnley to the Queen', which has little artistry but much controlled intelligence. Eileen told Agatha to send her own work to the *Poetry Review*, to whom she sold the odd thing – including her Commedia dell'Arte poems – for a guinea.

'Eileen was rather plain, but she had a remarkable mind.'[12] Her brother was the schoolmaster, but Eileen herself was the very model of one of Agatha's sharp-brained, distinguished, energetic teachers. 'She was the first person I had come across with whom I could discuss *ideas*.' Agatha herself had a different type of mind, more fluid and diffuse; although she held strong opinions, it was her writerly strength to be able to doubt them. Nor did she trust concepts, theories or ideologies, being always of the opinion that human nature did not fit easily into them. Yet with Eileen she liked to talk about these things. It was perhaps the unaccustomed freedom within their friendship that led to this speech, in Agatha's first novel *Snow Upon the Desert*: Rosamund Vaughan, who measures her worth solely according to male values, suddenly speaks with a new and wholly honest female voice.

'It seems to be an accepted idea that every woman will strive to live up to a man's ideal of her – that she will be grateful for his idealisation of her. It's not a bit true! One has, if anything, a contempt for people who can't see you as you are! . . .

'Oh! One gets sick, tired, *bored* of being admired for impossible imaginary qualities! I'm not a cross between an angel and a hospital nurse. What respect can I have for the brains of anyone who thinks I am? I've got *some* good points. Why don't they admire those?'

Those thoughts had lurked somewhere within the nineteen-year-old Agatha, as she danced in her pink dresses and made dutiful, decorously flirtatious conversation; somewhere she felt the desire for a different kind of life, a true liberation. But she was too happy, as a young girl, to care about it. She had no urge to 'be herself' in the modern sense. 'You are lovely and interesting and sweet to everyone,' Archie wrote to her, and this was what she wanted to hear. 'You are lovely and perfect in every way.' If he thought this because Agatha presented herself to him as an impossible ideal, that was fine by her: she knew he would not have written such things to a girl who looked or expressed herself as Eileen Morris did. Agatha was glad of her superior attractions, her success as a female, however strong the lure of Eileen's superior mind.

The irony is that, of the two, it was Agatha who forged the career; this despite her lack of formal education, her indifference to the notion of sexual equality, her complacent contentment with the status quo. But it was Agatha's very imperviousness to the way she *ought* to be thinking that, in the end, made her such a surprising and singular talent.

Of course she absorbed, she observed, she listened. She was susceptible to the powerful personalities of her mother, of Madge, of Eileen. Her early writings bear the imprint of what she had been reading: Poe, Sinclair, D. H. Lawrence.[13] 'I was trying things, like one does.'[14] Yet in some way she was always proof against outside influence. All her life she would – with only the most occasional exceptions – ignore any suggestions made about her writing. She followed her instincts with a rare certainty.

Agatha herself would probably not have understood what she was doing; or why, as a merry young girl leading a life of infinite pleasure, she was at the same time seeking the solitude in which to write stories, poems and a full-length novel; why, when deep in love with a young man whom she longed to marry, she was pursuing the ambition of publication. She saw no contradiction in any of this. Women today are tormented by the separation between work and life, between private and social fulfilment, between individuality and biology; it did not occur to Agatha to think in such a way. She had a simplicity that resolved her complexities.

But a letter from Eden Philpotts – who had been so generous about *Snow Upon the Desert* – hinted at the conflicts that might later arise. Agatha had shown him a further story entitled 'Being So Very Wilful', a quotation from the Elaine section of *Idylls of the King*. The story no longer exists but Philpotts was impressed by it, so much so that he dignified it with this remarkable reply:

All is going exceedingly well with your work and should life so fall out for you that it has room for art and if you can face the uphill fight to take your place and win it, you have the gifts sufficient. I never prophesy; but I should judge that if you can write like this now you might go far. However life knocks the art out of a good many people and your environment in the time to come may substitute for the hard road of art a different one. The late Mrs Craigie[15] was about the only woman I know who stuck to hard work for love of it. But then circumstances combined to make her do so.[16]

The prescience of Philpotts's letter was extraordinary, although not quite in the way he intended. The blissful state in which life and art co-existed would indeed come to an end for Agatha, when her world changed so completely in 1926. After that, there would be separation. Her dreams and imaginative delights would no longer weave through the whole of her life, but only through her work. Like Vernon Deyre in her first Westmacott novel, *Giant's Bread* – or like Pearl Craigie, whose marriage broke down hideously – Agatha would tread the 'hard road of art'. She would become, definitively, a writer; and, incidentally, a working woman of independent means, with a life entirely transcendent of her calm and closeted upbringing.

The girl who longed to marry Archie Christie foresaw nothing of this; not a shred. 'I had the normal comfortable ideas about a married life,' she said in an interview almost sixty years later. And in her autobiography she described her longing for Archie in simple terms. A young girl like any other, on the prowl for a mate, had found 'The Man': a charming and commonplace story.

But the soft meandering prose of *Unfinished Portrait* shows Archie to have touched deeper nerves. He was Agatha's dream come true, in every sense: the living expression of her ineffable yearnings: 'Something you want so much that you don't quite know what it is.'[17] He was the unknown, the dark, the free. She fell in love with him so deeply because she sensed that life, with him, would be like a piece of music or a poem. She would be an Isolde, an Elaine ('. . . he kissed her face/At once she slipt like water to the floor').[18]

The sensible part of her wanted the daily life of marriage, the housekeeping and the 'receipts' book; but in her artist's mind these were hallowed by the extraordinary fact of Archie himself. Such a contrast between the ordered breakfast table – folded copy of *The Times* with its personal columns on the front page, polished silver teapot, Cooper's Oxford marmalade – and the man who sat behind it; between the immaculate corners of the fresh linen bed and the mysteries that took place within. The way he looked, long and loose-limbed and unconsciously romantic; his air of doomed vulnerability; the strange purity of his desire, so unlike the practised urgency of Bolton Fletcher: these things ranged around Agatha's imagination, which in essence had not grown up at all. Despite her womanly craving for Archie, something in her remained childlike. 'Then to her tower she climbed . . . and so lived in fantasy'.[19]

Clara knew her daughter's nature, and intuited what Agatha saw in Archie. 'That young man – I don't like him' is the thought attributed to her in *Unfinished Portrait*; it was not completely true, but his powerful appeal alarmed her because she realised – as Agatha did not – that other women would see it too ('He is attractive to women, Celia, remember that . . .'). However much Clara had wanted a happy marriage for Agatha, she had dreaded this kind of attachment. Reggie Lucy was one thing; Archie was quite another, and he made her fearful: for Agatha and herself.

She had recognised the situation immediately, when he turned up at Ashfield on his motorbike. 'She did not tell herself that this all might come to nothing. She believed, on the contrary, that she saw events casting their shadows before them.'[20] And it was selfishness, in a sense, that made her uneasy. To be supplanted in Agatha's affections was alarming, painful. She recognised that Archie was as strong a character as she herself was, and that he had sex on his side. Nevertheless her sustained opposition to the marriage means that she surely believed she could win the day. It was extraordinary, unprecedented, for Agatha to go against Clara's counsel, but she was so deep in desire that the mother she adored was almost ignored. Her guilt at this periodically showed itself, as when, for instance, she broke off with Archie on account of Clara's failing eyesight. It was easy, though, for Archie to talk her round with reassurances. Clara could only look on and hope that the delays outlasted the passion.

Her misgivings were not just about her own jealousy, or even Archie's lack of money. Nobody knew Agatha as Clara did: she knew

her innocence, her childlike confidence in love, her 'dangerous intensity of affection', and she believed that her deep emotional capacity
should be left unplumbed, fulfilled only in the realm of imagination.
Was she right? 'It is never a mistake to marry a man you want to
marry – even if you regret it,'[21]Agatha would later write, but such a
thing is easily said and less easily endured. She also wrote this, in a
letter to her second husband: 'Mere love is rather an idiotic business
– approved of by Nature, but capable of inflicting a lot of unhappiness on individuals.'[22] As always, she was honestly uncertain: years
after her marriage had ended, the artist in Agatha would continue to
ponder the mystery of it.

Certainly she would have been spared a vast amount of anguish
had she allowed Clara to prevail against Archie. She would, though,
have missed much else beside; things of incalculable value. In her last
Westmacott novel, *The Burden*, she describes how the protective older
sister, Laura, tries with all her might to dissuade Shirley from marrying
a man who will hurt her. Yet Shirley would not have lived without
that love, for all the misery it brings her. 'I think he's utterly selfish
and – and ruthless,' says Laura to her clever old friend, Mr Baldock.
'I shouldn't wonder if you weren't right,' he replies.

'Well, then?'
'Yes, but she *likes* the fellow, Laura. She likes him very much.
In fact, she's crazy about him. Young Henry mayn't be your cup
of tea, and strictly speaking, he isn't my cup of tea, but there's
no doubt that he *is* Shirley's cup of tea . . .'

Later, Shirley accuses Laura of jealousy. 'You don't want me to love
anyone but you,' she says. 'You'll never want me to marry *anyone*.'
And she takes on Laura's accusation of Henry's ruthlessness: 'It's one
of those things that attracts me in him.' Agatha would never have said
– or thought – any of this at the time; as always in the Westmacotts
she is uncovering the perceptions that had lain within, understood in
a way that went beneath acknowledgement. 'Don't worry about Henry,'
Shirley says to Laura. 'He loves me.' Which is what Agatha undoubtedly believed back in 1913; and rightly so; although forty years later
she realised that love was not so simple. '"Love?" thought Laura.

"What is love?"' Not an immutable entity, as Agatha had once thought, but the possession of two separate people; who, however much they 'love' each other, have a different capacity for feeling.

Meanwhile Clara clung to the hope that this was 'not love: but love's first flash in youth', as Lancelot says to Elaine. Again, might she have been right? Elaine dies of love but it is absurd that she does so; she did not know Lancelot; she could not really have loved him. Normality could have broken through and told her that this was 'illusion – nothing but illusion', as Agatha later wrote as Mary Westmacott. 'The illusion that mutual attraction between man and woman breeds. Nature's lure, Nature's last and most cunning piece of deceit . . .'[23]

But Elaine's imaginative capacity was such that this, for her, *was* love. And the pressure of Tennyson's poetic world ensures that escape is not possible, that youthful passion must push itself towards a fateful intensity. Thus in 1913: when opposition to the marriage, rupture and reunion, made the love between Agatha and Archie ever more precious and necessary. And the following year: when the thick feel of death in the air, terrible and almost glamorous, helped twine love so tight around Agatha's soul that she would never quite be free of it.

So this was love, then. 'I do really love you,' wrote Archie to Agatha. 'No one else would be the same to me. Never desert me darling and always love me.'[24] His letters were kept in one of the leather cases in the chest of drawers at Greenway House: the case marked with Agatha's initials, which among other things contained the notebook in which Archie recorded the events of his life, his Royal Flying Corps badge, and a card sent from No. 3 Squadron, Netheravon, Wiltshire, on which he had written 'To Miss Miller in memoriam Christmas 1912'. There was also a photograph of Archie in uniform, on the back of which Agatha had written: 'There shall no evil happen unto thee; Neither shall any plague . . .'

When war broke out it was as Agatha said in *Unfinished Portrait*: 'War, for most women, is the destiny of one person.' She did not notice the curtain fall upon the world she had known: the afternoons on croquet lawns, the tea-tables and picture hats casting their shadows, the scent of rose in the air. Simply she knew that the man she loved was going to France and might never come back. Thus the hot, sultry summer of 1914 ended, for Agatha, on 3 August, when she and Clara took a train journey to Salisbury to say goodbye to Archie, who left for France nine days later.

> Dermot in khaki – a different Dermot – very jerky and flippant, with haunted eyes. No one knows about this new war – it's the kind of war where *no one might come back* . . . New engines of destruction. The air – nobody knows about the air . . .
>   Celia and Dermot were two children clinging together . . .[25]

Agatha had moved from her bedroom window at Ashfield, down the steep hill of Barton Road, towards the gleaming bay of Torquay. She had tripped on her high heels to garden parties, house-parties, racing parties. She had wandered through the sunlit gardens and dark forests of her imagination. Beyond that, there was nothing; and she had felt the need for nothing. She had smiled and tonged her hair, danced and dreamed, and that life was all the life there was. The campaign for women's suffrage; the birth of the Labour Party; Lloyd George and his People's Budget; the Parliament Act, which rendered the House of Lords essentially impotent; the movements of the great imperial powers, like lumbering chesspieces on a vast board: these passed over her. 'A murdered archduke, a "war scare" in the news-papers – such things barely entered her consciousness.'[26] Through her father, the haunted look she had seen in his eyes when the family returned from France at the end of the century, she had felt the first intimations that told her society was changing, that it would no longer be owned by the leisured, the easeful, the disengaged. But she was never a political animal. She absorbed the world by more instinctive means. 'No civilised nations went to war' was the thinking of the time, as she wrote in her autobiography; until, all of a sudden, they did; and Agatha, whose life up to that point had been wrapped as tenderly as a baby in its swaddling, was dropped like a stone into this stark new world.

As ever, the Westmacotts lay bare the fear she had felt, without expressing it, at the time. 'Oh, God, let him come back to me . . .'[27] Meanwhile the autobiography shows the Agatha who could face facts squarely. It describes the dreadful parting with Archie at Salisbury – 'I remember going to bed that night and crying and crying until I thought I would never stop' – but then passes on to describe her hurrying off, full of energy, to begin service as a VAD in Torquay. The impression is of a young girl taking her changed circumstances in her stride, uncomplaining and unquestioning. This is reinforced by the recorded interview that Agatha gave, in vibrant old age, to the Imperial War Museum. 'I thought oh well I'd like to become a VAD. And so I started orf on that . . . I was engaged then, to the young man who became my first husband, and he had just been accepted in the RAF [in fact the RFC] . . . so that I felt, you know, mixed up in it completely and wanted to have a part in it.'

More than fifty years' distance lent a degree of objectivity to Agatha's spoken reminiscences of the war. Nevertheless she described her nursing duties in a peculiarly realistic, pragmatic way; it is hard to grasp that this girl had emerged from so utterly protected a life, that she had gone with such a lack of fuss from her silly, jolly garden parties into the death-scented hospital wards. Of course no other kind of behaviour would have occurred to her. What had to be, had to be. Only Mary Westmacott thought to cry out in protest.

On attending her first operation, for example, Agatha described in the Imperial War Museum recording how she 'began to shake all over. And Sister Anderson took me outside and she said, "Now listen to me. You know what really makes you feel faint is the fact that you're going into an atmosphere of ether – you can't help but feel faint. But everything in life, one gets used to. Look in a different place – at somebody else's toe. And in the end that will be quite all right . . ."' Similarly with amputations: 'I went into one or two . . . If there had been an amputation and there had been things lying around – the legs or the arms – some of the youngest girls had to take these things down and put them in the furnace.' One of those girls, aged around eleven, had been grievously upset (although 'she got all right by the end'). So Agatha helped her 'clean up the floor down there – and stuck it in the furnace myself. There are so many odd things that you have to do in hospital.'

So complex was Agatha that, despite her extreme sensitivity, she could take the necessary attitude towards nursing – efficient, sensible, kindly, detached – and enjoy what she was doing. After the war she said that she would have liked very much to become a nurse, and might have done so had she not got married – 'I would have been very good at it.'[28] Again she suffered none of the frustrations shown in Vera Brittain's *Testament of Youth*, which portrays VAD work as innately, pointlessly horrific: wasting one's own life looking after young men whose lives had been wasted. Agatha, conversely, saw nursing as 'very satisfactory'. She did her duty, smilingly. She found humour in her days: in the love letters that she helped her young men to write to their girlfriends – 'they usually had three' – and in the trips to the X-ray unit at the other hospital across town. 'They said to me, "Mind you keep an eye on your little bunch, when you take them out. You do realise what they're looking for, don't you?" And I said, "Well, what are they looking for? One of them was looking at shoes." "That wouldn't have been next door but one to the Goat and Compass?" I said, "Well, I think there *was* a public house!" They learned very soon where all the pubs were . . .'[29]

If she was tormented by the wreckage, the beautiful boys with their missing limbs, the dirt and blood and phlegm, she did not say so. She must have been shocked, not least because she was plunged into intimacy with male bodies at a time when, as a young virgin, her knowledge of men would have derived from reproductions of Michelangelo's *David*. Suddenly she was dealing with bed-baths and bed-pans ('There was a special thing, you know, that they pushed on *that*') and, because she had a fiancé, was regarded as sufficiently worldly to handle the more harrowing tasks. 'They said, "It's better for you, because you're married" – I said, "No, I'm not married yet," but they said – "It's better, really".' The fact is that nobody could have been more innocent than the Agatha of late summer 1914. And she dealt with it easily, that sudden transition into reality; in some mysterious way, she remained untouched by it.

Stella stood meekly by the side of Sister [she wrote in a fragment of an early unfinished novel]. Her hands, freshly scrubbed, held the pile of sterilised dressings . . . What would it be like, Stella wondered, to have someone belonging to you out there? Most girls had, she supposed. She herself was one of the exceptions. She had been studying music in Paris when war broke out . . . Stella was a solitary creature. Her mind fed on itself to a large extent. She read a great deal and thought profoundly. She was serious – with the pathetic earnest seriousness of the young.

For all that she saw and experienced, Agatha still lived in her dreams. In *Unfinished Portrait* she does not work as a VAD but stays at home, looking after her grandmother (Margaret Miller did come to live at Ashfield, having almost lost her sight), and remembering her imaginary childhood friends: 'How keep herself from thinking of Dermot – out there?

'In desperation she married off "the Girls"! Isabella married a rich Jew, Elsie married an explorer. Ella became a schoolteacher . . .'

Of course the real Agatha grew up a good deal. Walking every day to the hospital set up in the old town hall; hearing every day of the death of some former dance partner, wondering every day if this would be Archie's last; making the long, lonely walk home to Ashfield, either heavy with thoughts or plagued by 'rather drunken' soldiers. 'My grandmother didn't like it – "Not at all suitable," she said, "you ought to have someone to come down and meet you and chaperone you." I said, "Well, they can't spare anyone to do things like that . . ."'[30]

It was a desperate time for Agatha, yet she did not feel it as entirely desperate. Eventually it would be over and her world restored. Not the world around her – that, she knew, would be changed – but *her* world. As long as she was young and pretty, as long as Archie was writing letters of adoration, as long as Ashfield bloomed safe and home to Clara, then life would still be Agatha's plaything. Like Nell Vereker in *Giant's Bread*, who becomes a VAD, she would still be 'Nell – Nell with her golden hair and her sweet smile'.

Nell marries Vernon Deyre just after the outbreak of war.

Lots of girls were doing it – flinging up everything, marrying the man they cared for no matter how poor he was. After the

war something would turn up. That was the attitude. And behind
it lay that awful secret fear that you never took out and looked
at properly. The nearest you ever got to it was saying defiantly:
'And no matter *what* happens, we'll have had *something* . . .'

And so Agatha married Archie, on Christmas Eve 1914. He was on
his first leave and Agatha told Clara that she thought now was the time
to get married; Clara, no doubt recognising that control had been
wrested from her by circumstances – she supported Agatha's VAD
work, for instance – said that she would feel exactly the same in Agatha's
situation. It was Archie, this time, who was against the idea. He was
flippant, which Agatha failed to realise was his way of dealing with fear,
and fed her what was then the RFC line on marriage: 'You stop one,
you've had it, and you've left behind a young widow, perhaps a child
coming – it's selfish and wrong.' Agatha did not care for this. Nor did
she care for Archie's Christmas present to her: not a ring or even any
kind of jewellery, but a luxuriously impersonal dressing-case, which she
refused, somewhat hysterically, to accept. Then, on the night of 23
December, everything changed again. Archie strode assertively into her
bedroom at Peg Hemsley's house in Bristol, where they were staying
for Christmas, and said they must get married the next day. 'I've
changed my mind.' It frightened Agatha a little, this sudden decisiveness of Archie's, the way it could override a different view of which
he had previously been equally sure. 'But – but you were so *certain.*'
    'What *does* that matter? I've changed my mind.'
    The following day was exciting, unnerving, a confused rush upon
fate. The marriage seemed impossible. Peg wailed in horror at the
idea; nobody could perform the ceremony without notice; and all of
this made Agatha and Archie all the more determined to do it. Finally
they were married in Archie's local parish church, at a cost of eight
pounds for the licence. Agatha wore her street clothes. The music was
played by an organist who happened to be practising. The witness was
a friend who – in what must have seemed a benign coincidence – was
passing the church at the time. 'It made us both laugh,' wrote Agatha,
of this odd wedding. She told Clara about it only when it was over.
The news was accepted, as of course it had to be, and in the light of
Peg's reaction it was agreed that Agatha and Archie would spend

Christmas Day at Ashfield, after their one night of honeymoon. It was late by the time they took a train to Torquay. Agatha held her new dressing-case in one hand, Archie's hand in the other as she walked the few yards from the station to the Grand Hotel, perched high above the seafront, overlooking the calm, dark bay.

Christmas was a happy day spent with Clara and Madge (who had been furious with Agatha over her bombshell – 'You are absolutely unfeeling!' – but got over it). On Boxing Day Agatha went to London with Archie, there to say goodbye to him for another six months, before returning to the hospital and a good deal of teasing from her patients. 'I heard some little knot of soldiers saying, Well, I think Miss Miller's done very well for herself. She's married an officer in the RFC.'[31]

Archie went back to France. His notebook logged his movements throughout the war, beginning: '2nd August First day of mobilisation. Dined in Salisbury on 3rd and 4th.' Then: '21st December Went on first leave. 24th to Bristol later Torquay. 26th Back to London. 30th Went to 1st Wing Headquarters.' This was the controlled side of Archie, who – like Major Despard in *Cards on the Table*, decisively crossing out his bridge scores as he goes – 'likes to know at a glance where he stands at every moment'. There was another Archie though, fragile and childlike, who touched Agatha's soul in a way that was not maternal but something more complex and poetical. Later in the war he wrote to her:

> Back again. The train journey was alright. I lay dazed in my corner . . . I got here about five had a cup of tea at the county cottage and am now facing war. I feel weak as a kitten but will go to bed straight after dinner.
>
> I am sure you don't know, my darling, how I love the way you cheered me up especially yesterday. If I had not had you I should have quite broken down.
>
> Write often. I would have loved to have found a letter here from you tonight.[32]

In *Giant's Bread* Nell wears Vernon's wartime letters against her heart: 'the indelible pencil came off on her skin'. So Archie's words had rubbed into Agatha beneath her crisp VAD uniform. 'It was so wonderful, so very wonderful, to be loved.' And Archie did love her: 'I love you much too much – more than ever now – to take any risks, for death only means to me being separated from you.' He loved her air of unassailable serenity, her sweet voice, her long pale hair and cool fresh slimness. He loved the way she held his hands when he stretched them out towards her like a lost little boy. He felt that she understood the Archie who lay beneath the Clifton head of school, the glamorous officer pilot; she knew his weak stomach and poor nerves, his neediness, his fear; she would always be there to help him.

The letters sent before the war show Archie's innate vulnerability. 'My dearest Angel,' he wrote in March 1914, from his RFC base in Netheravon, 'Your letter and the violets were most consoling though I am still unhappy inwardly – despite the fact that I have finished a bottle of tonic since you finished the dregs of the last bottle. You are full of pluck and courage . . .' Later he asked Agatha: 'What I want most is a letter from you to say you are quite well and not worried about all this flying.' This was to reassure Archie himself, of course, that *he* had nothing to worry about. More than obviously he did – photographs of his Cody biplane show it as insubstantial as one of the houses that Poirot would later build from a deck of cards – but the pragmatist in him was still determined on success in a piloting career.

> For your sake, more than for my own, I am taking no risks
> and feel perfectly confident that no harm can come to me.
> That poor fellow who was killed was not safe in any machine.
> He hated flying the Cody but did not like to refuse when he
> was asked to; showing a lack of moral courage. I am terribly
> sorry for his family – so much so that I will give up the Corps
> if you are really very unhappy about it but I know I am
> perfectly safe – I always carry St Christopher with me.

Before the war Agatha was not, according to her autobiography, particularly worried about Archie's job. 'Flying was dangerous – but then so was hunting, and I was used to people breaking their necks in the hunting field.' This may have been true, but at the same time Agatha had a rather self-conscious attitude towards physical risk: she thought it aristocratic to take it on. She liked the idea of Archie as a daredevil. It was grand; it was as it should be. 'That disposition to take risks was what she admired most about Dermot,' she wrote in *Unfinished Portrait*. 'He was not afraid of life.' She always attacked the bourgeois doctrine of 'Safety First' ('In my opinion all the people who spend their lives avoiding being run over by buses had much better be run over and put safely out of the way. They're no good.')[33] And she applied this philosophy to women – the best kind – as well as to men. She herself had gone up in an aeroplane at an exhibition in 1911, when planes 'were crashing every day'. Her books, particularly the early ones, are full of girls who show class by refusing to show fear. 'Just a moment she paused, then, with a little gallant toss of the head, the same toss of the head with which her ancestors had gone into action in the Crusades, she passed through . . .'[34]

But, for all this, Archie's letters show that Agatha *did* worry about his flying; how could she not? 'There is no machine for me to fly at present (Don't say hurrah or words to that effect because I am going to take more care than ever now),' he wrote to her from Netheravon. He continued with an expression of his own concern. 'Do take care of yourself. You hate being told this I know but you are so very precious to me that I can't bear to think of you being ill or unhappy or wanting anything you could possibly have.' In fact Archie hated the realities of misery, as he had told her early on in their relationship: 'It spoils everything for me.' Because of this Clara had feared his lack of consideration, his ruthlessness.

'But he was not ruthless to her,' Celia says of herself in *Unfinished Portrait*, thinking how wrong her mother had been. 'He was young, diffident, very much in love, and Celia was his first love.'

The first leave after the wedding – logged in Archie's notebook: 'July 1915 London' – was naturally a let-down. Too much pressure on too little time made relaxation impossible. 'It was like some queer delirious dream,' wrote Agatha of the same situation in *Giant's Bread*.

They were in some ways like strangers to each other. He was offhand when she spoke about France. It was all right – everything was all right. One made jokes about it and refused to treat it seriously . . . When he asked her what she had been doing she could only give him hospital news, and that he didn't like. He begged her again to give it up. 'It's a filthy job, nursing. I hate to think of your doing it . . .'

This was not entirely Archie's view. He did not interfere to that extent in Agatha's business. But he probably liked to think of her as a precious dream of home, untouched by war: the open-hearted girl who at the start of the year had sent him 'The A A Alphabet for 1915'.

> A is for Angel, by nature (?) and name
> And also for Archibald, spouse of the same.
> B is his BATH!!! Most important of matters . . .
> Z, for the Zest of that wonderful pair
> The Archibald Christies, who make their bow here!

Her heartrending lack of embarrassment was matched by Archie's in 1916, when he sent to Agatha an analysis of her character by – as he called himself – 'The Omniscient One':

A kindly and affectionate disposition
Fond of animals except worms and cockchafers, fond of human
    beings except husbands (on principle)
Normally lazy but can develop and maintain great energy
Sound in limb and eye, wind not good up hill
Full of intelligence and artistic taste
Unconventional and inquisitive
Face good, especially hair; figure good and skin excellent.
    Can wheedle well.
Wild but if once captured would make a loving and affectionate wife.

By the time of his first leave Archie had been seconded into the Royal Field Artillery, where he was promoted to captain. His sinuses – which had played him up from the first and caused intolerable pain in the air – eventually prevented him continuing as a pilot. Later he moved into administration, at which he was able: a 1917 letter described how he was

> glued to a telephone till 11pm last night and my temper is not so sweet in consequence. I sentenced a man to 28 days of what the Daily Mirror used to call 'crucifixion' i.e. being tied to a tree, and undergoing other punishments and fatigue, because he refused to work, went absent without leave, and pretended to be sick when he was not.
>
> The only person I care about today is you. And I do really love you . . . Never desert me darling and always love me.

Agatha worried less about Archie when he was no longer flying, probably believing that his sinuses had saved his life. But as one military historian wrote: 'The war of 1914–1918 was an artillery war: artillery was the battle-winner, artillery was what caused the greatest loss of life, the most dreadful wounds, and the deepest fear.'[34] And Archie was a determined soldier, as his record shows. His notebook logged his 'Promotions etc', which included being mentioned in despatches four times (by General Sir John French in October 1914), receiving a DSO and the Order of St Stanislaus 3rd Class ('So beautiful I would have liked to have worn it myself,' wrote Agatha), and ending the war as a colonel.

He had been through it, in other words. But when he came home in September 1918 – a little early because he had been posted to the Air Ministry – he was alive and sound and apparently the same as ever. For Agatha, it was a simple miracle ('O the Ovation that husbands receive/From affectionate wives when they come home on leave'). She did not need – or want – to think about it. Only after the Second World War, with which she was far less intensely engaged, did she consider what the first had actually meant to men like Archie. *Taken at the Flood*, *4.50 from Paddington* and the Westmacott novel *The Rose and the Yew Tree* ponder the question of the soldier's post-war life. The fiercely tormented David Hunter; the lost boy Bryan Eastley; the charming pragmatist John Gabriel: they were all created by Agatha after 1945 and they all have something of Archie in them: they all knew what it was like to sleep and wake with death, to live with it as intimately as with a wife, then come home to a world that expects them to return, gratefully, to their former selves. By then Agatha understood the terrible energy that these men carried with them. In 1918 she had scarcely a clue.

Her creation Captain Hastings had been invalided home in *The Mysterious Affair at Styles*, but in fact the war made scant appearance in the book. Agatha wrote it in 1916, between Archie's leaves and her hospital work. That she should have done so is a great and glorious mystery in itself. But there it is: out of almost nowhere, almost the complete article.

One can explain it, up to a point. Agatha had been writing all her life. She had already completed a novel, *Snow Upon the Desert*, which hinted at the themes of her detective fiction (although it was poorly structured, which augured badly). She had enjoyed Gaston Leroux's *The Mystery of the Yellow Room*, Poe's *The Murders in the Rue Morgue*, Leblanc's *Arsène Lupin* stories and, of course, Conan Doyle: the genre was modish in the early twentieth century, so it is perhaps not so hard to imagine that a clever girl might have a shot at it. And then there was the factor of Madge, always a thorn in Agatha's competitive side. According to the autobiography, the sisters had discussed the recently published *The Mystery of the Yellow Room* and Agatha had said she would like to write a detective story; to which Madge replied that she, too, had thought of doing so, and did not believe that Agatha could pull it off. 'I should like to try.'

'Well, I bet you couldn't.'

Leroux's novel was published in 1908 so, if this was indeed how the seed was sown in Agatha, it waited eight years before flowering. But in all probability this *was* the starting-point. To do something that Madge could not; how sweet that would be.

Then there was the job at the Torquay dispensary, which kicked Agatha's imagination to a new and more decided place. After a bad bout of flu in 1916, she found on her return to the hospital that a dispensary had opened, with her friend Eileen Morris in joint charge. It seemed sensible to take a job there, on a salary of sixteen pounds per annum, as the hours were shorter than on the wards and as Agatha's home duties were considerable (her grandmother was quite a handful, and there were now only two elderly maids in the house). In fact she preferred nursing to dispensing. Eileen's organised and scholarly brain left Agatha way behind when it came to the theory of chemistry, and in 1917 she received just 50/100 – 'average' – in her practical pharmacy exam with the Society of Apothecaries in London.

But dispensing, for all that Agatha found its principles elusive and its practice monotonous, interested her in other ways. The people interested her. She immediately saw that doctors prescribed according to their own ideas rather than the individual needs of their patients (her books were often unflattering to doctors: she had seen too much of them to be impressed).[36] And she was appalled, although again fascinated, by the arrogant little Torquay pharmacist who made a serious error – misplacing a decimal point – in Agatha's presence. She knew he would refuse to acknowledge this, so 'What was the young student to do? I was the merest novice, he was the best-known pharmacist in town. I couldn't say to him: "Mr P., *you have made a mistake.*" Mr P. the pharmacist was the sort of person who does *not* make a mistake . . .' In the end Agatha pretended to stumble and upset the tray of suppositories that Mr P. had made so toxic, then squashed them firmly with her shoes. 'That's all right, little girl,' said the pharmacist, patting her shoulders 'tenderly', as was his horrible habit ('I had to put up with it because I was being instructed,' wrote Agatha in her autobiography: an interesting throwaway). This man – who carried a lump of curare in his pocket because it made him feel powerful – reappeared more than forty years later in her book *The Pale Horse*, transmuted into the chemist Mr Osbourne.

What she also absorbed was the fascination of poison: the beautiful look of the bottles, the exquisite precision of the calculations, the potential for mayhem contained within order. The original idea for *The Mysterious Affair at Styles* was a method for murder. It came from Agatha's dispensing work and could not have come to her otherwise, as it entirely depends upon a knowledge of poisons. In fact it is impossible to reach the solution to *Styles* without this knowledge: the reader may guess right as to the culprit, but the guess cannot be proved without knowledge of the properties of strychnine and bromide. So Agatha's first detective novel was, in a sense, her only 'cheat'. But as it is, in every other way, so typical, so instinctively marked with her particular genius – so *nearly* the finished article – this seems to have gone unremarked.

Right from the start she realised the potential of the idea that she would always use to such effect: that of fastening suspicion so firmly to one person that the reader eliminates him or her, only to find that here, indeed, is the culprit. She deployed this device as no other writer has since, with the utmost logic and liberality: the murderer is absent from the scene of the crime (as in *Styles*), or appears to be the intended victim, or is the narrator of the story, or a person incapacitated by a gunshot wound, or is a child, or a policeman; the key, with Agatha, being that blessed element of the *ordinary* which gives the device an illusion of reality. That she had a gift for plotting coups was undeniable. The genre had a magical effect upon her ability to structure; although this was not achieved without a great deal of work, which interested her in the manner of wrestling with an intricate mathematical equation, as she had done as a child with her father.

But plot, for Agatha, meant distillation of character. It did not exist in a vacuum. It is not enough that the husband in *Styles* should be suspected because he is sinister, and rejected as a suspect because he has an impregnable alibi. What lies at the root of her solution is character: the truth about men who marry rich elderly wives. It was the people who interested her, always. 'Human nature. That, I think, is perhaps the real answer as to why I am interested in this case,' as Poirot later said.[37]

Clara, of course, was unsurprised when Agatha told her what she was doing. Why not a detective story? What couldn't her girls do? It was Clara who told Agatha to go away to Dartmoor for her fortnight's holiday and finish the book quite undisturbed; she wrote all morning then, in the afternoons, tramped the moors blissfully, becoming one character after another as she muttered dialogue out loud. This became a lifelong habit. 'My sister used occasionally to say to me, "You really look like an idiot walking along the street talking to yourself,"' Agatha recalled in an interview in 1974.[38] 'But when you first start to think out a book, the nicest thing to do is to go for a long walk somewhere. *The Mysterious Affair at Styles* I wrote going along and talking as I went . . . You can't do anything until you have thought of the characters and you can feel they are real to you. Not necessarily to anyone else but to you. And you can go walking about the garden with them.'

Chief among the characters of *Styles* – and central thereafter to Agatha Christie's life, an additional husband of sorts, albeit demanding in a very different way – was Hercule Poirot: the mythical Belgian with his fanatical neatness, his egg-shaped head, his grey cells and ink-black moustache. Unreal, unbelievable, yet mysteriously alive from the moment of his irruption on to the page, and with that indefinable literary quality of *connection* with the reader. This was Agatha's writerly instinct in action: pure, unteachable, defiant of analysis. She herself did not really know how she had come to create this extraordinary little being. In her autobiography she tried, rather helplessly, to eluci-date the thought processes that were the building blocks of Poirot. 'I remembered our Belgian refugees . . . Why not make my detective a Belgian, I thought? . . . Anyway, I settled on a Belgian detective . . . Hercule – Hercule Poirot. That was all right – settled, thank goodness.'

Quite possibly her thoughts *had* run very much along these lines, but in the end this does not explain why they did so, why other thoughts were rejected along the way and the right thoughts alighted upon: this is the mystery of creativity, after all. Far less creative was the relationship between Poirot and his friend Captain Hastings, which is straightforwardly that of Holmes and Watson and downright harm-less theft. But Poirot *solus* resembles Holmes only in his absolute indi-viduality. Both characters are like fabulous line drawings: always themselves and always recognisable.[39] Provenance can be pondered but is, in the end, almost meaningless.

Doubtless fashion led Agatha to make Poirot a foreigner like Poe's Dupin or Leroux's Rouletabille, and it has been said that he was created in direct imitation of Marie Belloc Lowndes'[40] Hercules Popeau. The name hints, again, at larceny but the characters were not alike. More similar was the conceited Eugène Valmont, who appeared in stories in the early twentieth century: a would-be biographer, who made a polite nuisance of himself in the 1960s, suggested to Agatha that Poirot might have been part-inspired by Robert Barr's creation, to which she replied, 'I think nothing of Valmont . . .' Significance has been found in Poirot's physical resemblance to a dandified Satan; in the fact that Agatha, the lover of food, gave him a name so similar to the French word for 'leek' (*poireau*), and in a good deal else besides, this being the kind of benign madness that surrounds celebrity of the magnitude achieved by Poirot. The strange and beautiful truth is that he was created in a way that not even his creator perfectly understood: a felicitous stew of things she had heard, things she had read, things she remembered, things she invented: mixed and dreamed in the spaces of Agatha's life, among the medicine bottles in the Torquay dispensary, along the uphill roads to Ashfield, over the Devon moors.

And although Poirot would develop, acquiring certain depths as and when Agatha felt the need of them, he is true to his own creed of character in that he never really changed. Here he is, scuttling neatly around Styles Court in Essex (a county of which Agatha knew next to nothing), utterly and instantly himself, although at this point he needed the wretched Hastings to show it.

> 'We have found in this room,' he said, writing busily, 'six points of interest. Shall I enumerate them, or will you?'
> 'Oh, you,' I replied hastily . . .'

And:

> 'It is certainly curious,' I agreed. 'Still, it is unimportant, and need not be taken into account.'
> A groan burst from Poirot.
> 'What have I always told you? Everything must be taken into account. If the fact will not fit the theory – let the theory go.'

The moment in the book when Poirot's shaking hands 'mechanically' straighten a pair of candlesticks – in which a vital piece of evidence has been hurriedly hidden, hence the crookedness – is essence of Christie. This is no mere clue: its unearthing is absolutely rooted in

Poirot's obsession with symmetry. At her very first attempt Agatha had understood – or intuited – that a clue based upon character has double the value. She also gave Poirot the rather charming sexlessness that allows him to be wise in a manner that is almost feminine, albeit disinterested in a way that women rarely manage to be. Here, for example, he responds as Hastings clunks his way to the wrong conclusion:

'I happen to know for a fact that, far from being in love with her, he positively dislikes her.'

'Who told you that, *mon ami?*'

'Cynthia herself.'

'*La pauvre petite!* And she was concerned?'

'She said that she did not mind at all.'

'Then she certainly did mind very much,' remarked Poirot. 'They are like that – *les femmes!*'

The original ending of the book – scrawled in excitable pencil in one of Agatha's many writing notebooks, all of which were kept at Greenway House – shows the naïvety she had hitherto kept so admirably at bay: perhaps for the last time she is back in the amateur land of *Snow Upon the Desert*, writing a court scene in which Poirot gives the entire solution of the murder in the form of sensational evidence. 'M. le juge, the temperature that day was 86 in the shade'; 'Read it, M. le juge, for it is a letter from the murderer . . .' All the lines that would later appear in the revised version of *Styles* are written as dialogue between Poirot and the court judge: impeccably worked out, absolutely unfeasible. 'I think in *Styles* I wrote a court scene out of my head which just could never have taken place,' she said much later.[41]

It was a minor flaw. In every other way the book was supremely sophisticated; not least in its blithe treatment of marital boredom. Without feeling the need to moralise or even comment, Agatha presented a couple – John and Mary Cavendish – whose love for each other is foundering on his dalliance with a pretty village gypsy, and her sombre flirtation with Dr Bauerstein ('I have had enough of the fellow hanging about. He's a Polish Jew, anyway,' says John, to which Mary replies, 'A tinge of Jewish blood is not a bad thing. It leavens the' – she looked at him – 'the stolid stupidity of the ordinary Englishman.') Hastings himself is half in love with Mrs Cavendish, loathes Bauerstein on this account, and seeks at every turn to be in a married woman's company. This, too, is presented as normal behaviour. Twenty years of listening to the worldly whispers of Margaret Miller had done their work. But Agatha – like many writers before and since – was more astute in her art than in her life; and saw a good deal more clearly with the eyes of her mind.

According to her autobiography she showed *The Mysterious Affair at Styles* to Archie, who liked it very much, and encouraged her to send it to a publisher. They had not seen each other – she wrote – for two years since that first, unsatisfactory leave in July 1915, when he was so nervy and she so tense. This time all was happiness: they went to the New Forest for a week. 'We walked together through the woods and had a kind of companionship that we had not known before.' Archie said that he wanted to follow the path that led to 'No Man's Land', so they did. It took them to an orchard full of apples, which they ate as they wandered through the trees.

> All around and below her were trees, trees whose leaves were turning from gold to brown. It was a world incredibly golden and splendid in the strong autumn sunlight.
>
> Henrietta thought: 'I love autumn. It's so much richer than spring.'
>
> 'And suddenly one of those moments of intense happiness came to her – a sense of the loveliness of the world – of her own intense enjoyment of that world.
>
> She thought: 'I shall never be as happy again as I am now – never.'
>
> She stayed there a minute, gazing out over that golden world that seemed to swim and dissolve into itself, hazy and blurred with its own beauty.[42]

In fact Agatha had remembered it wrong. As Archie's notebook makes clear, the New Forest leave was in October 1915, before she had even begun to write *Styles*, and there was at no time a separation of two years during the war. This, though, was how she had remembered that particular week. 'One of the oddest things in life, I think, is the things one remembers. One chooses to remember, I suppose. Something in one must choose.'[43]

The Child

'To love anyone,' I said, 'is always to lay upon that person
an almost intolerable burden'
(from *The Rose and the Yew Tree*, by Mary Westmacott)

'L'amour est une réalité dans le domaine de l'imagination'
(quotation from Talleyrand, written on slip and kept by Agatha Christie)

In autumn 1918 Archie came home from the war to take up his post at the Air Ministry, and Agatha's real married life began. Her husband had been a creature of fantasy since they met, they had lived at a distance for six years, so her ideas about marriage were 'limited in the extreme', as she wrote in *Unfinished Portrait*. 'When people loved each other they were happy. Unhappy marriages, and of course she knew there were many such, were because people didn't love each other.'

The book describes the brief and hallowed months before the Armistice. 'Celia and Dermot were so happy together.' Their life had a fresh, young ecstasy. They explored their new world of rented flats and legitimised passion like two children in a garden. 'Married life to them was a game – they played at it enthusiastically.' After dinner the two would 'sit in front of the fire before going to bed, Dermot with a cup of Ovaltine, Celia with a cup of Bovril', and these were the happiest times of all. Having been – as Celia put it to herself – a little afraid of the stranger in her husband, she now found he was her perfect companion. He was not demonstrative, but she knew he

loved her. Sometimes he would clutch her to him and stammer: 'Celia
– you're so beautiful – so beautiful. Promise me you'll always be
beautiful.'

'You'd love me just the same if I weren't,' she replied.

Married life began in London. Agatha had gone house-hunting as
soon as Archie came back to England. At the age of twenty-eight she
left Ashfield at last for a flat in Northwick Terrace in St John's Wood,
with a bed 'full of large, iron lumps' and a rent of two and a half
guineas a week. Although the Christies had so little money it did not
occur to them to live without staff: they were looked after by Archie's
batman, Bartlett, and the general caretaker Mrs Woods, who did the
'serious cooking' and handed out advice. She was one of those competent, confident women whom Agatha always found impossible to resist.
'Fishmonger done you down again, love,' Mrs Woods would say sadly
as Agatha – who had never shopped for food in her life – returned
with her ladylike basket of sub-standard groceries.

She learned quickly, though. It was fun to learn: fun to scour the
shops for fresh fish and juicy oranges, fun to take her classes in shorthand and book-keeping (which might, in some unspecified way,
prove useful), fun to be a wife. Even poverty was fun, in a way.
Agatha saw herself and Archie rather like the couple she would
portray in her second novel, *The Secret Adversary*, who end the story
engaged to be married. Tommy is an ex-soldier, Tuppence an
ex-VAD. Their bright spirits are undimmed by the fact that he is
out of work and she, whose appearance represents 'a valiant attempt
at smartness', must sate her 'thundering good appetite' on dinners
of buns.

In 1918 there was no thought of a second book, however, as the
first – *The Mysterious Affair at Styles* – had been swiftly rejected. Various
publishers turned it down, including Methuen and Hodder &
Stoughton,[1] and what they thought about this later can only be imagined; certainly somebody might have seen past the immaturities and
picked up on this young woman's unusual facility for making plot so
accessible, so readable. But Agatha's deceptive simplicity would always
cause her to be undervalued. In her autobiography she wrote that she
'hadn't expected success' and, in her usual way, made light of the
writing lark. It is true that she had no acknowledged thought of being

anything other than an amateur who wrote whatever took her fancy: a poem, a little piece of music, a detective story. Nevertheless she did not give up on *Styles*, and eventually sent it to John Lane at the Bodley Head.

But first and foremost she was Archie's wife. Gentlemen, as she had been taught all her life, required a good deal of looking after. Food was not plentiful at the tail end of war – in her autobiography, Agatha remembered Archie's surprise at her greed when he brought home a vast joint of rationed beef – but she tried hard to replicate the kind of delicacies that had been written into the 'Receipts' book ('the orange and lemon are placed on hot rashers of bacon, which have been cooked in the <u>meantime</u>' . . .). She went to cookery classes, and learned to prepare meals for her husband. It was unfortunate that the long, lean Archie could not face Agatha's food when he came home from the Ministry in Whitehall: the soufflé would slump as he succumbed to stomach pains, writhing on the bed in agony then suddenly demanding golden syrup or treacle. Agatha had always been strong, and attracted to the fragility in Archie, but she was baffled by the forms it took. He had come home looking the same as ever. The post-war realities were not something for which she was prepared.

And she was a little lost, away from Torquay. Almost everyone she knew lived in Devon, and her one friend in London – Nan Watts, Madge's sister-in-law, who had married in 1912 but whose husband, Hugo Pollock, had walked out – was so much richer than she that it seemed impossible to socialise with her, although eventually she did visit Nan at her Chelsea home.[2] It was not that Agatha particularly craved friends. She was not the kind of woman to sit and chat with other wives: despite her pleasure in playing at home-making she 'scorned "domestic women"', as she wrote in *Unfinished Portrait*, 'absorbed in their children, their servants, their house running'. She wanted her companionship with Archie, which was magical and precious. But he worked all day and the days had to be filled. Agatha had always loved the slow stretch of free time, the growth of her imagination within silence and space. But she had been used to thinking and dreaming within the arena of Ashfield, with the hills and sea around her, not on the war-dulled streets of NW8.'[3]

This was a very different London from the one she had known as a child, visiting her grandmothers in Bayswater and Ealing. Like 'Jane Marple, that pink and white eager girl', she had trundled through the streets in a four-wheeler and gazed at the china displays in the Army and Navy Stores. Now she no longer looked out from behind a protective screen. Just to walk the streets and go shopping were new to her. So too were the impersonality, the anonymity, the crowds of people and the harsh voices. Torquay life had been warm, familiar, structured; Agatha had known everyone, or known people who knew them; she had been 'Miss Agatha', 'Miss Miller', with all that that entailed. 'Mrs Christie' was somebody else, unknown even to herself, part of a couple but also – as a married woman – out on her own. The freedoms were unnerving. Agatha later wrote about the day that peace was declared; she left her shorthand class and

went out into the streets quite dazed. There I came upon one of the most curious sights I had ever seen – indeed I still remember it, almost, I think with a sense of fear. Everywhere there were women dancing in the street . . . One felt that if there had been any Germans around the women would have advanced upon them and torn them to pieces. Some of them I suppose were drunk, but all of them looked it.[4]

Lack of control always terrified Agatha. She hated it more than almost anything, having not yet experienced the lethal chill that came when control was absolute, impenetrable. She had seen wayward behaviour during the war when, at the end of her shifts at the hospital, she had had to walk alone at night past the drunken soldiers. But then she had been going home to Ashfield and, once through the garden gate, she had been safe.

She was powerfully homesick at the start of her life with Archie. For all that she was deep in love, and treating marriage as a grand adventure ('a damned good sport', as Tommy calls it in *The Secret Adversary*), she yearned for 'dear home'. She dreamed of 'the beech tree – and the grass – growing – growing – against her cheek'[5] as she lay in the garden, gloriously idle, her head full of thoughts and possibilities and imaginary worlds. 'I *was* slightly lonely' is how she described her feelings in the autobiography. It was in *Unfinished Portrait* – as always – that she roamed the dreamscape of memory and touched the deeper truths.

After the Armistice, she and Archie went back to Ashfield. 'It was lovely to be home – home looked so much lovelier than she remembered. It was so clean – the spotless cloth for lunch, and the shining silver and the polished glasses. How much one took for granted!'[6] She was like a schoolgirl going home for the holidays: chatting excitedly about her life in London, sitting on her mother's bed as she told her about Mrs Woods and the joint of rationed beef, turning her loneliness into something small and distant. Probably she had never been happier. Such was her delight in being with her husband, for whom she felt a dark and disturbing passion, in this place of sanctuary.

She wrote poems at this time. They would be published in 1924 as *The Road of Dreams* collection, together with earlier works like 'A Masque from Italy', the youthful verse sequence on the characters of the Commedia dell'Arte. Among the later poems was 'Progression', which began:

> Love comes as the Spring comes
> Fearing . . .
> Dreading . . .
> The brown boughs are in blossom;
> A breath of frost,
> A wind from the leas,
> And the blossom would fall . . .
> But close to the earth
> The tiny common flowers
> Blossom unheeded . . .

It was during the stay at Ashfield that Agatha discovered she was pregnant. The year 1919 was a busy one, beginning with a search for a new home, large enough for a baby, a nanny and a servant. Decisive as ever, Archie resigned his commission. He was still ambitious for advancement but took the view – contrary to his previous one – that there was no future for him in the Royal Flying Corps, and that he should instead go into the City. Above all he was keen to make money. No doubt he looked forward to proving Clara wrong. Relations with his mother-in-law were perfectly good ('Miriam told herself that she had been unduly hostile and suspicious,' wrote Agatha of the mother in *Unfinished Portrait*), but Archie would not have been human if he had not resented that implacable opposition to his courting of Agatha.

When he set his mind to a thing, it tended to happen. Although he wisely did not resign until he was assured of a job, Archie quickly found work with a man he described as 'fat and yellow' – like the financier Mr Robinson, who would later feature in several of Agatha's books – and a salary of £500 per annum. This, plus his eighty pounds, and Agatha's own hundred[7] gave them sufficient funds. Accommodation was scarce at this time, but eventually they took possession of a four-bedroom flat at 96 Addison Mansions, near Holland Park, for which they paid ninety pounds a year. It was light and airy, which Agatha loved, and she threw herself into the excitement of decorating it for her new family. Home-making of this kind would become a passion. Even then she had clear ideas about what she wanted – pale paper in the sitting room, a black ceiling covered with hawthorn blossom; 'it would make me feel, I thought, that I was in the country'[8] – and she set to cheerfully with her paste and brush. A rented flat in West Kensington was hardly Ashfield; even less was it Abney Hall, with its sumptuous tapestries and green satin walls (but then Archie was so much more attractive than James Watts, and Agatha's marriage so much more lover-like than Madge's). 'We were a very ordinary couple,' wrote Agatha, with a certain pride. This was down-to-earth London living, buses and trams, bustling along with one's fellow men, an occasional night out at the Palais de Danse in Hammersmith. Money was spent in the ways that seemed natural: inconceivable to take a taxi or own more than one evening dress, equally odd to live without servants and the precious hours of leisure that they brought. That was the way things were, and they were very good. 'We were happy. Life seemed well set up for us.'[9]

Summer!
And love . . .
Stillness
And at the heart of the Stillness
A throb . . .

Archie had not wanted the baby, though. In her autobiography Agatha wrote that he had wanted a daughter rather than a son, and only girls' names were discussed; there had been, she said lightly, 'great arguments'. In *Unfinished Portrait* the conversation about her pregnancy is odder, the sense of threat deeper. 'I hate the thought of a beastly little boy . . . I shall beat him.' And: 'I don't want a baby. You'll think of it all the time and not of me. Women do. They're forever becoming domestic and messing about with a baby. They forget about their husbands altogether.' And: 'I can't bear it. I've done this to you. I could have prevented it. You might even die.'

Agatha was violently sick through the whole nine months. 'Sickness means girls,' said Mrs Woods. 'Boys you go dizzy and faint.' Perhaps it was a secret relief to believe this. Agatha wanted Archie to be happy, after all. He was extremely kind to her through the pregnancy, despite his dislike of illness; on one occasion she found a lobster on her pillow, delicious and very expensive, with which he had hoped to tempt her appetite. She devoured the lobster (always one of her favourite foods) and enjoyed it so much that she hardly minded losing it afterwards.

In her autobiography she wrote that she was 'thrilled' about the pregnancy – the conventional, sensible attitude – although she admitted having been very scared. The baby would be born at Ashfield, which was a reassurance. A sensible Torquay doctor (not one with whom she had worked as a VAD: 'I felt I knew far too much about them') told her not to worry about anything. Death in childbirth was a greater risk at that time, but Agatha was a healthy girl and nature would take its course.

But in *Unfinished Portrait* Celia's very nerves are sick. She drifts into pregnancy in a state of quiescence, lying back in a chair and listening as Dermot's hatred for his unborn child breaks over her like waves.

> 'I was just imagining that the doctor said to me, "We can't save both the mother and the child". And I said, "Hack the child in pieces."'
>
> 'Dermot, how brutal of you.'

Celia is touched in her deepest soul by what she sees as Dermot's anxiety for herself. She does not see his own fear. He craves stability rather than change; he wants Celia to care for him rather than a baby. He needs her to hold his hands and soothe away unspeakable memories. So he is possessed with resentment of the child and, perhaps, of Celia for allowing it to grow inside her.

Yet Celia knows that 'no child could replace Dermot in her heart'. She craves her mother at this time – craves what she still thinks of as home – but she is determined to stay with her husband in London. She feels that she might die, and 'she wasn't going to miss a minute of her time with Dermot . . . Sick as she was, she still loved Dermot – more than ever.' Meanwhile Dermot waits for her to regain the ethereal beauty of her youth, and become again the girl for whom he fell.

> 'Look at Gladys Cooper. She's had two children, and she's just as lovely as ever. It's a great consolation to me to think of that.'
>
> 'Dermot, I wish you wouldn't insist so on beauty. It – it frightens me.'
>
> 'But why? You're going to be beautiful for years and years and years . . .'

Eventually the time came to remove to Ashfield. The baby was due on 5 August; Agatha, still sick, travelled to Torquay with Archie. At home she found Clara and the nurse who had been employed as midwife, 'like two females caught up in the rites of Nativity: happy, busy, important, running about with sheets, setting things to order'. Agatha herself was lost in the middle of it all, waiting to be initiated into the world of motherhood, feeling not just unready but unreal. On the night the baby was due[10] she wandered into her beloved garden, hand in hand with Archie, as if she would have stayed there with him for the rest of her life.

Nurse called from the house.
    'You'd better come in now, my dear.'
    'I'm coming.'

The next morning, when her daughter was placed in her arms, she wrote that she 'was now definitely playing the part of the Young Mother. But she did not feel at all like either a wife or a mother. She felt like a little girl come home after an exciting but tiring party.'

This is the person at the heart of *Unfinished Portrait*, who deals in adulthood and remains a child. She does not engage with life, except in her imagination: she lives as if she had invented herself as one of 'the Girls', whose fate is to marry a mysterious man with whom she will be happy ever after. That does not mean life will not touch her. Her vulnerability to life is acute precisely because she is so remote from reality.

Much later, in the Mary Westmacott novel *The Rose and the Yew Tree*, Agatha considered the difference between those people who live their lives and those – like Celia – who watch themselves living them.

I remembered vaguely as a child going carefully and unsteadily down a big flight of stairs. I could hear the faint echo of my own voice saying importantly, 'Here's Hugh going down-stairs . . .' Later, a child learns to say '*I*'. But somewhere, deep inside himself, that '*I*' doesn't penetrate. He goes on not being '*I*' but a spectator. He sees himself in a series of pictures. I had seen Hugh comforting Jennifer, Hugh being all the world to Jennifer, Hugh going to make Jennifer happy . . .

Then Hugh – the narrator of *The Rose and the Yew Tree* – thinks about other people he knows, who similarly see themselves as figures in their own emotional dramas: falling in love with people for whom their feelings are illusory, being kind to people about whom they do not really care, playing at life.

Finally he thinks about his sister-in-law Teresa who, although young, is wise, brave, and willing to deal in realities. 'Here's Teresa marrying Robert, here's Teresa –

No, that wouldn't work. Teresa, I thought to myself, was adult – she had learned to say "*I*".

Agatha did not say 'I'. She knew that she did not, which was why the idea fascinated her so much in *The Rose and the Yew Tree*. Back in 1919 she gave birth, she found a flat in which to live, she decorated it, she interviewed nannies, she found a competent woman named Jessie Swannell, she created a grown-up world in which to live with Archie. And she saw it all, still, through the veil that had been flung so magically across the whole of her childhood. Here is Agatha cooking for her husband. Here is Agatha smiling at her daughter Rosalind. Here is Agatha sending out cards: 'Mrs Archibald Christie returns thanks for kind enquiries and congratulations.' Here is Agatha walking up the four flights of stairs to her family home.

Only when she had been lying in bed at Ashfield, with the baby in the care of the nurse, and her mother by her side – only then had she been 'I'. She had held Clara's hand as she fell asleep.

'Don't go away, Mummy.'

'No, darling. I'm going to sit here by you.'

Perhaps no writer learns to say 'I'; perhaps if they did they would no longer be writers. But the Agatha of 1919 had lost all thought of writing. She had, as she wrote much later, 'quite given up hope of ever having a book published':[11] the letter from the Bodley Head, asking her to visit the office and discuss *The Mysterious Affair at Styles*, dropped out of the sky as from nowhere. It arrived just after the birth of Rosalind.

Eighteen months after the manuscript had been sent out, there she was, this attractive young mother, this ladylike figure, quite the most unlikely person to know about the properties of strychnine and bromide, sitting opposite John Lane, a real-life publisher, who 'looked to me like an old-fashioned Sea Captain, with his small grey beard and twinkling blue eyes'.[12] And here he was, saying that her manuscript 'might have – I only say *might* have – possibilities'. The court scene would have to go, of course, and some other rewriting would be needed. Then publication might just happen.

John Lane did a clever job on Agatha, recognising both a talent and an easy touch when he saw one. By making her feel grateful –

and emphasising the need for alterations – he tied her into a contract for five more books with the Bodley Head, at a royalty rate only slightly above the one being offered for *Styles*, which was 10 per cent on any English sale of more than 2,000 copies. She barely noticed this clause, as she had absolutely no thought of writing five more books. Later she wrote, 'It was the beginning of my career,' but she really did not see it that way at the time. Her life now was with Archie and Rosalind. She was a wife and mother with a home to run. She would remain an amateur, writing for fun, when and if she chose. That night the Christies celebrated her piece of luck at the Palais de Danse; the next day it was back to the park with Rosalind.

Agatha did not especially enjoy the long walk through Kensington with the pram. It was tiring and 'when you got there you couldn't sit still and rest and make your mind a blank'.[13] But she was proud of Rosalind, a beautiful dark-haired child, very much like Archie in looks. The name came from *As You Like It* – Agatha later named herself after Celia in the same play – and was the choice of both parents, although before the birth Agatha had wanted Martha, after her father's American mother, while Archie had shown himself a reader of *Idylls of the King* in favouring Enid and Elaine. But Rosalind was no lily maid of Astolat, living in fantasy. She was practical, pragmatic, with almost no use for imagination. Like her Shakespearean namesake she had a near-masculine boldness of character; she was, in fact, her father's daughter. And Archie, who had taken no interest in Rosalind as a baby ('Once she can talk and walk, I daresay I shall like her', says Dermot in *Unfinished Portrait*), found himself drawn to this intelligent and self-possessed little person, whose natural delight was to engage with reality.

From the first, Rosalind was able to say 'I'. Always she took life as it was. She had no need or desire to dream of other worlds. This fascinated Agatha, but at the same time confounded her. In *Unfinished Portrait* she dreams of the day when she will take 'Judy'[14] home to her own mother: 'Judy would play in the garden and invent games of princesses and dragons, and Celia would read her all the old fairy stories in the nursery bookcase . . .'. When she takes Judy home, however, there are no invented games in the garden:

Judy wasn't any good at make-believe. When Celia told Judy how she herself had pretended that the lawn was a sea and her hoop a river horse, Judy had merely stared and said: 'But it's grass. And you bowl a hoop. You can't ride it.'

It was so obvious that she thought Celia must have been a rather silly little girl that Celia felt quite dashed.

But for all her admiration of the bright-spirited Judy, Celia's own mother thinks differently: 'She's not you, my precious . . .'

This was how Clara thought of Agatha: their relationship was one of absolute understanding, unconditional acceptance. Clara loved the 'silly little girl' in her daughter. She had not wanted her to marry Archie, partly because she had sensed that he would be ruthless with Agatha's 'silliness'. At the same time she wanted Agatha to be happy, which meant accepting the marriage to Archie.

Now, with the birth of Rosalind, Clara tried to give Agatha advice on how to hold her husband. She warned her not to leave Archie alone, to put him first, to make him feel the most important thing in her life. 'Remember, a man forgets . . .' She spoke the words of Margaret Miller, knowing they were not cynicism but sober sense. Agatha knew it too, but she felt no need to apply them to her own life. It was not that Clara expected the marriage to go wrong. She simply worked in the interests of Agatha's happiness, seeing as she did that her daughter's 'dangerous intensity of affection' required the same in return. Agatha was not mature or realistic enough to live with a mere formal family union, the kind of marriage that Madge now had. She needed love.

In *Unfinished Portrait* the mother says more: she tells Celia to put Dermot before Judy. She tells her that there had been struggles, even in her own marriage, between her love for her children and for her husband. 'You care for Dermot so much – and children take you away from a man. They are supposed to bring you together, but it isn't so . . . no, it isn't so.' It was the Clara character who spoke these words. But it was Agatha's own view that was being expressed. This was the irony: it was Archie who had feared the birth of their child, and Agatha who probably should have done so.

Agatha already had two intense relationships in her life, with her husband and her mother. Although she would never have admitted it, she had little emotional room for a child. She had married a man with whom she was passionately in love; like Caroline Crale in her novel *Five Little Pigs*, she had an unusually attractive husband and a small daughter, and the daughter inevitably came second in her heart. As the governess Miss Williams put it, 'Mrs Crale was really completely wrapped up in her husband. She existed, one might say, only in him and for him.' The Crale child is treated with affection but, says Miss Williams, a child in such a marriage 'hardly seems very real' to its parents. Hence Archie's inability to get to grips with Agatha's pregnancy and Agatha's own passivity throughout; not fully acknowledged in the autobiography, laid bare in *Unfinished Portrait*. Later, of course, Archie's attitude changed. Rosalind became a companion to him, cleaning his golf clubs with an intent frown and sharing his dry sense of humour. She was, he told Agatha, 'perfect'.

But Agatha did not need a perfect child: she herself was perfect to Clara. And so in love was she with being a daughter ('A daughter's a daughter all your life . . .') that she was unable to find true fulfilment as a mother. Just as Clara had reacted to being given away as a child by becoming a possessive, powerful force in the lives of Agatha and Madge, so Agatha reacted to all that maternal love by detaching herself from her own daughter. Could she ever have conjured again the close perfection of her relationship with Clara? Would she have wanted to? Rosalind's independent spirit, her reluctance to be hugged, her disdain for imaginative play were almost a relief to Agatha. They removed the obligation to try to replicate the bond between herself and Clara, which would have been impossible anyway. Instead, Agatha could view Rosalind at an affectionate distance, telling herself that they were simply unalike. And as Rosalind's self-sufficiency developed, so too did Agatha's objectivity. With a son she might have been different, although of course Archie had not wanted a son.

A child, she wrote in her autobiography, 'is yours and yet is mysteriously a stranger . . . it is like a strange plant which you have brought home, planted, and can hardly wait to see how it will turn out.' This is wildly at odds with contemporary thinking, which tends to believe that a child's development is within the control of its parents; an idea that even Clara Miller, so dominant an influence upon the lives of her daughters, would have balked at. She knew very well the importance of leaving a child to occupy its own imaginative spaces.

Agatha felt more strongly still. 'Many children, *most* children, I should say, suffer from over attention on the part of their parents,' says Miss Williams in *Five Little Pigs*. 'There is too much love, too much watching over the child . . . The best thing for a child, I am convinced, is to have what I should term healthy neglect on the part of both of its parents.'

This was Agatha's considered opinion. There was nothing in her of the sentimental mother, although through her communion with Clara's emotions she could feel sentimental about herself. Such was her complexity that she could be in love with her own childhood, yet turn a cool eye upon children in general, and her own daughter in particular. At the age of thirteen she had written in the Album of Confessions of her desire to be 'surrounded by babies and cats'. As an adult she believed – or so she wrote in her autobiography – that an honest mother would treat her offspring as a cat does: take satisfaction in giving birth, nurture for a little, then move back into her own life. 'Is it really natural to go on caring about your young once they're grown up and out in the world? Animals don't.'[15] The idea was in *The Moving Finger*, which has a character disliked by her own mother. 'Only mothers can't say they don't want their children and just go away. Or eat them. Cats eat the kittens they don't like. Awfully sensible, I think. No waste or mess. But human mothers have to keep their children . . .'

This is a continual refrain in her books, so much so that it takes on a faint note of defiance. 'Lots of mothers don't like their children,' she wrote in *The Moving Finger*, and, in *Crooked House*, 'Again and again a mother takes a dislike to one of her children.' She consistently refuses to take the orthodox line, as expressed by this character in *Hallowe'en Party*: 'I like all children. Most people do.' Agatha agrees with Hercule Poirot, who replies: 'Ah, there I do not agree with you. Some children I consider are *most* unattractive.'

The person who likes 'all children' has, in fact, murdered a girl of twelve by sticking her head in a bucket full of water; in Agatha Christie there is no shirking the fact that children are killed, even by their own mothers. 'There was Mrs Green, you know, she buried five children – and every one of them insured. Well, naturally, one began to get suspicious.'[16] They can also kill. Agatha created two child murderers, a child suspected of murder and, in *Peril at End House*, a child who happily tells Captain Hastings that 'I seen a pig killed. I liked it.'

In other words she sternly refused to see children as different from adults: their character was formed at an early age, it did not really change and it was just as likely to be nasty as nice. 'We are all the same people as we were at three, six, ten or twenty years old,' as she put it in her autobiography. If a child was as charming as Miranda Butler in *Hallowe'en Party*, then both she and Poirot said so. If not, not. The haze through which Agatha saw her own young self cleared instantly when she looked at other children; her views on motherhood remained utterly separate from her feelings for Clara. Exemplary maternity is as thin on the ground in Agatha Christie as it is in the plays of Shakespeare. 'Julia's quite an ordinary sort of child,' says a mother at the girls' school in *Cat Among the Pigeons*. 'I think she's got reasonably good brains, too, but I daresay mothers usually think that about their children, don't they?'

'Mothers', said Miss Bulstrode grimly, 'vary!'

In fact Julia Upjohn's mother is one of the few of whom Agatha approves. 'Mummy's gone to Anatolia on a bus,' Julia tells Miss Bulstrode – 'The child said it exactly as though she were saying her mother had taken a seventy-three bus to Marshall and Snelgrove's' – when Mrs Upjohn disappears on a tour of the East. This was very much the sort of thing that Agatha herself would later do ('when are you coming home' the ten-year-old Rosalind wrote, resignedly, from her boarding-school). So Mrs Upjohn is presented as perfectly normal, a refreshingly sane contrast to the kind of mothers who loom too large in the lives of their children. 'I think, when your children have grown up, that you should cut away from them, efface yourself, slink away, *force* them to forget you,' says a character in *Crooked House*. Her view is portrayed as extreme but not completely unacceptable, since Agatha makes clear that the family in *Crooked House* has been damaged by its stifling closeness.

'Motherhood – unrelenting!' she wrote in *N or M?*, in a tone not unlike that which described her deep unease at the street celebrations on Armistice Day. Motherhood, too, implied a lack of control, a lack of rationality; as her own mother-in-law had proved. Agatha had near-contempt for the way in which biology could take over personality. Bella Tanios in *Dumb Witness* is despised as 'definitely a dreary woman.

Rather like an earwig. She's a devoted mother. So are earwigs, I believe'; Gerda Christow in *The Hollow* is equally devoted and equally dull. They are like the women described in *The Man in the Brown Suit*, who 'talked for hours of themselves and their children and of the difficulties of getting good milk for the children . . . they *were* stupid – stupid even at their chosen job'.

In the Westmacott novels, Joan Scudamore in *Absent in the Spring* is a 'perfect' mother, the kind that would be admired today: she involves herself in every aspect of her three children's lives, and not one of them can wait to escape her well-intentioned clutches. 'She'd wanted her children to have the best things – but what *was* the best?' Then there is Ann Prentice in *A Daughter's a Daughter*, who turns down her chance at a second marriage because her daughter, Sarah, dislikes the man. Ann makes the sacrifice for Sarah but finds herself filled with uncontainable resentment:

Why do you hate me, Mother?' . . .

'I've given up my life for you – given up everything I cared for. You were my own daughter, my own flesh and blood. I chose you.'

. . . 'And ever since then, you've hated me.'

Women who sacrifice their own lives for their children fail to understand, as the infinitely wise (and childless) Dame Laura Whitstable says in *A Daughter's a Daughter*, that a sacrifice is not merely a gesture. It is something 'you have to live with *afterwards* – all day and every day'. This can only lead to unhappiness. Detachment is therefore the better choice. 'Mother are the devil! Why have they got to brood over their children? Why do they feel they know all about their children? They don't. They *don't*!'[17] Perhaps the supreme example of this is Rachel Argyle in *Ordeal by Innocence*. She is haunted by her own infertility and adopts five children in an attempt to sate her longings. 'Mrs Argyle had been blinded by her intense maternal possessiveness,' thinks her house-keeper, Kirsten Lindstrom, who had seen the adopted children not as angels of innocence, or extensions of her own egotism but as individuals – as themselves – with all their faults and virtues . . .

Women like Mrs Argyle were difficult for her to understand. Crazy about a lot of children who were not her own, and treating her husband as though he were not there! . . . a kind of living walking embodiment of MOTHER KNOWS BEST. And not really even a mother! If she *had* ever borne a child, it might have kept her humble.

This last sentence shows Agatha's sombre respect for the realities of motherhood, and for those women who recognised them: like Renisenb in her ancient Egyptian novel, *Death Comes as the End*, who says of her daughter: 'She is not me and she is not Khay – she is herself. She is Teti. If there is love between us we shall be friends all our life – but if there is not love she will grow up and we shall be strangers. She is Teti and I am Renisenb.'

What enraged Agatha was the diffuse emotionalism that mothers tended to throw around the subject, the pretence that fulfilling a biological function somehow turned them into so many Virgin Marys. Even worse were the Rachel Argyles who thought that they could buy into these feelings from the outside, as it were. 'I know heaps of mothers who hate their daughters like poison,' says Sarah in *A Daughter's a Daughter*: her defiant petulance is Agatha's, too.

But the real anger went deeper, and was to do with Agatha's own self. She was no longer the child. She was no longer at the centre of her own life. And she wanted to be, although the sensible side of her knew this was absurd. So she was enraged, too, by what she knew to be her own shortcomings. She was unable to be the kind of mother that Clara had been to her. Her insistence upon objectivity was, in a sense, self-justification: it was right not to be blinded by love for one's children, right not to give up one's life to them, right to see them objectively. So her books kept telling her. They also, of course, told her that Clara's adoration of herself and Madge was wrong-headed, even dangerous; but the paradox did not bother her. Her relationship with Clara was perfect. Her relationship with Rosalind was compounded of love, regret, bafflement and jealousy – ironically, the jealousy that Archie had expected to feel – and no maternal instinct arose to resolve these ambiguities. The emotional capacity that lay within Agatha could never quite direct itself towards her daughter. In 1930 she sent a letter from Ashfield to her second husband, Max, full of news about Rosalind and Peter, her wire-haired terrier. 'Peter is my child, you know!'

Agatha's second book, *The Secret Adversary*, was written for money at Archie's suggestion. He was not the kind of man to object to a wife who wrote books, although this was really very unusual in 1920. He did not interfere in Agatha's private thoughts and doings; in fact in *Unfinished Portrait* she wrote that she wished he had interfered more.

> 'Do you mind very much, Dermot, my being dreamy and fancying things and imagining things that might happen and what I should do if they did?'
> 'Of course I don't mind, if it amuses you.'
> Dermot was always fair. He was independent himself, and he respected independence in other people . . . The trouble was that Celia wanted to share everything.

This was not absolutely true of Agatha, who had her own cravings for solitude. But she loved her companionship with Archie and did not want to lose it, even as the layers of self-sufficiency grew around the man who had written, in 1913, of 'feeling so lonely. I miss you more than ever this time and feel so lost without having you near me.'

But in *Unfinished Portrait*, after the birth of their child, Dermot takes Celia to bed and says in his old, diffident way, 'I – I still love you frightfully, Celia.'

'Lovers – yes, they were still lovers,' thinks Celia.

A photograph taken at the end of 1919, on the day of Archie's investiture at Buckingham Palace, shows the Christies walking down a London street together. Agatha is in a dark suit, Archie in a long overcoat; both are tall and slim and rather glamorous. They look alike, in the way that close couples do, although they walk some distance apart.

(Flame!
Flame in the Forest!
Flame in my heart!
Lover of mine
Never was love such as ours
Ecstasy . . .
Joy . . .
Passion . . .
Pain . . .)[18]

So if Archie had become more controlled, less emotional, this was merely inevitable in the course of a marriage. As 'Grannie' reminds her in *Unfinished Portrait*, it was unreasonable to expect too much: '"the men" were not like that'.

Agatha remembered Margaret Miller's phrases, her robust wisdom, long after she died, aged ninety-two, soon after the birth of Rosalind; Mary Ann Boehmer had died in 1916. The deaths of these two women may not have caused Clara much grief, but without Margaret's presence Ashfield seemed very empty. Archie was probably justified in telling Agatha that her mother would do better to sell the house, and spend the extra few hundred she had inherited on something other than household bills. As always, Agatha was appalled by the idea. And in *Unfinished Portrait* her mother is equally determined to hold on to her home: '"You may need it yourself one of these days – when I am gone. I should like to feel it was there to be a refuge to you." Celia thought refuge was a funny word to use, but she liked the idea of someday going to live at home with Dermot.'

In which case – said Archie – why did she not write another book, and earn some money? She had made twenty-five pounds from *The Mysterious Affair at Styles* when it was serialised in the *Weekly Times*; hardly a fortune, but she was sure to make more this time, and yet more the time after that. Agatha was flattered, encouraged, and pleased to have a husband who took pride in her talent. John Lane, who had wanted another detective story rather than a comedy thriller, did not much like *The Secret Adversary* but it made fifty pounds in serial rights and sold better than *Styles*, thus proving Archie right. '"Now," thought Celia, "I'm pretending to be a writer. I think it's almost queerer than pretending to be a wife and mother."'

The Secret Adversary had the quality peculiar to almost everything that Agatha ever wrote: readability. The hero and heroine may send some readers for a metaphorical shotgun but Agatha's delight in them is evident. She especially loved her ex-VAD Tuppence, every bit Tommy's match in courage and resourcefulness, although the feminist angle would not have occurred to her creator. Tuppence is a sunny-natured little pragmatist – as was Agatha, at times – with a childlike greed for both food and money. Money, indeed, is the real theme of the book. The lack of it was much on Agatha's mind. 'Money, money, money!' says Tuppence. 'I think about money morning, noon and night! I dare say it's mercenary of me, but there it is!' Agatha was never penniless like Tuppence but she gets under the skin of her heroine's poverty – the cheap cheerful clothes, the tea-shop meals – and shares her ecstasy in spending a windfall on a sumptuous lunch at the Piccadilly Hotel.

Yet Tuppence, like Agatha, prefers love in the end. She turns down a millionaire in order to marry Tommy: 'What fun it will be,' she says, accepting his proposal. He is her soulmate and will be until the very last book is written. *Postern of Fate*, published just before Agatha's death, showed Tommy and Tuppence still in love in vigorous old age, having moved to a house full of Ashfield's furniture and with the Millers' rocking-horse, Mathilde, in the conservatory.

Agatha did a good deal of writing in the years after Rosalind's birth. Although she had Jessie Swannell and a maid, Rose, she still had a home to run; yet she always possessed the gift of switching instantly from everyday life to the world of her books. She never fussed about it. There was nothing of the method actor in Agatha. She could think at the washing-up bowl and write at the kitchen table. The only thing that distracted her was motherhood. In her autobiography she would tell of the irritable horror of trying to write *The Man in the Brown Suit* while a subsequent nanny, Cuckoo, chirped outside the door that 'We mustn't disturb Mummy, must we little dear?' and of struggling on a beach with *The Mystery of the Blue Train* while Rosalind demanded her constant attention ('I can stay here, can't I? I can just stand here. I won't interrupt').

But in the early 1920s Agatha's productivity was gathering apace:

she wrote *The Secret Adversary*, then *Murder on the Links*, then a clutch of short stories. 'It was by now just beginning to dawn on me that perhaps I *might* be a writer by profession. I was not sure of it yet. I still had an idea that writing books was only the natural successor to embroidering sofa-cushions.'[19] In fact her amateurism showed most in her style, which was professional in itself but not yet that of 'Agatha Christie'. She felt no obligation to give her public what it expected, since she still felt that she was writing for herself. Therefore she continued 'trying things, as one does'.

Murder on the Links was as different from its predecessor as that had been from *Styles*. It is very French; not just in setting but in tone, which reeks of Gaston Leroux and, at times, Racine ('Paul! Husband!'). Agatha admitted that she had written it in a 'high-flown, fanciful' manner. She had also based the book too closely upon a real-life French murder case, which gives the story a kind of non-artistic complexity. A highly remarkable sub-plot has Hastings in hot sexual pursuit of an auburn-haired acrobat; this, though, can be forgiven since it has the effect – greatly desired on Agatha's part – of parcelling off Hastings to wedded bliss in the Argentine.

But Poirot is magnificently himself. What originality there is in *Murder on the Links* comes straight from his thought processes. For example he deduces the *modus operandi* of the crime because it is a repeat, essentially, of an earlier murder; this proves his favourite theory that human nature does not change, even when the human in question is a killer: 'The English murderer who disposed of his wives in succession by drowning them in their baths[20] was a case in point. Had he varied his methods, he might have escaped detection to this day. But he obeyed the common dictates of human nature, arguing that what had once succeeded would succeed again, and he paid the penalty of his lack of originality.'

The singularity of Poirot was beginning to be noticed, and Agatha was asked by the editor of the *Sketch* magazine to produce a series of twelve short stories with him at their centre. 'At last I was becoming a success.' At last she was doing as Madge had done years earlier when she had sold her clever, funny 'Vain Tales' to *Vanity Fair*. Now it was Agatha ('So terribly *slow!*') who was being chased by a publisher and a magazine; she may not have intended to be a success but, now that she was one, she realised that she had wanted it. As Eden Philpotts had said back in 1909, 'A little print is very encouraging.' These first Poirots[21] were nothing like as good as the short stories she would later produce, but it was remarkable that Agatha was able to construct twelve plots to order, and probably a very good exercise for the development of her talent.

Some of these first stories were sent for publication from abroad. Throughout 1922 Agatha and Archie did a remarkable thing together: they embarked upon what was then called an 'Empire Tour', travelling to South Africa, New Zealand, Australia and Canada. The opportunity had arisen when Archie was offered a job as financial adviser to the tour, whose purpose was to promote the Empire Exhibition[22] planned for 1924. The Christies had always wanted to travel but due to lack of money – no cheap flights in those days – they had managed just two short European holidays since their marriage. Now they grabbed at this chance.

It was a risk, of course ('a sport!'). Archie would almost certainly have no City job when he returned, and his thousand-pound fee for the trip would only just cover Agatha's expenses and a month off together. In fact they were probably about ten years too old for such a gloriously irresponsible venture, but Archie was willing to do it – his job was not advancing him as far as he had hoped – and Agatha was set on fire by the thought of cutting loose, leaving family life behind, roaming unknown continents hand in hand with her husband. Not to go would have been agony. She was like her heroine Anne Beddingfeld in *The Man in the Brown Suit*, who so despises those 'stupid' women who, despite their wealth, want only to stay at home and talk about 'the difficulties of getting good milk for their children'. 'The whole wide beautiful world was theirs to wander in and they deliberately stayed in dirty dull London and talked about milkmen and servants!'[23]

She handed over Rosalind to the care of her mother and sister. Clara had encouraged her daughter to accompany her husband ('Remember, a man forgets . . .'), although Madge tried to persuade Agatha that her duty lay at home: not so much with Rosalind as with Monty, who was coming home from Africa. 'You ought to be with your brother,' she said. Perhaps aware that Madge's motives were tainted with pique, Agatha was upset but in the end did as she wanted.

On 20 January 1922 the Christies left England on the *Kildonan Castle*, and did not return for almost a year.

The Empire Tour provided most of the material for Agatha's next book, *The Man in the Brown Suit*, which she wrote on her return. It overflows with Agatha's love of travel: her craving for new sights, configurations, sensations that stretched her very soul to its limits.

> I don't suppose that as long as I live I shall forget my first sight of Table Mountain [she wrote, in the voice of Anne Beddingfeld]. It made me catch my breath and have that curious hungry pain inside that seizes one sometimes when one comes across something that's extra beautiful . . . I knew well enough that I had found, if only for a fleeting moment, the thing that I had been looking for ever since I left Little Hampsley . . .
>
> 'This is South Africa,' I kept saying to myself industriously. 'You are seeing the world. This is the world. You are seeing it.'

Anne – the 'gypsy girl', as she is called – is a version of Agatha. She is the girl who danced beneath the drifting ghost of *Unfinished Portrait*, the one who strode the seven hills of Torquay with her hand clasped to her hat and the sea air fresh on her face, the one who could seize life without fear.

> 'Starting off alone with practically no money . . . I couldn't do it, Anne, and I've plenty of pluck in my own way,' [says Suzanne, her shipboard friend]. 'I couldn't start off gaily with a few pounds in my pocket and no idea as to what I was doing and where I was going.'
>
> 'But that's the fun of it,' I cried, thoroughly roused. 'It gives one such a splendid feeling of adventure.'
>
> She looked at me, nodded once or twice, and then smiled.
>
> 'Lucky Anne! There aren't many people in the world who feel as you do.'

Anne falls for a man on the ship that takes her to Africa, and this too is a version of Agatha's story. Harry Rayburn is the Archie of her dreams: lean and beautiful, daring almost to the point of murderousness,

helplessly passionate in the face of Anne's bold gypsy spirit. 'Damn your
French frocks,' he says to her. 'Do you think I want to put frocks on
you? I'm a damn sight more likely to want to tear them off . . .'

This love affair is the most vital and sexy that Agatha ever described.
It is full of abandonment, pleasure, optimism, and it thrives within
the wild poetic world of Africa. *The Man in the Brown Suit* considers
the nature of love, rather as the Westmacotts would do later, but
unlike those novels it does so from a position of strength; so sure is
Anne that love will make her happy, even when it makes her suffer.
So sure is she of Harry.

'I shouldn't dream of marrying anyone unless I was madly in
love with them. And of course there is really nothing a woman
enjoys so much as doing all the things she doesn't like for the
sake of someone she does like. And the more self-willed she is,
the more she likes it . . . Women like to be mastered, but they
hate not to have their sacrifices appreciated. On the other hand,
men don't really appreciate women who are nice to them all the
time. When I am married, I shall be a devil most of the time,
but every now and then, when my husband least expects it, I
shall show him what a perfect angel I can be!'

Harry laughed outright.

'What a cat and dog life you will lead.'

'Lovers always fight,' I assured him. 'Because they don't understand each other. And by the time they do understand each other
they aren't in love any more.'

This meant nothing, really, beyond Anne's delight in saying it, although
it was true that Archie remained a mystery to Agatha, true that she did
not understand him, and true that she was still in love with him.

(Closer, O heart of mine . . .
Closer yet . . .
Your lips . . .
In the Forest the leaves are on fire,
Spendthrift and reckless their joy!
Riot of life!)[24]

Of course the Christies were not like Anne and Harry, who end the book living in Africa, their son crawling happily between them and their passion for each other undiminished. Archie crossed London to the City every morning; Agatha pushed a pram, chatted to shopkeepers and servants, bashed at her typewriter. At weekends they took trains out of London. Occasionally they had a round of golf at East Croydon. Agatha had not played since her days on the Torquay course with Reggie Lucy, and had never been much good, but she liked the walk, and it pleased her to see Archie enjoying himself so much ('At weekends Celia got her comrade back'). It was all very typical, very ordinary. Normal life, beneath which lay powerful emotions. A photograph from the early 1920s shows Archie sitting on a wooden bench – possibly outside Ashfield – with a pipe in his right hand. To one side of him is Rosalind, serious-faced beneath her abundance of dark hair, and on the other Peter the dog, attentive to the click of the camera. The tableau could not be more conventional but it is entirely beautiful, because of the beauty of its subjects. There is love in the picture too; love, as Agatha wrote in one of her poems, which 'for a while, made magic common things . . .'[25]

A companion photograph shows Agatha in a similar tableau, with her daughter to her right, her dog to her left. Again the picture is charming – Rosalind smiles her father's smile, Peter lifts shining eyes to the camera – but Agatha, by this time, seems some years older than Archie. Here she is again, embarking upon the *Kildonan Castle* with the travelling dignitaries of the mission, photographed for *The Times*, looking assured and social in her hat and furs. Who would have guessed what imaginings lay within?

There is no Empire Tour in *Unfinished Portrait*, because it was a different Agatha who went round the world: free and bold and confident. Celia merely dreams 'that if the chance were to be given her she would leave Dermot and Judy and Aubrey [the dog] and everything and dash off into the blue . . .'

Of course the reality of the Empire Tour was a disappointment in many ways. Ordinary life continues, even in unknown continents, and human nature does not necessarily transform itself. To an extent, Agatha was at the mercy of Archie's job, not that there was any real point to it, or indeed to the whole trip. It had been organised by a man named Major Belcher, assistant general manager of the 1924 Empire Exhibition, who was leading a mission to the Dominions to promote the exhibition among political leaders and businessmen. This sort of thing was very much to Belcher's taste; so much so that the trip was probably conceived as a promotional mission for himself.

Belcher's presence dominated the tour, to an extent that Agatha could not have imagined, that she found insufferable at the time and comical in retrospect. He was a very modern type, for all his old-school-tie manner. He would have thrived on quangos or talking impressive-sounding nonsense on television; he was one of nature's politicians, although not from any sense of public duty: again, his sense of duty was directed towards his own advancement. In the First World War he had had the non-job of Controller of Supplies of Potatoes, which he did extremely badly before sailing on to his new post with the Empire Tour. He was childish, mean and somehow addictive as a personality: 'Never, to this day, have I been able to rid myself of a sneaking fondness for Sir Eustace,' wrote Agatha of the fictionalised Belcher, whom she put into *The Man in the Brown Suit*. 'I dare say it's reprehensible, but there it is.'[26]

Belcher liked Agatha too, although this was not always apparent. He had known Archie for years, having taught him when he was briefly a master at Clifton, and held him in such high regard that he had offered him the role of financial adviser to the tour (or, as Archie was billed in an overseas newspaper, 'Governor of the Bank of England'). Again, this sounds like a post that could easily not have existed. In fact Archie's chief job was to handle Belcher through his moods, and to defuse the situations they might create. For this he was far from overpaid, since Belcher was as difficult as a fractious two-year-old. Meanwhile Agatha bandaged Belcher's septic foot while he shouted at her like an aged Henry VIII, bought him socks and linen for which he never reimbursed her, and generally kept him as soothed as possible (the nurse in her now came in handy). He was tremendous material, of course. Although Agatha always claimed not to put real people into her books this was not completely true: Sir Eustace Pedler was Belcher to the life. It was Archie's suggestion that Agatha should give him a title, and Belcher's own that he should be the murderer.

Agatha had wanted to make him the victim. His behaviour was a constant nightmare, particularly to someone who, as she did, valued manners. 'We went into the Town Hall,' she wrote to Clara from Melbourne in May, 'and were kept waiting a few minutes while they looked for the Mayor. Fresh explosions from Belcher. When found, he genially asked Belcher who and what he was – I thought he would have apoplexy! He really does think he is a King, or Lord Northcliffe . . .'[27] Later, when he found himself sitting surrounded by notables in the Governor's Box at the races, he became 'complacent' and started to purr with snobbish pleasure. Later still his temper disintegrated again: 'I console myself by the thought that I have had nearly £200 of free railway travel, and one must put up with something for that! I speak to him as little as possible now, am just quietly polite!'[28]

This was all very well, but not every day for almost ten months. The itinerary, too, was exhausting. The mission spent February to April in South Africa, at one point becoming caught in the middle of a revolution.[29] 'They hoisted a red flag and proclaimed a Soviet government,' Agatha wrote to Clara, as she might have described a music-hall turn. Remembering that she must disdain fear, she refused to be alarmed when the mission was trapped in Pretoria (although Clara might well have been when she read the letter). Martial law was proclaimed, bombs fell and trains ceased to run, but Agatha's sole admitted concern was that she might 'miss the [Victoria] Falls after all with this strike trouble'.

The mission left Africa in May, travelled to Australia then Tasmania, and spent July in New Zealand. August was the holiday month in which Agatha and Archie went to Hawaii (this annoyed Belcher a great deal, even though they were paying for themselves). September and October were spent touring Canada – Victoria, Calgary, Edmonton, Regina, Winnipeg and Toronto, with two days in each city – culminating in a visit to Niagara Falls. From Ottawa Archie continued on northwards with Belcher and his secretary, Bates,[30] while Agatha went south to stay with her godmother Cassie in New York. 'Home on

November 30th!' she wrote to Clara, with the air of one who could scarcely wait.

It was not so much the travelling, more the relentless socialising that had taken its toll. A constant procession of people joined and met the mission. Agatha kept a diary of activities for her mother, and this was a typical week in South Africa: an evening spent in the tedious company of Mrs Hiam, whose rich husband was a friend of Belcher's – 'they are quite attached to me. I iron their clothes for them . . . deal and shuffle for them when we play cards'; a day's surfing; a tour of a museum in the company of its director, who explained to her in detail about early human skulls 'from the Pithecanthropus downwards'; a tour of fruit farms – 'I was by then rather weary of seeing fruit dried, it's the same everywhere, and it was scorchingly hot. The Hiams were so done to the world that they wouldn't get out of the car'; the Opening of Parliament ceremony 'to which we went dressed in our best', followed by more battles with surfboards – 'I believe one could have great fun with them at Paignton on a rough day'; an archbishop's garden party; a climb up Table Mountain; a foursome of golf with another couple; an evening of bridge; and so it went on, and on.

Agatha's stamina was always remarkable (which she attributed to the fact that she had spent her youth doing nothing), and she would never need it more than on this tour, which required her to be continually chatting, smiling, dressing up and taking an interest in things that must often have been intolerably boring. 'Companionship is not a thing that one needs every day,' she had written in her autobiography, adding that it 'sometimes becomes as destroying as ivy growing round you'. Here she had it unceasingly. She described, for instance, having to talk to unidentified royalty at a Government House lunch in Cape Town: 'A terrible five minutes ensued during which the Princess and I tried to keep up a conversation. She is known through South Africa as being only capable of saying 'oh, yes . . .' Later, Archie had charge of the princess and 'quite cheered her up. She and Archie agreed that they both hated getting up early and could never remember people's names, to which Archie added cheerily, "But that must be rather awkward for you in your line of business."' Meanwhile Agatha was coping with the prince, admiring his 'rather ill bred Sealyham' and laughing politely as he defined an optimist as 'a man who runs away with someone else's wife'.[31]

In later life Agatha would claim to be paralysingly shy, and to hate parties and conversation with people she did not know. Yet she showed no sign of this on the Empire Tour. She even made a speech, 'hanging on firmly to Mr Pecksniff's advice "Take care of the sounds and the sense will take care of itself."' On the whole she was a highly successful social animal. Duty, of course, kept her going. She was there to represent her country, the mission, her husband. She would therefore be as charming, cheerful and groomed as she could be; she needed to be, as she was under considerable scrutiny. A cutting from a newspaper in Canterbury, South Africa, described a 'delightful little impromptu morning tea' given in Agatha's honour: 'Mrs Christie, who is the author of several successful detective stories, wore, over her mole coloured marocain frock, a charming loose Paisley wrap, with mole collar and a small mole hat of hatter's plush . . .'

Agatha was also intensely grateful for the chance to make this trip, so she was never going to be anything other than gracious. And she was a good-humoured woman, not a complainer like Mrs Hiam; as she had written in the Album of Confessions at the age of thirteen, she would always seek 'to make the best of everything'. She must, in fact, have been a consoling presence on this long tour. Even when her passion for surfing brought on neuritis – 'like toothache all down your arm' – she tried very hard to keep up appearances. 'I'm getting the pain much less often now,' she wrote to her mother, in between the usual round of dinners, bridge tournaments and endless chat.

The compensations were immeasurable. She was seeing the world in the company of the man she loved and, as she later wrote in *The Man in the Brown Suit*, this was a wondrous thing. 'We have arrived!' she wrote to Clara from South Africa on 6 February. 'I had no idea there were so <u>many</u> mountains.' Lake Louise was 'the loveliest place we've been to yet'. The Victoria Falls were so beautiful 'I can't bear to leave'. On the Zambezi 'we saw a crocodile straight away, which cheered us very much'. In New Zealand, 'I have never seen anything in my life as beautiful as Wellington Harbour'. So it went on. She poured her enthusiasm on the many pages she wrote to Clara and, like an earnest schoolgirl, made determined attempts to describe everything:

> All Australian scenery that I have seen has a faintly austere quality, the distance is all a soft blue green and sometimes almost grey – and the white trunks of the blue gums give a totally different effect, and here and there great clumps of trees have been ringbarked and have died – then they are ghost trees, all white with white waving branches. It's all so – virginal – if there were nymphs in the wood, they would never be caught . . .[32]

Agatha was not a natural descriptive writer: as in this letter to Clara she became self-conscious, touchingly effortful. In her books she could give a sense of place in a phrase or detail, although there is a translucent quality to her descriptions that leaves them imprecise and generic. 'She was by nature remarkably unobservant,' she wrote of herself in *Unfinished Portrait*, and despite her acute ear it was true that she saw imaginatively rather than accurately. But with these letters from the Empire Tour she was trying to pin down her memories with words (she also took a good many photographs): she would not have expected to return to these places, and she did not want to forget them.

She also wanted to bring them alive for Clara. Despite her mother's blessing she felt guilt at being away, and she tried to assuage this by keeping her mother informed about all that she did. Ostensibly the guilt was over Rosalind: 'my little Teddy', as she and Archie called their daughter. 'I think of my little Poppet such a lot and get more and more homesick for her,' Agatha wrote to Clara, and a good deal more in similar vein. 'My baby must be <u>so</u> sweet. I'm dying to see her – so is Archie.' From Pretoria Agatha wrote to her daughter, then staying at Abney with Madge (or 'Punkie', as Rosalind called her). 'I suspect you love Uncle Jim and Auntie Punkie very much now, but if anyone asks you "who do you love?" you must say "Mummy!"' This was equally for Madge's benefit, as Rosalind was as yet too young to read.

As always, though, the weight of Agatha's feelings was bent towards her mother. She wrote to her in a pencilled scrawl immediately she boarded the *Kildonan Castle*: 'Darling Mummy – Everything very comfortable – Nice cabin with lots of room – I <u>do</u> love my violets. Take care of yourself, darling – I <u>do</u> love you so much.' She also sent many typed pages of her 'diary' and lots of photographs: shots of kangaroos, a pineapple farm, and two black children standing on their heads with 'Little Boys' Pastime' written carefully on the back. It worried Agatha to be away for so long. '<u>If you want me home earlier I can come</u>. I can come right away any time.' With her ability to inhabit Clara's emotions she felt her mother's vulnerability, solitude, fear of ageing more painfully than if they were her own; and she sought constantly to reassure Clara that she was in her thoughts. 'Lots and lots and lots of love, my precious Mummy'. On arrival in South Africa, Agatha had 'bought a 1/- basket of peaches, great yellow ones, five we thought, but discovered there were lots underneath and really about fifteen. We ate them juicily in the garden, and little Natal pineapples at 5d. each . . . I do wish you could be here. We would have a lovely eat together! Darling Mummy, it would be nice.'[33]

From Australia she wrote in May that the river Tamar 'for most of the way is almost exactly like a rather bigger Dart, with the wooded hills sloping down each side. It made me feel quite homesick.' This might have been true, but at the same time it was intended to please. Agatha also reassured her mother (and Madge) that her books were flourishing: 'Two splendid batches of cuttings from John Lane were awaiting me here – Very good ones,' she wrote of *The Secret Adversary*. 'I really feel Tommy and Tuppence is going to be a success – so don't worry about money.'[34] Among the letters sent from the Empire Tour were scraps of paper relating to the small investments that Agatha had made: 'Chinese Bonds: 4 at £2.5.0, 2 at £1.2.6 . . .' Money was still tight, and worrisome. 'Remember I have 200 in my deposit at home if you want it,' Agatha told Clara. 'Very glad you've got an invalid chair for Monty . . . I feel rather awful being away enjoying myself and living off the fat of the land here.'[35]

But Clara loved Agatha to be happy, and was pleased by her buoyant letters. She also received, from her son-in-law, a souvenir from Honolulu: 'Some Scenes from the great Cinema Picture entitled Agatha goes Surfing', a book that Archie had made containing captioned photographs of Agatha in her swimsuit (a little thick in the thigh, but confident and attractive), carrying her surfboard, sitting on it in deep water and finally 'entering a drug store for an ice cream soda'. The front page of the book read: 'Scenario by Archibald Christie; Produced by Archibald Christie; Directed by Archibald Christie'. So Archie was making an effort for Clara ('Dear Mrs Miller'), and he and Agatha clearly enjoyed their month off in Hawaii. They were not alone together. They chose to be almost constantly in company – 'Lord Swenfen and St Aubyn', also members of the country club, where they played golf – but they were spared Belcher, and they made the most of their freedom to bathe and surf. 'The first day's bathing so burnt us that we were in real agony! Archie was much the worst . . .' In fact Archie's health was starting to break down under the strain of travelling and socialising. He had a 'bad cold' in Honolulu, then in Ottawa collapsed with severe bronchitis and nettle-rash

so that he was almost screaming with the pain and frustration. It started at Winnipeg when he went over one of the big grain elevators and returned with streaming eyes and wheezing . . . I'm terrified of his getting pneumonia. It's been snowing all today and yesterday the wind was cruel. We are both sick of the Mission and longing to get home.[36]

Archie lacked Agatha's resilience. On the voyage out, back in January, he had looked after his wife when she was seasick, then played deck quoits with her against a pair of Belgians ('Everyone kept coming up to us and saying 'I hear you've knocked out the Dagoes! Splendid''). But as the tour wore on so Archie's strength wore out. He was 'not a sociable animal'.[37] His weak nerves and stomach craved respite.

In May the mission sailed to Adelaide. Agatha wrote to her mother that she was 'sea sick for the first half of the voyage', but that afterwards she

had rather a merry time. There were several young people on board and we played silly games every evening or else danced – and the last three nights we had supper parties with the Captain or one of the other officers and got to bed about 3 a.m. I loved it (Archie, needless to say, retired punctually at 10.30, as usual – but fortunately had no objection to my being gay even if he wasn't – though marvelling at my taste). Then we got up a jazz band – also played balloons in which game everybody banged others on the head with a large balloon . . .[38]

At which Clara surely longed to say: Remember, Agatha. Don't leave a man alone too much. Don't ignore a husband. Put him first.

One night in Sydney Agatha was dining alone in the hotel, Archie having gone off on an official outing, when she was swooped upon by a Major Bell and his sister Una. The mission had been invited to stay with the Bells at Queensland but had other commitments, so it was arranged that Agatha should stay with them for a week, then be joined by the men. She went off that night. 'We arrived about 10.00 after motoring five miles, and the room seemed full of tall energetic girls cooking scrambled eggs over the fire and all talking at once!'

The Bells, who owned large parts of Queensland, were 'rather like a Royal family', as Agatha wrote to Clara. The sisters treated her as one of their own. She helped them organise a local show, sang in it to great acclaim, and generally revelled in their admiring company. They reminded her of the merrily confident Lucy sisters ('"One of us" as the Lucys say – the first people I have met out here who were!') And as with Reggie Lucy, with whom Agatha had had a serious flirtation, so it was with one of the Bell brothers, Frick. 'I really lost my heart,' she wrote in her autobiography. In later life Frick's son Guilford would redesign Greenway House for Agatha, and become a close friend to both her and Rosalind.[39] 'I felt quite one of the family by the time I left! And quite sad to leave. We left Brisbane the next day and sail for New Zealand on the 29th. Archie has an awful cold and is very done up . . .'

But when Agatha wrote of having 'lost her heart', or of playing a balloon game on board ship until three in the morning, or of being 'snapped' with a camera by a young man who had watched her surfing, there was nothing but simple pleasure in the tales. She had no eye for anyone but Archie. Her flirting was merely that of Anne Beddingfeld with the 'strong, silent' Colonel Race, whom Anne finds attractive in a way that does not impinge upon her desire for Harry Rayburn. Similarly she took no notice of the woman in New Zealand who, on a drive to Lake Kanieri, took an 'immediate fancy to Archie' and insisted that he sit in her car. Agatha and Archie were married; they were in love; there was nothing more to consider.

> (What was that strange dry sound?
> A leaf that crackled beneath my feet
> Withered and brown . . .)[40]

In her next book, *The Secret of Chimneys*, Agatha would again portray a joyful and passionate couple.

> 'Marriage, the kind of marriage I mean, would be the biggest adventure of the lot.'
> 'I like that,' said Virginia, flushing eagerly . . .

Chimneys was perhaps the happiest book that Agatha ever wrote. A comedy thriller published in 1925, it steals from *The Prisoner of Zenda* and P. G. Wodehouse but has a soufflé quality all of its own. The hero, Anthony Cade, is long, lean, daring and passionate: another dream Archie. The heroine, Virginia Revel, is clever and charming, with her 'delicious and quite indescribable mouth that tilted ever so slightly at one corner in what is known as "the signature of Venus"'. The politician George Lomax is a cleverly drawn monolith of pomposity: 'Not that I approve of women in politics – St Stephen's is ruined, absolutely ruined, nowadays. But a woman in her own sphere can do wonders.' The owner of Chimneys (a house very much like Abney) is one of nature's nobodies whose misfortune it is to have a position in life, and his perpetual petulance is exquisitely done. '"Omelet," said Lord Caterham, lifting each lid in turn. "Eggs and bacon, kidneys, devilled bird, haddock, cold ham, cold pheasant. I don't like any of these things. Tredwell, ask the cook to poach me an egg, will you?"' Agatha was not an especially humorous woman – something deep in her took life very seriously – but *Chimneys* bubbles deliciously with laughter. 'For a moment or two, no one spoke. Superintendent Battle because he was a man of ripe experience who knew how infinitely better it was to let every one else speak if they could be persuaded to do so . . . George because he was in the habit of having notice given him of the question.' Very possibly Agatha had seen a George Lomax or two on her travels round the world during one of those interminable official dinners she had attended with Archie; had observed, with silent amusement, his worried desire to control the world.

Chimneys is what nowadays would be called a snobbish book. Almost all its characters are upper class and those who are not are described as such. 'I certainly know her face quite well – in that vague way one does know governesses and companions and people one sits opposite to in trains. It's awful, but I never really look at them properly. Do you?' And when Virginia first meets Anthony in bizarre circumstances, nervous of asking for his help,

'Excuse me,' she said, 'but are you – I mean—'
'Eton and Oxford,' said the young man. 'That's what you wanted to ask me, wasn't it?'
'Something of the kind,' admitted Virginia.

Agatha was too relaxed, in *Chimneys*, to bother to see round the class question in the way that she would later do, although probably never to the satisfaction of modern sensibilities. In her Westmacott novel *The Rose and the Yew Tree*, set at the time of the 1945 Labour election victory, she would look hard at the 'old ideas' and consider their validity ('The ruling class. The governing class. The upper class. All such hateful phrases. And yet – be honest – something in them?'). In *Towards Zero*, written in 1941, she would show sympathy with a young man who is despised by his social 'superiors' because he has no money and lives off his looks.

'You're happy and superior in your little roped off enclosure shut off from the common herd. You look at people like me as though I were one of the animals outside!'
'I'm sorry,' said Mary.
'It's true, isn't it?'
'No, not quite. We are stupid, perhaps, and unimaginative –

but not malicious. I myself am conventional and, superficially, I dare say, what you call smug. But really, you know, I'm quite human inside . . .'

'You're a nice creature,' he said. 'But you don't know much about the animals prowling about outside your little enclosure.'

Impossible to deny that Agatha lived in an enclosure, that of the upper-middle class into which she was born. Her letters home from the Empire Tour take a similar tone to *Chimneys*. A hotel room in Sydney 'reeks of stale commercial traveller'; a woman on the ship to Adelaide is 'rather common – but amusing – and when at a fancy dress evening she actually came as a "very fast chorus girl" we could hardly contain ourselves!' She also threw out the odd, casually xenophobic remark. 'It was a relief to get away from the "Australian voice",' she wrote to Clara from Wellington. 'The New Zealand people really are like English people.' In *Chimneys* she describes the rich banker, Isaacstein, as being dressed 'in very correct English shooting clothes which nevertheless sat strangely upon him. He had a fat yellow face, and black eyes, as impenetrable as those of a cobra.' In fact Isaacstein turns out to be a sympathetic character. Even more so is the Jewish Sebastian Levinne in the 1930 novel *Giant's Bread*, which – as always with the Westmacotts – takes a rounded view, and examines anti-Semitism in some depth. Nevertheless this kind of jaunty remark, typical of *Chimneys* – 'Like all Dagoes, he couldn't swim' – can only be explained away by saying that every class and every era has its own prejudices: a Tory MP in the late twentieth century might have been described with just as much contempt, and just as little general outrage, as a foreigner in early Agatha Christie.

As only a highly complex person can, she created simplicity in *The Secret of Chimneys*. She created a world that she longed to inhabit, full of people from a class slightly higher than her own, who took life easily; the kind described here by Superintendent Battle.

'You see, the majority of people are always wondering what the neighbours will think. But tramps and aristocrats don't – they just do the first thing that comes into their heads, and they don't bother to think what anyone thinks of them. I'm not meaning just the idle rich . . . I mean those that have had it born and

bred in them for generations that nobody else's opinion counts
but their own. I've always found the upper classes the same –
fearless, truthful and sometimes extraordinarily foolish.'

That was not Agatha. She was not fearless, she was not always
truthful and she learned the hard way not to be foolish. She was also
self-conscious to a degree that was not aristocratic at all. Perhaps it
was that very quality which she yearned, at times, to be free of: to be
a wife and mother, lead a happy woman's life, nothing more.

> (Closer, O heart of mine.
> I am afraid . . .
> Your lips . . .)[41]

The Secret Adversary

'To Lloyds Bank Torquay, 16th March 1926: to pay Wentworth Club £8.8/-
every year, Mrs A. Christie, Styles, Sunningdale, Berkshire'
(bankers' order form, signed and kept by Agatha Christie)

'What did Roddy know of Mary Gerrard? Nothing – less than nothing! . . .
It was the old story – Nature's hoary old joke!'
(from *Sad Cypress* by Agatha Christie)

I n 1943 Agatha wrote her third Mary Westmacott novel, *Absent in the Spring*. She wrote it very quickly – in less than a week – as the idea had been burning in her for a long time.

The central character, Joan Scudamore, whose life has been lived in pleasantly sheltered environs, is travelling home to England from a visit to her daughter in Baghdad. When her train fails to arrive due to bad weather, she is left alone in the desert for three days. During her time in the wilderness she comes to realise that her marriage, which she had believed to be entirely happy, is a lie: her husband, apparently so devoted and respectable, has for years been in love with another woman. Alone in the desert Joan understands all this. She reads the signs that should have been clear. She sees what she had been too obtuse, too complacent and too innocent to see before.

. . . Tony's scornful boyish voice:
'Don't you know anything about Father?'

She hadn't. She hadn't known a thing! Because, quite determinedly, she hadn't wanted to know.

When Agatha and Archie returned from the Empire Tour, having finally
docked at Southampton on 1 December 1922, life was harder for them
than either had anticipated. They had known that they would return
to problems but had been too excited by the idea of change – or 'risk'
– to take the realities seriously. Now they were back in a wintry London,
tired and broke. Rosalind would hardly acknowledge their presence ('I
want my auntie Punkie'). Jessie Swannell had fallen out with Clara and
been replaced with an annoying new nanny, known as Cuckoo ('Now
then, little dear . . .'). Monty's erratic behaviour had driven Clara to
breaking-point. And Archie, whose job in the City had of course been
given to somebody else, now found it impossible to get work.

He probably wished he had never embarked on the tour. Agatha –
who had enjoyed it immensely, on the whole, and retained her eager
zest for life – now stayed with him in London as he trailed through
the days in pursuit of employment, even though he urged her to go
away with Rosalind while he was in such a depressive state. 'I'm no
good in trouble. I can't stand trouble.' She refused to stay with Clara
or Madge, remembering that a man should not be left alone, even if
he wanted to be. It did not occur to her that she should put her
shorthand and book-keeping to use by getting a job – married women
of her class did not do that – but as the Christies no longer had a
maid she had work to do around the house. 'I want to share this with
you,' she said to Archie, although she was sorely tried by his irri-
tability and melancholia, which her presence seemed to exacerbate.
Later she wrote a version of this time in her Westmacott novel *The
Burden*, in which the glamorous young Henry is stricken with illness
and takes out his frustrations on his wife, Shirley, who similarly sticks
it out by his side.

'I don't want to leave you.'
'I don't care whether you go or not. What use are you to me?'
'I don't seem to be any use,' said Shirley dully.

Life was catching up with Archie, in fact. The trip abroad and the toll it had taken upon his health, the humiliating search for work, the knowledge that his mother-in-law would consider him to have failed her daughter, the constant background babbling of Cuckoo, the penetrating eye of Rosalind, the anxious smiling face of his wife and, beneath it all, the memories of death and blood and terror: his nerves felt as exposed as wounds. The Christies were not mentally robust. Peg was volatile in the extreme and in 1963 her younger son, Campbell, would be found dead in his gas-filled kitchen. Archie's air of masculine decisiveness, his charm and his extreme self-control kept his vulnerability hidden. But the effort cost him. He was later described as looking 'tied-up inside'.[1] Agatha knew her husband's fragility – she had found it powerfully attractive – but now she longed, above all, for it not to be exposed. She dreaded Archie's unhappiness because he coped with it so badly, almost in the manner of a small boy who demanded that things be made better. 'I can't stand not having what I want.' She prayed that he would quickly find a job. Eventually an offer of work was made, albeit from a firm of dubious reputation. 'It was employment and brought some money in, and Archie's mood improved.' No more evenings spent across the table from a tense white face staring down into an uneaten dinner, without television or even radio to divert the attention ('. . . on the hearth dead embers lie/Where once there burned a fire of living flame').[2] It had been hellish, Agatha could not help but admit to herself. But now life was back to the happy normality she craved. And her work – which thrived on that normality – was going wonderfully well.

She was free of the Bodley Head, having moved to another publishing house, Collins, on greatly improved terms. She had been vexed with John Lane for some time, believing that he had taken advantage of her inexperience when he tied her into a five-book deal. She had brooded on this during the round-the-world trip, encouraged to do so by the news that Madge's play was being considered for production: 'It seems as though there was such a thing as an agent who is some good,' she wrote snappishly to Clara. On her return she hastened to Hughes Massie – the literary agency to whom Eden Philpotts had recommended her back in 1909 – and this time was welcomed with open arms by the agency's new head, a young man named Edmund Cork. He could not have known quite how lucky a day it was for him when Agatha Christie walked through his door in Fleet Street, but he certainly treated her with serious respect. His manner, which was gentlemanly but direct, made him a person that Agatha could do business with; he would handle her affairs until the end of her life.

For all her dreaminess Agatha was tough when it came to selling her work. Cork encouraged this, and helped her write the terse, cool letters that would extricate her from the Bodley Head contract.[3] But the toughness was there anyway: she was, after all, the descendant of her businessman grandfather, Nathaniel, and of his wife Margaret, who always emphasised the importance of money in a woman's life ('Keep £50 in five-pound notes somewhere safe, you never know when you might need it'). In 1924 Agatha was offered five hundred pounds by the *Evening News* for serialisation of *The Man in the Brown Suit*, a sum that greatly astounded her husband and sister although not, of course, her mother. From around that time she realised that her writing had a measurable worth, and put a price on herself. Only very rarely could she be prevailed upon to do something for love rather than money.

This was not a particularly English literary attitude. It surprised people, not least the BBC, which was stunned by Agatha's refusal to accept that it had the right to pay less than anybody else. 'Her entire approach was commercial,' bitched an internal memo in 1948.[4] The BBC was not really Agatha's kind of set-up; she never liked anything state-controlled, and she certainly disliked low wages. She occasionally worked for BBC Radio but in 1932, in a letter to the producer, she refused to write a series of short stories: 'They really are not profitable. I don't mind an odd one now and again, but the energy to devise a series is much better employed in writing a couple of books. So there it is!' This would always be her attitude. She worked extremely hard and, in return, she expected her fair reward.

She had seen her father lose the Miller fortune through sheer blithe ignorance and, however much she had admired Frederick, she could not share his aristocratic airiness about money. She always understood that money had a value beyond that of simple currency and she was, instinctively, a capitalist. She approved of the banker Alastair Blunt in

Clara Miller

Archie *(2nd left)* as an officer
in the RFC

Agatha and Rosalind

THE DAILY NEWS, SATURDAY, DECEMBER 11, 1926

MRS. CHRISTIE DISGUISED.

Mrs. Agatha Christie as she was last seen (centre), and (on left and right) how she may have disguised herself by altering the style of her hairdressing and by wearing glasses. Col. Christie says his wife had stated that she could disappear at will if she liked, and, in view of the fact that she was a writer of detective stories, it would be very natural for her to adopt some form of disguise to carry out that idea.

The newspapers were ingenious in their search for new angles on the 'disappearance'

The searchers of the North Downs on a lunch break

Dredging the mill pond at Albury

Agatha's flight from Harrogate was on the front page of almost every newspaper; here, on the left, she is pictured with her sister Madge

The hotel in Harrogate where Agatha was discovered

Agatha and Max in 1933, outside her house in Cresswell Place and about to leave for the East

Max and Barbara Parker

The house in Baghdad where Agatha stayed

Excavations at Nimrud

Agatha and Max on site at Nimrud.
Behind them are the tents in which
they and their colleagues slept

Agatha and Max outside Greenway *(and below)*. The lawn at Agatha's left slopes down to the river Dart

In the library at Greenway, 1946. Above Agatha's head is the frieze painted by officers of an American flotilla, who occupied the house during the war

In the kitchen at Winterbrook, 1950

Agatha and Max, 1969

In the library at Winterbrook. This was Max's favourite room, in which he wrote his book on Nimrud; he would scarcely have noticed the state of the ceiling

JOHN HEDGECOE/TOPFOTO

St Mary's Church, Cholsey, where Agatha is buried

Max following Agatha's coffin, 1976

Max and Rosalind at Agatha's funeral

Agatha's grave

One, Two, Buckle My Shoe for his belief that a country should be governed by the same economic principles that apply to a properly run household. This was Agatha's kind of thinking: those who despised it as petty-bourgeois were indulging in mere adolescent fantasy. 'Yes, but how can you be satisfied with things as they are?' Alastair Blunt's niece says to him. 'All the waste and the inequality and the unfairness. Something *must* be done about it!' To which Blunt replies, in the voice of his creator: 'We get along pretty well in this country, Jane, all things considered.'

Jane Olivera is rich – not least thanks to Alastair Blunt – as is the upper-class David Angkatell in *The Hollow*, who has the similar luxury of despising his relations for their lack of political principle. 'I must have a talk with you, David, and learn all the new ideas,' says his cousin Lucy. 'As far as I can see, one must hate everybody, but at the same time give them free medical attention and a lot of extra education (poor things, all those helpless little children herded into schoolhouses every day) . . .' David's socialist ideals are laid bare by Midge Hardcastle, who as a worker lives what David merely talks about, and has a justifiable – far more ambivalent – resentment of her idle relations with their protective layers of money.

Money is central to Agatha's writings. It can override any other consideration in the minds of her characters. As both Poirot and Miss Marple are aware, it constitutes the prime motive for crime: of her fifty-five full-length detective novels, murder for financial gain is at the centre of thirty-six. But it is not just killers who like money: nice girls like Tuppence, or Jane Cleveland in 'Jane in Search of a Job';[5] clever women like Lucy Eyelesbarrow in *4.50 from Paddington*; sweet old ladies like Dora Bunner in *A Murder is Announced* – they are obsessed with it. The lack of it dominates lives. For all her own supposed obsession with the privileged classes, Agatha had plenty of sympathy for the desperate. 'I've heard people say so often "I'd rather have flowers on the table than a meal without them." But how many meals have those people ever missed?' says Dora Bunner. 'They don't know what it is – nobody knows who hasn't been through it – to be really *hungry*. Bread, you know, and a jar of meat paste, and a scrape of margarine . . . And the *shabbiness*.'

Agatha had a fear of poverty, deriving from her memory of the sudden downward swoop of the Miller fortunes. It alarmed her just to think of the way money had trickled like sand through her father's hands. In later life she too would have money problems, which she attempted to treat with *hauteur* but which in fact completely terrified her; the difference was that these came about through no fault of her own. Although she loved to spend, she always treated money with absolute respect.

And it was money that changed her attitude towards her work. She was no longer writing for the love of it. She was a professional. That was how it happened. She signed a three-book contract with Collins at the beginning of 1924, which gave her an advance of two hundred pounds per book and an improved royalty rate, negotiated by Edmund Cork, although she still had to deliver one more book to the Bodley Head, *The Secret of Chimneys*, published in 1925. John Lane had told Cork that Collins were welcome to Agatha if they were willing to pay that kind of money. The Bodley Head had wanted to keep hold of her and had offered another contract, but Agatha felt no obligation to them for giving her a first break. She had something of the smiling grandeur of her sister, Madge, who breezed through rehearsals of her West End play *The Claimant* with the air of a duchess ('You're quite emphatic, Mrs Watts!'); these two were ladies, after all, with a core of impregnable assurance. From early on Agatha was confident in the sphere of her work. She treated the Bodley Head with disdain, she 'bullied Edmund Cork'[6] – albeit politely – and she always stood her ground on issues like blurbs and book jackets (in 1922 she had had an altercation with her publishers over the cover of *Murder on the Links*, which showed the victim 'having apparently an epileptic fit, and as he had never had an epileptic fit in his life, it seemed to me rather . . . Well, they made rather a fuss about that.')[7]

In 1924 she used her own money to publish her poems, *The Road of Dreams*, under the imprint of Geoffrey Bles; the sales were negligible, and the works had clearly been written for the poet's own pleasure, but Agatha liked the idea of them being in print. She was enjoying her success, which was as new and miraculous as a sudden spring sun. Through 1924 to 1926 she wrote stories not just for the *Sketch* but for other magazines, including the *Grand*, the *Novel*,

Flynn's Weekly and the *Royal*: they would be published later in collections like *Poirot Investigates*, *The Mysterious Mr. Quin* and *The Listerdale Mystery*. Even her first story, 'The House of Beauty', which she had written as a teenager convalescing in bed, was published in 1926. It seemed that every piece of prose she wrote – or had ever written – was wanted.

With the money from the serialisation of *The Man in the Brown Suit* she bought a grey Morris Cowley car. Her pleasure in it is impossible to comprehend in these days of instant travel: she could scarcely believe the rapture of being able to go to places beyond where her feet or a bus route would take her. Many years later, in her autobiography, she was still possessed by the sense of amazement that this first car had brought (she compared the excitement with that of dining at Buckingham Palace with the Queen).

The Morris was hers: did Archie resent this? Surely not, as it had been his idea to buy it, and he who taught her to drive it. Why should he have cared? It has been suggested[8] that he *did* care, that he was increasingly disturbed by Agatha's career, the independent income and the attention it brought her. However his own career was now flourishing. A friend in the City named Clive Baillieu had invited him to join his firm, Austral Development Ltd; this made Archie 'immediately, wonderfully, completely happy', wrote Agatha. He was now properly established in the world of finance, for which he had a decided aptitude. Things were good. Money was no longer a worry. Agatha received irregular but satisfying sums; Archie was earning around two thousand a year, and surely even Clara would be satisfied with that?

Nor was it just his new job that delighted Archie. He had fallen in love with golf. Agatha had introduced him to it after the war, during their weekends spent in East Croydon, and from the early 1920s onwards it became for him a way of life. He played every weekend if he possibly could on any nearby course and then, as his game improved, at Sunningdale. 'I was,' wrote Agatha wryly in her autobiography, 'becoming that well-known figure, a golf widow.' In *Unfinished Portrait* she is unable to hide her sense of loss, saying, 'We've always spent the weekends together, you and I.' He is patiently reassuring in reply.

'It isn't that I don't love you. I love you just as much as ever. But a man likes doing things with other men. And he needs exercise. If I was wanting to go off with other women, well, then you might have something to complain about. But I never want to be bothered with any other woman but you. I hate women. I just want to play a decent game of golf with another man. I do think you're being rather unreasonable about it.'

Yes, probably she was being unreasonable . . .

And so it was that Agatha agreed to live at Sunningdale. She had wanted to leave London for some time but Archie would only countenance a place near a good golf course. Like Anne Beddingfeld in *The Man in the Brown Suit*, Agatha gave in for the sake of her own happiness: 'There is really nothing a woman enjoys so much as doing all the things she doesn't like for the sake of someone she does like.' Of course the dark-leafed Surrey-Berkshire border was not her idea of the country. Having been brought up in Devon, having known pink and gold hills and the gleam of the sea every morning, Sunningdale looked to her cramped and meretricious. But Archie's upbringing had been very different. He had never lived with space and relaxed grandeur, and he liked the comfortable feel of the Home Counties. He could get along with the people – City types such as he himself was now becoming – although Agatha found them alien, cautiously social in a way that she had never before encountered. So unlike the families she had known in Torquay, ranging happily around their large villas with the peeling paint and the good old furniture.

The Christies found a flat in a house called Scotswood, which seemed to Agatha typical of Sunningdale: a vast jumble of gables, half-timbering and mock Tudor. It stood at the end of a short drive, behind trees, off one of the well-tended avenues. At night, the lights in all the differently shaped windows gave it a disoriented look. But it cost little more than Addison Mansions, which decided the question, and Agatha set to decorating it. With her usual creative delight in home-making, she hung curtains, patterned with different flowers: tulips for the dining room, buttercups and daisies for Rosalind's room, bluebells for the main bedroom 'which was not really a good choice'. They looked 'grey and dispirited', as the room received almost no sun. Like a little girl she cheered herself up by writing a poem about 'Bluebell, wild Bluebell, who dances in the wood'.

She was happy, having made Archie happy. Her newly contented husband was the person she wanted to be with. 'We had been through so much worry since we came back from our world tour that it seemed wonderful to enter on this halcyon period.' Everything seemed set fair. She had her dog, her daughter, her writing, her man. She even had Clara – now aged seventy, dividing her time between Ashfield and her daughters – staying in the other top-floor flat at Scotswood. 'Wandering out into the garden in the early morning with Aubrey at her heels, Celia felt that life had become almost perfect. No more dirt and dust and fog. This was Home . . .'

The first book that Agatha wrote for Collins was the one that changed her reputation for ever; no doubt she knew, as through 1925 she turned the idea over in her mind, that here she had a winner. *The Murder of Roger Ackroyd* is the supreme, the ultimate detective novel. It rests upon the most elegant of all twists, the narrator who is revealed to be the murderer. This twist is not merely a function of plot: it puts the whole concept of detective fiction on an armature and sculpts it into a dazzling new shape. It was not an entirely new idea – Agatha had played with it before, when she had Sir Eustace Pedler narrate part of *The Man in the Brown Suit* – nor was it entirely her own idea, since it was suggested to her by both James Watts ('Why not have a Watson do the murder?') and in a rather self-important letter sent by Lord Louis Mountbatten, which did not merely offer the device but explained exactly how it should be used.[9] Agatha very rarely took advice on her plots – although a great deal was offered in the course of her career – but here, she realised, was an idea worth having. And only she could have pulled it off so completely. Only she had the requisite control, the willingness to absent herself from the authorial scene and let her plot shine clear.

'The artist is only the glass through which we see nature and the cleaner and more absolutely pure that glass, so much the more perfect the picture we can see through it . . .' So wrote Eden

Philpotts to Agatha, back in 1909. The manner in which she took his advice was perhaps not quite what he had intended, as he had been thinking of her as a straightforward novelist, whose model should be Flaubert. But she applied the Flaubertian principle to her detective fiction. In *Roger Ackroyd* she revealed for the first time her natural quality of translucency: her ability to control every sentence of her books, yet allow them to breathe free. Agatha did not impose. Nor did she interpose one atom of herself between her writing and her readers. Her words communicate exactly and only what is required; which is not the same as saying that they have no life beyond what is on the page. They have, in fact, the mystery of simplicity. They are the conduits for her plots, which are also ultimately simple. And her plots are the conduits for her ideas of character; which are complex.

In fact, in *Roger Ackroyd*, character is not yet as important as it would become when Agatha was writing at her peak, in the years between 1935 and 1950. By then she would know fully how to integrate character with plot, how to make plot an immaculate distillation of character. Thus a novel such as *Five Little Pigs* – one of her very best – is a mystery resolved into simplicity by an understanding of human complexity. A beautiful process, and a beautiful book. The beauty of *Roger Ackroyd* is of a different kind: that of a diamond whose every facet gleams, whose geometry is perfection. Every line, every angle leads towards resolution. The plot progresses not in linear form, as a story with a beginning, middle and end, but by the architectural construction of a shape that eventually reveals its true dimensions. It is masterly: exquisite. And although the book is more of a mathematical exercise in ingenuity than a full-blown novel, it does hint at profundity. The character of the narrator, Dr Sheppard, is shadowy because he is, by definition, obfuscating. Yet this reticence translates into a sense of a hollow man, a man whose extreme self-control conceals guilt, grief, emotions that he can never express. 'I have lost the quality of resilience long since myself,' he says. And his sister, who knows more about him than he would wish, tells Poirot that he is 'weak as water. You *are* weak, James . . . With a bad bringing up, Heaven knows what mischief you might have got into by now.' These are clues; they are also truths. At the end of the book Sheppard kills himself in order to spare his sister suffering. His last words are bleak, bathetic, and somehow very real.

> 'Not that I take any responsibility for Mrs Ferrars' death. It was the direct consequence of her own actions. I feel no pity for her.
>   'I have no pity for myself either.
>   'So let it be veronal.
>   'But I wish Hercule Poirot had never retired from work and come here to grow vegetable marrows.'

How did Agatha develop from the amateur, 'trying things, as one does', into the creator of this dazzlingly accomplished book? By degrees. By intelligence; by instinct; by confidence; by courage. By trusting her own judgement about what made her writing work. By having a mind uncluttered with received ideas, and an imagination that naturally ran so free she could enjoy the exercise of its restraint. It was a relief, in fact, to trammel it within a genre. Although the structural work of a detective novel was very difficult, there was joy in the discipline. She was ordering her brain like a well-run establishment. Like Lucy Eyelesbarrow in *4.50 from Paddington*, she was shining the silver and scrubbing the kitchen table and making a Spanish omelette with the leftover potatoes. She was living in a world where all could be known, all motives uncovered, all ambiguities penetrated. Where mysteries were within her control.

In her novel *A Pocket Full of Rye*, Agatha described the home of her murder victim:

> This place, this pretentiously named Yewtree Lodge was just the kind of mansion that rich people built themselves and then called it 'their little place in the country'. It wasn't in the country either, according to Inspector Neele's idea of the country. The house was a large solid red-brick structure . . . with rather too many gables, and a vast number of leaded paned windows. The gardens

were highly artificial – all laid out in rose beds and pergolas and pools, and living up to the name of the house with large numbers of clipped yew hedges.

Thus she remembered the house in Sunningdale – 'Styles', as she and Archie renamed it – to which they moved from Scotswood at the start of 1926. Yewtree Lodge is similarly set in the commuter belt. 'Baydon Heath was almost entirely inhabited by rich City men. It had an excellent train service, was only twenty miles from London and was comparatively easy to reach by car.'[10] It also had 'three well-known golf courses'. Sunningdale had two, having newly developed the course at Wentworth, in which Agatha bought a debenture share so that she could play there at weekends.

Despite her authorial control she cannot help giving a dark quality to *A Pocket Full of Rye*, which derives from its setting and the smart, vulgar, 'very unpleasant people' who live there: a ruthless City man with a sexy young wife, the wife's lounge-lizard lover whom she meets when pretending to play golf. Agatha can scarcely hide her contempt for Baydon Heath. This was how, thirty years earlier, she increasingly felt about Sunningdale. At first there was intense pleasure in walking among trees and feeling clean air on her face, although in fact there were so many cars in Sunningdale that the air was positively choked compared with the high, fresh breezes of Torquay. Archie had suggested that they buy a second car – something glamorous like a Delage – as their finances continued to improve. Agatha suggested instead that they have another baby, but to this Archie replied that there was plenty of time (although Agatha was coming up to thirty-five) and that anyway he did not need another child, Rosalind being 'perfect'. They bought the Delage.

Perhaps Agatha had thought that another child – a son? – would arouse in her the maternal instincts that as yet remained dormant. Perhaps she thought that she would have 'her' child, Rosalind being indubitably Archie's.

'Judy was so aloof – so unattached – she was like Dermot.'[11]

The mere fact that Agatha could write this about her daughter shows her own detachment. She knew that Rosalind would read the book, after all. She would learn that her mother had seen her as 'a complete puzzle', full of 'depressing' common sense, with an almost repellent love of her father's 'rough' games. But *Unfinished Portrait* was written by somebody unable to stop themselves, heedless of pain or shame or damage, and, half hidden as she was behind her pseudonym, Agatha felt compelled to write the truths of that time as she saw them: the growing subterranean despair, the creeping sense of disengagement.

They had a good many neighbours there – most of them with children. Everyone was friendly. The only thing that made a difficulty was Dermot's refusal to go out to dinner.

'Look here, Celia, I come down from London tired out, and you want me to dress up and go out and not get home and to bed till past midnight. I simply can't do it.'

'Not every night, of course. But I don't see that one night a week would matter.'

'Well, I don't want to. You go, if you like.'

'I can't go alone. People don't ask you to dinner except in pairs. And it sounds so odd for me to say that you never go out at night – because, after all, you're quite young.'

'I'm sure you could manage to go without me.'

But that wasn't so easy. In the country, as Celia said, people were asked in couples or not at all . . . So she refused the invitations, and they sat at home, Dermot reading books on financial subjects, and Celia sometimes sewing, sometimes sitting with her hands clasped . . .

This was not the whole truth, of course. It was the underside. Agatha had a successful and fulfilled life: her books were admired, her family was healthy and handsome, her future prospects were good. In fact it was all most enviable. Agatha felt this herself. But beneath it lay Celia, fearful and questing and unable to make this grown-up life her own: desperately in love with Dermot yet only truly herself with her mother ('She could say "I am so happy" without having to catch back the words at Dermot's frown . . .').

Nobody would have believed Celia to exist within the confident, clever woman of substance (a little too much substance, by then) whose stories and photograph appeared in the *Sketch*, whose *The Murder of Roger Ackroyd* would soon be published to acclaim and controversy (there was a body of opinion that considered the novel a cheat, although in fact it plays entirely fair).[12] Celia writes just one book – not a detective story – purely as an outlet for her powerful imagination; she never becomes a professional at anything. She remains a dreaming, drifting girl. She does not grow up in any way. 'She didn't look like a writer – this young creature with her Scandinavian fairness,' thinks the man who publishes her book. She remains young, not just emotionally but physically.

Inside that was how Agatha still thought of herself, as the lovely nymph who had danced through Torquay and into the arms of her husband. She is Jane in *The Secret Adversary*, who has 'a wild rose quality about her face'; she is Anne in *The Man in the Brown Suit*, with the beauty that 'drives men mad'; she is Flora in *The Murder of Roger Ackroyd*, who with her 'real Scandinavian pale gold hair' has exactly the looks of the young Agatha. But Flora Ackroyd was dreamed into life by a woman who, only in her thirties, had become middle-aged. She was not unattractive – her smiling charm did not show itself in photographs – but she had lost her particular quality of beauty. Her masculine features needed lightness and youth to offset them; these had disappeared with the birth of Rosalind. So she created lovely girls, whose looks she had once shared, and although there was pleasure in doing so it also caused anguish. Meanwhile Archie remained lean, intense, attractive as ever. Perhaps Agatha should have done more about this physical disparity. 'I hope I am getting thinner with all this walking!' she wrote to Clara, from an Italian holiday in 1924.

Agatha's tone on this trip was very much that of the Empire Tour, enthusiastic and blithe: 'We got ourselves to Milan, spent the afternoon of Wednesday there, and on to Bologna . . .' As he had on the tour Archie fell ill, 'had a temperature and went to bed whilst I jeered at him and said it was liver!' They would be home soon, Agatha told her mother. 'Archie has an "Autumn Meeting" of golf at Sunningdale the first week in October . . .'[13]

The golf was becoming a nightmare for her, although she pretended it was not. So trivial was it, in itself, she could never quite believe the extent to which it asserted its importance: it was as if her life were dominated by train-spotting or kites. But any childlike optimism that Archie's passion would blow itself out was misplaced. His obsession continued to grow. She was unable to invite friends from London to stay unless the man played golf, otherwise Archie resented giving up his free time. This meant that Agatha herself was often left alone, having scarcely seen her husband during the week. She had her writing to think about, of course, and did so increasingly. One of the stories published during the Sunningdale period was 'Philomel Cottage',[14] which appeared in *Grand* magazine in November 1924. It is the story of a woman, Alix, who throws over a devoted suitor in order to marry a man of whom she knows nothing and who, she gradually realises, is planning to kill her.

A solution of sorts came to Agatha's solitary weekends. Nan Pollock, sister to James Watts, was now on her second marriage to a man named George Kon: a golfer. Nan and Agatha had liked each other from Madge's wedding day. Now they would sit and chat while Rosalind and Judy (three years the elder) played together in the garden, or they themselves played a few incompetent holes on the ladies' course. Afterwards they met their husbands at the club house for drinks. Agatha chose not to take alcohol, although the official line that she was a lifelong teetotaller is not quite true: on the Empire Tour she had enjoyed the odd glass of burgundy. But despite her weight gain – and, perhaps, Archie's embarrassment – she now preferred the comforting glasses of mixed cream and milk that she had drunk, as a girl, when staying with Nan at Abney.

By this time Agatha got on better with Nan than she did with her sister, although she was intrigued to have Madge stay for weekends at Scotswood in 1924, during the rehearsal period for *The Claimant*. Although by then Agatha was decidedly the more successful, her sister still fascinated and irked her. She was so wildly assured, so appallingly charming. 'The head of the Press Bureau approached me for an interview,' wrote Madge to her husband, 'and I said I didn't <u>want</u> to be known . . . All I told him was that I was Mrs Agatha Christie's sister. And he simply <u>revels</u> in Styles and has read all her books! So perhaps we'll have to be the Dolly

Sisters after all!' This easy generosity – of which Agatha herself would not have been capable – was even more annoying, since it somehow implied that Agatha's acceptance by the press was within Madge's gift. Of course she and Archie attended a performance of *The Claimant*. And it was fun, in a sense, to be writers together with Madge; particularly when it became clear that *The Claimant* was not quite the work of genius she had been led to believe. Madge planned to write a play about Warren Hastings but despite the enthusiasm of her producer, Basil Dean, this did not happen. Agatha remembered it, though. In *Absent in the Spring* Joan Scudamore meets an old schoolfriend, Blanche, and asks – somewhat condescendingly – if her husband 'ever wrote his book on Warren Hastings?' He had; it was never published.

Archie was on perfectly friendly terms with Madge, although he may have had his fill of Agatha's family by the mid-1920s. Monty continued to be a nuisance. On his return from the Empire Tour, Archie had found a flat for his brother-in-law and offered to install him in it; instead he ended up escorting him to a favoured hotel in Jermyn Street, saying to Agatha, 'It seemed so reasonable, the way he put it.' Then Agatha had helped Madge buy the cottage for Monty on Dartmoor: James Watts was always annoyed by the way his wife threw money at this problem, but in Agatha's case the money was her own and there was nothing Archie could say.

Meanwhile Clara was just along the corridor, no doubt encouraging the purchase of the cottage. She was not permanently at Sunningdale, as she still had Ashfield (and Abney), and to preserve her sense of independence Agatha arranged for her to stay in rooms with some friends in London. But she was often at Scotswood and in her frail old age she had become – as even Agatha admitted – 'difficult to get on with'. Not that Archie had ever found her especially easy. Although he had expected to be jealous when Agatha had a baby, this had not in fact been the case. Yet he remained jealous of Clara. Agatha's devotion to her mother, her near-obsession with Ashfield, the letters she had written from abroad to her 'precious mummy': it was hardly usual behaviour in an adult woman. And Clara's adoration of Agatha was another irritant. Of course Peg Hemsley thought the same way about Archie (and was similarly hard to avoid, having moved to Dorking in Surrey). The difference was that Archie took no notice of his mother while Agatha remained under Clara's spell. Now Clara was taking a hand in the education of Rosalind. She was a natural teacher, and Rosalind responded well to her. 'She knows and understands her Grandma and her Grandma loves and understands her Rosalind,' Clara wrote from Abney in early 1926. It was not quite interference.. But from Archie's point of view Clara was always too much of a presence in his life, with her unnerving quickness and penetrating eye.

'I was wrong about Dermot' [says the mother in *Unfinished Portrait*]. 'When you married him, I didn't trust him. I didn't think he was honest or loyal . . . I thought there would be other women.'
  'Oh, Mother, Dermot never looks at anything but a golf ball.'

At which Miriam smiles; then says:

'He's very attractive – he's attractive to women, Celia, remember that . . .'
  'He's a frightfully stay-at-home person, Mummy.'
  'Yes, that's lucky.'

It was true that, aside from his golf, Archie had no wish to be out and about: he liked a normal, controlled family life. He craved a wife who bestowed constant reassurance with a light, quiet touch. Agatha's success was not particularly intrusive – although it had gone beyond what either of the Christies had expected – and she still put Archie first, even if he did not think so. Her marriage was by far the most important thing in her life. That was why she had moved to Sunningdale, bought her debenture at the golf club, agreed to the plan of building a house on the Wentworth Estate when, in her heart, she yearned to leave this tight little gin-drinking society behind her and live somewhere large and free.

('Let me see.' Shirley's eyes half closed. She spoke dreamily. 'I'd like to live on an island – an island rather far away from anywhere. I'd like to live in a white house with green shutters . . .')[15]

Archie knew her longings: he knew that there was a wildness in Agatha that did not belong in Sunningdale. He had fallen in love with her dreamy poetic aspect, although he had not fully understood it. He had seen bliss and safety in the girl with whom he had danced amid the pink stone of Ugbrooke. How sweet she had been, how soothing, with her cool hand in his. How beautiful, too, his Elaine, with her slim body in its long skirts, her magical quantities of pale hair that she took down at night for his eyes alone ('You are lovely and perfect in every way').

But what had been adorable in a young girl was now faintly repulsive. Agatha's artistic soul had once expressed itself with discretion; now there was something uncontrolled about her eagerness, her zest for life, her childishness ('Dermot hated you to say what you were feeling. He felt it, somehow, to be indecent'). The Agatha of 1912 was the same woman as the Agatha of 1926, but to Archie she seemed a different person. Louder, larger, uglier. 'Yes, more difficult to disguise that you were silly as your looks left you.' (A sudden flash of memory: 'Don't ever grow less beautiful, will you, Celia?')

'Yes, but that was all over now. They'd lived together long enough for such things as the beauty of a face to have lost its meaning. Dermot was in her blood and she in his.'

'Styles' was not the house that either Agatha or Archie had wanted, but they were tired of the flat at Scotswood and felt it was time to buy. The plan to build a new home on the Wentworth Estate came to nothing, although according to Agatha's autobiography the Christies had spent 'happy summer evenings tramping over Wentworth looking out for a site which we thought would suit us'. The quality of the numinous, so essential to Agatha, bloomed on those walks as she dreamed a house – *her* house – into life. But in the end it was deemed too expensive (£5,300) and too complicated. Easier to take on something ready-made, with a nice garden for Rosalind, conveniently near to the station for Archie. The Christies looked around for a year or so before they took out a mortgage on Styles, and had plenty of time to find something they really liked. Instead they acquired the house described in *A Pocket Full of Rye*: large, modern, red-brick, with leaded windows like small black eyes and a thick shroud of trees.

It is impossible to imagine Agatha living in this place. Compared to Ashfield, which had light and magic and homeliness, Styles was as immutable as a stockbroker's fortress. Inside it was 'decorated regardless of expense', with panelling, gilt and 'quantities of bathrooms', although the plan was to change all this when it could be afforded. Outside could not be changed. Styles was handsome but it had a cold, dead look. During the war a woman had been murdered in the copse behind it. Agatha hated the house, Rosalind liked it for its garden, Archie was indifferent to it.

'I am sorry for you settling in,' Clara wrote to Agatha from Ashfield. 'It is always so full of unexpected worries.' Chief among these was money: the Christies had overstretched themselves and were running two cars and three servants. There was also Charlotte Fisher, employed to look after Rosalind and to act as Agatha's secretary-typist. Rosalind had previously had an excellent nanny – Miss White, known as 'Site' – and a hopeless Swiss governess, Marcelle. She now attended Oakfield School in Sunningdale but Agatha felt the need for help with her daughter, and so it was that Charlotte, or 'Carlo',[16] as she was later known, came to live with the family. She was young, highly intelligent, the daughter of an Edinburgh chaplain and – as one of her nieces later described her[17] – 'a very splendid person'. There was in her something of Katherine Grey in *The Mystery of the Blue Train*, the novel that Agatha began to write after *Roger Ackroyd*. Katherine has both judgement and humour, despite being obliged to earn her living as a companion; as Charlotte did Clara, she handles old ladies with patient kindness. Charlotte also commanded instant respect from Rosalind and, despite the ten-year age gap, got along very well with Agatha. She was the kind of person with whom Agatha felt comfortable. Like Katherine Grey, she said little and listened a good deal. She could size people up with her cool Scottish eye, and she thought the world of her employer.

Styles was bought by Archie and Agatha together. His income was obviously more stable than hers, although she was earning quite well.

The suggestion has been made[18] that Agatha had become possessive about her own money, spending it on herself and her blood relations rather than sharing it with her husband. But even if that were true – which it was, in the case of Monty – what would it mean? Men supported the home in the 1920s; Archie would not have expected to do otherwise, and would certainly not have wanted money from his wife unless in real need of it.

Nevertheless it is true that Agatha's earnings were giving her the appearance of an independent being. The Christies shared a home and a child, but in other ways their lives had become quite separate. Archie had his golf and his City friends like Sam James, a smiling, successful businessman who lived with his wife, Madge, at Hurtmore, near Godalming. Agatha had Nan, Carlo, her family. Archie loved to stay where he was; Agatha yearned to travel again. In 1925 they went on holiday together to Cauterets in the Pyrenees, where she had stayed as a child with her parents; happy memories had made her want to return. No doubt the shadow of Agatha's family cast itself upon Archie's willingness to enjoy himself, and he did not especially do so. As on board ship during the Empire Tour, he went to bed at ten thirty while Agatha stayed up, watching the music-hall show at the Kursaal, her mind half on her husband. The next year she wanted to go away again, but Archie did not, so she went with her sister for a short break to Corsica. Her relationship with Madge was not perfect but there was a level of understanding between them that Agatha craved. They could talk together about the past, about Monty, about their parents. They could share the delight in life they had both felt before marriage, motherhood and housekeeping had claimed them. They could alleviate each other's concerns about Clara, whose health had been precarious for some time now.

The first months of 1926 were crammed and exhausting for Agatha. She was moving to Styles with her family, she was buying a first home with her husband, she was awaiting the publication in May of *The Murder of Roger Ackroyd*, and all the time her heart was with her mother at Ashfield.

Clara had written in February, her hand by this time somewhat wild but still firm.

The coat is lovely just right. I did not expect to live to wear
it, but I think I shall now!!! The worst is over, and my heart
is getting stilled down . . .

I took off nightie today, and put on clothes and Dressing
gown (yours), both windows wide open, no fire, and the sun
streaming in. Such a hot glorious day . . . I have really had a
beautiful birthday. Miss Butler went in Motor Boat to Brixham
and was happy – I have asked her to stay for the present and
she seemed very pleased about it. I am still too weak to
bother about getting a gardener, and she is doing the garden
very well . . .

My firm love and devotion to Archie and Rosalind.[19]

And instantly Agatha was transported back to childhood: the
windows pushing open to the taut smell of the sea, the boat to
Brixham along the coast from Torquay, the cry of gulls scratching
the sky, the garden at Ashfield. She had a yearning to go back, a
yearning to escape.

On her return from Corsica she went down to stay with her mother.
Clara had contracted bronchitis: 'Her mother looked so small and
pathetic. And she was so lonely in that big house.'[20] But Ashfield still
sang its siren lure. The border needed tending and the rooms had
become shabbier; it made not a whit of difference to Agatha, who
loved this house, and the kind, clever little woman in it, with an inappropriate and indestructible passion.

Clara kept to just two rooms now, where she and Agatha talked
together like the mother and daughter in *Unfinished Portrait*. Miriam
tells Celia that she seems happy. 'I want you so much to be happy,
my darling'. She also tells her that she has been wrong about Dermot.
'I've been jealous. I haven't been willing to recognise his good qualities.' Then she says: 'Don't ever leave your husband too long alone,
Celia. Remember, a man forgets . . .'

So Agatha returned to Archie, and the dark house at Sunningdale.
Madge took her place at Ashfield, and at the end of March brought
their mother home to Abney. Again Clara kept to her room, but she
seemed over the worst. 'Darling Agatha, Going on about the same,
a little better I think. Lovely weather here and I expect you are all

sitting in the garden and Peter digging, the precious naughty one. My love to Rosalind . . . Did you back Jack Horner?'[21] she wrote, in a reference to the 1926 Grand National winner.

She died on 5 April, soon after this letter was sent, while Agatha was on the train to visit her at Abney. In her autobiography Agatha wrote that her mother had longed to be free of the 'prison' of her ageing body and that she herself had felt Clara's sense of release. Her tone is sad, reasonable, resigned.

Unfinished Portrait came closer to the truth of that time. Agatha writes of 'her little gallant mother . . .' whom all her life she had found 'wonderful and satisfying . . . And now her mother had gone . . . The bottom had fallen out of Celia's world.'

Even this, though, does not begin to express the unbearable sense of loss: it was, quite literally, beyond words. That is why every sentence ends with ellipsis. There are no words with which to end the sentence.

For Archie, Agatha felt the love of a woman for a man, she loved him passionately and occasionally to distraction; however much the comfortable appearance of middle age shrouded her emotions they were there, still, burning inside her.

But Clara had been the love of her life. It was Clara who had laid Agatha's heart bare with her courage, her earnestness, her indomitable spark. The thought of her mother alone at Ashfield, her spectacles slipping from her nose as she fell asleep over Dickens in front of the fire, had aroused in Agatha all the sweet, poignant, tender emotions that probably should have gone towards her child, that kept her child-like ('Lots and lots and lots of love, my precious Mummy'). Without Clara she was like Joan Scudamore in *Absent in the Spring*, alone in the desert and unsuccoured. How would she live without the know-ledge that, whatever happened, she could go to Ashfield and be with her mother? That exquisite relaxation, that sense of sinking into soft familiarity, that perfect smiling communion. Her mother's hand in hers. Her luminous gaze, which saw Agatha as she was and thought what she saw quite perfect.

'How lovely to be at home . . . Celia loved the feeling of stepping back into her old life. To feel the happy tide of reassurance sweeping over her – the feeling of being loved . . . It was so restful to be your-self . . . Oh, dear home.'

What was home now? Was it the dark prison of Styles, where Agatha must try to be for Rosalind – cool-eyed Rosalind – the person that Clara had been for her? Or was it still Ashfield, where memory bloomed in the empty rooms like rose scent?

Agatha clung to the thought of Archie's return from Spain, where he was on business. He knew how she had loved her mother. He would hold her. He would fill some of the terrible space inside and around her in this shadowy house. Rosalind was useless: although she had been sad about her grandmother she was too young and self-possessed to give sympathy. Carlo gave it, in her dignified way. So did Peter the dog, whose eyes seemed to shine with the same understanding that Clara had once bent upon Agatha. She clung to him as if his warm, woolly body held all the love in the world. 'My little friend and loving companion in affliction',[22] she later called him.

It was Archie, though, whom Agatha needed. Her man, her love. Like a drowning person she held to the thought of him as she put on her black clothes and stood, frozen, at Clara's graveside. Belief in God was a theoretical consolation: Clara would have felt that she was now with her maker. But this did almost nothing to help the thirty-five-year-old woman who simply wanted her mother. She wanted Clara to make it better, as she had done thirty years earlier, when Agatha had cried silently all the way home from the day trip in France and Clara had said, looking at her daughter, 'I believe she doesn't like that butterfly in her hat.'

Then Archie came home. The sound of him entering the hall at Styles was beautiful to Agatha ('Now do I surely know that I shall awake! Return once more to love and delight').[23] Now she would no longer be alone. She would be understood and cared for. Agatha had forgotten her husband's nature: he had always hated illness and distress, it disarmed him, and now in his embarrassment he assumed an air of jollity. Everything all right? Not yet? Ah well, time heals. He suggested that Agatha come back with him to Spain, where he had more business to transact; it would take her mind off things. How about it?

She reacted with horror. It was as if he were asking her to abandon her mother, which in a way he was. The jealousy he had felt for Clara in life was there still. Agatha's grief was excessive, unseemly. Would she have been reduced to such a state for him?

He had made his offer of a holiday, the best thing he could think of. There was, he felt, nothing more he could do for his wife.

'In the end Celia went to sleep holding his hand, which he withdrew with relief when he saw she was really asleep.'

Later Agatha wrote of how wrongly she felt she had behaved towards her husband. 'My life with Archie lay ahead of me. We were happy together, assured of each other, and neither of us would have dreamed that we could ever part.'[24] She should have gone with him to Spain, and dealt with Ashfield – which was now her property, and needed cleaning and sorting – on her return. She should have recognised the nature of the man she loved.

'My mother left my father alone,' said Rosalind.[25] 'Grannie always said, don't leave a man alone.'

So Archie went to Spain and Agatha went with Rosalind to Torquay, to clear her family possessions. The estate – such as it was – had to be settled, and a decision made as to whether to sell Ashfield. It was arranged that Styles would be let (not least because the money was needed). Archie would stay at his club in London and then, when Agatha had finished her task, the Christies would take a holiday together in Italy. This was something to look forward to. Again, it was a thought to which Agatha clung.

The smell of Ashfield was the same, within the smell of damp and decay. The roof was falling in, water was dripping through the ceilings. It was a sad house now, although every cupboard held the memory of happiness.

'No man ever had a wife like you,' read the letter that Frederick had written to Clara shortly before his death. In one of the drawers was the purse Clara had embroidered with the entwined initials F and C, and the line 'Set me as a seal upon thine heart, for love is strong as death'.

There was the letter to Agatha from Clara: 'Darling little girlie, Mother is longing to kiss and love her sweet pea again. Auntie-Grannie sends you much love . . . Tell Jane to please get a partridge to make you some potted meat for tea or breakfast.' And from Frederick: 'I hear your Grannie is going to have your picture painted. I think it is a most lovely idea and I want you to put your little arms around Grannie's neck and give her a hug and kiss for me. You must always be good and gentle to her and I am pleased to think you are . . .' These things were like dead flowers, like the edelweiss Clara had kept from her honeymoon in Switzerland: as they were uncovered the faint scent of love arose and grew strong again.

The house had become almost like an immense store-room, with all but the two rooms Clara used crammed with furniture, trunks, books, cases. Margaret Miller's possessions were also there, transported when she moved from Ealing. In her old home Margaret had wept as her life was unearthed around her: a moth-eaten velvet dress from 'Madame Poncereau's', lengths of silk from the Army and Navy Stores, print for servants' dresses, a clothes-basket full of weevilly flour, thirty-six demijohns of home-made liqueur (five of which had been stolen by the removal men, to Margaret's flattered delight), packets of sugar and butter stored for future Christmases, which would never now be eaten. Letters, papers, an old envelope full of five-pound notes: Margaret following her own advice. A diamond brooch slung inside a stocking. A wax-wreath memorial to Nathaniel Miller. Such were the things Agatha now had to go through.

It is beyond endurance, the continued life of things, when the owner of those things is dead. So it was with Clara's clothes, bought with busy plans for when they would be worn. Or the Album of Confessions, filled in with a seventeen-year-old's solemn concentration. The humble accretions of a life. At some lost moment, every one of these things had been the most important thing in the world to Clara. Perhaps it would have been better, as Archie had suggested, to burn them at once.

Peter bent his friendly eyes upon Agatha as she pulled out dress after dress from her mother's wardrobe. He wagged his wiry tail every time she moved, and was at her heels as she made incessant trips up- and downstairs with boxes of hats, clothes, books. He may even have been slightly annoying, in his relentless determination to stick with her, but he would not be deterred. Meanwhile Rosalind helped her mother to carry boxes, in between playing in the garden. Agatha felt she should keep her grief away from her daughter and tried, much of the time, to suppress it. Only the dog saw its manifestations.

Agatha worked through Ashfield with the intensity of a woman possessed: as she was, in a sense. One maid helped her in the morning, another in the afternoon, but the work went on and on. Madge could not leave Abney until August. Carlo would have been a consoling presence but she had her own concerns: she had been recalled to Edinburgh where her father was believed to be dying (but at least she would be by his side). The weeks passed, solitary and strange. *Roger Ackroyd* was published. Summer bloomed in the garden. The warmth and light grew outside as Agatha sat in the house among her family's things, burying herself deeper in her past, which lay around her in heaps, like earth. 'To have been so happy and not to have known it!' she wrote in *The Hollow*, when her character Henrietta thinks of the house she had loved as a child. '*If I could go back.*'

'One can't go back,' says Henrietta. 'That's the one thing one can't do – go back.' And soon Archie would be there, just before Rosalind's seventh birthday on 5 August, and then they would go on holiday together to Italy ('Summer! And love . . .'). She was slim again, as he liked her to be, although she was also worn and tired, because she was unable to eat despite the physical work she was doing. Sometimes she was not quite sure *what* she was doing. Would she sell the house? Would she let it? Would she ever be finished? She could do nothing with Ashfield until she had cleared every room, some of which had been locked up for years. 'Still, another six weeks or so, and I would get it all finished,' she wrote in her autobiography. 'Then I could begin to live again.' She collapsed in uncontrollable sobs one day when she was unable to start her car. 'That worried me.' She also worried that Archie did not come to Ashfield for an occasional weekend, despite the fact that she could not visit him at his London club, as she had nobody to look after Rosalind. He said he was helping in the General Strike, and that anyway it was a waste of money as they would see each other soon. It occurred to her that he did not want to miss his golf. The thought upset her so she tried to dismiss it. She heard Clara's voice telling her that Archie could be ruthless. 'Celia thought: "He's *not* kind . . . he's *not* . . ."

'A great wave of loneliness passed over her. She felt afraid . . . How cold the world was – without her mother . . .'

But then there were the memories of Archie at Ashfield: infinitely lovely and precious. Chugging up Barton Road on his motorbike. Rising from his chair in the drawing-room when she had tripped home from Rooklands across the road. Turning to her in the schoolroom upstairs, saying, 'You've got to marry me, you've *got* to marry me.' Walking hand in hand with her in the garden before Rosalind was born, kissing her beneath the summer night sky before the nurse called and she went back into the house.

Almost to the day, it was seven years since that night when Archie returned to Ashfield. Madge had arrived already. She was to look after Rosalind during the Italian holiday, and her presence had lifted some of the blight from Agatha, who was wrapping her daughter's birthday presents when Archie came into the house. As soon as she saw him she knew something was wrong. It was as if somebody else inhabited his body and looked out through his eyes. He was the Gun Man of Agatha's childhood nightmare, who came to Ashfield in the guise of a beloved person but, as became apparent, was a stranger filled with murderous intent.

'Archie seems very queer – is he ill, or something?' Madge asked her sister. Perhaps, thought Agatha, that was it. Perhaps it was cancer, even. Or perhaps there was a problem at work, something to do with money. Because he looked almost criminal in his shiftiness.

It was none of these things.

Archie told Agatha that he had done nothing about organising the holiday in Italy. She said it didn't matter, it would be just as nice to stay in England. No, that wasn't the point.

'You know that dark girl who used to be Belcher's secretary? We had her down for a weekend once, a year ago with Belcher, and we've seen her in London once or twice.'

Agatha could not remember the dark girl's name, although she knew whom he meant.

Nancy Neele. Well, during his summer alone in London he had seen rather a lot of her.

'Well,' said Agatha, 'why shouldn't you?'

She felt such relief that it was not cancer, not embezzlement, not something that would threaten her future with Archie. Just a flirtation. Not the sort of thing she would have expected from her serious-minded husband, in whom she had always placed complete trust ('Dermot never looks at anything but a golf ball'). But then, her grandmother would have reminded her that any man was capable of that sort of thing, particularly if he was left alone. How right Margaret had been! And how awful of him, really, to flirt with that girl, while his wife of twelve years was going through such hell. But of course he had never been able to stand illness, or unhappiness. She would forgive him for his silliness. He was the silly one this time.

He was still talking, sounding impatient, and guilty about being impatient. He was saying things that could not be believed.

'You still don't understand. I've fallen in love with her and I want a divorce as soon as possible.'

As Agatha asked him to do, Archie stayed at Ashfield for Rosalind's birthday, so that it should not be spoiled for her. The next day he went back to his club and, not long afterwards, his wife and daughter returned to Styles. Carlo's father was less seriously ill than had been feared; in response to Agatha's distress she came back from Edinburgh, and her stalwart presence made the days a little easier. At night only Peter brought comfort. Sleep did not come for Agatha, who wandered through the corridors of the black and terrible house, crying for her mother.

> Love passes out into the silent night,
> We may not hold him who has served our will
> And, for a while, made magic common things . . .
> Now, like a bird, he spreads his wings in flight,
> And we are left in darkness – listening still
> To the faint far-off beating of his wings . . .

The poem 'Love Passes' was in the *Road of Dreams* collection. As this was published in 1924, the possibility that Archie was no longer in love with her may have occurred to Agatha some time earlier, before he had even met Nancy. She may have thought that she, too, had fallen out of love.

Of course the poem is not a factual record, although outside her detective fiction (and, occasionally, within it) Agatha wrote from the heart.

> Love passes! On the heart dead embers lie
> Where once there burned a fire of living flame,
> Where we, starved children, sheltering in shame,
> Stretched out our hands, and let the world go by . . .

The truth is that Agatha was playing with her very real emotions: pushing her fear to the point of exorcism, to the point where she no longer believed it. She must have been thinking these things, in however deep a part of herself. For all her obtuseness, something in her had sensed change. While she was bringing life to the merry love affairs in *The Man in the Brown Suit* and *The Secret of Chimneys* – those ecstatic pairings between the Archie she wanted and the Agatha she wanted to be – she was also writing her own future in poems like 'Love Passes' and 'Progression'.

> Springtime will come again,
> The almond trees blossom once more . . .
> *And yet I weep,*
> For never again shall I tread love's way with you . . .
> Farewell, O Lover of mine,
> Our day is done.

But she did not really think that the Christies' day was done: she had played with fear, in her art, in a way that was almost a luxury, until the moment the truth came out of Archie's mouth. Agatha knew Nancy Neele. She quite liked her. Nancy was twenty-six, still living at home with her parents in Hertfordshire, working as a secretary in the City.[26] Her great friend Madge Fox, with whom she had trained at the Triangle secretarial school in South Molton Street, later married Archie's friend Sam James. Thus Nancy had come into Archie Christie's orbit.

At some point in 1925 she stayed a weekend at Hurtmore Cottage, the James's home near Godalming and found Archie there alone. He needed a golf partner, as Sam did not play. Nancy did, rather well. In the course of things she came to know Agatha, who chaperoned her at a dance and asked her to stay at Styles for a weekend. It seems, although there is no absolute proof of this, that Nancy accepted at least one invitation. According to the autobiography Archie 'objected to my asking her down to stay, he said it would spoil his golf'. Which was, of course, a remark that could be interpreted in two very different ways.

Agatha took the view that this meant he had had no particular interest in Nancy until after April 1926. At that point he was left alone in London; he did not wish to visit his wife at Ashfield because he could not cope with her uncontrolled grief; his boredom and solitude had driven him into Nancy's arms. As Agatha put it, her own absence 'left him open to other influences'.[27]

This was the view also held by Rosalind, whose loyalty to her father was staunch. 'He wasn't that kind of man. They'd been married a long time. But my mother went away. Naturally he wanted someone to play with, play golf with.'[28]

'Well, that's a generous interpretation,' says Rosalind's half-brother, Archie.[29]

Because the more cynical view, of course, is that Archie Christie did not want Nancy Neele at Styles because he had an interest – to say the least – in her, and would have found it both embarrassing and distasteful for his wife to receive her at their marital home.

There is no way of knowing exactly when Archie fell in love with Nancy, neither is there any proof that they had an affair. Indeed Madge James was 'absolutely adamant' that Nancy was never Archie's mistress, writing in a letter in the 1980s that 'In those days we did not pop into bed at the "drop of a hat" as they do today – I was Nancy's most intimate friend and I am prepared to swear that nothing of this occurred.' Another source[30] states that the affair had been going on – and off – for eighteen months before Archie visited Ashfield in August 1926. But this information is at three removes, coming as it does from Judith, daughter of Agatha's friend Nan Kon. It assumes that Archie told the details of his affair to Agatha, who then relayed them to Nan – both of which are unlikely in the extreme – and that Nan repeated every single detail to her daughter (who was only ten at the time of these events).

Judith's account states this timetable. Archie was sleeping with Nancy from the time he met her in early 1925. In the summer he went to Cauterets with Agatha, having broken off the affair. On his return from the holiday he resumed with Nancy, and led a double life until August 1926. His obsession with playing golf was, in fact, an excuse to be with his mistress; his weekends were for her and her alone; and the Jameses, who knew that he was unhappy with Agatha, provided a useful bolthole at Godalming. Archie refused to go to Corsica with Agatha because he wanted to be with Nancy. During his months alone in London after Clara's death, he took the opportunity to consolidate the relationship.

Such a version of events is completely uncorroborated, and cannot possibly be taken as fact. Nevertheless Nan Kon might have known *something*. She was on the Sunningdale scene and her husband George was a friend of Archie's: a photograph taken by Nan on a golf course in 1926 shows George with Archie and a slightly defiant-looking Nancy. It seems reasonable to think that there was gossip, which does not necessarily mean there was also a love affair. People are quick to see attraction between others – to scent scandal in the air – and close societies, which Sunningdale was, thrive on rumour.

Yet the fact that Archie chose to buy a house with Agatha at the start of 1926 suggests that he had no serious thought then of leaving her. It would have been insane to move from rented accommodation into that large place, with its huge mortgage, if he had been planning to get away. Even if the urge to buy had been Agatha's, the Christies had already delayed doing so for a year or more before they took Styles. Perhaps this was due to Archie's friendship with Nancy; perhaps he was thinking of her when he trod the Wentworth Estate with

Agatha, pretending to plan a new home. That is pure conjecture, though. What is certain is that it would have been easy to wait a little longer, to stay at Scotswood until Archie had finally made up his mind to leave.

More likely he was attracted to Nancy from the first and, to some unknowable degree, the two became close throughout 1925. Certainly Archie was not happy during the holiday to Cauterets, so he may well have wished himself back on the golf course with another woman. But by 1926 he had taken the view that his responsibilities lay with Agatha and Rosalind. He was prepared to stick with the life he had; possibly with the addition of a mistress on the side.

Then, during the summer in London, he grew close enough to Nancy to want to marry her. To that extent, Agatha was right in her analysis of the situation. It is entirely possible that Archie began an affair while Agatha was at Ashfield. It is equally possible that Nancy held out for marriage, in the manner of an Anne Boleyn. But some sort of pressure was brought to bear upon Archie – who was, undeniably, willing to be pressurised – to make him want to leave his family. The removal of Clara from the scene, which left Agatha with nobody to fight her corner and shame her husband, would have made it easier for Archie to announce his decision.

How could Agatha possibly have remained ignorant? Because her intuition was not quick when it came to real life; it worked only in her art. The shock of Archie's betrayal was absolute. That is beyond question.

Yet *Unfinished Portrait* makes clear the changes in her husband, evident since the birth of Rosalind. According to that book, he had become withdrawn, unemotional, cold. Contemptuous of Agatha's eager, childlike ways, which seemed so inappropriate in a grown woman. Controlled to an extent that was worse, even, than the lack of control she so disliked. Such detachment from his wife might be seen to indicate earlier, less serious affairs; as might the growing obsession with golf, which took Archie so completely away from his wife; and, of course, the poems in *The Road of Dreams*. In fact there is no evidence whatever of Archie's infidelity. But something in Agatha intuited the death of love, the death of the fervent young man who had returned so apparently unchanged from war. 'I will always love you more than anything on earth,' he had written to her in 1914. 'You are so very precious to me that I can't bear to think of you being ill or unhappy or wanting anything you could possibly have'; 'One day we will have our cottage which will be heavenly happiness and will never say goodbye again.' She had kept these letters: kept them until she died. This was the Archie she had loved, still loved, still saw within the man who had looked at her with that furtive, shifty-eyed expression, which meant he was about to betray her. He was not just taking away the life she had hoped to have. He was taking everything: the dances at Ugbrooke House, the honeymoon night at the Grand Hotel in Torquay, the wartime fear and passion, the foolish things they had written.

> (Q for the Quarrels that end so 'demurely'
> Each apology binds them together securely!)

She knew, of course, that they had not been 'in love' with each other for some time now. But in her obtuse and childlike way she did not grasp the reality. Her vision of Archie was so deeply fixed in her imagination that she did not see how incomplete it was: the beautiful soldier Lancelot, 'bruised and bronzed', with his air of romance and fragility, was no more than a man. Like Elaine, Agatha had lived in fantasy. Having spent six years dreaming an illusory Archie into solid life, she had played, with complete sincerity, at being a wife. She had lovingly cooked food he could not eat; had accompanied him round the world, then had more fun without him; had tried to 'share' his life while failing to understand him. He was vulnerable in ways both more complex and more banal than she had realised. The war had left terrible marks. The fear he had felt during Agatha's pregnancy showed his need for undivided love. His nerves were bad: and, throughout the 1920s, Agatha had made them worse. Her work as a writer gave her assurance that expressed itself as a kind of excitable talkativeness, unlike her previous quiet serenity. Her enthusiasms – for books, music, travel, Devon – were not his. And her growing independence was a threat because it made Archie feel she could do without him. Perhaps Agatha herself sometimes felt this way. Perhaps the problem was that she was a writer, and he was not.

> . . . they'd go on and on and on – probably at Dalton Heath or somewhere like it . . .
>
> Little shivers ran over her . . . If one could be free – quite free – nothing, no belongings, no houses, or husband or children, nothing to hold you, and tie you, and pull at your heart . . .[31]

The desire for freedom was always there, and the prison of Sunningdale had pushed it to a pitch; Archie might have been falling out of love but he did so, partly, because he feared Agatha would do so. He saw in her the need for something more than he could give. He had once stretched out his hands to her, like a little boy, knowing that she would hold them. Now she was clothed in the accoutrements of success, and he could no longer reach her. He did not know that she felt the same way about him: that she was chilled to the bone by his self-control, which had grown like a skin over the heart of the man she loved.

There was another factor, though: the oldest one in the history of betrayal.

> The golden green light, the softness in the air – with them came a quickened pulse, a stirring of the blood, a sudden impatience.
>
> A girl came through the trees towards him – a girl with pale, gleaming hair and a rose flushed skin.
>
> He thought, 'How beautiful – how unutterably beautiful.'

Nancy Neele was beautiful. She did not look at all like Agatha, being dark, with a face full of sweet, seductive curves, but she had what Agatha had once had and had now lost.

'That's what I remember about her,' said Sam James's daughter. 'As a child, I remember that Nancy was so beautiful.'[32]

Thus Agatha wrote, in her detective novel *Sad Cypress*, of how Elinor Carlisle is taken away from the man she loves by a young girl,

Mary Gerrard, whose beauty renders him helpless. 'They would have been together *here – now*,' thinks Elinor, 'walking side by side in gentle proprietary pleasure, happy – yes, *happy* together – but for the fatal accident of a girl's wild rose beauty . . .'

Left alone in London with this lovely girl, while his wife wept her heart out down in Torquay, Archie was unable to resist. Why had Agatha allowed her looks to go, after all? Did she not realise that a man wanted beauty in his wife? And why must she mourn her mother so wildly? Had she not heard him say that he could not bear illness or distress, he simply could not cope with it? Why could she not have remained the girl with whom he had fallen in love, slim and fair, the steady smiling presence who made him feel safe? ('I miss you more than ever this time and feel so lost without having you near me.')[33] Nancy seemed like everything Agatha had ceased to be. She was lively in a way that did not irritate, she consoled and reassured with a light touch, she played golf, she did not write, she was grown-up, she was beautiful, she needed him: she was the wife and the woman Archie wanted.

'I must in some way have been inadequate to fill Archie's life,' wrote Agatha in her autobiography. 'He must have been ripe for falling in love with someone else, though he perhaps didn't even know it himself. Or *was* it just this particular girl?'

With love, who knows? There is always illusion, the illusion that makes one person seem more magical than any other in the world. The question is of degree: is there enough reality within to sustain love when it can no longer feed upon 'Nature's lure, Nature's last and most cunning piece of deceit'?[34]

When Archie no longer felt passion for Agatha, it was just a matter of time before love evaporated. 'Archie was a good chap,' said Agatha's son-in-law, 'but you could never have imagined two people who were less compatible.'[35]

And yet. Although Agatha knew that Archie was not the man she had believed him to be – he was not Harry Rayburn or Anthony Cade, not Tristan, not Lancelot – she felt for him a passion that refused to die, however much she might wish it to. 'O lover of mine that I loved, Farewell . . .'[36] She simply could not believe that the letters Archie had written to her belonged to another time, a time that was as dead now as her mother. They seemed as real and alive as ever. 'Never desert me darling and always love me . . .' What had that meant when Archie wrote it? Had it meant something then, but not now? How could that be?

For Agatha – who spent the rest of her life trying to understand what love means – the illusory Archie did not die: he was fixed in her imagination at the very point of his leaving. Had the marriage lasted longer, she herself might have fallen out of love. As it was, she would never do so. A part of her would always be stuck at the moment when she had sat at Ashfield with Clara's things around her, and heard Archie's voice telling her that he loved another woman.

'He loved Celia, I think, for her beauty and her beauty only . . .' says the narrator of *Unfinished Portrait*. 'She loved him enduringly and for life. He was, as she once put it, in her blood . . .'

Agatha begged Archie to stay, if not for her sake then for Rosalind's. She was tormented by the thought that she had lost him through her own fault, and she begged for another chance. Knowing that he ought to stay, he gave in. After a couple of weeks at his club he returned to Styles, and Agatha's heart soared: he had not really meant it. Everything would be all right again. Archie had just been looking for a fling. Hadn't her grandmother always told her what 'the gentlemen' were like? Agatha simply had to be more realistic, more adult.

She made plans for the future. She would take a house in town to be nearer her husband, they would let Styles, they would take the holiday that had been deferred (the Pyrenees again, perhaps?). They would spend a wonderful Christmas at Abney, where the sight of the stockings, the magnificent table, Rosalind's starlit face would make Archie realise how much he was abandoning. Madge reassured her. Yes, Archie would get over it. But James Watts never thought he would; neither did Charlotte Fisher. This quiet, clever girl watched events at Styles and, as she burned in sympathy for her employer, saw how wrongly Agatha was behaving with Archie. Her distress made him feel guilty, and guilt made him cruel. She drove him quite mad and filled his head with thoughts of young, fresh, beautiful Nancy. According to the Nan Kon version of events the Christies rowed continually at the time and, on one occasion, Agatha threw a teapot at Archie. But it is hard to see how Nan could have known this (she was not there, after all, and the deeply private Agatha would hardly have confessed to such behaviour, particularly as – according to Nan's daughter – she had 'cast herself as the innocent victim').[37] Far more convincing is Charlotte's testimony, later offered to Rosalind, that Agatha was tearful, depressed, passive to a degree that alarmed Charlotte and played desperately on Archie's nerves.

'Everybody can't be happy,' he said to Agatha. 'I can't stand not having what I want, and I can't stand not being happy.'

He had not, perhaps, understood that Agatha would mind so much; he might have believed that her independence would sustain her. She had money, a career, Rosalind, Carlo, Madge. She could travel if she wanted to. She had so much more in her life than a husband. That was part of the problem for him, after all: that she had so much else besides him.

Yet here she was, white and distraught, as if losing him were a death blow. If only her mother were still alive. Then she would have been all right, perhaps.

Archie had agreed to try a three-month reconciliation period. He went away with his wife to the Pyrenees and, although this was even less successful than their last holiday together, Agatha saw it as a sign of his willingness to stay. In fact, being alone with her in France merely underlined for Archie how little suited they were. 'Slowly things went worse and worse,' she wrote in *Unfinished Portrait*. 'If Celia came into a room, Dermot went out of it.' She began to be scared of her husband's hatred. She feared he wanted her dead. This, after all, was what happened in her books: men killed their wives. 'He must wish her dead; otherwise she wouldn't be afraid.' Peter at her heels was like a little woolly lion. Agatha took him everywhere. One day he was knocked down by a car and left stunned and immobile; after a few minutes he came round but Agatha, gibbering with grief, was unable to take in the fact that he was alive.

Archie was theoretically living at home between August and December 1926, but in reality he was of no fixed abode. He stayed at Styles, he stayed at his club, he visited the Jameses at Hurtmore

Cottage. Madge James had recently had a baby, so the weekend parties were less social than usual, but if Archie saw Nancy it would be there, although ostensibly she was simply one of a party. This was important to Archie. He wanted to marry this woman – more than ever now – and he wanted no scandal attached to her name. To this end he intended that she should not be named in a divorce: a piece of middle-class propriety that Agatha despised. She held out. She would not agree to divorce Archie, would not accept that her marriage was over. There was Rosalind to consider, after all. The bond between father and daughter was so strong.

'Daddy doesn't like you much,' says Judy in *Unfinished Portrait*. 'But he likes *me*.'

Yet he was prepared to leave his daughter as well as his wife. How could it be possible? Agatha clung to the thought that it was *not* possible. But she was losing her grip upon that belief, upon everything in fact. She had not written since her mother died. This worried her. She needed to write, needed to finish *The Mystery of the Blue Train*, especially if she no longer had a husband. Although it was impossible that she should have no husband, that Archie should leave her. Not Archie. 'You are much much too good for me,' he had written to her during the war, 'but I will do anything to try and keep your love.' So everything would be all right. If only she had Clara to talk to. What would Clara have said? That she had warned her about Archie's ruthlessness, his attractiveness to women? That she had told her not to leave him alone? No, she would not have said those things. She would have looked at Agatha in her luminous way and held her hand as she fell asleep.

If only Mummy were there. If only she were at home at Ashfield, with Mummy and Peter, lying on the grass beneath the beech tree, dreaming stories into life.

It was the night of 3 December 1926. Agatha sat inside Styles as the house grew dark. She was waiting for Archie to come home. They were going to spend a weekend away together in Yorkshire.

('We shall meet again soon but till then we will be happy, eat, smile and grow very fat. I have your photograph to look at, letters to read. I know that you love me almost as much as I love you and nothing else matters.')[38]

Rosalind was in bed, Carlo in London. Peter slept calmly. The servants whispered in the shadows. If he did not come home tonight, if instead he went to Godalming, he was never coming home again. The words of Elaine.

> Sweet is true love though given in vain, in vain;
> And sweet is death who puts an end to pain:
> I know not which is sweeter, no, not I.

The Quarry

Time for a new story.

On the evening of Friday, 3 December, Agatha had dinner in the big dark house with the yew trees outside. As she ate she waited for the sound of Archie's car. She had made a chink in the curtains and every so often she saw lights approach. Not this time. She smiled at the maid, Lilly, who cleared the plates and looked concerned at how much was left on them. Silly to sit down to dinner when you had no desire to eat. The clock ticked heavily. Peter sighed at her feet, and as the shadows grew round her she continued to wait.

Upstairs on her bed was the dressing-case she had begun to pack for the weekend with Archie in Yorkshire. She did not understand the obduracy of men, their ability to make a decision and not be swayed from it. Few women do. They look for cracks. Surely he would be sorry for her. Surely he would remember how they had loved each other. Surely, surely. The room was becoming colder. The fire was dying in the grate. She had told Lilly not to bother stoking it, she would do it herself.

She sat on and on. The road outside grew quiet. Her head opened and shut like a trapdoor. Something had always been going to happen today, that must be why she had sent Carlo to London this morning. Carlo was due back at around eleven. Now it was almost nine.

Peter lifted a sleepy head as suddenly she stood, found her pen and some paper, sat down again with a foot against the dog. The position in which she usually wrote. She wrote a letter to Carlo, then a letter to Archie. As she did so the black windows seemed to watch her. Perhaps Archie was outside one of them. It was the long narrow one beside the front door that she had always feared. It had a sly, malevolent look, like a goat's eye.

She finished her letters and went into the hall to leave them. She dared herself to look through the goat's eye window. Nothing. No, he was not coming home again. The house was silent at its centre. Beyond were the discreet sounds of the servants and the soft breaths of Peter. The stairs were striped with shadow. She climbed them. Her bedroom was chilly and flooded with moonlight. She collected her dressing-case from the bed, put on a fur coat and a hat. She slipped into Rosalind's room, watched her daughter sleeping. Archie's face on a porcelain doll. Rosalind's favourite Blue Teddy was falling out of the bed so she tucked it in again. Then she went back down to the hall. Peter wagged his tail. She loved him, but the house was sending her out into the blackness, she could not stay in it. 'I'm going to London,' she said to Lilly, whose white face had appeared in the hall. She kissed Peter. He looked baffled that she was going out without him. His body was warm as she held him, so tight that he gave a brief whine. Then she went out of the house to her car. Her feet crunched as she pushed her way through the night, moving fast now to escape the terror.

That morning she and Archie had stared at each other across the breakfast table, such a naked look of estrangement in their eyes that it was almost like intimacy. He had told her, before he went to catch his train to London, that he would be spending the weekend with the Jameses at Godalming.

If only she were a different kind of woman, if only she could raise hell rather than sit, heavy-eyed, with not a clue as to how to make her husband stay with her. When you come back I shan't be here, she said, and in his eyes she saw a glimmer of hope.

After he left she took off her wedding ring.

She sent Carlo out for the day, having told her that all was well. Carlo's cool eye had looked at her penetratingly, lovingly, but Agatha had insisted. You have a good time in London.

A neighbour, Mrs de Silva, had telephoned at around midday. Would she like to come over for tea and bridge? No, she said, she had to visit her mother-in-law at Dorking, she was taking her little daughter. But how kind. Yes, they had had a pleasant day in London that week, hadn't they? On Wednesday, 1 December, she had gone shopping in the West End with Mrs de Silva. Planning for Christmas. The shops were full of festivity, how Margaret Miller would have enjoyed seeing it all. Debenham & Freebody, Swan & Edgar, Harrods, Selfridges, Whiteleys, the Army and Navy, all full of women like herself, with husbands and fur coats and handbags.

She had packed her week with activity. A normal week. Wednesday night she had spent at her club, the Forum in Grosvenor Place. The next day she had visited her literary agent. Her writing was going well enough, she told him. Yes, it had been a little difficult after her mother's death, a great deal to sort out, yes indeed, how kind, but all was now in hand. She would not say anything to Mr Cork. She smiled and she showed good spirits.

She was very tired when she reached Styles, late on Thursday afternoon. Every night her sleep took her to Ashfield, then woke her after two or three hours; sometimes she wandered through the house looking for Clara, or for Jane in the kitchen. Nevertheless she went out with Carlo on Thursday night, to a dancing class at Ascot they attended every week. Sunningdale–London–Sunningdale–Ascot–Dorking–Sunningdale. Chat–smile–eat–drink–two no trumps–yes perfectly well thank you–wash–teeth–face–cream–bed. Who would know, who knew what went on inside.

It was cold in the car. But it started all right. A mild night for December.

The little black eyes of the house watched her as she drove away. At the end of the road was a crossroads. She thought, not clearly, then turned right. The road she had taken that afternoon to visit her mother-in-law. Rosalind had chatted about Christmas while Peter sat in the back, alert as a kindly sentry.

Bagshot, Woking, Guildford. Names so familiar in daylight. Meaningless now that the black sky dipped upon her. A funny thing. The contempt in which she held Surrey had vanished. In the dark its shapes had power, an ancient English mystery.

An animal shot across the road in a formless streak. She braked in time. What had it been? A fox? A deer? As a girl she had gone hunting with the Ralston-Patricks. Their car, she could see it still. And the man she had met at the Barttelots near Goodwood – Mr Ankatell? – who had given her and Clara a lift to London. 'Beastly things, trains,' he had said, as he bundled them merrily into the vast open machine. How cold that drive had been, despite the rugs piled around them, and how exciting. She had smiled at her mother in pure happiness as they powered along. Why, they must have driven at fifty miles an hour through the Sussex countryside!

She was a good driver, but she would not dare go fast now. It made no sense, but she was being careful. She clung to the steering-wheel and from time to time lights roared behind her as if in anger. Past Guildford, she was coming now to the Epsom road that she had taken earlier, the way to her mother-in-law. On her right, Newlands Corner. She had seen it that afternoon, people walking their dogs across the stiff green slopes: a beauty spot so-called. She passed it, went on to the turning that led to the Silent Pool. In fact there were two pools, she knew. She had never seen them but she had heard they were fearful. She turned right. Down she slipped, down to roads that were less familiar. Albury, Chilworth. Water all around, a millpond, a fishing stream. The air damp and grey.

Now she was nearly at Godalming and she could see that it was pretty, even in the dark. Not her world, of course. Too careful, too ordinary. You are not an ordinary woman, Mrs Christie. On she drove, through Godalming, on to the little village of Hurtmore.

It took a long while to find Hurtmore Cottage. The lanes were winding and leafy. She went up and down them three times and then suddenly – how had she missed it? – she was opposite the house, a nice relaxed house, far more her kind of house than Styles. She sat there staring at it. Suddenly a dog barked and refused to stop. A big dog, she thought. Perhaps inside they would guess why it was making that terrific noise. But it needn't have bothered. She did not want to look in through the windows. She did not want to see Archie's car. She drove on through the dark. Her head had begun to open and shut again. She had to stop it. At the end of the road she seemed to see the river she had once dreamed of in the garden at Ashfield.

Ah, now, if she were driving to Ashfield. The beech trees, the croquet lawn, the rock cakes for tea.

She drove back along the road she had taken, the one that went past Albury Mill Pond. Then she climbed the hill to the Silent Pool. Deep, they said, as deep as death.

That slow, sweet drag into forgetfulness.

No. Not yet. She wanted to see the sky again. She turned left, back towards Newlands Corner. She stopped the car on the grass verge. The North Downs sloped away from her, great stretches of colourless ground, like invitations to the end of the world.

She got out of the car. A pure vast starless black. The silence of the night, with its own sounds and magnitude.

'Where am I myself, the whole man, the true man? Where am I with God's mark upon my brow?'

Archie. Mummy. She began to walk down the hill.

She was nothing any more, no thoughts, no feelings. She was just a shadow moving towards the edge. She found a rutted path. It led to a quarry, a round bowl of chalk, white and faceless beneath the moon. A blank circle. She stood staring down into it, grasping a bush with one hand.

'They came round the last corner – came to the deep pit and to something lying in it that had not been there before, the body of a woman lying in a wonderful pose, arms flung wide and head thrown back.'

She would write that, quite soon, in a story called 'Harlequin's Lane'. In the story she was a great dancer who gave up her art for love. At the end she danced along the lane with her husband, an illusory figure who leads her to death.

Her first thought, after an unknowable space of time, was that the lane did not end at the quarry but led beyond it, down the hill and out towards Albury. She was not, in fact, at the edge.

*   *   *

Archie had once teased her for her dislike of walking uphill. 'What about Barton Road?' he had said, as she puffed and laughed beside him. She could hear her breath now, hard and loud in the silence. She kept to the path but it was rough. Her feet were never sure where they were going. Her hand had been pierced by the bush and hurt. She cried like a child, sobbing and puffing as she stumbled upwards. It wasn't fair. That was what she had written in the letter to Archie. Not fair, not fair. Not fair that she had to be scared like this, that she had to climb this horrid hill in the dark.

Surely those were shadows, moving across the grass. The Gun Man was waiting for her.

She would make for the car. The ground flattened at last and she began to run, tore at the door, flung herself into the driver's seat and crouched in it. The keys were in the ignition. After two attempts she turned them and shunted the car a little further on. By lifting her left wrist to the sky she could see that it was ten past two. How long, she wondered, had she stood looking into the quarry?

A sin, of course, she had always known that. But it had got to a certain point.

'She was up against reality. The reality of herself and what she could bear, and what she could *not* bear.'

She would write this many years later, in a book she called *Destination Unknown*, having forgotten nothing.

'Escape, escape! That was the refrain that had hummed incessantly in her mind ever since she left England. Escape. Escape . . .' It was from herself that she longed to escape, herself and her pointless grief. And yet the woman in the book did not kill herself. She assumed another identity, gladly, as an alternative to death.

'You have had an experience. I should like the experience of having come so near to death. To have that, yet survive – do you not feel yourself different since then, Madame?'

Wrapped in her fur coat, she felt ready for sleep. There was a hotel across the road, but time for that tomorrow. How tired she was. A light from one of the rooms burned dimly through her shut eyes, like the lamp in the nursery. She tucked the coat round her and with her good hand held the cut one tight.

I am sure there is more to know
Something to love
Something to dream of
Something to make
And with that you can walk
You can walk in the wood
In the cool of the eve
And when God walks beside you
You are not afraid.

It was years later that she wrote this, on a scrap of paper, as a very old woman at the end of her life.

When she woke the light had changed. There was a lift within the darkness and she knew that it was morning. Around half past five. She was still very tired but it seemed a miracle to have slept. She decided to thank God for it.

In her mind was a story. The woman who lay dead in the pit. She was an artist, whose husband had loved her for her artistry although he did not understand it. Then, because he was really very ordinary despite his air of romance, he fell in love with a pretty young girl, because it was easier for him.

Did it have to end that way? Well, she would begin to write it, and she would leave the ending up to her husband.

Of course, she could make up stories. Wasn't that what she did? Better than anyone, she could write her own story.

But she began to cry again when the car refused to start, because unless the car started she could do none of it. The engine had gone solid cold while she had slept inside her coat, dreaming of the wood at the end of the garden. Oh please, she said to it. That day at Ashfield after Mummy died when it wouldn't start, that same obdurate sound. She took off her coat in despair and got out and cranked at it. She was so tired though. Her arms seemed full of shifting stones. A man dressed like a farm-worker came up on his bike and she smiled at him graciously, as if she were back on the Empire Tour, accepting his offer to start the car. Her voice sounded a little strange. 'Oh *do* help!' But she had not spoken to anyone for so long, for days it seemed. The thick grey air held on to her words.

Whatever would Mummy have said? Worse yet, her grandmother? Such an odd situation. She almost laughed, thinking of it. 'Stone cold it's gone,' he said to her, shaking his head, looking at her, expecting an explanation that she was not, of course, going to give. She had no doubt that he *would* start the car; that was what men like him did. So she just waited. But she had not wanted to see anyone so when he finally got the engine going – telling her what to do, what not to do, although it made not a stitch of difference any more – she drove back towards Guildford to throw him off the scent. She knew that he would be watching as she went. Annoying he had been, although kind. Should she have offered him some money? She drove a bit further to shake away the thought of him. Still almost nothing on the road. Imagine if she now had to drive back to Styles. That black fortress opening its door to claim her. No no no no never again.

She turned the car round and drove the other way, back towards Newlands Corner. Nothing on the road as she slipped the car on to the grass. Careful now. Concentration. This had to be done right.

Pink streaks across the sky. Do it, now.

She let out the clutch and bumped along slowly, slowly, down she goes, easy does it, on to the rutted lane and – a moment of lost control, something in the path? No, it was all right. Slow, slow, nearly there, it was only a couple of hundred yards after all, nothing really, yet it had seemed so far in the middle of the night. Down she goes and round to the right. Careful, very careful. Straighten up.

The bush she had grabbed, the one that overlooked the quarry, there it was again, a few yards down the hill. Gear in neutral, brakes off. She got out of the car, taking her big black handbag with her. She had removed all the money from her dressing-case. Also a sheet or two of writing paper. Everything else she left. She no longer felt tired, or even cold without her coat. She pushed hard and the car rolled smack into the bush, obediently, just as she had planned.

The sky was lifting into lightness as she walked past the quarry and looked up to where the car perched over the edge without her. Its lights stared at nothing. You clever girl, she said. She almost ran as the lane sloped downhill. Houses at last. People inside them drinking tea and reading the newspaper, but today she preferred to do what she was doing. 'Water Lane', she read, on a sign at the end of the road.

She turned right into Albury and walked at a clip past the fishing waters, past the mill pond, on for another mile or so, on towards Chilworth station. She had noticed it on her drive to Godalming. The seven-thirty London train was just arriving. Well, that was luck. She sat in a corner seat with her hat pulled down, writing another letter. She watched Surrey fly past and felt a little sleepy.

The train reached Waterloo at nine o'clock. She bought a stamp and a *Daily Mail*. She could see that she needed a coat because it looked odd not to have one. She took a taxi to the Army and Navy Stores. Before going in she posted her letter. It was addressed from Styles to her brother-in-law, Campbell Christie, at the Royal Military Academy in Woolwich. Campbell was someone she liked and trusted. He was the only person to whom she could write what she wanted to say. He alone took no sides in this matter. So she explained to him something of what she was doing, and why she was doing it. She was going away to Yorkshire, as planned, although not to Beverley. She was going on her own to a spa. She was in need of respite, her health was not good. In fact she was very distressed, and he would understand why. She was pleased with the letter. It was less excitable than the ones she had left for Carlo and Archie, but she had been in a different state of mind then. When Campbell arrived at work on Monday he would read it.

In the ladies' room at the Army and Navy she washed her cut hand and tidied herself. She looked respectable again, not a fugitive at all as she clinked a shilling into the attendant's plate. She trod the thick carpets of the store as she bought a small case, a nightdress, a hot-water bottle and a coat. She drank a cup of coffee.

London was bustling with pre-Christmas shoppers as, in her new coat, she took a taxi to Harrods. In the ground-floor jewellery department she left a ring to be repaired, giving a name and address for it. Mrs Neele, the Harrogate Hydro. It felt good to say it. Then she took the Piccadilly line to King's Cross. In the station buffet she drank another cup of coffee and read her newspaper. Nobody noticed her. Everything was going right. At one forty she caught the train, which was due to arrive at Harrogate at six thirty-eight. On the long peaceful journey, in her warm first-class carriage, she slept again.

Thorp Arch, she remembered, as the train drew close to Harrogate. The house near Wetherby, owned by the Matthewses, where she had stayed for a house-party. They had gone to the St Leger. She liked the St Leger, a crisp English sporting occasion. Who had won it that year? Someone had put five shillings for her on Lord Derby's horse, which came in third. Such an enjoyable visit it had been. The train journey had been amusing because she had been wearing a wonderful new tweed coat-and-skirt, so smart that the station master had assumed her to have a maid and a jewel-case, although she could not even afford to travel first class. Archie had admired that coat and skirt but, really, it had belonged to the life before him. It was at Thorp Arch that she had met Arthur Griffiths, the man who had told her to look out for his friend Christie when she went to the dance at Ugbrooke House.

The north was different. She liked its clean airy skies and dark colours. The look of Harrogate reassured her as the taxi took her through the streets. Grave, stately buildings, grey stone in the moonlight. She could stay here and feel safe. How nice it was to sit back in the seat and be driven. She looked out of the windows and saw the opera house, the Crown Hotel, the White Hart Hotel, the Pump Rooms. Hills and spires and beech trees. The grand scale she had been missing.

The taxi swept respectfully up Swan Road. Calm and wide in the darkness, edged with handsome houses. Muncaster Lodge, Britannia Lodge. Lived in by people with solid, indestructible lives. Yes, she could move among them like a shadow.

The Hydro was spread across the end of the road, dark stone again, ivy-covered, deep windows and, behind them, warm forgiving light. She thanked the driver as she tipped him. Up the stone steps. It was just before seven o'clock when she entered, smiling.

Mrs Teresa Neele of Cape Town took room five, on the first floor, at five guineas per week.

She slept long and late and the next day was like a holiday. Sunday, after all. Still a special day. And she could do whatever she wanted; she would no longer worry that her soul was in danger. How she had feared for Daddy's when he played croquet instead of praying! Silly, when she thought of his goodness.

As a precaution she did not let the maid see too much of her face in the morning. A nice pretty girl, a maid of the old-fashioned kind, who tended the coal fire and brought breakfast. It was delicious. She enjoyed her food and her bath. Boring to have to wear the same clothes, but there was nothing to be done about it until the next day. So she again put on the grey and green outfit that she had dressed in, on Friday, before driving to see her mother-in-law.

By the evening these clothes would form part of a police description, circulated to the fifty stations closest to Albury: 'grey stockinette skirt, green jumper, grey and dark grey cardigan and small velour hat'. Charlotte Fisher had given the description with her usual efficiency. 'No wedding ring,' she had said, having found it in her employer's bedroom. 'Hair, red, shingled part grey.'

Her beautiful hair, once as fair as light itself. She would go a hairdresser in Harrogate. Thirty-six was not so old.

Late autumn sun fell through the window of her bedroom and her face shimmered in the glass. Pale skin, pale eyes.

'Odd if one had got into a train with a ghost!' She would write that soon. A fragment of a short story about a young widow with 'haunted frozen eyes', unable to move past the moment when she had found her husband lying dead on the study floor. 'Of course, she hadn't really gone on. She'd stayed there. In the study.'

But no writing for now. Just this story of her own, whose ending she did not know.

Harrogate pleased her. She liked the certainty of the wide streets, the strong crescents and the manly, elegant houses. They said to her: wrecked hearts and lost identities mean nothing to us. Whatever you have done, whoever you are, we stand above it. We keep life's mysteries in their place.

She lunched among women like herself at Betty's tea-room. The food was wholesome and very good. Then she walked all afternoon. The light fell and the beech trees rattled their leaves as she went across West Park. More dark grey houses. Beech Grove, Stray Lodge. A tall Victorian church. Perhaps she should? No, she did not want to. She preferred to walk among these straight shapes and northern colours, with the leaves over her head and beneath her feet, the sun seeming to expand as it dropped in the sky, flooding the grey with its dying yellow, the stone translucent in the brief powerful glow.

And she a striking figure, glimpsed from windows as she strode across the green, her hat down and her collar up. Something odd about her, perhaps. Illness, bereavement, loss?

The time went slowly but she did not mind. The time was hers again.

For how long? she wondered, as she walked up Swan Road. Tomorrow Campbell would read her letter and then something would happen. She had said a Yorkshire spa: well, he would know that Harrogate was the sort of place she would go, it was full of upper-middle-class women like herself. And he would say to Archie, look, she is distraught, she needs you, what are you doing? So that would be all right.

Of course they would have found her car by now. The police would be rapping on that great dark door at Styles, alarming dear Carlo, and then, a bit later, on the door at Hurtmore Cottage. Poor Archie, really. He would be worrying about her dreadfully. Perhaps she had said too much in the letter she wrote to him, in fact she had hardly known what she was writing. She had wanted to die, that was certain. She had said so, she was sure of it, to Carlo. Carlo would be frantic beneath her calm quiet demeanour, which she would maintain in front of everyone and especially Rosalind. But tomorrow Carlo would know that she was not dead after all.

Except that she *had* died, in a way. She had died looking down into the blank face of the quarry. It was a smiling ghost who walked up Swan Road and looked through the windows at the people in the

Hydro lounge, real people, pouring tea from silver pots: warm, magical, configurative.

She nodded to a couple as she went past ('Not human – not a bit human').[1] She chatted to Mrs Taylor, the very pleasant manageress, told her that she had come back from South Africa just three weeks earlier and had stored her large luggage with friends at Torquay. Well, she smiled, she would enjoy herself buying a few new things! Quite right, Mrs Neele. Bentalls on Oxford Street is very good.

Into her room. Out of the window she stared at the sweep of the drive, the road that led to the town, the trees, the stone houses, the fallen light.

Dinner. She liked this big handsome room, although the night before she had been so tired she had found the ceiling somewhat disorienting. It had a big square panel that reminded her of a dungeon roof. In fact what had looked like an iron grille was dark stained glass, rather nice really. She sat in a quiet corner. A little embarrassing, to be in the same clothes again and not evening clothes either. Still, she had made her speech to Mrs Taylor. Books were what she needed. Difficult to have none. But tomorrow she might well be having dinner here with Archie, or might not be here at all, who knew.

She stopped thinking about all that. She listened to the chat of the other guests, who were the kind of people with whom she felt at ease (people like us), she looked at the menu, she sipped the water that was supposed to be so good for you. Cleaner-tasting than Sunningdale water, that was for sure. A few people had wine, she noticed, but not many. They were here for their health, after all. Perhaps wine would have helped, back at Styles? She found it strange to think about Styles. In fact she could scarcely believe that the place existed. It lay inside her head like a distant nightmare.

After dinner she went with the other guests into the Winter Garden Ballroom where she drank her coffee and did a crossword, having picked up a newspaper in the lounge. Then she fell into conversation with the couple she had nodded to earlier. Mr and Mrs Campbell, up from London. Ah, how nice. The theatres. Well, yes, it *was* rather exhausting at this time of year, she had passed through to catch her train and she could understand that they liked to get away! No, she *had* lived in London, but of late she had been in Cape Town. Oh yes, marvellous scenery. No, she had lost her baby, that was why . . . Yes, she found them relaxing, stimulating too; she had always enjoyed puzzles.

Pleasant people. Easy to be with. And a pleasant room. Almost like a conservatory on the side of the hotel, looking out on to the gardens. Cloudy night sky outside the window. What was Archie doing now. He seemed very remote, somehow, as though he had been killed in the war and in her mind she was seeing the photograph of a dead man. But tomorrow she would hear from him, or perhaps the day after that. He had to find her, it was not so easy as all that. Still, he had done it before. Chugging up the hill on his motorbike to Ashfield. Mummy's voice on the telephone, calling her home.

She drank her coffee, smiled, and thought of all the nice things she would do tomorrow. A new dress, for a start.

Monday, 6 December, and her own face on page nine of the *Daily Mail*. 'A beautiful woman,' they called her.

Her car had been found at eight o'clock on the Saturday morning, she read. 'It is believed that it was allowed deliberately to run down from Newlands Corner with its brakes off.' All weekend they had searched for her on the North Downs. They had dredged the Silent Pool and visited cottages in Albury. There was a small picture of 'Col. Christie'. Archie said that she was suffering from a nervous breakdown. 'She is a very nervous person.' He had returned to Sunningdale on Saturday. He would be at work now, perhaps. Campbell would be at work too, and he would tell Archie about her letter.

She got up and went out into the streets of Harrogate, hat down, collar up. Oxford Street, Cambridge Road, Parliament Street. She enjoyed looking at clothes, trying things on, especially now she had lost weight. A dress of pink georgette would be wonderful for the evening. Archie would surely like it. Shoes to go with it, underclothes and – why not? – a new hat as she was very bored with the one she was wearing. Yes, that *was* becoming, wasn't it? No, from South Africa, actually. Yes, a very pleasant stay.

She joined the W. H. Smith library. That was a relief. She went to Handford and Dawson the chemists, bought face cream, *papier poudré*, lavender water. How nice to have these things again. She bought a *Sketch*, a *Pearson's*.

Cold Bath Road, how amusing. Westminster Arcade, full of antiques, that would be interesting. And the Royal Baths for the therapeutic treatments. Her neuritis had come back, pushing that car would have done it no good, and she remembered how much the salt water had helped it on the Empire Tour. Perhaps she would try a treatment tomorrow. Assuming she had heard nothing by then. Of course she had not told Campbell exactly where she was going: she had not been sure, had she. So Campbell had to tell Archie and they had to work it out between them that Harrogate was the likeliest place and then Archie had to find her. He had to work out that she was Mrs Neele. It was a game, really. And think of the trouble he had gone to, finding her house in Torquay.

She asked for everything she had bought to be sent to Mrs Neele at the Hydro. When she got there, perhaps there would be a message from Archie.

She did not ask, they would tell her, and they said nothing as she walked in. The day suddenly yawned at her.

Oh, Mrs Neele? Her heart leaped. Archie, thank heavens.

A parcel for you, from London, Mrs Neele. Her ring. Well, that was good service.

And all her Harrogate parcels would arrive later. A cheering thought. There were therapeutic treatments here as well, something to do this afternoon. Lunch and then perhaps a massage. Into the dining room she took one of her library books, a collection of mystery stories called *The Double Thumb*. She had taken out six books. Perhaps, as she had done this, she had known it might take him a couple of days to find her.

She was pleased with her appearance at dinner that night, and Mrs Campbell complimented her on the georgette dress. She gave her little speech about the luggage being stored with friends. At dinner she read her book and finished it.

After dinner a band played in the Winter Garden Ballroom. We call them 'the Happy Hydro Boys', one of the elderly resident guests said to her, and she smiled. It was a six-piece band. A lady called Miss Corbett sang with them, quite well. People got up and danced. As she sat there it occurred to her, quite suddenly, that she could do anything she liked. She could sleep with one of these men, if she really put her mind to it. There were two or three who were apparently unattached. One was looking at her, admiringly it seemed. Of course she would not do it. But she sat with her coffee and meditated upon freedom, gazing through the window of the ballroom to the black grass and trees.

Tuesday, the seventh, and having woken early she went down to breakfast. She felt well. In the mirror she looked different already. As she entered the dining room she smiled and chatted to a guest. Mrs Robson, such a nice lady. Yes, all the way from South Africa!

Up in her room she learned that the *Daily Mail* was getting worried about her. The man who had started her car had come forward. He said that she was 'moaning and holding her hands to her head' when he had found her at Newlands Corner. Had she been doing that? Surely not. 'As I approached the car she stumbled against me.' No, she had not done that. She had not particularly liked that man at the time, so these exaggerations did not surprise her. Although of course she had been most grateful to him.

The policeman in charge of her case was called Superintendent Kenward. He had theories, which he gave to the newspaper. He believed that she had driven her car inadvertently off the road at Newlands Corner, got out of it when she came off the track then watched, 'terrified', as it ran down the hill and crashed into the bush over the chalk pit. She had stumbled away and become lost. Although he did not say so, he believed she was dead.

Archie, she read, was a 'pitiful figure' who, 'driven to distraction by the mystery, finds comfort only in the presence of his little daughter, Rosalind'.

Perhaps Campbell had not gone into work on Monday? Because she could not account for any of this. She was here, for heaven's sake, waiting for them!

Mrs de Silva had given an interview about her. 'Mrs Christie is one of the sweetest women who ever lived.' Oh good Lord. On and on it went, full of detail about the past year: her grief about Clara, her worries about work, her poor health, her day with Mrs de Silva in London, her holiday with Archie in France. 'They have always been a most devoted couple and both idolise their little daughter.'

The maid was coming into the room. She bundled up the paper and turned to her with a smile. Going out soon, she said. The maid had noticed the picture of Rosalind that she kept on her dressing-table, across which she had written 'Teddy', which her daughter had liked to be called.

Downstairs she saw her face on the cover of the *Daily Express*. It was one of those pictures with Rosalind that had been taken by the *Sketch*. She nodded to the woman at Reception and went out into the Harrogate streets. Today she would buy some more clothes (thank heavens for Grannie's advice about money!). And tonight she would hear from Archie. Campbell would read her letter, telephone Styles, and everything would be all right.

She returned to the Hydro with a beautiful new evening shawl that she planned to wear at dinner. She felt happy, excited. She read all afternoon, another mystery called *The Phantom Train*, but found it hard to concentrate. She looked out of her window as the light fell. At any moment a car might come along. Or perhaps a taxi, if he had taken the train. A long drive, after all.

When she came down the stairs the telephone was ringing at Reception and Mrs Taylor was looking at her as she answered it. News, she felt, surely news. She lingered until Mrs Taylor put the receiver down.

Good evening, Mrs Neele, she said, what a lovely shawl.

She went in to dinner with *The Phantom Train*.

That night in the Winter Garden Ballroom she did *The Times* cross-word and calmly read the column about herself in the middle of the paper. They had dragged Albury Mill Pond, she read. She had been sighted at Milford station, a few miles south of Godalming. 'On inquiry at Colonel Christie's residence at Sunningdale yesterday morning it was stated that so far no news had been received as to the where-abouts of the missing woman.'

So she would not see Archie tonight after all. Whatever had happened to Campbell's letter, it was not what she had planned.

She smiled at Mrs Robson and sipped her coffee. Mrs Robson came over to her table. Your price tag is still on, Mrs Neele. Is that all you are worth? I hope not, she said, I hope that is not all. They talked some more. When Mrs Robson asked about her husband she changed the subject, rather cleverly, she thought.

Wednesday, the eighth, and the mystery was solved, as she read what had happened to Campbell's letter. Oh, oh, for heaven's sake, she said to herself, drinking her tea in bed and grappling with the *Daily Mail*. Campbell had received her letter on *Saturday* afternoon, she read. How could that be? He must have gone into Woolwich at the weekend rather than waiting until Monday. So that was not what she had planned, for a start.

More to the point he had entirely ignored what she had wanted him to do, which was to contact Archie immediately. Why had he not done that? Did he not care that Archie was leaving her? Did he think it had nothing to do with him? Perhaps she should have written the letter differently. She had thought it well done.

He had thrown the letter away. 'In it Mrs Christie is said to have dealt with her health and to have stated that she was going to a Yorkshire spa to stay with friends and to recuperate.' Well, not quite. These newspapers, they could not be trusted, and they proclaimed their knowledge with such authority! For example, she had *not* made arrangements for the Forum Club to post her letter to Campbell when she stayed there on 1 December. What nonsense. She posted it on 4 December and she had meant what she said in it. Why did nobody believe her? Why did nobody, that is to say Archie, come and find her?

Her head began to open and shut in the old way. That maid would be in soon.

A lady never shows her feelings in public, however much she may give way in private.

She disappeared to the bathroom. She thought and thought and thought. She came to no conclusions.

When she returned to her room the tray had been taken and the bed made. She dressed in a warm new twinset and went down to the lounge. She picked up *The Times* and looked at it with a casual air. 'It was learned late last night that a brother of Colonel Christie living in London had received a letter written by the missing woman since her disappearance, and that in it she stated that she was in ill-health and was going to a Yorkshire spa.'

A man walked into the lounge and bowed at her. She recognised him as having sung with Miss Corbett the other night. A foreign gentleman, with courtly manners and a pleasant tenor voice. She lowered her head to the page.

'The Surrey police, however, have communicated with certain centres in Yorkshire, and as a result are satisfied, it is understood, that Mrs Christie is not in that county.'

She rose and went out into the Harrogate streets. Hat down, collar up. She walked for hours. So she was not here, Mrs Christie was not here. Here instead was a ghost who walked through the Valley Gardens, looking up to the stone buildings that rose behind the trees. She liked the hills, they reminded her of Torquay. So the ghost had memories. She remembered how flat Sunningdale had been. How deathly.

She walked and walked. She was a ghost but she felt quite happy, walking through the gardens, feeling strong again in her body. How silly it would have been to kill the body of a strong, still-young woman, striding beneath the trees and feeling the air on her cheeks.

She thought of *Peer Gynt*. 'Where am I with God's mark upon my brow?' But she thought about it as at a distance, not really minding where or who she was.

She went into the Royal Baths and saw that people did see her as a ghost. The eyes of the women at the desk alarmed her. That was silly too, though, so she smiled and said she would like a Turkish bath. She was here for her health, after all. To make things better.

At dinner she would wear her beautiful shawl again and afterwards she would not sit with the newspaper crossword. She did not want to read the newspapers any more today. She would chat and have a nice time. She might sing to Miss Corbett's accompaniment, as she had seen the male guest do; she loved to sing and had not done so for a long time. Why, she might even dance. She and Archie had enjoyed dancing together. How tiresome of him not to have understood what she was saying to him, through the letter to Campbell. He could have been with her now. Everything could have been different.

Instead she accepted the invitation of the man who had sung the other night, and stood up to dance the waltz with him. When he asked her about South Africa she deflected the conversation. Gentlemen, her grandmother had always told her, much prefer to talk about themselves. Mr Pettelson, as he introduced himself, was a refugee from the Russian Revolution. He was in Harrogate for his health, too, and enjoying it very much. Particularly the band at nights. Yes, he loved to sing. He had wanted to sing opera. Is that so, Mrs Neele? Well, perhaps we shall make a little music together!

Thursday, the ninth, breakfast in bed again and she knew now to turn to page nine of the *Daily Mail*, although not of course when Rosie the chambermaid was in the room. A nice, pretty, friendly girl. She had asked her name when she came in with the tray.

A rather strange photograph of herself – a 'composite', as they called it – that had been put together with the help of Carlo. Poor Carlo. What a time she must be having. She had never liked Archie and there the two of them were, thrown together by circumstance. Archie, said the report, was 'harassed and bewildered' and had asked for a police presence at Styles.

Her mother-in-law had been talking all about how depressed she had been of late. She had told the story of how Peter had been hit by a car and she had refused to believe he was alive. Well, that was true. Peg obviously believed her to be dead. Or perhaps she was just being dramatic and hysterical, which was nothing new.

She saw Rosie look at her a little strangely when she came back for the tray.

She smiled at her and told her that today she would take the waters. She ought to do it, oughtn't she? Rosie told her that she thought that healthy water tasted horrible, like rotten eggs though she shouldn't say so! But she knew some of her guests swore by it. It would perk

Mrs Neele up, she was sure. She was looking a lot better already, though, said Rosie. She'd looked a little bit tired at first.

Yes, she agreed, she had been very tired when she arrived.

As she walked down Swan Road and around Promenade Crescent, she wondered if people were looking at her through their windows. Those deep, formal, respectable windows.

They might well have been looking. She had, after all, asserted herself with this story. She was chief character again. No longer side-lined, as she had been for too long.

And plot was a function of character, she knew that now beyond dispute. The first thing she would do that day was place an advertise-ment with *The Times* newspaper in the post office at Harrogate. She had mentioned to Miss Corbett, with whom she had chatted the night before, that she was going to do this, because she was a little concerned that some of her relations did not know where she was. What a good idea, said Miss Corbett, who reminded her of a smart young nursery governess.

She marked out the words: 'Friends and relatives of Teresa Neele, late of South Africa, please communicate. Write Box R 702, The Times, EC4'. She paid fifteen shillings.

The story had not gone the way she expected, but she was trying to regain control of it.

At dinner that night she wore a new dress and read a new book, *Ways and Means*. Afterwards she dodged Mr Pettelson and took coffee with the Findlays: Mr, Mrs and Miss. Mrs Findlay, who had a side-long look that she did not altogether care for, waved a copy of the *Express* at her and asked what she thought of this Mrs Christie story? Did she think she was dead? Did she think, as Mrs Findlay suspected, that she had been murdered by her husband? Just the sort of thing that Mrs Christie herself might have written! Was that not droll? Mr Findlay laughed, so evidently he thought it was. Then he said: You look very much like the missing lady, Mrs Neele.

Do I?

Mrs Christie seems to me rather an elusive woman, she said. I really don't know where she is or whether she is alive. She poured more coffee.

*   *   *

Friday the tenth, and in the *Daily Mail* a statement from Archie. He knew that she was alive. He knew, and she knew it.

'It is quite true,' he said, 'that my wife had discussed the possibility of disappearing at will. Some time ago she told her sister, "I could disappear if I wished and set about it carefully."'

Had she said that? Had she, really? But what had that to do with what was happening now. She had not meant to disappear. This was all meant to be over by now. It had all gone beyond the place where it was meant to have stopped.

'I do not believe this is a case of suicide. She never threatened suicide, but if she did contemplate that, I am sure her mind would turn to poison.'

No, that was not true. She knew about poison, that was not the same thing.

'If she wanted to get poison, I am sure she could have done so. She was very clever at getting anything she wanted.'

Rosie the maid had come into the room. She did not smile at her. For the moment she could not do so. Yes, take the tray, she said.

'Curiously enough, Peter, our little dog, which I took over there this afternoon, made straight down the hill from the place where the car was found. He did that of his own accord and then stopped.'

Oh Peter, her friend.

'It is absolutely untrue to suggest that there was anything in the nature of a row or tiff between my wife and myself on Friday morning.'

So the servants had been talking. Well, that is what servants do. Perhaps Archie did not know that?

'I strongly deprecate introducing any tittle-tattle into this matter. That will not help me find my wife which is what I want to do. My wife has never made the slightest objection to any of my friends, all of whom she knew.'

Which was not true either.

She read that '500 Police' were searching for her. She had told them where she was, where she had gone, and none of them believed her. It was all so silly. Perhaps, as sideways-looking Mrs Findlay had said last night, they really did believe that Archie had murdered her. It was all mad.

On the back of the newspaper were the usual pictures. Today it was of Archie leaving the house in his Delage, Rosalind and Carlo with him, Peter in the back. Also one of this fool policeman Kenward, looking for her on the downs.

She went out into the streets and took a train to Leeds. She was sick of herself, today. She did not return until evening, having shopped all day and eaten an indifferent Welsh rarebit. It was very nice to be back in Harrogate. No doubt about it, she did feel safe here. Have you had an enjoyable day out, Mrs Neele? She smiled and went up to her room, not a thought in her head to speak of.

Saturday the eleventh, a week of it all now. Oh, she sounded quite peculiar in the *Daily Mail*, thanks not least to her mother-in-law, telling the world about her behaviour when she had visited with Rosalind for tea. 'She seemed very cheerful'; 'But a few minutes later she became very depressed'; 'I am certain that her brain refused to function when she sat down to complete her novel'; 'Before she went she repeatedly muttered, "These rotten plots! Oh! these rotten plots."'

Had she really done that? No, she could not believe she had done anything so ridiculous.

'It has been hinted that Archie and Agatha had a quarrel or tiff on Friday morning. They were a devoted couple.'

Still protecting him, then.

'I believe she is dead and on the Surrey Downs.'

Wrong, and wrong again. As usual, Mrs Hemsley.

One thing, though, for which she was grateful to her mother-in-law. She remembered how Peg could sometimes be kind, even perceptive. 'The general public can be quite certain that her disappearance has not been staged by her for any purposes of self-advertisement.'

So that was what people thought, was it? If they only knew. The longing to escape: to be elsewhere, to be not herself. And yet. She had written this leading role. It had not turned out the way she wanted but, somehow, she did not want it to end just yet. She could end it, after all. She could go downstairs and end it now. She did not quite want to do that.

People were leaving when she went downstairs to go out for the day. Mr and Mrs Campbell, Major Brigg and his family. Going home to prepare for Christmas, no doubt. Goodbye, goodbye! Yes, and to you too!

She edged her way into the lounge and glanced at the cover of the *Daily Express*. 'Mrs Christie "Still Alive",' it read. She shifted her hand to see *The Times*. Her advertisement. Yes, it was there, second from top in the Personal columns, Friends and Relatives of

Mrs Neele, good morning. The voice came from behind her shoulder. Mrs Findlay. She smiled. Good morning, she said. A nice mild day, it looked, didn't it? And how were her husband and daughter? She had been out all day yesterday but she hoped they would see each other this evening. She was looking forward to Miss Corbett and the band.

She walked and read and ate lunch and had a massage and dressed herself for the evening. At night, after dinner, she played the piano for Mr Pettelson to sing and then she sang herself, to much polite acclaim. The bandsmen, who had watched her closely, applauded. Miss Corbett declared that she would lose her job!

Sunday, the twelfth. She felt bored with newspapers. Bored with the whole thing. They were searching for her across those wretched North Downs, police and aeroplanes and dogs and sensation-seekers. She could only think them idiotic for not believing her letter to Campbell, for trying to say that it was a blind, somebody else had posted it, she was dead, Archie had murdered her. It was silly and she was bored with it. A woman like her grandmother, she thought, would have worked out days ago what was really going on.

She dressed in some of her new clothes and walked the familiar streets. Swan Road, Promenade Crescent, Parliament Street. She went into a church, St Peter's, and prayed for her mother. Then she walked across West Park, beneath the beech trees and within the edging of dark grey stone. Those deep, formal, respectable windows.

She could dream what was behind them into life.

She began to conjure words, lines, ideas. They rose up out of her, and she played with them as she walked.

A woman deeply in love, whose fiancé falls hopelessly for a beautiful girl of whom he knows nothing. The woman dreams of killing the girl . . .

('I know the story. She offered Fair Rosamund, did she not, the choice of a dagger *or a cup of poison*. Rosamund chose the poison . . .'

Elinor said nothing. She was white now.

Poirot said:

'But perhaps, this time, *there was to be no choice* . . .')

A woman whose fiancé marries a rich woman. He plans to kill his wife for her money before returning, in triumph, to his old love.

('So I had to come into it, too, to look after him . . .'

She said it simply but in complete good faith. Poirot had no doubt whatever that her motive had been exactly what she said it was. She herself had not coveted Linnet Doyle's money, but she had loved Simon Doyle, had loved him beyond reason and beyond rectitude and beyond pity.)

A man with a beautiful young mistress. She begs him to leave his home even though, as he tells her, his wife loves him too.

('I said I understood that, but if she loved him, she'd put his happiness first, and at any rate she wouldn't want to keep him if he wanted to be free.'

He said: 'Life can't really be solved by admirable maxims out of modern literature. Nature's red in tooth and claw, remember.'

I said: 'Surely we're all civilised people nowadays?' and Amyas laughed.

'. . . Don't you realise, Elsa, that she's going to suffer – *suffer*? Do you know what suffering means?')

A woman in love with a married man, whose wife has the white-skinned, provocative looks of Nancy Neele. The girl betrays her husband with a lover. The other woman, 'fresh and pleasant and very English', learns about the affair. She threatens to expose it. She induces the girl to kill herself.

('Suicide needs a lot of courage.'

Vivien flinched back as though she had been struck.

'You've got me there. Yes, I've got no pluck. If there were an easy way—'

'There's an easy way in front of you,' said Claire. 'You've only got to run straight down that green slope.')[2]

A woman on a train with a face like that of a ghost.

So many stories.

'Harlequin's Lane', for instance, in which the woman flung herself into the moonlit pit.

And Mr Satterthwaite, who found the woman's body at the end of the lane, which leads either to love or to death. He 'had a vista of something at once menacing and terrifying . . . Joy, Sorrow, Despair'. He knows that he will never, now, experience these emotions. 'But I see things,' he cried. 'I may have been only a looker-on at Life – but I see things that other people do not.'[3]

That evening after dinner she sat in the Winter Garden Ballroom with her head bent to a crossword. The room was emptier than it had been since she arrived. Quiet, calm, soft piano music. The light was dim and forgiving, gleaming low.

Perhaps she could live this way for ever. Without love, without grief.

She smiled at Mr Pettelson as he came across and asked if he might join her for coffee. He had heard that she might be leaving, also? Was this true? It had been Mrs Findlay, he thought, who had told him this.

She did not know where Mrs Findlay had got that idea. She did not know when she would be leaving, in fact, she had no plans at all.

Might he interest her later in a game of billiards? He had heard that she played. Too well for him, no doubt!

The band did not play that night but earlier in the day two of its members had gone to the police. They suspected, as did other members of staff at the Hydro, that the nice lady who called herself Mrs Neele was, in fact, Agatha Christie. It was almost over.

She smiled at Mr Pettelson and said that would be delightful.

Monday, the thirteenth. Rosie looked at her a little shamefacedly as she brought in breakfast.

Are you all right this morning, she asked. Oh yes, ma'am. Your newspaper as usual, ma'am.

Five thousand people had looked for her yesterday.

She felt somewhat tired today.

A man named Max Pemberton gave his expert theory to the *Mail* that she was dead. 'Should happily I be wrong, then I will bow to her as to a great mistress of a staged drama. But I should still think it very wicked of her to have awakened so much public sympathy in so poor a cause.'

She felt unusually reluctant to go out. She sat in her room and read for a while. When Rosie came back to do the room she apologised for being still in her dressing-gown. Always make life easy for servants, her mother had said.

Oh Mummy. What would you have thought of all this. The journalists had gone to try to find her at Ashfield, had walked up to the dear front door and poked around the garden. She should not really have let that happen.

Downstairs the papers were full of the Sunday hunt.

Another woman had disappeared. Miss Una Crowe. She had walked out of her home in Chelsea and not been seen since. A girl really, poor thing, suffering from a nervous breakdown after the death of her father. How pitiful it sounded.

Meanwhile it was suggested that she herself was living in London, disguised as a man like Ethel le Neve. How ridiculous it all was.

She heard a newspaper rustle in the corner of the room. Quite a handsome man. So many people were leaving, she had seen Miss Findlay saying goodbye to Miss Corbett and had felt a certain relief at the thought of no more sidelong looks from Mrs Findlay. Not that she had minded so much. In fact she would miss the Findlays, their inevitable presence at the corner table of the Winter Garden Ballroom. Mrs Findlay guiding her husband in a well-trained waltz and their daughter's faintly resentful gaucheness. She had enjoyed them.

She smiled at the new guest and went out into the streets. Hat down, collar down.

Tuesday, the fourteenth, and Mrs Taylor smiling more brightly than ever as she broke off her conversation with Mrs Robson and said, Good morning! How well you are looking, Mrs Neele. Harrogate seems to agree with you.

Are we still going to the dance at the Prospect Hotel tonight, asked Mrs Robson, I do hope so. Oh yes, of course. They had discussed this a few evenings ago. Mrs Robson had suggested it and she had thought, why not.

Well, do enjoy yourselves, ladies, said Mrs Taylor.

Pleasant, polite, utterly normal. Yet in the *Daily Mail* an ex-policeman had written this about her: 'One great difficulty is that the search is for a woman with certain attributes that are not common to the ordinary individual. She is talented. She is a woman who by the very nature of her work would have an exceptionally elastic brain. Consequently one would expect her, consciously or subconsciously, to do something extraordinary.'

Well that, she thought, was really rather nice.

'Soon some most interesting development must occur, but its nature cannot yet, in my opinion, be even guessed at.'

She smiled at that. Everything else was more nonsense. On and on it went. How very famous Mrs Christie had become. How absurd it was when she was here, simply here, as she had told them. They were going to send divers to search all those pools she had driven past. So apparently she was no longer living in London in her musical-comedy male-impersonator costume, well that was good to know.

This girl, this Una Crowe, she was surely dead. Poor young thing. She had lived at Elm Park Road, how odd, that was just by her friend Nan Watts. Why, they might have passed each other in the street.

She went out for her walk, through the Valley Gardens today. Past the Majestic Hotel, a vast red-brick building, unusual for here. She looked at it, at the people inside drinking their morning coffee and smoking. Contained within their lives.

How lovely it all was. How safe she felt.

She enjoyed her lunch. It was quiet in the dining room and she read some poetry she had taken out from the library. Later she had a massage. Afterwards she played billiards again. She signed a piece of sheet music for Mr Pettelson of the song 'Angels Guard Thee', which he had sung to her piano playing. Teresa Neele, she wrote. He was a charming man, certainly. Perhaps a little smitten with her? A pleasant thought, no more. My dear Mrs Neele, how very kind. I shall treasure this always.

Afterwards she went for her bath and changed for dinner. She put on the georgette dress she had bought when she first arrived, heavens, more than a week ago now. She glanced at her newspaper again in the darkening room. A woman with certain attributes that are not common to the ordinary individual.

She looked out of her window. The sweep of the drive, the road that led to the town, the trees, the stone houses, the fallen light.

She looked at herself. Pale hair, pale eyes. She smiled.

As she did every night at this time she walked down the corridor, which creaked a little, then down the short flight of stairs that turned and led to the lobby. Outside the hotel doors something seemed to be massing in the black air. New arrivals? She went to glance at a copy of *The Times*.

Archie was in the lounge, sitting by the fire.

They looked at each other. Archie and Agatha again.

She sat down opposite him.

Then an extraordinary thing, Mr Pettelson came up to her with his little bow, and she was saying, look, do you see, my brother has arrived. And then suddenly there was a small bustle of activity, and she saw how tired and sad Archie looked, and she knew that she loved him now, always, for ever, that she had done this for him and he was here too late, too late.

He was touching her arm to lead her into dinner.

Yes, that is my wife, she heard him say, to the man she had seen in the lounge the day before. The man was talking to her. He was a policeman. A nuisance. What had policemen to do with her? She explained to him that she remembered nothing of what had happened since she left her home eleven days ago, was it really so long? and that only now was she beginning to regain her memory. Yes, my wife remembers nothing, said Archie.

They were going into dinner together. On the way she saw

Mrs Robson, oh, she was so sorry about tonight, my brother has arrived unexpectedly, would she forgive her? Of course, Mrs Neele, how very nice for you.

They sat. Archie again, opposite her at a table. How white his face was.

But could it not, now, be just all right? The menu, the food, perhaps even a glass of table wine?

How was Teddy, she asked.

She knew nothing about any of it, he said, so she was perfectly all right.

Missing me?

At that moment the waiter came up and he turned his head away to give their order.

Are you all right, Agatha? he said, when he had finished.

I don't know, she said, am I?

He looked at her.

She had gone away but she knew that it was he who eluded her, then, now and for ever.

She had grown up at last.

> But ten slow mornings past, and on the eleventh
> Her father laid the letter in her hand,
> And closed the hand upon it, and she died.[4]

She smiled at the waiter and began to eat.

From that point on, she became public property.

The journalists poured into the Harrogate Hydro. Mr and Mrs Taylor were powerless against them. Agatha was what the press wanted but she had gone up to her room after dinner. Archie, who had taken a separate room for himself, was left to cope. Although he wished to say nothing he took the advice of Superintendent McDowell of the West Riding Police, the man who had spoken to Agatha before she went in to dinner, and agreed to speak to one newspaper. In a statement to the *Yorkshire Post* Archie put forward for the first time the official line on Agatha's disappearance, which for many years her family stuck to resolutely.

'There is no question about her identity. She is my wife. She is suffering from complete loss of memory and identity. She does not know who she is. She does not know me, and she does not know why she is in Harrogate. I am hoping to take her to London tomorrow to see a doctor and a specialist, and I hope that rest and quiet will put her right. Great credit is due to the police for their untiring efforts in the matter, and for the inquiries which have led to her discovery.'

The idea that this would put an end to speculation is, in retrospect, almost comical. But Archie did not have a clue about what he was doing, what he had become mixed up in. He could only dimly understand the mysterious motives of a wife who was, as he had told the *Daily Mail*, 'very clever': far cleverer than himself. He had been through pretty good hell during the past week or so, suspected of adultery at best and murder at worst, and his relief that it was over was complicated by anger, anxiety and guilt. As always, his instinct was to bury his feelings. It was a good idea, but he did not do it very well. He held himself on a rein so tight it was always liable to snap, and the reporters knew it. He had something to hide. 'Mrs Neele' indeed! They knew all about what that meant. If Archie was covering up for his wife, he was also covering up for himself.

After giving the statement Archie sent a telegram to Charlotte Fisher at Styles. He suggested that she arrange for his Delage to be driven from Sunningdale to King's Cross, where he and Agatha could pick it up before going home. Charlotte had been rung at around midday by the Surrey police, who gave her news of the possible sighting that they had received from Yorkshire. She was asked to travel to Harrogate but could not go, as Rosalind was in her care. Instead she contacted Archie at his office and he caught the one forty from King's Cross, the same train that Agatha had taken.

Charlotte too had gone through hell. She had been under a certain degree of suspicion: not just that she knew more than she was telling, but that for some unknown motive she had murdered her employer. Reporters had clustered round Styles, lurking beneath the little black windows, taking her photograph every time she emerged. For support she had had her sister, Mary, to stay with her, and between them they had looked after Rosalind. Under intense pressure, Charlotte's loyalty to Agatha had remained absolute.

Now she rang family and friends, giving them the official 'amnesia' line. Meanwhile Archie changed his mind about the arrangements for getting Agatha away from Harrogate. It was obvious that they could not catch a train to London tomorrow then go on to Sunningdale: the journalists would simply follow them and camp outside the house. So he contacted Madge and James Watts and made a new arrangement. The pretence would be maintained that the Christies were going to Styles; at Leeds, they would change trains and travel to Abney. There Agatha could hole up. No reporter could get past those vast iron gates.

Accordingly the Wattses arrived at the Hydro early on Wednesday morning, where they were met by Archie. Madge had known absolutely nothing of Agatha's thoughts before she had left her home on 3 December, although she might have made a better guess than most at her sister's state of mind. James, who was fond of Agatha and a practical, competent man, took charge of the arrangements to get her away.

At around 9.15 a.m., Agatha left the hotel that had been her home for ten days. How reluctant she must have been to drag herself back from the forgetful depths. The sheer number of journalists made escape very difficult so a decoy car had been arranged, a landaulette, which drew up at the entrance and attracted a crush of photographers. Meanwhile a taxi had arrived at the goods entrance, around the side. The *Mail*, having guessed the ruse, was there to take a picture of Agatha as she walked down the few steps to the car: beneath the brim of her hat her face is entirely blank.

At Harrogate station she again used the goods entrance. There were too many people on the platform for the journalists to identify Agatha with certainty. She and Madge managed to hide in their compartment – taken for 'Mr Parker's party' – while their husbands kept discreet watch outside. Meanwhile some reporters were running across the tracks to reach the King's Cross train. At Leeds the whole performance was repeated, when it was realised that Agatha was changing trains rather than going on to London. Her photograph was taken by many of the newspapers as, smiling bizarrely, she led the way towards the Manchester train. By the time it arrived, a vast crowd of journalists had amassed to meet them. Archie lost control briefly when he pushed away a man who tried to talk to Agatha, saying, 'This lady is ill.' Madge's chauffeur-driven Wolseley was waiting outside the station and more photographs were taken as Agatha got into it. Again, she was smiling. She also appeared to be wearing her wedding ring.

A convoy of press chased the Wolseley all the way to Abney Hall, where the gates were padlocked. The crowd at King's Cross, waiting for the arrival of the Harrogate train, sighed and shoved as Agatha failed to appear; then the train driver shouted, 'We have not got her!' and they went home disappointed, clutching their newspapers, talking of Mrs Christie.

Something of the mystery will always remain. The blank face of the quarry will never give up all its secrets. The facts may now be known, and much of the intention behind them, but in the end what is left is a story. A mystery story. Her finest, because it cannot be solved.

Of course there have been many attempts to do so, but these fail, because the mystery Agatha created was so much more than merely a puzzle. Questions can be asked. Did she plan it all? Did she lose her memory? Was it a publicity stunt? Was she after revenge, or pity, or an end to it all? Indeed these questions have been asked repeatedly, in the hope of a simple answer. But such a hope is not relevant: it is reductive. Her eleven days in the wilderness are a myth, a poem. They exist in a different sphere from that of theories and solutions.

The eleven days are the creation of an artist, a writer; and writers live life differently. Their motives are always mixed, because to them everything is a story. That is their escape, their freedom. That is their way.

But because the story is that of Agatha Christie, the temptation has been to treat it as a detective story: to work it out. Oh for Poirot! Somebody who could simply take the facts – the letters, the abandoned car, the train journeys, the *Times* advertisement – and by a miracle of reasoning make them cohere.

In a sense, they *do* cohere. As has been shown, there *is* a solution that clears the tangle from the forest. But it can only do so, in honesty, by acknowledging the dark areas, the ambivalences, the unknowable. Agatha herself barely understood what she had done throughout those eleven days: how, then, can they be rendered, except as a story?

All biography is story-telling. No life is a code to be deciphered: there will always be gaps and inconsistencies, and it is stories that make the missing connections. Omniscience is for Hercule Poirot. Real life knows less; it has the beauty of mystery; and this, despite the books that she wrote, was something that Agatha understood very well. She must have known she had created a puzzle of a different order, with all the geometric complexity of *Roger Ackroyd* – how to work it out? Turn it this way? That way? – and yet with this twist in the tale: it was true, and therefore it could never be solved. It was perfect, in fact. The perfect metaphor for human mystery. What could be more impenetrable than the woman who moved through Harrogate like a smiling ghost, reading newspaper reports about her own vanished self?

And so the story endures, infinitely fascinating; and those who would lay it to rest, who would destroy its beauty by 'solving' it, are defeated at every turn.

Perhaps the best comment of all was written on 16 December, two days after Agatha had been found at Harrogate, when the newspapers were still simmering about the affair and the faintly foolish part they had played in it. It came from a columnist in the *Daily Sketch*, who wrote as 'The Man in the Street'.

Many citizens who, like me, have neither met Mrs Agatha Christie nor read any of her novels must have felt immensely relieved when the police at last ascertained her new address . . . Whether such facts as were available regarding this matter from the start ever justified the subsequent efforts at fiction in which so many people indulged, not to mention the resulting impressive expenditure of energy and money, is a little doubtful.

Shortly after Mrs Christie had left home a letter from her was received by a brother of Colonel Christie stating that she was in ill health and was going to a Yorkshire spa, which, apparently, is precisely what she did. So all that can be said now is that various people have had a good run for someone else's money.

This is the sublime joke about the Agatha Christie 'disappearance'. Separate the intention from the effect, and it is clear that there *was* no disappearance. At least, not an intentional one. Certainly there was never any intention to disappear for eleven days. It just looked that way, to the people who were searching so hard for Agatha they were blind to the fact that she had told them where she was. As the Man in the Street so unarguably put it, Agatha did exactly what she had said she was going to do; and more fool the police and the press for not having believed her.

So here, in plain text, is Agatha's story. She drove away from Styles with the vague intention of looking for Archie, or killing herself, or both. She then drifted into a highly particular state of mind: she was in command of herself, to the extent that she could plan and think and function, and yet the self that she commanded was no longer really there. She had not killed herself, yet in a sense she had died.

This ghost Agatha created her pathetic *faux* puzzle of the abandoned car overhanging the quarry, the case, the driving licence, the fur coat: the clues. And she sought to do the one thing that might reclaim her husband. She absconded, in the belief that giving Archie a weekend of agony, making him fear that she was dead, awakening his buried feelings, might restore him to her. She appealed to the one person who could intercede on her behalf – her brother-in-law – and told him that she was going away to Yorkshire, making it plain that she was unwell and unhappy. Her hope was that Campbell would receive her letter on Monday, 6 December, get in touch with Archie, and make him go and find her. 'Mrs Neele' was another clue, both a sign of her presence and a prick to Archie's conscience.

Yet to explicate is, in the end, to confuse. What Agatha did made sense, and yet it made no sense. That is why the two most familiar 'solutions' to the disappearance are not just wrong, they are meaningless. Agatha did not lose her memory, as the official line had it for many years. Nor did she plan a set-up, as certain commentators have cynically insisted. The truth lies somewhere between those two theories, in the realm of ambiguity, in limbo; like the consciousness of its creator, whose identity slipped away into the dark sky as she walked down to the quarry.

But of course, it was not only Agatha who wrote the story of her disappearance. Alongside her version was the far more familiar one created by the police and the press. There were two stories, in fact, the private and the public, and in the divergence between them lies infinite fascination. Agatha drifted silently beneath the beech trees while, as it were in another universe, the busy people of England pondered her fate.

She always saw the story as a private one, right up to the moment that she was found at the Harrogate Hydro. Considering how famous her name was to become, it is hard to realise how little known it was at the start of these events (the *Daily Mail* of 6 December referred to the disappearance of 'A Woman Novelist', a 'writer of detective stories' including *Who Killed Ackroyd?*).[5] She was an entirely private person and, even in her right mind, she would never have dreamed that her actions would become public property. Thus it was that she believed she could abandon a car over a quarry and cause serious alarm to just one person: her husband. The idea that her behaviour might reverberate beyond her own circle would simply not have occurred to her. She was not that kind of person.

Nor would it have reverberated – at least, not to the extent that it did – had it not been for the attitude of the police; or, to be precise, the attitude of Deputy Chief Constable Kenward of the Surrey Constabulary, a man who fell in love with his theory about the case, and with the attentions of the journalists who wanted to hear it.

It was around 11 a.m. on Saturday, 4 December, when Kenward

first learned that a car – established as Agatha's property by the driving-licence left inside it – had been found at Newlands Corner. In an interview given after the event to the *Surrey Advertiser*, Kenward said: 'It seemed probable that . . . the occupant or occupants had met with disaster.' As Agatha lived in Sunningdale, the Berkshire Constabulary was informed, and the two forces were then obliged to work together. Therein lay a difficulty. From the first, Deputy Chief Constable Kenward was convinced that Agatha was dead and that her body lay near the site of her car. Superintendent Goddard of Berkshire was equally certain that she was alive.

Goddard was a sensible man, whose instinct told him that an emotional upheaval had caused Agatha to take flight. Shorn of complications, this was pretty much what had happened. However chief responsibility for the case lay with Surrey, so Kenward's will prevailed. The case of Agatha's disappearance, which could have been handled with tact and intelligence, became wildly overblown: a focus for nation-wide publicity, extensive press involvement and numerous searches of the area around Newlands Corner. Obviously Kenward was sincere in his belief that Agatha was dead; but the less likely it became that her body would be found in the environs of her car, the more dogged he became in his desire to be proved right.

'What have I always told you? Everything must be taken into account. If the fact will not fit the theory – let the theory go.' The words of Poirot in *The Mysterious Affair at Styles*, but Kenward – like most people with ideas about this case – ignored them. Rather as in the investigation of the Yorkshire Ripper murders, which in the late 1970s became fixated upon a hoax tape-recording and thus missed the culprit as he passed repeatedly through police interview rooms, Kenward went in such single-minded pursuit of his own ideas that he ignored the one real clue to Agatha's whereabouts. 'It was the clear duty of the police, from the point of view of humanity alone, to endeavour to find Mrs Christie if she was wandering about, out of her mind because of nervous collapse, in the woods or surroundings of Newlands Corner,' said Kenward to the *Surrey Advertiser*. 'Having failed in this direction, it was again the duty of the police to satisfy themselves that it was not a matter of foul play, and that no crime had been committed.'

This was the nub of it: Kenward believed there was a strong possibility that Agatha had been murdered by her husband. That was why he failed to pursue the clue of the letter that had been sent to Campbell Christie. Instead of taking its contents at face value, and accepting that its postmark – '9.45 a.m., London SW1' – almost certainly proved that Agatha had been alive on Saturday morning, he clung to his own theory. He decided that the letter had either not been posted by Agatha herself, or that she had posted it in London before returning to Newlands Corner. There was, therefore, insufficient investigation of Agatha's statement that she was going to a 'Yorkshire spa'. The problem was that the letter had been destroyed – although its envelope had not – and there was only Campbell's word for its contents. Kenward might have believed that Campbell was shielding his brother by lying about what was in the letter; or he might have thought that Archie himself had posted it.

From quite early on, the newspapers knew what was in Kenward's mind. They sensed that he was itching to cuff the hands of that arrogant Colonel Christie. Several other theories were put forward in their pages, but it was the possibility of wife-murder that kept the story bubbling so fiercely. It has led some commentators to suggest that Agatha had wanted Archie to be suspected or even arrested. This is an entirely absurd notion – Agatha was trying to get her husband back, not to alienate him for ever – but, in order to see this, it is again necessary to separate intention from effect. Agatha meant no such thing to happen to Archie; nevertheless, it became a very real possibility. As one of the journalists who reported on the case, Ritchie Calder of the *Daily News*, later wrote: 'If her body had been found in the Silent Pool, say, I have no doubt from what I knew of the police attitude, that Colonel Christie would have been held, on circumstantial evidence.'

So it was that, because of Kenward in the first instance, then because of the newspapers, Agatha's private story became public. The police and the press were entangled in a *folie à deux*, which led to a deeply personal crisis becoming the property of the nation. Anyone who believes that an intrusive and judgemental media is a recent phenomenon should look at the reports of Agatha's disappearance: back in 1926, newspapers were making exactly the same assumptions about the hunger of their readers for sensation, disaster and scandal. But the press cannot really be blamed. The bones that Kenward held out were too juicy to resist: it was, and remains, a cracking story.

It started quite small, on Monday, 6 December, alongside news of the death of Claude Monet. By the next day it was the stuff of headlines. It was reported with a decent level of accuracy, which would later be compromised, as newspapers became competitive and claimed exclusive information for themselves. On Tuesday, the seventh, however, certain facts were established.

Agatha's Morris had been found at Newlands Corner, a vast expanse of the North Downs that stretches away from the A25, near Guildford, towards the village of Albury. The car was found about three hundred yards down the hill, at the edge of a quarry, with its bonnet jammed in a bush. It was close to one of the paths – now called a byway – that leads from the top of Newlands Corner. About half-way down this path becomes a rutted track, Water Lane, which passes to the left of the quarry, then leads out towards Albury. The car was seen on Saturday, 4 December, by a gypsy boy named Best, who had been walking along Albury's main street at around 8 a.m.

In 1926 Newlands Corner was far more open than it is today. There was no barrier, as there is now, between the main road and the sloping grassland, and drivers did occasionally career off on to the downs. A good many trees are now planted across the hills but there was little, then, to impede a car's descent. Nevertheless, Agatha's car was a long way down, and as there were no signs of the brakes having been applied it seemed unlikely that she had skidded there by accident.

A little after eight a man named Frederick Dore, who worked with cars, examined the Morris more closely. According to most reports, he found it with a flat battery and the brakes off. He was variously quoted as to how the car had got there: in the *Surrey Advertiser* he said it was as though 'the car had been allowed to run down the hill' and in the *Daily Sketch*, more strongly, 'It appeared to me that it must have been given a push at the top of the hill.' But the car had suffered very little damage, considering its extraordinary position, and was later capable of being driven to a garage on the Epsom Road. It contained around two gallons of petrol; also Agatha's dressing-case, some items of clothing including a fur coat, and an out-of-date driving licence.

In some reports, Dore also made reference to a gypsy girl, whom he met nearby on Saturday morning, who said that she had heard a car at about midnight being driven along the top of Newlands Corner. He walked up the hill to the refreshment kiosk run by a Mr Alfred Luland, who was given charge of the car while Dore went to the nearby Newlands Corner Hotel to telephone the police (Luland told the *Daily News* that he was certain the brakes were on, adding that it was 'difficult to see how it managed to run down the hill').

The newspapers also reported a sighting of Agatha herself. Early in the investigation a man came forward to say that he had started a car at around 6.20 a.m. on Saturday the fourth, near Newlands Corner, for a woman answering her description. This man was named first as Ernest Cross, then as Edward McAllister – a discrepancy that was never resolved – and there were inevitable deviations within the reporting of his story. The *Daily Express* described the woman he had helped as having 'hoar-frost' in her hair, and putting her hands to her head 'as if in distress'. The *Surrey Advertiser*, who talked to McAllister direct (and whose reporting was generally excellent), wrote that 'The woman did not seem distraught, or particularly distressed, but seemed a little strange, which he put down to the worry of the car.' It was, indeed, almost as though there were two different men involved, since 'Cross' described the car radiator as 'quite hot' and square-shaped (Agatha's Morris had a bull-nosed radiator) while McAllister stated that it was stone cold. In every report the woman is said to have worn no hat or coat, and to have driven off in a direction away from Newlands Corner.

At this point the newspaper reports would have caused readers to believe that Agatha had killed herself. 'Hatless Woman Met on the Downs', was the headline in the *Express*, giving an impression of a semi-dressed lunatic who had wandered through the night to her doom. Emphasis was given to the proximity of the abandoned car to the Silent Pool, which the police were draining and which was described (rightly) as an extremely creepy place. From the first, and not just because of what Agatha did for a living, the case was treated as a dark and sinister mystery.

The big story on Wednesday, the eighth, was the letter that Agatha had sent to Campbell Christie. 'SAID SHE WAS GOING FOR WEEKEND VISIT TO A YORKSHIRE SPA' was the headline in the *Daily Sketch*. Then, dismissively: 'No evidence that she went there'. How could the story have so simple a solution? With regard to the SW1 postmark – which also presented a threat to the 'Corpse at Newlands Corner' scenario – it was suggested that Agatha might not have posted the letter herself, or that she might somehow have arranged for its posting when she stayed at her club, the Forum, on the night of 1 December. 'How and by whom it was posted in London is a question that has not yet been elucidated,' wrote the *Surrey Advertiser*. Never was there any suggestion that the letter might be taken at face value: it was merely another snort of a drug to which police and press had become quickly addicted.

For example, it was reported that Agatha had visited her local chemist in the past couple of weeks to get sleeping pills, and that she had had a conversation with him about the poison hyoscine,[6] saying: 'I should never commit suicide by violent means when there is such a drug as hyoscine available.' Some of the papers also stated that Agatha might have been in possession of a revolver.

But although the strong implication was that Agatha was dead, the newspapers also printed reports of several sightings. Most of these were in the area of Newlands Corner. Mrs Kitching, who lived near Albury, had 'met a strange woman on the road at noon on Saturday', whom she was convinced was Mrs Christie. A cowman had seen her car at around 4 a.m. on Saturday, the fourth, driving through the nearby village of Shere; a Mr Brown offered her a lift at about 11.15 a.m. on the same day ('She seemed to be in the kind of mood when she did not care what happened'); and a Mr Richards reported seeing her on Saturday afternoon in a parked car, up a lane a few miles from Guildford, with a man sitting beside her.

On Monday Agatha was seen in Plumstead, south-east London, when she burst into the house of a Mr Daniels waving a pound note and demanded change. On Tuesday she was seen by a Mrs Bisshop boarding a bus at Piccadilly and alighting at Bayswater, 'in a very distressed condition'.

Meanwhile, on Wednesday the eighth, the *Harrogate Herald* printed its weekly list of visitors to the town. The name of 'Mrs Neele, Cape Town' appeared as a guest at the Harrogate Hydro.

The police had, of course, taken some note of Agatha's letter to Campbell. A small paragraph in the *Daily Express* of 9 December referred to them making 'careful inquiries' in Harrogate. 'It was reported that an unknown woman, about the same age as Mrs Christie, went to the Royal Baths yesterday': the one true sighting among the mass of false ones. Journalists from the *Express* and the *Daily Chronicle* did the rounds of the Harrogate hotels but, finding no woman registered under Agatha's name, concluded that she was not there.

Yet the clue that might have found her was published on the ninth, with the first mention of 'Miss Nield', as the *Westminster Gazette* called her: 'the only other person' at the house in Godalming where Archie had spent the previous weekend. There were also reports of police interviews with the Christies' household staff. 'I understand', wrote the *Gazette*'s Special Correspondent, 'that there is "no truth in the rumour" that there were "high words" between them at the break-fast table.'

In other words the Special Correspondent believed that there *had* been high words; and had a pretty good idea as to what those words had been about. The press had the scent by now. They knew what Kenward thought about Archie and they knew why he thought it: the story had acquired a luscious new dimension. Having been an object of considerable pity ('driven to distraction by the mystery', as the *Mail* wrote on the seventh), Archie was becoming more like an object of suspicion. He had requested, and obtained, a police guard at Styles, in order to protect both himself and his daughter (a policeman accompanied Rosalind to school every day) from the jabbering attentions of the press. Yet he was unable to resist talking to them. 'I am in a bad state of health,' he told the *Daily Express*, 'and suffering from the anxiety caused by the continued lack of news. Frankly, I cannot stand it much longer.' To the *Evening News* he said even more: 'I left home on Friday to spend the weekend with friends. Where I stayed I am not prepared to state. I have told the police. I do not want my friends to be dragged into this. It is my business alone. I have been badgered and pestered like a criminal, and all I want is to be left alone.'

The next day, the tenth, brought extensive reports and photographs of the searches for Agatha at Newlands Corner: '500 Police Search for Mrs Christie' was the headline in the *Daily Mail*. Less sensationally, *The Times* reported that nearly 250 police had taken part in the search, assisted by volunteers including Archie Christie. With him was Agatha's dog Peter (or 'Patsy', as some of the papers called him). Two civilian aeroplanes were used to scour the area. Earlier in the week Albury Mill Pond had been drained, and the beagles of the Guildford and Shere Hunt had been used by Kenward as an unofficial search party. Nothing had been found, except for a hoax message – dutifully reported in the newspapers – which read: 'Ask Candle Lanch. He knows more about the Silent Pool than . . .'

But the big news on 10 December were the words of Archie Christie, who had given in and talked extensively to the newspapers. The *Mail* quoted him at length. Doubtless encouraged by the sympathetic demeanour of yet another Special Correspondent, he revealed something of his thoughts: not just about the disappearance, but about Agatha herself. He did not lack understanding of her nature; he knew that her mind worked in unusual ways. Nevertheless the theories he put forward were deeply coloured by the desire to cover his own tracks.

To this end he said that Agatha

'had discussed the possibility of disappearing at will. Some time ago she told her sister, "I could disappear if I wished and set about it carefully." They were discussing something that appeared in the papers, I think. That shows that the possibility of engineering a disappearance had been running through her mind, probably for the purpose of her work.

'Personally, I feel that is what happened. At any rate, I am buoying myself up with that belief.'

Archie went on to give his reasons as to why he did not believe Agatha had committed suicide: she would have used poison, he said, had she done such a thing, and anyway, 'If a person intends to end his life he does not take the trouble to go miles away and then remove a heavy coat and walk off into the blue before doing it . . . I think she walked down the hill and off – God knows where. I suggest she walked down the hill because she always hated walking uphill.'

Some of this was amazingly near the mark, especially the passage about walking downhill. Archie's motive for saying it, however, was affected by self-interest. He wanted to emphasise that Agatha was still alive because her only credible reason for killing herself was his relationship with Nancy Neele.

He gave details of the last three days before Agatha had disappeared, including the visit to Edmund Cork in London. It is surprising, in the light of their estrangement, how much he knew about the progress of Agatha's writing. Obviously they had maintained some sort of relationship, or perhaps it was simply that Agatha had pretended to carry on with him as normal.

'She told me that they had been talking about her new novel, *The Mystery of the Blue Train*, which she could not complete . . . I think she was also rather worried about turning another series of hers, *The Big Four*, into book form. It did not, however, appear to affect her, for after dinner on Thursday evening she went off with her secretary, Miss Fisher, to a dancing class or something at Ascot.'

This was all very interesting, but the point of the interview lay elsewhere. 'I directed Colonel Christie's attention to certain rumours which have gained currency in Sunningdale and elsewhere.' Archie strenuously denied that there had been a row between him and Agatha on the morning of Friday the third.

'She was perfectly well – that is to say, as well as she had been for months past. She knew I was going away for the weekend; she knew who were going to be the members of the little party at the house at which I was going to stay, and neither then or at any time did she raise the slightest objection. I strongly depre- cate introducing any tittle-tattle into this matter. That will not help me to find my wife which is what I want to do.

'My wife has never made the slightest objection to any of my friends, all of whom she knew.'

How badly this reads; how much wiser Archie would have been to say nothing. Yet he would not be the last person to be seduced by the press into 'explaining' himself. People with infinitely greater media awareness have been convinced that silence is more liable to misinterpretation than words; only clever, watchful Charlotte knew that Archie was doing the wrong thing. It was not the job of the journalists to exonerate him. Their loyalty was solely to the story, and the best story of all was Archie's guilt. One reporter, Stanley Bishop of the *Daily Express*, was absolutely convinced that this was a case of uxoricide. Ritchie Calder theorised that Archie had left the Jameses' house in the middle of the night, met Agatha at Newlands Corner and killed her. As the 1922 trial of Edith Thompson[7] had shown, the English public was willing to condemn an adulterer for murder, however shaky the proof. Evidence against Archie was non- existent, but his character had been similarly blackened; even if he had not actually murdered his wife, the press believed that he had probably driven her to suicide. So he should not have talked. But perhaps because he *was* innocent of the greater crime – and because he was sure, knowing her as he did, that Agatha was alive – his instinct was to defend himself.

In truth, Archie could not believe the situation in which he had been placed. He was the type of man to think that journalists and policemen belonged to a different caste; and now here he was, at the centre of both a headline story and a possible criminal investi- gation. The cosy comfort of his weekend with Nancy – relaxation, respite, golf, Madge and Sam playing happily with their new baby – had been shattered by the calm voice of Charlotte. Possibly he knew then that life would never be the same again, for any of them.

Reports differ on whether Charlotte contacted Archie on Friday night, when she returned to Styles from London, or on Saturday morning after Agatha's car had been found. According to Ritchie Calder's recollections – by no means error-free – it was on Friday that Charlotte, 'whether at Mrs Christie's suggestion or because she was in a panic', telephoned to warn Archie that Agatha had gone missing. 'A dinner party was in progress,' wrote Calder, 'what the household described as an "engagement" party for Colonel Christie and Miss Neele.' This was gossip from the servants, relayed to the press via the police. It is unsubstantiated, but it helps to explain the attitude towards Archie. It also backed the theory that Archie had left the Jameses that night, driven to meet Agatha nearby and murdered her. But none of this is clear, as other reports have Charlotte tele-phoning Archie on Saturday morning, when he returned to Styles and met the police.

Nancy, meanwhile, had retreated into the fastness of her parents' house in Hertfordshire, where Archie prayed she would remain undis-turbed; if only Agatha could be found before Nancy's name was known! It was a mercy that Charlotte was so discreet, although the servants could not be similarly trusted. Charlotte remained self-possessed even when the police threw the occasional dart of suspi-cion her way. She and her sister Mary moved in their dignified, Edinburgh way about the house, keeping things organised, keeping them normal. Charlotte dealt beautifully with Rosalind, who had been told that her mother was away writing a book. She dealt with Madge Watts, who believed that *somebody* must have an idea of what had happened to her sister. She dealt with the constant telephone calls and with the press who lurked outside the house; they knew that they would get little change from Miss Fisher, however hard they tried. Archie was a different matter. In his 10 December *Daily Mail* interview he had yet more to say about what Agatha might have done.

'I only know what I have been told by the servants. I imagine, however, that she got into such a state that she could not sit down quietly to read or work. I have got into that state myself many a time and have gone out for a walk just aimlessly. That, I think, is what my wife did, but instead of walking she took the car, a four-seater, and drove off . . .

'The servants did not notice anything particularly strange about her, and when Miss Fisher, who had gone to London, rang up in the evening to see if she was wanted, my wife was all right. She left a note addressed to Miss Fisher in which she asked for the arrangements for the Yorkshire visit that weekend [to Beverley] to be cancelled, adding that she was going for a run round and would let her know on the morrow where she was.

'That is all I know, and I need hardly tell you that the suspense of the uncertainty is terrible.'

The letter that Agatha had written to Charlotte was in the posses-sion of the police by this time. There was also the letter that Agatha had left for Archie, which he had burned before anybody else could read it. Almost certainly it made reference to his relationship with Nancy Neele; although not according to the *Daily Mail* of 11 December, which had Archie's own assurances as to the letter's contents. 'They have nothing whatever to do with my wife's disap-pearance,' he explained. 'It was certainly not a goodbye letter, nor did it make the slightest complaint. It was a note which, I am sure, my wife wrote when she recalled something she wanted to tell me long before the impulse overtook her to go out in the car.'

Not surprisingly, Kenward took a somewhat different view of Agatha's letter to her husband. Obviously Archie himself would not have told Kenward about the letter; it is possible that Charlotte did so but far more likely it was one of the maids, who would have seen it in the hall.

Subsequently there was a conference between the Surrey and Berkshire forces at Bagshot police station, 'in the course of which the discovery of the new letter was discussed', wrote the *Daily Sketch*. The newspapers also pondered the contents of the letter left for Charlotte, which Archie discussed with the *Mail* in his by now customary fashion: the one that led readers to believe precisely the opposite of what he said. 'It had nothing whatever to do with my wife's disappearance. It certainly made no allegations against anyone.'

Clearly thinking it would help his cause, he went on to say that he and Agatha 'did not quarrel about our individual friends or anything else. You must remember that we have been married for some years and, like other married couples, led to a certain extent our own lives.'

Some of the 11 December newspapers would have made uncomfortable reading for Archie. The *Sketch* informed its readers that 'Colonel Christie was today invited to call upon Deputy Chief Constable Kenward' in order to discuss the letter that he had destroyed. The *Westminster Gazette* wrote that 'important developments were pending' as a result of the Bagshot conference and described Archie as showing signs of 'anxiety' when he left his meeting with Kenward. The averagely astute reader might well have thought an arrest was imminent. However the *Express* took a different tack, stating that the police now believed Agatha to be alive (certainly this was true of the Berkshire force). Meanwhile the reporters had inevitably been badgering the Jameses' household in Godalming. The *Mail* had managed to get a somewhat fractious interview with Sam James, whose loyalty to Archie read unsympathetically.

'Suggestions have been made that Colonel Christie was called up by his wife while he was here, or that he went out to meet his wife, or that she came here to meet him. Nothing of that kind happened.

'I believe that Mrs Christie returned home and found that the Colonel was spending the weekend with us, and that she then drove off in a fit of pique.'

This was not the general belief. Although the *Daily News* printed three doctored photographs purporting to show Agatha in possible disguises, and although there were new rumours that she was in a south-coast hotel or possibly in Rhyl, it was Kenward's theory that held popular sway. So it was that on 12 December the public decided to go looking for Agatha's corpse. 'Great Search Today by Public for Mrs Christie,' wrote the *Sunday Pictorial*. 'Motorists asked by police to join in hunt on Downs – appeal for bloodhounds.' Rather in the way that thousands of people would descend upon Kensington after the death of Diana, Princess of Wales, motivated as much as anything by the desire to be part of an event, from early Sunday morning the excited crowds came to Newlands Corner; among them was the crime novelist Dorothy L. Sayers.

As advised by Kenward and his force, the public came dressed in hardy clothes ('A police officer said it was no use people turning out in patent leather shoes') and carried sticks. A half-dozen bloodhounds duly made their appearance. Large areas were covered by the search – horses were used to carry instructions to far-flung groups of people – although inevitably some of the volunteer hunters were more energetic than others, and Alfred Luland's refreshment kiosk was popular. Rumours of discoveries were rife: the best find was a number of handbags, which the *Daily Express* strove to present as potentially significant.

Estimates varied as to the size of the crowds. The *Daily Mail* said there were five thousand people, the *Daily Sketch* ten thousand, the *Express* and the *Westminster Gazette* fifteen thousand. *The Times*, more judiciously, had the crowd at just two thousand, although even so 'The roads were blocked with traffic, and parked cars covered the whole of the plateau where the abandoned motor car was found.' Around four hundred cars had turned up (or 'three thousand', according to the *Sketch*). A jolly good time, it would seem, was had by all. It was perhaps unsurprising that Archie – who had not taken part in the great Sunday hunt – should have told the *Daily Express*: 'I am sure she will not return until all is quiet.'

The back pages of the newspapers were covered with pictures of the search at Newlands Corner. Also reported was the disappearance of twenty-year-old Una Crowe, who had walked out of her family home in Chelsea on the morning of Saturday the eleventh. 'Daughter of a Famous Diplomat Missing' ran the headline in the *Express*. 'Another mystery of a missing woman has been added to that of Mrs Agatha Christie.'

On 13 December the newspapers reached the height of their madness. Was Agatha dead? Was she alive? Was she in Hindhead, as suggested by the manager of the Royal Huts Hotel, which had entertained her to lunch at the weekend? Was she 'in London disguised as a man'? This was reported, with all apparent seriousness, as the latest police theory; the *Daily News* revealed that Archie had 'made a prolonged investigation' to check if any of his clothes were missing.

The *Westminster Gazette* referred back to the letter left for Charlotte Fisher – 'Sealed Note in Christie Case To Be Opened Only if Body is Found' – then quoted from Mrs Hemsley, Agatha's mother-in-law, who had suggested that the half-written novel *The Blue Train* (*sic*) might contain the solution to the real-life mystery. The paper also made mention of a 'white-clad figure' which had been seen haunting Newlands Corner, an area that became deadlier by the day.

The *Daily Sketch* informed readers that 'séances have been held in the open air on the downs and in incense-laden rooms in Guildford and adjacent towns'. A journalist attended one held by a 'well-known medium', whose spirit guide, Maisie ('an African girl, tribe unknown'), told him that Agatha had been waylaid by two men in Bayswater. The journalist was a sceptic; nevertheless he got his story, and incidentally showed the extraordinary lunacies that Agatha was leading people to commit.

The fourteenth brought reports of a hut at East Clandon, barely a couple of miles from Newlands Corner, that bore signs of habitation. The reliably sensationalist *Westminster Gazette* described it as 'a kind of eerie Hansel and Gretel house in the loneliest part of the Surrey Hills'. It contained a postcard, the end of a loaf and a fur coat; also an empty bottle 'labelled Poison, lead and opium'. The police, it was said, had strewn powder on the floor of the hut so that they would know if anybody entered it. 'This morning there were clear traces of a woman's footprint over the powder.' All, however, was not as it seemed: a rogue reporter had scattered the powder, then asked the barmaid of a Guildford hotel to put her foot in it. The 'opium' was a medicine for the treatment of diarrhoea. The few belongings that had been left in 'the hut' – a perfectly normal, if remote, cottage – were the possessions of its owners.

Meanwhile Kenward was off again, telling the *Daily Mail* of his plans for another huge search around Newlands Corner: 'All ravines, streams, and ponds in this area will be combed.' He reiterated that a body would be found, and sought to regain the backing of the reporters (by now slightly bored with this unproductive theory) in his quest. 'The newspapers are suggesting that Mrs Christie is alive. If this is so, why has she not written to her bankers, her agents, or her solicitors, or to any of her relatives – without divulging her address? . . . She has not written any such letter for a reason which is obvious – that she is dead.'

Unfortunately for Kenward's subsequent reputation, Agatha had written just such a letter – to Campbell Christie – and he had chosen to ignore it. Yet even as Kenward was speaking to the *Mail*, the mystery was being quietly solved.

On Sunday the twelfth, two members of the band at the Harrogate Hydro, Bob Tappin and Bob Leeming, had gone to the local police station to report their suspicions about the quiet, smiling Mrs Neele, who so resembled the photographs of the missing Mrs Christie. The next day, officers of the West Riding Police went to the hotel and, after observing the woman, were of the opinion that Agatha had been found. They contacted Kenward, who took no notice and continued with his plans to search the area around Newlands Corner.

First thing on Tuesday, the Yorkshire police were again in touch with Kenward, emphasising to him that, whatever his own doubts, Agatha's household should nonetheless be informed. Accordingly he telephoned Charlotte Fisher at Styles and asked her to travel to Harrogate in order to establish if this was indeed her employer; she then contacted Archie, who took the train north. According to the *Daily Express*, Kenward was still expressing scepticism barely an hour before Agatha was identified. 'I do not think there is anything in the Harrogate end,' he said. Later he claimed that Archie, too, had had doubts about the sighting.

Tappin and Leeming were not the only people in the hotel – or, indeed, in the Harry Cobb Band – to have recognised Agatha. Rosie Asher, who had acted as her chambermaid throughout her stay, had done so early on. Much later she said that she had not dared to go to the police: 'I suppose I was one of the first to know, but it was more than my job was worth to get involved.' She had found Mrs Neele 'a bit odd' from the start, with her one small case and her withdrawn, ghostly air. Among her few possessions were the unusual buckled shoes reproduced in a newspaper photograph of Agatha, and the zipped handbag described by the police. 'Then it dawned on me.'

Mrs Taylor, manageress of the Hydro, also had her doubts, which she mentioned only to her husband. 'I took on a certain responsibility in not informing the police,' she told the *Mail*. 'Someone outside the hotel informed the police, although some of the servants here had said that there seemed to be a great resemblance between the woman and the pictures. I told them to say nothing.'

Certain of the guests had also wondered, but the suspicions never led to action; the people at the Hydro were not that kind. Nor were the people of Harrogate. 'Of course, we knew it was her, but we didn't say anything,' a town resident said many years later. If Mrs Christie wanted to be there, on her own, wandering around and buying clothes, that was entirely her business: Harrogate would not worry, so long as she fitted in. It was aristocratic, discreet, impregnable. An incongruous place for this particular journey to have ended and yet, for Agatha, the obvious one. Harrogate was the Torquay of the north. It was where 'people like us' went; even when they disappeared.

And it could not have been more removed from the world of obsessive policemen and news-hungry journalists who, for all their frenetic pursuit, had failed to find Agatha; who had ignored the one clue, given by the woman herself, that could have taken them to her.

Small wonder the press found it so hard to forgive her, when she was finally discovered, in the place where she had said she was going.

It was not her fault that she had made a fool of so many people. She had not asked them to search the undergrowth of the North Downs, or to drain pools, or to espy her on London buses. She had not wanted to become the headline story in almost every newspaper for the past week. She had become public property despite herself, and now there was not a single thing she could do about it. The press felt that she had led them a dance; this was true, although again she had not asked them to be led. So, too, with those members of the public who had speculated endlessly about Mrs Christie's fate: she had aroused their pity on false pretences, had made them think that she was a hapless corpse when in fact she was a sleek and well-fed resident at a swell hotel (all right for some!), had caused them to behave in ways they would not otherwise have done. She had made them look silly. Now she would suffer for it.

On the evening of Monday the thirteenth, the reporters were tipped off that their quarry might be found. Some travelled up to Harrogate immediately, and spent Tuesday trying to identify the hotel at which Agatha was said to be staying. The *Evening Standard* took the plunge and, in its 14 December afternoon edition, stated that a woman was awaiting identification by Colonel Christie.

Archie arrived in Harrogate just after six thirty and, with Superintendent McDowell of the West Riding Police, went to the Hydro where he met the manageress, Mrs Taylor. 'Mrs Neele' was upstairs dressing for dinner. Her handwriting in the register was Agatha's, slightly disguised.

At around seven thirty Agatha came down the stairs and saw Archie, who confirmed with McDowell that this was indeed his wife. Outside, the press waited. Soon they would be let loose upon Colonel Christie; no longer a wife-murderer, now participating in a whole new cover-up.

The newspapers of 15 December splashed the discovery. Amid the Christmas advertisements for Derry & Toms, Whiteleys, Bourne & Hollingsworth, the headlines blazed: 'Mrs Christie Found at Harrogate'. And then Archie's desperate lie, given to the press the night before: 'She does not know who she is.'

Details were given of Agatha's stay at the Hydro. Inevitably there were discrepancies, as each newspaper found its own source for information. The *Daily Mail* went to the top of the tree and spoke to Mr Taylor, manager of the hotel, whose wife had suspected that the missing woman was in their midst.

'Mrs Christie arrived at the Harrogate Hydropathic on the Saturday in a taxicab [he said]. From the first her life in the hydro was exactly similar to that of our other guests. She took her meals in the public dining room, only occasionally having her breakfast in bed.

'In the evening we sometimes have singing and dancing in the lounge. In this Mrs Christie took an enthusiastic part. She sang several songs – what they were I do not remember, for I am not musical – and she danced often, mixing freely with the young people staying in the hydro . . .

'What account of herself she gave to them I cannot tell you, but, although I understand they remarked several times to each other on the resemblance between their fellow guest and the missing woman, they did not really believe she could be Mrs Christie.'

The *Mail* also said that she bought a good many clothes while staying in Harrogate. At the Hydro she spoke little at first, then made some friends; another guest, Mrs Robson, was given to understand that her child had died and she was recovering. She played billiards occasionally although 'rarely made more than five or six at a time'. The *Westminster Gazette*, however, spoke to 'an employee at the hotel' who had seen Agatha play and

'although she had told her opponent, a foreign gentleman staying at the hotel, that she could not play, some of us who were watching at the game remarked that she must have been "kidding" him . . .

'She is a fine, good looking woman,' he said, 'and was looking cheerful, often joking with the members of staff. She did not hide herself at all from the public gaze, but on the contrary took quite an active part in the life of the hotel, being very fond of singing and playing in the lounge . . . There was certainly nothing to suggest that she was in ill-health.'

The *Daily Express* spoke to the hotel's lady entertainer, Miss Corbett, who was full of after-the-event wisdom: 'We have all been saying it was Mrs Christie, but we hardly liked to do anything. She has done a great deal of singing to my accompaniment. She has a very high soprano voice and she sings very nicely.' One of the hotel guests, a shipping merchant named Mr Pettelson, described to the *Express* how he had seen 'Mrs Neele' the previous evening before dinner, and she had said to him: 'Oh, fancy, my brother has come.' Mr Pettelson said that other guests at the Hydro had thought she was Mrs Christie, although he had 'never dreamed' it. She seemed, he said, to be 'always thinking. I said to her once, "Where do you come from; do you live in London?" She replied, "No, I do not live in London. I live in South Africa." I did not like to pursue the matter further, as she did not seem to want to encourage the conversation.'

The next day Mr Pettelson talked some more, telling the *Daily News* that he and Agatha had become great friends. 'Perhaps it was because we were both interested in music.' He described how she had bought and signed for him a copy of the sheet music to 'Angels Ever Guard Thee', which they had played together. He also elaborated upon the meeting with Archie. 'It seemed at the time strange to me for a brother to be as despondent as he was.'

The next day, in fact, a good many things had started to seem strange. On the fifteenth the newspapers had dutifully parroted the amnesia theory, describing the 'pathetic' little scene of reunion between the Christies, and Archie's attempts to get Agatha to recognise him. They had done this with a fair degree of sympathy and compassion. Now cynicism began to stream back into the reporters' hearts.

'No Evidence of Lost Memory,' scoffed the headline in the *Westminster Gazette*,[8] which had 'consulted leading mental specialists' on the subject. It was not possible to lose one's memory and continue to act in such a normal manner, showing no signs of distress; nor was it feasible that Agatha would have failed to recognise her own name in the newspapers. Archie clung to his theory, however, and told reporters that although Agatha knew nothing of how she had arrived at Harrogate, she was beginning to regain her memory.

'This morning,' he said, 'she has a faint idea that she is Mrs Christie.' The reporters had been struck by Agatha's demeanour as she took the train from Harrogate to Leeds, thence to Manchester. 'She chatted gaily with her sister and once laughingly patted her on the shoulder.' This looked a little like mockery, and the newspapers began to get vicious. They knew that their readers felt similarly aggrieved, so they were on safe ground, especially when they brought up the issue of money. How much had the search for Agatha cost? The *Daily Sketch* gave estimates of between a thousand and three thousand pounds, although the figure would go up dramatically, eventually reaching the ludicrous heights of twenty-five thousand. The *Daily Mail* started a correspondence on the subject of the 'remarkable and (it seems to some of us) unjustifiable concentration of the police of two counties on the disappearance of Mrs Christie,' wrote one reader. 'I see no reason why the police should have expended thousands of pounds which could not be collected from anyone connected with the missing novelist.'

Then there was the question of the name Agatha had assumed in Harrogate: 'a name which coincides with that of the young woman who, in addition to Colonel Christie, visited Hurtmore Cottage, the Godalming home of Mr and Mrs James', as the *Westminster Gazette* somewhat pointedly put it. The *Daily Express* was also alert, writing that Archie had 'requested particularly that this name his wife had used at the hydro should not be divulged'. It then informed readers that Archie had no intention of contributing to the cost of the search. 'I did not ask them to search for her,' he said. 'I knew all the time that she was alive, and I told them so.'

This, of course, was unanswerable. But logic no longer had much to do with the way that this case was reported. The public story of the disappearance had been created in the minds of thousands of people; yet it was Agatha herself who had written it; and it was not the story that people wanted. The subtleties of what she had done were beyond the public grasp. It was therefore decided that her mysterious creation was nothing more or less than a 'set-up'.

She had eluded everybody for eleven days; now she eluded them again, locked as she was behind the gates of Abney Hall;[9] and frustration poured out. 'Millions of fine fellows were killed in the war and practically no notice was taken of them,' said Mr Mitchell-Hedges, 'the well-known explorer', to the *Sketch*. 'Yet paralysis set in when one woman disappeared.' If loss of memory could be proved, wrote the *Express*, then sympathy for Agatha would flow; meanwhile the joke was on 'the police who argued that she was lying dead near Newlands Corner, the willing crowds who tramped the downs in search, the good people who saw her at various irreconcilable times and places . . .'

The *Surrey Advertiser*, which took a proprietorial interest in the case, summed up the general mood:

> Mrs Christie has been found, but the mystery surrounding her disappearance is very far from being cleared up. Indeed, to many people the whole business gets 'mysteriouser and mysteriouser' with successive explanations. We all rejoice that Mrs Christie is alive and well – or was well, to all appearances, until the arrival of her husband at the Harrogate Hydro on Tuesday evening. But, frankly, the public are puzzled and bewildered.
>
> When did memory loss kick in? When she left her car at Newlands Corner? If so, it is passing strange that one so afflicted should have been able to find her way to London, cross the City from one terminus to another, book to Harrogate . . . Medical men may be familiar with such cases; the layman, in his ignorance, simply wonders.
>
> Another puzzle almost, but not quite, as great is how Mrs Christie came to remain unidentified for so long. Just think of it! For ten days she was the most talked about person in the country . . . All the while the cause of this sensation is pursuing the normal life of a normal person at a hotel where there were numbers of guests, talking to them, even singing to them, yet unidentified . . . We withdraw the qualification in the first sentence in this note: the one puzzle is as great as the other, if not greater.

On 17 December, the last day that the case was headline news, Archie faced the reporters outside Abney Hall and handed to them a medical bulletin. It was signed by Dr Donald Core, lecturer in neurology from Manchester University, and the Wattses' family doctor, Henry Wilson, and it read: 'After a careful examination of Mrs Agatha Christie this afternoon we have formed the opinion that she is suffering from an unquestionably genuine loss of memory, and that for her future welfare she should be spared all anxiety and excitement.'

Archie added his own statement, reported in *The Times*:

'My wife is extremely ill, suffering from complete loss of memory. Three years have dropped out of her life. She cannot recall anything that has happened during that period . . . She has not the slightest recollection of going to Newlands Corner or of proceeding eventually to Harrogate.

She now knows who I am, and has also realised that Mrs Watts is her sister. It is somewhat remarkable that she does not know she has a daughter. In this connexion, when she was shown a picture of herself and Rosalind, her little daughter, she asked who the child was. "What is the child like?" and "How old is she?"'

In conclusion Archie made a plea for privacy. 'All the worry has been terrible, and all we want now is peace and quietness. I have been offered £500 to tell how my wife came to Harrogate. I do not know, and she cannot tell me.'

'And I hope,' he said to the *Daily Sketch*, 'that ends the matter.' But, if nothing else, Archie's own inability to evade questioning would ensure yet more coverage. The *Sketch* asked him about the suggestion that Agatha's disappearance had been a publicity stunt, 'all arranged to sell her books', which he fiercely denied. 'It has been nothing of the sort. The doctors' report proves it.'

The reporters also asked about the even more dangerous subject of Agatha's use of the name 'Neele'; that of a 'mutual friend', as Archie had told the *Daily Mail*.

'She inserted the advertisement in *The Times* under the name of Neele, asking her relatives to communicate, because she was in the extraordinary position of being in a strange hotel for no purpose that she could think of and with no knowledge of who she was other than the conviction that Teresa Neele was her real name. The doctors told me that such an action was compatible with the action of a person suffering from loss of memory.'

The *Mail* then proceeded to print a few paragraphs about our mutual friend, Miss Neele, whose father had given a brief interview from his home in Hertfordshire. 'I cannot hazard any theory why Mrs Christie should have used my family name. It is unfortunate,' he said, 'that Nancy should have been a member of the house-party of Mr and Mrs James during the weekend that Mrs Christie disappeared, and that Colonel Christie should also have been a member of that party.'

To the *Westminster Gazette* Mr Neele said a little more. 'It is most unpleasant, both for my daughter and for all of us in the family, to have her name dragged through the mud, and, furthermore, it is quite unnecessary.' Mrs Neele told the reporter that Nancy was a friend of the Christies, 'but she has never been especially friendly with the colonel'. Her daughter, she said, was 'very distressed over the whole affair'.

The *Gazette* also alighted upon the incident of the ring that Agatha had left for repair at Harrods on Saturday the fourth, giving to the store the address of the Harrogate Hydro, to which the ring was sent. 'It is accordingly established beyond doubt that "Mrs Neele", en route for Harrogate, was in the West End on the Saturday morning of Mrs Agatha Christie's disappearance, making purchases like any normal woman.'

However much Archie insisted that Agatha was 'extremely ill', and that it would take weeks for her to recover, his statements were received with almost complete disbelief. As 'Lady Pontifex' wrote to the *Daily Mail*: 'Many of us would also like to know how the statement that she has lost her memory squares with the fact that she has stayed in an hotel, paid her bills, danced and sung, and played billiards.' The money question also continued to rankle: Archie had stated that the additional expenses incurred by the search were no more than twenty-five pounds, and that as a ratepayer he was under no obligation to meet them. 'A Surreyite' wrote to his local newspaper, the *Advertiser*, that

the best thing Colonel Christie can do to show his gratitude for the restoration of his wife is to pay all the expenses connected with that search. It is sad enough to know that one of our Surrey beauty spots has had to suffer by being trampled down and disfigured unnecessarily. Perhaps when Mrs

Christie's memory returns she will make what reparation she
can by seeing that the ratepayers do not suffer for her
disappearance.

Agatha, and to a lesser extent Archie, had become a focus for public
opprobrium. She was regarded as a devious woman whose husband
was defending her in inappropriate and possibly self-serving ways. She
was attacked in a manner characteristic of the British public: enviously,
resentfully, pruriently and with a strong dash of 'who does she think
she is?'. A letter was sent to the *Mail* from 'An Ordinary Woman',
saying that she would like to know what would happen if *she* disappeared. Would she get the same preferential treatment as Agatha
had received? When the body of poor Una Crowe was found on the
twenty-first – suicide after a nervous breakdown – it was quite obvious
what people were thinking: here was somebody who had really done
what Agatha had pretended to do. Here was a good person, truly
deserving of sympathy, not a jumped-up attention-seeker.

Newspaper coverage sensed the mood and did not hesitate to
inflame it. Probably the reporters shared it. Female hate figures are
a common feature in the press today; it is almost as though society
needs them as a repository for its less-elevated emotions. 'The world
is not charitable in what it says about women,' Agatha would later
write.[10] She was subjected to something scarcely less cruel than a
modern tabloid witch-hunt for having committed the crime of allowing
her private anguish to move into the public arena. In February 1927
questions were asked in the House of Commons about the cost of
the search. Sir William Joynson-Hicks, the home secretary, answered
that the total additional cost to Surrey Police was about twelve pounds
ten shillings, but other MPs were not going to let this go so easily.
'Who', it was asked, 'is going to compensate the thousand of people
who were deliberately misled by this cruel hoax?' Joynson-Hicks's
reply, which was that people had simply joined the search out of
curiosity, was of course the truth; but nobody wanted to hear it. As
always with populist stupidity, there was absolutely nothing whatever
to be done about it.

*   *   *

The theory that Agatha had known exactly what she was doing all along, that she had disappeared voluntarily and led both police and public a deliberate dance, remains attractive to many; people still emerge from time to time with tales of how they once met someone who was staying at Harrogate when she was there and, oh yes, she was *definitely* up to something.

The sceptical view appeals, in part, for the same reason as it did back in 1926. It is a reaction against the 'amnesia' theory that was initially propounded by Archie and upheld for years by the family. So unlikely is it that Agatha lost her memory, so unconvinced is almost everybody that she did, that the official insistence upon this explanation tends to irritate. It makes people think that something is being hidden: something detrimental. And it sends theorists in precisely the opposite direction. Those who do not believe that Agatha lost her wits when she disappeared tend to think, instead, that she was in full possession of them: planning a plot, as she did with her stories. But this was not that kind of story.

Despite what he said to reporters after the event, Archie himself believed that Agatha had known what she was doing. A letter sent to Rosalind many years later said that, according to his friend Madge James, he had 'felt that the disappearance was a publicity stunt'. So too did Madge and her husband; and so, presumably, did Nancy Neele. The phrase 'publicity stunt' implies that Agatha had disappeared to advance her career as a mystery writer, but this was not what Archie meant: rather, that she had tried to create publicity against him. She had tried to generate a furore of sympathy that would lead him to be discredited, and jeopardise his relationship with Nancy.

It was inevitable, perhaps, that Archie saw things this way. Undoubtedly he would have felt guilt about Agatha, and guilt always hardened his heart. Also he had been through hell, and blaming Agatha was the easiest way of dealing with it. Possibly, deep down, he did not entirely believe his own words to Madge James. Possibly he was using this simplistic explanation of the 'stunt' as a shield for deeper feelings, which it was his instinct to hide.

The theory of deliberate intent was laid out in a famous piece of journalism in the *New Statesman*, written just after Agatha's death by Ritchie Calder.[11] He described the way the story had taken possession of the newspapers – 'even the sedate *Times*' – and the hints from the police that this was a murder case: 'In those days, crime reporters and police were very much in cahoots.' He aired various rumours from the time as if they were fact, including the idea that Archie and Nancy had been attending an unofficial engagement dinner on the night that Agatha disappeared.

He also wrote about Agatha's demeanour on the night she was discovered at the Harrogate Hydro. 'She was not flustered. She answered to "Mrs Christie" and when asked how she had got there she said that she did not know and was suffering from amnesia.' There is no evidence at all that Agatha spoke to the press on 14 December – the newspapers would certainly have reported it if she had – and this throws doubt upon Calder's piece. He was quite right, though, in his conclusion. 'Emotionally disturbed, yes. Suffering from amnesia, no.'

Closer to the truth, in a way, was the 1979 film *Agatha*[12], which caught something of her dreamlike state as she drifted, ghostlike, through Harrogate. The actual plot is absurd – Agatha concocts a means to kill herself by Nancy Neele's hand – and, although the film is extremely sympathetic to her mother, it is understandable that Rosalind sought to stop it being made.[13] Yet it grasped the essential truths: that Agatha might have been 'planning' without being in control of her thoughts, and that throughout the eleven days she was 'writing' her own story.

Far more brutal to Agatha was Jared Cade's 1996 book, *Agatha Christie and the Eleven Missing Days*, which purported to solve once and for all the mystery of the disappearance. It was based upon a version of events told to the author by the daughter of Agatha's friend, Nan Kon. As has been emphasised, Nan's daughter Judith was ten years old at the time of the disappearance; therefore her account came entirely from her mother, who must have told her everything in remarkable detail. For some reason she waited a very long time to allow this story to be told, despite its apparent newsworthiness.

According to Judith, Agatha planned to disappear to Harrogate in order to punish Archie for his affair with Nancy, and she did so with Nan's help. On the morning of Friday the third, she drove to London to visit Nan and discuss the plan, before returning to

Styles for lunch. She left Styles at nine forty-five on the evening of 3 December, drove straight to Newlands Corner, pushed the car down the slope, then walked to West Clandon station in Surrey and caught a train to London. She stayed the night with Nan at her house in Chelsea. In the morning the women rang hotels in Harrogate asking about vacancies but, being told that none was full, they decided that Agatha should turn up unannounced at the Hydro. This would give credibility to the amnesia theory. Nan gave Agatha some money, went shopping with her at the Army and Navy Stores for clothes and a case, then lunched with her and put her on the train to Harrogate.

This theory is at first quite compelling. Some things about it are perceptive and accurate: for example, the importance it gives to the letter that Agatha wrote to Campbell Christie. But there is a flaw in the theory that renders it impossible.

The distance between Styles, at Sunningdale, and Newlands Corner is not great: just under twenty miles. To drive it nowadays would take between thirty and forty minutes. Obviously in 1926 cars were slower and less agile, and Agatha was driving on a dark winter's night. Nevertheless it is possible – for the sake of argument – to assume that she drove at full speed to Newlands Corner and arrived at ten thirty.[14]

She then had to manoeuvre the car on to the plateau at the top of the hill and – again in pitch darkness – give it an almighty shove that would send it down the slopes. Steep though these are, they are not vertiginous, and to push the Morris would not have been an especially easy job. Nevertheless it can be assumed – again – that this went without a hitch, and took no more than five minutes.

Agatha then had to walk along unlit, unfamiliar roads to reach the station at West Clandon, approximately two and a quarter miles away. Assuming that she went at the brisk pace of four miles an hour, assuming even that she broke into an occasional run, this journey would still take more than thirty minutes. So Agatha would have arrived at the station a little after eleven o'clock. This at the very earliest, assuming a quick and straightforward journey along dark and bending roads, an untroubled shove of the car down the hill and a sprightly walk (in high heels) through the night.

And here lies the central flaw in the Jared Cade theory: according to the *Bradshaw Railway Guide* for December 1926, the last London train from Clandon left at 10.52 p.m.

There are other problems, too. Even if one accepts the theory, why on earth would Agatha have made things so difficult for herself? If this was part of a plan, why leave so little time to accomplish all that she had to do? Why not leave at nine o'clock instead? And although there is logic to the idea that she wanted to abandon her Morris near Godalming, thus implicating Archie and drawing attention to his whereabouts, it is barely conceivable that Agatha would have chosen the arduous task of shoving the car down a hill when there were so many other tempting places in that area to suggest misadventure. Why not leave it by the Silent Pool? If she did push the car she would have had no idea where it would end up. There was no guarantee whatever that it would become stuck in so peculiarly sinister a position, overhanging a quarry. In fact the shape of the landscape makes it almost impossible that it would have done so, since it followed the track of Water Lane then took an unnatural right-hand swerve. There was also the question of how it travelled downhill for three hundred yards, constantly gathering speed before it hit the bush above the quarry, and yet suffered so little damage that it could be driven away to a garage.

Added to the extreme unlikelihood of Agatha deciding that this was the best way to deal with her car, there is then the amazing fact that, amid all the many sightings, nobody should have remembered the lone female answering the police description who took the last train from Clandon to Waterloo, and that no taxi driver should have remembered picking her up at around a quarter to midnight.

There is something more, though: and this is the fact that renders all talk of deliberate intent quite meaningless. Newlands Corner on a December night is a fearful place. To stand there alone, in the silence, under the black winter skies, and look out over the vast empty slopes, is a terrifying thing to do. No woman, especially a woman of imagination, could do such a thing out of malice, or revenge, or any such petty motive: the place annihilates such a possibility. Those who have not been to Newlands Corner in the dark may accept the idea that Agatha could have got out of her car, pushed it away and skipped off to the railway station. To go there is to know, instinctively, that this is not possible; that nobody could endure that place without the mysterious insulation of mental agony.

On a more pragmatic level, in his book Cade extracts the facts he requires from accounts of the disappearance and dismisses those that do not fit. For example, he takes Janet Morgan's authorised biography to task (while making much use of it) for a minor mistake about train times to Harrogate, but completely ignores the fact that his theory puts Agatha on a train from Clandon that she could not possibly have caught. He also disregards the sighting of Agatha at around 6.20 a.m. on Saturday the fourth, by the local man, Edward McAllister, who said he started her car. Admittedly this is not corroborated evidence, and is complicated by the newspaper references to 'Ernest Cross'. But McAllister came forward very early, before publicity had muddied the investigative waters, and his description of Agatha to the *Surrey Advertiser* is convincing. The police (not just Kenward) always took the story seriously, and it seems far more likely than not to be true: 'unless', as the *Advertiser* wrote, 'by a coincidence so improbable as hardly to be worth entertaining, another woman closely resembling her was the person the man McAllister saw'. That was the fact of it. Not many women drove through the early mornings alone back in 1926.

Cade also uses what was reported in newspapers, representing it as corroborated evidence when this suits his purposes. He repeats the words of Agatha's Sunningdale friend, Mrs de Silva, without benefit of quotation marks, so that her self-important witterings to reporters become unarguable fact. Yet when Mrs de Silva told a newspaper that she had telephoned Agatha around midday on Friday, the third, asking her to tea, he ignores it as it would clash with his theory that Agatha was not at home at that time, having driven to London in order to meet Nan Kon.

This is a small example of the book's fundamental naughtiness. Throughout, the author describes scenes that he cannot possibly know about – such as the conversation between Agatha and Archie on the morning of the disappearance – as if he himself had been present. The omniscience of his interviewee Judith, or more precisely of her mother, is boundless. There is nothing about Agatha that they did not know. Nan, to be sure, was a good friend. Judith, too, was close to both

Agatha and Rosalind, until some strange impulse led her to collaborate on a book that could only cause Rosalind great pain. But they were not the repositories for Agatha's secrets. This role was filled most closely by Charlotte Fisher.

It has, therefore, been suggested that Charlotte was Agatha's accomplice in the disappearance. The advertisement placed in *The Times* was part of a code between the two women, and the letter Agatha left told Charlotte what she intended to do. However, as the letter was in the possession of the police throughout the inquiry, this cannot be so. The advertisement placed in *The Times* does look like a message (and, if so, for whom but Charlotte?); but Charlotte was simply not the kind of woman to practise such a level of deceit. If she had known anything, she would have said so. What is true is that she learned a good deal after the event, and this she told subsequently to Rosalind.

It is understandable, laudable indeed, that Rosalind should have clung for so long, and so obstinately, to the 'official' theory. Her mother had driven off into the night and left her, her father was willing to leave her for good, but her loyalty to both was absolute. She wanted to protect them. So she adhered to the line that they had taken from the very first: Agatha had become ill during 1926 and, at some point during the traumatic night of 3–4 December, had lost her memory.

It was said that Agatha did not recognise her daughter when she saw her again at Abney. This is impossible to believe, although it is very easy to imagine Agatha pretending to do such a thing. Like her character Jane Finn in *The Secret Adversary*, she may have feigned memory loss as a means of protecting herself. She would have felt the deepest shame about what she had done, and never more so than in the presence of her daughter. 'Amnesia' was a way out of the responsibility.

But the official theory has never held water, and it could never be proclaimed indefinitely. It ignores too many facts, not least about the way in which amnesia works. Certainly it is a mysterious affliction, but it does not take possession of a person for a couple of weeks and then go away again, never to return.

To explain Agatha's movements between 3 and 4 December, which have a degree of design about them, it is said that she drove around for much of the night, so distraught that she did not know where she was going. Yet two gallons of petrol were left in her car, so she cannot have driven very far. Then it is said that she careered off the road at Newlands Corner and ran into the bush overhanging the quarry, perhaps concussing herself as she stopped. This, too, is unlikely, since she would surely have tried to apply the brakes during a descent, and there were no signs that she had done so. Although it was entirely possible for a car to come off the road, it was almost impossible for it to end up three hundred yards down the hill unless intent of some kind was involved.

Despite being in a state of extreme physical distress, Agatha is then said to have made her way to Guildford station – almost four miles away – which meant climbing the steep hill to get to the main road. She took a train to Waterloo, thence to King's Cross, thence to Harrogate. Posters for Harrogate were prominent in railway stations at that time: the suggestion is that this put the idea into Agatha's head. Once she had arrived, the idea of going to the Hydro also occurred to her, perhaps because there were at that time cars at the station taking guests to the various hotels (although Agatha was actually reported to have arrived at the Hydro in a taxi).

According to the official theory, she did not take part in the activities of the hotel: dancing and singing were off the agenda for a woman in Agatha's condition. Yet the evidence that suggests she did these things is considerable. Of course some of the reporting of her behaviour at the hotel is highly dubious, and the words of some of the guests were doubtless exaggerated or misrepresented. But the fact is that the sheet music to 'Angels Ever Guard Thee', signed 'Teresa Neele', was indeed in the possession of Alexander Pettelson; his daughter offered it to Agatha's publishers in the 1970s[15] (Collins turned it down on Agatha's behalf, saying that she was ill and no doubt thinking it would upset her).

The advertisement that was placed in *The Times* – which the conspiracy theorists regard as Agatha seeking to validate her claim to have lost her memory – is inconvenient to the amnesia theory. So too is the ring Agatha left at Harrods, which was subsequently posted to 'Mrs Neele'. And why should Agatha have abandoned her car so near to Godalming, if she had not been thinking directly of Archie? There are many questions that the official theory simply fails to answer.

Yet it was created for reasons that are far from ignoble; not, as has often been suggested, to conceal, but to protect a fragile woman who had suffered immeasurably, in ways too complex for any theory to encompass. And it comes infinitely closer to the truth than any talk of 'stunts' or 'schemes' ever could. It understands that Agatha had been in a state of breakdown, that the cumulative effect of her mother's death and her husband's betrayal had sent her to the edge. But not over it.

The aftermath was sombre: a sad and drawn-out hangover, in which several reputations were subjected to an unforgiving scrutiny. Nancy Neele was sent on a round-the-world trip by her parents, in the hope that she would live down the press attention and get over Archie. He himself had to face his colleagues in the City, in those days a gentlemanly world that did not deal in open scandal: company directors did not come close to being accused of murder, and closer still to adultery; neither did they have hysterical wives who became front-page news. Archie left Agatha at Abney Hall on 17 December, before returning with Rosalind for Christmas. Afterwards he went back to Styles, and began the process of selling the house.

The Jameses were left to contemplate the part they had played in allowing Archie and Nancy to meet at their house. Madge James, said to have been a 'silly woman',[16] had assumed Archie's marriage to be over in all but name, but she should not have put the interests of her friend Nancy above those of the inconvenient wife. It must have been a shock to realise that Agatha did not share Archie's view of their marriage. Sam James, who was not silly at all, may have understood Agatha's grounds for distress, but he was a loyal friend and took Archie's side throughout. The two couples came to the tacit conclusion that the only way to deal with the whole affair was to dismiss Agatha as a hysteric and get on with life. They were all holidaying together in the South of France, just before the outbreak of the Second World War, when Sam died of sunstroke; for a time after this, Archie and Nancy lodged in the grounds of Madge's huge house at Godalming.

The friends always remained close; they had been through a lot together.

After Agatha was found, it was said – rather debatably – by the *Westminster Gazette* that 'Perhaps the chief sufferer has been Mr Kenward, a responsible and reliable officer.' In 1927 Kenward was obliged to make a report to the Home Office, explaining his much-criticised handling of the case. 'I submit,' he wrote, in a tone of muted defiance, 'that the circumstances fully justified me in taking the action that I did.' He denied the claims about large numbers of police being diverted from other duties. Only three dozen regular police were employed in the search, he said. There were also 'innumerable Special Constables', who were unpaid, and a great many 'civilian helpers'. Inquiries in other parts of the country were made by Berkshire Police.[17] No other forces were used and, contrary to rumour, Scotland Yard was never called in. The expenses amounted to about twenty-five pounds, 'made up chiefly of hire of conveyances, and refreshments for the Special Constables', a sum which Colonel Christie had been asked, and refused, to pay. This sum is double the one quoted in the House of Commons but it still seems very low; as does the number of officers involved in the case.

Kenward's chief defence, for having stuck to the belief that Agatha was dead, was 'the disquieting nature of certain information that had come to my knowledge'. Many years later Kenward's daughter would state that this referred to a fourth letter, written by Agatha, in which she said that she was in fear for her life.[18] This assertion has been roundly discredited. In fact the letter that had influenced Kenward was the one written to Charlotte, which was hysterical, suicidal and accusatory towards Archie. It is not surprising that it loomed large in Kenward's mind, and he was quite right to say that, had he taken insufficient notice of its contents, he would have been vilified.

But in a long interview with the *Surrey Advertiser*, he went further still. He had, he said, believed that this was a murder case because 'It was suggested very freely by people who knew her, including some of her own relations, that perhaps something of this nature had occurred.' Now, this remarkable statement may well have been the words of a man trying to justify himself, knowing full well that he could say rather more outlandish things to a newspaper than he could to the Home Office. Nevertheless it gives pause for thought about the role of Madge, Agatha's sister, in all of this. It was unlike her to keep quiet, yet she seems to have done nothing until she gave Agatha sanctuary at Abney Hall. Surely, though, she would have had ideas of her own about what had happened? It is impossible to imagine her telling Kenward that she suspected Archie of murder: for all her confident eccentricity, she was as reticent as Agatha in the public sphere. But she must have realised that Agatha had disappeared – possibly killed herself – because of Archie's behaviour; in other words, that this was all his fault; and she would have been staunchly on Agatha's side. She might, therefore, have said something to Kenward that helped lead him towards his wrong-headed theory.

In the end, though, there can be little excuse for the fact that Kenward ignored the clues that did not fit his own ideas: notably, the letter to Campbell Christie. He was guilty of forcing facts to fit a theory. He had been a good officer, but this particular case had done for him. Five years later he retired from the force, and died, aged fifty-six, in 1932.

As late as February 1928 Agatha's disappearance was still in the news, her behaviour having become a byword for duplicitous conduct. During a libel action (issued, coincidentally, by the same Mr Mitchell-Hedges who had criticised Agatha back in 1926), reference was made by the prosecuting counsel to 'a woman who played a foolish hoax on the police'.

Deeply hurt and provoked by this, Agatha gave an interview to the *Daily Mail* that purported to give her version of the disappearance: that is to say, the 'official' theory. She also instructed her lawyer to make a statement on her behalf at the libel trial. Accordingly Mr Stuart Bevan, KC, asked the indulgence of the judge to present, in defence of her reputation, the medical certificate that had been issued at Abney Hall. The exchange between lawyer and judge was reported in *The Times*. The Lord Chief Justice stated that there was not time to spare 'to hear applications about persons who happen to be referred to in the course of cases'. Mr Bevan replied that 'When reference is made to a woman who is not here, is not represented here, and is unable to protect herself grave injustice is done unless the full facts are known.' To which the judge said, 'I think that, having said so much, Mr Bevan, you have probably accomplished your purpose.'[19]

But Agatha had failed to accomplish hers. The actions that had been taken out of love for Archie had, by cruelly uncontrollable means, become the surest way to kill any love he had for her: she had wanted him back, she had dreamed that he would come to Harrogate and be restored to her, and instead she had ensured that he would want never to lay eyes on her again. The ending of the story had been wrenched from her grasp.

When she saw him at the bottom of the stairs at the Harrogate Hydro, hope must have raged in her heart. Yet that night she had gone to bed alone to lie sleepless, facing the wreck of her dreams that she herself had brought about. The next morning she had left the hotel with Archie, she had travelled with him, they had walked side by side, he had defended and protected her against the terrifying assaults of the press. And yet it had meant nothing. He was doing it for himself, for his future life with Nancy Neele. He wanted more than anything not to be with her. Having, as she thought, helped to destroy her marriage by leaving Archie alone while she grieved for her mother, she had now delivered its death blow by making herself an object of public ridicule, and Archie an object of public loathing. They were both private people, intensely so. How had she let this happen? How had it happened?

She was back to herself now: the drifting, smiling ghost of Harrogate was gone. She was in the real world. She stayed at Abney and watched the contempt in Archie's eyes, the disdainful exhaustion after he had spoken to the press. And then he left.

Those days were the worst of all.

> You were a king, my love, and I
> In the far North lie nightly down to die . . .[20]

* * *

'It was an appalling, not just distress, but a shock to her – so much so as to mentally unhinge her. There is a woman whom life has treated very well. Very loving mother, handsome and loving husband, and psychologically she could not take this upsetting. I don't think she ever did get over it. I think that the breaking down of any relationship in which a woman has invested so much, it's one of the universal griefs. And, therefore, she took pleasure in doing books in which, although there is a complete upsetting of normality, in the end order is restored. It was a psychological need to bring order out of disorder, which may have mirrored her own life. I think maybe every one of them is a kind of catharsis. All of them, a little catharsis' P. D. James

'People still think there's an ulterior motive. Having known her, there's no way she would have done anything like that' John Mallowan, nephew to Agatha

'She was in shock, and she was driving her car, and she's got the most inventive mind. She says: Sod this. I'm going to disappear' Charles Vance, producer of Agatha's plays

'It was the unspoken subject. Agatha refused to talk about it. To anyone. It was a real no-go. I was told once in Baghdad that someone had broached the subject, and she wouldn't speak to that person again' Joan Oates, friend of Agatha

'I think we all operate on a secret, and if we were to let that secret out, we'd no longer be able to live – at least not in the way that we're used to living' Kathleen Tynan, author of *Agatha*, in an interview with *Woman's Wear Daily*

'I was stupid. I lived in a world of my own. Yes, I was stupid' Agatha, writing as Mary Westmacott in the autobiographical novel *Unfinished Portrait*

'She continued to love him throughout it all, but it shattered the world of fantasy in which her spirit – her genius – lived. This is what led to her breakdown' A. L. Rowse, friend of Agatha, in *Memories of Men and Women*

'Christie was a shit' Charles Vance

'You mean detective stories have to end with everything explained? Part of the rules?'

'The unreality.'

'Then if our story disobeys the unreal literary rules, that might mean it's actually truer to life?' John Fowles, *The Ebony Tower*

'I know what happened, because I was there' Rosalind Hicks, daughter[21]

'Although I am now quite well and cheerful, I have not quite that utter happiness of Mrs Neele' Agatha Christie, in an interview with the *Daily Mail*, 16 February 1928

The Second Husband

'For it is not an open enemy, that hath done me this dishonour:
for then I could have borne it.
Neither was it mine adversary, that did magnify himself against me:
for then peradventure I would have hid myself from him.
But it was even thou, my companion: my guide, and mine own familiar friend'
(from Psalm 55, copied and kept by Agatha Christie)

'. . . from then on it was as though a knife fell, cutting my life into two halves'
(from *Endless Night* by Agatha Christie)

From this point the deepest mystery was Agatha herself. She had grown up at last, and with adulthood came concealment: a new self worn like protective colouring. She had lived in the world of her dreams, had been the heroine of her life and books for more than thirty years. Now she merely dreamed her dreams. Youth and beauty had gone, as had love and contentment. In their place came something else: the life of a writer.

In the dark year of 1928 Agatha wrote her first Mary Westmacott novel, *Giant's Bread*. The protagonist, Vernon Deyre, serves in the war and is reported killed. A mistake has been made but, believing the news, Vernon's wife remarries. It is when he reads the notice of this wedding that Vernon tries to kill himself in earnest. He walks out into the road and is hit by a lorry. When he recovers from his injuries he has become a man called George Green, as whom he is completely happy.

Later he is brought back to the old self he wanted to escape. 'It's been rather hell – getting back, remembering things. All such beastly things. All the things that – really – I didn't want to face.' He thinks vaguely that life as Vernon Deyre might be the same as it was before he went away. But his wife no longer wants him, and eventually he is free of emotional ties.

'There was nothing now to come between him and his work.' Vernon realises that his calling is that of a musician – an artist – and that the life he has lived, however real and absorbing, is nothing but material. 'That was what it meant to be a creator.' Having lost his old identity, having travelled through the happy limbo period as George Green, he has finally come to the place where he is supposed to be.

Similarly, Henrietta Savernake in *The Hollow* is an artist – a sculptress – who cannot help but experience life at one remove. When her lover is murdered she turns her deepest feelings into an alabaster work entitled *Sorrow*. 'I cannot love – I cannot mourn – not with the whole of me.' She asks what the word 'integrity' means, wondering if she herself can possibly possess such a quality. She considers the quotation from *Peer Gynt* that haunted Agatha all her life:

'Where am I myself, the whole man, the true man? Where am I with God's mark upon my brow?'

This was what Agatha had become: a Vernon, a Henrietta. The dream period spent as Mrs Neele rearranged her personality in a fundamental way, and through the dark years of 1927 and 1928 she became the person she would not otherwise have been. She became a writer. Her dreams became her work, and her work became everything. She wrote too much, and too compulsively, for anyone to doubt that this was where the real Agatha now lived.

It was the way to survive the great rupture of 1926: either that or go under. The life she had had before no longer existed, so she became an onlooker, an outsider. It was not what she had wanted, but it was the right thing. As her friend A. L. Rowse wrote, the wound left by that nightmare year was 'so deep . . . it left its traces all through her work. It also made her the great woman she became.'[1] Why else did she begin to write *Giant's Bread*, if not as a sombre celebration of a new beginning?

Without the burden of normal female expectations, she found herself free. There was no longer an obligation to be a certain kind of woman: slim, pleasing, feminine. She could absent herself from these restraints. She could formulate a persona and wear it like a suit of armour – present it to the world in place of herself – and inside she could be whatever she chose. This was the freedom of the creator. She had lost everything and found everything: because everything was material.

As 'Agatha Christie' she could write as much as her facility would allow, and from the end of the decade the books poured forth: seventeen full-length novels between 1930 and 1939, shaped with the geometrical perfection she had first shown in *The Murder of Roger Ackroyd*. The murderer who pretends to be the victim; the murderer who pretends to be a serial killer; the murderer who is the investigating policeman; the cast of suspects who are all innocent; the cast of suspects who are all guilty: magnificent, bold ideas that did not merely reinvigorate detective fiction but redesigned it as a gleaming hall of bright new mirrors. So impregnable was the construct that, although the world of the books was Agatha's to create, she never had to reveal anything of herself. That, never again. 'Agatha Christie' wrote the books: the clever, controlled, sensible woman who knew all about human emotion but who dealt with it, every time, and kept chaos at bay. Agatha herself was 'Mary Westmacott', the sensitive, secret creature who had been born of the drifting ghost of Harrogate; and who could never have existed without the strange freedom that came from using another woman's name.

Mary Westmacott wrote about love and its mysteries. She wrote about Archie Christie; he was her primary inspiration. In *Giant's Bread* she pondered the idea of love at first sight, its absurdity and its peculiar power. Vernon is in love with his wife, Nell, because he always sees her as she first appeared to him: magical and moonlit. She is also weak-natured, but this does not stop Vernon loving her. He is unable to separate the force of his emotions from the person towards whom they are directed.

Similarly with Agatha and Archie. She wrote about their marriage in her second Westmacott, *Unfinished Portrait*, and her conclusion is simple. Whether or not her husband – 'Dermot' – is worthy of her love, that love exists. In order to keep it alive for herself, she should have recognised the truth about Dermot. 'I loved Dermot – and I didn't keep him. I ought to have seen what he liked and wanted, and been that . . . I ought to have known and been on my guard and not been so cocksure and pleased with myself. If a thing matters to you more than anything in life, you've got to be clever about it . . . I wasn't clever about it . . .'

She had been brought up to believe that marriage mattered more than anything to a woman, and that a man had to be held by a wife. Her grandmother, her mother: they had both told her so. Yet she had failed to keep her husband. Her flight to Harrogate, which had been her last desperate throw of the dice, had ensured that he would never return. Every day she had spent as Mrs Neele had banged another nail into the coffin of her marriage. This was the knowledge she now had to live with: that by her own actions she had brought about these terrible consequences.

This was what she went through in 1927 and 1928, all the time turning her agony into material, all the time wishing that she simply had her husband back.

Of course she could say to herself that Archie would have left anyway, in the end, and possibly this was true. But there would always be the doubt that, if she had behaved differently, he might have stayed.

Throughout the bleak months Agatha had to bear public opprobrium and mockery. These were bad enough in themselves. Worse, though, was that this public attention – which it was widely believed she had sought – was the thing she had least wanted: the thing that had destroyed her private, precious world. It was a ghastly, shaming irony. She did not know what Archie thought, how much he blamed her for the wreckage of his own life, but obviously she feared the worst. This, then, was another irony: that the guilty party in all of this was now causing Agatha to feel guilt on his behalf.

A small part of her still hoped, faintly, that he might come back. She had moved to a flat in Chelsea with Rosalind and Carlo; Archie was living at Styles while trying to sell it, and the thought of him in the house – a hated place, but it had been *theirs* – must have taunted her. 'It's all the little shared intimacies of life that hold you so with a husband and tear you to pieces when you part,' she wrote in *Unfinished Portrait*. She knew, really, that even if he did come back, they could never be happy again. She was not the kind of woman – wry, adult, realistic to the point of cynicism – to live with a man who longed to be elsewhere. Her kind brothers-in-law, James Watts and Campbell Christie, both helped her to understand this. But later in 1927 she saw Archie again, a polite and dreadful meeting at which 'we talked of ordinary things', and she asked one last time if he might not be persuaded to stay: for Rosalind's sake. 'I said once again that he knew how fond of him she was,' wrote Agatha in her autobiography, 'and how much she had been puzzled by his absence.'

The answer was no. He still loved Nancy and Nancy, despite having been away for the last ten months, still loved him. Of course he owed a debt to Nancy – albeit far smaller than the one he owed his wife – for the damage to her reputation. Being the man he was, decisive and sudden and unwilling to admit mistakes, he was always going to stick with the woman who had caused all this in the first place; to have said to Agatha, 'Yes I was wrong, yes I should stay with you,' would have been impossible. So Agatha accepted it was over. She never saw Archie again, although she kept his love letters and photographs. She went to court on 20 April 1928, listened to the fake evidence of adultery with an unknown party in the Grosvenor Hotel and, in October, was granted her divorce. Two weeks later Archie married Nancy.

After her divorce Agatha never again took communion in church. Always she felt shame and guilt, especially towards her daughter, for having 'given in' to Archie's demands for a divorce. 'I don't even know why I did give in' she wrote in *Unfinished Portrait*, '– because I was tired and wanted peace – or because I became convinced it was the only thing to be done, or because, after all, I wanted to give in to Dermot . . . I think, sometimes, it was the last . . . That's why, ever since, I've felt guilty when Judy looked at me . . . In the end, you see, I betrayed Judy for Dermot.'

Archie's second marriage lasted until Nancy died of cancer in 1958. Agatha wrote to Archie to condole with him, and he wrote back thanking her for giving him thirty years of happiness with Nancy: an apparently benign exchange which nonetheless, hums with undercurrents. Was Agatha really so altruistic, or was a small part of her reminding Archie of the luxurious, splendid life he could have had with her? And was Archie's reply entirely tactful, in the light of the suffering that his love for Nancy had caused Agatha?

The marriage of Archie and Nancy – whose son was born in 1930 – must have been shadowed with memories. Agatha was not a person they could escape. Her fame grew, her name was constantly in the newspapers, her books were everywhere: how odd for the Christies to see *The ABC Murders*, say, in the window of the local bookshop, and to know that its celebrated author had been willing to go to such lengths on their account. At home Agatha's name was not mentioned, nor were the events of 1926 (indeed Archie's son knew almost nothing about them until he reached maturity). Like Agatha herself, these were people who believed in the value of concealment and reticence. Whatever either Archie or Nancy thought or felt about the strange beginnings of their relationship, they pushed it aside and dealt with the realities.

It is generally agreed that their marriage was a success. Nancy, it was said, was 'fun and full of life. I'm sure theirs was a happy marriage because she was such a happy woman.'[2] Yet Agatha, too, had had a vast capacity for joy, and her zest for life had ended by irritating Archie greatly. He was 'not a sociable animal', said his son; 'although my mother was'.[3] So Nancy was not exactly Archie's soulmate, any more than Agatha had been. And he fell for her in the same abrupt way that he had fallen for Agatha. The difference, of course, was that while Agatha had been beautiful, Nancy was beautiful still. And she was a wife, in the way that Archie craved: she did not have that quality of obtuseness which Agatha had displayed towards her first husband, and which seemed, unjustly, like selfishness.

After their separation, the lives of Archie and Agatha diverged so completely that it is hard to believe they ever thought they would grow old together. Archie did well in the City and acquired several directorships, including one in the Rank Organization. Although in a 1958 letter to Rosalind he admitted that 'Twice I have been down to zero and that may happen again', he left upwards of £90,000 gross when he died in 1962. Before the Second World War he had a home in London's smart Avenue Road, and later acquired a house in Godalming (which apparently had 'no taste').[4] By that time he had given up golf. He lived quietly. 'He was a good chap,' said Agatha's perceptive son-in-law, Anthony Hicks, who met Archie with Rosalind on a few occasions. 'Rosalind didn't want to meet Nancy so I didn't meet her very often. She was quite dull. And Archie became duller.'[5]

Meanwhile Agatha glittered and shone and became one of the most famous women in the world; she bought houses with abandon, living as she chose in Kensington, South Kensington, Oxfordshire or Devon; she travelled to glamorous, faraway lands; she married again, a man of intellect who had no fear of her brilliant, fertile mind but had the sense, instead, to revel in the fruits of its labours. She learned a different way of life.

Archie weathered the shame of the police investigation, the embarrassment of the scandal, the near-total rupture with Rosalind. He acquired the life with Nancy that he had craved throughout 1926. The pain of getting rid of his wife had, it seemed, been worthwhile. But some years later he had a breakdown of his own, requiring hospital treatment of a serious nature, from which he recovered well. Like his mother and brother he had always been fragile, although his self-control was remarkable.

Ever blunt in his opinions, A. L. Rowse had little doubt that Archie had done the wrong thing in leaving Agatha, and that he must have known it. 'Poor Mr Christie – what a story he would make, looking at it from his point of view! What a mistake he made!'[6] A friend of Agatha's told Rowse that Archie had had 'reason to regret his conduct since'; in other words, that he knew he should have stuck with his first wife. This is speculation, of course. But it is the sort of question that Agatha would repeatedly ask: whether Archie might not have been happier, in the end, had he stayed. And whether she herself would have been happier, had she lived until death with her 'own familiar friend'; had the lifelong compensations for his absence been unnecessary.

*   *   *

'What did Roddy know of Mary Gerrard? Nothing – less than nothing! . . . It was the old story – Nature's hoary old joke! . . . Didn't Roddy himself – *really* – want to be free of it?'

So wrote Agatha in *Sad Cypress*, and indeed, when Mary Gerrard dies, Roddy emerges from her spell with the easy bewilderment of a man waking out of a dream.

Of Elinor Carlisle, the girl who loves Roddy so deeply, it is said: 'She'll forgive him the Mary Gerrard business. It was only a wild infatuation on his part, anyway.'

But Hercule Poirot speaks with the wisdom of his creator, and says: 'It goes deeper than that . . . There is, sometimes, a deep chasm between the past and the future. When one has walked in the valley of the shadow of death, and come out of it into the sunshine – then, *mon cher*, it is a new life that begins . . . The past will not serve . . .'

In 1927 Agatha did not understand this yet; or understood it only in theory. Her life, on the surface, was as grey and dreary as a prison exercise yard, her mind prey to a daily succession of torments. She lived in London, hating it. But to hate was easier than to be at Ashfield, where she would remember love. Madge had suggested she live quietly in Devon but, as she wrote in her autobiography, 'Something that reminds you of a *happy* day or a *happy* thing – that's the thing that almost breaks you in two.'

She thought, on the whole, that she would prefer to be dead (but those who had failed to kill themselves 'didn't do it again'. So she wrote in *Towards Zero*). She could not bear her notoriety, the fact that every time she went out, or gave her name, she was waiting for a reaction: recognition, curiosity, contempt. She was an acutely sensitive creature whose wrenching griefs had been exposed to national ridicule. She had been condemned for something she had not done. In 1929 she wrote in the *Sunday Chronicle* about the 'Croydon murders', as they were known, in which three members of the same family were poisoned: the murderer clearly came from within the family circle but the case was – and remains – unsolved. It always fascinated Agatha, not least because 'It is a case where the innocent suffer most horribly for sins they have never committed. They live in a haze of publicity; acquaintance and friends look at them curiously; there are continually autograph hunters, curious idle crowds. Any decent happy private life is made impossible for them.' The idea in this article would later be written into one of her best detective novels, *Ordeal by Innocence*.

She knew, of course, that Rosalind was bewildered and upset. When Agatha's own mother had been devastated by the death of her husband, she had been told to 'live for her children', but this was not Agatha's way. 'The bright spot of my life was Rosalind,' she wrote in her autobiography; in fact it was not quite that simple. She was too much of a child herself, she still missed her mother too much, and she was torn by her complex feelings towards her daughter. 'She never said anything, but I thought that, secretly, she blamed me for the loss of her father,' she wrote in *Unfinished Portrait*. 'I failed her.' The guilt that Agatha felt made her deeply uncomfortable: she was sorry for her daughter, but not always sympathetic, particularly as Rosalind remained so determinedly keen to see Archie.

This was not a modern divorce, so Archie did not have 'access'. He did not turn up at Agatha's door to take his daughter off for weekends. Rosalind did not meet Nancy; she did not even meet her half-brother until Archie's funeral; Archie, for his part, never met Rosalind's son.[7] The lives of Rosalind's parents became entirely separate, which would nowadays seem odd, but it is hard to imagine how Agatha would have coped with Archie's constant presence in her life. For Archie, too, it would have been quite impossible.

As an adult Rosalind was discreet about her meetings with Archie, the boxes of whisky he sent her at Christmas. 'I certainly always saw my father myself, we were very fond of each other,' she wrote in a letter not long before she died. She was pragmatic enough to accept what he had done, and loyal enough to proclaim her affection. 'I hate the image of him as someone cold and unfeeling,' she said.[8]

And as a child she missed him badly. She had been uprooted from Sunningdale – the big house, the proper family – and moved to a London flat full of women, around which her mother drooped like a dying bird. Although barely nine she was glad to go to the Caledonia boarding-school in Bexhill, where both her parents could visit her (when Agatha was away, as increasingly she would be, Carlo or Madge would go in her stead). The letters that Rosalind sent home to her mother were cool, funny and occasionally barbed: 'Thank you very much for the letter you sent me although it was very short. Rose May Lever was sick all over the passage the other day. She is going out today. Her mother came to church to take her out. She looked rather nice.'[9] And: 'I am getting a bit tired of writing to you so I will now write a short letter to Daddy.'[10] And, after Agatha's second marriage: 'Don't be late for sports will you!!! Don't come in your black and white dress come in an ordinary dress. Who are you bringing to the Sports this year. I would rather you brought only Carlo.'[11]

This was utterly remote from the relationship that Agatha had had with Clara, all that 'darling Mummy' and 'pigeony pumpkin'. Rosalind had never been easy for her mother to deal with; something about this marvellous, bright, sharp-edged child seems to have shrivelled Agatha's maternal impulse in the bud, and the break with Archie ensured it would never flower. Always there would be tension, a kind of tough, joshing bonhomie between the two that precluded simple affection.

'I don't know whether she loves me or doesn't love me,' wrote Agatha in *Unfinished Portrait*. 'The kind of person I am is no good to the kind of person she is . . . I love her, just as I loved Dermot, but I don't understand her.' In fact there was love on both sides; and a neediness that for some reason neither could show. When Agatha was trying to write again, on a holiday to the Canary Islands in February 1928, she was nearly driven mad when her daughter would not leave her alone. Had Peter the dog been standing there, Agatha would have melted. So she did, subsequently, with her grandson. With her daughter, though, it was different: always there was the barrier, the gulf.

Agatha sensed that she had let Rosalind down but, more obscurely, she felt that Rosalind had contributed to the death of her marriage. She believed that a child came between a man and a woman, and she had no compunction about writing this in both *Unfinished Portrait* and *A Daughter's a Daughter*. So Rosalind knew her mother's feelings and, it was said, 'felt in some way responsible for the divorce'. There was guilt on both sides; there was resentment of this guilt. And there was the irreducible fact that Agatha had been prepared to abandon Rosalind when she disappeared in 1926. Hardly surprising that both mother and daughter should have taken refuge in the 'amnesia' theory;

although Agatha's books told Rosalind a good deal that was otherwise left unsaid.

'I have always thought how singularly lucky you were to have her for a mother and I have no doubt at all that you share this opinion,' wrote a family friend to Rosalind after Agatha's death. Her reply would have been exemplary; her feelings were a good deal more complicated.

The book that Agatha had been writing on her 1928 holiday was *The Mystery of the Blue Train*. The year before she had finished cobbling together some Poirot short stories, previously printed in the *Sketch*, into a book entitled *The Big Four*. In her autobiography Agatha emphasised how difficult it had been to finish these two books, although what she did not say was that she had actually been half-way through both at the time of her disappearance. Nor was *Blue Train* in need of much original thought, as, like *The Big Four*, it was derived from a short story ('The Plymouth Express').

The difficulty was that she had never before had to write when she did not want to. Writing had always been a happy activity. It had been hard work, but the work had been her choice. Now she *had* to write.

She was not quite as destitute as her autobiography implies: she had been left something in the region of thirteen thousand pounds by her mother, and although she had sunk all her capital into Styles, the house was on the market. A flat in Chelsea, a home in Devon, a child at boarding-school and a personal secretary does not sound like penury. But when Agatha wrote about her financial fears – 'I had no money coming in from anywhere' – what she was really describing was her state of mind. She was utterly panic-stricken about the future. Like most women who have been protected all their lives – looked after by their family, then their husband – and who suddenly find themselves completely alone, Agatha was frightened. Who would look after her now? Even if writing *The Mystery of the Blue Train* seemed like the most hideous job in the world – which it did – she had to do it. Simple as that.

In her autobiography she described the transition in straightforward terms – she had been an amateur, she was now a professional – but what had happened was far more subtle and profound. There was a fundamental difference in the way she engaged with her work. And even in *Blue Train*, which she professed to detest,[12] this came across: she was writing it not just because she had to, for money, but because she *had* to: for herself.

Some of the book is, indeed, workaday Christie. But she created in it a character called Katherine Grey, and this calm, observant, attractive woman was balm to her shattered spirit. Katherine is alone in the world, albeit with money, and is described as being in the 'autumn' of her years: a situation terrifying to her creator but which Katherine handles with a quiet, humorous assurance that Agatha must have longed to possess. It soothed her to dream it into life.

'Don't think you'll get married, my dear, because you won't,' says an old lady friend, before Katherine leaves for the Riviera. 'You're not the kind to attract the men. And, besides, you're getting on. How old are you now?'

'Thirty-three,' Katherine told her.

'Well,' remarked Miss Viner doubtfully, 'that's not so very bad. You've lost your first freshness, of course.'

'I'm afraid so,' said Katherine, much entertained.

On the Blue Train Katherine dines with a fellow traveller, Ruth Kettering, who is coming to the end of a bad marriage ('You may have a hankering after the fellow still. *Cut it out,*' her father says to her, urging divorce as the only possible solution. 'I might find ways of whistling Derek back to you, but it would all come to the same in the end.') Ruth intends to meet a lover in Nice, and asks Katherine whether she should go ahead. 'It seems to me an awfully silly thing that you are going to do,' is the unarguable reply. 'I think you realise that yourself.'

Throughout much of this book Agatha is talking to herself, reassuring herself about the divorce, allowing the integrity of her heroine to console her. Katherine might have hankered after Archie still, but her instinctive sense of self would have come to her rescue, and she would not have longed for what could not be. She would have faced facts.

Hercule Poirot, too, admires Katherine Grey; and by allowing a friendship to develop between the two, Agatha gave a new quality to her detective, hitherto a mere charismatic assemblage of moustaches and bombast. On the Blue Train Poirot is wise as well as clever, his eyes penetrate emotion as well as facts. He has, in his way, a *tendresse* for Katherine;[13] and this, too, was oddly comforting to his tired and sad creator. "Well, Mademoiselle, how goes it?" She looked at his twinkling eyes, and was confirmed in her first impression that there was something very attractive about M. Hercule Poirot.'

Later Poirot is talking to the daughter of one of his contacts. They are standing beside a bridge, and the girl says to him that it is a favourite spot for suicides. 'So it is said. Men are foolish, are they not, Mademoiselle? To eat, to drink, to breathe the good air, it is a very pleasant thing, Mademoiselle. One is foolish to leave all that simply because one has no money – or because the heart aches. *L'amour*, it causes many fatalities, does it not?'

This was the attitude that Agatha yearned for: again, there was consolation in writing it into life.

But perhaps the greatest solace of all was the Blue Train itself. Murder scene it may have been, yet it bloomed in Agatha's mind as a symbol of order and escape. She had always wanted to travel. However much she had loved Archie she had known, in her heart, that they were very different people; that while he moved with apparent contentment between Sunningdale and Waterloo and the City, day in day out, she craved the sight of the unknown ('. . . they'd go on and on and on – probably at Dalton Heath or some-where like it . . . She'd never see things – faraway things – India, China, Japan – the wilds of Baluchistan – Persia, where the names were like music: Ispahan, Teheran, Shiraz . . .'). She had longed for freedom and for love, and she was beginning to learn that the two rarely went together.

Now she had exchanged the one for the other, and she had that other thing: writing. She would write her books – including the special, secret one, *Giant's Bread*, which was all about the things that fascinated and perplexed her – and she would travel. Carlo and Madge would visit Rosalind at school and she, Agatha, would go to the West Indies. She booked her tickets, excited at the prospect of spending the winter of 1928 in the sun. Then came a push from fate. A day or two before she was to leave, she went to a dinner-party in London and sat next to a man just back from Baghdad. Oh, she said, that was somewhere she had always dreamed of visiting. He seemed unsurprised and was full of information. You could get there, he told her, by train: the Orient Express. Oh, how wonderful that sounded! You could see the archaeological dig at Ur, which was then all over the *Illustrated London News*: its leader, Leonard Woolley, was making spectacular claims to have found the site of the biblical Flood. Oh, yes, said the man, you should certainly go to Iraq some time.

The next day Agatha went to Cook's and changed her tickets. She would take the Orient Express to Stamboul, then go on to Damascus in Syria and finally to Baghdad. Carlo expressed concerns – the East, a woman, unaccompanied? – but for the first time in more than two years Agatha felt alive again. She would travel alone to new worlds. She would dare. Her course was set.

'One of my pet theories (quite unrealisable, of course, that's the pleasant part about theories) is that everybody should spend one month a year in the middle of a desert . . . With enough to eat and drink, and nothing – absolutely nothing – to do, you'd have, at last, a fairly good chance to make acquaintance with yourself.'

Thus speaks Laura Whitstable in *A Daughter's a Daughter*. Nothing, she says, is more important than that people should know themselves ('a man should have *knowledge* of himself and *belief* in God'). Yet this was an extraordinarily hard thing to achieve, as Agatha herself now recognised. And what did it mean? In early 1927 she had gone, at her sister's suggestion, to a psychiatrist in Harley Street; did she believe that this would help in any way? As much as anything she went to maintain the fiction that she had lost her memory and needed to recover it: in other words, she was lying about herself to find out the truth about herself. According to Agatha's *Daily Mail* interview in 1928, she had been told that 'for the health of my mind there should be no hiatus of any kind in my recollections. That is why I can now recall at the same time my existence as Mrs Christie

and as Mrs Neele.' This, of course, was a kind of nonsense. Agatha
may well have duped her doctors – she was quite clever enough to
do that, to fake confusion like Jane Finn in *The Secret Adversary* –
yet at the same time being forced to talk, to remember, was genuinely
painful.

> Vernon was listening, trying to understand what the doctor was
> saying to him. He looked across the table at him. A tall thin
> man, with eyes that seemed to see right into the centre of you
> and to read there things that you didn't even know about your-
> self.
> And he made you see all the things you didn't want to see.
> Made you bring things up out of the depths. He was saying:
> 'Now that you have remembered, tell me again exactly how you
> saw the announcement of your wife's marriage.'
> Vernon cried out: 'Must we go over it again and again? It was
> all so horrible. I don't want to think of it any more.'

Agatha was interested in psychiatry – she was interested in almost
everything – but her own means to self-knowledge was self-reliance.
For all that she engaged with twentieth-century ideas she was, in the
deepest sense, a creature of her Edwardian upbringing. And by 1928
she knew that she had to strike out on her own.

She was not alone in the desert when she went east – this fate
would befall another of her characters, Joan Scudamore in *Absent
in the Spring* – but it was the first time that she had been thrown
completely on her own resources. As a girl, solitude had been her
secret delight, its pleasures enhanced by the sense of protection all
around her. As a woman she had sacrificed solitude to the demands
of adult life. Now she did not know how she felt about it. It was
necessary for her imagination; but the loneliness of the past two
years had been so great. 'I should find out now what kind of person
I was,' she wrote in her autobiography, of her trip to Baghdad,
'whether I had become entirely dependent on other people as I
feared. I could indulge my passion for seeing places – any place I
wanted to see. I could change my mind at a moment's notice, just
as I had done when I chose Baghdad instead of the West Indies. I

would have no-one to consider but myself. I would see how I liked that.'

She entered a different world: in every sense. All at once she was a grown woman of means, sitting alone on the Orient Express, taking her pleasures as she chose. She threw off the hunted, haunted creature of London and lifted her eyes to the new things around her. The Cilician Gates, for example, which form the passage through the Taurus Mountains into Turkey, and take the traveller from the Mediterranean into Anatolia: Alexander the Great and Paul of Tarsus had passed here, and now Agatha, at sunset, disembarked from her train and confronted this 'indescribable' beauty. 'I was so glad then that I had come – so full of thankfulness and joy.' At the entrance to the East she began to find her way back to her Christian God, in whom she had always believed but had doubted of late. And something else. Later she described the Cilician Gates as 'like standing on the rim of the world and looking down on the promised land . . . a land one will never reach'. This was her most precious, private dream: of the numinous, of the world that existed outside reality. She was back in the imagination of childhood, when she had dreamed a river at the end of the garden at Ashfield.

The last thing she needed was the Englishwoman who shared her *wagon-lit* compartment on the Orient Express, and who instantly set herself to the task of directing Agatha's itinerary. 'You can't possibly stay in a hotel in Baghdad. I tell you what you must do: you must come to us!' Baghdad, in those days, was thirty years away from the revolution that would change Iraq for ever. It was a city where the British traveller could find racing, tennis, clubs and no doubt Marmite on toast; in the pre-war years it was not at all unusual to find people of Agatha's class in such places. But Agatha was possessed with the spirit of adventure, not of colonialism. She had gone to the East to avoid her fellow-countrymen, not to socialise with them. At the end of her magical journey she found herself in what she called Memsahib Land: 'I felt ashamed of myself for the caged feeling from which I suffered.'[14] To sit in Baghdad among the kind of people she had known all her life was not merely pointless, it was painfully retrograde: here was the world she had inhabited before 1926, but with worse food and without Archie at her side. Everything had to be new and different.

She would go away from this thin, bare, polite society to the city of Ur, below the confluence of the Tigris and the Euphrates in what had once been the land of Sumer, where civilisation had begun; although, like a good memsahib, she carried a letter of introduction to the dig.

As shown in her novel *The Man in the Brown Suit*, Agatha had been interested in antiquity for some years; she had visited anthropological museums on the Empire Tour, and had written to her mother that looking at early human skulls 'was altogether one of the best afternoons I have ever spent!'. But archaeology became modish in the 1920s, and her interest was kept alive. It was in 1922 that Leonard Woolley began his work at Ur, for which he obtained a level of publicity rivalling that of Lord Carnarvon and Howard Carter, who had unearthed the tomb of Tutankhamun in Egypt. Woolley was a good journalist and a clever salesman, although his work was so fascinating that, really, it sold itself. 'It is', wrote Woolley, 'with the third Dynasty of Ur that connected history begins.' The excavations were from the late third millennium BC – the kingdom of Ur fell in around 2000 BC – and were of great importance. From Sumer (or southern Mesopotamia) had come the first recognised work of 'literature', *The Epic of Gilgamesh*, and the earliest concept of religion: the pyramid-like ziggurats, or temple towers, such as Woolley was excavating, were believed by the Sumerians to be homes to their gods. Agatha's knowledge of the Old Testament gave her some grasp of the mythical history of Mesopotamia. This was the land of the biblical patriarchs, of the ten tribes of Israel that had been swept away by the Assyrians, of the Babylonian empire and its last king, Nebuchadnezzar. But Nebuchadnezzar, who had reigned in the sixth century BC, was absurdly recent in this context: Woolley's dig unearthed houses dating back to his time and, beneath them, to the time of Abraham. Agatha was mesmerised. It was the idea of history itself that gripped her, the fact that 'then' could be 'now' if one chose to make the connection. Again this was a world away from Archie, in every sense.

As a young girl in Egypt Agatha's attention had been on men rather than pyramids, but men were now out of the picture, and she exerted herself to engage with the life of the mind. Like many autodidacts, she wanted to carry on learning, but this was a decision that she took in the late 1920s: not to go under, not to lose interest. 'I have been struck by the extraordinary number of things she did know, the sheer range of her experience,' wrote A. L. Rowse.[15]

She was an honoured guest at Ur. Woolley normally found visitors a terrible nuisance but his wife Katherine was a fan of *The Murder of Roger Ackroyd*, and that decided the matter. What Katherine wanted, happened. Subsequently Agatha would realise that this beautiful woman was also strange, controlling and dangerous, but on her first visit Katherine was extremely charming. It was a wonderful thing for Agatha to be known not as the troublesome hysteric of 1926 but as a writer, a celebrity, a person worthy of respect. *Roger Ackroyd* had, after all, been rather special. Katherine thought its creator a remarkable person; although she quite obviously preferred the company of men, she took to Agatha and invited her to return to the dig. This, too, was a healing thing. What had half killed Agatha was the reality of how the world – and Archie – saw her, which was so different from how she saw herself. Now at Ur she was viewed in a new way. It was unfamiliar, it still felt like a disguise, but she was quietly inclined to accept it. There may have been a hollow where her heart had been but at least her life was *interesting*, in a way that it could never have been with Archie: he would not have thrilled to the sight of the Cilician Gates, nor of black buffaloes watering on the road into Baghdad, nor of the colours of the desert, 'pale pink, apricots and blues'. He would not have eaten the strange food – greasy meat, leathery tomato omelettes, huge cauliflowers – without falling ill. He would have stood on the dig at Ur, watched 'a dagger slowly appearing, with its gold glint, through the sand', and thought of the golf he was missing at Sunningdale.

So Agatha told herself, as she sought to remake her life, to collect experiences. It was a brave venture; for she *was* a wounded creature, damaged, hardened and highly suspicious ('If *Dermot* could be treacherous, then anyone could be treacherous. The world itself became unsure. I couldn't trust anyone or anything any more . . .') Yet for all her vulnerability she had a latent strength. The men of her family – Frederick, Monty – were lovable and weak. The women could see life for what it was and bear it. Agatha was not innately of that type;

she was a dreamer, a child; but she had studied these women and, with her artist's temperament, she was able to assume something of their character for herself.

'Things have to happen to all of us . . . That's the way life is. You just have to take it. Some of us can, some of us can't.' So Agatha wrote in *The Mirror Crack'd from Side to Side*; and, having been one of the people who couldn't 'take it', she thereafter remade herself into one of those who could. At the root of this shift was her writing. That was her refuge, her protection, her outlet: her real life.

It was also increasingly successful. In 1928 a new contract with Collins gave her a £750 advance for her next six books, while an American contract with Dodd Mead gave $2,500. *The Secret Adversary* became the first of her books to be filmed (in German), as was a story, 'The Coming of Mr Quin'. A theatrical version of *Roger Ackroyd* was staged in 1928 as *Alibi* (this, too, would soon be filmed), with Charles Laughton the first of several superb actors to be miscast as Poirot.[16] Agatha enjoyed the novelty of *Alibi*, attending rehearsals with her dog Peter, but she was sufficiently irritated by the changes to the original to want to write a play of her own: *Black Coffee* would be produced in 1930. This, as A. L. Rowse later wrote, was the irony about the disappearance: 'Everybody thought it a publicity stunt; but it was genuine – so much better than the best of jobs. After that every book was a bestseller, everything fell into her hands.' *The Big Four* was one of the worst pieces of writing she ever published but in the wake of 1926 it sold well, as did the other offerings of the 1920s: *The Mystery of the Blue Train*, *The Seven Dials Mystery* and *Partners in Crime*. These last two are, respectively, a thriller and a series of short stories. It is easy to see that Agatha's real creative attention was on *Giant's Bread*; although *Seven Dials* has a dry wit that reveals a slightly acid state of mind. It has the same setting as *The Secret of Chimneys*, but comparing it with that wonderfully joyful book shows, albeit obliquely, the road that Agatha had travelled in between. The country house Chimneys has been let by Lord Caterham to a rich businessman, Sir Oswald Coote, and these are the thoughts of Lord

Caterham's daughter: 'She had a nightmare vision of England with innumerable Cootes in innumerable counterparts of Chimneys – all, be it understood, with an entirely new system of plumbing installed . . . A hundred delicate appreciations of life which Lord Caterham could and did enjoy were a sealed book to Sir Oswald.'

But Lord Caterham has all the pragmatism of his class, and remains one of Agatha's finest creations. 'Coote got me in as a director of something or other. Very good business for me – nothing to do except go down to the city once or twice a year . . . and sit around a table where they have very nice new blotting paper. Then Coote or some clever Johnny makes a speech simply bristling with figures, but fortunately you needn't listen to it – and I can tell you, you often get a jolly good lunch out of it.'

Seven Dials is proof that Agatha could be very funny (a young man describes his new showgirl conquest as 'one of the eight girls who made the living bridge'), although this is hard to believe when reading the ghastly *Partners in Crime*. Tommy and Tuppence are back, jollier than ever, enacting parodies of other detective writers in appallingly twee fashion: back in 1929 these may have had a certain *élan* but, as with many of Agatha's early short stories, they hold almost nothing of her essence.

The Murder at the Vicarage, however, is all essence, all assurance. With the arrival of Miss Marple[17] centre stage (she had appeared in a series of six short stories in 1927, later used in *The Thirteen Problems*), Agatha found the means to convey a complete world-view. It was not quite her own view, although it has been seen as such. Nor was it quite her own world, although she knew it very well. But it was her own creation; and if in real life she would have grown wildly irritated with her generic English village, in her imagination she lived there most happily: among the hierarchies, the familiar roles, the morality that can be both petty and solid. St Mary Mead, where Miss Marple lives and where *The Murder at the Vicarage* is set, is the prototype. There are also Lymstock in *The Moving Finger*, Chipping Cleghorn in *A Murder is Announced*, Wychwood-under-Ashe in *Murder is Easy* and Much Deeping in *The Pale Horse*: all of these are as defined, and as real to the author, as the world of Highbury was to Jane Austen. 'Real to the author' may imply that Agatha's England is anything but real to anyone else. This criticism is often levelled, yet it is actually meaningless. Art does not reflect reality, it creates it: in that sense, the world of St Mary Mead is real. It must be, else people would not believe in it as they do. It is said that the trick of Agatha's England is that it so lacks a proper sense of place, readers from anywhere can rewrite it in their heads with a setting familiar to themselves. This is not quite true (nobody who has read the accurate trot along the main street of Long Basing in *Third Girl* can complain of deficit of detail), nor is it quite the point. Agatha was not a 'descriptive' writer. But she could sketch an atmospheric setting, by means so direct at times that it almost goes unnoticed (as, for example, in *And Then There Were None*, when she took the brilliant step of staging mass murder in a bright-lit, modern house with no atmosphere at all).

'She has', says P. D. James, 'the ability to conjure a world without actually describing it.'[18] Her villages are especially alive; and what is rarely appreciated is that they move with the times. *A Murder is Announced*, written in 1949, is full of post-war uncertainty ('Fifteen years ago one *knew* who everybody was. The Bantrys in the big house – and the Hartnells and the Price Ridleys and the Weatherbys . . .'), while *The Mirror Crack'd from Side to Side* opens with an unusually precise evocation of a 1960s housing estate ('It was like a neat model built with child's bricks. It hardly seemed real to Miss Marple'). But the village essence remains: 'The new world was the same as the old. The houses were different, the streets were called Closes, the clothes were different, the voices were different, but the human beings were the same as they always had been.'

This is the reassuring wisdom of Miss Marple: to see past what is frightening and unfamiliar and find the sanity, the common bond, the truth. Miss Marple knows that 'there's a great deal of – well, *queerness* about'. But she would have agreed, on the whole, with a remark Agatha made in 1955: 'Do you know, people always fall back on madness as an explanation when they don't understand a criminal's behaviour.' What interested Miss Marple and her creator was the way in which behaviour relates to normality, even when it is murderous. Agatha was intrigued by the Croydon case because she saw in it a complex family puzzle, a recognisable pattern pushed to an extreme.

Although in her 1929 article she touched upon the idea that the murders had been committed because of a 'strange lust for killing', such a solution would not have interested her at all. Motive, for her, was everything.

In *The Moving Finger* Miss Marple realises that the crime is not, as everybody else believes, motivated by something weird and impersonal. In fact it is all too human. This book is perhaps Agatha's most wholly satisfactory, and was admired by clever friends like the epigraphist Sidney Smith, who called it Marple in her best vein.[19] The setting is magnificently drawn, a Christie village in all its abundant life: hearty Aimée Griffith bounding unwanted up to front doors ('Hello, slackers!'), organising the Girl Guides while her heart burns for the local solicitor; the little aesthete Mr Pye, whose 'voice rose to a falsetto squeak as he narrated the exciting circumstances under which he had brought his Italian bedstead home from Verona'; the vicar's wife, Mrs Dane Calthrop, with her lean greyhound face and her eccentric perceptiveness. Perhaps the setting comes across particularly well because it is narrated by an outsider, a London man who has something of Agatha's own detachment. 'I have much business to transact,' he says. 'I shall call in at the baker's and complain about the currant loaf.' And later, when murder comes to the village: 'Just for a moment I hated Lymstock and its narrow boundaries, and its gossiping whispering women.'

This, too, Agatha could see: the danger in villages, the lack of outlets, the way inhabitants can turn in on themselves and fester. In *Murder is Easy* the sinister undercurrent is made explicit. Again the book is narrated by a male outsider, who has returned from the East and finds himself, initially sceptical, falling under the spell of a village whose comfortable face glints with danger. 'The sky was dull and menacing, and wind came in sudden erratic little puffs. It was as though he had stepped out of normal everyday life into that queer half world of enchantment, the consciousness of which had enveloped him ever since he came to Wychwood.' There is devilry in this village – sacrifices to Satan, a girl like a witch – but, as always with Agatha's detective fiction, the real evil is all too human. The serial killer is a person whom life has thwarted and who, in a village, has nothing to do but brood on it. Class also plays a convincing part in this book; not because Agatha was an irredeemable snob but because class *did* – still does – loom large in closed communities.

Murder is Easy is not a Miss Marple (although it contains a substitute of sorts) but it is born of her world. Miss Marple herself was cast in the mould of Caroline Sheppard, the doctor's sister in *The Murder of Roger Ackroyd*. Miss Sheppard has a gift for unearthing information – usually from servants – and a terrific curiosity: offered two separate snippets of gossip to pursue she visibly wavers, 'much as a roulette ball might coyly hover between two numbers'. But her deductive powers are wayward. Miss Marple tries far less hard because her innate wisdom is so much greater. In *The Murder at the Vicarage*, though, she is decidedly Carolinian: 'I must admit that her rapid appearance on the scene and eager curiosity repelled me slightly,' says the vicar, who narrates the book. The later Miss Marple would never behave in such a way, which teeters upon the unladylike. Nor would she be described by the vicar's wife, Griselda, as 'that terrible Miss Marple'; although the later emphasis upon her 'fluffiness' is deceptive. As *Books and Bookmen* put it in an essay published after Agatha's death, 'Jane Marple is a tough old boot. If she was a "nice old knitting lady", so was Madame Defarge.'

Miss Marple shows her mettle early on in *The Murder at the Vicarage*. She is the only one of the elderly ladies – congregating at the vicarage for 'tea and scandal' – to realise where the attentions of the local glamour boy are directed ('Not *Lettice*. *Quite* another person, I should have said . . .'). She also reveals her creed: her way of looking at the world that makes her a natural detective. Griselda says that Miss Marple ought to be able to solve the case,

> 'like you did the time Miss Wetherby's gill of pickled shrimps disappeared. And all because it reminded you of something quite different about a sack of coals.'
>
> 'You're laughing, my dear,' said Miss Marple, 'but after all, that is a very sound way of arriving at the truth. It's really what people call intuition and make such a fuss about.'

Now this, of course, was straight from Agatha's grandmothers. Like Miss Marple, both Margaret Miller and Mary Ann Boehmer managed to hold a Christian faith in human nature with a realistic knowledge of its dire capabilities. Expect the worst, because the worst is so often true, but have belief, have faith, have compassion. That was the way of such women: upright, wise, Victorian: infinitely consoling to Agatha.

She was not yet forty. Yet she took comfort in the creation of a woman who was far older, and whose relationship with life was serene, not disturbing as her own had been. Miss Marple's emotional experience was almost non-existent, although her knowledge and understanding was immense; she was at a remove from life and happy to be so. Wisdom brought contentment. Agatha was wise in her books, less so in life. An exchange from the collection of short stories *The Thirteen Problems* shows the difference between Miss Marple and her creator. The character speaking is a painter, Joyce Lempriere:[20]

'I am an artist . . . I see things that you don't. And then, too, as an artist I have knocked about among all sorts and conditions of people. I know life as darling Miss Marple here cannot possibly know it.'

'I don't know about that, dear,' said Miss Marple. 'Very painful and distressing things happen in villages sometimes.'

This was what Agatha liked: the distillation of life into a containable microcosm – such as St Mary Mead – from which the answer to any problem could be deduced. She knew that it was, in a way, nonsense. She had lived through her own personal mystery story and she knew, none better, that there are no true solutions: that reality always has an unfinished, untidy quality. At the same time the world of her creation both fascinated and soothed her.

Omniscience is the greatest gift that the fictional detective can offer to readers: what infinite reassurance there is in the idea of the brain that understands everything, that sheds light on every dark area. But this quality is a gift, too, for writers. Agatha found support in her detectives, in their omniscience and detachment, which showed itself differently in Poirot and Marple. It is frequently said that Agatha disliked Poirot, although there is no real evidence for this; in later life she sought to protect him against misrepresentation as powerfully as if he were her own flesh and blood; but she had a deeper involvement with Miss Marple. 'Miss Jane Marple does not exist in the flesh and never has,' she wrote. 'She is entirely a creation of the brain.'[21] But this was not entirely true. Post-1926, Agatha intensely disliked any implication that she wrote from life; nevertheless it was the reality of Miss Marple – her resemblance to those strong, wise, benign women of Agatha's childhood – that gave her creator the greatest succour. Agatha enjoyed Poirot, but she *needed* Miss Marple. She craved the sound of that quiet, ladylike voice. Like detective fiction itself, it was a bulwark against the mad and intrusive world beyond: a voice from the grave, from the Army and Navy Stores, from Ashfield.

So comforting was Miss Marple that, in one of the stories from *The Thirteen Problems*, Agatha had the confidence to plant her in a 'Hydro'. This was an oblique reference to Harrogate, made very shortly after the event, and one of the male characters helps to lance the boil of memory by declaring that hydros are 'absolutely beastly! Got to get up early and drink filthy-tasting water. Lot of old women sitting about. Ill-natured tittle-tattle.'

Miss Marple freely admits the truth of this (as if *she* would not have known that Mrs Christie was sitting opposite her in the lounge! And exactly why she was there!). Then she launches into a very characteristic defence:

'Talking scandal, as you say – well, it *is* done a good deal. And people are very down on it – especially young people . . . But what I say is that none of these young people ever stop to *think*. They really don't examine the facts. Surely the whole crux of the matter is this: *How often is tittle-tattle*, as you call it, *true*! And I think if, as I say, they really examined the facts they would find that it was true nine times out of ten! That's really just what makes people so annoyed about it.'

'The inspired guess,' said Sir Henry.

'No, not that, not that at all! It's really a matter of practice and experience . . . What my nephew calls "superfluous women" have a lot of time on their hands, and their chief interest is usually *people*. And so, you see, they get to be what one might call *experts*. Now young people nowadays – they talk very freely about things that weren't mentioned in my young days, but on the other hand their minds are terribly innocent. They believe in everyone and everything . . .'

Agatha herself had believed, had trusted. She had suspected nothing; how she had needed Miss Marple by her side, to hint delicately that a man who wishes to play golf *quite* so often, well, of course, one *wonders* . . . Now it was too late. And, although she would never have guessed it, Agatha was about to plunge again.

She returned to Ur in February 1930, at the end of the digging season, having forged a firm friendship with the Woolleys. The previous May the couple had stayed at her new London house, a charming little mews at 22 Cresswell Place, off the Old Brompton Road, which she had bought in 1928 ('a radiantly green spring tree among grey roofs' was how the *Star* described it). The house still had its stables until Agatha had it redesigned: a large room downstairs, and above, a tiny kitchen, dining room, bedroom and marvellous green bathroom painted with dolphins. Soon she would buy another house, at 47–8 Campden Street in Kensington, then three more in the 1930s. The pre-war years were indeed, as she later said, her 'plutocratic period', before taxation prevented her keeping the better part of the money she earned.

In 1929 Agatha's brother Monty died and she herself was very ill after a vaccination (which she believed to have been double strength) against Rosalind's measles. However, after spending the end of the year at Ashfield she felt ready for more adventure. Travel was in her blood now: much as she loved her home, she became restless if she stayed in England too long.

This time at Ur she met a member of the expedition who had been away the previous season with appendicitis: Max Mallowan. 'If he had been there the year before, it would have been too soon for her after Archie,'[22] says his biographer. When Max met Agatha he was twenty-five, the same age as her nephew Jack Watts, whose contemporary he had been at New College. Max was so much younger than Agatha that she viewed him from a benign distance, although she noted his tact with the Woolleys and thought him clever. She got to know him better when Katherine, in typical autocratic fashion, ordered him to take Agatha on a tour of the local sights on the way from Ur to Baghdad. Agatha was somewhat embarrassed, thinking that this poor young man was being imposed upon. Max, however, was unperturbed, and the two discovered that they got along.

Katherine Woolley was, by now, revealing the oddity of her character. She had had an unusual life: half German on her father's side, she had gone up to Somerville in 1910 to read history (although she did not take her degree) and met her first husband while working in a prison camp during the First World War. Within six months of the wedding in 1919, Colonel Keeling shot himself. After this Katherine – who was highly intelligent, and a gifted artist ('nearly an artist', wrote Agatha in her autobiography, a trifle cattily) – gravitated towards archaeology, which was at that time a small, amateurish and gentlemanly world. She became part of the set-up at Ur as a volunteer assistant, but women were rare creatures on digs and, after a while, pressure was put on Leonard Woolley to regularise the situation. He and Katherine were married in 1927.

Although two years older than Agatha, Katherine looked far younger and was still extremely beautiful. Yet she lacked all normal sexual feeling. Her first husband's suicide may well have been linked to this. The extent of Woolley's congress with his wife was, apparently, to watch her having her bath at night (the fact that he did this gives the lie to the bizarre rumour that Katherine was, in truth, a man).

However, if Katherine had no desire to sleep with men she still wanted them in her thrall. The young men on the dig at Ur – including Max – would be commanded to brush her hair: 'They actually found this really embarrassing, oppressive, but impossible to refuse,'[23] says Agatha's friend, Dr Joan Oates. 'It was really very, very peculiar.' Katherine would also ask them to walk ten miles or so to the *souk* and buy two kilos of her favourite Arab confectionery. This had its advantages, however, as the sweets would keep her quiet for a day or two. 'She used to eat the whole lot, and then be sick.'

Hardly the behaviour of a *femme fatale*, yet such Katherine undoubtedly was, and it fascinated Agatha, so much so that she wrote her friend into *Murder in Mesopotamia* as the victim. 'We all thought that was a marvellous way of getting back at someone that you couldn't get back at any other way,' says Joan Oates. The portrayal of Louise Leidner is, unusually for Agatha, absolutely that of a real person, and this knocks the book slightly off-balance; not least because the actual solution is one of Agatha's weakest. What interests her is not the detective puzzle but the mystery of this singular woman, an *allumeuse*, as she is called, whose delight is to inflame passion, not to experience it.

'I was convinced', says Poirot, 'that Mrs Leidner was a woman who essentially worshipped *herself* and who enjoyed more than anything else the sense of power. Wherever she was, she *must* be the centre of the universe . . .'

Another character says of her that 'She didn't really care a damn. And that's why I hate her so. She's not sensual. She doesn't *want* affairs . . . She's a kind of female Iago. She *must* have drama. But she doesn't want to be involved herself. She's always outside pulling strings – looking on – enjoying it.'

This, then, was Katherine Woolley: beautiful, clever, fiercely independent, destructive. But Agatha's writerly instinct made her push the character further. She imagined what would happen if Katherine were to meet her match and fall helplessly in love. She imagined, too, a streak that was fatalistic to the point of *self*-destruction: beneath the detective-fiction ending there is a strange, subtle hint that Louise Leidner has placed herself in a situation that invites her own death. Simple in plot, complex in characterisation, this book – like two or three other Christies – would have made a magnificent Mary Westmacott.

Its narrative voice, that of Nurse Amy Leatheran, is determinedly prosaic: a foil to Mrs Leidner's weary allure. She sounds a little death knell for Archie Christie when told that Mrs Leidner's first husband was killed in the war: 'I think that's very pathetic and romantic, don't you, nurse?' To which she replies: 'It's one way of calling a goose a swan.' In other words, if the man had lived – if Archie had stayed – there would have been time for glamour to fade into curmudgeonly middle age.

So Nurse Leatheran speaks for a side of Agatha, the plain and sane side. This can also be seen in the character's reaction to the East – 'Frankly, what had struck me was the *mess* everywhere' – and to archaeology: 'Would you believe it, there was nothing to see but *mud*! Dirty mud walls about two feet high and that's all there was to it. Mr Carey took me here and there telling me things . . . all I thought was, "But how does he *know*"?' This was not, of course, exactly what Agatha thought. She was entranced with the work on the dig, sporting in her attitude to 'so-called bathrooms' and non-European hygiene. There was nothing parochial about her whatsoever; yet she understood the parochial mind – this, indeed, was part of her genius – and relished its homely good sense. She, too, would have had her sceptical moments in the face of Leonard Woolley's blind assurance that he was digging at the site of the Flood (but how did he *know*? He did not: he was wrong). What she liked about archaeology were the moments – despised by intellectuals like Woolley – when past came to meet present, and the buried fragments of human daily life were magically lifted into the air.

Also in *Murder in Mesopotamia* there is a hint of how Agatha perceived the young Max Mallowan, semi-portrayed as David Emmott, the quiet American who refuses to be bullied by Mrs Leidner and earns her grudging respect. 'I may say that of all the expedition, *as far as character and capacity were concerned*, Mr Emmott seemed to me the most fitted to bring a clever and well timed crime off satisfactorily,' says Poirot: an oblique semi-compliment. In fact Max was rather more under Katherine's spell than his fictional counterpart. The portrait of David Emmott was somewhat idealised, although Agatha shared Amy Leatheran's view that 'There was something about him that seemed very steadfast and reassuring.'

She enjoyed her time sightseeing with him in Iraq. A kind of friendly intimacy was established, not least because of what she described as the 'strenuous way of living': Max was required to escort Agatha to the lavatory when they stayed the night at the police post at Kerbala (sleeping in separate cells), and on the dreary road to Ukhaidir they sang songs before stripping off to their underwear to bathe in a desert lake. Agatha was relaxed with Max from early on, probably because the age difference dispersed the usual male-female tensions. Her joy of living returned during this strange journey through hot, exotic, dreamlike landscapes. The whole thing was *fun*, which was not something Agatha had experienced for a very long time (dashing and handsome though he undoubtedly was, Archie had never been fun). It felt like an interlude: surprising, serendipitous and, she felt, not to be repeated.

Yet there would be a further opportunity. Agatha was travelling through Greece with the Woolleys (Katherine somewhat vexed at her friend's closeness to her *protégé*) when a bundle of telegrams arrived at Athens to say that Rosalind was extremely ill with pneumonia. Agatha panicked – no doubt from guilt – then fell over and sprained her ankle. Whereupon Max announced that she would need a companion on her journey and he would return to England with her.

Throughout the four-day train journey (no flights in those days), the two got to know each other properly. Max knew a certain amount already, of course, but the whole Archie-Harrogate business would have sailed over his head. Not so for the rest of the world, whose judgement upon her had turned Agatha defensive and brittle: a woman who met her at the time wrote in her diary, 'Mrs Christie is actually *Agatha*!! Rather nice, very hard.' But Max divined the childlike vulnerability within. He understood her very well, in fact. He set about gaining her confidence.

Max himself was an extremely assured person, despite his lack of apparent advantages: he was short, physically unimpressive, and his background would not have been considered *comme il faut* by the people with whom he wished to mix (the Woolleys, as he wrote in his memoirs, were both snobs).[24] Yet people of this kind tend to work harder at making themselves liked, and this was Max's great gift. He could handle anyone. 'I foresee that you will always be able to manage me!!!' Agatha wrote to him in 1930. He took the trouble to understand what every situation required, then supplied it. When he first met Agatha he perceived that she was raw and bruised and, without being in any way obvious about it, soothed her. He made himself indispensable, although he never made himself cheap. His nephew, John, has described him as 'a lucky person, in general';[25] but, as the cliché has it, he made his own luck. Unlike those who are more naturally attractive, who tend to assume that luck will come their way, he set himself to do the right thing with the right people and thus rose high.

As an adult Max was very much the Englishman, with his membership of Boodle's and collection of eighteenth-century silver, but his lineage was wholly continental. His clever manners were not those of a typical Englishman, neither were his instinctive tastes: he had, for example, a passion for Prokofiev and Rachmaninov. He also had what A. L. Rowse called 'Austrian charm'. His grandfather – also named Max – was 'of Slav origin', and lived as a refugee in Vienna until 1879, when he was naturalised. By this time he had married a Czech girl and become a mill-owner, but when the mill burned down the family was left nearly destitute. In 1897 his son Frederick – Max's father – cut his losses and came to London. He had served in the Austrian army, from which he only obtained his certificate of release in 1913, but by that time he had become entirely British in his loyalties.

In 1902 he married a French girl, Marguerite Duvivier, who had come to London as a companion. Her background was also unusual: her mother, Marthe, had been an opera singer, performing Salome in the first production of Massenet's *L'Hérodiade*. The Mallowans were not, in fact, especially well suited. Marguerite was an emotional woman, religious and highly devoted to her three sons: Max the eldest, Cecil and Philip. Frederick was far more disciplined in his attitude to life. He had a duelling scar on his skull and, although he became a businessman, he remained very much the foreign soldier.

Max was extremely close to his mother, as Agatha had been to hers (later she would envy him his relationship with Marguerite – 'I went away horribly jealous of you having a mother to meet you'[26] – and later still be somewhat irritated by it). But he certainly did not enjoy the childhood that would support – and occasionally torment – Agatha with its idyllic memories. He grew up in London and his life lacked what he termed 'domestic peace'. His parents argued a great deal. 'I am indebted to both father and mother,' he wrote, 'for inclining my temperament towards peaceful companionship.'[27] Just as the happy marriage of Agatha's parents had led her to take her own for granted, so Max learned by example that marriage required courtesy and effort.

He went to Lancing, where he was a contemporary of Evelyn Waugh and Tom Driberg ('a very exceptional generation', Waugh later wrote), then read Greats at New College. 'The transition from Lancing to Oxford University where I spent four years, 1921–1925, was a step from purgatory to paradise.' Max belonged to the Brideshead era, and within his means he behaved accordingly. He got a fourth in mods and a third in finals; he threw what he called 'Derby Winner Parties', backing the right horse three years in succession; and he met his own Sebastian Flyte, a glamorous and aristocratic Catholic with whom he had a deep, powerful friendship.

Esme Howard, eldest son of Lord Howard of Penrith, was not Max's lover, but he was the closest that Max came to this relationship before he met Agatha. 'I feel', he wrote to her in 1930, 'that my love for you is the perfect continuation of that friendship with Esme that I thought I should never recover.' Like many clever, inexperienced young men, he found it easier and more congenial to fall in love for the first time with another man. Certainly Esme was a far more romantic figure than the average female undergraduate. He was brilliant, sweet and fatally sick; he died aged twenty-five of Hodgkin's disease. Max visited him for the last time at Portofino, 'in the Dowager Lady Carnarvon's villa', as he wrote in his memoirs. Coincidentally he endured a dark night of the soul at around the same time as Agatha – Esme had died five days before Agatha disappeared from Sunningdale – and found the same remedy for grief in intensely hard work. He also made a deathbed promise to Esme that he would take on his friend's religion. Technically Max was a Catholic through his French mother but he had never taken communion, and refused to be confirmed when a pupil at Lancing. Now love overcame rationality. Having seen the strength that Esme – 'the true saint' – derived from his religion, Max was convinced that he too should seek faith in God. The irony was that Agatha, who had always attended church, would no longer take communion after her divorce; the further irony was that Max reneged on his promise to Esme when he learned that the Catholic Church would not recognise his marriage to Agatha.

In fact his nature was never that of a devout Catholic. 'I always have a feeling that God is good and giving me his divine protection,' he wrote to Agatha during the War, and that was the extent of his religious feeling. He was a questioner, a lover of high-table talk rather than contemplation, a 'lover of beauty'[28] in art, history, flesh, rather than in the spiritual realm. He was also ambitious. Like Charles Ryder, he had to use chance and connections to get on in life. When his casually expressed interest in archaeology led, via the Dean of New College and the Keeper of the Ashmolean Museum, to an interview with Leonard Woolley in the summer of 1925, he determined to make as much as possible of the meeting. With Woolley that day at the British Museum was Katherine Keeling. Max was sharp enough to realise that he had to impress them both; his gift did not let him down, and he began work at Ur in the autumn.

Four years later, he had the sense to make friends with the lonely, likeable, well-to-do Mrs Christie. He did not move too fast. He simply established himself as the companion Agatha needed. He told her she had a 'noble' face: a charmingly tentative compliment of the kind that clever young men offer to older women. After a hurried parting at Paris, where Max met up with his mother and Agatha went home to Rosalind, she found herself – as he had intended – unable to forget him. In the spring of 1930 Max was working with Woolley at the British Museum. He wrote to Agatha at Ashfield, asking her to visit London (the pretext being that objects excavated from Ur were on display at the museum and she might like to see them). Her reply was intriguingly passionate, flustered and childlike.

> My Rosalind was much worse than they had told me – it wrung my heart to see her – skin and bones and pitifully weak . . . Oh! Max – everything has been beastly – like coming back into the worst kind of unquiet dream! . . . Can't you come down here some weekend, Max? I can't have parties or ask ordinary people – but you're such an angel.[29]

The letter ended with an invitation to breakfast at Cresswell Place; Agatha was visiting London for a series of meetings. In her autobiography she wrote calmly about the reunion with Max, saying that she felt shy seeing him again but was very pleased not to be 'losing touch'. The tone of her letters, however, is different. 'I feel quite homesick for you,'[30] she wrote, and gave away secrets that she told nobody else; for example about the Mary Westmacott pseudonym ('Don't tell anyone, will you? Not even your mother. [*Giant's Bread*] has been awfully well reviewed which is rather marvellous for me, isn't it?').[31] Quite plainly she had feelings for this young man, although she might not have been aware of them. She purported to have felt absolute surprise when, not long after the London meeting, Max visited Ashfield, and – just as Archie had done almost sixteen years earlier – marched into her bedroom and proposed to her. 'It had never occurred to me that Max and I would be or ever could be on those terms. We were *friends.*' Yet within no time at all she had accepted the idea of a second marriage.

She had not been without male attention since the split with Archie. Her husband might have wanted youth and unblemished beauty, but other men were less fussy; indeed the sexual culture as a whole was, in some ways, more robust than it is today. It was less obsessed with physical perfection, more with straightforward availability. As a divorced woman, Agatha was assumed to be in the market. A male acquaintance made a remark to her that found its way into *Unfinished Portrait*: 'You'll have either to take a lover or lovers. You will have to decide which it's to be.' In the book, Celia thinks that 'Lovers would be best. You'd be – almost safe – with lovers!' In other words a procession of men could not get close enough to hurt her in the way that Archie had done. That must never happen again.

There is no evidence, however, that Agatha succumbed to any of the passes that were made in her late thirties. It is as certain as it can be that she slept with only two men in her life. *Unfinished Portrait* says that after 'Dermot' she 'tried to learn to be alone', and the book would not lie about such a thing; if there was an affair to confess, this would have been the place to do it. In her autobiography Agatha wrote, very openly, that she was pleased about the passes (she always had an uncomplicated liking for men, and got along with them easily so long as there was no real emotional attachment). She told a rather charming story about a Dutch engineer whom she met on her first journey on the Orient Express. After they had had dinner together one night, he looked at her and said: 'I wonder now . . . No. I think it will be wiser if I do not ask.' To this she replied: 'I think you are very wise, and very kind.' But the question had been in the air. It was like the hotel scene in *Destination Unknown*: 'A good looking young Frenchman came out of the bar and across the terrace, cast a swift discreet glance at Hilary which, thinly disguised, meant: "Is there anything doing here, I wonder?"' Agatha took all this on board; in some ways she was very worldly, utterly unlike the grandmotherly image she later cultivated. 'You know, you're the sort of woman who ought to be raped' is a line spoken to the prim Joan Scudamore in *Absent in the Spring*. 'I'd rather like to rape you myself – and see if you looked the least bit different afterwards.' Agatha (or Mary Westmacott) could write this kind of thing without embarrassment and – more to the point – without inducing embarrassment in her reader.[32]

Yet with Max Mallowan, fourteen years her junior – Agatha was almost as senior to him as he was to Rosalind – she became as defence-less as a child. 'I think you *will* marry me, you know,' he said when he left her bedroom at Ashfield, after what Agatha described in her autobiography as hours of talking. He had made the running and prepared the ground, and he was fully confident as to the outcome. 'Of course I'm wise,' he wrote to her soon afterwards; 'wisdom is my chief defence and that's why I've yanked you out of the stalls as you put it.'[33]

For her part, Agatha began writing to Max like an excitable young girl. She seemed instantly seized by the idea of spending her life with him: an idea that had, according to her autobiography, come as a complete shock.

'Dearest – Do I really mean what you say to you? I've just got your letter – oh! my dear. I would love to mean that to you. And I, too, feel the same – that being with you *is* a kind of freedom.'[34]

This was an example of Max's extreme cleverness at providing Agatha with what she needed from a putative relationship: some-thing utterly unlike her first marriage (luckily for Max, as he could not have competed with Archie in the romance stakes). She wanted to feel both liberated and reassured. 'When we are companion dogs the world seems a wonderful place . . . a rich freedom . . . there is *no* feeling of restraint or captivity or being "tied down" – I would never have believed anything could be like it.'[35] Her willingness to write these things was desperately touching, in the light of the terrible betrayal she had suffered. Yet there was a sense in which she was writing *for* Max, as a thank-you; it is almost impossible that he should have unleashed such intense feelings so incredibly quickly. The love letters that lead up to the marriage are, in fact, a performance on both sides. 'It is obviously decreed that you should be my sunflower' was the kind of thing that Max wrote to Agatha. Not exactly insincere; but not the usual tone of love letters (such as the ones that Archie wrote, which labour under an exquisitely male sense of strain).

Of course Agatha and Max were not usual lovers. Nothing about this courtship was normal. The most interesting irony was that the dominant partner should have been Agatha – she had the money and the experience, Max had not a penny and was almost certainly a virgin – yet it was he who took charge. He assumed the parental role. He did not need a mother figure, having a perfectly devoted mother of his own; but this was exactly what Agatha needed, and Max knew it. He was not so much an emotional substitute for Archie as for Clara, the person whom Agatha missed more than any other. With Clara she had been completely herself, free of any demands to restrain her nature, able to let her imagination take flight in the secure knowledge that her mother was there, at Ashfield, the centre of the real world. With Max she recaptured something of this feeling: the sense that life was safe. He enabled her to behave like a child again. This suited him very well, as he was a natural teacher and delighted in telling Agatha that she should learn Greek, read Gibbon and take drawing classes to help on the dig. He wrote to her about Rosalind, saying, 'She is more grown up than you isn't she ange?' And, knowing very well what she most wanted to hear: 'Agatha, I don't love you merely with the glorious eyes of the blind, but I see you as you are.'

'I do believe you love me for what I am,' she replied, before adding this note of sobriety. 'Mere love is rather an idiotic business – approved of by Nature, but capable of inflicting a lot of unhappiness on individuals. But you are my friend, Max . . .'[36]

In a strange way the age difference made Agatha better able to cope (even though it was minimised to six years on the marriage certificate: Agatha was '37', Max '31'). She lamented it loudly – 'your damnably silly age!!' – but in fact it rendered Max less threatening. Nothing about him would resemble her marriage to Archie, who would never have written to say 'If you feel serious my ange remember that life together will be a glorious joke if only we choose to make it so'. She was anxious, however, that the joke should not be on her. She had already been made to look ridiculous in the eyes of the world. Her sister was adamantly against the marriage and did not hesitate to tell Agatha so (Max never really forgave the Wattses for this).[37] Two weeks before the wedding Madge sent a present of handkerchiefs: 'It is not suggested that they will be useful for mopping tears let it be clearly understood.' She hoped that Max would take care of her sister; if not, 'one of his old mummies will arise and deal with the matter which I have been led to understand that the said mummies thoroughly understood'. Jack Watts, who was very fond of Agatha, had never liked Max at Oxford; both he and Madge were suspicious of Max's motives and viewed him as a fortune-hunter. This thought must have occurred to Agatha herself, particularly when she read his letters about their honeymoon, which he was planning and for which she was paying. They were heading for Venice ('I am having a white blazer made in anticipation of a warm séjour') through what was then Yugoslavia, and on to Greece ('I wish I had time to learn to play the shepherd's pipe'). Meanwhile Max wrote to Agatha about the registrar's fees for the actual wedding, 'because it's right that I should pay for all that'.

The ceremony was due to take place in September, at St Columba's Church in Edinburgh. The religious question was resolved, quite easily on Max's side, less so on Agatha's: 'You *are* still sure of yourself, aren't you? I mean about the religious side. You've no qualms of conscience or guilty feeling?' She continued to dither through the summer of 1930. 'One moment a bit of blind panic . . . I feel "I won't – I won't – I *won't* marry anybody. Never again" . . . But it's Max. It's being with Max and having him always – to hold on to when I feel unhappy.'[38]

This pattern was repeated even as plans for the wedding advanced. At the end of August, she went on holiday to Skye with Rosalind, Carlo and Mary Fisher (who would be witnesses), then moved down to Edinburgh. From Skye she wrote of 'the madness of exchanging mediocre but safe happiness for great happiness but possible disaster. You see, Max dear, I do so hate being unhappy . . . Oh! my dear – be very very sure – We could always be friends, you know, even if we didn't marry.'[39]

Again this has the slight air of the performance, although the feelings beneath it were genuine. But it was designed to get a response of the type at which Max excelled: 'You are to go on being brave for another fortnight so that you may be the happiest ange in all the world.' In fact, Max never really doubted that Agatha would go through with the wedding. The one time that she did seem to want to call it off he played the man's trump card and withdrew contact. 'You are a *pig* – Max – three days since you left and not one word from you . . . You know – you can't really care. Oh! Max.'[40] Which resolved the situation.

Max's greater worry before September was probably the Woolleys' reaction. He still needed their patronage, even if only for one more season; and he craved the goodwill of Katherine, however much he disparaged her to Agatha. It is impossible to know what he felt towards her during the years at Ur. But the portrait of Louise Leidner in *Murder in Mesopotamia* is of a deeply alluring woman, and an inexperienced young man such as Max might well have been susceptible. Agatha had had an inkling of this after her first sightseeing tour with Max: she returned to Baghdad, longing for a hot bath; Max drew one for her then offered it to Katherine. As late as 1943 Agatha would write to him on 14 February, saying, 'Have you remembered to send your Valentine to K. Woolley?!!!' She made a joke of it, but was Max's behaviour really so funny?

In May 1930 he was insistent that he and Agatha should both write to Katherine with the dire news of their engagement. Her reply was gracious: 'It is lovely to know that two people I love so much as you two are going to be so happy', although revenge would come later. Katherine did say that Max should be forced to wait before the marriage, as it would be bad for him to get everything he wanted so quickly. This was a perceptive, if outrageously rude, remark, but keeping men keen was not Agatha's style. As she wrote to Max: 'It's no good – I shall never have proper K. like Olympian attitude towards the male sex. I shall either think they are <u>pigs</u> or else perfect darlings.'[41]

She had had 'K. like' allure once, of course, in the days when men like Reggie Lucy had fallen at her buttoned boots. Now she was tired, lonely and intensely grateful. Somehow she knew that, despite everything, this alliance with Max would suit her. It would restore her wrecked confidence – see, Archie, I can still get myself a husband! Fifteen years younger than you! – and it would allow her the freedom she cherished. It would not interfere with her writing, as Max was far too sensible to do such a thing and far too confident to be jealous of her success. It would not oblige her to change herself in any way, as she so obviously should have done with Archie. She worried, nonetheless, about her fading looks and her weight, although she tried to make a joke of it. 'Perhaps I am (little Piglet!) your favourite size!! Do say I am!' Later Max would tease her a good deal about this. But now he wrote, 'I know you are very beautiful', and she loved him for the lie.

Above all, marriage would provide companionship. For this she would take the many risks. She craved solitude, but not infinite solitude. And those bleak, sad years of the late 1920s had nearly killed her, going to bed alone, seeing her ageing face and body in the mirror, trying to make a life out of friendships and parties, remembering life as it had once been, clinging to Peter as if only his love came between her and nothingness. Now this little smiling man had come along to save her. 'Bless you my love,' he wrote to her on 6 September, five days before the wedding. 'I want you to be as happy as I am and I think you will be, my darling.' This was kindness, and she drank it in like water in the desert. She would be a better wife to him than she had been to Archie, because she was not in love with him. Nor was he in love with her. They were together for reasons other than love; and this, she thought, might very well make for greater happiness.

She wrote as much a year after their marriage, when she was working on *Lord Edgware Dies*. The words are Poirot's, the reasoning Agatha's.

'And suppose he marries a girl who loves him passionately, is there such a great advantage in that? Often I have observed that it is a great misfortune for a man to have a wife who loves him.

She creates the scenes of jealousy, she makes him look ridiculous, she insists on having all his time and attention. Ah! *Non*,
it is not the bed of roses.'

So she became, in a way, a realist. She compromised. After the happy
honeymoon ('so many lovely things') she accepted the call of the
Woolleys upon Max, and his instant jump to their attention. They
behaved very badly, in fact, as they had done all along. 'The devils
are going to do their best not to make it easy for us', as Max put it.
Agatha recognised that Leonard was merely weak, and she blamed
Katherine. She also wrote: 'K. I think is jealous not of happiness, but
simply and only of *money*!'

Woolley extracted the last ounce of work from Max before the
wedding ('Made him sit up and draw pottery practically the night
before they were married,' says Joan Oates),[42] then recalled him to
Baghdad on 15 October. This would have been all right, but Agatha
had fallen ill in Athens on the last days of the honeymoon. It was a
kind of food poisoning, apparently brought on by 'joyful eating of
Crevettes and Langoustines', and it was very serious. Agatha was taken
into hospital and Max left for work. 'The doctor has just been,' she
wrote to him from Greece, where the treatment cost her a fortune,
'and there is no doubt, from the coldness of his manner, that he
regards you as a brutal and inhuman man . . . My poor Max – and
you so kind and tender to your Ange.'[43]

What she really thought, it is impossible to know. Of course the
Woolleys – Katherine – were to blame for terrorising Max into such
craven obedience (especially as they themselves did not turn up at
Baghdad for another week), but should he not have said that his loyalties now were to Agatha? She herself insisted that he return to Baghdad.
Nevertheless she would surely have liked him to insist that he stay
with her. 'Don't forget to tell me exactly how you are and whether
you really are free from all traces of that poisoning,' he wrote, in his
precise way, then: 'I don't think I dread meeting the Woolleys half as
much as I did, I feel more aloof and independent now that I have
my ange to think of.'[44]

She kept wisely silent on the subject for five years before referring, in *Death in the Clouds*, to 'an Englishman whose wife had been taken ill. He himself had to be somewhere in Iraq by a certain date. *Eh bien*, would you believe it, he left his wife and went on.' The English girl to whom this story is told replies, 'One's work has to come first, I suppose', but the mere fact that Agatha brought up the incident suggests it had rankled.

Despite Max's dutiful return from his honeymoon, relations with the Woolleys were unsalvageable. 'It was Katherine who not only forbade Agatha to come to Ur, but said she was not allowed to come to Iraq at all,' says Joan Oates. 'Because Max had suggested that she should stay in a hotel in Baghdad and he could go off on the occasional weekend and see her.' This, it was made clear, would not be possible; Woolley himself had hinted as much when dining with Agatha before the wedding. It was quite mad, but it really did not matter very much. Max was in a position to get work elsewhere and this would be his last season at Ur. He had gained experience with Leonard Woolley; he had gained a wife; through his marriage he became a man of means. The future was bright for him. For Agatha, who wrote to him from London where her journey finally ended:

It is the first time for several years that I have arrived in England without a feeling of such misery.

My dear, you have lifted so much from my shoulders – so much that I didn't even know was there – I can feel the wounds healing all over. They are still there – and very little would open them again.[45]

This was, perhaps, a reminder to Max that she was still vulnerable. Back at Ashfield – where Rosalind had coolly accepted her mother's new status, saying, 'I think it's rather a good thing having two sets of parents' – she wrote:

I couldn't bear you ever to be less nice than you are now . . . I think men often are their best at about your age. They have a finer vision and a bigger ideal of life. And then, very often, life narrows them – they get egotistical, self-centred, petty,

self-indulgent and censorious – you mustn't – you must always
be Max.[46]

She was happy, though. 'Everyone has said I look very well
and ten years younger and that being married to you suits me.'
What also suited may have been that she was married but had her
own life while Max was away. She was free but she was safe, just
like in the old days. A letter from November 1930 bubbles over
with effervescence.

> Have just had a most exciting and reprehensible day – I have
> been to a SALE! . . . Oh! I have enjoyed myself . . . A lovely
> Chippendale Tallboys went for £8 10/-, I just didn't get there
> in time. Just as well perhaps – for where I should have put
> that I really do *not* know! What fun life is. I do think archae-
> ology is the most fascinating thing in the world . . .
>   I am still doing my best to be a worthy wife. Have drawn
> one super pot [she was taking art lessons, as suggested by
> Max] . . . *Black Coffee* coming in on December 8th – so I
> shall have to go up to town for rehearsals next week – I'm
> really *very* busy just now . . . Six *eminent* detective story
> writers have been asked to broadcast again[47] – we're all getting
> together on December 5th to plan the thing out a bit –
> Dorothy Sayers will begin on January 10th, I shall follow on
> 17th and again on 31st – all rather fun.
>   Another thing I'm doing is embroidering a peacock – I
> started it when I was nineteen and found it the other day . . .
> I feel as though I'd gone back to nineteen again!

In December she wrote from the Ladies' Army and Navy Club –
both her houses were let –

> just to say that you are my own darling Max and that I love
> you frightfully and I might fill up the page with kisses like
> children do – !! *Very* sweet kisses . . . I really am *frightfully*
> happy, darling. And that's what gives such a zest to everything
> and makes me feel life is so wonderful.

Max replied in kind: 'Ange, shut your eyes now and pretend that you are in my arms and that I am returning your kisses.'

The opening of *Black Coffee* was a particular delight – Madge was there, as Agatha had been at the opening of *The Claimant* back in 1924, so were Nan and George Kon – and the reviews were good. 'I like Francis Sullivan better than Charles Laughton as Poirot. He makes him much more lovable,' she wrote to Max. On the strength of this success, a play version of *The Secret of Chimneys* was scheduled to be staged, although this did not happen:[48] 'but it's *exciting* any way'. There was even a possibility of work from Hollywood: 'We might clean up a nice little sum and with it we'd raze a mound to the ground!', which must have sounded like music in Max's ears. 'Darling Max – why are you so far away? Or why am I? But Rosalind is very pleased to have me.'[49]

On Christmas Eve she wrote more soberly. 'It's my old wedding day today. It's always been a sad day for me – but not this year. Bless you, my darling, for all you have done and given back to me.'

Agatha went out to Ur for the last time in the spring of 1931. 'I have written to Katherine and hope all will be well.' Rather oddly – but Agatha tended to enjoy displays of forbearance – she dedicated *The Thirteen Problems* to the Woolleys. By this time Max had a new job lined up, with Dr Campbell Thompson at Nineveh (the eighth century BC capital of the Assyrian empire). 'CT', as he was called, was not an especially clever archaeologist, although he and his wife were easier to deal with than the Woolleys. Still he too thought it his business to 'vet' Agatha before she could be permitted to visit the dig. He also remonstrated with her when she bought a writing table to use at the sparsely furnished dig house at Mosul. Economy was his passion, and he could not understand why Agatha should not write her books on a packing case. What business this was of his, the Lord alone knows, although Agatha did not say so. Her good humour in the face of her husband's strange colleagues – who had the dry, petty, rather childlike belief in their superiority that often characterises the 'intellectual' – was remarkable; perhaps she simply drifted away from it, secure as she was in her own creative world. Anyway she did not want to make trouble for Max. She strove to get along with CT and his wife, Barbara, making an effort she had never bothered with when it came to Archie's golfing friends. Max went out to the Nineveh dig in the autumn and Agatha went alone to Rhodes, where she worked on *Lord Edgware Dies* before joining her husband at the end of October and finishing the book (dedicated to the Campbell Thompsons) on her table.

Her letters to Max had become more lover-like. Before the honeymoon there had been no talk of the sexual delights that awaited, if indeed these were anticipated. 'Don't forget your hot water bottle,' Max wrote; and, in his innocence, 'I can promise you stiffs all through life'; he meant the dead bodies that emerge from archaeological digs. But a year later Agatha wrote: 'Max – sometimes I want to sun myself on a hotel beach and bathe with nothing on – in daylight – and then I want to lie on my face in the sun and have you kiss me all down my back. Can we ever do that? Is there any place? We could have in Greece, I believe, only we weren't like that then, were we?'[50]

This letter rather gives the lie to A. L. Rowse's theory that Agatha and Archie's marriage ended, in part, because she lacked sex drive.[51] Agatha was proper, but she was not at all prim. 'Slip in, and gently in/Till breast and neck and arms/Are kissed and swung . . . ,' she wrote, in a wonderfully sexy poem called 'The Evening Bathe'. Swimming was always a voluptuous experience for her; as, in 1931, was her second husband. 'I go to bed so sleepy I haven't even the energy for sensual thoughts!' she wrote in December, when back in England for a hectic Christmas.

In Rhodes, meanwhile, she had gone into a cathedral and 'said a prayer to (I think it was!) St John the Baptist. Not perhaps a very good person to pray to for a son.' She wanted a new family, or so she believed. Her own – 'restless Punkie, indefatigable Rosalind' – exhausted and exasperated her. But she was past forty, and her sole pregnancy ended in miscarriage in 1932. Just as well, perhaps, as when Rosalind's child was born Max would write to Agatha saying how relieved he was not to have a baby, and to have all his wife's attention to himself.

Not that she had all *his* attention. In Rhodes, she began to feel that their separate lives might be a cause for concern.

Darling are you real? Or just a dream I had . . . I'd like you to be here to laugh at me when I come out of the sea all happy like a dog . . . Suppose I never saw you again? As soon as one loves anyone one gets afraid, doesn't one? That is why dogs go about growling with a bone. They're convinced it will be taken from them by other dogs. Are there any other dogs at Mosul, darling? Perhaps you'd better not tell me if there are![52]

In fact Max was far more concerned about his career at this time. But what Agatha had called 'the wounds' were opening again: just a little. She had had one unfaithful husband and was preparing herself for the possibility of another (so much younger, after all), although she showed no outward sign of insecurity. She remained the happy, busy, successful 'Agatha Christie', with her theatrical triumphs and her procession of acclaimed novels: *The Sittaford Mystery, Peril at End House, Lord Edgware Dies, Murder on the Orient Express* and *Why Didn't They Ask Evans?* were published between 1931 and 1934, with two sets of short stories, *The Listerdale Mystery* and *Parker Pyne Investigates*. This last is an interesting one. Parker Pyne is a specialist in happiness: he runs a business that supplies happiness to discontented people. Although not a detective he has the quality of omniscience that Agatha found so irresistible, and he is both wise and kind. He is visited, for example, by a middle-aged wife whose husband is straying with a pretty young secretary. The situation is presented as too familiar to be distressing – a consoling idea in itself – and the solution is simple: the wife must smarten herself up and conduct a harmless romance of her own. This works so well at bringing the husband back into line that Agatha must have wondered whether she should have done the same thing with Archie.

For it was Archie who was on her mind. Why otherwise should she have written *Unfinished Portrait?* She had been busy enough already in 1933; in that year alone she had produced *Orient Express, Why Didn't They Ask Evans?*, some of the stories in *The Listerdale Mystery* (others were reprints from magazines) and *Parker Pyne*

Investigates. Her urgent desire to write, which had relaxed its grip in the first two years of her marriage, was burning again. And what she wanted to do was revisit memory. She wanted to be the one to open 'the wounds'. She was a writer. Only a writer would behave in such a way.

So out it all came again: the idyll of childhood, the beloved mother and husband, the end of her world. How could she bear to write it? She bore it because that was what Mary Westmacott did.

She had helped Max achieve the goal of his own dig. After a season at Nineveh he was now in charge at Arpachiyah in Iraq, which he excavated – for one year only, due to the political situation – in 1933. Agatha did drawings and described herself as 'bursting with happiness' when 'our pimple of a mound' proved to contain some magnificent pottery. She enjoyed herself, although her son-in-law described her attitude to archaeological life thus: 'Max liked it, so Agatha liked it.'[53] Meanwhile she planned *Unfinished Portrait*, that hymn of love to the past.

At the end of the book she described the man who wanted to marry her after her divorce:

> He told me that what I needed was gentleness . . . he'd been unhappy too. He understood what it was like.
>   We enjoyed things together . . . we seemed to be able to share things. And he didn't mind if I was myself. I mean, I could say I was enjoying myself and be enthusiastic without his thinking me silly . . . . He was – it's an odd thing to say, but he really was – like a *mother* to me . . .

A part of her wants to marry the man, 'Michael', but in the book she does not do so. Her fear of being hurt is too great. She tries again to kill herself and is rescued. Then she goes out into the world to face an unknown future. 'She went back at thirty-nine – to grow up,' writes the narrator of the book. 'And she left her story and her fear – with me . . .' This, perhaps, was how Agatha felt when she reached the end of *Unfinished Portrait*. The past was now the past, buried within words. But of course it was not so simple.

I am tired of the past that clings around my feet,
I am tired of the past that will not let life be sweet,
I would cut it away with a knife and say
Let me be myself – reborn – today.

But I am afraid of the past – that it will creep back to my feet
And look in my face and say, 'You laugh and eat
But I am here with you yet . . .
You would not remember – but I will not let you forget . . .'
What is or is not courage? Who shall say?
Shall I be brave or base if I cut the past away?[54]

War

'It's not the crisis, it's the Christie, that is keeping people awake at night!'
(newspaper advertisement for *Murder is Easy*, 1939)

'I am not very young, darling, and three years is a big gap'
(from a letter sent to Max Mallowan in December 1944)

The years around the war, between 1937 and 1949, were the most fertile period of Agatha's writing life. A handful of her books had an emotional content, shadowed by their author's experience, which put them in a subtly different class: *Death on the Nile, Sad Cypress, Five Little Pigs* and *The Hollow*. Others have an unusual depth beneath the surface cleverness: *Hercule Poirot's Christmas, Murder Is Easy, And Then There Were None, Evil Under the Sun, N or M?, The Body in the Library, The Moving Finger, Towards Zero, Taken at the Flood* and *Crooked House*. Within this period Agatha also wrote her finest collections of short stories, *Murder in the Mews* and *The Labours of Hercules*. Finally she produced two superb Westmacotts: *Absent in the Spring* and what is probably her best book of all, *The Rose and the Yew Tree*.

It cannot be said too often: Agatha was a writer. To say otherwise is, as Poirot would have put it, to deny the evidence. (Who else wrote so much? Blyton? Wodehouse? Both of whom, like Agatha, created a world of solid artistic reality.) At the same time there is no denying that she was under intense pressure to produce books throughout the war. Her financial situation changed and, for a time, she was effectively living hand-to-mouth. Yet this does not fully explain the insatiable creativity of her middle years: the brilliance of these books produced under duress, the fact that when she had a bare few days at her disposal – a precious holiday during the war – she completed *Absent in the Spring*. She had to write for money; but she also had to write. It was as simple as that.

'Do you think of me as successful? How funny,' says Henrietta Savernake in *The Hollow*.

'But you are, my dear. You're an artist. You must be proud of yourself; you can't help being.'

'I know,' said Henrietta. 'A lot of people say that to me. They don't understand – they don't understand the first thing about it . . . Sculpture isn't a thing you set out to do and succeed in. It's a thing that gets at you . . . so that you've got, sooner or later, to make terms with it. And then, for a bit, you get some peace – until the whole thing starts over again.'

The way in which Agatha wrote – with apparent ease – and the kind of books she produced – mostly lightweight – have led commentators to take her extraordinary output for granted. But what she did *was* extraordinary, and although she herself did not choose to see it that way it *was* the most important thing in her life. 'One never saw that in life, she was so modest,' wrote her friend A. L. Rowse. '[But] her persona as a writer was something quite different, almost as if there were two personalities.'[1]

Two, yes: because Agatha wanted her ordinary life as well. She fed off it. She enjoyed it for its own sake, and it was essential to her writing; her drug, in a way, since unlike most writers she used no others. As Rowse wrote, 'Outwardly she had a full and normal social life, family, two marriages, friends, hospitality, entertainment, housekeeping (at which she was very good), shopping (which she much enjoyed) . . . All ministered to Agatha's life of the imagination.'

'[Henrietta] had learned the trick, years ago, of shutting her mind into watertight compartments. She could play a game of bridge, conduct an intelligent conversation, write a clearly constructed letter, all without giving more than a fraction of her essential mind to the task.'[2]

In the 1930s Agatha's life acquired a pattern that then fragmented into war, separation, anxiety, death. There was not the intensity of suffering she had known in 1926, but her determined joy of living might have been shaken had she not, in some inner part of herself, been insulated against reality. The easy answer is that her marriage had brought security. In fact it was not quite that simple. More subtly, her marriage allowed her to be the person she had been when she *truly* felt secure: a child, in other words, whose imagination now roamed through adult lands, and dealt in adult mysteries.

There were real things in her past that she did not want to lose, but in the 1930s they both quit the scene. Peter was immortalised in *Dumb Witness* (*'brave chien, va!'*) and died the following year, 1938. 'My little friend and loving companion in affliction,' Agatha had written to Max in 1930. 'You've never been through a *really* bad time with nothing in the world but a dog to hold on to.' Peter had been her 'child', and later in a letter she remembered him 'jealously pushing between us'. Max liked dogs, but Agatha adored them: for their goodness and loyalty, the qualities she valued above all others.

Max also liked Ashfield, or so he had said in the early days. 'You need not worry as to whether I shall find Ashfield like home for any abode will be home with you and I shall like to think that you have not lost the older memories that you love.'³ Yet Agatha was sensitive to Max as she had not been to Archie, and she knew that he was uncomfortable with the weight of memory in that house.

There were other reasons why she sold Ashfield at the end of the 1930s. 'Once it had been all countryside out of Torquay,' she wrote in her autobiography, 'three villas up the hill and then the road petered out into country. The lush green fields where I used to go to look at the lambs in spring had given way to a mass of small houses. No one we knew lived in our road any longer. It was as though Ashfield had become a parody of itself.' Perhaps it would have been too painful for Agatha to see these changes inflicted upon her home: it had lived so powerfully in her memory. But when Max said, 'You've been getting worried about Ashfield, you know', this was a coded message, and she knew it. She sold. At the time it felt like the right thing, but when the house was finally demolished in the 1960s she cried like a child. 'Sometimes I feel very homeless,' she wrote to Max in 1944. 'I find myself thinking "I want to go home" and then it seems to me I have no home – and I do long for Ashfield. I know you didn't like it – but it was my childhood's home and that counts.'[4]

She had bought a very different kind of house – Max's house, as she called it – at the end of 1934. Winterbrook House at Wallingford (convenient for Oxford, described in *Dumb Witness* as Market Basing) was an elegant yet homely building, with a very lovely long garden that stretched down to the Thames. The façade was Queen Anne, close to the main road but screened by thick dark holly; the back of the house was Georgian; a staff flat and stables were seventeenth century, and there was a walled kitchen garden. The main bedroom overlooked the lawn with its spreading cedar tree and deep, calm shadows. Max also had this view from his library, a double-length room thick with cigarette smoke, comfortably piled with archaeological journals and volumes of Herodotus: 'the best gossip in antiquity,' in Max's phrase.

A. L. Rowse often went to lunch at Winterbrook: 'a cosy, warm, hospitable, upper middle-class interior', as he wrote in his diaries, 'with all the comforts and amenities, the pretty china and good furniture that Agatha's prosperity has bought . . . that sunny house where the living rooms at the back look over their flat water-meadows to the river'.[5]

The essence of middle England, like Wallingford itself, and surely the perfect home for Agatha Christie. But Agatha was about to acquire the house of her dreams.

Greenway House, that magical white box set above the gleaming Dart; Greenway, with its wild romantic gardens; Greenway, rooted in its Devon history and yet, with its ghostly pallor, looking as if it might at any moment vanish into the air. 'I sat on the seat overlooking the house on the river,' wrote Agatha to Max in 1942. 'It looked very white and lovely – remote and aloof as always – I get a kind of pang over its beauty . . . "Too dear for our possessing" but what excitement to possess it! I thought tonight, sitting there – it is the loveliest place in the world – it quite took my breath away.'[6]

The house she had dreamed into life at Ashfield – the river at the end of the garden, the vast unknown rooms that opened out from familiar doors – was now a reality. Agatha bought Greenway in 1938 for six thousand pounds: an unbelievable sum, it would seem, equivalent to not much over £200,000 in today's values, but not everybody wanted to take on such a property and its thirty-three acres. With the help of architect Guilford Bell (nephew of her friend, Aileen, with whom she had stayed in Australia during the Empire Tour), Agatha rediscovered the perfect Georgian proportions of her new acquisition. Wings had been added in 1815 but Guilford took them down, leaving the house symmetrical and exquisite. The main rooms opened out from a central hall: library, dining room and sitting room, which itself led to a drawing room with long, white windows giving on to a small, secret lawn. The first floor had five main rooms, with a large handsome master bedroom and a vast lavatory with a wooden surround, the kind that Agatha favoured. Above were more bedrooms and a bedsitting room for Rosalind; behind was a complexity of servant quarters, a pantry downstairs and a huge high-ceilinged kitchen. Everything was high, deep, rightful. Everywhere was secrecy, enchantment, mystery. A glamorous house on the grand scale, yet relaxed and full of ease, even if its beauty was too great for it to be a home of the kind that Ashfield had been.

The original Greenway House was built around 1530 and destroyed, probably by fire, around two hundred years later. Agatha kept notes on the history of her possession (her mother had had a similar habit of scrawling down facts on scraps of paper): 'Named because on the "grain way" across the Dart. Belonged to Gilbert family. Sir Humphrey Gilbert, discoverer of Newfoundland, born there *c*.1537. His mother's second husband was a Raleigh . . . Rebuilt 1780s . . .' It was a famous house, like glorious Ugbrooke near Exeter, where Agatha had met Archie Christie. It was her Devon past, where her soul lived. As a girl she had seen it from the Dart; Clara had pointed it out to her; now it was her own. Agatha was too intelligent to take for granted that she was living in a house her imagination might have conjured. She tramped around the gardens, an overgrown tangle of rare plants that she and Max had begun to cultivate, and felt that she was, indeed, inhabiting a dream.

She would write about this in later books, the place that seemed too beautiful to be real: it was there in *Endless Night* ('The house isn't enough, you see. It has to have the setting. That's just as important') and in *Hallowe'en Party* ('If you wished, what could there not be?' 'A garden for gods to walk'). Yet in both these books the desire to create beauty leads to evil. Beauty alone is not enough: it needs humility and warmth and humanity. 'But, alas, there would be no garden blossoming on an island in the Grecian Seas . . . Instead there would be Miranda – alive and young and beautiful.'

Earlier she had used literal representations of Greenway in *Five Little Pigs* and *Dead Man's Folly*, and in both books it is the setting for a murder. One victim dies on the battery overlooking the Dart, another in the rather sinister boathouse.[7] The house is portrayed as incredibly beautiful, although there is no sense whatever of Agatha's own relationship with it. 'It was a gracious house, beautifully proportioned,' is her simple description of 'Nasse House' in *Dead Man's Folly*. 'Mrs Folliat went through a door on the left into a small daintily furnished sitting room and on into the big drawing-room beyond': precisely the configuration of Greenway.

Nasse House is the family home of the Folliats and, although the former lady of the house now lives at the lodge, she has a relationship to Nasse that Agatha could not share with Greenway. Poirot comments on the 'superb and noble mansion', and Mrs Folliat nods 'in a matter of fact manner. "Yes. It was built by my husband's great-grandfather in 1790. There was an Elizabethan house previously. It fell into disrepair and burned down in about 1700. Our family has lived here since 1598."'

A part of Agatha envied Mrs Folliat this casual grandeur. 'Mrs Folliat of Nasse House, daughter of a long line of brave men . . .' She herself was more like her clever little detective, standing and gazing in half-bewilderment: 'It is a beautiful place,' said Poirot. 'A beautiful house, beautiful grounds. It has about it a great peace, great serenity.'

Agatha took a deep, quiet pride in having acquired this miraculous home by her own means. Yet she remained fascinated by those who did not need to buy, to work, to strive; those who do not change or doubt, who cannot be other than themselves. Mrs Folliat belongs at Nasse House as surely as the trees in its grounds, yet she is the same person living in the lodge as she would be in the big house. This was the idea at the heart of *The Rose and the Yew Tree*.

> . . . it was nevertheless a sordid room. In the middle of it, sitting with her feet tucked up under her, and embroidering a piece of silk, was Isabella . . . She and the room had, I felt, nothing to do with each other. She was here, in the midst of it, exactly as she might have been in the midst of a desert, or on the deck of a ship. It was not her home. It was a place where she happened, just at the moment, to be.

As a child, Agatha had longed to be 'Lady', and now in a sense she was. Later she would become 'Lady Mallowan' through her husband's knighthood, then 'Dame Agatha' in her own right.[8] Now she was mistress of Greenway House. But her idea of aristocracy was something different: it could not be acquired, achieved or learned. This is the spell exerted by Isabella, the 'Princess imprisoned in the ruined castle', over John Gabriel, the dynamic and brilliant man who falls in love with her.

> 'I didn't want to be a common little boy. I went home and said to my father, "Dad, when I grow up I want to be a Lord. I want to be Lord John Gabriel."
> '"And that's what you'll never be," he said. "You've got to be born that kind of a Lord. They can make you a Peer if you get rich enough but it's not the same thing." And it isn't the same thing. There's something – something I can never have – oh, I don't mean the title.'

The Rose and the Yew Tree is complex: it deals with class, but more than that it deals with the mystery in human beings. In middle age

Agatha was still in love with the ineffable, the numinous. She grew older and coarser, grander and greedier, contented and assured. But her dreams did not change.

Meanwhile Max's life was going according to plan. After his season at Arpachiyah, the first in charge of his own dig and officially paid for by his sponsors, the British School of Archaeology,[9] in 1935 he went with Agatha to Chagar Bazar in Syria. Two years later they also began to excavate Tell Brak, around twenty miles away. 'He worked alone and his talents were given full rein,' it was later said of him. 'Success followed success.'[10] To say the least: full charge of his workforce through the winter months then home to Greenway, or Winterbrook, or the new house that Agatha had acquired at 58 Sheffield Terrace in Kensington (the only house, she claimed, in which she ever had a designated room for writing). Yes, it was a grand life for young Max Mallowan.

It has been said that he was not an especially good excavator, but he had other gifts. He had had the sense to keep his mouth shut and learn on the dig with Woolley, and now he had the confidence to take charge. 'He played the role,' says Joan Oates, who worked with him after the war. As might have been expected, he was a terrific handler of his workers: Arabs mostly, also Kurds, Turks and Armenians. These were the days of cheap labour when as many as two hundred men might be employed simultaneously. 'He was very good with the workmen. Shouting at them. There was a strike at the beginning of one of the seasons, they wanted more money. And Max actually got up on a large wooden packing case and *harangued* them – and they all stood there, and in the end they all nodded their heads, and off they all went to work! I mean, he really enjoyed that.'[11]

Agatha too enjoyed herself. 'She liked being at Chagar Bazar,' says Joan Oates. 'She liked the flowers. If you look at the films she made on digs,[12] they are full of wild flowers, which she had a passion for.' She did, indeed, photograph fields of soft, luscious marigolds swaying in the wind; also, at Tell Brak, a little dog wagging its tail as it watched a lorry being laboriously unloaded. 'Yes, dogs and children, and the lovely house they lived in at Chagar Bazar. But the dig, no. Her interest was in being there, being the devoted wife, enjoying the countryside, which she did enormously.' In a letter to Max written during the war, Agatha remembered Chagar Bazar: 'that fresh untouched feeling of the empty smiling country. How lovely it all was . . .'[13]

It was also, often, extremely uncomfortable, but Agatha was tough and healthy, and always despised complaining women. In her memoir of life in pre-war Syria, *Come, Tell Me How You Live*,[14] she wrote of terrible heat, sudden rains that weighed as heavy as coins, nights spent in tents that 'look drunken, a little out of true', meals 'swimming in grease' and sleep interrupted by

> mice across one's face, mice tweaking your hair – mice! mice! MICE! . . . I switch on a torch. Horrible! The walls are covered with strange, pale, crawling cockroach-like creatures! A mouse is sitting on the foot of my bed attending to his whiskers! Horrible crawling things are everywhere!
>
> Max utters soothing words. Just go to sleep, he says. Once you are asleep, none of these things will worry you.

The endless difficulties – getting about the desert, finding accommodation, communicating with the houseboys and cook – sound frankly oppressive; but in her book, at least, Agatha's good humour is relentless. She also emphasised the joy of archaeology, the spell that bound her still.

> These autumn days are some of the most perfect I have ever known [she wrote of her life in 1935]. Here, where nowadays only the tribesmen move with their brown tents, was once a busy part of the world. Here, some five thousand years ago, was the busy part of the world. Here were the beginnings of civilisation, and here, picked up by me, this broken fragment of a clay pot, hand-made, with a design of dots and cross-hatching in brown paint, is the forerunner of the Woolworth cup out of which this very morning I have drunk my tea . . .

A different view comes across, however, in *Death in the Clouds*, which she wrote in 1934, probably while staying in Beirut (or 'Beyrout', as she spelled it) *en route* to Syria. She allowed one of her characters to take a sceptical view of her husband's profession:

> As I look at it an archaeologist is a poor kind of fish. Always burrowing in the ground and talking through his hat about what happened thousands of years ago . . . Well, there they are – liars, perhaps – though they seem to believe it themselves – but harmless. I had an old chap in here the other day who's had a scarab pinched – terrible state he was in – nice old boy, but helpless as a baby in arms . . .

This, of course, would be reiterated by Nurse Leatheran in *Murder in Mesopotamia*, although in *Clouds* there is a trace of real contempt. In other words, despite the easy temper with which Agatha treated Max's colleagues, she was in fact noting every quirk of their behaviour. In *Come, Tell Me How You Live* she describes a young architect called Robin Macartney ('Mac') whose air of taciturn superiority reduces her, she says, to a state of 'nervous idiocy'. She makes polite conversation and is rebuffed at every turn:

> 'I expect you'd like to explore the town,' I suggest. 'It's fun poking round a new place.'
> Mac raises his eyebrows gently and says coldly: 'Is it?'

Agatha is portrayed as a socially inept twitterer; but in fact it is Mac who looks bad. Similarly with the 'odes' that Agatha would later write on digs for members of the expedition. They were very jolly and clever, and meant to amuse but, as Joan Oates says, 'There was often a sting in the tail with them.'

But *Come, Tell Me How You Live* reads as if it was written to please one person, at least: her husband. It has a slightly manic style, as different as can be from that of her fiction, although in its way the book is equally artful. As with her letters, it has the air of a performance: what fun, Max! Oh! I *am* enjoying myself! She was not going to lose touch with him as she had with Archie, that was for sure. She had a profound desire to make this a happy marriage. The power in it was hers, but so was the willingness to please; and she wanted to prove to Max how much she enjoyed sharing his life.

She did have a genuine love of the East, and a genuine liking for some of Max's colleagues, from whom she could, if she chose, withdraw herself mentally. Perhaps the greatest attraction of all was that, when the pressures of her life in England grew too much, she could simply jump ship and escape every year. 'Mrs Mallowan is in Syria/Iraq' became Edmund Cork's constant refrain, when asked if Agatha would appear on the BBC, or answer a mad fan letter, or allow an amateur playwright to adapt one of her books, or agree to Miss Marple appearing on American television.[15] It was another layer of protection. On the dig she was not 'Agatha Christie', she was not even Agatha: she was 'Mrs Mallowan', wife of the man in charge, the smiling figure who kept to the background and kept life sweet. Yet the impression given by her book, that she devoted her every waking thought to Mesopotamian pottery, is false; she did a good deal of writing in Syria. She had her little typewriter and her blissful solitude. As war in Europe drew near, as the dogs barked and the workmen shouted, 'Yallah, yallah!' she sat at her sharp-lit table in the desert and dreamed into life the world of *Murder is Easy*. 'England! England on a June day, with a grey sky and a sharp biting wind . . .'

And then: September 1939. Agatha was at Greenway when war was declared and she realised that her delightful life would be put on hold. There was not the desperate anxiety of the first war, when Archie had been on active service, although now she understood what he had gone through. But there would be upheaval, deprivation, loneliness and – remarkably – a creative outpouring of work of the very highest quality. Agatha was almost compulsively occupied during this period, which sat at the centre of her life and was as important, in its way, as the years around 1926.

The last book she wrote before the war was *Sad Cypress*, that sombre story of love and loss. Elinor cannot live without Roddy, but Roddy has fallen for Mary. 'Tell me, honestly,' says Elinor, 'do you think love is ever a happy thing?' To which her dying aunt replies:

'To care passionately for another human creature brings always more sorrow than joy; but all the same, Elinor, one would not

be without that experience. Anyone who has never really loved
has never really lived . . .'

The girl nodded.

She said:

'Yes – you understand – you've known what it's like –'

Elinor is a cool, aloof creature who hides her feelings, while
Jacqueline de Bellefort in *Death on the Nile* is an impassioned little
hot-blood, but they are sisters under the skin: hopelessly in love
with men who cannot quite return their feelings. Jackie loves Simon
Doyle, who is 'dazzled' by the rich and glamorous Linnet Ridgway.
Jackie behaves badly, makes a public spectacle of herself. Linnet
complains to Poirot, who says, 'There are times, Madame, when
pride and dignity – they go by the board! There are other – stronger
emotions.'

Poirot has an intense sympathy for both Jackie and Elinor. He is
on their side. When Simon, in the authentic voice of Archie Christie,
asks, 'Why can't Jackie take it like a man?', Poirot says, 'Well, you see,
M. Doyle, to begin with she is not a man.' In *Sad Cypress* Elinor says
that she has always loved red roses, while Roddy preferred white; and
that, says Poirot, is the difference between them. 'It explains Elinor
Carlisle – who is passionate and proud and who loved desperately a
man who was incapable of loving her.' Poirot does not approve of
murder. He says so all the time. Yet he feels for these women: if despair
has blinded them to morality he will not condone, but he will
understand.

Then there is Bridget Conway in *Murder is Easy*, thrown over by
a man whom she loved so much 'that it hurt'; and Vera Claythorne
in *And Then There Were None*, who murders for the love of a man
('So you did drown that kid after all? . . . There was a man in it probably. Was that it?'). Love, as the doctor says in *Sad Cypress*, is the
devil. He himself is in love with Elinor, who is on trial for the murder
of Mary Gerrard. 'She might have done it, yes! *I don't care if she did*,'
he says to Poirot. 'I don't want her hanged, I tell you! Supposing she
was driven desperate? Love's a desperate and twisting business.'

These were the books – interspersed with more straightforward fare,
like *One, Two, Buckle My Shoe*[16] – that Agatha was writing before the

war, and in 1942 came the best of them all. *Five Little Pigs*, the story of Caroline Crale, whose painter husband Amyas takes his beautiful young model, Elsa, as his mistress, is not that of Agatha's first marriage,[17] but it is perhaps the closest she came to telling it: in her detective fiction, that is. It has an intimacy, a 'felt' quality. It gives a very real sense of the disrupted household: the quarrelling couple, their neglected daughter, and the governess who is totally loyal to Caroline.

'I'm a very primitive woman,' Caroline says. 'I'd like to take a hatchet to that girl.' Meanwhile the girl, Elsa, tells Amyas Crale that his wife should let him go. 'If she loved him, she'd put his happiness first, and at any rate she wouldn't want to keep him if he wanted to be free.' To which he replies: 'Don't you realise, Elsa, that she's going to suffer – *suffer*? Do you know what suffering means?'

Five Little Pigs is a masterly piece of writing: its motivations are complex, intertwined and, in their resolution, entirely satisfying. At the centre of the book is the relationship between art and real life. Amyas sees the world differently from his wife and mistress: like Vernon Deyre in *Giant's Bread*, he sees it through the prism of his art.

'With women, love always come first . . . Men, and especially artists – are different.' So says Poirot. But Agatha was a woman *and* an artist. She understood the artistic sensibility, the fact that Amyas Crale has fallen in love not with Elsa herself but with the subject of his painting. At the same time she understood Elsa, the depth of her feelings for the real man; and, of course, she understood Caroline. In this book, as in *Giant's Bread*, she set the claims of art against those of ordinary life, and was able to give them equal weight. Rare stuff for a book that also works on another level entirely, fitting the template of the detective novel as neatly as a lid on a jar. In fact *Five Little Pigs* has a fair claim to being Agatha's finest; its chief rival is *The Hollow* which, through the character of the sculptress, Henrietta Savernake, has a similar central theme.

But what an extremely complicated woman Agatha was; because, even as she was shaping these really quite beautiful books, which were both perfect geometric puzzles and perfectly distilled meditations upon human nature, even as she was writing back into life the memories of lost love; even as she was letting the shadows of the past drift across her imagination; even as she was dedicating *Five Little Pigs* to another man: so, at the same time, she was writing to Max Mallowan like an eager little girl, telling him how much she was longing to see him again. Oh! Max . . . !

Max, for whom the war came as a wretched interruption to his career, seized the opportunity to obliterate the fact of his lineage by serving his country. His father's Austrian military career hampered him in his early attempts to get war work, as did his age (thirty-five), and at first he joined the Home Guard at Brixham, near Greenway ('One of my companions in arms', he wrote to Rosalind, 'is Professor of Greek at Bristol University . . . our experience in Hellenic warfare is second to none').[18] Not until 1940 did he find occupation, helping to organise an Anglo-Turkish Relief Committee. In 1941 – after constant pressurising of the authorities[19] – he joined the Air Ministry with his friend, the Egyptologist Stephen Glanville, in what became the Directorate of Allied and Foreign Liaison. Finally, in early 1942, he got a job that made use of his abilities. He went to Cairo as a squadron leader, there to establish a branch of the Directorate, moving to Tripolitania in 1943 and working in administration. As an Arab linguist he was very useful. He ended the war 'number three', as he put it, 'on the civil side out here', and attained the rank of wing-commander.[20] 'Administration is probably rather bad for one and you would say I am getting pompous,' he wrote to Rosalind at the end of 1944, 'but I try not to be.'

In fact he enjoyed the work. 'I know that I am doing a man's job, pulling my weight and not wasted,' he wrote to Agatha in October 1943. 'It has been a leavening for my life, which always tends to take the easy path.' He was, nonetheless, very nicely set up. At first he shared a flat with his brother, Cecil, who, coincidentally, was in Egypt. 'I often imagine you sitting here,' he wrote to Agatha. 'One particular armchair is yours. Do you eat as much as I do when you are alone or are you wasting away?' Then, in Tripolitania, he lived in 'a house on the sea, a beautifully built Italian villa', which by comparison with England at that time must have sounded like heaven ('Who likes the sea? *I* do. Oh! the unfairness of life,' wrote Agatha). 'My room,' wrote Max, 'is snug and cosy and somehow it has become full of books.' Rather charmingly, he added: 'That is what you have done for me – given me a feeling for making a room homely and comfortable.'[21]

Meanwhile in 1942 Greenway had been requisitioned by the Admiralty, and Agatha was braving the bombs in London. Not that Devon had been much of an oasis: in September 1940 she wrote to Edmund Cork that 'We had a good invasion scare last week – house swarming with soldiers so dressed up they could hardly move!' She had also coped briefly with a number of evacuated children, two of whom came under fire from a fighter plane when sailing on the Dart. It seemed reasonable for Agatha to join Max in London. Cresswell Place and Campden Street were let; Sheffield Terrace was bombed in October 1940. Despite Agatha's giant property portfolio she became itinerant, living in Half Moon Street, then at a service flat in Park Place, then in the Bauhaus block at Lawn Road[22] in Hampstead (whose windows were broken by a blast in 1940). 'But how odd,' Agatha wrote, 'to think that as I pass a funny old building like a liner I shall always look up at it and say to myself, "I was happy there!" No beauty to speak of . . . but oh darling I did have so much happiness there with you.'[23]

She stayed at Lawn Road Flats for much of the war. It might seem an unlikely setting for cosy, chintzy 'Agatha Christie', with its contemporary philosophy of designed living in near-identical flats. But Agatha was a more daring creature. She rather liked her fashionable block. She took little part in the life of the Isobar dining club – something of a social centre during the war, also used as a bomb shelter – although she would occasionally go down in search of company. She liked to be near Hampstead Heath, where she walked the Sealyham, James, that she had semi-appropriated from Carlo Fisher.[24] She also enjoyed the convenience of living in a furnished flat – found the modernist 'Isokon Long Chair' strangely comfortable – where tenants were looked after by the management ('Will you please look into the question of these knickers which have not been returned,' they wrote on Agatha's behalf to the local laundry. 'If they have been lost, send Mrs Mallowan the necessary coupons'). Some years later she recalled that her 'chief memories are of the fascination of finding a place where, like the wood in *Dear Brutus*, trees really seemed to have moved close up to the windows. That, meals in the garden, and one particularly beautiful white blossoming cherry tree are the things I have never forgotten.'[25]

No wonder her possession of Greenway seemed barely real: she had lived there less than two years before clearing it for the Admiralty. 'My heart sinks, darling, at the thought of more turning out, packing etc. However I hope I shall have Ros to help me. Run her down there by the scruff of the neck if necessary!'[26] ('It makes me quite tired to think of all the work you have done moving,' wrote Max, 'and that devil Rosalind mainly thinking of how to unlock the tantalus!')[27] It was a huge job. 'The two garden boys have been a godsend. They practically never see the garden but live in the cellar carting up dinner services and silver etc – It was in such an awful state that I started to clean it,' she wrote in October 1942. Then, two weeks later: 'Goodbye to wonderful Greenway. I have used the last colour film so that we shall have a remembrance of it in case anything happens.' In fact the house was in very good hands, those of the officers on an American flotilla, who treated it with great respect and painted a blue and white frieze around the cornices of the library ceiling in memory of their wartime exploits.

And London had its compensations: friends, theatres. Agatha had a large acquaintance – the Hon. Dorothy North; Sybil, Lady Burnett;[28] Allen Lane of Penguin Books and his wife Lettice; Max's colleague Sidney Smith and his wife Mary; Max's friend Stephen Glanville – and she maintained a determinedly active social life. She went to the ballet, seeing contemporary productions like Robert Helpmann's *Hamlet*, and she indulged her passionate love of Shakespeare. In 1942 she saw *Othello* at the Old Vic; this provoked a long correspondence with Max who announced his intention of reading all the plays (a task he gave up half-way through). Agatha's attitude towards Shakespeare was an interesting one. It was typical of its time, but it was also typical of her: she saw his characters as psychological studies, looking for clues in the poetry, rather than viewing Hamlet or Iago as an unparalleled accretion of words and rhythms. Iago, in particular, obsessed her. For Agatha he was a fixed entity, almost a reality; she took little account of the way the pressure of the play magnifies his initial intent, but her analysis of what she saw in the character was brilliant. 'Iago suffered, poor devil,' says John Gabriel, in *The Rose and the Yew Tree*, who understands exactly what it feels like to 'hate the human being who's up amongst the stars' (in his case, Isabella; in Iago's case, Othello). Iago features too in *Curtain*, where he is described as the perfect murderer because he instils in others the desire to kill. Poirot – in the voice of Agatha – says this:

'I have always been of the belief that already present in Othello's mind was the conviction (possibly correct) that Desdemona's love for him was the passionate unbalanced hero worship of a young girl for a famous warrior and not the balanced love of a woman for Othello the man. He may have realised that Cassio was her true mate and that in time she would come to realise the fact.'

This is terrific stuff, true to the spirit of Shakespeare, whose poetry allows characters to be and feel more than one thing at the same time. What she wrote in August 1942, after her visit to the Old Vic, was closer to the Freudian school of literary criticism:

Iago and Emilia are really a couple of common swindlers, or confidence tricksters. That is borne out (I am now being Hercule Poirot!) by the opening of the play when Iago enters with the present fish that he is playing and Rodrigo is saying, 'Thou, Iago, who hast my purse' . . . On this theory where comes Iago's intense hatred of the Moor? I think that plain sexual jealousy is the crux . . . He has suffered through Emilia again and again. The joy of seeing Othello suffer as he has suffered – and finally the sex maniac's suggestion 'strangle her'. That is what he would like to do but hasn't ever had the courage . . .

Later Agatha discussed Ophelia,[29] offering to Max the real *aperçu* that Shakespeare, with his female characters, 'was feminine enough himself to see men through their eyes'. Then she asked the impossible question: '*Why* does she go mad?'[30] A little later she believed she had her answer. After a performance of *Henry IV part II* she dined with Robert Graves and met a friend of his, a doctor. 'I said

I found Ophelia the most difficult to understand. He said, "Oh! no, you would find Ophelia in any schizophrenic ward of a mental Hospital."'[31]

Agatha was, at this point, almost in love with Shakespeare: 'I cannot think of anything else.' (By comparison she found Greek drama disappointing: 'What astounds me in these dramas is the lack of any ideas – or *concepts*,' an opinion that would not have gone down well with Max). Shakespeare's sonnets featured in *The Moving Finger* and *Absent in the Spring* ('From thee have I been absent in the spring . . .'), while the title of *Taken at the Flood* is from *Julius Caesar*. Later she hinted at a *Lear* reference with the name 'Edgar' in *They Do It with Mirrors*, and used *Macbeth* as a base for the plot of *The Pale Horse*,[32] which also contains an inspired disquisition on how the play should be staged. *By the Pricking of My Thumbs* is, of course, a direct quotation.

In a letter to Max she imagined the man himself. 'I don't believe he had much what you call "personality",' she wrote, which was true of Agatha herself. 'A quiet little man, I see him – rather vain – eaten up with longing to play the lead – but with some disability – did he stammer?' She pictured him drinking in the tavern with Ben Jonson and the rest, not saying much, then leaving: 'and in the tavern they wouldn't notice he had gone. But he would walk home in the moonlight with words singing and dancing in his head – lovely sequences of them and he would *see* them being said on stage . . . Why aren't you here to talk to?'[33]

Max was impressed – perhaps a little surprised – by Agatha's knowledge, which has the slight air of being offered to a teacher for approval. In February 1943 he wrote to suggest that she 'write a short and simple book on Shakespeare the Man. You have the imaginative penetration of the writer and creative artist yourself, and the solution of the many problems in his life and his work is partly if not largely detective work! So put old Poirot on the job and get down to it. If you want any help on the scholarship side I will do what I can to keep you on the straight path.'

If this struck Agatha as condescension, she showed no sign of it. Nor did she accept Max's suggestion: 'No I couldn't write a book on Shakespeare, all my remarks are just Mrs Puper and for you only!!'

(She and Max addressed each other in private as 'Mr and Mrs Puper'; as with most intimate nicknames, the origin of this is unfathomable.) She was annoyed when Max's mother told her that she should deploy her talents in writing more serious books, like 'biographies'. Yet Max's remarks about her work – which occasionally verge upon interfering – seem not to have bothered her. He was not jealous of her success, and in this he was probably unusual: most men (Archie?) would have found it difficult to act as consort to a woman of Agatha's renown. 'Well, Max was very conceited,' says Joan Oates. But his self-assurance also made him competitive. He liked to assert his opinions, the worth of his own work, his claims to the intellectual high ground. This, for example, was the critique that he sent of *The Murder at the Vicarage* back in 1931:

> Ange I think you are terribly clever. I think my only objection to the story was that it was too clever . . . I think your manner of writing is perfectly adapted to a detective story because one forgets the printed page and is transported straight into real life and breezy life at that, rather like a whiff of ange, and one feels that the narrative and conversation is all spoken and not written – exactly as it should be, it seems to me; I understand now why you don't bother about semi colons. Well done!

Later he took Agatha to task for a grammatical error in *Five Little Pigs*, which he nonetheless considered to be 'in a class with some of your special masterpieces'. If only she had not used the word 'like' as a conjunction! 'Wrong: He doesn't know him *like* I do. Right: He doesn't know him *as* I do. This is a very usual mistake to make . . . But you see I read it carefully and enjoyed it' (in fact, as she told him, he had read it already in manuscript).[34] In his next letter he praised Dorothy L. Sayers's *Murder Must Advertise*, which he was reading and loving for its 'highbrow style'. Agatha fired back, telling Max that she had been typing in his library at Winterbrook: 'Heresy! Lowbrow stuff in the highbrow sanctuary of Mr Puper!' But on the whole she took absolutely no notice of her husband's patronising tone. Indeed, when it came to her work, she took no notice of Max whatsoever, and almost nothing of him appeared in her writing. Only with *Come, Tell Me How*

You Live, did she seek his opinion: this, after all, was his territory. Max read the manuscript at the end of 1944.

> I confess at first I thought it might be a shade embarrassing to publish such a book and perhaps there is rather a lot about us in it, but I don't think it matters really and the main thing is that it will I believe give pleasure and amusement to quite a lot of people. Also it is perhaps better that it should come out now during the war, than when I am actively at work, digging.

Max then told Agatha that she had

> become a very good writer, I mean descriptive writer, quite apart from your graphic conversational style at which you were always an adept . . . There are of course a number of mistakes or rather misspellings in the book on which I must try and send you a special letter tomorrow. MOHOMMED is consistently misspelled and should be MOHAMMED throughout . . .

Agatha wrote to Max how much she had loved writing the book, so much so that it had been an almost painful experience: 'I've been living all those days over again – and now it's like waking up in a cold and lonely world – what did I do before you were there?'[35] Living without her husband for more than three years, the buried fear of being alone and abandoned came to the surface, and the shared past became hallowed. Their letters are full of exchanged memories. 'I am doing a lot of writing just now – It's going well – but when I am tired and my back aches I would like to find a cushion . . . and put it on your lap and lay my head on it as I used to do long ago at Cresswell Place. Do you remember?'[36]

In turn, Max wrote: 'I like to think of you with the woolly Jaeger's dressing gown I gave you before leaving England. Do you use it often? My woolly bear! Do you remember the woolly bear coat you were wearing in the cab at Baghdad that day in March was it when we were on the way out to dig at Arpachiyah?'[37] More than once he reminded Agatha of an evening at Lawn Road when she was ill, and 'I cooked the meal while you issued instructions from the bed! Great fun that was.' He also hit an occasional lyrical vein, a legacy of his youth, perhaps, when he had written the occasional, rather laborious poem.[38]

> Odd things that come back to me . . . planning the garden
> at Greenway, sitting under the limes and looking over the
> green lawn at Wallingford, my books in the library, talking
> archaeology. These are only a few of the things that flash
> across the mind like the yellow marigolds that are specially
> yours, gleaming in the sun . . . What I treasure in you is
> your imagination, that has been a continual stimulus to me,
> needful to the scholarly side, your love and affection
> without which life is a drab thing, your enthusiasm, fresh-
> ness and vitality, your capacity for sharing my interests and
> enjoyments . . .[39]

This was a wonderful thing for Agatha to read: that Max appreciated in her all the things that Archie had shunned. 'I am so glad that you can write that to me darling.' Her insecurity was almost palpable, nonetheless. However much Max reassured her, the fact of physical separation unnerved her. Perhaps she remembered what had happened when she spent those weeks at Ashfield sorting through her mother's things. 'Oh! darling – I hate these November days,' she wrote in 1942. 'I want to be with you – I feel so afraid sometimes that we shall grow outwards' (she drew two lines moving apart) 'instead of a nice parallel track . . . Think of me a good deal, please, and write often, because I need cheering when there are no sunny days.'

Small wonder Max had confidence in himself. This woman had given him so much, yet she was the supplicant for his affections. He could write to her 'of course use our joint account for anything you want', and get away with it. He could count on the fact that she would visit his mother – and subsidise her through the 'joint account' – even though Agatha and Marguerite were now rather ragged with each other. 'I was very tired when I went there and your ma's criticism of England got me on the raw and I flared up – I daresay it will all blow over!! . . . Don't be cross with me – I really *have* been very nice all these years.' ('Hope you will try and patch it up,' he replied). He could answer in all seriousness when Agatha asked his opinion as to whether she should accept an offer of four thousand pounds for Winterbrook, pretending that the decision was in any way his to take. He could tell Agatha to write more legibly (it was true that her hand-writing sometimes resembled 'hieroglyphics'); to number her letters ('Lazy Puper!' he wrote, when she forgot); to consider a certain actress for a part in one of her plays, because he happened to know the girl's fiancé (this, Agatha only pretended to go along with); to remember, when she dramatised her books, 'not to make the detective part of a play too difficult for the man in the street'. He could do all these things, because he had the power to make Agatha happy or unhappy.

Sometimes he revelled in this. 'Wouldn't you have been a very foolish Mrs Puper if you hadn't married me and aren't you pleased you did and do you remember how A.P. [Madge][40] tried to dissuade us and what a foolish thing that was to do', he wrote in February 1945.

Yet there can be no doubt of their real closeness. 'In many ways we are so unlike,' Max wrote in March 1943, 'but our hearts are the counterpart of each other.' For their different reasons, each wanted the marriage to work. Their private world together had therefore been a careful construction, not an evolution, but for that reason it was all the more solid.

In March 1944, Agatha conjured it to express her longing for Max.

Sometimes my need for you is worse than others. It's a feeling like an ache in one's middle going round and round – Do you ever feel like that? Or it is purely a Puper reaction? I have had all sorts of dreams of you lately – really very erotic and rude ones!! Extraordinary after all the years we've been married! I wouldn't have believed it! Nice – except that it's annoying to wake up – I miss your nice coarse conversations too!

Yes, Puper dear, I do miss you a great deal [Max replied], but the corkscrew motion you speak of is definitely a Puper motion – with me, it is a feeling of emptiness, of being unfilled, not unlike being hungry – I want to eat and hug Mrs

Puper; but then one fine day that will happen . . . and there
will be a great deal of wagging of tails, continuously. I am
glad that you miss nice coarse conversations! I have plenty of
that saved up for you – rude Mr Puper!

This was what Agatha would have thought of as 'being herself'.
'You do love your funny Puper as she is,' she wrote. She could tell
Max to 'think of your porpoise Puper every time you are in the sea',
and write about eating so much she 'almost burst', knowing that he
would not shudder in horror. Similarly she wrote to him about the
joy of their reunion:

What lovely times we will have when we are together again
and how we shall eat!! There will be your socks with holes in
them!! and things strewn everywhere and chairs covered with
books and a lot of laughing – And we will talk and talk and
talk. And you will pick your nose and I shall yell at you – and
you will say 'Puper' to me very sternly when I . . . ??!! . . .[41]

This was a long way from the slender, fairy-like girl who had married
Archie Christie: between those two there had been the mystery of physical allure, which Agatha still conjured in her books but had deliberately
destroyed for herself. She had, indeed, coarsened. She did not merely
hide behind the public persona of 'Agatha Christie'; she sheltered within
a shroud of flesh, dense and unwieldy, a symbolic defence against the
sharp agonies of the past. Her fatness also made her sad, although she
made light of it. She described in *Come, Tell Me How You Live* the embarrassment of trying to buy clothes for the Syrian heat ('Oh, no, Modom,
we do not keep *out*-sizes') and of being asked by Max to sit on their
overfilled trunks ('If you can't make them shut, *nobody* can!'). But she
had grown resigned to the loss of her looks, and she truly loved to eat.
She also loved the fact that she could do so with Max, who had been
thin when they met ('That was before I fattened him up,' she told Joan
Oates) but who now described himself as 'an awful gourmandiser'.

It was childlike behaviour again, in a way: the gleeful tearing away
of adult protocol. It was the equivalent of the absolute relaxation she
had felt at Ashfield, lying beneath the beech tree, knowing that Clara

was somewhere nearby. 'The years we have had together have been the happiest of my life since I was a child.' But no man could ever be quite what Clara had been. At times Max's letters became far less frequent. In October 1943 he went on leave and did not write for a month. 'You are a dirty dog . . . I can *see* your face saying: "Naughty Mr Puper!" and then I should have to laugh if you were here. You are not really contrite you just know you can make it all right.' In July 1944 she was unable to stop herself writing repeatedly. 'Still no letter from you, damn your eyes – or damn somebody's eyes!' Three days later: 'It's hell not hearing from you – What are you *doooi*ng?' And four days later: 'Please, darling, don't leave me without a word – I know you get lazy fits – but just a word or two would do . . .'

'I feel very guilty dearest at my lapse in not writing to you,' he wrote eventually. She had tried to be sanguine about what Max might do, left so long to his own devices. 'I *ought* to be able to share your leave,' she wrote in October 1943. 'Have a good time, darling, and do *anything* you want and that you need – just so long as I am held in your heart in deep friendship and affection and very close . . .' But in 1944 she tried to get herself sent out east. 'When exactly do you get your two months' leave?' she asked, several times. 'I still think it possible that I might do a writing job in Egypt . . .' This plan did take tentative shape – 'Prospects of Middle East good,' she wrote in August – although Max did not encourage it particularly. 'I think I ought to get home first for as you know my time is up at the beginning of April next year,' he replied; then, in September: 'You don't want to risk getting stuck out there for a long time and Mr Puper back in England and you in Egypt!' This was undeniable, although Agatha might have preferred it if Max had been desperate to see her *immediately*. She would not be reassured until they were in the same country. 'I had a horrid dream that I had come to visit you somewhere abroad . . . they told me that you no longer cared or wanted me and had gone away and I woke up in a panic and had to say over and over – 'It's *not* true – it's *not* true – I've got his letter.'[42] The terrors of 1926 did not go away.

*   *   *

This desperation was odd, as Agatha wrote about it at a time when her friendship with Stephen Glanville was deepening in intimacy.

Stephen was ten years her junior, and had been a friend of Max since 1925. An intellectual through and through, his career as an Egyptologist had taken him first to the British Museum, thence to London University, then back to Oxford where he had taken his degree. He served in the Air Ministry during the war, working in Whitehall and living in Highgate, near Lawn Road Flats. After the war he took up a professorship at Cambridge; it is testament to his abilities and popularity that he became the first Oxford man to become provost of King's College, a position to which he was unanimously elected in 1954. A person of great substance, he nonetheless had a gift for lightness. Like Agatha, he had a joy for living.

He was bespectacled, not handsome, but he had immense charm and was attractive to women. It was said of him that 'Stephen fell in love with every woman he met.' Certainly he was unable to resist a close friendship with somebody like Agatha, whom he found intelligent, humorous, splendid and above all *sympathique*. In this relationship she was the grown-up, he the troubled and unhappy party who sought reassurance. 'Of course, he isn't really *adult* like you,' Agatha wrote to Max. But something in Stephen's vulnerability may have reminded her, distantly, of the early days of her courtship by Archie Christie, when he had loved her soothing voice and sweetness.

Agatha and Stephen became friendly because both were alone. His wife, Ethel, and the two daughters he adored were in Canada, so he and Agatha began to see a good deal of each other. In 1941, she dedicated *Five Little Pigs* to him. From overseas Max gave his blessing to Agatha's new friendships with his old colleagues: 'How nice of Stephen and the Smiths – Sidney (not Sydney!) to have been so kind,' he wrote in August 1942. In fact they were not being kind at all; but Max always had a slight air of condescension when imagining his wife in the sphere of academia ('Clever Puper!' he wrote, after she told him that she had caught out Sidney Smith in a conversation about free will. 'You had him nicely there . . .').

In November 1942 Agatha went to hear Stephen lecture – 'Didn't realise what an attractive *voice* he has,' she wrote to Max – then invited him to Greenway, which she was in the process of clearing. 'Stephen seems to have revelled in Greenway,' wrote Max. The two men were in regular contact, although occasionally Agatha had to push Max to write. 'The one person you must keep up with is Stephen, Max – he really is very fond of you and I think will be really hurt if you don't keep in touch with him – He's a sensitive person and minds about things – And he has been endlessly kind to me – always tells me when he has heard from you and news about you.'[43]

The friendship between Agatha and Stephen intensified in 1943, when he used what she called his 'serpent's tongue' to persuade her to write a murder mystery set in ancient Egypt. 'Rather a fascinating idea but can I do it?' Max's reply was that it sounded a 'most interesting experiment, and, as you say, if Rosalind can't see anything wrong with it, then it must be pretty good! Stephen I am sure must be much intrigued.'[44] It would have been surprising, however, if Max were completely happy about it. He would not have thought Agatha likely to betray him: he was too sure of himself – and of her – for that. But Glanville was *his* friend, whom she had appropriated, and Agatha was *his* wife, with whom Glanville was intending to collaborate; moreover, it was almost unprecedented for her to accept a suggestion about her work. She had used James Watts's idea about the narrator-murderer in *The Murder of Roger Ackroyd*, but this was very different. She knew almost nothing about ancient Egypt, so the book would necessarily be a joint enterprise.

When *Death Comes as the End* was finished, Max wrote to both Agatha and Stephen, expressing concern about the book in a manner that suggested more general perturbation. 'I am not clear,' Glanville replied, 'whether you are afraid that the book will damage her reputation as a detective story writer, or whether you think that archaeology should not demean itself by masquerading in a novel.' The tone softened thereafter – 'It was an extraordinarily difficult thing to do, and she's brought it off. Incidentally, it's a damn good murder story' – but the rivalrous note had briefly flared.

The book was by no means one of Agatha's best, as the solution was so easily guessed. In that sense the setting limited her. Her source material was a series of letters by an Egyptian landowner –

discovered at Luxor in the 1920s and known as the Hekanakhthe Papers – and understandably she stuck to them very closely. But the evocation of Egypt was well done. She had a talent for finding the present in the past, for grasping the ideas of a distant civilisation and finding in them a core of relevance. It was, in effect, her talent for the ordinary. She wrote, for example, about the spread of literacy within Egypt: 'The writer and the scribe will come to despise the man who ploughs the fields and reaps the barley and raises the cattle – but all the same the fields and the cattle are real . . . when all the records and all the papyrus rolls are destroyed and the scribes are scattered, the men who toil and reap will go on, and Egypt will still live.'

Perhaps the most interesting part of the book was Agatha's depiction of the Egyptian home: the 'houseful of women – never quiet, never peaceful – always talking, exclaiming, *saying* things – not *doing* them!'. Through this close community – wives, grandmother, concubine – she explored her own ideas about femaleness, its power and pettiness and mysteries. 'What are men anyway? They are necessary to breed children, that is all. But the strength of the race is in the women,' says one of the wives, who is blind to everything except her children. This, of course, was not Agatha's way. She spoke through the character of Renisenb, a subtle creation, a young widow who seeks a life beyond the constraints of the home. Renisenb likes to sit in thought, doing nothing, 'drowsily content with the men's murmuring voices as a background'.

Agatha wrote a letter of thanks to Stephen Glanville at the front of *Death Comes as the End*. She had sent him several painstaking 'models' of this letter to ask which he preferred. 'I was very touched,' he replied, 'and am a little embarrassed in my conscience . . . for, as you know, just as well as I do, the "fun" was equally shared between us.' He ended: 'I am very proud that a suggestion of mine should have resulted in a book by you. (If I had a coat of arms I would like to choose for my motto: 'By Agatha out of Stephen' – despite the physiological improbability implied).'

Throughout 1943 the two saw a good deal of each other. In March 1943 Agatha told Max that she had given Stephen dinner at Lawn Road to celebrate the publication of *Five Little Pigs*, standing the wine 'by your photograph to give it luck and prestige . . . You were duly toasted in it by Stephen.' Another dinner elicited this letter of thanks: 'Charles Sorley', wrote Stephen, 'has a verse, in a pleasant description of Homeric days, "And then the grandeur of their mess!" The phrase has been gently calling – like the spring notes of one of the rarer warblers! – in my head ever since I left you on Friday night . . . What a meal! What hospitality!' He had told friends, he said, about the wonderful food she offered, 'but have found myself shy of undertaking to convey the subtler delight of the talking that completed our evening'.[45] This was a lovely letter, full of its writer's own charm; as was this, in July, after a visit to Winterbrook. His wife and children were now back in London and Agatha had invited them all to her home. 'Yours is a quintessential hospitality', he told Agatha, praising her 'personal charm, great kindness, tolerance, catholicity of interest . . . all added to the physical delights, comfort, ease, idleness and lovely things to touch and see in and out of doors. It was a banquet . . .'[46]

In November Stephen accompanied Agatha and Rosalind to the West End first night of *Ten Little Niggers*. From the Athenaeum he wrote:

Agatha darling – Last night was really something to remember . . . The whole thing was FUN – it was delightful to make a party with so many altogether enjoyable people . . . But best of all was the diverse experience of Agatha: Agatha really nervous (as she must be until the show is over) – not just shy – even in the midst of close friends: Agatha in the moment of triumph, quite radiant, but still asking only for her friends, and incredibly unegotistical; at last, and perhaps most precious, Agatha still quietly excited, but beautifully poised and content, balanced between the success of the immediate achievement and the purpose to achieve more . . .[47]

If not exactly a love letter, this comes very close. Reflected in it is the image of a very different woman from the Mrs Puper conjured by Max: this Agatha is infinitely more attractive, more adult and, indeed, more natural. It is not surprising to learn that Stephen confided to one of his friends that he was in love with Agatha, or that Agatha kept his letters with those from her husband. In his letters to Max, Stephen made semi-serious references to his attraction to Agatha. For her own part, she told Max about their meetings, qualifying her open fondness for Stephen with adoring references to Max himself: 'Just back from first night of *Niggers* – I felt *awful* of course – It *is* an agony – but Stephen came again and was very kind and soothing and he and Rosalind pulled me through. I *do* wish you had been there.'[48]

In 1944 Stephen helped Agatha again, this time with Arab dialogue for her play *Hidden Horizon*. He was, she told Max, 'really longing to come to Dundee himself and have a finger in the pie'. He did not go as he was looking after his sick father: 'Mrs G. is apparently "afraid of nursing" (convenient!) – one doesn't expect anyone as plain as that to be bone idle,' wrote Agatha with unusual cattiness. Then she returned to the familiar refrain. 'Oh! Max, how I would like a good *laugh* with you. I use Stephen a good deal – but it's not quite the same thing. No Max. Boo hoo.'[49]

Later that year, Stephen moved to a flat in the Lawn Road block. Agatha had predicted that the return of his family would 'cramp his style a little!!'. In fact it precipitated a crisis; he decided to leave his wife. He had one extra-marital affair going already but now, living on Agatha's doorstep, he talked a great deal about his unhappiness and confusion. When Agatha was out of London he wrote her loving and impassioned letters. Meanwhile he was conducting an affair with his designated mistress (about whom Agatha was also critical: 'Margaret's way of life and friends and background are not Stephen's.').[50]

The situation made Agatha extremely uneasy, as it rekindled memories of Archie Christie. She wrote to Max in a state of near-turmoil: 'I keep thinking of the wretched Ethel . . . She has been, I think, a very inadequate wife to him – but then he had known her all his life and must have realised her mental inadequacy. It is hard after eighteen years to find your husband can no longer stand having you in the house.' Of the children, she wrote:

It seems so sad for them – yes – and *wrong* – that their home should be broken up. Stephen is a most lovable person – so very sensitive and vulnerable in many ways – and yet with an odd streak of cruelty . . . Oh darling – life is *cruel* – cruel and separations are the most cruel things of all . . . seeing other people's lives break up frightens me. Not us – not us . . .[51]

Insecure as she was with Max – whom she must have known in her heart would never leave her – Agatha could not have coped with a man like Stephen, who was bound by his nature to hurt her. She would never have embarked on an affair with him, even if he had really wanted it. She was an innately moral woman, deeply attached to her husband and wary of attractive men. By the end of 1944 her relationship with Stephen had lost its intensity: his mistress spent more time at Lawn Road and Agatha was anticipating the return of Max (who was badgering Stephen for a job in the Air Ministry). Once again Stephen became a friend of the Mallowans, remaining so until his premature death in April 1956. His obituary in *The Times* was succeeded for some days by contributions from colleagues, who had loved him for 'the generous magnetic warmth of his personality'.[52] He had burned out, it was said: his nature was always to do too much – work, socialising, acts of kindness – but this was what Agatha had admired in him most. After his death she wrote to his daughter, Lucia, saying that Stephen had had 'the art of living' more than anybody she had ever known.

In *The Hollow*, written in the summer of 1944, there is a character called John Christow: a man of deep vitality and personal magnetism, dedicated in the sphere of his career, with a dull wife and a complex love life. He is entangled with three women at the same time, although the one with whom he is most relaxed, because she understands him best, is the sculptress Henrietta Savernake.

The Hollow is charged with an unusual depth of feeling, and its central characters feel peculiarly alive. Their love affair is intense, moving, utterly believable in its unsatisfactory nature. The character of Henrietta is possibly the most interesting in any of the detective novels; she is rendered with authorial sympathy and, insofar as this is possible, the story is seen through her eyes. She is not Agatha, but she is an Agatha who might have existed, had she retained her emotional independence and her looks. 'Henrietta is a very lovely and satisfying person,' it is said in *The Hollow*, which was exactly what Stephen thought of Agatha.

Only very rarely in her detective fiction did she write from life, and she certainly did not do so in this book. Yet there is a shadowy sense of the relationship that might have been, if almost everything had been different.

Agatha's guilt about Rosalind had come out in her letter about Stephen's children: the emphatic declaration that what he was doing was *wrong*. Yet her own daughter continued to take second place. The pattern of their relationship had been set when Agatha went on the Empire Tour with Archie back in 1922. Her mother and grandmother had said, 'Don't leave a man alone'; but she had ignored their advice, although not on Rosalind's account, and she knew that she could not pay that price again. After marrying Max she never doubted what she should do. Rosalind was sent to Caledonia, then to Benenden (which she disliked, although Agatha used it as the basis for the estimable Meadowbank school in *Cat Among the Pigeons*). Agatha was left free to travel with her husband.

'Where are you?' wrote Rosalind in 1931. Then: 'I am glad you have arrived safely at Nineveh. What are you going to do . . . will you go on somewhere else, do write and tell me.'[53] Meanwhile a typical letter from Agatha began, 'I suppose you are back at dear old Benenden – We got shot up last night – at least not quite as exciting as that – a couple of roving bandits were trying to rob the house next door':[54] hardly reassuring reading. It was Carlo who filled the gaps, sending Rosalind a regular stream of what were called 'Bonzo' postcards[55] and checking that she was informed about Agatha's activities. 'Missus has written to you today so I expect you have heard about the new house!' she wrote in 1934, referring to Winterbrook. 'You will see me next weekend, isn't that a treat for you?'

By 1936 Rosalind was living in Paris with a French family, the Laurins, having begged to be rescued from two Swiss *pensions*.

If I meet some nice people I think it may be alright, if not I don't know what I shall do [she wrote to Agatha in her familiar dry tone]. I expect I shall see quite a lot of good theatres. Otherwise I can't help feeling that it is an awful waste of money, my being in Paris. Give my love to Max and tell him they still think he is my father. They asked me what he was like, meaning Max and I said he was tall and like me. They will get muddled soon.[56]

This was the kind of thing that Agatha found difficult in Rosalind. She refused to recognise what was going on beneath Rosalind's *brusquerie*: the desire to be, if not the centre of her mother's attention, then at least somewhat further from its outer edges.

'Do hurry up and spend all your money and come home,' she wrote from Paris. 'You don't know what kind of brains these people have got, the silly ideas they have.'[57] (Madame Laurin was driving her mad: 'Poor woman she is having nearly as bad a time as I am except that she is making some money,' she wrote to Carlo. 'She didn't know my name was Christie until the day before yesterday and she speaks of Daddy always in the past as though he were dead.')[58] Rosalind wrote to ask if Agatha was 'staying a few days in Paris on the way home? I hope so as I have got a good many ideas as to what you could do.'[59] But Agatha did not come to Paris: instead she arranged for her daughter to go on to another family in Munich. In May Rosalind wrote to Max, her tone of fake rage barely concealing her real emotions:

Before I forget, tell Mummy she is really a pig!! I have just had a letter from Carlo in which she says Mummy has let Ashfield until March. How could she! It makes me absolutely miserable. This will be the first time I haven't had my birthday there. I believe it is all your fault too with your archaeological conferences and things. I just hate you all but perhaps I shall get over it.

Also tell Mummy that I went to a good tea party at the Baronne's today. The Baronne was awfully nice and told everyone how marvellous Mummy was: '*l'intelligence rayonne d'elle*' (I don't think so!) . . . Don't spend all June touring about out there. Just remember you have got a stepdaughter dying of heat, shut up in this Town.

And, to Agatha: 'Would you mind telling me *when* you are coming home. You seem to tell Carlo and not me.'

The next year, 1937, was Rosalind's débutante season: as a divorced woman Agatha was unable to present her at court (her friend Dorothy North did the job in her stead), but in the spring she brought her daughter out to Tell Brak, where Rosalind did some drawing on the dig. Both she and Agatha viewed the 'season' as somewhat absurd,[60] but it would not have occurred to them to bypass it. 'No good saying you don't want to go to Ascot now,' wrote Agatha from Sheffield Terrace. 'Everything is in full swing – Missis has been really active! Your dance is fixed for May 10th . . . I suspect you will live a gay and hectic life and by July will only pray to be allowed to sit at home with your knitting!! Whether you enjoy it or not I think it will be an interesting experience and you'll probably find it quite funny!!' In fact Agatha had gone to a certain amount of trouble for Rosalind, but she could not drop the jaunty tone that kept affection at bay. She had bought her daughter two dresses, she wrote: 'If you don't like them I shall GIVE THEM TO CARLO!'[61]

Rosalind was amazingly beautiful. This must have caused Agatha pain as well as pride, not least because her looks were Archie's: long lean body, chiselled little face. Her portrait picture appeared at the front of *Tatler*, which described her as 'very attractive'. She was photographed by Lenare, posing like a mannequin, but these gorgeous shots also show the vulnerability in Rosalind's cool dark eyes. Like her mother she was sensitive, she formed powerful attachments, she had a deep love of her home and her animals but, unlike Agatha, she had no creative outlets. She could not, or would not, show her feelings. They had to be divined in her, and in this Max did a better job than Agatha. From the first he made sincere efforts with his stepdaughter, despite her occasional gibes about 'tall' fathers. When she was a child he took pleasure in teaching her, and introduced her to the rudiments of philosophy.

She had a quick and penetrating intelligence, although she does not seem to have considered any particular career. After her season she was at a loose end. She became great friends with Dorothy North's daughter, Susan, and together they thought they might become models (an idea instantly vetoed by Agatha, who viewed it as *déclassé*, although this was as nothing compared to the scandal when, in 1942, Susan went to live in sin with 'a doctor down in Bourne End'. Agatha's sympathy for Dorothy was boundless; in some ways she was very conventional.) The two girls spent a lot of time lounging around Agatha's London home: 'Do you remember Sheffield Terrace with Ros and Susan in the drawing room?! The *chaos*!' she wrote to Max in 1944.

Something of Rosalind was written into the Westmacott novel, *A Daughter's a Daughter*. Beautiful Sarah – 'a tall dark girl' who resembles her father – is a 'tempestuous influence' upon her mother's calm flat, which she strides around with a cigarette in one hand and a drink in the other. Sarah's attitude towards her mother, Ann, is also familiar: 'The one thing that Sarah – and all the other girls of her age – seemed to insist upon was an attitude of casual indifference on the part of their parents. "No *fuss*, Mother," they said urgently.'

Sarah is a destructive force in her mother's life, coming between Ann and the man she wishes to marry. Ann is unable to forgive this: she encourages Sarah to marry a man who cannot possibly make her happy, and goes through a phase of actually hating her daughter. Sarah is indeed a 'creature of temperament', but what Agatha also shows is that she is intensely vulnerable and terrified of being displaced in Ann's affections. 'I don't want to be on my own. I want to be with you. Don't send me away, Mother.' As always when she wrote as Mary Westmacott, Agatha saw what she chose to ignore in real life; not least the intrinsic value of her daughter's character. 'She's got backbone,' says wise old Dame Laura Whitstable. This, by the time the book was written, Rosalind had been called upon to prove.

She was at Greenway when war broke out and looked around vaguely for work. The first inkling that something else was in the air came in the spring of 1940, when Agatha noticed the vast number of cigarette butts beside the upstairs telephone, where conversations could be held in privacy. Nevertheless it came as a shock when Rosalind announced, in her usual nonchalant way, that in a few days' time she was going to marry Hubert Prichard of the Royal Welch Fusiliers. She had met Hubert, who at thirty-three was twelve years her senior, when he was attached to the regiment of her cousin, Jack Watts. He had visited Abney, and had also come to Greenway in the company of Madge. He himself had a large and lovely home, Pwllywrach in Glamorgan (although his mother was firmly ensconced in it at the time), and by all accounts was a remarkably nice man. It has been suggested that Rosalind married him so suddenly because she had no idea what else to do with herself; it has also been said that she fell in love and anticipated a life of great happiness. Perhaps there is truth in both these suppositions. At any rate she had her quiet, quick wedding on 11 June 1940, and Agatha wrote to Edmund Cork from the Grosvenor Hotel, Chester, that 'he is very nice and I am very happy about it'.

Rosalind's life again became somewhat aimless. '[She] leads the life of a Wandering Jew nowadays,' wrote Agatha to Max in November 1942, 'has just been passing through London on her way to join Hubert.' In January 1943 Rosalind took on an administrative job. 'I am working quite hard here this week stocktaking, pages and pages of stuff, tinned food, everything in the kitchen,' she wrote to Max. 'There still seems nothing to do. I can't conceive what people find to do in an office all day.'

In May Agatha informed Max that 'She has unwillingly let slip the information that she is having a baby in Sept.!! I am so happy about it . . . Secretive little devil – but I'm glad I didn't know before.' Agatha was in fact extremely anxious about Rosalind's pregnancy. Her letters imply that there had been an earlier miscarriage (and of course Agatha had lost a baby). The two women spent time together at Winterbrook, then travelled to Abney where the baby would be born. 'I shall be so thankful when the baby has come safely – I get (all mothers seem alike) so panicky sometimes . . . It's silly, I know, but her lifeline is broken in both hands – and I think of it sometimes. It's the one thing I want for her happiness. I know she'll be happy with a child.'[62]

Mathew was born on 21 September, 'looking so like Hubert to my mind that all he needs is a monocle!'. Agatha had 'chucked' her first night of the dramatised version of *Ten Little Niggers* – 'Plays don't matter' – and gone to Abney straight after the dress rehearsal. 'H. ringing up and asking anxiously "Does she like it?" "Tell him it's a monster," said Ros. "Far too big." "Is she getting cross again yet?" asked Hubert. "I'll feel she's all right then!!" Oh darling Max – I am so happy. Thank you for all your help and love,' she wrote, although it is unclear what he had actually done. After so much talk of her daughter and grandson, Agatha clearly felt her attention should be back on Max. 'You are all the world to me,'[63] she wrote at the end of her letter; an odd phrase, in the circumstances.

Meanwhile Max was writing his own letters to Rosalind, and in a very different tone from the 'Mr Puper' one he adopted with Agatha. With Rosalind he was droll, relaxed; intimate, even. He was still a relatively young man, only three years older than Hubert Prichard. Now that Rosalind was an adult, it was impossible to ignore that he was almost equidistant in age from his step-daughter and his wife. In 1940 he was thirty-six. Agatha was nearly fifty; Rosalind a lush twenty-one.

Her own letters to Max were those of a pert younger sister, full of bone-dry teases about Max's 'conceit' and the size of his head. 'I might make you a godfather but am not sure yet,' she wrote before Mathew's birth (she did; Max sent a five-pound note saying, 'You might tell me if it is possible to spend a fiver on Mathew all at one go'). Nor, in his turn, was Max especially fatherly, although there can be no denying that Rosalind meant a great deal to him.

He did not write very often but, as he put it in 1941: 'I am more really your friend than you might think from the little action I take to write to you and do things for you . . . The trouble is, you see, that to those of whom I am really fond I find it difficult, really diffi-cult to write, because I want to give them the things I cannot express. But as we are so bloody confused we have to act as humans do.'[64] In 1942 he again admitted his laxness: 'You say you were hurt that I had not written', then attempted to atone:

Long may I live to shake you, argue with you, criticise you,
eat with you, quarrel with you, laugh with you, exchange ideas
with you and find life more and more exciting because of you
. . . you are one of the people and things (for you are a thing)

that I valued, and found good in life . . . I wonder if this embarrasses you at all. I enjoy trying to embarrass you very much indeed, but I don't think I ever really succeed. My privilege. Devilish conceit. In that letter I wrote I answered a long tick off of yours about my conceit. What I said I can't remember.

At the end of the letter he struck a more paternal note: 'Keep your philosophy and a metaphysical outlook in life. Don't be afraid of yourself. Go on loving flowers and green fields.'[65]

In 1943 it was Rosalind who had failed to send him a 'birthday letter' in May.

Maybe I didn't deserve one because I have not written to you for so long . . . Do you ever feel prickly because I don't write to you, or don't you mind? This sounds like one of our old arguments. As a matter of fact I am still crackers about you and I think of you surprisingly often, just about every day! . . .

How are you? What do you feel and think now – I know your pretended answer. 'Nothing.' I would like to come along and give you a good shaking. Is your face really as incredibly small as ever and will you ever look any older? . . . I always miss you.[66]

Agatha might have been considerably surprised by these letters, having written to Max about her recollection of life at Greenway: 'you and Rosalind having rows . . .' Rosalind herself seems to have taken Max in her stride, as she did most things. She was preoccupied now with her husband and baby, about whom Max wrote: 'I am glad to know you are going to have a brat it ought to be a pretty good type with you and Hubert as ancestors. I can imagine you when you have produced it putting it down by the scruff of the neck like a cat in a box of rusty nails, not unpleased . . .' The arrival of Mathew was, he wrote,

the best news from home I have had in this war. Though why indeed there should be cause for jubilation at the birth of an unfortunate brat into this world, handicapped with the prenatal sins of its parents and hidebound with their virtues it is indeed hard to say and I expect that you with your cantankerous and philosophic outlook will already have thought of that . . . I am fearfully pleased about it all, the Lord alone knows why; but there it is.[67]

While Max pontificated, Agatha worked herself to the point of exhaustion. She found it strange to have no proper staff; she had enjoyed cooking at Lawn Road Flats, but this was very different. 'I need a Carlo or two about – a dogsbody, that's what I need!' Charlotte was doing war work, living with her sister in a house provided by Agatha. 'No, I just need Max . . . Yes – I want *Max*. And I can't have him.'[68] She prepared Campden Street to receive the new mother and baby. Furniture was sent to London from the squash court at Winterbrook, 'No one to clean or help . . . my hands are like nutmeg graters from soda and soap – and my knees are sore – and my back aches . . . I'm so *tired*, darling . . . Of course they took these things out of Sheffield Terrace in a rush – Result *nothing* is together.'[69] Agatha stayed with Charlotte, nearby on Ladbroke Terrace Mews, then arrived every morning 'like a daily' to help Rosalind. When Mathew's nurse was recommended to see *Ten Little Niggers* by Agatha Christie, her reply was 'I know – she's our cook.'

In November 1943 Agatha was laid low with flu, and Christmas at Pwllywrach nearly finished her. 'I must say, darling, that I am glad not to be a mother – I don't think I could cope with it!! One needs to be young and strong . . . I have felt very tired and depressed ever since I had 'flu. I shall get over that – shan't I?'

In fact 1944 would be a very difficult year. Agatha was now working at a pitch that verged upon the masochistic. Since 1940 she had, much of the time, given a number of days each week to the University College Hospital, where she worked at her old game of dispensing and was described as a 'tower of strength'.[70] She had cleared Greenway for the Admiralty, dealt with the bombing of Sheffield Terrace, cleared Campden Street for Rosalind, moved from Half Moon Street to Park

Place to Lawn Road. She had lived through the 1940 blitz and the flying bombs of 1944 ('I sometimes worry a bit at the thought of your being in the raids in London, and not being with you, because it is lonely being bombed by yourself so to speak!'[71] wrote Max). This was what happened in war, of course, but on top of this she had written a staggering amount.

The first book of 1940 was the undervalued wartime thriller *N or M?*. She had been promised a good serial sale for it in America, only to be fobbed off with the incredible excuse that 'editors are afraid that such a strongly anti-Nazi story would upset a substantial section of their readers'; 'I am FURIOUS,' she told Edmund Cork, although the book was sold in 1941. In 1940 she also wrote *Evil Under the Sun* and two extra books, insurance against unforeseen events such as her 'sudden demise': *Sleeping Murder* and *Curtain*, final cases for Miss Marple and Poirot, given to Max and Rosalind respectively. In 1941 she wrote *The Moving Finger, The Body in the Library, Towards Zero* (which she also thought might be left in reserve; she was remembering how, after 1926, she had longed for a finished book to throw at her publishers) and *Five Little Pigs*. In 1942 came *Absent in the Spring*, in 1943 *Death Comes as the End*, with much of *Come Tell Me How You Live* written in between. Fewer books, but more activity: in 1942 she had written her dramatisation of *Ten Little Niggers*, which, with its new 'happy' ending, went into rehearsal in 1943, as did a version of *Death on the Nile* (later retitled *Hidden Horizon*). Although her friend Francis 'Larry' Sullivan longed to play the part again, she took Poirot out of the script and instead gave him a 'good part as Canon Pennefather[72] – a kind of budding Archbishop of Canterbury and Sir William Beveridge rolled into one', as she told Max. 'You sound very much the play Puper,' he wrote to her.

A great deal of rushing around was involved with these plays. In January 1943 Agatha was in Dundee with *Ten Little Niggers*, then involved in a vexing saga as to when – if – the play would open in London. This finally happened in September, at Wimbledon, after a dress rehearsal in which 'they had altered the whole of the end and made it quite idiotic'. The play moved to the St James's Theatre in November (where it was attended by none other than the Woolleys).

Three months later the theatre was bombed and the play went to the Cambridge Theatre, then on tour, then to New York.

In between all of this Agatha was also travelling back and forth to see Rosalind who, she wrote, 'never sits down – and is infuriated if anyone else does. "Now mother, what are you doing just wandering about, *singing* too!? There's lots to be done – we must *get on!*"'[73] It was a miracle – perhaps a miracle of politeness – that the vicar who christened Mathew should have said to the exhausted Agatha: 'You – the *grandmother* – Impossible!' Agatha adored her grandson. 'Ros. is going to be a very jealous mother!' she wrote. 'She doesn't like his *looking* at anyone else!!' Max wrote to ask how Rosalind treated the baby: 'Is she as good to him as she was to her dogs.' Then, in somewhat appalled sympathy: 'But by Jove it all sounds like hard work running a house and a baby! Don't overdo it dear Mrs Puper, till Mr Puper is there to look after you in case you need attention, e.g. cook you an omelette in bed.'[74] It has been said[75] that Max would have liked children, and felt the lack of them in his life, but his own words seem to contradict this. In September 1942 he wrote to Agatha that he was thinking of Greenway and of 'the young incoming trees that we planted with our own hands. These are our children, yours and mine . . .'[76]

A week earlier Max had written in more prosaic vein. 'How are your financial affairs,' he asked. 'You never speak of them. I hope it isn't because you don't want to worry me because I want to share your troubles if you have any. And anyhow one doesn't worry about money now. Help yourself to anything in my bank if you need it.' Agatha's reply was a blithe lie, told to protect Max from alarm and embarrassment. 'Worries, darling? As long as you are all right and happy I have no worries. My debts get more and more enormous but it doesn't seem to matter and I don't care!'

This was not quite true, however. The fact was that throughout the war Agatha had grappled with another problem, which she chose scarcely to mention, and about which Mr Puper could do nothing. It had all begun in 1938 – ironically, the year Agatha reached the plutocratic heights by acquiring Greenway – when the revenue authorities in America began to probe into her earnings, which had been substantial in the 1930s: in the tax year 1935–6, for example, she earned more than seventeen thousand pounds from American magazines. The serial market was hugely lucrative for her (hence the alarm when *N or M?* failed to sell), and had formed the basis of a trust for Rosalind. On top of this came advances, fees for translation rights, film and play options; all of this made additionally complex by, for example, the reprinting in new collections of stories that had already been published, and the ensuing multiplicity of contracts.

Until 1938, Agatha had been classified in America as a 'non-resident alien author' and, as such, the tax on the sale of her copyrights was payable only in Britain. This changed, however, when what became known as 'the Sabatini case' was heard in the US Court of Appeals. Rafael Sabatini was a British subject, a successful author living in London but making a large income from American sales. The court's judgment was that he was liable to pay American tax on the sale of his American copyrights. The same judgment, if applied to Agatha – as seemed inevitable – would cost her thousands in back tax, although at the time it was not established how retrospective it would be.

Harold Ober, her US agent, employed a tax lawyer, Howard E. Reinheimer, to handle the enquiries and prepare statements for the US Revenue Board. This was no easy task. Many of the relevant records were missing, and it did not help that both Hughes Massie, Agatha's London agent, and Collins, her publisher, had suffered bomb damage; although, in a sense, the lack of material evidence was helpful to the case. Reinheimer was expected to plead that Agatha and her advisers had taken all possible steps to fulfil the tax authorities' requirements, as known *at the time*. This sounds like a reasonable defence; but when government officials have a scent they are reluctant to let it go. 'The tax people here are being very active in looking up tax payments of English authors and they are now demanding to see Agatha Christie's accounts from the very beginning,' Ober wrote to Edmund Cork in June 1940. 'I'm going to stall on this as long as possible . . .'

Ober stayed cool throughout. Cork remained gentlemanly; but he found it hard to conceal his alarmed revulsion at the rapacity of the tax authorities. He was quietly fond of Agatha, he respected her and knew how extraordinarily hard she worked. What she had, she had earned. When it transpired that she would not receive any revenue from serialisation sales in America until the situation was settled, he relieved his feelings by writing to Ober ('rather a warm letter', he later admitted).

> The point is that owing to the necessity of paying for the war, Mrs Christie will have to pay during 1941 in British Income Tax and Surtax alone an amount equal to four-fifths of her total receipts during the twelve months ending 6th April last, and as you know, more than four-fifths of her income comes through you . . . The obvious reply is that she is a wealthy woman, and should have no difficulty in borrowing the income, but war conditions have altered all this . . . in any event Mrs Christie's assets, apart from her copyright, are in real estate, which is a drag on the market now.
>
> I entirely agree with you that this is a most unfortunate time for the US government to try to get back tax out of people in England, and I do think the strongest possible appeal ought to be made on every ground . . . I am sure Mrs Christie would be the last person to evade improperly any taxation that was rightly due, but this desperate state of affairs can only be met by desperate remedies. I really feel very badly about this. It is against all our ideas of justice that anyone should be penalised to this extent . . .[77]

The 'extent', according to a letter that Cork sent to Agatha in August 1940, could be as much as $78,500,[78] assuming the ruling backdated her liabilities to 1930. 'I really don't think this could happen,' he wrote, stressing that, anyway, $42,000 was owing to her from serial payments. Nevertheless the sums involved must have shaken her badly. Certainly they shook Cork rather more than he showed Agatha; how, he asked Ober, could Agatha possibly pay these sums as well as her British tax? 'It is just like a nightmare having to produce for the Tax gatherer no less than three-quarters of those very monies you have to retain for American taxation.'[79] Naturally enough, the authorities at home had started to get busy, and were making their own trouble about the money that was being held in America. Cork wrote drily to Ober: 'I can quite understand your finding it hard to believe that Agatha will have to find money for Income Tax on monies she has not received . . .'[80]

Agatha was working like a demon so she continued to receive an income, even though she was unsure how much of it was actually hers. Her advance from Collins was £1,150 per book (increased to £2,000 in 1945), from Dodd Mead $4,000 (an attempt to reduce this went down very badly with Cork). A typical British serialisation fee was the £300 paid for *The Moving Finger*. The plays also generated money: *Ten Little Niggers* was a solid source, bringing in an average £200 a week on tour: 'but alas! How much shall I get out of it?' she wrote to Max.

In her uncertain situation Agatha felt the absurdity of owning both Winterbrook and Greenway (as well as two London houses). In August 1942 she told Max: 'We must decide sometime which house we're going to stick to – I don't believe we can keep both.' Max's advice was that she should sell one if it would get her 'absolutely clear'. The next year she wrote of the 'great relief' of not having to run Greenway, then in the hands of the Admiralty – 'no rates, repairs or *gardens*!' – but the thought of actually selling it made her very sad. However, as no buyer was likely to come along in the middle of the war, nothing could happen to resolve the situation.

On and on it dragged, with no end in sight. By 1944 Cork was receiving tax demands on Agatha's income dating back to 1930, plus huge amounts of interest, despite what he called 'the honest doubt' about whether the money was owed in the first place. 'Mrs Mallowan is particularly interest-conscious at this time,' he wrote to Harold Ober, 'as she is having to pay vast sums in interest on the Bank loans on which she is living during the hold-up. I am sure you must wish for the final settlement of this matter as much as we do.' But in November 1944 Ober informed Cork that it 'had been put on the reserve calendar'; probably until the war was over. By that time more than $188,000 of Agatha's money was being held, the majority of it impounded by the government and none of it available to her. 'I realise', Ober wrote, 'that this whole business may seem inexplicable to Mrs Mallowan and to you, and I hope it can be straightened out before many years.'

As she had done all along, Agatha kept working. At the start of

1944 she was back at Dundee with *Hidden Horizon*. Perhaps unsurprisingly, she viewed this interlude as restful. Despite what she often saw as the idiocies of actors, she always enjoyed the company of Larry Sullivan and his wife Danae. 'Oh! it does make me so mad that you have not been with me for my plays,' she wrote to Max. 'I shall probably never have a play on again [sic].' But ideas were already rolling around for dramatising both *Appointment with Death* and *Towards Zero*. She completed the first by March, then wrote two books: *Sparkling Cyanide* and *The Hollow*.

In September she told Cork, 'I have finished *The Hollow* must get down to *Towards Zero*.' But it was, as she said, 'a cruel time'. On 25 August she learned from Rosalind that Hubert had been reported missing in France. 'Poor child,' she wrote to Max. 'How I hope he will turn out to be a prisoner . . . I am going down there right away . . . How I wish you were here . . . I must be very offhand and confident with Ros. The only way to help her.'

A week later she wrote again:

It is terrible for Ros – She is wonderful – never turns a hair – carries on exactly as usual – with food, dogs, Mathew – we act as though nothing has happened . . . But I can't bear the unhappiness for her. If only he is not killed. They were so well suited and would be so happy here in Hubert's house which he loved. Oh! darling, how sick I am of war and misery.

So deep was her sickness that the very next week she was debating with Max whether or not she might go to Egypt: 'My longing to see you is so very great,' she wrote on 6 September. So too was her longing for straightforward escape. 'I am so dreadfully tired, Max darling, I could sleep and sleep and sleep . . . If only I do get out to Egypt how wonderful it will be and if you come we can sleep a lot!! . . . I wish Rosalind could get some permanent help here.'[81]

Surely she would not have left Rosalind at this time? The idea was dangerously alluring, nonetheless. Agatha had pretty much reached the end of the line; her stamina was extraordinary, but she was fifty-four, and weary in her very bones. Returning to Greenway and 'getting it habitable again is a task one rather dreads – I couldn't do it alone without any help'. Turning *Towards Zero* into a play 'lies heavy on my conscience as I promised to deliver it by end of October – sometimes feel I just can't write anything ever again'; 'I get deadbeat here and my feet ache and my back hurts.' Perhaps it was not so strange that she yearned to be elsewhere. This had been her instinct back in 1926; although the circumstances now were very different, the impulse remained the same.

But of course she stayed at Pwllywrach, where news of Hubert's death came in October. Rosalind 'let it make no difference to her – took Mathew out to tea with some people as arranged – eats her meals well and calmly makes arrangements about obituary notices, etc. That stoical temperament is wonderful.' Agatha was left helpless, uncomprehending and admiring, but said: 'I sometimes think too much bottling up must be bad.'[82] In fact, the wound went very deep with Rosalind. Her outward appearance did not change – she had always been dry, direct and brusque, and she remained these things to the end – but her outlook on life became fundamentally pessimistic. This was another difference between herself and her mother, whose determination was always to find the joy in living.

But for a time things were even more nightmarish: fate became vicious and mischievous, and a mass of complications entangled Agatha's misery. One of her uncles died, and she and Madge were charged with handling the arrangements. She returned to Pwllywrach for Hubert's church service, only to learn that it had been postponed. A call came from University College Hospital asking her to be on hand for emergency cover. Dispensers were scarce, duty called, so at the end of October she left Rosalind and went back to her seven-hour days at the hospital. Meanwhile the play of *Towards Zero* had to be finished. 'Everyone keeps saying I look ill and tired and I feel worried that you may think I look very plain and much older.'[83]

Her depression was brief but very real. Her London confidant, Stephen Glanville, was now too engrossed in his affair to be of much use to her. 'I have never felt like it before,' she told Max. 'Write me some words of faith and courage so that I shall have them to read if another bad spell comes.'[84] 'Cheer up lovely,' he wrote in reply. And this, for Agatha, seems to have been consolation.

As the year ended she found herself dreaming of a future utterly unlike the cold grey life she was living. 'I don't think, darling, that our happiness is a selfish thing,' she wrote in January 1945. Greenway was reclaimed in February ('chaos'), *Appointment with Death*[85] opened at the Piccadilly in March. 'Notices haven't been very good . . . Even if it's not a success I don't care – Max is coming home – that's the great thing and *nothing* else matters *at all*!'

It was on 9 April 1945 that Max finally wrote to say, 'My time is up now hooray!' Agatha – described as 'expectantly wagging your tail for master to come home' – sent a list of telephone numbers, as she was roaming around England with *Hidden Horizon*[86]. 'Won't it be exciting ringing you up and saying, Mr Puper calling.' In fact he simply arrived at Lawn Road one evening in May. For Agatha, the war was over.

She remembered it, though, in her books. *Taken at the Flood* and *The Rose and the Yew Tree* deal with the aftermath of war. The strange thing is how restless these books feel. For all Agatha's delighted anticipation of reunion and restoration, a sense of dissatisfaction pervades her post-war writing.

'Lynn thought suddenly, "But that's what's the matter everywhere. I've noticed it ever since I got home. It's the aftermath war has left. Ill will. Ill feeling. It's everywhere," wrote Agatha in *Taken at the Flood*.

Lynn Marchmont is returning home from work overseas. She had longed for the end of war and now finds herself prey to inner turmoil. 'When I was out East, I longed for home,' she says to Hercule Poirot, who replies, 'Yes, yes, where you are not, there you will want to be!' It is this state of mind that lays Lynn open to the advances of David Hunter, a sexually desirable misfit, dealing in his own way with the post-war world.

Of David it is said: 'In wartime, a man like that is a hero. But in peace – well, in peace such men usually end up in prison. They like excitement, they can't run straight, and they don't give a damn for society – and finally they've no regard for human life.' Through this character (and, later, that of Bryan Eastley in *The 4.50 from Paddington*), Agatha understood at last the disorientation felt by her first husband when he returned, apparently whole and unchanged, from the horrors of France. She understood that he could so easily have shared the fate of Hubert Prichard, whose 'gallant but senseless' death still haunted her. Men like these, brave and unpredictable and, in David's case, not quite straight, fascinated Agatha. That is why she has Lynn Marchmont so bored with the fiancé that she left behind, the farmer Rowley Cloade, who feels himself less of a man because he did not go to fight. Later Rowley reveals that he, too, can be something of a savage. His actions, which are genuinely violent, reawaken Lynn's interest in him. 'I've never, really, *cared* very much for being safe,' she says.

Taken at the Flood is a dark book: its mood is that of grey, confused, bomb-wrecked England. There is a sense that hitherto normal people are living by the law of the jungle. When a character says that 'There have been dreadful things in the papers lately. All these discharged soldiers – they attack girls', the reply is 'I expect the girls ask for it.' It is as though the rules of behaviour have changed for ever. Criminality has become commonplace. The roots of society have been torn out and thrown about and anything – including murder – might be acceptable if it leads to individual advancement. Identities are fluid: the tricky old Christie device of having, say, Miss Durrant pretend to be Miss Barton – 'the whole thing hinged upon one old woman being so like any other old woman'[87] – now has a real resonance.

'*Can* you love someone you don't trust?' asks Lynn; to which Poirot replies, 'Unfortunately, yes.'

These unsettled and troubling emotions had been stirred by war, and they suffused *The Rose and the Yew Tree*. This book was written in 1946 and is set at the time of the post-war election won by Attlee. Although Collins criticised it for mistakes in its depiction of an election campaign,[88] its wider view was both acute and prescient. The Labour victory symbolised, very obviously, the end of an era for Britain, but although Agatha used this metaphor she also made subtler points about both class and politics. St Loo, the Cornwall constituency where the novel is set – a Conservative stronghold – is won by John Gabriel, a 'downy fellow' who belongs to the thrusting new world. He is a salesman, 'positively slick, if you know what I mean': a Blair, but a Blair with self-knowledge. 'Oh, I've no beliefs,' he tells Hugh Norreys, the crippled young man who narrates the book. 'With me it's purely a matter of expediency.' His natural home is the Labour Party, but he knows that his natural gifts will shine brighter amid the Tories.

What John Gabriel says about politics is almost shocking to read, it is so cynical and accurate. He is in it for himself, he admits:

'And you can thank your stars that's all I *do* want! Men who are greedy and self-seeking don't hurt the world – the world's got room for them. And they're the right kind of men to have governing you. Heaven help any country that has men in power with ideas! A man with an idea will grind down the common people . . . But a selfish grasping bloke won't do much harm – he only wants his own little corner made comfortable, and once he's got that, he's quite agreeable to having the average man happy and contented. In fact, he prefers him happy and contented – it's less trouble. I know pretty well what most people want – it isn't much. Just to feel important and to have a chance of doing a bit better than the other man and not to be too much pushed around. You mark my words, Norreys, that's where the Labour Party will make their big mistake when they get in . . . They'll start pushing people round. All with the best intentions.'

Of course Agatha herself was a Conservative voter, but the things she was saying went deeper than mere Attlee-aversion.[89] They were about the relationship between politician and voter, and what this said about human vanity. 'Now don't make any mistake, Norreys, I probably *could* become Prime Minister if I wanted to. It's amazing what you can do, if you just study what people want to hear said and then say it to them!'

But John Gabriel – a brilliant character, attractive and repellent at one and the same time – is also vulnerable. Too intelligent for the life he has decided upon, he fools most people with ease but comes up hard against the world of St Loo Castle, where Isabella lives with her grandmother and two great-aunts. ('Did it with an eye on the gallery, of course,' is Lady St Loo's amused reaction, when John Gabriel sees a chance to help his election campaign by saving a drowning child.)

'I know they don't count,' he says. 'I know their day is over. They're living, all over the country, in houses that are tumbling down, on incomes that have shrunk to practically nothing . . . But they've got something that I can't get hold of – some damned feeling of superiority. I'm as good as they are – in many ways I'm better, but when I'm with them I don't *feel* it.'

He seizes upon Isabella, taking the opportunity to drag her down when she falls in love with him. She is compelled by what *he* represents: vitality, ambition, sex. For all that he is a 'common little man', as the Conservative Association describes him, he sweeps aside Isabella's other suitor, her cousin Rupert, heir to the castle and a 'verray parfit gentil knight'. To Isabella, Rupert is dying blood. With the certainty of an animal she moves towards John Gabriel instead: thus Agatha shows the changing class structure, while saying something more profound about the aristocratic instinct for renewal. But John Gabriel gets no pleasure from his prize. 'All the things I'd wanted and minded about all my life seemed to crystallise in her.' He destroys her, although Isabella is proof even against death. 'You persist in seeing Isabella's life as a thing cut short, twisted out of shape, broken off,' Hugh Norreys is told. 'But I have a strong suspicion that it was a thing complete in itself . . .'

Isabella is the heart of the book: the 'rose' whose life is shorter, but no less fulfilled, than that of the 'yew tree' (the title is from T. S. Eliot's 'Little Gidding'). One afternoon she is sitting in the sun with Hugh. He has railed against his fate after the road accident that crippled him; he has planned his own death. Now he sits silently with Isabella, and watches as

across the terrace came running a brown squirrel. It sat up, looking at us. It chattered a while, then darted off to run up a tree.

I felt suddenly as though a kaleidoscopic universe had shifted, setting into a different pattern. What I saw now was the pattern of a sentient world where existence was everything, thought and speculation nothing. Here was morning and evening, day and night, food and drink, cold and heat – here movement, purpose, consciousness that did not yet know it *was* consciousness. This was the squirrel's world, the world of green grass pushing steadily upward, of trees, living and breathing. Here in this world, Isabella had her place. And strangely enough I, the broken wreck of a man, could find my place also . . .

It is like a description of a primitive Italian painting, a Pisanello, where animals of different species inhabit the same dreamscape. It is also like the mysterious garden at Greenway, which became Agatha's home again at the end of 1945.

'The feeling did not last,' says Hugh. 'But for a moment or two I had known a world in which I belonged.'

English Murder

'To Hercule Poirot there was only one thing more fascinating than
the study of human beings, and that was the pursuit of truth'
(from *The Hollow* by Agatha Christie)

'All I can say is, dear Francis Wyndham, that if I die and go to heaven,
or the other place, and it so happens that the Public Prosecutor
of that time is also there, I shall beg him to reveal the secret to me'
(from a letter written by Agatha in 1968 to the editor of the *Sunday Times*
magazine, on the subject of the Croydon murders)

I t was around the middle of the twentieth century that Agatha became
the phenomenon that is 'Agatha Christie'. In 1945 she was a
successful author whose books would sell out a UK hardback print
run of around twenty-five thousand copies. By 1950 she was esti-
mated to have sold fifty million books worldwide, and from then on
her sales simply grew and grew.

It is a paradox, although perhaps not a surprise, that Agatha's
popularity should have increased as her powers declined. After 1950
she wrote a handful of brilliant and unusual books – *Destination
Unknown, Ordeal by Innocence, The Pale Horse, Endless Night* and
Passenger to Frankfurt – but she produced her best work in the
twenty previous years, particularly in that period of intense, sustained
creativity around the war which marks the high point of her career.
In 1950 she published *A Murder is Announced*, and this set the standard for much of what followed: supremely accomplished, utterly

readable, but the product of 'Agatha Christie' the phenomenon, rather than Agatha the writer.

A further paradox is that the leap into fame did not really come about from the books. It was the adaptations that did the trick; particularly the stage and film versions of *And Then There Were None*. The conceptual daring of this book had been recognised by readers back in 1939, but a whole new audience was hooked with the wartime dramatisation and, in 1945, with the 20th Century Fox film directed by René Clair. This was Agatha's first big cinema release, a much larger-scale affair than, for instance, the 1937 British film of *Love From a Stranger*. Agatha later called it 'bad' – although it was far better than the two subsequent films of the book[1] – and it did good box office. The play of the book also ran on Broadway where it caught the attention of the theatrical impresario Lee Shubert, who took an interest in the dramatised versions of *Towards Zero* and *The Hollow*. Later Shubert proved to be a nightmare (he delayed horribly over *The Hollow* while refusing to let anyone else near it; only his death in 1953 released the rights), but that was not the point. The fact was that Agatha was now moving in a different world, the world of success, where everything a writer produces has value and possibilities. Hercule Poirot had become a feature on American radio (although Agatha despised these weekly broadcasts, and turned down repeated requests from television; including those from her former Poirot, Francis Sullivan, extremely persistent on the subject). The play *Hidden Horizon* flourished after its initial difficulties and it, too, went to New York; in 1949 Agatha's version of *Murder at the Vicarage* opened in London, followed by *The Hollow* in 1951, which according to Edmund Cork 'almost burst the Fortune Theatre'.

And so it went on, reaching a golden peak when a story entitled 'Witness for the Prosecution', originally titled 'Traitor Hands' and published in 1925, was dramatised for the West End stage. Out in Iraq in early 1953, Agatha wrote a new ending for the play which she knew to be sensational. Cork had his doubts about the additional twist; but she was right. Produced by Peter Saunders – the architect of Agatha's theatrical career, who had launched *The Mousetrap* to minimal fanfare a year earlier – *Witness* was a staggering triumph. 'The play is the biggest success we have had for years,' wrote Cork to Harold Ober in December. 'It was put on at the worst time of year in the worst theatre in the West End [the Winter Garden, Drury Lane], and it is just packing out.' At the beginning of 1954 Agatha threw a party at the Savoy to celebrate the play's success: among the guests was Campbell Christie, her former brother-in-law, himself now a West End playwright in partnership with his wife, Dorothy.[2]

On Broadway *Witness* caused the same furore, and received a New York Drama Critics Circle award for best foreign play. 'We are receiving numerous inquiries about the play for motion pictures,' wrote Ober. After detailed and often excruciating negotiations – 'the best we could do – with blood sweat and tears', as Cork wrote to Ober – the rights were sold for the then newsworthy sum of £116,000, which was given to Rosalind in a tax-evading Deed of Gift.[3] The film was made by Billy Wilder[4] and starred Charles Laughton, Tyrone Power and Marlene Dietrich. Stylish, caustic and relentlessly entertaining, it was the only cinematic version of her writing that Agatha ever liked. It was also a raging hit.

Here, though, was another paradox: the greater Agatha's success, the more disastrous became her financial situation. In 1948 she had written to Edmund Cork: 'I shall go on enjoying myself and have a slap-up bankruptcy!!!' If this had been meant as a joke, the fact is that it was anything but. How could such a thing have happened? There was now a possibility of the US tax authorities returning to Agatha some of the money that had been impounded since 1941, but as soon as it reached her it would be taxed into nothing by the British government, even though she needed the American money precisely in order to meet the demands on her depredated British income. 'The British tax authorities are becoming very difficult indeed, and there seems to be very little likelihood of Mrs Mallowan avoiding bankruptcy,' Cork wrote to Harold Ober in September 1948. 'It seems almost incredible to a layman that she should be liable for tax on income which arose in a foreign country, and which could not be transmitted to her.'

The insane fight to avoid bankruptcy would drag on for years yet; the logic of the position was that the British authorities would prefer to destroy Agatha's powerful work ethic – or oblige her to move to a tax haven – rather than see reason about her liabilities. In March 1949 Agatha wrote to Cork from Baghdad: 'Anyway, what the hell, is what I now feel about income tax.' Later she would buckle under the strain of the situation, but at that time she refused to do so (perhaps refused to believe it could be true). Cork sent her a steady stream of cheques for serial rights, play receipts and so on, and in an act of rather splendid defiance she behaved as though the shadow of the taxman did not exist, living in the grand style of what she had called her 'former plutocracy'. She no longer thought of selling Greenway – although for tax purposes it was run as a 'market-gardening' business – and, as well as Winterbrook and Cresswell Place, Agatha acquired a new flat in Chelsea's Swan Court,[5] decorated with what she described as 'paintings that can be lived with'. She loved her homes, she loved her gardens, she loved travel, she loved good food, she loved bathing, she loved selective company, she loved freedom and space and munificence, and she continued to revel in these pleasures. They flowered around the work that was the core of her life.

She did write less than before, and this caused Cork to panic, as he attributed it to her dislike of working in order to enrich Stafford Cripps: 'We are very worried indeed that this anxiety about the tax position has had such a bad effect on Mrs Mallowan,' he wrote to one of her accountants, Norman Dixon, in 1948. Cork's agency, Hughes Massie, had come to rely upon 'by far our most remuner-ative client' and her miraculous ability to deliver irresistible manu-scripts. But throughout 1948 she wrote nothing. When the war ended she had had a burst of creativity, almost like an aftershock, which produced three of her best books: *The Rose and the Yew Tree*, *Taken at the Flood* and *Crooked House*. Then: a spell of silence. Her next full-length book was *A Murder is Announced*, written in early 1949 and a very different kind of beast. Thereafter came books like *Mrs McGinty's Dead*, *They Do It with Mirrors*, *After the Funeral* and *A Pocket Full of Rye* – all highly competent, Agatha Christie on majestic auto-pilot – and a great deal of theatrical activity: most notably, the adaptation for the stage of the radio play *Three Blind Mice*, which had been written to honour the eightieth birthday of

Queen Mary in 1947, and in 1952 would open at the Ambassadors Theatre as *The Mousetrap*.[6]

Agatha loved her theatrical successes of the mid-twentieth century. 'I ENJOYED writing plays,' she later wrote, in a tribute to her friend and producer Sir Peter Saunders, whom she had first met when he produced *The Hollow*. 'Not a life project by which to support oneself like books – but enormous fun because of the interesting technique.' Despite the extreme popularity of what she wrote, however, Agatha's plays were lightweight things on the whole. Only *Akhnaton*, set in ancient Egypt, written in 1937 but not produced in her lifetime, and *Verdict*, a failure when produced in 1958, have any real depth. The dramatisations of the novels show an understanding of the medium – Agatha always knew what 'worked' when it came to writing – but they leech all the subtlety from the originals: *The Hollow* and *Five Little Pigs* (or *Go Back for Murder*, as it was retitled) are greatly enfeebled as plays, almost as if Agatha herself did not realise what had made them such good books. The Westmacott novel *A Daughter's a Daughter* was also first conceived as a play. Although the book does not manage to cut loose from its inherent 'staginess', it has vastly more light and shade than the theatrical version.

But through the 1950s it was the theatre that engaged much of Agatha's attention, in between producing what Collins began to call its 'Christie for Christmas' (a slogan that, in 1961, William Collins said was 'good for an extra 26,000 copies'). If the profound and compassionate *Crooked House* had marked the end of an era, then nobody much noticed; least of all the public, which would have been most surprised to learn that a woman reported to earn two thousand pounds a week was a prospective inhabitant of Queer Street; and which could not get enough of Agatha Christie.

It wanted to read her thoughts in newspapers, hear her voice on the radio, study her photograph, collect her autograph, learn her opinions, plague her with fan letters, abusive letters, begging letters, worshipping letters. 'It gives me such a respectable feeling to write to a person I adore,' a young girl wrote from Pakistan. 'You are the second best author in the history of the Human Race and only Shakespeare, whom I regret to say I have hardly read though of course

I should have done, is better than you,' wrote another fan. A letter came from a woman in Stockport: 'I have had another shock this morning, my electric bill came and it is over £6, where the money is coming from to pay it, I do not know. Do please be an angel and help me.' More forceful was the man who wrote: 'Two days ago I tried to rob the bank in Brecon in Wales . . . I have written to no less than forty rich people, even the richest man in the world, not one of them would even see me, I feel there must be something wrong with me. Only you can save me.' From Aberystwyth a man wrote to protest about a joke remark from Mrs Oliver – 'I never trust the Welsh' – in *Cards on the Table*: 'Your veiled attack on the people of Wales has done and will do you and your books much harm.' Another man wrote to tell her to 'lose that insufferable Belgian; he had become very wearisome'. A young man in Hong Kong ('I am of the height of Hercule Poirot') wrote to say, 'I *admire* you and *respect* you and *love* you, Miss Christie, *more than anything else in the world!*' She was asked for her thoughts on America ('Have you ever met any anti-Americanism in England?'; 'No'); on 'les grands sujets feminins' ('Nothing I'd hate more – tell them so!'); on the early life of both Poirot and Miss Marple. She was asked where Lapsang Souchong tea could be bought ('Fortnum's,' Cork replied). Editors of quotation anthologies asked to use her alleged remark that 'An archaeologist is the best husband a woman could have, as the older she gets, the more interested he is in her.' (Cork: 'Agatha did not in fact say this, and nothing infuriates her more than to have it attributed to her.') *Vogue* asked if she would tell them what Christmas presents she most wanted to receive ('NO,' she scrawled on the request). The BBC hoped to televise a series of 'famous people in their homes' and film her at Greenway. Literary societies wanted her to speak, the organisers of fêtes wanted her to cut ribbons, writers wanted her to read their manuscripts. 'What silly letters one does get,' she wrote to Edmund Cork.

> 'People wish to interview her, to know what she thinks about such subjects as student unrest, socialism, girls' clothing, should sex be permissive, and many other things that are no concern of hers.'

'Yes, yes,' said Poirot, 'deplorable, I think.'[7]

Almost all of this she shunned. Occasionally she gave in to a demand or a plea, as when a company of Dutch ex-PoWs wanted to stage a production of *Ten Little Niggers*; during the war they had had a copy of the book and dramatised it for performance at Buchenwald concentration camp. This was clearly a very special request. The more usual response was 'Get me out of this unless you strongly advise it', which Agatha scrawled to Cork in 1951 when asked to do a feature with the *Pictorial Press*. 'The *Sunday Express* are threatening to telephone you to ask you to contribute to a new publicity feature,' wrote Cork in the same year. '(One of the questions is "What do you dislike most about your career" – which is, I suppose, publicity.)' A photographic session in 1953 was reluctantly agreed to and instantly regretted. 'Look here, Edmund, have I got to stand for this? Just about fit for the psychopathic ward, is what I should say . . . from now on, photography is OUT. I don't see why I should be constantly humiliated and made to suffer.' ('We seem to deal with about three photographers a week!' Cork wrote to her the following year.) In late 1953 an invitation to appear on *Panorama* was turned down: 'I am afraid Mrs Christie feels that she would definitely not like to appear on television, under any circumstances whatever. She is, as I have told you, very shy, and she hates publicity of any kind.' It drove her American agency, Obers, to distraction. 'Will Agatha Christie *ever* consent to be interviewed?' they asked in 1965.

This, then, was yet another paradox. The more famous Agatha became, the more she retreated into her private world: her gardens, the dig house with the view across the desert, her intimate circle, her writing. What the public saw instead was the construct of 'Agatha Christie'. In the eyes of the world she became an entity rather than a person.

She allowed occasional photographic shoots, such as the sixtieth birthday pictures taken by Angus McBean, and she appeared, beaming radiantly from inside the collar of one of her fur coats, at openings of her own plays ('Best you've written yet, dearie,' she was told as she emerged on to Drury Lane after the first night of *Witness for the*

Prosecution). She gave occasional interviews in which she said almost nothing. And she encouraged the image of the 'Queen of Crime', the 'Duchess of Death', the woman who looked like a bridge-playing pillar of the community yet had 'made more money out of murder than Lucrezia Borgia'.[8] What a useful creature this Agatha Christie was! Even when she revealed the inner emotions of her creator, which she frequently did in the years around the war, nobody really noticed. The world was too smitten with the persona.

Agatha further complicated the situation by inventing a character, Ariadne Oliver, who is a fictional take on 'Agatha Christie'. Mrs Oliver, who first appeared in *Parker Pyne Investigates*, is a large grey-haired woman who writes murder mysteries, eats apples and is saddled with an imaginary detective – the Finn, Sven Hjerson – whom she cannot bear ('Of course he's idiotic, but people like him'). It is a wonderful joke, and Mrs Oliver is a wonderful creation, but she is not Agatha; although occasionally she does speak in her authentic voice:

> A deal table, her typewriter, black coffee, apples everywhere . . . What bliss, what glorious and solitary bliss! What a mistake for an author to emerge from her secret fastness. Authors were shy, unsociable creatures, atoning for their lack of social aptitude by inventing their own companions and conversations.
> ' . . The truth is I'm not very good with people.'
> 'I adore people, don't you?' said Robin happily.
> 'No,' said Mrs Oliver firmly.
> 'But you must. Look at all the people in your books.'
> 'That's different . . .'[9]

But Agatha's famed 'shyness' was of a different order from Ariadne Oliver's. Like most things in her older life, it traced back to the events of 1926. As a young married woman she showed very little evidence of being shy; quite the opposite, in fact, if her behaviour on the Empire Tour is anything to go by, when she socialised will-ingly and went off without a qualm to stay with the Bell family in Australia, even though she knew none of them beforehand. She also did photographic shoots for the *Sketch* (including some pictures with the very young Rosalind) and showed no dislike of publicising her books. She enjoyed it, in fact. At this point, admittedly, her fame was of a minor order. Nevertheless it is easy to imagine that, if she had remained married to Archie, she would have been less retiring in later life. Her hatred of publicity derived almost entirely from the period of her notoriety, when journalists had written a story that was not merely wrong but that would not have existed at all, had it not been for their desire to create it. Also, and more subtly, it was not enough for her to hate publicity: she wanted her hatred to be made public. In so doing, she was continuing to suppress any lingering belief that she had 'disappeared' in order to advance her career.

Of course if Agatha had remained married to Archie – that great imponderable – she might never have become 'Agatha Christie' at all. Almost certainly she would not have looked like her. Her large, comfortable physicality was a defence against wounds, and after the war it grew more massive still. She lost the last trace of the attraction she had held, until her early fifties, for a man like Stephen Glanville. Her weight rose to nearly fifteen stone, her legs swelled immensely and she became extraordinarily sensitive about photographs. Those taken at Greenway show a relaxed, rather splendid woman with a sweet smile, a penetrating eye and, as often as not, one of Rosalind's Manchester terriers[10] perched upon her like a tiny black-and-tan deer. These images are charming, but they were intensely private. The wider world was less forgiving; as Agatha was only too aware.

So her shyness may have arisen partly from a desire only to be seen by people who knew her well. A friend of Stephen Glanville's daughter met Agatha at lunch in the 1950s, at the Provost's Lodge at King's College: 'I know I thought the sight of her surprising, with a fat, somewhat uncoordinated body and messily applied lipstick.' This was the truth, as Agatha herself knew. But seeing it confirmed in photographs saddened her, as she confessed to Edmund Cork. 'One doesn't really (thank the Lord!) know just how awful one looks,' she wrote in April 1957. 'Oh well, good for one? No.' It was the same feeling she had had after 1926: of a terrible divergence between the way she was seen and the way she saw herself. She felt its poignancy as she created girls like the radiant Gina Hudd in *They Do It with Mirrors*, who says of her beauty: 'It doesn't last very long, you know.' In her secret imaginative self Agatha was still in touch with the Gina she had once been: sitting in her garden at Greenway she felt the presence of the young Miss Miller, sunlit and joyful, within the massive, becalmed woman she had become. Out in the world, this illusion was not really possible. Too much reality obtruded. Thus the fame that exposed and constrained Agatha's life also became necessary to her, because it brought her the means to be private and free.

She was secretive too, however, about the cause of the fame: her writing. 'How on earth is it done?' said her Penguin publisher and friend Allen Lane,[11] in *Close Up*, a radio programme about Agatha broadcast in 1955. This was, indeed, the question. 'The time came when we reprinted ten Agatha Christie titles – a hundred thousand of each. We sold something like two and a half million of these ten stories alone. I know, from her output alone, that she is a prodigious worker; and yet I've never been conscious of her having done any work at all.'[12]

Even her family knew nothing of her writing. 'She would just announce, at dinner, that she had something to read to us,' said her son-in-law Anthony, 'and we'd all groan.'[13] Unlike most writers Agatha had no desire to inflict her creative anguish on those around her. She simply disappeared to a room – rarely at Greenway: her books were chiefly written at Winterbrook or in the East – and got on with it.

It was impressive, to achieve such a separation, and it had never been Agatha's way to mystify what she did. Yet somehow this made it all the more mysterious. Although she never again wrote with the fervour of the years around the war, she was still possessed by a creative compulsion; what she called lazy (one book a year) was what most writers would consider highly industrous, particularly when aged over sixty. Writing was the centre of her life, a demonstrable truth that she sought always to deny. In *Come, Tell Me How You Live* she portrayed herself as a dutiful archaeologist's wife, and in her autobiography as a very normal person who *lived* her life, with delighted gusto, and wrote books on the side – such a nuisance! – in order to pay for her pleasures. Dear Agatha, the talented amateur who happened to hit the jackpot and who never thought of herself as a *real* writer, just a lucky and hard-working craftswoman! What did books matter, compared with cooking meals and going for drives and cleaning ivories with Pond's cold cream on Max's digs?

But this was disingenuous: another facet of the construct of 'Agatha Christie', the nice ordinary lady who happened to have a talent to deceive. 'I can't imagine why I do so much,' she said, in her 1969 interview with the *Observer*. 'Especially as I say, "This is the last one I'll ever write," whenever one is finished.' She also spoke on the 1955 *Close Up* programme (a safe piece of publicity, presumably, since trusted people like Allen Lane and Richard Attenborough were contributors), saying: 'I do find that one's friends are curious about the way one works. "What is your method?" they want to know. Well, the disappointing truth is that I haven't much method . . . And if you lead a pretty busy life, as I do, it's very difficult to find a couple of weeks without any interruptions.'

The guardedness about her writing went deep and was, in its way, another by-product of 1926. She wanted to keep herself hidden from view, in every possible sense. She wrote as 'Agatha Christie', which was a formidable protection, and she wrote as 'Mary Westmacott', which was a protection until 1949, when the Atticus column in the *Sunday Times* revealed that she and Agatha were one and the same. This had not been a state secret. Agatha must have known that the story would come out at some time, but she had not wanted it to: the Westmacott reviews tended to be far better than the reviews she got as Agatha Christie, but she did not want them for herself. Up until the end she always insisted that the Westmacotts were marketed separately, as if by a different author; never under the name of Agatha Christie. That would have brought them too close to home.

She had felt an absolute freedom writing those books. She could go wherever she wanted, into every idea that had ever fascinated her, even into the recesses of her own past. Although she wrote two inferior (but no less interesting) Westmacotts in the 1950s, *A Daughter's a Daughter* and *The Burden*,[14] there was a sense that the revelation of her identity had closed a door: the one that opened into her most private and precious imaginative garden. 'It's really all washed up,' she wrote to Cork. Almost all her best writing was done between 1930 and 1950, the years when she sheltered behind the name of her mysterious other self.

'I think people should be interested in *books* and not their authors!' So Agatha wrote to Edmund Cork's daughter, Pat, in 1964. When she spoke about her writing in interviews, it was in the broadest terms. 'I suppose it's just like making sauce. Sometimes you get all the ingredients just right.'[15] She was giving nothing away – and, indeed, why should she? The only real clues to what she did, and how she did it, come from the evidence of her own writing notebooks. Almost seventy survive and they show that, beneath the pose of ease and amateurishness, she worked extraordinarily hard to shape her plots.

It is typical that Agatha did not buy notebooks specifically for her own use, but would scribble her ideas anywhere. She used her daughter's school exercise books ('Rosalind Christie, Scotswood, Devenish Road, Sunningdale 1925') and a '*Cahier d'Agatha Miller*', dated 1907, from her finishing-school in Paris. She jotted ideas between shopping lists, bridge scores or diary entries ('out to dinner – 8 o'clock Morton's'). Thoughts on *A Caribbean Mystery* are interrupted by '<u>Peter Jones</u> – kettle, cutlery, two pans'. Before sketching the plot for *Curtain* she wrote these lines on Peter: 'You are no longer with us and the days shall go more soberly, my well beloved dog and dearest friend'. 'Get Petrol Coupons,' she reminded herself, before launching into a chapter breakdown of *Sparkling Cyanide*.[16] In the middle of detailed notes about poisons she printed pairs of names with the matching letters crossed out to see what remained, and whether the couple was compatible. 'Archibald Christie' is paired with 'Agatha Mary Clarissa Christie', 'Archibald' is paired with 'Agatha'. She also paired 'Reginald Lucy' with 'Agatha Christie', perhaps to see if that half-regretted suitor might still prove a good bet as a husband. Among the notes for her very last book, *Postern of Fate*, she wrote 'Next make a list of characters', as if reminding herself of what Agatha Christie did. In between her thoughts is a passage from Psalm 84 and a note about a 'Paisley dress, hip size 46', advertised in the *Daily Express*: essence of Agatha.

Agatha was not ritualistic, or 'writerly', about her notebooks. She had always been able to write anywhere – on the kitchen table at Addison Mansions with Rosalind in her cot; in a hotel bedroom; on a table in a dig house – and she could write in any kind of exercise book. She never needed a special pen, a particular typewriter, the props that most writers use to ease themselves in. Despite the external separation that Agatha made between work and life, inside there was a constant flow from one to the other.

Ideas came easily to her: she saw them everywhere. But she went surprisingly round about to find her plots. A reader might imagine that at the heart of her books lay one central twist, or trick, around which a structure was built. In fact the process was more haphazard and empirical. Structure did not come naturally to Agatha; her first book, the teenage novel *Snow in the Desert*, showed that she could write dialogue and understand human motivation with no trouble at all, but had no idea whatever of how to construct a story. This she learned; but the prevalent belief that she did it mathematically, as if working out an equation, is not really accurate. The finished product might give that impression. The workings out do not. She arrived at her structure rather in the manner of a bird building a nest: taking this, rejecting that, recognising what was needed when she saw it, by some means ending up with a smooth and watertight whole.

'Foreign girl (Yugoslavian) looks after old lady who lives with niece and husband or nephew and wife – She leaves her money to girl (Sonia) – Anger – Suspicion – Evidence against Sonia found.' Thus Agatha jotted the origins of *Hallowe'en Party*, adding at the end: '<u>Good</u> idea. Needs working out.'

She collected possibilities, of course. With her notebooks are various cuttings: notes on poisons – pilocarpine has 'no post-mortem appearance', thallium 'similar to chronic arsenical poisoning'; a letter in the *British Medical Journal* about a patient living for hours after being stabbed;[17] a letter from her own solicitors, Hooper and Wollen of Torquay, giving an opinion on the Legitimacy Act 1926;[18] a letter from Madge in 1935, giving information she had obtained about insulin – 'I am very glad, by the way, that your need to know is professional, not personal.' There are also letters from Agatha's doctor friends, the McLeods, whom she met in Iraq: 'Peter is a bit dubious about the Evipan murdering being correct,' wrote his wife Peggy, in response to a query about *Lord Edgware Dies.* 'He says that probably after death it won't be eliminated and so would be discovered. It is used as a sleeping draught . . .'

In a notebook from the late 1930s Agatha wrote the heading 'An Alphabet of Ideas', an oddly touching challenge to herself to come up with twenty-six possibilities. Some were more substantial than others, but all show that she could see the potential in anything. 'C', for example, reads 'Débutantes – Teas etc – Mothers killed off in rapid succession', which sheds light on what was going through Agatha's mind during Rosalind's season. 'D. Dangerous drugs stolen from Doctor's car' played a small part nearly twenty years later in *Hickory Dickory Dock.* 'E. Poirot asked to go down to country – finds a house with a dead man in it and various fantastic details' was a visual image used in *The Hollow.* 'F. Legless man' and 'I. Arsenic taken – looks like caviar' were ideas to which Agatha repeatedly returned, although she could never make them work. 'J. A murderer – after execution evidence proves he was innocent' was the central premise of *Five Little Pigs.* It is interesting that some of her thoughts were extremely macabre – a stabbing through the eye; a steel window shutter acting as a guillotine; a cat with its throat cut – and that they were all discarded.

Ideas took various forms. Some related to Agatha's knowledge of poison: 'The poison that makes everything yellow – applied to dress. V. misleading as another girl had yellow dress.' Some were connected to place: 'Caribbean – Miss M – after illness . . . Bogus Major – like a frog. He squints', which became *A Caribbean Mystery.* Others were about motive. 'The Rubella Idea' lay at the heart of *The Mirror Crack'd from Side to Side;* 'Death-Broker idea' became *The Pale Horse.*

Some books came easily. The notes on *Lord Edgware Dies* are almost identical to the finished article. So too with *Evil Under the Sun* ('Scene. Hotel on Island – Bigbury),[19] which Agatha sketched to perfection, then tussled with various complicated plot permutations before returning to her original. This was something she did frequently. Her energetic mind was not easily satisfied. What would be best? This?

That? Some books cost her agonies before arriving at their eventual form; among these was the boldly conceptual *The ABC Murders*, whose central idea seems so simple but emerged only from a good deal of muddly thought. *They Do It with Mirrors* went through several different forms along the way, two of which branched off to become *A Pocket Full of Rye* and *A Murder is Announced*. *Third Girl* is not an especially complicated book, but Agatha went through pages of notes – even drawing a family tree – in her attempts to build a plot. Among her many thoughts was a twist about a forged will. This was discarded for *Third Girl*; recycled in *Hallowe'en Party*.

Little was wasted, even when Agatha was in her seventies. A 1966 notebook has an idea for 'The Cyanide Murder' which was not developed, although its 'National Trust tour' setting was used in *Nemesis*. This was the sensible side of Agatha, completely at odds with the reckless person who travelled the world first-class and owned the majestic Greenway while owing thousands in back tax; the side she had inherited – or learned – from women like her grandmother Margaret Miller, and wrote into her character Lucy Eyelesbarrow, the Oxford graduate who becomes a housekeeper and makes use of leftover potatoes in a Spanish omelette. Agatha refused to be profligate with ideas. She was once asked by a jovial Cecil Day-Lewis (a sometime writer of detective fiction) if she would sell him a few of the 'seventeen plots' he believed her to have in hand. 'Certainly not!' she replied in the same spirit. 'I intend to write them myself.'

She did not need to be given ideas – although on two occasions she accepted them – because they came to her from anything. *Taken at the Flood*, for example, was another book that went through many changes; its starting-point, noted at least twelve years before the book was written, was simply the name 'Enoch Arden'.[20] Such a slight thing – a quotation, a phrase – could become a hook from which to hang a plot. Ideas in a notebook from February 1937 included: 'A. "Rose without a thorn" and 'D. "I'm afraid of being hanged", which became *Sad Cypress* and *Towards Zero* respectively. 'H. "old lady in train"??' was probably the origin of *Murder is Easy*. So, a single page contained the germ of three books. Fragments of dialogue also abound in her notes; they were the connective tissue in her construction, as in these notes on *Curtain*:

H[astings]. at Styles – has heard about P[oirot]. from Egypt – his arthritis . . .

'I am here because a crime is going to be committed.'

'You are going to prevent it.'

'No – I can't do that . . . It is certain to happen because the person who has made up his mind will not relent. *Listen* . . .'

H. stupefied.

Agatha did not necessarily know who her murderer would be until some way into the planning of a book. She had worked out much of her plot for *Crooked House*, for example, before considering where to point the finger of guilt; her old friend the 'legless man' also made an appearance:

Does Lawrence do it – a cripple – really no legs – therefore is always different heights. Better for *Pocket Full of Rye* – brother who comes from abroad.

Or shall it be Clemency –

Dorcas? No. Clemency – Yes. Her motive. Fanatical – slightly mad.

Edith – Yes – possible . . .

Emma – Yes – Interesting . . .[21]

Similarly with *Hickory Dickory Dock*: 'Hickory Road – Who is killed? And why?' Then, when she had her victim: 'Why did C. have to die? What did she know?' Her notes on *Dead Man's Folly* were even blunter: 'Who wants to kill who.' With *Mrs. McGinty's Dead* Agatha had her central idea but again no culprit:

Try-outs. Maureen's husband did it. His wife – EK's daughter . . . Does young woman – EK's daughter – prevail upon Robin Upward to kill Mrs McGinty – says she is blackmailing her . . . Maud is Lily Gamboll or Craig child – How about *Maud*?

Under the title *One, Two, Buckle My Shoe* she simply wrote: 'Who? Why? When? How? Where? Which?'

Neither was Agatha always sure which of her detectives to use in a book, and quite often she replaced Miss Marple with Poirot: this argues against the prevalent belief that she grew to loathe Poirot. No doubt he was easier to use because, as a proper detective, he could be called into any situation, although the original idea for *Cat Among the Pigeons*, that Miss Marple should have a relation at the girls' school where the book is set, was entirely plausible. *Death on the Nile* was originally a Marple, but this book changed almost completely from its early form and eventually became *Appointment with Death*.[22] *The Pale Horse*, which has no detective, was also conceived as a Marple story.

Occasionally Agatha changed her titles – alternatives to *The Hollow* were 'Tragic Weekend' and 'Return Journey' – and some of her characters acquired new names along the way. Jacko Argyle, in *Ordeal by Innocence*, was originally 'Albert'; Ruby, in *The Body in the Library*, was 'Queenie'; Judge Wargrave in *And Then There Were None* was 'Mr Justice Swettenham'; Miss Arundell in *Dumb Witness* was 'Miss Westmacott'. There was even a 'Mrs Pooper' in the original *Nile/Appointment* plot, a 'cheap novelist' who became the character Salome Otterbourne.

'I can't start writing till I can get names that I feel *fit*,' she wrote to Edmund Cork; and one of her minor talents was her instinct for the right name, the right book title. Nick Buckley, Elinor Carlisle, Caroline Crale, Lucy Angkatell, Bess Sedgwick, Franklin Clarke, Alistair Blunt, Boyd Carrington, Sir Stafford Nye, Ratchett, Blore: these are all marvellous names, flavoursome but not overdone. She rarely used the names of people she knew – although she did use Devon place names, 'Luscombe', 'Christow' – but Inspector Neele is an interesting exception;[23] he investigates both *A Pocket Full of Rye* and *Third Girl*. This went unnoticed, although a Monsieur Nicoletis in France accused Agatha of libelling his mother with the portrayal of the drunk, aggressive Mrs Nicoletis in *Hickory, Dickory Dock*. ('I *invented* the name of Nicoletis!! It's terrible that if you invent a character it should come out so true to life. Positively uncanny!')

Even her apparently banal titles have a power that helped to establish her position as the definitive crime writer: *Murder on the Orient Express*, *Lord Edgware Dies*, *Death on the Nile*. But the title *Towards*

Zero is masterly, as are *Dumb Witness, Evil Under the Sun, A Murder is Announced, After the Funeral, Ordeal by Innocence* and *Nemesis* (her titles were frequently changed for the American market, and invariably for the worse). Of course many of her titles are quotations, from Shakespeare, Tennyson, Blake and the Book of Revelation; or from nursery rhymes, a clever idea of which she made considerable use. It tapped into the desire in readers to have murder placed within a contradictory context: the vicarage, the country house, the luxury train. It reassured, but it had a sinister aspect, hinting as it did – literally, in the case of one of her books – at evil lurking within the world of childhood.

It was also *simply* clever: clever in a simple way. This was what Agatha could do, and where she differed from a contemporary like Dorothy L. Sayers, who was clever in a complicated and ostentatious way. Sayers would never have invented the murderer who pretends to be a serial killer in order to commit a single murder, or who makes a particular bid in bridge to distract attention from a crime. These coups of Agatha are almost blinding, they are such direct hits; and they cut to the heart of her art. Sayers has coups of her own – the haemophiliac whose condition misleads as to the time of death; the arsenic eater who dines with his victim – but they are presented to the reader in a completely different way, with, as it were, the workings-out still visible. Simplicity sets Agatha apart. It was hard won, as her notebooks make clear, but she knew that it was the desired end. The finished product had to be impregnable. Its geometry had to be capable of being turned this way and that, like a jewel in the sunlight. It had to be constructed so that it could be satisfyingly dismantled. Then everything had to be hidden from view.

Because of her simplicity she has been misunderstood. The removal from her books of any trace of authorial presence; the refusal to admit of any interference between the reader and the genre; the unfathomable gap between the artistic sphere in which her plots have reality, and the real world: these are the things that give her work its translucent, almost mythic quality. And yet, seen from another angle, these qualities become defects: a lack of depth and substance. Nevertheless they were deliberate on her part. She knew perfectly well how to write books that grappled with unfinished, insoluble, raggedy real life; Mary Westmacott has an honourable walk-on part in the story of the twentieth-century novel. But Agatha Christie did not choose to write in that way.

Among the writers of 'classic' detective novels – Sayers, Margery Allingham, Ngaio Marsh – Agatha Christie was the only one who did not allow herself to intrude upon her books. Ngaio Marsh, for example, was probably more interested in theatre than in detective fiction, and did not hesitate to make this plain in many of her novels. The books of Dorothy L. Sayers are full of knowledge that is obviously and proudly her own – campanology in *The Nine Tailors*, the advertising industry in *Murder Will Advertise*, academic life in *Gaudy Night* – and while this may delight or bore, according to taste, it is also obviously the knowledge of a woman who is amusing herself by writing in a genre when she could (and later would)[24] do something more artistically strenuous. Agatha was also capable of doing other things, but she never felt the need to hint at them in her detective fiction: she kept to its limits and never patronised them.

Nor did she invent a detective who was anything other than a function of the genre. Hercule Poirot has a mysterious artistic reality but he is also, and only, a detective: an omniscient brain, a *deus ex machina*, an emblem of impersonal truth. Because of his profession he has a detachment from life (which he is once heard to regret, after reading the first lines of Homer's *Odyssey* in *The Labours of Hercules*: 'Was there, here, something that he had missed? Some richness of the spirit? Sadness crept over him'). Miss Marple, too, lives aside from the world. She is essentially an observer, although she does play a recognisable social role in a way that Poirot does not.

The other detectives of the classic murder mystery are not so much detached from the world as from the genre they inhabit. They are all surprising people for the job; unlike Poirot, who is a natural. Margery Allingham's Campion and Ngaio Marsh's Alleyn are gentlemen, set above their genre by class and, in Alleyn's case, by an encyclopedic knowledge of Shakespeare and a powerful sex appeal

The young Agatha: 'I was a lovely girl', she wrote in her autobiography

In Paris in 1906, when she dreamed of a career in music

During her first marriage; and (inset) in 1932

In 1924; the bizarre object on the desk was probably acquired on the Empire tour she had undertaken the previous year

PENGUIN
BOOKS

MYSTERY & CRIME

THE MURDER
ON THE LINKS

AGATHA
CHRISTIE

PAN-Books

THE SECRET
ADVERSARY
Agatha Christie

THE SECRET ADVERSARY

Christie

PAN

357

Agatha Christie
Murder is Easy

Agatha in 195

A 1937 BBC radio production of Agatha's story *The Yellow Iris*; centre right is Anthony Holles, who played Poirot

With Patricia Jessel, going over the script of *Witness for the Prosecution*, 1953

With Margaret Rutherford in 1961. The first MGM Marple, *Murder She Said*, was about to be released; although Agatha liked Margaret Rutherford very much, her facial expression is indicative of her opinion of the film

Agatha's friends, Richard Attenborough and his wife Sheila Sim, in the original 1952 cast of *The Mousetrap*

The Ambassadors Theatre – note the House Full sign. The play moved to the St Martin's Theatre in 1973

A 1958 party to celebrate the 6th anniversary of The Mousetrap. The actress Mary Law is to Agatha's right; to her left is Peter Saunders, so influential upon her career as a playwright

Some of the many faces who have played Poirot and Miss Marple..

Charles Laughton

David Suchet

Peter Ustinov

Joan Hickson

Angela Lansbury

Helen Hayes

Ann Harding and
Basil Rathbone
from *Love From
a Stranger,* 1937

*And Then
There Were
None,* 1945

Tyrone Power and
Marlene Dietrich
in *Witness for the
Prosecution,* 1957

Albert Finney in
*Murder on the Orient
Express,* 1974, with his
stellar cast of suspects

In bridge-playing matron mode, at a 1957 party for *The Mousetrap*

This marvellous portrait was from a 1969 shoot by John Hedgecoe

Agatha near the end of her life; and *(inset)* in her prime

Outside the door of her publisher in St James's Place. Agatha was attending a party given to celebrate her eightieth birthday (nobody has ever met a policeman quite like him). Lord Peter Wimsey is also a gentleman, but so much else besides: Balliol scholar, war hero, glass of fashion, advocate of equal rights for women and highly accomplished lover. Midway through his career Sayers gives him a passion for Harriet Vane, an independent-spirited woman who writes detective fiction. A version of her creator, of course, although there is also an intriguing – subconscious? – hint of Agatha. In *Strong Poison* Harriet is accused of murdering her lover; she is triumphantly acquitted, but her reputation suffers for some years afterwards. At the time of the trial it is said that 'The wretched woman's sales are going up by leaps and bounds', and another character offers the opinion 'that the whole thing is a publicity stunt gone wrong'. Being tried on a capital charge is not at all the same thing as disappearing for eleven days, but in both cases the women were innocent of the central charges against them and guilty of more minor sins. And there is something of Agatha during the period after 1926 in *Have His Carcase*, which depicts Harriet's life after her acquittal: in that book she is portrayed as 'scathed and embittered', bracing herself for recognition every time she gives her name. At the same time she has never been more successful: 'Harriet Vane thrillers were booming.'

Wimsey, who falls in love with Harriet despite the scandal, is Dorothy L. Sayers's ideal man (her crush on him caused much mirth among her fellow members of the Detection Club), and it seems that the female crime writer does tend to invest her detective with the qualities she admires in a man. She also uses him as a symbol of her own literary ambition, which goes way beyond the limitations of the genre. Wimsey is far too deep and sensitive a person to inhabit the world of detective fiction; so is P. D. James's Adam Dalgleish, a highly romantic figure with a tragic past and a poetic gift; so, too, Ruth Rendell's Wexford, a broad-minded liberal with a complex family life and a deep love of English literature. They are all too good to be detectives; all too good for the genre; all, that is, except Poirot. He alone is happy in his world.

So was his creator. This was not lack of ambition on Agatha's part: it was simply her instinct. She could always do more than she let on, but she did not want to draw attention to the fact. For reasons that were both personal and artistic, she liked to subsume herself within the genre. When she invented complex characters – like Henrietta Savernake in *The Hollow* or the Crales in *Five Little Pigs* – she did not allow them to cloud the shining simplicity. When she dealt in complex themes – like the nature of justice in *Murder on the Orient Express* – she refused to explore them outside the geometry.

It is, very often, women who write (and read) these books; but Agatha, for all her genteel settings, domestic detail and unwillingness to describe physical violence, was probably the least feminine of any of the writers of classic detective fiction. Usually there is a sense that female crime writers are using the genre because it is fantastical and safe. It enables them to go so far, in their contemplation of death, and sex and darkness, then to be thankfully reined in again; it enables them to explore relationships within a grid, a pattern, rather than in the vast expanses opened up by ordinary fiction; it allows the creation of an idealised figure, the detective, whom they can colour in with whatever characteristics they choose; it allows them to transcend the genre as much and as cleverly as they wish in the comforting knowledge that it will, in the end, provide a literary safety-net. However much depth is put into a piece of detective fiction, it will never have the power that it would within a straight novel: it will always be bound within the rules of its world. That is the delight and limitation of the genre; for both writer and reader.

Agatha worked with it rather than against it. She accepted and embraced its impersonal structure. She did not want to be like Dorothy Sayers, making herself vulnerable, even ridiculous, as she paraded too much of her knowledge and her unfulfilled passions. If Agatha revealed herself she would do so either under another name or within a highly controlled environment: the impregnable world of 'Agatha Christie'.

In 1966, Francis Wyndham wrote in the *Sunday Times*, 'Agatha Christie epitomises the "cosy" school of crime fiction.' All classic detective fiction is 'cosy', up to a point, but there is no doubt that she came to symbolise the genre. She acknowledged as much when she wrote *The Body in the Library*, a title that comes close to being ironic. She was also, of course, a mystery in her own right. Although it had not been her intention, the 1926 disappearance had fixed her in the public mind as a woman whose smiling façade concealed impenetrable depths.

This was the real point about her image. It became synonymous with what she wrote. 'Agatha Christie' became the living definition of classic English mystery fiction: the respectable veneer that hides the mayhem beneath. 'While Mrs Christie looks and dresses like a happy provincial matron who has experienced nothing worse than the thunderstorm which wrecked the flower show, she has, in fact, been getting away with murder,' wrote the *Daily Express* in 1950. This was the way she wanted to present herself, because it protected her so completely from view. But the image took on a greater significance. It came to embody the very idea of English murder.

Raymond West waved murder away with his cigarette. 'Murder is so crude,' he said. 'I take no interest in it.'

That statement did not take me in for a moment. They say all the world loves a lover – apply that saying to murder and you have an even more infallible truth.

So wrote Agatha Christie in *The Murder at the Vicarage*, published in 1930, five years after the period delineated by George Orwell as the golden era of murder: 'our Elizabethan period', as he calls it drily, in his essay 'Decline of the English Murder'.[25] For him English murder was at its most fascinating between 1850 and 1925, a span of time that takes in cases like those of Constance Kent, Charles Bravo, Madeleine Smith, Frederick Seddon, Hawley Harvey Crippen, George Joseph Smith, Herbert Armstrong and Thompson–Bywaters.

Orwell viewed such murder cases with a mesmerised artistic eye, as a perverse symbol of middle England. He saw in them an irreducible paradox, because they used the ultimate act of disorder as a means to maintain the status quo: for example, murder committed in order to get money to maintain the life one had before the murder. This was murder for gain, the favoured Christie motive. Like Orwell, though, Agatha was also intrigued by the notion of guilty passion leading people into an impossible situation from which the easiest means of escape becomes murder. The motivation is the desire to preserve appearances, to keep everything as it was; as Orwell put it, 'not to forfeit one's social position by some scandal such as a divorce'.

Crippen is the template of the Orwellian murderer. Married to a lascivious harridan, he fell for his quiet and ladylike secretary, Ethel le Neve, but divorce in 1909, from a partner who was determined not to agree to it, was a near-impossibility. Crippen took the other escape route. After burying his wife under the cellar he told their friends that she had gone on a trip to America and, yes, of course, he would send her their regards. Then he looked forward to a life of bliss with Miss le Neve. This would have been the kind of murder of which Archie Christie was suspected in 1926; and which, according to *Unfinished Portrait*, Agatha feared briefly he might commit.

The Thompson–Bywaters murder was born of a similar situation. Edith Thompson, whose husband was stabbed in 1922 by her young lover, had no hand in the actual crime. But she was certainly guilty of wanting to keep up her respectable lifestyle while conducting a romantic affair; an untenable situation which eventually led Bywaters to commit his *crime passionel*. Unless her husband had been amenable to divorce – which, like Cora Crippen, he emphatically was not – Mrs Thompson could not leave him without losing her reputation, her job and, although she earned more than her husband, her comfortable Edwardian villa in the then genteel suburb of Ilford. She was stuck, because divorce was simply too difficult to deal with. It required her to lose too much. And, human nature being what it is, she was not prepared to give up her lover either. For those who wanted – in the cheap phrase – 'to have it all', murder was often quite simply the only option.

'He wanted to marry the girl, you see. She's very respectable and so is he. And besides, he's devoted to his children and didn't want to give them up. He wanted everything, his home, his children, his respectability and Elsie. And the price he would have to pay for that was murder.' So says Miss Marple in *The Moving Finger*, in a passage that might well be called the sacred text of English murder.

It is the ordinariness that is at the heart of it: Crippen standing outside his front door in Hilldrop Crescent, waving to his neighbours, chatting politely about the wife whose body lay a few feet away from them. 'Most of the interest and part of the terror of great crime are due not to what is abnormal, but to what is normal in it,' wrote Filson Young in his essay on Crippen.[26] That is what fascinated Agatha, the same tension that Orwell described, between the life that goes on as before and the terrible unseen rupture at its heart. George Joseph Smith marrying yet another wife, standing at the altar, smiling happily, one part of his mind fixed upon the moment when he will drag her feet up from the bottom of the bath and let her head go under; Herbert Armstrong strutting along the streets of Wye, the local solicitor saying his good mornings, with a neat little packet of arsenic in his pocket. It is called 'cosy', this distancing of death by turning it into stories, dressing it up in frock coats and cloche hats, focusing on the quotidian to accentuate all the more the one moment in the day that is not ordinary, not familiar, that is a small black impenetrable mystery. It is childish, in a way: Grimm's fairytales for grown-ups. Real death, real murder, is not English murder: it is dirty and smeared and grief-stricken. We know that. But the other is irresistible because it *is* a story: a story that follows the rules of behaviour so perfectly in every way bar one, and leaves the human dynamic so beautifully plain to see.

In English murder, motive is always at the heart of the matter. It is money, or it is passion, or it is fear: it is the ordinary made extreme. This was what interested Agatha. Murder without recognisable motive, human motive, ordinary motive, meant nothing to her.

Hence her lifelong obsession with the Croydon murders – the members of the Duff family, in and out of the kitchen, talking about everyday things, one of them with the hidden intent to kill – and, later, the unsolved Bravo case, about which she wrote a letter to Francis Wyndham which was published in 1968, in the *Sunday Times* magazine. 'I myself think it was Dr Gully who killed Charles Bravo.' There were two other chief suspects, the wife Florence and the companion Mrs Cox. All three had opportunity, so Agatha considered the far more interesting question of human nature: 'I've always felt that he [Gully] was the only person who had an overwhelming motive and who was the right type: exceedingly competent, successful, and always considered above suspicion.' Agatha dismissed Florence Bravo because she 'had all the money' and thus no motive: 'She always had the whiphand.' Mrs Cox was 'an obvious suspect at first glance, but not when you look into it – a timid and prudent character'.

'The Bravo idea – would entail woman widow having affair with a doctor' was an idea jotted in one of Agatha's notebooks, but she did not develop it. However, both the Croydon and the Bravo cases were in Agatha's mind when she conceived *Ordeal by Innocence*, the story of a family thrown into turmoil when a murder case, considered solved, is reopened and they are forced to consider which of them might have killed Rachel Argyle, wife and adoptive mother to four children.

> It reminds me, you know, of the Bravo Case . . . no one now can ever know the truth. And so Florence Bravo, abandoned by her family, died alone of drink, and Mrs Cox, ostracised, and with three little boys, lived to be an old woman with most of the people she knew believing her to be a murderess, and Dr Gully was ruined professionally and socially – Someone was guilty – and got away with it. But the others were innocent – and didn't get away with anything.

Agatha also alluded to the Crippen case: directly, but glancingly, in one of the short stories in *The Labours of Hercules*, which contains the line 'I've always wondered if Ethel le Neve was in it with him or not.'[27] Perhaps the answer to this question is given in *Mrs. McGinty's Dead*. Mrs McGinty is murdered because she has recognised someone in her village from a newspaper cutting, a 'Where Are They Now?' story relating to four murderesses. One of the cases in the newspaper is clearly based upon Crippen and le Neve. 'Craig' kills his wife, is hanged for the crime and protects his mistress, 'Eva Kane', throughout the trial, but the story makes plain that she had encouraged the idea of murder.

In *Crooked House* there are echoes of the Thompson–Bywaters murder: an actress, Magda Leonides, hopes to play the part of Edith Thompson in a new play. Occasional references are made to this and it becomes a delicate motif throughout. When a cache of love letters is found, written by Brenda, the young wife of the victim, anyone familiar with the Thompson–Bywaters case will recognise the allusion: Edith Thompson was convicted of conspiracy to murder almost solely on the evidence of her letters to Frederick Bywaters.

I was thinking of the desperate terror on Brenda's face. It had seemed familiar to me and suddenly I realised why. It was the same expression that I had seen on Magda Leonides' face the first day I had come to the Crooked House when she had been talking about the Edith Thompson play.

'And then,' she had said, '*sheer terror*, don't you think so?'

A detective novel by Dorothy L. Sayers, *The Documents in the Case*, is also – as the title implies – reminiscent of the Thompson–Bywaters case. In it, a character makes this remarkable little speech:

'The suburbs are the only places left where men and women will die and persecute for their beliefs . . . the blessed people of the suburbs – they do believe in something. They believe in Respectability. They'll lie, die, commit murder to keep up appearances. Look at Crippen. Look at Bywaters. Look at the man who hid his dead wife in a bath and ate his meals on the lid for fear somebody should suspect a scandal. My God!'

It is not entirely superficial, this idea of the English murder. It is not merely cosy, this fascination with an ordered universe in which a disordered act is committed and hopes to go unnoticed. It is a fascination with people, in the end. People are not just their emotions: they are the interplay between their inner and outer selves; and this is what English murder distils to its essence. It is what Agatha Christie distilled.

She did have a 'knack' for creating puzzles. She had a brain that seized upon potential plots. She had a conceptual daring that enabled her to imagine a different kind of solution, wherein the culprit was not simply one of a set of possible suspects, as in almost every other example of crime fiction. With her, the solution was not merely a question of one guilty party among a cast of innocents: it could be everybody, or nobody, or a child, or the apparent victim: the surprise was not in 'who did it', but in the possibilities within the very idea of the solution.

Because of her facility – which nonetheless did not come easily – and her unusual clarity of exposition, Agatha Christie has been regarded as a craftsperson rather than a writer. She herself used this description in her autobiography. When she was awarded the CBE in 1956 ('It ought to have been at least a damedom!' wrote Edmund Cork), she replied: 'I feel it's one up to the Low Brows!!' But this was another example of the disingenuous persona that she adopted, very much at odds with the possessive pride in her work that she displayed in much of her correspondence with her literary agent. 'I'm not just a performing dog for you all,' she wrote in 1966. 'I'm the writer.'[28]

But it is as the performing dog that she is seen. 'Agatha Christie writes animated algebra,' wrote Francis Wyndham, in his essentially admiring and perceptive 1966 piece. '[She] keeps her distance, according to the rules of a craft which she herself laid down and seldom breaks. This best of all sellers is abstract, enigmatic, logical and completely ruthless.' Other commentators have said the same thing in less flattering terms. 'Who cares who killed Roger Ackroyd?' was the famous question posed by Edmund Wilson in 1944, who wrote an essay dissecting the entire genre and – according to a *Times* column written by Bernard Levin in 1977 – 'found not one of the books worth the time of an intelligent adult. Nor are they, for they are really nothing more than a verbal equivalent of those bent-steel puzzles in which the two bits of tangled metal look inextricably joined until you twist them so . . . when they come apart without further difficulty.' Agatha Christie, wrote Levin, was the best of them, but such praise meant quite literally nothing. He would have agreed with Agatha's so-called friend Robert Graves (who in fact preferred the company of Max Mallowan), who praised her books to her face and behind it stated that 'her English was schoolgirlish, her situations for the most part artificial, and her detail faulty'.[29]

In 1958 Raymond Chandler wrote to a French literary critic, Robert Campigny: 'The idea that Mrs Christie baffles her readers without trickery seems almost impossible for me to believe. Isn't it true to say that rather she creates her surprises by destroying the portrait of a character or of a person in a novel whom she has up to this point depicted in colours completely opposed to the finished portrait?' Chandler was irritated by Agatha Christie, whose *And Then There Were None* had been sold to him as 'the perfect crime story' but which he found full of impossibilities.

> I'm very glad I've read the book because it finally and for all time settled a question in my mind that had at least some lingering doubt attached to it [he wrote to a friend in 1940]. Whether it is possible to write a strictly honest mystery of the classic type. It isn't. To get the complication you fake the clues, the timing, the play of coincidence, assume certainties where only fifty % chances exist at most. To get the surprise murderer you fake character, which hits me hardest of all, because I have a sense of character . . .

Since then Agatha has been described by other crime writers in similar terms. According to Julian Symons, she wrote 'riddles rather than books'. H. R. F. Keating said of her: 'She never tried to be clever in her writing, only ingenious in her plots.' Even admiration was expressed with reservations. But in 1992 the criticism got nasty, reflecting a growing view that she was outdated to the point of offensiveness: a Channel Four television programme, *J'Accuse*, took the view that Agatha Christie had murdered the genre, no less. She 'was a killer, and her victim was the British crime novel', as the writer Michael Dibdin put it.

> Her aim was to fool the readers, and she sacrificed everything to achieve it. The plots in Christie's novels were all basically the same – an ill-assortment of people gathered at an out-of-the-way place where a murder takes place. The characters were all generalised types. There were never any complex psychological characters. They were devoid of any emotional depth. Her books were artificially pure, and she ignored the problems faced by society.

He went on to make the accusations of snobbery and xenophobia that have frequently been levelled. On the same programme, Ruth Rendell said: 'When I read one of her books, I don't feel as though I have a piece of fiction worthy of the name in front of me. With death, I do feel there should be an element of shock and horror and pain – but pain and passion aren't there in Agatha Christie novels.'

Agatha had a cold eye, for sure. The 'Rubella Idea' that she jotted in her notebooks is one whose real-life origin can be identified: it came from the pharmacist with whom she worked in the Second World War, whose daughter was registered blind, the victim of German measles. Agatha was extremely kind to this child and gave her as a gift a Manchester terrier bred by Rosalind; at the same time, part of her mind was ticking away on what would later become *The Mirror Crack'd from Side to Side*. This book – in which a child is born imbecilic as a result of its mother having contracted German measles – was uneasily received by her American agency, which thought the subject matter potentially offensive:[30] 'It was out for the women's magazines,' Edmund Cork wrote with reference to the serialisation market. But this would not have stopped Agatha writing the book. 'She was a tough old lady in that regard,' says P. D. James.[31] 'She's perhaps the only writer who would have a child as a murderer, and quite happy to have a child murdered. Most of us would shy away from that. But she doesn't. Anybody could be murdered in Agatha Christie, and anybody was.'

P. D. James does not take quite the same view as most of the crime-writing fraternity – or sorority – although she does see Agatha Christie's plots as frequently absurd. 'I particularly like – from the point of view of incredibility – *The Body in the Library*. Now here we are expected to believe that this blonde dancer who they wanted to get out of the way (and they could quite easily have murdered the old man, put a pillow over his face) – instead we have this extraordinary plot in which they kidnap a Girl Guide who doesn't look anything like her . . . For one thing the time sequence is impossible. Any woman would know that to dye a brunette blonde you've got to bleach the hair first, and it would take hours and be quite a skilled job. The pathologist would know just by looking at the other hair on her body that this is not a natural blonde! But of course there isn't a pathologist . . . But that doesn't matter, because we are in Christie Land. We're not dealing with reality. We're dealing with a different form of reality.'

This, of course, is the point; and a rather more subtle point than it is generally allowed to be. 'Christie Land' is all too often understood in the most banal possible terms, not as an artistic construct but as a stage set. Agatha Christie is stuck for all eternity at a tea-party in a country vicarage, sticking a fork into her seedcake as the bank manager's wife chokes on a strychnine sandwich. Around her the real world turns, but she remains fixed in 1932: a time when servants were adenoidal, ladies never showed their feelings in public and Jews had to be asked for the weekend, damn them.

The *J'Accuse* criticisms are not without substance. Ideas that range free in the Mary Westmacott books are clipped to the demands of detective fiction; while *The Rose and the Yew Tree* examines the issue of class with an open, questing mind, Agatha Christie deploys what would now be called snobbishness without a second thought. In *The Body in the Library*, for example, a young hotel dancer is taken up by a rich old man in the weeks before her murder, much to the horror of the old man's family, to whom she was a 'common little piece' on the make. When her body is found, the dead girl is wearing an old white dress; from this Miss Marple deduces that she was not prepared to go on a date, else her clothes would have been new. 'A well bred girl', she explains, 'is always very particular to wear the right clothes for the right occasion. I mean, however hot the day was, a well bred girl would never turn up at a point to point in a silk flowered frock. [But] Ruby, of course, wasn't – well, to put it bluntly – Ruby *wasn't* a lady. She belonged to the class that wear their best clothes however unsuitable to the occasion.'

In real life Agatha probably *was* something of a snob; even people who liked her will say so. She was not offensively snobbish, and she could empathise with those who, like working-class Michael in *Endless Night*, see life from the other side. But she had grown up with social hierarchies and preferred to maintain them ('Life is so hard without SERVANTS!' she wrote in the 1950s). Fond though she was of both Charlotte Fisher and Edmund Cork, in a sense she still saw them as staff.

More serious are the frequently levelled accusations of xenophobia, even racism. This last chiefly derives from the original title of *And Then There Were None*: somewhat absurd, as in 1938 'Ten Little Niggers' was simply the name of a nursery rhyme. But by the 1960s the title had become decidedly offensive – as, albeit less so, was its replacement title, *Ten Little Indians* – and when the play of the book was staged in Birmingham in 1966, placards reading 'Contemptuous Reference to Coloured People' were held outside the theatre.[32] More damningly, Agatha's books do harbour some highly unfortunate references to black people. 'I'm not a damned nigger,' says a drunk young man in *Lord Edgware Dies* and, in *Death in the Clouds*, a young couple agree that they 'disliked loud voices, noisy restaurants and negroes'. *Hickory Dickory Dock* also has a 'Mr Akibombo' whose primitive speech patterns would certainly offend modern sensibilities, although Agatha herself had no such intention ('There's no feelings of that sort [racial] here amongst the students, and Sally certainly isn't like that. She and Mr Akibombo have lunch together quite often, and nobody could be blacker than he is.')

When Agatha was a child her father, Frederick Miller, wrote a short story called 'Jenkins Gives a Dinner'. It contains, within its depiction of New York club life, a description of a game in which the young blue bloods of the Union Club gamble on the number of black people walking up or down the street outside: the game is called 'Nigger Up, Nigger Down'.

In other words, Agatha was born into a world that thought this way and said such things. 'It really is so silly!' she replied to Edmund Cork, who before the 1962 revival of the play had written, 'We have had a spot of bother over the title.' But a late poem called 'Racial Musings' proves that her casual prejudices had no real or lasting substance; in it she takes issue with the white man for his 'unpigmented pride'.

It was probably her remarks against Jews, however, that got her into most trouble. After the war, complaints were made to both Collins and Dodd Mead, her American publishers, and in 1947 an official objection was sent to Dodd Mead by the Anti-Defamation League.

Edmund Cork did not tell Agatha of the extent of the problem although in 1953 he wrote to his American counterpart, Harold Ober, saying, 'Yes, by all means authorise Dodd to omit the word "Jew" when it refers to an unpleasant character in future books.' It has been noted in Agatha's defence that the Westmacott novel *Giant's Bread* presents a sympathetic Jewish character, Sebastian Levinne, who 'had always had that curious maturity of outlook which is the Semitic inheritance'. Two years later, however, in *Lord Edgware Dies*, she had a character make reference to 'the fair (I beg her pardon, dark) Rachel in her box at Covent Garden', whose 'long Jewish nose is quivering with emotion'.

In real life Agatha was no serious anti-Semite; she would not, like others of her class, have enjoyed the ambassadorial hospitality of von Ribbentrop. In 1933 she had met a Nazi in the unlikely setting of Baghdad. The Director of Antiquities, an apparently highly civilised man, was playing the piano when he suddenly reacted to a casual reference to Jews: 'They should be exterminated. Nothing else will really do but that.' She was shocked to the core by this although, rather amazingly, it did not put a stop to the cheap anti-Semitism in her books: *The Hollow* contains a lisping 'Whitechapel Jewess with dyed hair and a voice like a corncrake'. Perhaps this proves, as nothing else could, how meaningless such references really were.

Of course Agatha was not alone in writing these things ('Mr Antoine . . . was rather surprisingly neither Jew nor South-American dago, nor Central European mongrel,' wrote Dorothy L. Sayers, in the Wimsey novel *Have His Carcase*). But she fails when measured against contemporary levels of prejudice, which we believe to be lower although they are, on the whole, merely different. According to modern judgements, a person is the sum of their opinions; Agatha might have made crass remarks about Jews or blacks or servants but it would never have occurred to her that conclusions about her own character might be drawn from this, any more than from her relaxed and 'liberal' portrayal of a lesbian couple in *A Murder is Announced*. To her, life was not so simple. She loathed what would now be called – in the convenient shorthand – political correctness, the belief systems that give the illusion of thought to stupid people ('Don't you think you go in too much for labels?' says Hilary Craven in *Destination Unknown*, as another character spouts about Communism and Fascism). Agatha knew that human nature would always, in the end, resist ideology and false solutions. As a very old woman she tried to vote against British entry into the European Community, believing the whole thing a doomed and unnecessary enterprise; an opinion that many now share (although at the time Max convinced her to change her mind). In 'Racial Musings' she wrote: 'Some think, and more than one/That coffee-coloured children meet the case'. But she could not bear the vision of a future in which the divine human muddle has been tidied up in the name of 'progress'. 'Oh, coffee-coloured world/You'll be a BORE.'

For all that she was a product of her background, Agatha was also a creature of her time: she engaged deeply with the middle years of the twentieth century. 'Agatha Christie' may be fossilised in time but Agatha herself was not. She wrote about the world she lived in: about class mobility in *Endless Night*; political fanaticism in *One, Two, Buckle My Shoe, Destination Unknown* and *The Clocks*; the effects of war in *Taken at the Flood, The 4.50 from Paddington* and *A Murder is Announced*; social engineering in *They Do It with Mirrors*; virtual reality in *At Bertram's Hotel*; café culture in *The Pale Horse*; drug culture in *Third Girl*; changing attitudes towards the death penalty, heredity, the nature of justice, guilt and criminal responsibility. She did not draw attention to the fact that she was writing about these things. That was not her way. Nor did she particularly agree with much contemporary thinking, even though she engaged with it. She was still, at root, a late Victorian who believed in God and the human spirit rather than 'ideas'.

In *Appointment with Death*, for example, she dealt in some depth with the fashionable notion of the subconscious mind. An eager young doctor sees it as a problem to be solved – the 'modern' view – but her older counterpart knows better.

'There are such strange things buried down in the unconscious. A lust for power – a lust for cruelty – a savage desire to tear and rend – all the inheritance of our past racial memories . . . They are all there, Miss King, all the cruelty and savagery and lust . . . We shut the door on them and deny them conscious life, but sometimes – they are too strong.'

Then he goes on, developing his theme to take in the dangerous political nonsense spoken in the pre-war years:

'We see it all round us today – in political creeds, in the conduct of nations. A reaction from humanitarianism – from pity – from brotherly goodwill. The creeds sound well sometimes – a wise regime – a beneficent government – but imposed by *force* – resting on a basis of cruelty and fear. They are opening the door, these apostles of violence, they are letting out the old savagery, the old delight in cruelty *for its own sake*! Oh, it is difficult – Man is an animal very delicately balanced. He has one prime necessity – to survive. To advance too quickly is as fatal as to lag behind. He must survive! He must, perhaps, retain some of the old savagery, but he must not – no definitely he must not – *deify* it!'

This, in 1938, was really rather prescient. But because it was written by 'Agatha Christie', it was not noticed as such. It was subsumed within the whole, the construct. Yet this was one of the moments when Agatha herself was briefly glimpsed from behind her persona. There are many such examples – most of them, again, hidden from view – such as this in *One, Two, Buckle My Shoe*:

'If I was ruined and disgraced – the country, *my* country was hit as well. For I've done something for England, Monsieur Poirot. I've held it firm and kept it solvent. It's free from Dictators – from Fascism and from Communism . . . I do like power – I like to rule – but I don't want to tyrannise . . . We're *free*. I care for all that – it's been my life work.'

These were Agatha's beliefs, unchanging within the fluidity of her imagination and the upheavals of her century. They are the still centre of 'Agatha Christie': without them the construct would have crumbled long ago, like the fake Edwardian façade of Bertram's Hotel.

But at the heart was her fascination with human nature. This is the great joke: Agatha Christie was not interested in murder. She was interested in 'English murder', which is a different thing, relating to the human dynamic rather than the act of violence. She has been criticised for failing to show the effects of murder, the blood and gore and grief; but naturally she does not show these things, because they were not her subject. Similarly it has been said that the murders she describes could never happen in actuality. In real life, nobody would kill by dropping a quern through a window on to their victim's head; they would not give themselves an alibi by having their wife masquerade as a dead body; nor would they plan a murder by running around a ship deck then shooting themselves in the leg to appear incapacitated: these things cannot happen. But then, Agatha never thought they could. Why would anyone imagine that she intended these plots to be seen as credible events? They were 'animated algebra', a puzzle to be solved.

Raymond Chandler's criticisms of *And Then There Were None*[33] are totally accurate: 'It is as complete and shameless a bamboozling of the reader as ever was perpetrated. And I won't go into the mechanism of the crimes, most of which were predicated on pure chance, and some actually impossible.' All true. But all, in a way, sublimely irrelevant. The puzzle in Agatha Christie has nothing to do with the actual fact of murder: the fact that a murder might be a physical near-impossibility does not affect the puzzle. It is there to be solved, not to be compared with reality. And what is being solved is not the act of murder, but the human dynamic. *That* is where the reader seeks clarity: within the suspects, the characters, the people.

Now this, of course, is the opposite of the accepted view, which says that Agatha Christie writes brilliant puzzles devoid of insight into either emotion or character. Her books are still read because readers want to solve the puzzle; having done so, they do not read the book again; or, if they do, it is because they are guiltily fascinated by the image of a vanished era in which servants are adenoidal, ladies never show their feelings in public etc., etc.

And yet: how can this be true? How *can* these books have survived, when clever detective writers like John Dickson Carr (creator of the 'locked-room' mysteries), Margery Allingham (capable of a stylish phrase: 'He looked proudly puzzled, like a spaniel which has unexpectedly retrieved a dodo') and even Sayers (excellent, in her singular fashion) are no longer part of the common currency? Can it *really* be due to the quality of the puzzle, when half the world knows that the narrator did it, they all did it or the policeman did it? Might it not be due to something else, something within the puzzle, invisible most of the time and yet sensed, all the same?

Is it not that the quality of Agatha's imagination – so powerful in her other writings – underpins this disciplined geometric structure, and makes it durable? 'All the time, yes, we get the sense that there's rather more there than is apparent,' says P. D. James, whose book *A Certain Justice* is based upon an identical idea to *Murder on the Orient Express*. Both books turn upon the vexed question of justice versus legality: an insoluble question, within books that demand solutions. If the murderer of a child has escaped prosecution, do the child's connections have the right to exact justice? In *A Certain Justice* this idea is expanded into a novel – realistic, detailed, very fine – in which the solution of the 'puzzle' plays a minor and deliberately sidelined part; in *Orient Express* the puzzle and its solution *are* the novel, the mythic resonance of the theme barely sketched but present in the structure, the plot, the very bones of the book. Of course 'they were all in it': what other solution could be possible, or could give the necessary satisfaction, in this book of Agatha's?

When she is working at her best – by no means always the case – the satisfaction of the solution is intense and profound, because it solves the puzzle and resolves the human dynamic. In a book like *Five Little Pigs*, the plot shadows the characters so closely that the workings of the mystery are the workings of human nature, and the solution depends entirely upon the revealed truth of human nature. What a magnificent premise, that a painter should be killed because his model has fallen in love with him, and he is pretending to be in love with her because he wants to finish his painting! A remarkable, satisfying idea. Not real, but true.

And then the idea that lies within the plot of *Towards Zero*: the urge for revenge by a husband upon the wife who left him for another man. He commits a murder for no other reason than to have his ex-wife hanged for it. A powerful, violent, sick idea, not described as such because Agatha did not do that; she simply let the idea become the plot. *Towards Zero* (in which the film director Claude Chabrol[34] saw possibilities) is the sort of book that might have been imagined by Ruth Rendell, who would certainly have probed more deeply into the darkness and perversity of the motive. The character of Nevile Strange, the murderer, would have been written very differently. Ruth Rendell would have laid bare the inner workings of his psyche; Agatha Christie does no such thing, and because she merely presents a man like Nevile, rather than analysing him, she is said to be unable to create fully rounded people. With Nevile Strange she does indeed, as Raymond Chandler wrote, 'fake character'. Nevile is a gentleman tennis player, a rich and smiling amateur, the kind of person whom Christie's detractors would accuse her of favouring on purely snob grounds. In fact she is penetrating the gentlemanly persona with cool-eyed accuracy. Nevile uses his 'good-loser' act to conceal the fact that he actually cannot bear to lose; beneath layers of well-bred concealment he is desperate to settle the score with his ex-wife, and his public image helps him to do so. So it is not Agatha Christie, but Nevile himself, who is faking character; insofar as that phrase means anything at all.

Is character really only revealed through 'inner workings'? Surely not; surely this is an absurd idea, positively sixth-form, thrown at Agatha Christie by critics who disapprove of her on other grounds. 'She sometimes might be apparently simplistic in her characterisation, that doesn't mean to say that it's not true characterisation,' says P. D. James. Stereotypes, her detractors say: 'but then, many people *are* types', as Bevis Hillier wrote in his 1999 essay on Christie. And, as with Nevile Strange, the books are at least as intent upon subverting stereotypes as upholding them: in fact Agatha Christie often uses stereotypes to mislead us, because she knows that we believe in them, or at least that we believe *her* to believe in them. In *Evil Under the Sun* the line throughout is that the murdered vamp Arlena has been killed in consequence of her irresistibility to men. In fact, as Hercule Poirot realises, the opposite is the truth. 'I saw her very differently. It was not she who fatally attracted men – it was men who fatally attracted her. She was the type of woman whom men care for easily and of whom they as easily tire . . .' Arlena dies because she is rendered vulnerable by her need for male affirmation of her beauty: flattery renders her helpless in every sense.

It is *simply* clever, this inversion of the cliché, but it is so much more than that. This twist of Agatha's upon the *femme fatale* is also the truth: women like Arlena are not so much predators as prey. And so the twist slots the whole book into position. It solves the puzzle because it solves the character: *that* is why it is satisfying.

It also tends to go unnoticed, because the writer has no especial desire to draw attention to it. This, again, is a function of Agatha Christie's supremely deceptive simplicity. Whereas in Ruth Rendell – a writer whom the modern world admires – the mysteries of character are the object of morbid scrutiny, in Agatha Christie they are a given: she assumes we know the ways of the world. For all her so-called 'cosiness', she is a sophisticate. Adultery, for example, is taken for granted. Henrietta Savernake is not condemned in any way for her love affair with John Christow. In *The Mysterious Affair at Styles* it is accepted that both partners in the central marriage are amusing themselves elsewhere. In *Sparkling Cyanide* there is no question but that the young, beautiful Rosemary Barton will cheat on her older, duller husband ('He'd schooled himself to accept – incidents!'). Nor does being capable of adultery necessarily make somebody capable of murder. Agatha might allow her experiences to cast shadows in her books but she could always detach from them: they infused, but did not influence, what she wrote. It has been said that she had a tendency to cast Archie-types in the role of killer, though it is hard to see where this idea came from. It is simply not the kind of thing she did.

If Agatha Christie could accept human fallibility as a fact of life so, too, could her detectives. In *Five Little Pigs* Poirot says: 'Me, I lead a very moral life. That is not quite the same thing as having moral ideas.' In *Sleeping Murder* Miss Marple is accused of being a 'wonderful cynic', to which she replies: 'Oh dear, Mr Reed, I do hope not *that*. One always has *hope* for human nature.'

Both, however, are unambiguous in their condemnation of murder. Only in *Murder on the Orient Express* does Poirot decide that it is excusable to kill; only in *Curtain* does he display ambivalence. Otherwise it is as he always says: 'I do not approve of murder.' Miss Marple is stronger still. 'Really, I feel quite pleased to think of him being hanged,' she says, at the end of *The Body in the Library*.

Poirot is tempted by the arguments of the banker Alistair Blunt in *One, Two, Buckle My Shoe*, who pleads that he has committed murder for the sake of his country, and should be let off for the same reason: 'If *I* went – well, you know what would probably happen. I'm *needed*, Monsieur Poirot. And a damned double crossing, blackmailing rogue of a Greek was going to destroy my life work.' Poirot agrees. He believes in the politics of conservative solvency, and fears a world without them (this book was written in 1939). Yet he speaks in his creator's voice when he says that nonetheless Blunt must be called to account.

'You are a man of great natural honesty and rectitude. You took one step aside – and outwardly it has not affected you . . . But within you the love of power grew to overwhelming heights. So you sacrificed four human lives and thought them of no account.'

'Don't you realise, Poirot, that the safety and happiness of the whole nation depends on me?'

'I am not concerned with nations, Monsieur. I am concerned with the lives of private individuals who have the right not to have their lives taken from them.'

Poirot is troubled by the arrest of Alistair Blunt; he has real sympathy for Jacqueline de Bellefort in *Death on the Nile*.

'Don't mind so much, M. Poirot! About me, I mean. You do mind, don't you?'

'Yes, Mademoiselle.'

'But it wouldn't have occurred to you to let me off?'

Hercule Poirot said quietly, 'No.'

She nodded her head in quiet agreement.

'No, it's no use being sentimental. I might do it again . . . I'm not a safe person any longer. I can feel that myself . . .' She went on broodingly: 'It's so dreadfully easy – killing people. And you begin to feel that it doesn't matter . . .'

Jacqueline is not a killer by nature; the man she loves wants to commit a murder, and she knows that he is not clever enough to do it alone. 'So I had to come into it, too, to look after him,' she says.

'Poirot had no doubt whatever that her motive had been exactly what she said it was. She herself had not coveted Linnet Doyle's money, but she had loved Simon Doyle, had loved him beyond reason and beyond rectitude and beyond pity.'

Yet Poirot remains 'bourgeois' in his refusal to let moral ambiguity prevail. He will not weep for a murderer's doomed soul, as Peter Wimsey does in *Busman's Honeymoon*. Miss Marple, too, is understanding of frailty but obdurate in setting her face against it. They speak for their creator, who also took a utilitarian attitude towards murder: a killer must be eliminated because he or she affects the lives of the many. Agatha was unbending on the subject of the death penalty; here her toughness outweighed her sensitivity. 'I do think public hangings are very barbarous,' she wrote from Baghdad,[35] where she had seen a gallows being erected, 'but I suppose they have their effect in these parts.' If the punishment worked, that was what mattered. Similarly, Miss Marple says:

'I can suspend judgement on those who kill, but I think they are evil for the community; they bring in nothing except hate, and take from it all they can. I am willing to believe that they are made that way, that they are born with a disability, for which, perhaps, one should pity them; but even then, I think, not spare them – because you cannot spare them any more than you would spare the man who staggers out from a plague-stricken village in the Middle Ages to mix with innocent and healthy children in a nearby village. The *innocent* must be protected . . .'

This is the sort of comment that would inflame Agatha Christie's detractors, who use her support for the death penalty as a sign of her outdated attitudes, and find something overly schematic, even crass, in her refusal to admit moral ambivalence into her solutions. In so doing they ignore the fact that ambivalence does show its face, only to be shown the door. They also take insufficient account of the reader, who experiences the profound, subliminal satisfaction that comes with restoration and resolution. If writing these books was a little catharsis every time for Agatha, so too was reading them, for her public.

'There is a psychological need for that genre,' P. D. James says. 'I think the detective story, particularly because of its structure, provides a sort of psychological support. It is the bringing of order out of disorder. And it was particularly powerful in that Agatha Christie went through times of great social unrest, when it was possible to believe that the problems of society were beyond the capabilities of men to solve them. And there was a feeling that they can be solved, not by supernatural means but by courage and intelligence. And I think also they're affirmations of the belief that we live in a controllable universe. I think all those things operated very powerfully in her, and very powerfully in us when we read her.'[36]

So murder was a means to an end. In itself, it held little fascination for her. She was interested in the psychology of fear (as in *And Then There Were None*), and in suspicion (particularly in family dramas like *Crooked House* and *Ordeal by Innocence*). But when she described the psychology of murder, she was really writing about human nature; not something beyond the ordinary but the ordinary pushed to an extreme. There are very few killers in Christie who enjoy murder for its own sake: three, perhaps four. Most are like Seddon and Smith, who murdered for money (much the most common motive in her books); or Crippen and Bywaters, who murdered for love; or Armstrong and Constance Kent, who murdered out of jealousy. The other familiar motives are murder committed for self-preservation (as in *Roger Ackroyd*, *Cards on the Table*, *Mrs McGinty's Dead*), and murder for revenge (*Hercule Poirot's Christmas*, *Towards Zero*, *The Mirror Crack'd from Side to Side*). A more arcane motive – of unusual interest to the owner of Greenway – is murder committed in order to preserve, or create, a place of beauty (*Peril at End House*, *Hallowe'en Party*), although in the end this comes down to straightforward murder for profit. There is also murder in the name of justice, in

Murder on the Orient Express and *And Then There Were None*. There is even a murder committed to acquire the means to buy a tea-shop, which perhaps qualifies as Agatha's least convincing motive. Still, it is a reason, a reason that can be understood. And the reason is what matters.

'Human nature. That, I think, is perhaps the real answer as to why I am interested in this case,' says Poirot in *Taken at the Flood* and, as so often, he speaks for his creator. So too did Edmund Cork when he replied on Agatha's behalf to a fan letter in 1961: 'She considers that if a murder springs from characterisation and what has gone before there can really be only one possible solution.' When Agatha is writing at her best, the two separate components of her books – the puzzle and the people – achieve a perfect synthesis. Of course she did not achieve this every time: the characters do not always fall into place with those extraordinarily clean twists, and in a weak book like *The Clocks*, the human interplay bears almost no relation to the pattern of the puzzle. This is extremely rare, however.

'When I know what the murderer is like I shall be able to find out who he is,' says Poirot in *The ABC Murder*. 'I begin to see – not what *you* would like to see – the outlines of *a face and form* but the outlines of a *mind* . . . Crime is terribly revealing. Try and vary your methods as you will, your tastes, your habits, your attitude of mind, and your soul is revealed by your actions.' This is the way that Agatha chose to write about murder: as a paradigm of character. In *Death on the Nile* Poirot is asked: 'Do people interest you too, M. Poirot? Or do you reserve your interest for potential criminals?' To which he replies: 'Madame – that category would not leave many people outside it.'

In real life this is almost certainly not the case. Most people manage to experience jealousy, passion, envy and hatred without reaching for the arsenic. Nevertheless, Poirot's remark is true when applied to the world of Agatha Christie. She is dealing with the reasons for murder rather than the act itself, so almost everyone is a potential killer (this is, indeed, the whole premise behind *Curtain*). 'My dear, these things are very common – very common indeed,' says Miss Marple in *The Thirteen Problems*. What this actually means is that the *motives* are very common. Like Poirot – who finds people fascinating yet 'monotonous' – Miss Marple sees patterns in human nature, and similarities between people who on the surface appear to be very different. 'I always find one thing very like another in this world,' she says. It is this instinct for people, the ability to penetrate the complex surface and see the simplicity within, that makes Miss Marple such a natural detective. It is a gift very similar to that of her creator, who can cleave to the heart of her characters and find the detail, the truth, that illuminates.

'I don't find it spoils an Agatha Christie a bit knowing the end,' P. G. Wodehouse wrote to her in 1969, 'because the characters are so interesting.'

Not just in the very best books, with the brilliantly conceived families like the Angkatells in *The Hollow*, the Crales in *Five Little Pigs*, the Leonides in *Crooked House* and the Argyles in *Ordeal by Innocence* ('Just as magical as ever,' wrote Wodehouse, on rereading it). These people are drawn with evident depth, and even Agatha's detractors would find it hard to say otherwise, although they would undoubtedly try. But how memorable are some of her other characters, flooding the page with a sudden surge of life, conjured in a sudden easy phrase: Miss Bulstrode the headmistress in *Cat Among the Pigeons*, sitting 'cool and unmoved, with her lifework falling in ruins about her'; Valerie Hobhouse in *Hickory Dickory Dock*, with her 'nervous, rather haggard elegance', lying wearily on the sofa in her chic bedsitting room; Miss Hinchcliffe in *A Murder is Announced*, winking at the inspector as he prepares to question her sweet-natured lady friend: 'Where were you at the time of the crime, that's what he wants to know, Murgatroyd'; Megan Hunter in *The Moving Finger*, the gawky misfit with whom the narrator of the book falls stealthily in love, and whisks off to London for a transforming makeover: 'As the head waiter hurried towards us, I felt that thrill of idiotic pride that a man feels when he has got something out of the ordinary with him'; Philip Lombard in *And Then There Were None*, with his feline grace and defective conscience, coolly flirting with the child-murderer Vera Claythorne: 'So you did kill that kid after all?'; Jason Rafiel in *A Caribbean Mystery*, wildly rich, wonderfully rude and staunch in the face of death. '*Ave Caesar, nos morituri te salutamus,*' he says to Miss Marple, before she boards her plane for England.

These characters may not be deep but they are *there*: vivid as a splash of colour. So too is her writing style – so frequently and inexplicably criticised – with its felicitous clarity of expression, its natural sense of rhythm, its quick and zesty idioms. Examples can be picked from almost any of her books:

'There's a type of lady,' he said, 'that you can't force. You can't frighten them, or persuade them, or diddle them.'

No, Poirot thought, you couldn't force or persuade or diddle Mrs Folliat.

Lady Westholme entered the room with the assurance of a transatlantic liner coming into dock.

Miss Amabel Pierce, an indeterminate craft, followed in the liner's wake . . .

'The jealousy of wives is proverbial. But I will tell you something. In my experience jealousy, however far-fetched and extravagant it may seem, is nearly always based on *reality* . . . However little *concrete* evidence there may be, *fundamentally* they are always right.'

And quite suddenly another memory assailed him. One of many years ago. His Aunt Mildred saying, 'She looked, you know, my dear, quite *half-witted*!' and just for a minute her own sane comfortable face had borne an imbecile, mindless expression . . .

It was no moment for trying to seem English. No, one must be a foreigner – frankly a foreigner – and be magnanimously forgiven for the fact. 'Of course, these foreigners don't quite know the ropes. *Will* shake hands at breakfast. Still, a decent fellow really . . .'

'Well, he can't have been a real gardener, can he?' said Miss Marple. 'Gardeners don't work on Whit Monday. Everybody knows that.'

'We were young and virile and we looked the girls over we met and we appreciated their curves and their legs and the kind of eye they gave you, and you thought to yourself: "Will they or won't they? Should I be wasting my time?"'

'. . . he was Elvira's boy – I couldn't bring myself to say anything. Ah well, you're a righteous woman, Jane Marple, and right must prevail.'

'You can go to the rock, Cyril . . .'
　　That was what murder was – as easy as that!
　　But afterwards you went on remembering . . .

. . . she had loved Simon Doyle, had loved him beyond reason and beyond rectitude and beyond pity.[37]

What a gift Agatha had for those quick creative sweeps, and how well she hid that gift! So perfectly does she fit the genre of detective fiction that only the construct is seen; she herself is subsumed into it, and rendered invisible. And yet, when it is turned towards a different light, the translucent structure reveals the mass of stuff within.

There have always been people who divined what was hidden: illustrious admirers, not just P. G. Wodehouse, Clement Attlee and Stephen Glanville, but T. S. Eliot, whose *Four Quartets* had yielded the title *The Rose and the Yew Tree*, and who, in *The Family Reunion*, took the name 'Agatha' for the character who unravels the mysteries in the play.[38] There was also John Sparrow, the Warden of All Souls', Oxford, whom Agatha knew through Max, a fellow of the college from 1962. After the publication of *Endless Night* Sparrow wrote to Agatha that he had read the book twice: 'I particularly relished a number of calculated ambiguities that I had missed before.' He was impressed by the character of Michael, who narrates the book: 'His classlessness (or, rather, his between-classness, if I may put it so) and also his schizophrenia (or, rather, his practically dual personality – displayed especially in his ambivalent feelings about Ellie – absolutely convincing).' Later he praised *By the Pricking of My Thumbs*: 'Sheer joy, from beginning to end.' The dialogue had 'never a word, never an inflection, wrong', while 'the sad world of Old People's Homes can never have been more truthfully, more vividly rendered . . . And *village life* – it's all there!'[39]

In 1955 Agatha's old friend and kind mentor, Eden Philpotts, wrote to commend her 'splendid work': '[I] watch with admiration how you maintain your great gifts of invention, of character creation, for your people are as full of life still as they have always been. That is a rare quality in a novelist . . .' A remarkable and perceptive tribute came from Sidney Smith, the epigraphist, with whom Agatha had become friendly during the war. She dedicated *The Moving Finger* to Sidney and his wife, Mary, and he wrote to her from the British Museum:

> One of these days (it may be long after our time, but I hope much sooner), some critic will wake up to the fact that you are practising, and have perfected, an art of story telling which men like George Moore theorised about, and that your backgrounds, done with great economy and an elimination of all but harmonious detail, represent a social study with more truth than the longer efforts by the biographical school of novelists. Accept honest admiration for the skill that devises new effects.[40]

The Shakespearean scholar Robert Speaight knew Agatha after the war and, in 1970, wrote to inform her that she was all the rage in French intellectual circles.[41] The Catholic philosopher, Jacques Maritain, had called her 'la gloire' of the genre, and said: 'Son intelligence et son humeur sont depuis longtemps pour moi un précieux réconfort.' And 'Gabriel Marcel, the Christian existentialist, philosophically opposed to Maritain, admires you just as much!' wrote Speaight, who then went on to relay a somewhat spiteful compliment. Marcel had said of Agatha: 'C'est *presque* un grand écrivain.'[42]

But more straightforward praise came from A. L. Rowse, whose essay on Agatha described her as 'a better novelist than people realise', with a first-rate brain and an 'abnormal intuition about human beings'. He wrote: 'We must not underrate her literary ambition and accomplishment, as her publishers did, simply because she was the first of detective story writers.'

As so often, Rowse gets it right. The genre fitted Agatha to perfection, and she was its mistress. But inside those clean, clear mysteries there was much more; so much that had been distilled down to evanescence; and her books simply could not have survived for so long without that quantity of hidden substance.

'The woman herself does remain a mystery,' says P. D. James. 'So that may have affected the books.'

Part of what was hidden was 1926, the mystery that hovered over everything. Yet Agatha does make the odd, oblique reference to it, almost as if she is daring herself, like a child in a state of trepidation, to walk up to the forbidden subject. 'I had a Welsh nurse and she took me to Harrogate one day and went home having forgotten all about me. Very unstable,' says Mrs Oliver in *Cards on the Table*. Then, five years later, in *One, Two, Buckle My Shoe*:

'It is so extraordinary that she has disappeared like this. I feel sure, Monsieur Poirot, that it *must* be loss of memory.'

Poirot said that it was very probably. He had known cases of the kind.

'Yes – I remember a friend of one of my cousins. She'd had a lot of nursing and worry, and it brought it on. Amnesia, I think they called it.'

Poirot said that he believed that that was the technical term.

In *Destination Unknown* the central character, Hilary Craven, walks even closer towards the secret centre of Agatha's life. She prepares for suicide, having decided that she can take no more unhappiness. 'She had borne her long illness, she had borne Nigel's defection and the cruel and brutal circumstances in which it had operated.' But instead of killing herself she adopts the persona of a woman who has survived an accident. 'The last twenty-four hours before the crash are still quite vague to me,' she says, to which the reply is:

'Ah, yes. That is the result of the concussion. That happened once to a sister of mine. She was in London in the war. A bomb came, she was knocked unconscious. But presently she gets up, she walks about London and she takes a train from the station of Euston and, *figurez-vous*, she wakes up at Liverpool and she cannot remember anything of the bomb, of going across London, of the train or of getting there! The last she remembers is hanging up her skirt in the wardrobe in London. Very curious these things, are they not?'

This reads like Agatha excusing herself, peddling the official line about her disappearance; but of course Hilary is lying when she says she has been concussed – she was never in a 'crash' at all – so *Destination Unknown* is both honest and disingenuous. Hilary is told: 'You are to be envied. You have had an experience. I should like the experience of having come so near to death. To have that, yet survive – do you not feel yourself different since then, Madame?' Again, this comment refers to the crash that never happened. But Hilary did come near to death, when she prepared to take her own life; again, therefore, the comment is both true and untrue; again, it constitutes a complex reference to Agatha herself.

In *At Bertram's Hotel* an elderly clergyman disappears (genuinely, as it happens), and a senior policeman makes this throwaway remark: 'Of course,' he says, 'a lot of these disappearances are voluntary.' This was Agatha marching up to the forbidden subject in a different way; almost defiantly. In the book that followed, *Third Girl*, she took it on again. Poirot is talking to a man whose daughter has disappeared, and analysing for him the reasons why she might have done so.

'Your daughter dislikes her stepmother . . . It is a very natural reaction. You must remember that she may have secretly idealised you for many many years. That is quite possible in the case of a broken marriage where a child has had a severe blow in her affections . . . You went away. She wanted you to come back. Her mother, no doubt, discouraged her from talking about you, and therefore she thought about you perhaps all the more . . . And because she could not talk about you to her own mother she had what is a very natural reaction with a child – the blaming of the parent who remains for the absence of the parent who has gone. She said to herself something in the nature of "Father was fond of me. It's Mother he didn't like," and from that was born a kind of idealisation, a kind of secret liaison between you and her. What had happened was not her father's fault. She will not believe it!'

Later, Poirot is asked: 'Do you think she may have lost her memory? One hears of such things.'

Despite – because of – the limitations of the genre Agatha had a quite extraordinary freedom to write in this way: to reveal whatever she liked, knowing that she was hidden from view. For instance she referred to the reasons why suicide should always be resisted, however powerful the urge:

'I will put a case to you. A man comes to a certain place – to commit suicide, shall we say? But by chance he finds another man there, so he fails in his purpose and goes away – to live. The second man has saved the first man's life, not by being necessary to him or prominent in his life, but just by the mere physical fact of having been in a certain place at a certain moment. You take your life today and perhaps . . . someone will go to death or disaster simply for lack of your presence in a given spot or place.

'You say your life is your own. But can you dare to ignore the chance that you are taking part in a gigantic drama under the orders of a divine Producer? . . . You as you may not matter to anyone in the world, but you as a person in a particular place may matter unimaginably.'

This was written in 1929, in 'The Man from the Sea', one of the stories that would be published the following year in *The Mysterious Mr. Quin*. The speaker is Mr Satterthwaite: a recurring character in Agatha's work, an observer rather than a participant, with the soul of an artist and an instinct for human nature. 'Perhaps,' he is told, 'as a result of the price you have paid, you see things that other people –

do not.' So Mr Satterthwaite voices Agatha's thoughts on suicide, the long hard conclusions she had come to more than two years after she stood at the edge of the quarry. 'You've got to go on living whether you like it or not'; 'God may need you.' She wrote this again in *Towards Zero*, when precisely the instance conjured by Mr Satterthwaite takes place: a man who has botched a suicide attempt saves a woman from killing herself. And then, in *Destination Unknown*:

'You don't think of it as – wrong?'
Hilary said heatedly: 'Why should it be wrong? It's *my* life.'
'Oh yes, yes,' Jessop repeated hastily. 'I'm not taking a high moral line myself, but there *are* people, you know, who think it's wrong.'

Jessop then proposes that, rather than commit suicide, Hilary should assume the person of another woman: act as a spy, a role that might itself result in death, but at least carries the possibility of doing some good. And so Hilary chooses life. Like Celia at the end of *Unfinished Portrait* – also saved from death by a failed suicide – she carries on.

This, for Agatha, amounted to a philosophy. She never made direct reference to her own quiet religious faith – shared by Miss Marple who, like her creator, reads regularly from a 'small devotional book' – but having once committed the sin of despair she was determined to believe in the blessing of life ('And when God walks beside you/You are not afraid . . .').

That is why her books are innately virtuous: because they are on the side of the living. They take life – but not themselves – extremely seriously. They inhabit a world free of the creep of moral relativity. They exemplify harmony and order, clarity and optimism. 'I was asked what I read during my recent spell of captivity in South America,' wrote a man named Geoffrey Jackson to Agatha in 1971. 'My captors actually produced Spanish editions of your detective stories for me, which I read with vast enjoyment. What particularly helped was to be reminded by Miss Marple and Monsieur Poirot that there was indeed another world where absolute values still applied.'

This could scarcely be more inimical to the modern sensibility, which throws a veil of doubt and ambivalence over everything except its own politicised opinions. And yet Agatha Christie survives, to the point where it seems as if she is still, indeed, fulfilling a purpose.

Everything she stood for is devalued. Her books are still adapted for screen and stage, as successfully as ever, but there is scant under-standing of what she was actually saying: her stories are used merely as vehicles. A recent dramatisation of *Five Little Pigs*[43] seized upon the human drama and turned its power in all the wrong directions, creating a meaningless homosexual dynamic that destroyed the book's delicate emotional balance, and adding a semi-pornographic execution scene. In the television film a terrified Caroline Crale is hanged, in error, for her husband's murder. In the book she dies in prison, and is happy to do so. She believes that she is taking the blame for the crime on behalf of her younger sister, whom in youth she badly injured: she is therefore expiating a lesser guilt. That was Agatha's careful intention. She did not deal in injustice. Although in her plotting notebook she had the idea of a 'murderer wrongfully executed', which developed into *Five Little Pigs*, she modified the idea according to her own morality.

Yet it is hangings and couplings that the modern world feels it must bring to Agatha Christie: the realities of death and forbidden passion, the things she left out of her books. She did so deliber-ately, not because she knew nothing about them; she knew a good deal. But the belief today is that these gaps should be filled, and that poor old ladies born in 1890 need help to express what their uptight upbringing left them unable to say. That is why the most recent screen incarnation of Miss Marple[44] has been given a back story – a doomed love affair with a married man killed in the First World War – in order to flesh her out, to make her human and 'real'. Of course the books make it perfectly clear that nothing has ever happened to Miss Marple. Everything happens around her, and this is the point: she has become wise through observation, not through experience.

But the idea of innate wisdom is a hard one for the modern world to grasp. So it is that when, in the latest adaptation of *The Murder at the Vicarage*, Miss Marple realises that the crime was motivated by thwarted passion, she does so not because she is wise but because she recognises the situation. She empathises. She has been there.

Twenty years earlier, when Joan Hickson played Miss Marple on BBC Television[45] with a definitive, detached compassion, she could judge and still be magnificently human; but the intervening years have changed a great deal, including our relationship with Agatha Christie. They have rendered her finally and definitively at odds with the modern world. Not because she is a snob, or a racist, or a xenophobe, not because her characters live in well-ordered country houses and have maids who serve afternoon tea; but because she deals in constancy and certainty and fundamental hope, and those qualities are no longer ours.

Yet we seem to need her, still.

So, most mysteriously of all, did her own creator. In 1956 Agatha wrote her last Westmacott novel, *The Burden*, a diffuse and barely structured book (two ideas brought loosely together, to judge by her notes) into which she poured every question she ever asked herself. The central story is that of Laura who, as a child, is so jealous of her younger sister, Shirley, that she wants her to die. But when the chance comes to abandon Shirley in a house fire, Laura unaccountably saves her life, and thereafter is obsessed with her sister's happiness. Shirley marries a ne'er-do-well, Henry, who becomes an impossibly difficult invalid. In order to free her sister from a life of misery, Laura allows Henry to take (unwittingly) a fatal second dose of pills.

This is not an Agatha Christie murder: its consequences are unexpected and unforeseeable. There are no simple rules against what Laura has done, and no simple means by which she can atone for it.

The secondary story in *The Burden* is that of Llewellyn Knox, a former evangelist who has lost not his faith but the simplicity of his religious calling. He asks:

'What *is* doing good? Burning people at the stake to save their souls? Perhaps. Burning witches alive because they are evil personified? There's a very good case for it. Raising the standard of living for the unfortunate? We think nowadays that that is important. Fighting against cruelty and injustice?

'What is good to do? What is right to do? What is wrong to do? We are human beings, and we have to answer those questions to the best of our ability.'

After fifteen years as a 'messenger' for God, Llewellyn Knox now seeks a way to live in the world. How to do it? he asks himself.

It all came back, perhaps, to Kant's three questions:
What do I know?
What can I hope?
What ought I to do?

A strange echo of 'Who? Why? When? How? Where? Which?', the questions that Agatha Christie asked in her plotting notebooks, and to which she always knew the answers.

The Late Years

'Et s'il revenait un jour
Que faut-il lui dire?
Dîtes-lui qu'on l'attendit
Jusqu'à s'en mourir'
(verse written on a slip of paper, kept by Agatha Christie)

'The only people who really know what other people are like are artists –
and they don't know why they know it!'
(from *The Mousetrap* by Agatha Christie)

In *The Burden*, Shirley remarries after the death of her invalid husband, Henry. Her second husband is clever and kindly while Henry – who had courted Shirley by appearing at her home, unannounced, when she was out at a tennis party – was charming, handsome and unfaithful. 'I've been married twice,' Shirley tells Llewellyn Knox, who asks:

'Did you love your husband?'
He left it in the singular, and she answered without quibbling.
'I loved him more than anything in the world.'

It is often said of Agatha that from middle age onwards she never touched alcohol; the official line was that she hated the taste, but it would be truer to say that she disliked the way it made her feel. 'All it did, she said, was make her sad. Weepy. So that's why she didn't drink.'[1] In drink the emotions are no longer resolute. They shift into dangerous new positions, which sometimes have a clarity and beauty that sobriety does not see. Shirley is a brandy drinker and it is in a bar that she says to Knox, of her first husband: 'I loved him more than anything in the world.'

Agatha did not drink, but she reached an equivalent state in her Mary Westmacott novels. They have an emotional looseness, a poetic sweep, a recklessness that is not wholly controlled; they inhabit a highly adult state of confusion that she avoided everywhere but in her most private self.

'It's so hard to explain [Shirley tells Knox]. I wasn't very happy, but yet in a curious way it was all right – it was what I'd chosen, what I wanted . . . Of course I idealized him – one does. But I remember now, waking up very early one morning – it was about five o'clock, just before dawn. That's a cold, truthful time, don't you think? And I knew then – *saw*, I mean – what the future would become, I knew I shouldn't be really happy . . . and that I loved him, and that no one else would do, and that I would rather be unhappy, married to him, than smug and comfortable without him . . .

'Of course I didn't put it to myself as clearly as all that. I'm describing now what was then just a feeling. But it was *real*. I went back again to thinking him wonderful and inventing all sorts of noble things about him that weren't in the least true. But I'd had my *moment* – the moment when you do see what lies ahead of you, and you can turn back or go on . . .'

He said very gently: 'And you regret – ?'

'No, *no*!' She was vehement. 'I've never regretted. Every minute of it was worthwhile! There's only one thing to regret – that he died.'

That Agatha still had powerful feelings towards Archie is made clear in a letter written by Rosalind. 'I planned to see him and his family some years ago, but my mother got in a terrible state and although she felt no animosity towards him she just couldn't seem to accept anything more intimate between us.' This referred to a time soon after 1958, the year that Nancy Christie died and two years after publication of *The Burden*. By then the events of 1926 were long distant, and Agatha herself was immersed in her life with Max.

'Deeply happy' was how she described her state of mind in 1954, when she again filled in the Album of Confessions, which she had last done at Ashfield aged thirteen (in answer to the same question Max described himself as 'well contented'). But this simple statement is again thrown into doubt by *The Burden*, which asks what 'happiness' really means. Shirley had chosen unhappiness, in the knowledge that she would prefer life that way. Her sister Laura's attempts to make her happy, by letting Henry die, in fact destroy Shirley too. According to Llewellyn Knox, happiness is 'one of the foods of life, it encourages growth, it is a great teacher, but it is not the purpose of life, and is, in itself, not ultimately satisfying'.

A large part of Agatha's life operated in the everyday world of happiness: family, routine, travel, pleasures, the companionship and freedom of her second marriage. She knew that she had been given a second chance at life, and she always strove to delight in her magical good fortune. This, for her, was almost a question of duty. Not to do so would have been a sin – committed once only – against her deepest belief: that to be alive was a joyful thing.

But in her private imagination she allowed herself to wander through the darkness. She remembered. She dreamed other lives. Did she sit in the garden at Greenway – that place of incomparable beauty, with its brief-flowering camellias and the Dart gleaming like a mirror through a tangle of trees – and picture Archie at her side?

('When you look back on your life with him, what are the things that come first to your mind, the moments that you will always remember? Are they of the first time you slept together – or are they of something else?')[2]

What did she feel when she wrote to him in sympathy after Nancy's death? An odd thing to do, in the calamitous circumstances.

('His hat,' she said. 'On our honeymoon . . . I put it on, and then he put on mine – one of those silly bits of nonsense women wear, and we looked at each other and laughed. All trippers change hats, he said, and then he said: "Good Lord, I do love you . . ."' Her voice caught. 'I'll never forget.')³

Did she wonder what he thought, when he received her kind and magnanimous letter? If he regretted anything? He wrote back thanking Agatha for her generosity in giving him those years of happiness with Nancy; but then, what else could he say? He also wrote to Rosalind after Nancy died, saying, 'It did make me realise more clearly that death often comes unexpectedly', and that he had therefore gone to buy a present by which his daughter would remember him.

> What I should do conventionally is to leave you a small reminder of old father. But then I thought you would rather have your reminder now.
>
> So I went back to the ruby ring. You would have laughed to see me hurrying off to inspect those offered. Small, queer shapes, some like bits of pink glass. Perhaps in murder stories or if you are a maharajah you get them. Last week I gave up and picked a small one I had seen earlier and liked and as it was rather small, even for me, I threw in a diamond one as well.
>
> . . . Tearing up other letters, to prevent anyone seeing yours to me I read all that I had saved, from school, finishing places abroad, war work etc. Some were very good, with new ideas, and some were quite affectionate!
>
> So with all best wishes for the future you will get two small reminders and lots of love from Old Dad.⁴

Four years later, in December 1962, Rosalind attended Archie's funeral, and for the first time met her half-brother, Nancy's son. Did Agatha grieve that day, not just for Archie but the fragile, tenacious memory of their happiness? Did she wonder if he had ever grieved, for the life he had chosen to leave?

> I cannot say [Agatha wrote, as her sober self, in reply to a series of questions posed to her in 1971] that I have ever reflected on

whether I regret anything in life or not. Probably there are hundreds of things I regret but as one cannot go back and do anything about it it is not worth thinking about them. There was a charming play . . . where a man bitterly regretted the fact that once he had not managed to catch a train. He was allowed to go back and catch the train and lived his life through again and came to terrible grief through doing so. 'The fate of every man have we hung about his neck.' Do not let us forget that definition of Karma . . .

So her life from middle age onwards was with Max Mallowan, and she knew that it was better that way. She had security and she had freedom. She traversed countries, continents, ideas, civilisations, the span of her own century. Her energy and curiosity gave fullness to almost every year of her mature life. She saw India, Pakistan, Sri Lanka, Turkey, the West Indies, America; she saw the past brought back to life in Iraq; she listened to Wagner at Bayreuth, attended a passion play at Oberammergau, watched the Coronation of Queen Elizabeth II from a splendid vantage-point at 145 Piccadilly; she socialised with people of intellect, who respected her and with whom she could discuss any subject she chose, exercising the muscles of her powerful mind; she revelled in her comfortable Winterbrook and her glorious Greenway, the summers spent in her beloved Devon with its moors, its coasts, its hills, its English wildness: it was a good life, a magnificent life in truth, the kind that can scarcely be lived any more. And married to Archie she would not have had it. ('. . . they'd go on and on and on . . . She'd never see things – faraway things . . .')

Agatha was conventional: she always wanted marriage. At the same time she wanted a life of her own. During her years with Archie she had, in effect, confronted a dilemma familiar to many intelligent women, who almost always believe that love and independence can be reconciled and find, so often, that they cannot. In Agatha's case, reconciliation came about in her second marriage for two reasons: she was so outlandishly successful that she could make her own design for living; and her husband had the sense not to mind about this. Max Mallowan had a career of his own, less lucrative but with unassailable prestige and dignity. He was not bothered by being married to a phenomenon: hooray for it, was what he generally thought, not least because it was so immensely helpful to him. And he understood the depth of Agatha's appalling vulnerability, which redressed any imbalance caused by her wealth and fame. What really maintained the equilibrium in the marriage was that both parties wanted it like that. In their different ways they both wanted the marriage to succeed; and, paradoxically, this is far more likely to happen when neither partner is in love with the other. For love, as Agatha wrote over and over again, is 'the devil'.

'I think they were very good friends,' says Max's nephew, John, who stayed at Greenway for summers in the 1950s and 1960s. 'They genuinely liked each other, they enjoyed each other's company. They didn't kiss and cuddle all the time, but they always spoke affectionately. I don't remember them having rows. I don't think Agatha liked rows. I do remember my uncle having some tremendous arguments with Rosalind, but in a way later on she was closer to his age . . .'

The marriage was also observed by Agatha's friend Joan Oates, who worked with Max after the war on his dig at Nimrud. 'It was an odd marriage really. Odd. But very successful.'[5]

Nimrud, near Mosul in the north of Iraq, which Max and Agatha visited every spring from 1949 until 1959, was the heart of Max's lifework. He directed the excavation of the dig until the 1958 revolution in Iraq, when the Hashemite King Faisal II was assassinated and the republic established. Afterwards the dig was led by David Oates – Joan's husband – then by Jeffrey Orchard, until the cessation of work in 1963.

In 1966 Max's *Nimrud and Its Remains*, which he dedicated to Agatha,[6] was published in two volumes by Collins. The negotiations were handled free of commission by Hughes Massie: 'So glad you are going to help Max,' Agatha wrote to Edmund Cork. Max himself told Cork that 'Agatha is just as keen to see the book published as I am, never having missed a season at Nimrud,' and that the book was 'one to which prestige will be attached, for no richer or more spectacular discoveries have been made in ancient Western Asia during the last decade, and this will be the authoritative work on the subject'.[7] (Cork replied, in his gentlemanly way, that it was 'an honour' to handle the project. Obers in New York took a somewhat different tone, saying, 'Collins are publishing a book called *Nimrud* and something or other, I didn't get the rest of it, which I gather is on archaeology . . . Dodd Mead are agreeing to take 500 copies from Collins'.)[8]

Nimrud was a beautiful place, rippling stretches of green with the Tigris a ribbon of blue beyond. It had been one of the great cities of Assyria, inhabited from at least the thirteenth century BC. In the reign of Ashurnasirpal II (883–59 BC, a little after King Solomon) it became capital of the Assyrian empire, the all-conquering power that would stretch from western Iran to the Mediterranean. In the Bible it was called 'Calah' and, according to Agatha, it was 'a sort of Assyrian Aldershot, the military capital'.[9] Destroyed in 614–12 BC, when the Babylonians took control of Mesopotamia, Nimrud had been excavated in the mid-nineteenth century by Sir Henry Layard, although he had mistaken it for Nineveh. Since 1879 no archaeologist had really gone near it. A vast deal of potential therefore lay waiting for Max Mallowan, who knew Nimrud from his work with Campbell Thompson in the 1930s, and who in 1949 applied for permission to reopen the excavations there.

By this time Max was director of the British School of Archaeology in Iraq, and also professor of Western Asiatic Archaeology at the London University Institute of Archaeology, which had started up in 1934 and, from 1937, been based at Bute House in Regent's Park. At the end of the war Max had been concerned as to what he might do, and how he would pick up the threads of his career, although he must have felt secure in the knowledge that Agatha was behind him all the way. 'I hope we get plenty more archae-ology after the war,' he wrote to her from Tripolitania in 1943. 'That is the only pursuit that really matters.'[10] Sensitive as ever to what Max wanted to hear, Agatha frequently reassured him that he should continue with his work. 'You are right about the future,' he replied in 1944, 'clever Mrs Puper knows Mr Puper only wants to dig really.'[11]

In 1947 Max and Agatha went to the East together for the first time in ten years: 'It is obvious that there are hundreds of plums waiting to be pulled out of the rich Iraqi mud pie,' he wrote home to Rosalind. He was also writing up his report on the dig at Tell Brak, where he had spent one season in 1937, and Sidney Smith – to whom it was submitted, and who himself gave tutorials at the institute – set about trying to find him an academic post. As usual, things fell Max's way. Regent's Park suited him very well. It involved a certain amount of lecturing – at which he was said to be very good – and postgraduate teaching, but it allowed five months away every year for field work. Colleagues included Kathleen Kenyon, an expert on Palestine, Mortimer Wheeler, 'the last figure of the heroic age of British archaeology',[12] and Rachel Maxwell-Hyslop, a recent graduate of the course in western Asian archaeology, who covered for Max when he was away. At the end of the day he could return to the wonderfully comfortable flat in Chelsea that Agatha had newly acquired.

> I am now here and addressed as Professor Puper [he wrote to Rosalind in May 1947]. Hundreds of persons, mostly women, prostrate themselves to the ground as I enter the building . . . I think I am very lucky to have hooked this job. I will try to be a good professor by which I take it you mean that I must be in London, Wallingford, Pwllywrach and Greenway lecture and write books all at the same time . . . My head has definitely shrunk since I got here; my hats are positively spinning round my head as I realise how much my brain needs to expand if I am to cope adequately with all I am expected to do.

In fact it was said at Max's memorial service that his appointment to the institute had 'caused some misgivings; fears, that is, that, as was said at the time, it might prove to be like harnessing a racehorse to a plough'. Although in the circumstances Max was obviously eulogised, this speaks highly of the way his abilities were viewed. At any rate he had the confidence to seek to lead the excavation of a huge and neglected site. He visited the Director of Antiquities of Iraq, and wrote in his memoirs that 'any thought of caution which

I may have had, left me, and I was moved to ask if we might return to Nimrud'.

Permission was given by the Iraqi authorities, but of course money was needed. Archaeology was a different game by this time, still a world of its own although not so clubbish as it had been before the war; it was more professional, its practitioners were better trained, its attitudes towards the East were less imperialistic and it was funded, on the whole, by public institutions rather than private fortunes. Max was not especially in favour of these developments. 'I conclude that at its best archaeology is a private pursuit, not to be shared with the masses,' he wrote to Agatha, and it was lucky for him that she agreed. She gave a lot of help to the British School of Archaeology: 'What she gave didn't go into the accounts,' says Rachel Maxwell-Hyslop.[13] 'There was a fund, but nobody quite knows how much she put in.' What is certain is that in 1953 her book, *A Pocket Full of Rye*, was offered to the school as a gift. Edmund Cork wrote to Harold Ober that 'The Metropolitan Museum in New York have discontinued their support of the BSA in Iraq, which means that Agatha's husband's life work is threatened by lack of funds. Consequently we have devised a scheme by which Agatha – who cannot support the School directly because of her tax position – gave *Pocket Full of Rye* to the School, and I have bought it from them [for £7,500].'[14] The royalties also supported the BSA and, in part, the book on Nimrud. It was a difficult deal for Cork to pull off. 'With all this scrapping over legal technicalities,' he wrote to Agatha, 'probably no one has told you how wonderful your magnanimity appears to the average man.'[15]

Work at Nimrud began in March 1949. In what became their routine, Max and Agatha travelled first to Baghdad, where they arrived in January and where she, having taken much of the previous year off, applied herself again to work. This, too, became routine. Iraq was where she did much of her writing. In the mornings at Nimrud she would work in the dig house and, eventually, at a cost to herself of fifty pounds, had her own room built on the side. Square, mud-brick, with a chair and a table, two paintings by young Iraqi artists and her floppy-sleeved fur jacket for when she grew cold; this was 'Beit Agatha', or Agatha's House. In it she produced much of her

1950s work and began, in pleasurable and sketchy form, to write her autobiography.

Outside this little room there was constant noise of shouting, barking, braying: 'The roar of London's traffic was nothing to it.'[16] The focus of attention for the dig was the citadel mound. Although much ground was eventually covered – temples, a governor's palace from the eighth century BC, a complex of private houses, a fort – work began with what was called the North-west Palace, founded by Ashurnasirpal II and partly excavated by Layard. In it was a *stela*, covered with a cuneiform inscription that detailed the king's titles, works and military victories, with a description of a great banquet organised to celebrate these achievements: a remarkable find. Wells as deep as twenty-five metres were cleared and excavated with the help of equipment lent by the Iraq Petroleum Company, and these yielded unexpected treasures, such as a pair of ivory horse blinkers, decorated with sphinxes. In 1952 the *Illustrated London News* pictured on one of its covers a 'Mona Lisa of 2600 Years Ago', a female face carved from ivory tusk with slanted, sensual eyes and lips. Another ivory female had bulbous eyes and a mouth like a slit: 'the Ugly Sister'.

The ivories were very much Agatha's business (so too were photographs and typing the catalogues). She had a woman's good sense about these things, which most of Max's team did not, and advised – for example – that the Mona Lisa be kept under damp towels for several weeks, thus accustoming the ivory by degrees to a dry atmosphere. She did much of the cleaning:

> I had my own favourite tools [she wrote in her autobiography] just as any professional would: an orange stick, possibly a very fine knitting needle . . . and a jar of cosmetic cold cream, which I found more useful than anything else for gently coaxing the dirt out of the crevices without harming the friable ivory. In fact there was such a run on my face cream that there was nothing left for my poor old face after a couple of weeks!

In 1953 she reconstructed, almost single-handedly, more than thirty ivory and wood writing boards, which were recovered from a well in tiny fragments. This was 'her greatest contribution to archaeology', wrote Joan Oates, who had first met Agatha the previous year when, as a research student at Cambridge, she had stayed at the BSA house in Baghdad, 'which was basically a home for Max and Agatha when they were there'.[17]

The house was right on the Tigris, with a paved courtyard and a balcony above on which Agatha would eat her breakfast. It was a charming place, and by comparison Nimrud was truly roughing it, but into her sixties Agatha remained game about the leaking roof of the dig house, the nights spent in a tent through which rain would drop as if from a giant bucket ('no worse really than a burst hot water bottle'),[18] the water that had to be carried by two donkeys from the Tigris, the Thursday night bath ('in that Victorian hipbath, which still exists somewhere in Iraq'),[19] which might contain a frog or a fish. The weather, though, was difficult: the soft green calm of Nimrud could snap in a sudden fury.

I am sitting writing this in the middle of the fiercest hailstorm I have ever seen – cascading down [she wrote to Rosalind in April 1957]. Scene resembles a Channel steamer – buckets everywhere! Catching the drips from the roofs – Max's office would make quite a good swimming bath! No fine weather at all until ten days ago – then so stifling hot you really feel nearly dead and perspiration drips into photo developing and on to ivories – then two days terrific thunderstorms – the track washed away . . .

As for finds, however – Just *masses* of fine ivory carvings tossed in heaps into the rooms of this building . . . Joan and I exhausted – work on them all day – frightfully short of time – and they were so near the surface that they're in a very perishable state. My back – my back! (always something wrong – one's feet, one's teeth, one's back, one's blindness etc etc!)

Did she enjoy this? Yes, in a way; but it also served a purpose. 'She was relaxed on the dig,' says Joan Oates. 'She loved the flowers, she loved the scenery – and she never said, that's too much for me. That always impressed me. She was extremely friendly and generous, but she was very much in the background.

'She was a sort of mother figure, but not in any interfering way. Without her there it would have been a totally different sort of life. And Max would have been much more difficult to live with.' Max was in his element in every way, and success brought out the auto-crat in him. On the dig he could be confrontational – 'Max was very volatile, he used to flare up' – but the presence of Agatha acted as a balm. 'All she ever did would be to say "Now Max", a very quiet voice, and he would pause for a moment, and whatever he was raging about would drop.'

The presence of Agatha Christie was a draw, of course, bringing attention and prestige to the dig, and this suited Max very well. 'Max loved entertaining. They would have all sorts of archaeologists, ambas-sadors, government ministers – it was extremely interesting. But I remember Agatha on those occasions, she would retire into the corner somewhere and she would just sit. I don't think she was excluding us, she just didn't take part in the conversation. Max took care of all that . . . That was the life that Max was attracted to. I think she found it very difficult.'[20]

This, then, was evidence of Agatha's 'shyness', of which there are so many stories from her later life (including the famous example of when she allowed herself to be turned away from the Savoy for a 1958 party to celebrate *The Mousetrap*). Certainly she did become extremely retiring as she grew older, although her unwillingness to mix at social gatherings was not always in evidence. There was a lively embassy life in Iraq at that time – according to Joan Oates, this was what Max missed after the 1958 revolution – and Agatha was a part of it. 'We are going into Society tonight – Cocktails at the French minister's and dinner with one of the British Council people,'[21] she wrote to Rosalind from Baghdad. And: 'We dined at the Embassy last night and met the new Ambassador – very dynamic and amusing. They had taken their entire family, ranging in years from 79 to 11 to *Spider's Web* [her 1954 play][22] on Boxing Day and had loved it . . .'[23] Perhaps she did these things for Max: the world-famous Agatha Christie was his calling-card, after all. Or perhaps her shyness was a tool, as much as an affliction. It was useful to be shy, sometimes. Particularly if a person is subject to the kind of attentions that Agatha had to endure; as when, staying a few nights in Cairo (taking in 'two enormous dinner parties at the Embassy'), she was told by her hosts that three girls were visiting 'because, you see, they want to see Mrs Mallowan! When we said we had Agatha Christie staying with us, they wouldn't believe it!' She described the scene in a letter to Rosalind: 'They silently filed in after tea and more or less stood in a row to attention, their eyes fixed on me. *Very* embarrassing . . .'[24]

Out east, however, there was still a sense in which Agatha was at a remove from her fame. 'I think she probably was happy to be away from the pressures of England,' says Joan Oates. 'I remember once – we all hated taking visitors around – this car was sighted coming, and Agatha always went into her own little room and locked the door. And there were two young men from Finland. They'd come to see Agatha Christie, and they weren't being told no. They knew she was here, and they were going to see her. They went into the house and realised that there was this other room, and they actually went and banged on the door. And Agatha was on the other side. So if that sort of thing happens to you, you can imagine how nice it is to be in a place where it doesn't happen that often.'

This, indeed, was the point. Throughout the 1950s, the pressures on Agatha at home grew so intense that the East acquired an almost spiritual allure. 'It's lovely to crawl out into the sun on the terrace every day and look at the Tigris,' she wrote to Rosalind, 'rest – sit in the sun – think up a few fancy murders to keep the home fires burning and eat a good deal of rather rough meat!' For all the ambassadorial trappings, it was a simpler life. It had the primitive quality that Agatha had conjured at the end of her early novel, *The Man in the Brown Suit*, which ends with her 'gypsy girl' heroine living close to the gorgeous South African earth and caring not a jot for the cool, over-civilised West. Something in Agatha craved this: the sharp air, the forceful weather, the smiling Arabic fatalism. ('Sarah admired the easy swing with which he walked – the careless proud carriage of his head. Only the European part of his costume seemed tawdry and wrong.')[25]

She had responded to it when she first visited Baghdad in 1928, when it helped remake her after the death of her old life. Now it represented a different kind of escape. It brought clarity. When England threatened to overwhelm her she could pack her trunks and head east. The lunacies of fame had grown to the point that they could even follow her to the banks of the Tigris. But there were other things that she longed to leave behind every year; and it was lucky that she had acquired, by this time, a team of people at home who could look after her affairs in return for the financial protection she afforded them. The *quid pro quo* was that she was left free to do the work that earned their keep.

Edmund Cork now devoted the greater part of his life to running Agatha's life. He maintained what she called 'the Cork service': as well as managing Agatha's career he dealt with her tenants, arranged her travel and currency transactions, booked hotels, bought theatre tickets for a good many London shows (second row stalls, for preference), put on her bets for the Grand National (and for the Derby, if she was away in June), paid her bills and attempted – a near overwhelming task – to handle her tax problems. 'I'm *relying* on you, Edmund,' was the refrain. Looking after Agatha inevitably meant looking after Max too; not just his work on Nimrud but some of his personal affairs. When Max had business in Paris, for example, Cork booked him into the Hotel Montalembert. 'I don't particularly recommend it,' he was told for his pains.

Rosalind, too, was in her mother's service. In 1949 she had married again, a man of great charm named Anthony Hicks, who had been called to the Bar but now effectively worked for Agatha; an arrangement that suited them both. Anthony thought Agatha 'a wonderful mother-in-law' and, it was said, worshipped Max (in later life, when he and Rosalind had possession of the master bedroom at Greenway, Anthony insisted on sleeping in Max's narrow old bed at the side of the sumptuous double). He became an easy presence in the family with his light, dry humour, his ability to get along with everybody, his extreme cleverness which he kept, on the whole, to himself. He had withdrawn from the world, to an extent, and concentrated his considerable intellect on studying Tibetan; this was the way he liked it.

It was not a love match. Rosalind had written in her usual tone to inform Agatha of the ceremony at Kensington Register Office:

I don't suppose anyone will enjoy it much but you have got to be there and Max and then we will have to come back to look after the dogs. You mustn't look too smart . . . but I hope you are pleased. I think we will have rather a nice time here [Pwllywrach]. He has some money (more than me!) and he will give me £10,000, but he can't afford to live in two places at once . . . I think you will find Mathew will be pleased too. He is always pressing him to stay a long time and I don't think really he will be jealous.[26]

After the tragic experience of her first marriage, Rosalind had decided to marry for more pragmatic reasons. In this, as she perhaps realised, she was behaving very much as her mother had done. It had been a relief to find a relaxing companion – Rosalind herself was not a relaxed person – to share the burdens she had shouldered since Hubert Prichard's death in 1944: caring for Mathew, Pwllywrach and, increasingly, her mother. Agatha's attentions were always directed towards Max, what she saw as the necessary business of keeping her husband happy. Max, in his turn, allowed Rosalind and Anthony to keep Agatha happy. They were both sensible enough to see that this brought them considerable benefits, and that there was really no alternative to the arrangement, although for all her pragmatic acceptance Rosalind knew exactly what was going on. 'Anthony devoted himself to my mother,' she wrote towards the end of her life, 'helping her with all her affairs and taking over the running of the gardens because Max couldn't be bothered to do it.'

Throughout the 1950s, the problems that went with Greenway fell with increasing weight upon Rosalind and Anthony; only the financial side remained Agatha's worry.

While she was in Iraq it was left to the Hickses to run the house and gardens, which in practice meant trying to find decent staff who could be trusted. This was easier said than done. Agatha disliked the head gardener at Greenway, Frank Lavin ('Hitler-Lavin'), but he knew his job, and usually walked off with every prize at the

Brixham Flower Show. Other staff, however, came and went. No doubt this was partly why Agatha conjured the housekeeper of her dreams, Lucy Eyelesbarrow, when writing *The 4.50 from Paddington* at Nimrud in 1956. Her letters home constantly revert to the problem of servants, which fifty years on she still saw in the beatified image of the pre-war staff at Ashfield: Jane the cook, calmly presiding in her kitchen, the maids moving about the house with quick discretion. 'I am really very sorry about Maisie,' Agatha wrote in 1948 when Rosalind lost her own housekeeper at Pwllywrach. 'I really did hope she would be with you more or less for life – what a weary world it is.'

Winterbrook also required looking after: 'I must say it's nice to feel the Smiths are there,' she wrote in February 1953, 'she's so fat and comfortable and *loves* people coming – I think he does and will do some gardening in the intervals of talking.' But in the same letter she wrote: 'I *do* wish I could get Greenway settled.' In around 1954 she acquired a trustworthy couple called the Gowlers – cook and butler – but only after a period of upheaval, indirectly caused by Agatha herself. In 1952 she had employed a Mrs MacPherson to oversee both house and garden in her absence, and to take charge of the Brisleys, who had worked at Greenway for the past three years. Mrs MacPherson got along extremely badly with Brisley, who disliked being told what to do and let the garden go to such an extent that Rosalind was obliged to give notice to him and his (admirable) wife. Then she had to cope with Mrs MacPherson. 'I have been down to Greenway to help Rosalind deal with the nasty situation that developed there,' Edmund Cork wrote in April. 'Mrs MacPherson was not at all what you wanted. Her idea of her stewardship was that she should just play the lady of the Manor . . .' A month later Mrs MacPherson tried to kill herself in her home, Ferry Cottage, in the grounds at Greenway. When the police arrived it emerged that she was a full-blown con-woman who had reached a pitch of despair over her losses on the horses, and had meanwhile amassed bills totalling more than eight hundred and fifty pounds. 'The police want to know what Mrs MacPherson owned in the cottage,' Cork wrote to Rosalind. 'In view of the bills it is our opinion that she owned absolutely nothing apart from personal attire . . .'[27] Among the bills was a substantial order for drink, 'which is clearly a personal liability of Mrs MacPherson's'. Everything else was paid by Agatha. Quantities of 'Mrs Mallowan regrets . . .' letters were sent to Devon suppliers, together with cheques.

It was after this débâcle that Rosalind and Anthony took proper charge of Greenway, which had to be put on a commercial footing in order to offset taxation. In fact it was the terrible tax demon that had led Agatha to employ Mrs MacPherson in the first place. 'I have told her we *must* make money,' Agatha had written to Rosalind when the problems first began. 'How can I pay three men [garden assistants] out of income taxed at about 19 shillings in the pound with no income tax relief?'[28] Edmund Cork told Agatha that 'The Inspector of Taxes persists in asking awkward questions, obviously with the intention of showing that the Gardens are nothing more than a hobby.'[29] Eventually this particular problem was solved, and Anthony took charge of the Greenway Gardens Trust on which tax relief was allowed. Agatha actually sold Greenway to Rosalind in 1959 as a means of avoiding tax, although she continued to use it as her own home while the Hickses lived at Pwllywrach. But the Greenway problem was a side-show compared to the main event: the pursuit of Agatha for tax arrears in both America and the UK, which had begun in 1938 and which continued, more or less unabated, deep into her old age.

It was a bizarre and rather horrible business. The strength of character she showed, living and working for so many years beneath this massive shadow, was remarkable. Possibly Edmund Cork should have dealt with the problem more promptly, or more aggressively; but the fact was that he had been overtaken by the sheer sweeping success of his client, whose sales grew to staggering levels even as he was trying to cope with pre-war taxation demands which had come pretty much from nowhere.

Not until 1948 was a settlement reached upon the American tax arrears: a sum of more than $160,000 for the years 1930 to 1941. This was paid, with ten years' worth of legal and accountancy bills, but it was nothing like the end of the matter. The UK government staked a claim to the residue of Agatha's American income, frozen for a decade and now returned to her; she needed that money desperately, but the tax authorities fought her for it until the end of 1954.

Through the 1950s the same problem recurred, over and over again. There was simply no getting clear of it. Surtax was appallingly high at this time and in March 1954 Agatha wrote to Cork from Nimrud: 'An income tax return sent to me by Heaven [this, almost unbelievably, was the name of her accountant] has shattered me to the core! Did I really make £30,000 in one year? Where *is* it all?!!!'

'It is terribly shocking', he replied, 'to think that one can earn £30,000 and retain so little. It is not the sort of fact that encourages an author to get on with a book that the publishers are clamouring for [she was writing *Destination Unknown*]. The short answer to the question where is it all is Mr Butler . . . For the current year the tax would amount to £25,100 and for the two previous years £25,800 per year.' That year saw the settling of the UK end of the drawn-out American tax dispute; this meant that, although the tax paid in America was finally regarded as 'deductible expenses' – a considerable relief – there was still a good deal outstanding at home. In September 1954 Cork informed Agatha that she owed around £70,000 to the UK authorities. Sensibly, considering her innate lack of thrift, he had stowed away just about this much in what he called her 'No. 1 Deposit Account'. 'It relieves my mind of a great deal of worry,' she wrote to him, especially as she had believed the account to contain about twenty-seven pounds. 'Did you conceal riches of the No. 1 account for me on purpose? I wouldn't put it past you. And probably very wise too! I might have bought a racehorse and started a Racing Stable.'[30]

This was all quite cheerful, and despite the vast sum of money involved Agatha was happy enough to pay, in the belief that this would get the Inland Revenue off her back. Of course it did not. At the end of 1954 she wrote to Rosalind from Swan Court, saying she had just heard from Cork: 'I'm worried, Agatha, terribly worried! I'm terribly afraid you're going to make £100,000 next year!!' In the governmental climate this was, indeed, a serious worry. 'I think something ought to be done *and* quickly – and actually I've been saying so for years,' Agatha's letter concluded.

The plan – which Cork had been considering for some time,

perhaps for too long – was that Agatha Christie should be turned into a limited company, which would employ Agatha to produce her novels and from which she would receive a wage. Her income would be something like the one she was receiving after tax, but far less money would go to the government as the company itself would only pay profits tax at the standard rate. In 1955 the Christie Settlement Trust was formed. The trustees bought one hundred shares in a company called Agatha Christie Limited, controlled by Agatha, whose hundred pounds had bought the shares. In 1957 the Christie Copyrights Trust was formed to look after the copyrights of almost all Agatha's work (she kept the rights in just twenty books and stories). This avoided a potential problem after death, when her copyrights might otherwise have been assessed at something like £20 million if – as in the case of Bernard Shaw – the tax authorities chose to multiply the income from a top-value property like *Witness for the Prosecution* by the number of stories she had written.

Essentially Agatha had to give away as much as she possibly could, in ways that were more congenial to her than handing it to the Revenue. She had already assigned *The Mousetrap* and *They Do It with Mirrors* to Mathew, *A Pocket Full of Rye* to the BSA, and the magazine rights of the short story 'Sanctuary' to the Westminster Abbey fund, but all this was for reasons of simple kindness rather than tax avoidance. Now she gave the film sale of *Witness for the Prosecution* to Rosalind, and *Hickory Dickory Dock* to Max's two nephews, John and Peter Mallowan, establishing a trust for their school fees; she gave sums to members of the Boehmer family (relations of her mother), to godchildren and to Charlotte Fisher. She gave to a charity, Harrison Homes, which cared for the elderly, and later the Agatha Christie Trust for Children was established. She also assigned a story called 'Greenshaw's Folly'[31] to the Diocese of Exeter, with which to buy a stained-glass window for the church at Churston Ferrers, near Greenway, where she worshipped. Agatha was by nature an extremely generous woman, but now she was obliged to be.

She had had her doubts about the scheme from the first: 'I presume it's ethical? So difficult to know nowadays.'[32] Although she thought her tax bills absurd, exorbitant proof of government wastefulness, she never for a moment considered becoming a tax exile, or being anything other than above board with the Revenue. She was instinctively uneasy about the way she was obliged to dodge and shift with her money. Why did it have to be like this? Deep into her sixties she still worked so very hard; through no fault of her own she had to play this absurd game of catch-up, and try not to be the victim of her overwhelming popularity. She strove to remain valiant. 'All this money rolling in and a far harder working life than when we had £400 a year and I wheeled a pram to the Park every day!!'[33] she wrote to Cork.

He, of course, was acting in what he considered to be Agatha's best interests, and had striven for the best possible scheme. In this he was helped by Anthony, who put his good legal brain to use and who, along with Cork and Rosalind, was to be a trustee. Herein lay the problem, in a sense. The scheme – which in effect took power away from Agatha, and turned her into what she called 'an employed wage slave' – was not for Agatha's own benefit. 'It really concerns Rosalind and Anthony,' she wrote to Cork in 1956. And there was something distasteful about the fact that, in order for the arrangement to work properly, Agatha was told that she had to live for another five years. 'How awful that sounds,' wrote Cork, 'but tax machinations make everyone seem inhuman, but do believe me we are not where our dear Agatha is concerned.'[34] She was sensitive to his embarrassment – 'Dear Edmund, the Doll will do her best to live another five years' – but she disliked the whole thing, and her attitude was to dissociate from it.

> I leave all complications to you, and to Anthony who, I
> suspect, may even enjoy them. Rosalind can be counted upon
> as a brake lever, oiled with perfect pessimism.
>   Don't upset yourself too much over all this. I always feel
> that in taxes the dice are loaded against one.[35]

Agatha then wrote to Rosalind and Anthony, saying, 'The thing is undertaken for your benefit – not mine, since I gather that my means of livelihood (and luxury living!) are more or less unchanged. Therefore unless you really want it and think it a good thing, let it go. [But] if you both think the possible worry and fuss is worthwhile go ahead. I personally am not going to worry or even take much interest. I think it's your pigeon.'[36]

This was relayed back to Cork as evidence of Agatha's apathy: 'I am definitely not prepared to go ahead unless our schemes have your unqualified approval,' he wrote to her. 'The whole thing does involve putting an awful lot of trust in Anthony and me . . .'[37] He remained convinced that the company was a necessity but was desperate for Agatha to be happy about it, and knew that deep down she was not. Nevertheless she went along with the scheme.

> Stung by being called apathetic (by Anthony, not by you!) I sent an indignant telegram denying the charge. Agreeable, not apathetic . . . Now don't have qualms, Edmund, I know you are doing your utmost for my financial welfare (and peace!) and I repose complete confidence in you and Anthony, and anyway, I've always been urging you to try something of the kind, haven't I? So don't let anxiety sit too heavily on your brow.[38]

But she had been right to doubt the protection that the scheme would afford her. In 1957 the Inland Revenue started up again. It was disputing the tax position of Agatha's copyrights, which had produced about £120,000 in the hands of the trustees, and indeed the whole notion of the scheme, which said she had 'died as an author' in 1955 and become a mere company employee with a tax code number. The Revenue had initially accepted this change of status, then, as Cork put it, 'changed their mind as only the Crown can do'. As with the Sabatini case back in 1938, which had started the whole nightmare of Agatha's tax liability in America, this new problem was waiting upon a judgment: the decision as to the copyrights of the late author, Peter Cheyney. It would not be resolved until the end of 1964.

In the interim Cork decided to urge further action. After the success of *Witness for the Prosecution* there was a huge amount of film interest, and the prospect of a deal with MGM seemed a straightforward way to pay the taxman, should the need arise. It was not a good deal. According to Mathew, Agatha's books 'were simply handed over to the first person who offered for them'.[39] MGM paid $75,000 in early 1960 for the film and television rights to forty properties, and the expectation at this time was that the profits – to be shared fifty-fifty with Agatha Christie Limited – would be handsome. Again, Agatha had doubts; again she was proved correct. 'I hope there won't be "broken hearts" over the MGM agreement – but what will be – will be! And what one loses in cash one may gain in absence of worry. But don't break *your* heart over it, Edmund dear – .'[40]

MGM cast as Miss Marple Margaret Rutherford, who was physically quite wrong – large, galumphing, with what was once described as a 'face like a poached egg' – but had the requisite light voice and ladylike English charm. As Cork wrote to Rosalind, she was 'a lot more like Marple than some of the sophisticated American minxes that were proposed. MGM have an option on Rutherford for the future, and we hope that may mean a long and remunerative run for Miss Marple.' The first film, *Murder, She Said*, released in 1961, was an adaptation of *The 4.50 from Paddington*. It did good box office but Agatha had some justification in writing to Cork, after a family visit to the Regal at Torquay: 'Frankly, it's pretty poor! I thought so that evening in London, but I couldn't say so before Margaret Rutherford, especially as she herself was so good. I thought it might seem better if seen in a real cinema with people. But no, definitely not.'[41]

Agatha did have an admiration and liking for Margaret Rutherford, and dedicated to her *The Mirror Crack'd from Side to Side*. 'I can assure you that this is one of the proudest moments of my life,' wrote Rutherford, with a touching sincerity. 'I am glad you were really so pleased with my performance, as no one but yourself really knows what "Miss Marple" is like – I just put myself in her hands, with faith, and let her do the rest – and very happy she made me!' There was a poignancy about this letter because, even as the actress was expressing her desire to continue in the role, Agatha was doing her utmost to get the films stopped. If she had thought *Murder, She Said* 'pretty poor', this was as nothing to her feelings about *Murder at the Gallop* – an extremely free adaptation of *After the Funeral*, set for no fathomable reason in a riding school – and *Murder Most Foul*, an even freer rewrite of *Mrs McGinty's Dead*.[42] When she made plain her feelings about the gross liberties that were being taken, MGM's reaction was to come up with *Murder Ahoy!*, which put Miss Marple on a Royal Navy ship and bore no resemblance whatever to any Christie story.

After this MGM turned its attention to Poirot, whom it threatened to reincarnate as a moustachioed old lecher played by Zero Mostel. *The Alphabet Murders*[43] was made – in fact with Tony Randall as Poirot and, in a cameo role, Margaret Rutherford as Miss Marple – but after this both sides had had enough. At the start, Agatha had established friendly relations with Lawrence Bachmann, the MGM representative, who had visited her at Greenway and been very popular because he and his wife liked dogs (Agatha had by this time acquired a Manchester terrier of her own: Treacle, bred in 1955 by Rosalind and given to her mother because he fought with Rosalind's shih-tzus). Bachmann had reassured Agatha that the films – while inevitably deviating somewhat from her original stories – would not cause her pain or embarrassment. She had been prepared for substantial changes. 'Don't think I'm upset by *Murder, She Said* – I'm not!' she wrote to Cork. 'It's more or less what I expected all along.'[44] But she refused to go to the première of *Murder at the Gallop* and the riding-school setting led her to write, a little caustically, to Bachmann: 'Don't kill Margaret Rutherford by making her embrace too many outdoor sports.'[45] The title *Murder Most Foul* aroused her scorn, as did the predilection for putting Miss Marple into books written for Poirot. But it was *Murder Ahoy!* that caused her real distress. 'I return to you this farrago of nonsense!' she wrote to Pat Cork (Edmund's daughter), after reading the script in March 1964. 'Why on earth can't MGM write their scripts, engage Margaret Rutherford to play an old lady, "Miss Sampson", have plenty of cheap fun and leave me and my creations out of it?' This was unarguable. MGM had valued her books: why then did they do everything in their power to destroy what made them valuable?

The shock to me is to find that possibly MGM have the right to write these scripts of their own featuring my characters. *That*, neither I nor Rosalind seem to have known . . .

I don't suppose there could be any misery greater for an author than to see their characters completely distorted. After all, I *have* a reputation as an author . . . I really feel sick and ashamed of what I did when I joined up with MGM. It was my fault. One does things for money and one is wrong to do so – since one parts with one's literary integrity. Once one is in the trap one can't get out. It is one of the sickmaking things that happen all the time nowadays . . . I held out until seventy but I fell in the end.

If they can write limitless scripts of their own, we've really had it. But I still hope that isn't true.

She wrote to Larry Bachmann, who apologised for the 'difficulties over *Murder Ahoy!*' and attempted to reassure her as to *The ABC Murders*. 'Please be assured that our basic conception of Hercule Poirot is such that it will not diminish your pride in your creation of this world famous character . . . we will not make him a licentious, "girl-chasing", dirty or shabby character.'[46] ('Soft words butter no parsnips', began her reply, and if this flummoxed Bachmann then the rest of the letter was admirably clear: 'I still feel it questionable that you really have the right to act as you have done.') Cork did his best to restrain any future excesses on the part of MGM, but it was a losing battle and he knew it: 'No film company will surrender absolute control,' he wrote to Anthony in May 1964. But Agatha was also obdurate. The films had gone from bad to worse, in fact they had become demeaning, and there was no prospect that MGM would ever treat the books with any kind of respect. It was stalemate. In July 1965 Cork delivered the news that 'MGM have not scheduled any further cinema films, as they find it impracticable to proceed without some more flexible arrangement as to adaptation than we are willing to grant them.' To Rosalind he wrote: 'It is a relief to be free of MGM . . .' The company had also employed Agatha to write an adaptation of *Bleak House*, one of her favourite novels, for which she – or Agatha Christie Ltd – was paid ten thousand pounds in 1962. She found the work fascinating, but had been subject to constant interference. 'She said that she had never got headaches from worry over her work before, as with this,'[47] wrote A. L. Rowse. The film was never made.

So the MGM deal had not yielded the promised riches. And the Cheyney case, which had been awaiting judgment since 1957, went against her. In November 1964 Cork wrote: 'I need not say how sorry I was to have to tell you last night that we lost our case against the Special Commissioners.' She was now liable for a sum between £100,000 and £125,000, this being the tax arrears from 1955. 'Agatha may indeed be shaken when she comes to consider the amounts at stake,' Cork wrote to Anthony; he himself was extremely upset about it, and felt deeply frustrated at his own failure to protect her.

He attempted reassurance: 'In my view the copyrights that we reserved against contingencies are worth substantially more than these sums,' he told her, but of course they had to be sold without the proceeds incurring tax at eighteen shillings in the pound. The old spectre of bankruptcy raised its head: 'You would be gloriously solvent,' he wrote tentatively. Then he moved away from this frankly unbelievable idea. 'I am more than ever confident that a solution will be found that will not scrape the barrel and which should not *force* any alteration in your mode of living. If you decide you want to cut down a bit anyway, that is a different matter!'[48]

It was a desperate shambles. Although it was nobody's fault – except that of the rapacious Revenue – it was a cruel position for Agatha to be in. The decision was appealed and the appeal was lost. More money was paid; more demanded. As a younger woman Agatha had had the resilience to withstand the situation, the sheer relentlessness with which it drove back and forth across her life. But in her seventies she found it hard, although she put up a show of courage.

Now that the unmentionable financial year has come round again [she wrote to Cork in March 1966], will you send me my accounts so that I can keep up with my homework and know how I stand and why – I don't know how or what I am spending. And I find this worrying. So will you do this as you have the figures and I don't – I can't say 1966 has been a pleasant year so far . . . Thank you for enclosed accounts. I can't help grudging Medley! [one of her legal advisers]. Talk, talk, talk, object, and no good comes of it!

In October 1966 a meeting was held at Somerset House, at which her liability was assessed as somewhere near £200,000, but it was agreed that she could sell her retained copyrights for £150,000 to Agatha Christie Ltd without incurring tax. Agatha was in America at the time, and replied from Princeton:

Nice to receive your letter, though I must say I am far from sharing your inexplicable jubilation! . . . If the tax people can get me to sell my copyrights to the Agatha Christie company they are sitting pretty to collect nearly all of the sum received for ordinary income tax – and no doubt would! Why not? They are entitled to it. No – I'm not rejoicing yet.

We are enjoying ourselves very much . . .

Eventually a solution of sorts was found when 51 per cent of Agatha Christie Ltd[49] was sold in 1968. It was bought by Booker McConnell (the company that in 1972 established the Booker Prize), a subsidiary of which had bought a similar controlling stake in Ian Fleming and the James Bond books. The sum paid to Agatha Christie Ltd was unspecified, but reported as being 'very much more' than the £100,000 deal with Fleming. By 1972 Booker also acquired the interest in the copyrights that had been owned by the Christie Copyrights Trust.[50] The company then lent to Agatha the money she owed to the Revenue, the loan being secured by the copyrights she retained. So it was that, in her eighties, she was in personal debt to Booker McConnell but clear of her obligations to the Inland Revenue: relieved at last of a weight that had pressed upon her – horribly, by the end – for more than thirty years. What has been called the mystery of her will, the fact that she left only £106,000, was in fact no mystery at all. Everything else had been taken from her.

Throughout, Rosalind's attitude was complex; as always between her and her mother. For a start her views on her mother's writing was far from straightforward. Like Agatha, she loathed publicity – because she too lived with the fallout from 1926; because her nature was so down-to-earth and suspicious of flummery – and what conjured more publicity than the words 'Agatha Christie'? The plays, in particular, attracted a huge amount of public attention. The Mary Westmacotts were obviously autobiographical, which was why in later life Rosalind was at pains to stress that they were not. According to her son, she rather wished the Westmacott novels 'had never been published' and she hated the idea of first nights. 'She was not proud of her mother and what she did.'[51]

It was not so surprising if Rosalind felt resentment, too deep for acknowledgement, about Agatha's career. It had helped to make Agatha the absent mother she undoubtedly was. In Rosalind's eyes it may have contributed to the breakdown of her marriage to Archie ('She left him alone too much . . .'). And the portrayal of Rosalind herself, in *Unfinished Portrait* and, to a lesser extent, *A Daughter's a Daughter*, was appallingly clear-eyed: reading those books, there could be no denying that Agatha was writer first, mother second.

With Mathew, Agatha was very different. She had adored him from the first, for the happy optimist's nature to which the death of Hubert lent poignancy. Her effusive delight in 'the lovely boy' contrasted starkly with her cool, joshing relationship with Rosalind ('Mummy won't have got writer's cramp from writing to me,' she wrote to Mathew. 'Tell her this').

Subconsciously, this emphatic adulation of Mathew may have been aimed at Rosalind. Agatha would not be the first to use a beloved grandchild in this way: women who have been semi-detached mothers quite often become devoted grandmothers, almost as if to prove to their children that they *can* be maternal. And there is no doubt that Agatha found Mathew more congenial than she did Rosalind.

As a cheerful boy at Eton, as a handsome young man at Oxford, she loved his company: she took him to school in her Rolls-Royce, watched him play cricket at Lord's, whisked him off to Stratford ('I'm going to take Mathew,' she wrote to Rosalind; 'I'm TELLING you this – not asking – because you'll make a fuss and say no'), and indulged their shared love of Wagner at Bayreuth. In many ways he resembled Agatha far more than his mother (although physically he took after Rosalind and Archie). Rosalind did not exude joy of living. She could not help but be sardonic with her son: 'my poor little halfwit', as she called him in a 1944 letter to Agatha. She was not overtly maternal. 'Agatha was afraid that Rosalind would love her dogs more than Mathew,' says John Mallowan – somewhat ironic, considering that Agatha had called her own dog Peter 'my child' – but in fact, like many people with a demonstrative love for animals, Rosalind had strong emotions towards humans that she found difficult to show. As a child she had longed for her father but had been obliged to keep this to herself. She had tried to get her mother's attention with her droll, sad letters but had lost out to Max. Now, in adulthood, she continued to play a strange role within the family: a still young and highly attractive woman, living in what was – however agreeable – a marriage of convenience, with a father whose name could not be mentioned and a mother to whom she must act as perpetual handmaiden. Where, in the midst of all this, was Rosalind's own life?

At the same time she was an absolute pragmatist (another difference between her and her mother). She knew very well that Agatha's writing had bought them all a magnificent existence. If she and Anthony had the problems of Greenway, they also had Greenway; if they had the worry of how to deal with the money, they also had money. So the handmaiden existence was the only one possible.

But Rosalind's resentment glinted dangerously when it came to Agatha Christie Ltd, which had been brought into being for her own benefit (and that of her husband and child). The way the trust worked was for Agatha to be its employee and to be paid a yearly salary. In letters to Rosalind, Edmund Cork referred to 'our servant' in a joking way, as if thereby to emphasise that Agatha was still in fact her own mistress. Rosalind, however, had no such scruples. 'I am glad that Agatha Christie Limited is gathering some money and sincerely hope it won't all be paid to our Wage-Slave!'[52] This also reads like a joke, but it was not. 'I hope you won't pay too much of the £14,000 in salary to my mother!'[53] she wrote to Cork, who had told her that the company had collected this sum during its first year of operation. By 1958 the company had accumulated £45,000; Cork suggested that Agatha's salary be raised from £5,000 to £7,500. 'I think, of course, it is a very bad idea indeed – but if you think it won't be acceptable to the Income Tax at £5,000 with the £3,000 a year expenses it will obviously have to be considered . . .'[54]

It was true that, in a sense, the yearly salary was a formality paid to fulfil the conditions of the tax-avoidance scheme. Agatha still had the money from the sale of her copyrights although this, like everything else she owned, was potentially up for grabs by the Inland Revenue. But Rosalind's attitude was extraordinary, nonetheless, and Edmund Cork was baffled by it. When Agatha was paid £10,000 for her draft script of *Bleak House*, he wrote cautiously that 'It would be nice to show [the company's] appreciation by paying her, say, another £5,000.'[55] Back came the reply: 'I am not sure about my mother having extra money as I think Anthony told you on the telephone and will have to think about it – I'm glad you have got £10,000 though!'[56]

Rosalind did agree that Agatha might have a new car; Collins had previously given her a huge Humber which had been nothing but trouble. But it was quite some time before Cork prevailed about the additional £5,000.

And yet, for all this, Rosalind was powerfully protective of Agatha. In February 1957 she wrote to Cork about an article that had appeared in the *Daily Mail*: 'I was most upset to see a reference to her disappearance – It said [of a missing woman] "I'm not sure she's not doing an Agatha Christie on us." I don't know whether you can make some complaint about this – it makes me very angry and I know it will not please my mother . . . I really do feel very strongly about it.' The events of 1926 were always extremely sensitive for Rosalind; for mixed reasons, of course. She herself had a good deal to forgive about the behaviour of both her parents, and she was also obliged to maintain the semi-fiction of the 'official' theory. At the same time her instinctive reaction, when the subject arose, was to rise to her mother's defence. She could not bear Agatha to be defamed or ridiculed; she knew something of the agony that her mother had endured at that time, and it literally pained her to have this belittled. 'The unspoken subject', as Joan Oates calls it, was a test to be passed in order to be admitted over Rosalind's personal threshold. Anyone who regarded Agatha's behaviour as deceitful or attention-seeking would have the door shut upon them. Judith Gardner had been a childhood friend of Rosalind; her mother, Nan Kon, had been Agatha's friend, and when Nan died in 1959 Agatha wrote to Judith to say, 'If ever you need help or anything from an older person, I'm always there and you must consider me as a kind of mother.' Yet in 1996 Judith collaborated with Jared Cade on the book that purported to have solved the disappearance, unequivocally calling it a stunt. Rosalind – who viewed Judith's behaviour as a personal vendetta against her family – was distressed and disgusted. Oddly enough, Agatha herself had learned in 1960 that the journalist Ritchie Calder was preparing to write a book containing his 'memories' of Agatha's discovery at Harrogate; her reaction, as expressed to Edmund Cork, was sanguine. 'You may worry it's coming to my ears,' she wrote, 'but after all it's only what crops up from time to time every few years, and what does it matter after all this time?' This may, of course, have been partly bravura. At any rate Rosalind would have sought to keep such stories from Agatha.

She was also, perversely, protective of her mother's work. She reacted fiercely to attacks upon the books, of which there were many after Agatha's death, although such was their success that she could easily have left them to speak for themselves. But she felt that Agatha Christie was much misunderstood; as in the Channel 4 *J'Accuse* programme, which upset her greatly.[57] Until her own death in 2004, Rosalind felt an obligation to stand up for her mother's books. When she was no longer a power within Agatha Christie Ltd, and raged at some of what was done in its name, she would protest against what she saw as absurd, inappropriate, or insufficiently faithful adaptations. The accomplished BBC television series starring Joan Hickson as Miss Marple earned her delighted praise; the ITV series of *Poirot* was accepted, on the whole, but she could not understand its occasional lack of fidelity. The closer the adaptations stuck to the originals, the better, was Rosalind's belief, and on the whole she was right. But her belief was held out of loyalty, as well as conviction: she believed it because she knew that it was what Agatha herself had wanted.

She remembered, for example, the real misery that the MGM adaptations had caused her mother. Agatha had tried not to take this to heart, but she had minded very much indeed, and in March 1964 Rosalind wrote to Cork:

I feel personally most discouraged and ashamed about the dealings with MGM. Larry Bachmann knew he had been wrong both legally and morally over this film . . . You may say as you have done constantly over the last few days that it is all good money – but I do feel and I was really genuinely dismayed to see you did not share my feelings – that we have really let my mother down very badly over this whole deal.

The following year she wrote again: 'I am very worried about my mother's tax . . . the chief concern is for my mother. She is not looking very well and I know this is bothering her a lot.'[58]

It was as though Rosalind felt guilt about Agatha: not just about how hard her mother had to work for them all but about her own resentment of this work, for which she knew she had to be grateful. In order for Agatha to write, Rosalind had to help run the rest of Agatha's life. This was the way things were; and it aroused in Rosalind a complexity of emotions that, being the kind of person she was, she did not voice or even acknowledge. But the protectiveness that she showed towards Agatha was partly connected to her feelings of guilt: a way to expunge them, in fact, and to prove to herself how wrongful they were.

As Agatha grew older so Rosalind became more protective. After her mother's death she became as fierce as a lioness in Agatha's defence, and never wavered in her staunch support of both the woman and the writer. 'Even if I am her daughter, I think she was an exceptional person!'[59] she wrote. Like her mother, Rosalind was the product of an age that did not pity itself in public; unlike her mother, she had the unusual ability to accept whatever life threw at her and deal with it as simple fact. She was the daughter of Agatha Christie, and that brought with it things that were both good and bad. Fact.

She has been called 'damaged', 'difficult': terms that she herself would not have recognised, and that bear little relation to the warm, highly intelligent, straight-talking woman she was in old age. It is true that her childhood would nowadays be regarded as blighted – no regular contact with her father; left for months on end while her mother went travelling; sidelined in favour of a step-father of an age to be her own husband – and it is also true that her adulthood, after Hubert's death, was not really her own to enjoy. But it was also true that she had a glorious life through her mother's success. This, then, was the way things were. Rather than discussing them, it was better to have a large gin (unlike Agatha, Rosalind was no abstainer; it was said that life at Greenway revolved around drink) and get on with it.

For her part, Agatha found her feelings hard to express when it came to Rosalind. The letters that she sent from the East during the 1950s took their usual tone. 'It will probably make you gnash your teeth to read it, but I am having a very pleasant life', she wrote from Baghdad; and, after a visit to Tunis, 'Lucky for you you weren't born in the days of Carthage. They sacrificed all their first born children! There are thousands and thousands of holes full of little bleached bones!!' At the same time she wanted to hear from her child. 'Severe shock for the postman, bringing a letter from you'; 'Over *three weeks* here and not *one word from you* YOURS TRULY FED UP'.

In 1955 Agatha was taken ill on the dig, with what Max described to Rosalind as 'an internal chill' – in fact a very unpleasant infection – and driven for three and a half hours to hospital at Kirkuk. From there she wrote, 'What a rotten correspondent *you* are! I take it very poorly. Now that I'm only the servant of the company I shall have to be kept in a good temper and induced by a great deal of kindness to do some work!!! . . . Lots of love to you really, you horrid girl.'[60]

Agatha knew the debt she owed to Rosalind. She too felt a good deal of guilt: since 1926 her actions had influenced her daughter's life, by no means always in the way that Rosalind would have chosen. She still believed that her divorce was a very wrong thing, and that in some way she was to blame for it; she knew that Rosalind saw Archie, and was grateful for the discretion with which this was done; she realised that her second marriage had relegated Rosalind to a minor role, and that her daughter stoically stoked the home fires while she and Max lived pretty much as they chose.

At the same time Agatha was aware – as how could she not be? – that it was her money which paid for everything, and this made her autocratic. Although her façade was modest, she could be grand; not with everyone, but often with Edmund Cork, and sometimes with Rosalind. In the years of her great fame she tended to conduct her affairs with a rather irritable airiness, thus: 'Do go to Greenway sometimes to see how it's all going. (But don't go out of your way to 'make trouble' . . . !) The great thing is nobody writes and bothers *me*!' She left Rosalind and Anthony to deal with Greenway ('Tell Anthony bending the back to pick lettuces is the best cure for those aches and pains and stiffness,' she wrote from Nimrud), and a part of her thought that this was right and proper. Another part of her felt differently. On a visit to Pwllywrach a row erupted about Greenway, and Agatha, as she put it, 'blew her top' in its defence. Afterwards she wrote to Rosalind to apologise.

> The truth is I've got a guilty conscience about Greenway – you and Anthony and Mathew have Pwllywrach – a lovely home and garden and Max has his Winterbrook and its books and its river – and it's really only *I* who cling on to Greenway because I love it so . . . I feel a bit better since the Garden's done so well, thanks to Anthony, but of course I suppose it is pure selfishness on my part.
>
> There is no doubt that, far from being a rum baba, I am a Bloody old Bitch.[61]

She loved the house with a deep and private passion. It absorbed some of the feelings she had had for Ashfield. It could never quite replace that home: Ashfield would always be the place where she had been most entirely at ease, and most entirely happy. But Greenway laid a sharp, exquisite touch upon her imagination. In the summer it was often filled with people – names in the visitors' book include members of the Mallowan family, Allen and Lettice Lane, Billy Collins, Peter Saunders, Stephen Glanville and his daughter Lucia, Charlotte Fisher, Nan Kon, Edmund Cork, Stella Kirwan (from the 1950s Agatha's secretary and friend), A. L. Rowse – and filled with activity: tennis, croquet, clock golf, boats on the Dart, children playing in the sun, dogs scurrying everywhere. Yet it was a place where solitude could become something magical. The walled gardens, the tangled paths, the brief-blooming camellias, the sunlit shadows within the shuttered rooms, the lawn outside the front door dropping away to the Dart, a scene of configurative stillness rustled by trees. There was a serenity to the whole that was nonetheless disturbed by its beauty, a beauty so extreme that it did not quite permit restfulness. It demanded imaginative response. This was Agatha's dreamscape, and through it she walked, a fat and wrinkled lady with shrewd eyes and a black-and-tan dog at her heels; a country gentlewoman, it might be said; but in her head what mysterious thoughts.

So she was intensely grateful to Rosalind – and to Anthony, whom she adored – for the help with the house and, indeed, with everything. 'Oh! dear Rosalind – what a relief,' she wrote in April 1953, after hearing that the Hickses were taking charge of her affairs while she was at Nimrud. 'I can now apply myself to the important development of *After the Funeral.*' Beneath the dry surface of their relationship Agatha recognised Rosalind's worth; increasingly so, as she grew older. 'I feel you really must have a proper letter thanking you for the lovely Xmas you gave us . . . I know, too, that a lot of work and planning and thought has to be done to make everything seem so right and so effortless. And I *appreciate* it . . .'

At Nimrud she began to miss her English life: 'Days of whirling dust storms . . . have been sitting gasping and *longing* for home, crocuses, snowdrops, camellias at Greenway, river at Wallingford – You and Mathew at Pwllywrach – somewhere *green* where there is a flower or two. Can't think why I ever wanted to come to this stupid country . . .' In 1957 she wrote describing her attempts to type Max's catalogue with a tornado hurling itself against the door and panes of glass smashing into the dig house, then going to a bed partly protected by a mackintosh.

That, visitors, sandflies, peculiar beetles and now mosquitoes have curbed my enthusiasm a good deal. And to read of your daffodils makes me long for Pwllywrach and you and Anthony and possibly a Japanese poem or two!

Well, not long now.

*   *   *

But Agatha went to Nimrud to be with Max, as well as to escape the oppressions of England; there would no leaving Max alone out east. She would never leave a husband alone again. Rosalind knew the depth of Agatha's loyalty to her husband, the extent to which she used her own career to support his, and this played a part in her desire to protect her mother. It may, too, have influenced Rosalind's desire to cap the salary that Agatha Christie Ltd paid to her mother every year. This money, after all, was spent on Agatha's life with Max: the travel, the trips to Rome and Paris, the nights at the Hôtel Bristol and sumptuous French dinners ('a Château Latour 1924, bang on', as Max wrote to Rosalind in 1953, 'complete with Châteaubriand, sauce Béarnaise and all the French cheeses. Price of wine 1,600 francs . . .'). The more salary Agatha was given as spending money, the more she would do this kind of thing.

It is usually said that Rosalind was very fond of Max, although there is no particular evidence one way or the other. 'He didn't beat me, or my mother, not that I remember,' she said of him.[62] Certainly he had a liking for her, as shown in his letters during the war, and he got along very well with Anthony: both were intellectual men with a shared love of good conversation and wine. Rosalind's own feelings were more opaque. Her aunt Madge, who died in 1950, had never trusted Max; neither did Madge's son Jack, a tricky character but highly intelligent. They were wary of a young, impoverished man (and Catholic) who had sought to marry a much older woman of considerable means. There is no evidence that Rosalind shared their view. 'Arguably she might have resented the fact that Uncle Max took her mother off on digs, and she got popped into school and got looked after by Agatha's secretary, things like that,' says John Mallowan, although in fact she coped very well with the considerable upheaval of her mother's second marriage. But it does seem that she came, in later years, to distrust one particular aspect of Max's behaviour.

Nobody knows for certain if Max Mallowan had a long-term affair with Barbara Parker, the woman who organised the dig at Nimrud and whom he married less than two years after Agatha's death. Such a liaison, if it happened, was inevitably conducted with secrecy. It was also surrounded by rumour and gossip, some of which appears to have reached Rosalind's ears; and, very possibly, Agatha's also. Was it the case that, despite her best efforts to stay with her second husband and to keep him happy in every way, Max had betrayed her just as Archie had?

Although she was eighteen years younger than Agatha, and obviously far less of a personage, Barbara Parker was an interesting woman in her own right; highly singular, in fact. In Jared Cade's version of Agatha's life – which naturally takes the view that Max and Barbara *did* have an affair – Barbara is portrayed as somewhat pathetic: a hardworking spinster whose 'compliant nature and dog-like devotion [to Max] masked unfilled sexual needs'. This is presumably the view of Judith Gardner (and her husband Graham), but it is not the way she is generally remembered. 'Rather magnificent, Barbara,' says Dr Julian Reade, who was a young archaeologist in the 1960s. 'She had a reverberating whisper – so that "*He's one of them*" would go ringing across the room.'[63]

'I adored Barbara,' says Joan Oates, who shared a tent with her on the Nimrud dig. 'She was an unusual person. A bit of a character. You could almost put her on a list of extraordinary British women who spent a lot of time in the Near East, going back to people like Lady Hester Stanhope – she was in that mould. She was terrific. A little bit odd, but you had to be to live that sort of life.'[64]

The way in which Barbara fell into the world of archaeology shows how small it was – yet wide open to those with enthusiasm – in the pre-war years. She saw the announcement of a course in western Asian archaeology on a noticeboard at the Courtauld where she was studying Chinese. Before this she had worked as a mannequin at Worth and gone to RADA; now she decided to enrol upon this course. The only other student was Rachel Maxwell-Hyslop, who says: 'The course existed on paper only. Nobody had ever asked to do it!'[65] But with the encouragement of Stephen Glanville – 'bless his heart' – the two women went to see Sidney Smith at the British Museum, with whom they would study cuneiform. 'He was amazed. In actual fact he was so amazed he was marvellous.' Smith gave tutorials after hours at the museum, sending his students to sources that were only published in German, which neither of them read, although later they were joined by another female student who was fortuitously bilingual. Rachel Maxwell-Hyslop was a highly educated post-graduate, with a mind attuned to academic study; Barbara was nothing of the kind, but she completed the two-year course and although, according to Henrietta McCall's biography of Max Mallowan, she was never 'taken terribly seriously by her colleagues', she evidently possessed a good and inquisitive brain. 'Archaeology was so alive at that time,' says Rachel Maxwell-Hyslop, whose fascination with the subject had been fired by hearing Leonard Woolley lecture. 'He'd put up slides, say, "This is the Flood!" – very exciting. You never knew what was going to come up. And there were very few people in it. We all knew each other, and everybody had come in in odd ways.'

When Max was appointed to the Institute of Archaeology, Rachel Maxwell-Hyslop became his assistant lecturer and Barbara, who had worked in Palestine just before the war, was 'shot out to Baghdad' in 1949, there to run the BSA house. By then Max had known her for some time; a wartime letter to Agatha tells her to ask Barbara – then working for the fire service in London – to 'send my Herodotus' out to Tripolitania. When she arrived in Iraq she had very little Arabic, but she learned quickly, and she got on well with Arabs. Her connections within Iraq society were invaluable to Max Mallowan. 'You couldn't get anywhere in Baghdad without knowing the right person, and if things were ever difficult then Barbara would know the right person one should ask to dinner.'[66] So it was that Max reaped the benefits not just of Agatha's wealth and status but of Barbara's insider knowledge.

Barbara was lean and fine-boned, with an angular face and large eloquent eyes. She was the physical model for Valerie Hobhouse in *Hickory Dickory Dock*: 'Valerie rather like Barbara!' Agatha wrote in one of her notebooks. It has been said that Barbara was very alluring, although the general impression is that – unlike the rakishly attractive Valerie – she was not quite assured enough to be a *femme fatale*. John Mallowan remembers that at Greenway 'you'd try and keep her away from plates and glasses because she was a bit clumsy'. But a photograph taken on site at Nimrud shows a stark difference in the silhouettes of Barbara and Agatha; the one with the slightly drooping, heron-like stance of the former mannequin, the other massive as an ageing bull. 'Barbara wasn't really elegant,' says Joan Oates, 'she was a bit bizarre, she wore Kurdish trousers. But she was tall and very slim.' And she clearly had some attraction for the eminent Arabs with whom she mixed so easily. On one occasion in the 1950s she was taken to court in Baghdad, accused of flouting a new law, which said that sewage could no longer be dumped in the Tigris (although with houses like the BSA residence, whose drains ran into the river, there was no simple alternative). 'And then she was summonsed,' says Joan Oates, 'she had no lawyer, so she decided to defend the case herself. In her Arabic, which was quite good by then. And she defended herself in court, and she was found not guilty, and the judge took her out to lunch.' Similarly, Agatha wrote to Rosalind in 1951 of 'our Barbara, now on great terms of intimacy with Sheikh Abdullah, from whom she had collected twelve turkeys, a set of divan pillows with variegated satin ends and a prism . . .'

Joan Oates met Barbara for the first time in 1952, when they were both staying in the BSA house, awaiting the arrival of Max and Agatha. 'The previous year Max had told her to go and build a dig house. And she had gone up and built a house [in fact she extended what was already there]. Impressive. Back of beyond, she was on her own, she had to hire the labour – Max just told her to do these things. And anything difficult, she did beautifully. The simple things were always getting her sacked.'[67] This was the joke with Barbara: Max sacked her every day. She was, wrote Robert Hamilton, a classical scholar who worked on the dig, 'the good-natured butt of Max's occasional satirical humour'. She was also the target of his volatile temper. Although a capable epigraphist she was not a naturally concentrated worker – 'Her notebooks of the period have a harried look about them,' wrote Henrietta McCall[68] – and Max, for whatever reason, constantly blew off steam in her direction. In 1955 Agatha wrote to Rosalind that 'lots of imposing tablets' were turning up on the dig, and that Barbara was consequently 'very busy and full of gloom. "I knew this would happen if you had no epigraphist but me", actually doing very well with constant goading by Max.'

So she was capable of the hard scholarly work of deciphering cuneiform; but her real talents lay in her ability to understand and penetrate Iraqi society. Even after the 1958 revolution, the contacts

Barbara had made held good: 'The BSA owe her for that,' says Rachel Maxwell-Hyslop. 'It was a difficult job, starting off with being a woman in the first place.' But she did a good deal else beside, almost to the point of masochism. Max, it was said, knew the extent of her devotion (whether to the work or to himself) and used it. For example she would pay the workmen on the dig; once, it was said, she had forgotten to go to the bank, paid the first man then asked him if she could borrow the money to pay the second, borrowed again and so on to the end of the line. 'She was ingenious,' says Joan Oates. She would also do the accounts, although they never came out right, and would put in her own money (of which she had little) to make the totals fit. 'Whereas Max would come along and say, I need some money for the trip up to Kirkuk, to take some money off this oil company, about £200 will do . . .'[69]

It was in the winter of 1952 that Barbara took Joan on a trip from Baghdad to Mosul in order to get fruit trees for the terrace on the dig house. 'And then it starts to pour with rain. Really dumping rain. And once it starts to rain like this the roads were just impassable. But she had to do this, because Agatha wanted trees.' In the end Barbara persuaded two policemen to take her to Nimrud, about thirty kilometres from Mosul. 'And we get to Nimrud and Barbara gets the policemen to dig the holes for the trees.'

Agatha and Barbara were friends, although not intimates. They seem to have liked each other well enough: 'A Barbara type! – good company' read another note in one of Agatha's books. The two women travelled together each year from Baghdad to Nimrud – 'we go up like ladies' – a few days after the men. But as the story of the fruit trees shows, Barbara also worked for Agatha; and Agatha was always in the position to command. Back in England Barbara had a fairly solitary life, living as she did in her nephew's flat in Kensington. The visitors' book at Greenway shows that every year, almost without fail, she spent two or three weeks at the house from August to September. If she was there for Max she was also there at Agatha's invitation, beholden to Agatha's hospitality; rather as Nancy Neele had once been on her visit to Styles.

But was Barbara there for Max? Joan Oates says categorically not. 'I don't believe the story of the affair at all. I lived in the house at

Baghdad, and it was a house where all the bedrooms opened into the inner courtyard. I shared a tent with her at Nimrud, I really knew her quite well. The story actually originated with somebody who stayed in the house at Baghdad. It was a mischievous story.'

Joan Oates was married (to the subsequent dig director) in 1956, after which she would not, of course, have shared a tent with Barbara; nonetheless she is adamant in her belief that there was no affair, and so, too, is John Mallowan, who is clear and calm on the subject. 'I remember Judy and Graham [Gardner], and I think they just got it totally wrong. I don't think there was anything between Barbara and Uncle Max. They were good friends, and they shared an interest, so getting married after Agatha died was a logical thing to do. And Barbara helped Uncle Max with Agatha towards the end, and rendered genuine assistance. Barbara was always – she was a very faithful person. I think Uncle Max always tried to do his best for her workwise. I think he may have had some influence in what jobs she got. But I think that's as far as it went.'[70]

Other people who knew Barbara and Max are of this opinion, that they were friends and no more, and that they married in November 1977 to assuage each other's loneliness. A photograph of the two together does have a marital look, although it was taken in the 1960s; they are on a sofa in an unidentified sitting room (possibly out east), Max reading comfortably in his slippers, Barbara close to him, smiling at the camera, with a bottle of Gordon's gin on a cushion at her side. They look not exactly blissful, but familiar with each other. And there are those who say that this familiarity was born of a long-standing love affair, which after thirty years or so was finally regularised in marriage. One friend does not state that there was definitely an affair, but comes close to asserting his own belief in it. 'What people say [meaning those who deny the affair] may be the truth in their eyes. Which may have involved a certain amount of turning a blind eye.'

Judith and Graham Gardner did not go in for blind-eye turning. In the course of their collaboration with Jared Cade they regaled him with tales of Max's infidelity; and not just with Barbara. They say, for example, that Max conducted affairs with the young female students at the Institute of Archaeology after he was appointed

lecturer-teacher in 1947. There is absolutely no evidence whatsoever of this. According to Julian Reade, Max hardly had any students
anyway (he remembers just one of note, a talented young Iraqi whose
PhD was published with Max's help), so the idea that a cluster of
young girls was fluttering around him is entirely misleading.
According to the Gardners, however, Judith's mother Nan discovered that Max was conducting casual liaisons and 'broke the news
to Agatha . . . Nan had approached Max for advice after a friend's
daughter was uncertain how to pursue an interest in archaeology.
Max had offered to help by giving the girl a place in his class and,
although he formed no relationship with her, reports of his friendships with other female students got back to the girl's mother, who
in turn told Nan.'[71]

The omnipresence of Nan in Agatha's life – which Cade's book
requires the reader to accept, as Nan is the source of almost every
one of its stories – is simply not borne out by facts. The two women
were good friends, certainly. Nan's name is the first entry in the visitors' book at Greenway ('Good luck to Greenway and Agatha and
Max, lots of love Nanski'), but also there at the time was Dorothy
North, and Nan features no more than she in Agatha's correspondence. Max refers to her during the war, saying that he owes her a
letter; Agatha mentions her as an entertaining dinner guest who amused
Allen Lane into the small hours; but although Agatha wrote to Judith
'I shall miss her very much' after Nan's death in 1959, there is no
sense that she was an intimate friend of the kind that Jared Cade
implies. Agatha was simply not the type to have confiding relationships. For all her dependency on Max she was in many ways a proud,
grand, self-contained creature, and it is impossible to imagine her
having hushed little female discussions about her husband's infidelity
over the teacups in Chelsea.

It is said that Max 'had an eye for a pretty girl'. In Baghdad, for
example, he apparently became quite smitten with the glamorous wife
of an ambassador. But this is quite usual behaviour among men, not
necessarily meaningful, and certainly out east the shrewd eye of Joan
Oates saw nothing untoward.

Yet the very nature of the Mallowan marriage might well have led
Max towards other women. It was not just that Agatha was growing

old while he was merely middle-aged; it was something more subtle. The money was Agatha's, the houses were Agatha's, the patronage was Agatha's, and everybody knew it. In such circumstances – which, in less exaggerated form, are quite familiar – it is not uncommon for a man to take something that is definitively his own. That is to say, a mistress.

There were hints in Agatha's earlier letters that Max might want to look elsewhere from time to time, and that she would accept him doing so. Agatha knew the nature of her marriage. It was not a great romance, the age difference was very considerable and she was a woman without physical allure (although Max was not abundant in this quality). The truth was that Max simply did not have the power to hurt her as Archie had done. A dalliance or two, she could take. The only pain she could not endure was to be left alone again, and she did not ever really believe that that would happen.

Even if she *were* Max's mistress, Barbara was not a threat. She could offer nothing to compare with the life Max had with Agatha. 'Nevertheless,' writes Jared Cade, '[Agatha] still grieved over the loss of Max's love for her': a statement without a shred of supporting evidence, although the assumption must be that Agatha spoke of her grief to that all-knowing confidante, Nan Kon.

More concrete evidence (albeit uncorroborated) comes from Graham Gardner, who visited Baghdad with his wife in 1962; although the Mallowans were not there at the time, the couple stayed at the BSA house and Graham photographed some of the Nimrud treasures. According to his account, he went to Swan Court before leaving for Baghdad, to receive instructions from Max as to the photographs he was to take. At the flat he found that his arrival was unexpected, and that Max and Barbara were 'furtively ensconced' in a 'lovers' tryst'. The precise meaning of this is unclear. Barbara lived not far away in Kensington, and unless Graham Gardner caught her and Max *in flagrante* – which he would surely have mentioned – it is entirely possible that she was visiting Max as a friend and colleague.

Nor is there any evidence for the statement, made by the Gardners, that Max was 'keeping Barbara' (presumably with Agatha's money): as Henrietta McCall writes, she was 'Max's slave', his secretary and generally indispensable aide, so if he helped her in return this would be in the nature of things. The Gardners also say that the affair was conducted at Winterbrook House. This, again, is hard to prove. It was said – not by the Gardners – that on Barbara's visits to Greenway she and Max would shut themselves away for long periods in the library, leaving Barbara's plimsolls outside the door as a sign that they should not be disturbed. But the truth is that nobody knows what went on between Max and Barbara. As with the disappearance, so with the affair: Jared Cade's book presents a weight of unsubstantiated claims as if they were undisputed facts.

That said, Max's behaviour after Agatha's death was not quite that of a grief-stricken widower. It was said by the Gardners that he 'was impatient for Agatha to die so that he could marry Barbara';[72] in fact he had an eye elsewhere, notably on the wildly glamorous Baroness Camoys, who lived close to Winterbrook at the magnificent Stonor Park, near Henley, one of the great Catholic houses.[73] Jeanne Camoys Stonor was born in 1913, the product of an illegitimate mating between the daughter of an Irish viscount and a Spanish grandee. She was a genuine thoroughbred beauty, capable of dazzling men with her charm, but she had a lethal streak. She swore like a stevedore ('and you can eff orf out of it'), supported the Nazis unashamedly during the war ('*Olé* and Heil Hitler!') and treated her kindly husband with something close to contempt. She cultivated Agatha and Max – her rich and famous neighbours – and, when her husband died in March 1976, she saw in the recently bereaved Max a suitable replacement. Her calculation was that Agatha would have left him millions. The situation was, of course, rather more complex; but it seems that for a short time in 1976 Max did see himself as the likely husband of this lurid and exotic man-eater. Then, for whatever reason – perhaps his friends advised him that it would not look entirely suitable, perhaps Jeanne learned that Max was not so cash-rich as she had believed – Max quit the Stonor scene.

He had a less tricky companion than Lady Camoys in the young girl, D., aged around twenty, whom he befriended very soon after Agatha's death. She had asked if she could graze her pony in the grounds at Winterbrook; Agatha was very ill at the time but, after she had died, Max contacted the girl and they quickly became close. He drove her in his Mercedes[74] to lunch at Boodles – 'there was me, just in my scruffy clothes'[75] – and would suddenly whisk her off for ice-cream at Fortnum & Mason, where he parked outside 'practically on Piccadilly'[76]. Max's cars were always flamboyant – in the 1950s he drove a silver Rolls-Royce, 'a monster of a machine', according to John Mallowan, in which he would do around seventy m.p.h. on the curving road along Slapton Sands in Devon – and he was known for driving right in the middle of the road. In the end D. drove the Bentley, taking Max down to Greenway in it – 'stopping on the way for sherry and sardine sandwiches' – and resisting his urges to 'see if it would do a hundred and thirty m.p.h.'. So D. became a regular visitor to Greenway, and for about six months went to live in the mews house at Cresswell Place that Agatha had bought in 1928. Max was worried about squatters, so he said, 'Why don't you go and live in my house?'[77] He also suggested that she might go out to Iran with him and 'act sort of like a hostess, take him around, and all that'. This, for Max, was obviously in the nature of a dream; by that time, his days of swanning around the East were over.

There was nothing whatsoever improper about this relationship, although it was not perhaps what might have been expected at that time. It was in the nature of an innocent last fling. D. 'had the impression that Agatha was a bit tricky towards the end, that it was a bit of a relief to Max when she died. I would think the last two or three years of Agatha's life were tough on him.' So he conducted himself like an ageing, still frisky dog let off the leash. He enjoyed his old role of teacher – 'He was a mentor to me' – and particularly with this very young, direct, fearless girl, who was unimpressed by his considerable standing and knew nothing of his achievements. 'I'd just sit there and say, "Well, what did you do, then?"' Doubtless this amused him a good deal. After so many years of ingratiation and social-climbing and academic politicking, after a life spent as Mr Agatha Christie, how very refreshing it must have been to nip into the Bentley with this bright and unpretentious young thing, play King Cophetua and show her a jolly good time.

Certainly she remembers him with great fondness. 'Everyone should have a Max in their life. It was like a picnic.'[78]

D. knew Barbara, of course, who was 'always around' (Rachel

Maxwell-Hyslop remembers Barbara saying, 'I can't do anything at weekends,'[79] because she was looking after Max at Winterbrook). 'She was great. She was a real case. She drove Rosalind mad because she wouldn't eat this, she wouldn't eat that ... She had this wonderful old fur coat, it was quite raggedy but she'd wear it in the summer because she felt the cold – I think that used to annoy Rosalind as well.

'Rosalind', she says, 'used to like to talk about Agatha. But she was very possessive, very very possessive of her memory.'[80]

D. obviously detected Rosalind's antipathy towards Barbara; it was with some trepidation that Max told his step-daughter of his plans to remarry. 'No one will ever take the place of my dear Agatha,' he wrote in March 1977, 'but I think she would have approved for she used to tell me to marry in case anything happened to her ... It is lonely now, and will not be so with Barbara who has always been a devoted friend.'

'It was just obvious that he should marry Barbara,' says D. 'Because she was spending so much time there ... He said, "I'm tempted to ask you" – thank God he didn't! No, there was never anything ... I mean, I used to get teased.'

Jared Cade's book gives the impression that Barbara was desperate to marry Max but D., who was at Winterbrook much of the time, says, 'She wasn't bothered. I heard her saying, "It's so silly – so silly – I know he'll look after me." But Max wanted to marry her, as a thank-you.' Max and Barbara lived together for barely a year at Winterbrook House. Their companion was the dog Bingo, Agatha's second Manchester terrier, who, in her declining years, had been viewed by a watchful friend as 'her ally'.

When Max died in August 1978 Barbara was left £40,000, with which she eventually bought a house in Wallingford where she lived alone until her own death in 1993. Winterbrook was sold. This caused Rosalind a good deal of anguish, as the house was full of things that had belonged to Agatha – even to Archie – whose ownership she had constantly to prove. 'It must be understood that under the terms of my mother's will she left all her personal possessions to me,' she wrote to Cecil Mallowan, Max's brother, in 1981. 'Secondly under Max's will I was able to choose certain ornaments particularly associated with my mother after Barbara left the house. I have always known and agreed that Winterbrook was Max's house . . .'

Perhaps there is little wonder that D. remembers Rosalind at the lunch after Max's funeral, 'going round Winterbrook saying, "That's mine, that's mine . . ."'. Nor is it hard to understand why Rosalind became ever more protective towards Agatha as her mother grew older, and ever more alert to the fate of Agatha's legacy.

Yet Agatha's own attitude was rather different. Whatever she suspected about her second husband – that he had married her for money; that he was unfaithful; that he would quickly remarry if she predeceased him – she remained defiantly on Max's side. In 1971 she sent a long letter to Rosalind on the subject of her plays (Rosalind was urging her against a new production of *Fiddler's Five*, a late work that had been poorly received). The letter ended: 'I know you have my best interests at heart – as A.P. [Madge] had when she implored me not to marry Max . . . and even refused to come to the wedding – I'm thankful I didn't listen to her! Forty years of happiness I should have missed. If one doesn't take a few risks in life one might as well be dead!'[81]

This, then, was Agatha's stance. Max made her happy. Which may mean that Max was not having a long-term affair with Barbara Parker and that the Mallowan marriage was mutually devoted until the end. This is the way that Max portrayed it in his memoirs. Or it may be that Max was having an affair, and Agatha knew nothing of it (although the Gardners insist she was aware of it all along).

Or it may mean something more complex, more mature, more accepting. The evidence for this is in Agatha's writing: so often the key to her mysterious character.

Her play *Verdict*, which was produced in 1958, was not a success. It was booed on its first night and ran for just four weeks. It was not an 'Agatha Christie' play: there was no puzzle, no dénouement. It was a human drama. Karl, a middle-aged professor, is married to Anya, an invalid. One of Karl's young students, Helen, falls in love with him so passionately that she murders his wife, justifying it as an act of philanthropic euthanasia. Another woman, Lisa, is accused of the crime.

She is the wife's companion; she and the professor are in love, although their passion is suppressed and not acted upon. 'Every month, every year, she gets a little weaker,' Lisa says of the wife. 'She may go on like that for many, many years.'

'It's tough on him,' is the reply.

'As you say,' says Lisa, 'it is tough on him.'

Of Helen, the student, Lisa says, 'She has fallen in love with Karl, of course,' but she does not think that he will respond. Indeed he does not. 'How little you understand,' he says to Helen, when she makes her blatant play for him. 'You talk like a child. I love my wife.' The girl cannot understand this, saying that he may have loved Anya once but that, now she is old and her life as a sexual being is over, she is no longer the same person.

KARL: She is. We don't change. There is the same Anya there still. Life does things to us. Ill health, disappointment, exile, all these things form a crust covering over the real self. But the real self is still there.'

HELEN: I think you're talking nonsense. If it were a real marriage – but it isn't. It can't be, in the circumstances.

KARL: It is a real marriage.

Towards the end of the play, Karl confesses to Anya's doctor that he is in love with Lisa.

KARL: I love her. Did you know I loved her?

DOCTOR: Yes, of course I knew. You've loved her for a long time.

KARL: . . . It didn't mean that I didn't love Anya. I did love Anya. I shall always love her. I didn't want her to die.

DOCTOR: I know, I know. I've never doubted that.

KARL: It's strange, perhaps, but one can love two women at the same time.

DOCTOR: Not at all strange. It often happens. And you know what Anya used to say to me? 'When I'm gone, Karl must marry Lisa.'

The Times wrote of Verdict that, although the play contained no surprises of the familiar 'Agatha Christie' variety, it did have surprises of another kind: 'that people should behave as she makes them behave'. The reviews, in general, were catty and patronising. Yet the play has aged well, better than theatrical successes like *Spider's Web* or even *Witness for the Prosecution*. It is true that both Karl and Helen behave in ways that are not 'realistic'. Rather, they act according to their convictions: Karl seeks to protect Helen from an accusation of murder because, according to his philosophical belief, she lacked the capacity to realise what she had done ('Life has not yet taught her understanding and compassion'). But shielding Helen leads to Lisa being accused of murder instead. Thus Karl, who is a good man, is also dangerous. He lives according to ideas, rather than realities, and in some way it is the blinkered dedication of his mind that makes him attractive to women. Agatha sees his foolishness; she also sees his virtue; and if this was not the truth about Max Mallowan, it was almost certainly the truth as Agatha perceived it.

Was it also the truth about her marriage? Did Max love two women at the same time? Did he have feelings for Barbara, and did they – as in *Verdict* – remain unconsummated during the lifetime of his wife? It is impossible to know how far Agatha wrote the facts of the situation into her play. Not fully, is the most likely answer. Up to a point she might have been deceiving herself, writing what she wanted to believe; yet she faces a good deal in the play, and she does not give her life an easy ride. There is no reason to think she is sparing her own feelings about her marriage. She saw its realities, in all their ambivalence and, unlike Anya in the play, she lived with them.

During the war, she had described to Max a dream in which he no longer wanted her and she was left alone again: 'I woke up in a panic and had to say over and over – "It's *not* true – it's *not* true – I've got his letter."' One letter in particular was kept in a secret drawer of a little desk at Greenway. It had been written to Agatha for her to receive on the sixth anniversary of her marriage, and it made her happy.

> I think that sometimes, but not so very often, two people find real love together as we do, and then it is something that lies deep and intangible, not to be shaken by the wind.
>
> You are my dearest friend and my darling lover at the same time, and for me you remain beautiful and precious with the

passing of years. You have the sweetest face of anyone in the world. This is a lover's letter darling, and I won't add anything more to it except that I don't think anyone can know how much we mean to one another.[82]

God's Mark

I shall not return again the way I came,
Back to the quiet country where the hills
Are purple in the evenings, and the tors
Are grey and quiet . . .
(from 'Dartmoor' by Agatha Christie)

'Thank you for being Agatha Christie'
(fan letter sent from Maryland, USA)

Agatha was upset by the reception of *Verdict*. Its failure was to become the usual fate of her plays. The glorious period when she had dominated the West End – even Broadway – was coming to an end. Only *The Mousetrap* sailed on.

The Unexpected Guest did well enough in 1959 ('*Verdict* atoned for,' Agatha wrote to Edmund Cork), running for eighteen months. But *Go Back for Murder*, the dramatised version of *Five Little Pigs*, which opened at the Duchess Theatre in March 1960, was found severely wanting: 'Her dialogue is so strictly utilitarian that it hardly pretends to have the colour of life,' wrote *The Times*. In a letter to Rosalind, Edmund Cork warned of 'the most malicious press we have ever had – not even excepting *Verdict* . . . Agatha might be well advised to give the theatre a rest for a while, and get on with a new novel, for after all her novels are the basis of her success.'[1] In reply Rosalind wrote that the reviews for *Go Back for Murder* 'seemed quite a surprise for everyone. My mother is really very upset about it.' Post-*Look Back in Anger* the theatrical world had changed. The feebleness of Agatha's adapted plays, which had previously been obscured by the dazzle of her name, was now laid bare.

She was not done with theatre, though. She had wanted to take on its challenge ever since 1924 when she had played the supporting role to Madge during the brief run of *The Claimant*. Her 'shyness' was not so great that she did not enjoy the world of rehearsals, actors and first nights; although she always purported to hate the parties and publicity with which Peter Saunders so cleverly kept *The Mousetrap* alive, she went along with it all nonetheless ('See you at "Hell at the Savoy"!'[2] she wrote to Edmund Cork). It was as though the part of her that, as a girl, had dreamed of singing Isolde still yearned for expression, and bringing her writing to life on a stage was the way to achieve it. Why, otherwise, did she long for her plays to be produced, when the reception had become almost uniformly hostile?

Her belief was that the public still enjoyed what she wrote and it was just the critics who found her a soft, convenient target. 'Whatever I wrote in the play line would get nasty notices,' she wrote to Rosalind in 1971, 'chiefly because of *The Mousetrap*, which is much resented by the younger journalists.' There was truth in this, although Agatha was not entirely right: in 1962 the *Evening Standard* wrote that 'the public didn't care Then There Were None' when the play of *Ten Little Niggers* was taken off after twenty-four days, and *Verdict* had, of course, been booed on its first night (although this was partly because the curtain fell too early, cutting off the last two critical lines of dialogue and changing the message of the play entirely). There was, undoubtedly, a growing divergence between the reception of the books and the plays. After Agatha's death they would be revived frequently, become popular mainstays of repertory companies and appear from time to time in the West End ('You have to say one thing: Mrs Christie got away with murder,'[3] wrote Michael Billington after a 1987 revival of *And Then There Were None*). But they do not endure in any meaningful sense; not even *The Mousetrap*. The books do. That is why it is demonstrably absurd to talk about 'Agatha Christie' as a mere producer of plots. In the books, the plot really *does* thicken – with subtext, with resonance – but when the books are adapted for the stage it is stranded, like a jiggling skeleton, bereft of what gives it

artistic life. *Verdict* and *Akhnaton* are different altogether, being original works. They are not brilliantly theatrical but they are full of depth;
Akhnaton, with its representation of the idealistic, doomed Egyptian
king,[4] is highly unusual and was much admired by Max Mallowan.
Spider's Web, also an original work, has considerable charm. *Witness
for the Prosecution* was so changed from its source material that it
became *de facto* a new work and is Agatha's most accomplished play.
The rest, however, are shadows of the books, and the mystery is that
Agatha herself did not realise this.

But being advised to give up the theatre made her stubborn. She
knew that Cork wanted her to concentrate on books, with his not-
so-subtle remarks about the unpredictable fate of plays: 'No wonder
the theatre destroys so many authors, especially those who become
wholly dependent on it,' he wrote in April 1960. Yet the next year
Agatha produced three new playlets, clever but slight, entitled *Rule
of Three*. These opened in Aberdeen in November, while Agatha
was travelling in 'Persia' (as she always called it). Cork reported
that the reception for *Rule of Three* 'was on balance both friendly
and favourable', although the closer the plays came to London, the
less favourable the reception grew. At Blackpool they opened to
just thirty-eight pounds in box office receipts. Rosalind saw them
at Oxford; Mathew wrote to Cork saying, 'I hear frightful rumours
about *Rule of Three*: Mummy seems to think that everything is
"awful", but then she always does.'[5] No West End theatre was available to Peter Saunders, 'which', as Cork put it, 'solves one problem
for us'. But by the end of 1962 Saunders had managed to get the
Duchess, by now the usual home of Agatha's plays, where *Rule of
Three* opened to wretched reviews: 'I have never known a more
shameful running amok,' wrote Cork, on New Year's Day 1963.
The *Sunday Telegraph* wrote that 'the thriller is the lowest form of
drama. The better it is as a conundrum the worse it must be as a
play. But the bad thriller, which does not even obey its own logic,
is simply a tedious practical joke. The real victims at the Duchess
are the audience.' This particular review '*really* made me mad!'
wrote Agatha. '"Quite out of touch with today's beach life." I doubt
if anyone knows more about real life on the beaches than I do,
spending all my Augusts in South Devon!! Sacrificing myself for

the enjoyment of nephews and other children. I'm an AUTHORITY. What a spiteful ignorant lot critics are!'[6]

Within the newspapers, at least, it was becoming the accepted view that Agatha was a has-been. In 1962 *Ten Little Niggers* was disastrously revived and the failure of this dubiously titled play helped to reinforce the idea of her as a symbol of a vanished age, the one that contemporary history likes to believe was swept away when John Profumo lied to the House and the Beatles got the MBE. As if it were that simple; Agatha Christie's reign might have ceased over Drury Lane but, as Edmund Cork said, the theatre was not the foundation of her success, however much it had helped propel her towards stellar status. It was the books that counted. Maybe the 'Christie for Christmas' was bought partly *because* it symbolised a vanished age, but it was bought nonetheless, and Agatha's sales merely grew mightier. Through the 1960s she moved steadily towards a new and almost imperial standing, which culminated on her eightieth birthday in 1970. From that point onwards her position was unassailable. She was the best-selling author in the world, after the Bible and Shakespeare; as she remains.

Yet in 1961 the offices of both Hughes Massie and Harold Ober had issued to their staff a list of Christie manuscripts that might now be destroyed. 'The curve continues to rise,' Edmund Cork had written of her sales in 1955. Six years later it was thought that the curve had peaked. Even those who worked for her were unable to believe in the strength of the phenomenon.

Nor were her manuscripts necessarily greeted with boundless joy and respect by those whose living they helped to make; quite often there would be niggling little snipes at them. Harold Ober wrote to Cork of *A Pocket Full of Rye* that the use of the nursery rhyme seemed forced and that she had not been 'quite fair to the reader'; of *Destination Unknown*, 'I don't suppose she would consider doing another ending so we will do our best to sell it [as a serial] as it is.' Of *Curtain* he wrote bluntly: 'I did not like the story.' After Ober's death in 1959, Cork dealt with Dorothy Olding, a lively correspondent who sent gossipy little criticisms.[7] 'I don't know what to say about this story,' she wrote of *The Mirror Crack'd from Side to Side*, 'except that from the moment Mrs Badcock was murdered I read with the fear that Agatha might be using the effect of German measles on pregnancy as the main clue.' 'Don't quote me to Agatha but this isn't the strongest story she ever wrote, is it?' was her judgement on 'The Adventure of the Christmas Pudding', and when Cork asked her to try to sell an unusual short story, 'The Dressmaker's Doll', she said of a particular magazine editor: 'It will break his heart, I know, if he doesn't feel he can buy it. My guess is that his heart will break.' 'Has anyone wondered, as I did, how Miss Marple knew that Elvira Blake was Bess Sedgwick's daughter?' she asked chirpily, after reading *At Bertram's Hotel*. 'I wondered whether she was just so bright that she deduced it or what.' And, more strongly, on *Passenger to Frankfurt*: 'Confidentially, I was bitterly disappointed in the book. It seemed to me a bad imitation of a spy story and a damned weak one at that . . .'[8]

The key issue in America was whether Agatha's books were suitable for the serialisation market. In her younger days she would rewrite, if required, in order to sell to magazines like the *Saturday Evening Post*, but in later years she refused. Hence Ober's concerns about *Destination Unknown*, whose ending was indeed described by the *SEP* as 'utterly preposterous', and the general alarm about the subject matter of *The Mirror Crack'd*. It is somewhat extraordinary that the American magazine market should have been so picky at a time when Agatha's fame and popularity were so very great; before the war it had snapped up almost everything she wrote. Now she was seen as out of touch. In 1968 the *Saturday Evening Post* turned down *By the Pricking of My Thumbs*, saying, 'Not for us, I'm afraid. The plot is certainly ingenious, but the people are all so bloody decrepit,' and this kind of downright refusal was not uncommon. *Good Housekeeping* turned down *Curtain*: 'I wish I could be making you a nice fat offer . . . but I'm afraid I can't even make you a small or reasonably adequate one . . . I must admit I found it tedious. Everybody was so old and all the characters seemed to me to mesh into one Colonel Blimp . . .'

The modern world was speaking, loud and clear; yet despite itself the modern world kept reading Agatha Christie. And, in the light of this, Agatha rose up against what she considered casual treatment by both her literary agents and her publishers. She had always been critical of poor covers, idiotic blurbs and the like. Now she could get very irritated indeed. After reading the blurb for the US edition of

The Mirror Crack'd from Side to Side, she wrote to Cork: 'Having published my books for about thirty-odd years my publishers ought to know how to spell Miss Marple's village – St Mary *Mead*, not Meade.' Then, on New Year's Eve 1966, she exploded, rather as she would in the 1971 letter to Rosalind about her plays. She wrote to wish Cork a happy new year – 'if such a thing is possible for any of us' – before launching into a litany of distressed complaints: 'FIRST – I've got to have more strict control over the idiotic and *very* annoying things that my publisher and others seem to take upon themselves to do.' She was particularly annoyed about an edition of short stories, *Thirteen for Luck*, published by Dodd Mead and marketed as 'mystery stories for young readers'.

My books are written for adults and always have been.

I don't believe you realise in the least how much I mind having things slipped over on me – I *hate* the publishing of *Thirteen for Luck* – just when *Third Girl* ought to have had the field to itself . . . Haven't I got *any* control on how things I have written come into print? If I can forbid it, I say here and now I don't want *any* of the *Labours of Hercules* to appear separately again. They are a designed series . . . Both you and Harold Ober have *got* to consider *me* and what I feel . . . it's a misery to be ashamed of oneself – really for what I haven't asked for or wanted. You've got to keep a firm eye on Collins – I don't trust them . . . The same for Dodd Mead. When they next get one of their bright ideas, there is to be no going ahead until I have been consulted and agreed. I like Dorothy Olding very much indeed personally, but the firm has got to keep control over Dodd Mead on my behalf – otherwise how can I know what they are doing? . . .

Now then – any other complaints, Agatha?!

In 1960 Agatha had written to Cork from the 'Mount Lavinia Hotel, Ceylon' at the start of her travels around Sri Lanka, India and Pakistan. She had been bathing, she said. 'I feel almost girlishly carefree!!!'

But in December 1962 her health – always robust, sometimes

susceptible – showed the first signs of deterioration, although she recovered well. The newspapers reported that she had influenza while staying in Baghdad and had delayed her departure 'indefinitely'. In fact her flu had also comprised bronchitis and gastritis. She left, 'still rather fragile', just before the end of the year; her secretary Stella Kirwan wrote to Edmund Cork, saying, 'I will go to the airport myself with Agatha's mink coat to wrap her up in.'[9]

Agatha also suffered from psoriasis, a nervous complaint that afflicted her hands, and she wished, she said, that 'the Almighty would give me a new pair of feet'. But this was a sign of her desire to continue life as before. When she gave a series of little interviews in 1970 to mark her eightieth birthday celebrations, most journalists commented on how fit and spry she looked.

Max's health was less good. Although much younger than Agatha he had smoked and drunk all his life, as she had not, and suffered several minor strokes from the early 1960s onwards: 'He has suddenly come to look twice his age, and pretty feeble,' Cork wrote to Dorothy Olding in August 1961. Like Agatha, however, Max had a good deal of courage and vitality, and right until the end he carried on as if all his life was still ahead of him. The night before he died, in his bed at Greenway, he told his young friend D. that the next day he would teach her to play bridge.

But by 1967 the days of adventure were almost over. In spring the Mallowans went to Iran; this was Agatha's last visit to the East, the place that almost forty years earlier had given her the gift of hope, when she had dared to go to Baghdad and seek new worlds. The previous year she and Max had gone to America. Agatha had wanted to see the country of her father's ancestors: she had been 'driven through the town of Easthampton Mass. where the Millers came from', and a young woman from the Ober office took her to the grave of Nathaniel Miller, her grandfather, at the Greenwood Cemetery in Brooklyn. All the representatives of Obers and Dodd Mead were 'enchanted' by Agatha, as they had been when she visited America in 1956, although behind her back she was treated as a sweet and slightly tiresome old eccentric. 'Be warned Dorothy dear!' wrote Cork, somewhat infected by Dorothy Olding's jaunty irreverence. 'Agatha told me yesterday that the real object of her visit to America is to pick up

some outsize knickers . . . She recalled your prowess with the swimsuit, and I am awfully afraid sweetie you are for it.' There was a good
deal of this kind of thing by now. There had, for example, been a
drawn-out search for a certain kind of 'Gold Leaf Maple Sugar' that
Agatha had eaten in 1956, which Obers were obliged to try and find
for her: 'These chores for Agatha can be the devil, taking up so much
time and energy,' wrote Cork, although – as with Barbara and the
fruit trees – there was no question that they had to be done. Before
Agatha and Max arrived in America there had been a mass of commu-
nication between Obers and Hughes Massie about arrangements for
the two-month stay. 'Sorry, dear, to bother you,' wrote Cork to
Dorothy Olding, 'but it is probable your reply might make it easier
for me to stand up to the repetitive questions, which I am sure will
be my lot when the Mallowans come back from Switzerland.'[10]

Europe, now, was Agatha's destination of choice: Paris, Belgium,
Bayreuth, Oberammergau, Merlingen. 'Don't forward anything on to
me at Merlingen unless of such urgency it can't be helped!!' she wrote
to Cork in July 1966. 'No letters is the greatest joy in life to me!!'
A luxurious car was arranged for this Swiss holiday, although Max
asked for something 'more modest'. They also travelled economy to
America; as John Mallowan says, 'My aunt and uncle always said they
didn't have any money.'[11] The paradoxes remained extraordinary. They
stayed at the Paris Ritz but Max complained about the prices; they
lived much of the time at Winterbrook but 'hardly spent anything on
the house'.[12] When it was sold the roof was found to be in a terrible
condition. Greenway was better, because it was in the care of Rosalind
and Anthony. Mathew took over Pwllywrach after his marriage in 1967
and, in order to be on site at all times, the Hickses moved into Ferry
Cottage at the bottom of Greenway's gardens.

Agatha needed more looking after as she moved towards her eightieth birthday. Yet the books she produced during the 1960s were
arguably stronger, more creative, than those of the previous decade.
No longer writing on majestic auto-pilot, she was moving into new
areas, taking on the new world with which she was supposedly so out
of step. The quality of her work varied: *The Pale Horse* – stunningly
inventive – was followed by *The Mirror Crack'd from Side to Side* –
insightful, elegiac – which was followed by *The Clocks*: mystifyingly

bad. *A Caribbean Mystery* was straightforward Christie, as on the whole was *Hallowe'en Party*. But *At Bertram's Hotel*, *Third Girl*, *Endless Night* and, in 1970, *Passenger to Frankfurt* had a brilliant, confident grasp upon modernity, which Agatha looked full in its unfamiliar face.

Third Girl is set in Swinging London, the city of beatniks, casual sex and drugs, girls like 'unattractive Ophelias' and boys like beautiful van Dycks. 'Your editor is amazed at the way you have "got" the young people,' Cork told her admiringly in August 1966. Agatha wrote much of the book in the strong, clear voice of Ariadne Oliver – in fact she now used a Dictaphone – and in *Third Girl* this worked to her advantage. Mrs Oliver is openly intrigued by fashionable London and her thought processes, which are a simplified version of Agatha's own, bring the milieu to life. For example she shadows a young man ('the Peacock', as she calls him) to a ramshackle painter's studio in Chelsea. The scene is utterly convincing, as are the three people that Mrs Oliver finds there, who treat her with a typically youthful mixture of matiness, lack of respect and slight menace. Mrs Oliver is teetotal, like Agatha, and refuses a drink when it is offered. 'The lady doesn't drink,' says the Peacock. 'Who would have thought it?'

But there is far greater menace in *Endless Night*, perhaps the most remarkable Agatha Christie of them all. At the age of seventy-six Agatha took an extraordinarily audacious step: she chose to write a book from the point of view of a young working-class man, Michael Rogers, who is abundant in natural advantages and in thrall to dreams he barely understands. He longs for a life that is different and magnificent: a house of ineffable beauty, a girl like a goddess. He kills in order to help realise his dreams, and then killing itself becomes his dream. As he strangles his goddess-girl he says: 'I didn't belong to her now. I was myself. I was coming into another kind of kingdom to the one I'd dreamed of.'

Agatha spoke about the book as if it were not much different from anything else she had written: 'People shook their heads [when she told them what she was writing] as much as to say, "What is a county lady like that doing with such a character? She'll make a terrible mess of it!" Well I don't think I did – and it wasn't terribly hard. I listen to my cleaning woman talking and to her relatives. I've always loved shops and buses and cafés. And I keep my ears open. That's the secret.'[13]

She had had a natural ear from the very first, when she picked up the nuances and rhythms she had heard out in Egypt and wrote them into her teenage novel, *Snow Upon the Desert*. But the impressive thing about *Endless Night* is not the accuracy of Michael's speech, it is the rendering of his thoughts. Agatha understood instinctively the creed of the late twentieth century, so inimical to her own: the sense of entitlement that leads people to believe that anything they want they should be able to have. Mike Rogers is not merely a psychopath, he is a creature of his morally impoverished age, and Agatha – whose upbringing was steeped in ideas of duty and selflessness – realised him absolutely. She understood his charm, his casual urges, his rootlessness, his egotism; his belief that he can create his own destiny, and that achieving a desire is the same thing as fulfilment. The space where his soul should be is at the centre of the book: a confusion of desire and desolation pervade *Endless Night*.

Agatha had grown to mistrust young people. This was not a by-product of old age – despite what the American magazines thought of her – but a realistic appraisal of what she saw in the world. She knew that the cult of youth brought danger, since by definition it negated wisdom and experience: it had helped to make Mike Rogers what he was, since it said that strength and virility would get him what he wanted far more quickly than sense and virtue. Her late novels are full of warnings against youth, light and selfish and free of conscience. Elvira Blake in *At Bertram's Hotel* is 'one of the children of Lucifer'; the cool handsome creatures in *Third Girl* commit murder, assault and forgery; privileged young Michael Rafiel in *Nemesis* is convicted of assault, possibly rape (although 'girls, you must remember, are far more ready to be raped nowadays than they used to be').[14]

In *Hallowe'en Party* two children are killed and neither is much lamented: one was a liar, the other a blackmailer. This book is very much a meditation on the nature of youth, and on the credulousness of those who see it as inevitably innocent. 'It was not unknown in the present age for children to commit crimes, quite young children. Children of seven, of nine and so on . . .' *Hallowe'en Party* does contain a child who is as good as she is beautiful: the twelve-year-old

Miranda (a clear Shakespearean allusion in that name). But the feeling is very much that the innocence of the youth is not innate; that it is easily corrupted in a world that values youth too highly, and is too ready to excuse its faults. 'There are times when I get tired of hearing those words: "Remanded for a psychiatrist's report",' says a policeman, 'after a lad has broken in somewhere, smashed the looking glasses, pinched the bottles of whisky, stolen the silver, knocked an old woman on the head.'

But it was in *Passenger to Frankfurt* that Agatha's fear of the youth cult found its clearest expression. The book – disliked by Agatha's agents and her publishers – sold hugely in her eightieth birthday year, at least seventy thousand copies in hardback alone; admittedly it was backed by a lot of anniversary publicity, but it also touched a nerve. With her 'unerring instinct' (as Poirot says of Mrs Oliver), Agatha now gravitated towards themes of global terror, the growth of evil, the increase in violence for its own sake. Humanity had always been her subject matter. All her life she had looked for the recognisable, the familiar, within people who committed unusual acts. Now she perceived that the very things that made people recognisable to one another were being eroded and supplanted; were no longer even *necessary*.

She had hinted at this in *They Came to Baghdad*, whose villains are post-war believers in the Aryan ideal: 'Angels with wicked faces who wanted to make a new world and who didn't care whom they hurt to do it.' *Destination Unknown* has a similar theme, although this time the fight is with fanatical Communists. By 1970 the enemy is different, less identifiable. But its conduit is youth: 'Young people are much more easily influenced than older people,' she said, in reply to a series of questions about *Passenger to Frankfurt*, 'and evil can put on a better presentation of magnificence and importance than good can. Humility is and should be the first of the Christian virtues. I think nowadays that the worship of violence, and of cruelty, and the people who think that no aim can be achieved without it, is a very evil influence, and it is successful in many countries and in many places. At the present moment the things taking place in Ulster are the main expression of this . . .

'I have never been in the least interested in politics as such. My interest was aroused by the youth attitude of rebellion and anarchy, chronicled in news from all over the world.'

The hero, or anti-hero, of *Passenger to Frankfurt* is an unorthodox Foreign Office man, Sir Stafford Nye, whose faintly troublesome eccentricity has hampered his career, but gives him the ability to think for himself and resist the attractions of ideology. 'I wish I loved the Human Race; I wish I loved its silly face,' he says to himself. Indiscriminate love is as dangerous as hate; paradoxically, it is not 'human' to view the human race as lovable. Sir Stafford's morality is fallible, flexible, somewhat world-weary; it enables him to join the fight for humanity, a fight that Agatha is not sure can be won. In a sinister echo of Huxley's *Brave New World* it is suggested that the aggression in people will now be tamed only through the use of drugs. 'Benvo', as Agatha calls it, is a kind of soma, or Prozac: it calms to the extent that it induces 'artificial goodness'. Should it be widely used? *Passenger to Frankfurt* is ambivalent.

'Benefits to humanity are tricky things to deal with. Poor old Beveridge, freedom from want, freedom from fear, freedom from whatever it was . . . it hasn't made a heaven on earth and I don't suppose your benvo or whatever you call it (sounds like a patent food) will bring heaven on earth either. Benevolence has its dangers just like everything else. What it will do is save a lot of suffering, pain, anarchy, violence, slavery to drugs. Yes, it'll save quite a lot of bad things from happening, and it *might* save something that was important. It might – just *might* – make a difference to people. Young people.'

This, then, was Agatha's view of the future: prescient, courageous. *Passenger to Frankfurt* ends optimistically (if somewhat absurdly), for in her heart Agatha believed in the redemption of human beings. She had faith, after all. Nevertheless she accepted the passing of the old order and the introduction of disorder; accepted it, too, in a smaller and more personal way, in her novel *At Bertram's Hotel*.

In this book she relives her past; alongside her fierce engagement with the modern world this was something she would do, more and more, as she talked her memories into the Dictaphone. Bertram's

Hotel is an idealised version of Fleming's (not, as Dorothy Olding brightly guessed, the Connaught): a perfect Edwardian period piece. In an attempt to remember her own youth Miss Marple visits the hotel and finds it utterly unchanged. A fire still burns in the lounge where tea is served, immaculately, with seed cake and buttered muffins; a rosy-cheeked chambermaid brings a breakfast of properly poached eggs; the barman talks knowledgeably about the racing at Newbury; the clientele is good families, dowagers, clergymen; and the 'television room' is hidden from general view.

> It really seemed too good to be true. She knew quite well, with her usual clear-eyed common sense, that what she wanted was simply to refurbish her memories of the past in their old original colours. Much of her life had, perforce, to be spent recalling past pleasures . . . she still sat and remembered. In a queer way, it made her come to life again – Jane Marple, that pink and white eager young girl . . .

Miss Marple's memories are precisely Agatha's: the Army and Navy Stores, the drive to a matinée in a four-wheeler, the coffee creams at the theatre. Miss Marple traverses the London she once knew and finds it almost completely changed. It seems a miracle that Bertram's should survive intact; and it is, as she realises, indeed 'too good to be true'. Bertram's Hotel is merely a façade, a virtual reality re-creation of the past, peopled by characters like herself who add verisimilitude to a hollow stage set: mahogany fittings made of metaphorical cardboard and paste. '*Le five o'clock*', a Frenchman is heard to say appreciatively in the foyer of Bertram's; a passing policeman says to himself: 'That chap doesn't know that "*le five o'clock*" is as dead as the Dodo!'

What more perfect image could Agatha have used, for the disappearance of the world she had known? How wrong – how utterly wrong – were those who believed that Agatha Christie was a fossilised creature, suspended in an England that was forever 1932, comfortably taking tea in a firelit lounge: the very setting that Agatha herself was portraying as a sham.

She knew that the world had changed, although her critics – and her fans – thought that she had not changed with it. Like Miss

Marple, however, she could face facts that the modern world wanted to shun. The young girl in *At Bertram's Hotel*, Elvira Blake, has had every advantage, but she kills and lies without scruple. In the eyes of Agatha and Miss Marple, she is irredeemable: a sad fact, but a fact. Yet when the book was sent to *Good Housekeeping* for sale as a serialisation, the magazine wrote to Obers that, if they publish, 'they must indicate that the daughter will at least have some psychiatric help and guidance . . . there has to be some hint that she is salvageable'. Here was where Agatha and the modern sensibility parted company: not in her preference for Earl Grey over Coca-Cola, but in her willingness to see the truth about human nature. She had always known the wretchedness of which people are capable. She knew that the selfishness of apparently decent men and women knows no bounds, that the desire to be safe or rich or happy can override all but the strongest moral sense. She knew that murderers sometimes deserve compassion, but that it is the effect of this compassion that has to be considered. She understood – none better – that adultery may cause incalculable distress, but that it is committed by nice people as well as by rats. She understood that although children may appear sweet and innocent, they are capable of evil, and adults are capable of evil towards them. This was the kind of thing that she wrote, without comment and without the need for comment. It was her subject matter. And in her old age she saw a link between the naïvety of the modern world – its politicised belief in the perfectibility of human beings – and its love of ideology, anarchy and violence.

Meanwhile in her secret imagination, into which she increasingly withdrew, she conjured memories.

In *By the Pricking of My Thumbs*, Tuppence Beresford remembers her life as a VAD in the First World War. 'All soldiers, that was,' says Tuppence to herself. 'The surgical ward. I was on A and B rows.' And when the murderess is identified, the familiar quotation from *Peer Gynt* is spoken by her former husband:

> *Who was she? Herself? The real one, the true one*
> *Who was she – with God's sign upon her brow?*

In *Passenger to Frankfurt*, Sir Stafford's aunt Matilda recalls her distant youth: 'In the mornings, you see, girls were supposed to be doing something useful. You know, doing the flowers or cleaning silver photograph frames . . . In the afternoon we were allowed to sit down and read a story book and *The Prisoner of Zenda* was usually one of the first ones that came our way . . .' So Agatha had written in 1903, at Ashfield, in the Album of Confessions: her favourite male character in fiction had been 'Rudolf Rassendyll', the hero of *The Prisoner of Zenda*.

In *Elephants Can Remember*, it is Mrs Oliver's turn to recall Agatha's past. 'She then entered into what she thought of in her own mind, with vague memories of going to dancing class as a child, as the first figure of the Lancers. Advance, retreat, hands out, turn, round twice, whirl round, and so on . . .' Into the book Agatha wrote a character called Zélie, who is a governess and keeper of secrets. 'Lady Ravenscroft had been ill, and had been in hospital. Zélie came back and was sort of companion to her and looked after her. I don't know, but I believe, I think, I'm almost sure that she was there when it – the tragedy – happened. And so, you see she'd *know* – what really happened.' Here was something of Charlotte Fisher, that staunch young woman who had stood by and kept silent until the day she died: just two months after Agatha, at the little house in Eastbourne to which she had retired, having confessed to her niece that her heart had troubled her since the death of her former, much-loved employer.[15]

In *Nemesis* – Agatha's last masterpiece – the memories are different, more obscure. Yet the book is deeply personal. It is fraught with a passion that Miss Marple feels so powerfully she is barely at one remove from it. It is the story of Michael Rafiel, son of the Mr Rafiel whom Miss Marple met in *A Caribbean Mystery*. Mr Rafiel sends word after his death, through his solicitors Broadribb and Schuster, that Miss Marple should investigate a crime. Michael Rafiel is in prison for the murder of Verity Hunt, the young girl to whom he was engaged.

Miss Marple meets the archdeacon who was going to marry the couple, and he says to her:

'I know when a couple are really in love with each other. And by that I do not mean just sexually attracted. There is too much talk about sex, too much attention is paid to it. I do not mean that anything about sex is wrong. That is nonsense. But sex cannot take the place of love, it goes *with* love but it cannot succeed by itself. To love means the words of the marriage service. For better, for worse, for richer, for poorer, in sickness and in health. That is what you take on if you love and wish to marry. Those two loved each other. To love and to cherish until death us do part.'

At the end of the book, when Miss Marple has solved the case, she returns to the Archdeacon's words.

'He did not, I think, believe it would be a thoroughly happy marriage, but it was to his mind what he called a necessary marriage. Necessary because if you love enough you will pay the price, even if the price is disappointment and a certain amount of unhappiness.'

Nemesis is a beautiful book, despite its ramblings and repetitions; not really a detective story but a sombre meditation on the realities of love: 'one of the most frightening words there is'. It was planned in one of Agatha's plotting notebooks and, on the top of the page, she had written: 'Nemesis – January 1971 – D.B.E.'. As Edmund Cork had predicted she would back in 1956, she had received her damedom in the New Year's Honours List. Her life had reached a last glorious peak before the slow, inexorable descent.

In 1971 Agatha became old. She tried the theatre one last time, with the weak little play called *Fiddler's Five*, which was turned down by Peter Saunders. Back in 1962, after the *Rule of Three* débâcle, Saunders had declined a rough script that Agatha had written for Margaret Lockwood, and Edmund Cork had written to Rosalind with decorously concealed jubilation: 'I don't see any prospect of any more Christie plays being put on in London at the moment.' But *Fiddler's Five* opened in Bristol in 1971, while Agatha was on holiday in Paris. The reception, as expected, was generally poor. In an agony of protection Rosalind told her mother that the play should not go to London. Agatha, in the long letter sent from Winterbrook, replied with an agitation that was almost anger; and with an almost pathetic desire to remind Rosalind – and herself – of her achievements.

> I've not urged it specially – I can't see why you are so opposed to its being a commercial success on tour – if it does turn out to be so – I don't suppose you or Mathew or the Harrison Homes and the rest of those who benefit in the company will really refuse their cut of the takings . . . I knew I'd get bad reviews – and I've had several rather surprising good ones – and five curtain calls at many theatres. *The Mousetrap* – on tour originally – had only one criticism that could be used as advert – all the critics were somewhat unfavourable. *Verdict* was not a success in London – but I'm *very* glad it came on. I've had to put up with several plays and films that I hate to be associated with my name . . .

Agatha then wrote at length of how much she had disliked the early dramatisations of her books.

> It was because I hated them so much that I determined to adapt *The Hollow* myself – I did this at Pwllywrach and you did your utmost then to persuade me not to! If you'd succeeded in making me stick to books – there would probably have been no *Mousetrap*, no *Witness for the Prosecution*, no *Spider's Web* – I could have stopped any more adaptations of my books – but I should not have been a playwright and should have missed a lot of fun! . . .
>   All theatrical things are a pure gamble. If there's no London production I'll be quite glad for your sake!!

In June that year Agatha was taken into the Nuffield Hospital in Oxford, having broken her hip in a fall at Winterbrook. 'Things were critical for a day or two,' wrote Edmund Cork to her American agency, 'but I am delighted to tell you that she has made a miraculous recovery.'[16] On her return she wrote to her daughter in a different tone. Her writing was jumbled on a small piece of card, and looked very old and frail.

> Dearest Rosalind – It was wonderful to escape from Hospital and get HOME. You arranged that room beautifully and it was so cool – much cooler than the bedroom upstairs. The last nights in Hospital were deadly hot and sultry – almost impossible to sleep – was stuck to a bedpan that hadn't been powdered enough, practically tore bits of skin off. Flowers you had done everywhere are lovely – I'm so happy. You've been wonderful –
>
> I'm walking very well, doctors and sisters both said so. Max looks after me nobly at night. Commode absolute luxury after procession of innumerable bedpans waking one up – Mrs Belson [the housekeeper at Winterbrook] very good helping me dress and arranging my legs. Dear Rosalind – it was good of you to come up and do all you have . . .
>
> Bingo is beginning to forgive me for having left him.

Bingo had replaced Treacle, who died in 1969. He was desperately highly strung: 'You know Agatha, your dog's dotty,' A. L. Rowse would say to her when he visited Winterbrook. The sound of the telephone sent him mad – 'Agatha had a fantasy that Bingo believed there was a devil that lived in the telephone'[17] – and he bit everybody who came to the house. Occasionally he bit Max, who was nonetheless very fond of him. But Bingo worshipped Agatha. Rather as Peter had been forty years earlier, he was a necessary source of loyalty. 'New every morning was the love with which he snuggled under Agatha's eiderdown,' wrote Rowse of the little dog.

The sound of his manic barking can be heard on the recorded conversation between Agatha and Lord Snowdon, who visited Winterbrook in 1974 for a photographic session. Agatha herself sounds polite, amiable but grandly distant. Snowdon has to work hard for her replies; there is a faint echo of Poirot's effortful interview with the Princess Dragomiroff in *Murder on the Orient Express.* Also to be heard is Max, putting in the odd remark. At one point Agatha is asked about the filming of her books, on which subject she is unenthusiastic. She greatly disliked the film of *Endless Night*[18] and objected to the semi-pornographic violence: 'It had a very unpleasant scene which was written at the end, which was very unnecessary. I mean the bit where the other woman is strangled. It made it into a really horrible scene. Well, that of course I didn't like.' Max remarks that he thought the photography of the film was good. 'Well,' says Agatha, 'I think otherwise.'

Snowdon also asks about the forthcoming film of *Murder on the Orient Express*, and if the prospect of such a starry cast – Albert Finney, John Gielgud, Lauren Bacall and the rest – will annoy her. 'Yes, I think it will – if that is so.' In fact she had no objections to the film when she saw it. Having become so violently anti-cinema after the MGM experience – she repeatedly turned down a request from Hollywood to film *Passenger to Frankfurt*, for example – she had agreed to this partly because it was put to her as a direct, personal proposal from Lord Mountbatten, with whom she had corresponded in 1969 about *The Murder of Roger Ackroyd*, and whose son-in-law, Lord Brabourne, wanted to produce. 'As you know,' wrote Lord Mountbatten at the end of 1972, 'all my family are "Agatha Christie" fans . . . None of us feel that the films so far made do real justice to the "Agatha Christie" spirit.'

'I must tell you frankly that I am in a difficult position as regards films of my stories,' Agatha replied. 'They have been so painful to see, such awful scripts, and such bad casting . . . A firm refusal to anyone who makes films is a much easier attitude to take up and stick to, but in spite of all this I should very much like to meet your son-in-law.' The film was a massive hit in 1974, and generally a critical success also, although Dorothy Olding had disliked it ('but I had the sense to keep my mouth shut') and *Time* magazine's scathing review contained this snide, not wholly inaccurate comment: 'The idea is that everything will be more interesting if Sean Connery or Ingrid Bergman, rather than the characters they play, is suspected of having committed foul deed.' But the film led to a whole new style of adapting her books: *Death on the Nile* and *Evil Under the Sun* both became beautifully made blockbusters, with the highest possible production values.

Agatha recovered from her hip operation in 1971, and by the end of the year was walking again. She went to Madame Tussaud's to be measured for her model, and slowly she did some Christmas shopping. 'Most years I find it rather fun,' she wrote to Edmund Cork, 'but now I get tired and want to go home.' This was a new feeling. 'I am so tired,' she confessed to her housekeeper at Greenway, 'and they're waiting for every word I write.' Yet the words continued to come: in 1972 she wrote *Elephants Can Remember* and made changes to *Fiddler's Five*, now called *Fiddler's Three*. The play still failed to find a London theatre, although Agatha went to see it at Guildford.

By 1973 she was retreating ever more into her private, secret, imaginative world. On scraps of paper she wrote her thoughts.

I am 83 years of age. Do I want, being 83, to feel six years old – ten years old twenty-five years old? No. I don't. It would mean leaving an era of peace of mind, of tranquillity, of interesting reminiscences to go back to activity – or making it plural – activities which is worse – without having the necessary machinery . . .

I do not want, I myself, to be back there . . . I have different joys and pleasures – those of 1973 – delight in music, great joy in scenery – the red and gold autumn beauty of leaves and trees – the pleasure of the entry into sleep when it comes with the darkness that swallows light –

The excitement of morning when it comes – another day – and what will that day bring? Something? Or nothing – one does not know. But that day is MY day – it comes to me – I am alive and here – waiting –

It is as certain and true as the Past – the Past is with me – all of it – drifting by, with me always – I have only to open the secret coffer that all of us carry within us – My canary in its cage near my cot – my Yorkshire terrier dog . . .'

This sense of the past became slowly stronger, filling her mind like calm waters. In her last book, *Postern of Fate*, she moved Tommy and Tuppence Beresford into a new home, and filled it with her old possessions. The only thing in *Postern of Fate* that belongs to 1973 is a Manchester terrier, 'Hannibal', who follows Tuppence like a fierce little shadow.

'I read at five years old,' says Tuppence at the start of the book, as she sits in her comfortably disorganised new library.

'Everybody could, when I was young. I didn't know one even had to learn . . . if somebody had taught me how to spell when I was about four years old I can see it would have been very good indeed. My father did teach me to do addition and subtraction and multiplication, of course . . .'

'What a clever man he must have been!' says Tommy.

'I don't think he was specially clever, but he was just very, very nice.'

In the library are the books of Agatha's childhood: Mrs Molesworth, *The Cuckoo Clock, Four Winds Farm*. 'She couldn't remember *Four Winds Farm* as well as she could remember *The Cuckoo Clock* and *The Tapestry Room*.' Tuppence looks through them all, enraptured: 'Oh, here's *The Amulet* and here's *The Psamayad* . . . *The Prisoner of Zenda*. One's first introduction, really, to the romantic novel . . .' Finally she settles into a chair, curled up like a young girl, and loses herself in Stevenson's *The Black Arrow*.

The garden outside Tommy and Tuppence's house is the garden at Ashfield. There is 'K. K.' the greenhouse, Mathilde the rocking horse, Truelove the painted horse and cart. There is the monkey-puzzle tree. Tuppence rides Truelove down the garden and remembers playing a game, 'River Horses', for which 'you took your hoop out. Her hoop represented the horses. White horses with manes and flowing tails . . .'

'It's pretty ghastly, isn't it?' wrote Dorothy Olding to Edmund Cork. 'Much worse than the last two. I won't try serial even if there is time, unless someone requests it violently. Poor dear, I wish there was a way for somebody to tell her that this shouldn't be published – for her sake.'[19]

Since the 1960s the books had required a certain amount of polishing, partly because the Dictaphone made Agatha more prolix, but no editing could make *Postern of Fate* into a tight piece of detective fiction. Max tried to help; Rosalind did not want the book published at all. It contains the odd, sudden gleam, as when she describes Hannibal's 'extraordinary knack of altering his size when he wanted to [so that] instead of appearing somewhat broad-shouldered, possibly a somewhat too plump dog, he could at any moment make himself like a thin black thread'. But the plot is barely fathomable, indeed it is scarcely existent, and by now Agatha's voice on the Dictaphone meandered like that of an old, old woman as she crept along the distant paths of her life. 'Children nowadays who are four, or five, or six, don't seem to be able to read when they get to ten or eleven. I can't think why it was all so easy for us. We could all read. Me and Martin next door and Jennifer down the road and Cyril and Winifred. All of us . . .'

In one of her notebooks she wrote: 'October 1973 – Possibilities and Ideas. A cookery story. About: a meringue?' 'House said to be haunted. Ghost is a dog? A cat? Both –'.

She also had an idea about the ancient chalk horses that are carved into hillsides:

The White Horses – ideas for same. Alice and her friend Helen . . . go on tour to examine the various white horses of England. Alice stretched her neck and raised her chin so that her field of vision would include her view to the top of the hill. The outline of the White Horse was clearly defined. I love it, she said to her friend Helen, who stood beside her – I remember the first time I saw it . . . All the white horses on the hillsides are going to be done away with – it's a wicked shame. They'll scrap them all away and they are going to produce a picnic spot at each place. Our beautiful English white horses . . .'

And then her mind took flight one last time in the old, sure, questing way.

Jeremy – discusses with friends – murders. What difference would it make to one's character if one had killed someone? . . . No motive. For no reason. Just an interesting experiment. The object of the crime – oneself. One would have to commit homicide – observing all the time oneself – one's feelings – keeping notes. Do I feel fear? Regret? Pleasure?

What a marvellous book this might have been; yet it was obvious, to those around Agatha, that *Postern of Fate* would be her last. So it was that in 1974 a collection of stories, *Poirot's Early Cases*, was published instead of a new book. Every year had to have its Agatha Christie, after all. And in 1975 it was finally agreed that *Curtain: Poirot's Last Case*, which had been intended for posthumous publication,[20] should be published, prompting the famous *New York Times* obituary of the Belgian detective.

It has been said that there is an oddity about *Curtain*, deriving from the fact that it was written so many years before publication and has therefore no sense of real time, all references to period having been erased: it has 'a kind of historic weightlessness', as John Sutherland wrote in his essay 'Poirot's Double Death'.[21] This is true. For all that it was written when Agatha was in her glorious prime, *Curtain* is filled with the sense of the circumstances in which it was created: in the belief that it would only be seen when Agatha herself was dead. It has an air of displacement, of floating melancholy.

Poirot is dying, shrunken, with a wig on his head as black as a raven's wing. Hastings grieves for his diminished friend, for his dead wife, for the daughter whom he does not understand. Styles, the setting of the book, is a sad and sinister place. 'I don't like this house – there's some malign influence about it. Things happen here.' It was in 1940 that Agatha wrote this, when the memory of driving away from Styles on a December night was still near to the front of her mind; as perhaps it always was.

But the terrible sadness of *Curtain* lies, above all, in its lack of resolution. The murderer is a man who can never be accused and never be caught. He has perfected the technique of inducing other people to commit murder: he has perfected evil. Hastings's daughter, Judith, and the married man she loves, Dr Franklin, talk a good deal about how worthless lives should be brought to an end. 'I don't hold life as sacred as all you people do,' says Franklin. 'Unfit lives, useless lives – they should be got out of the way. There's so much mess about.' This is a motif that runs through *Curtain*. Almost every character in the book judges another to be supremely dispensable, and feels that the world would be better without them.

Yet the person who is called upon to enact this theory is Poirot.

His life has been spent in the service of justice; now, in order to prevent murder from being committed, he must commit murder. There is no other way. He knows this, but in the letter he leaves behind for his friend, he writes:

> *... I do not know, Hastings, if what I have done is justified or not justified ... I do not believe that a man should take the law into his own hands ...*
>
> *But on the other hand, I am the law! ...*
>
> *By taking Norton's life, I have saved other lives – innocent lives. But still I do not know ... It is perhaps right that I should not know. I have always been so sure – too sure ...*
>
> *But now I am very humble and I say like a little child, 'I do not know ...'*

Early in her marriage to Max Mallowan, Agatha had written, 'I think it would be very nice if at the end of our lives we could feel that we'd never done anyone any harm – don't you?'[22] As a child she had found comfort and safety in virtue: she believed that goodness had power, despite what the world was now telling her to the contrary. 'Remember that you have always a real job of work to perform in this world as you are one of the good and kind persons that matter,'[23] Max wrote to her during the war. He did, indeed, value her generosity, not just for what it gave him but for itself: despite everything, he had a profound regard for his wife.

At her memorial service, her publisher Sir William Collins said: 'Agatha knew what true religion means. The world is the better because she lived in it.' The son of her friends Sidney and Mary Smith wrote that she 'tried always to do good by stealth'.[24] The daughter of Stephen Glanville says: 'I know nothing about her that was not kind.'[25] And Joan Oates: 'She was a very, very nice person.'[26]

It was not that simple, of course. She was too clever for straightforward virtue, although she was clever enough to know what it ought to be. She had a sense of duty that helped her to live again after 1926, but it was a duty to life itself rather than to other people: she did not, as her mother had done, feel that she must recover for the sake of her child. Agatha's virtue lay in her vitality. That was what led her to cover the century with such zest and curiosity: hers was a life that refused to waste itself, and that is a noble thing. As an artist, too, she was on the side of virtue: her detective fiction dealt in justice and her Mary Westmacotts sought the humanity in her characters, not a single one of whom is dismissed as unworthy of consideration. But as an artist she was, in the end, a solitary being, for whom the concept of virtue is secondary.

She spent her last Christmas at Greenway in 1973. Magical Greenway, where Bingo ran around the chilly white house like a wind-up toy, and where the gardens had a different beauty in winter: bare, tangled trees shivered outside the bedroom window, and the Dart was a rustling grey ribbon. Devon was much in Agatha's mind. She received occasional letters from old ladies who had been childhood friends at Torquay. 'I remember you very well, and your dear mother,' wrote the daughter of Eden Philpotts. 'I remember quaint candle-lit tea parties with the Misses Ormerod . . . Torquay is much changed'[27]; 'I have often thought of you and the happy times we had in the old Torquay,' wrote another friend. 'Those guessing games we used to have at Mellis House! I am 87 now and am the only one left of my generation.'[28]

Agatha, now, was the only one left. As a vigorous sixty-year-old she had written this in *A Murder is Announced*, when an elderly woman says of her dead friend: 'She was the only link with the past, you see. The only one who – who *remembered*. Now that she's gone I'm quite alone.' She had written it, too, after the death of Nan Kon in 1959. 'She was the last of my friends – the one remaining person with whom I could talk and laugh about the old days – and the fun we had when we were girls.'[29] But fifteen years on Agatha had withdrawn so far into the past that she was no longer alone.

She attended the première of *Murder on the Orient Express*, arriving in a wheelchair but standing to greet the Queen;[30] it was one of her last outings. In October 1974 she had a heart attack, but not long afterwards made her final public appearance at the annual party for *The Mousetrap*.

I had heard [wrote Peter Saunders to Rosalind] that you were a bit upset at me getting your mother to come . . . I asked either

Agatha or Max whether she would *like* to be on the invitation as co-hostess. It wasn't just for publicity which was there in any case, but I felt that it would look nicer for her to be one of the "inviters" . . . I get her news from Edmund which one day is that she is very ill and the next that she has been presenting the Mousetrap trophy at the Exeter races. What a lady![31]

But Agatha was, in truth, very ill. Rosalind's desire to keep her from events like the *Mousetrap* party was intense. In December she fell into the French window at Winterbrook and split her head badly. She was thin now, shrunken like her little detective by the drugs she took for her heart, and her head loomed enormously above her body. Her eyes, behind their vast spectacles, were clouded, searching towards other worlds. 'Between you and me she is very frail,' Edmund Cork wrote to Dorothy Olding in July 1975.

She stayed at Winterbrook now. Her last Christmas was bleak ('Mrs Belson leaves on Tues December 23rd and is replaced by Barbara who would leave on Sat 27th,' wrote Max to Rosalind. 'Sat 27th we hope you would arrive and stay with us until Wed 31st'). Bingo sat at her side like a tiny black lion, while Max wrote his memoirs in the library with the view down to the Thames, and Barbara came to stay. Agatha was not always happy. One day, as if in a fit of desperate rage, she took up a pair of scissors and cut off her hair. A friend who came to lunch remembers that she talked about Jeremy Thorpe, then leader of the Liberal Party, but that what she said made no sense. On another occasion she suddenly offered: 'I wonder what *has* happened to Lord Lucan?' Her beautiful brain was fragmenting; or perhaps it was merely remaking itself in different shapes, sharp and sunlit in the darkening world.

> . . . that day is MY day – it comes to me – I am alive and here – waiting – . . .
>
> I might be a sculptor – or I might be a pianist – or I might train to be an opera singer. Perhaps I could compose music. So many things might come to pass. Most of them, of course, won't – One is coming to know that . . .

*   *   *

As the light faded Agatha held serenely to her faith. 'I'm joining my Maker,' she was heard to say, not long before she died at Winterbrook, on the afternoon of 12 January 1976. Bingo barked confusedly as the doctor arrived: he alone had not known the imminence of this death.

Four days later Agatha was buried at St Mary's Church, Cholsey, a few miles from Winterbrook, surrounded by calm and silent fields. According to her requests the burial service began with Psalm 23 and included a reading from the *Faerie Queene*: 'Sleep after Toyle, Port after Stormie Seas, Ease after Warre, Death after Life, Doth greatly please.' This was also engraved on her headstone. Agatha was laid in the still heart of England, many miles from the wild country of Devon, whose deep green slopes, winter mists and silver waters nonetheless hold her essence.

A few years before her death she had been asked her opinion on a vexed literary question. Kafka had requested that his works be burned after his death; did Max Brod do right in not destroying them, as requested? 'The literary output of an author is definitely his own possession and indeed part of himself, until the moment when he offers it to the world by asking for it to be published and offered for sale', she replied. 'I would agree that if some of the writings were creative works the destroying of them is a very unhappy thought. The destruction of the private personal correspondence, notes, diaries or letters I should do without regret.'[32]

Yet she had kept everything: she died, but her life was left behind. Not just the books, the fame, the indestructible London play, the autobiography that awaited posthumous publication, and that told her story in a manner both truthful and disingenuous. Her life was left in her houses, filling every cupboard, every attic, every secret drawer. The notebooks with their agonised jottings. The fur coats that smell still of distant scent. The soft pools of christening lace. The heavy satin robes, the jewelled bags. The attaché case that contained Archie Christie's love letters, and the wedding ring he gave her. The letter written by her mother, in which Clara folded sprigs of edelweiss from her honeymoon. The book with its carefully copied 'Receipts for Agatha'. The sheaves of elegant bills paid by her father for the chairs and china at Ashfield, some of which still furnish the rooms at Greenway. The photographs of Peter the dog, of Monty sitting in Truelove with a goat in harness, of her grandmother Margaret in a four-wheeler. She would have preferred – almost certainly? – that none of it be disturbed. But the immense and mysterious life is here; and out of it an elusive shadow, as carefree as a ghost.

She looked back from the door and she laughed. Just for one moment Mr Schuster . . . had a vague impression of a young and pretty girl shaking hands with the vicar at a garden party in the country. It was, as he realised a moment later, a recollection of his own youth. But Miss Marple had, for a minute, reminded him of that particular girl, young, happy, going to enjoy herself.[33]

The Works of Agatha Christie

Where a book has been published in the United States under a different title, this is given in parenthesis

1920 *The Mysterious Affair at Styles*

1922 *The Secret Adversary*

1923 *Murder on the Links*

1924 *The Man in the Brown Suit*

1924 *Poirot Investigates* (collected short stories)

1924 *The Road of Dreams* (collected poems)

1925 *The Secret of Chimneys*

1926 *The Murder of Roger Ackroyd*

1927 *The Big Four*

1928 *The Mystery of the Blue Train*

1929 *The Seven Dials Mystery*

1929 *Partners in Crime* (short stories)

1929 *The Underdog*

1930 *The Mysterious Mr. Quin* (collected short stories)

1930 *The Murder at the Vicarage*

1930 *Black Coffee* (play)

1930 *The Secret of Chimneys* (adapted play)

1930 *Giant's Bread* (Mary Westmacott)

1931 *The Sittaford Mystery* (*Murder at Hazelmoor*)

1932 *Peril at End House*

1932 *The Thirteen Problems* (collected short stories) (*The Tuesday Club Murders*)

1933 *Lord Edgware Dies* (*Thirteen at Dinner*)

1933 *The Sunningdale Mystery*

1934 *Murder on the Orient Express* (*Murder in the Calais Coach*)

1934 *The Listerdale Mystery* (collected short stories)

1934 *Why Didn't They Ask Evans?* (*The Boomerang Clue*)

1934   *Parker Pyne Investigates* (short stories) (*Mr. Parker Pyne – Detective*)

1934   *Unfinished Portrait* (Mary Westmacott)

1935   *Three Act Tragedy* (*Murder in Three Acts*)

1935   *Death in the Clouds* (*Death in the Air*)

1936   *The ABC Murders*

1936   *The Hound of Death* (collected short stories)

1936   *Murder in Mesopotamia*

1936   *Cards on the Table*

1936   *Love from a Stranger* (play)

1937   *Murder in the Mews* (*Dead Man's Mirror*)

1937   *Dumb Witness* (*Poirot Loses a Client / Murder at Littlegreen House*)

1937   *Death on the Nile*

1937   *Akhnaton* (play; published 1973)

1938   *Appointment with Death*

1938   *Hercule Poirot's Christmas* (*Murder for Christmas / A Holiday for Murder*)

1939   *Murder is Easy* (*Easy to Kill*)

1939   *And Then There Were None*

1939   *The Regatta Mystery* (short stories)

1940   *Sad Cypress*

1940   *One, Two, Buckle My Shoe* (*The Patriotic Murders*)

1941   *Evil Under the Sun*

1941   *N or M?*

1942   *The Body in the Library*

1942   *Five Little Pigs* (*Murder in Retrospect*)

1943   *The Moving Finger*

1943   *Ten Little Niggers* (adapted play)

1944   *Towards Zero*

1944   *Death Comes as the End*

1944   *Absent in the Spring* (Mary Westmacott)

1945   *Sparkling Cyanide* (*Remembered Death*)

1945   *Appointment with Death* (adapted play)

1945   *Hidden Horizon* (play adapted from *Death on the Nile*)

1946   *The Hollow* (*Murder After Hours*)

1946   *Come, Tell Me How You Live* (memoir by Agatha Christie Mallowan)

1947   *The Labours of Hercules* (short stories)

1948   *Taken at the Flood* (*There is a Tide*)
1948   *The Rose and the Yew Tree* (Mary Westmacott)
1948   *Witness for the Prosecution and Other Stories*
1949   *Crooked House*
1950   *A Murder is Announced*
1950   *Three Blind Mice and Other Stories*
1951   *They Came to Baghdad*
1951   *The Hollow* (adapted play)
1952   *Mrs. McGinty's Dead*
1952   *They Do It with Mirrors* (*Murder with Mirrors*)
1952   *The Mousetrap* (play)
1952   *A Daughter's a Daughter* (Mary Westmacott)
1953   *After the Funeral* (*Funerals are Fatal*)
1953   *A Pocket Full of Rye*
1953   *Witness for the Prosecution* (play)
1954   *Destination Unknown* (*So Many Steps to Death*)
1954   *Spider's Web* (play)
1955   *Hickory Dickory Dock* (*Hickory Dickory Death*)
1956   *Dead Man's Folly*
1956   *The Burden* (Mary Westmacott)
1957   *4.50 from Paddington* (*What Mrs. McGillicuddy Saw!*)
1958   *Ordeal by Innocence*
1958   *Verdict* (play)
1958   *The Unexpected Guest* (play)
1959   *Cat Among the Pigeons*
1959   *Go Back for Murder* (play adapted from *Five Little Pigs*)
1960   *The Adventure of the Christmas Pudding* (short stories)
1961   *The Pale Horse*
1962   *The Mirror Crack'd from Side to Side* (*The Mirror Crack'd*)
1962   *Rule of Three* (plays)
1963   *The Clocks*
1964   *A Caribbean Mystery*
1965   *At Bertram's Hotel*
1965   *Star Over Bethlehem* (short stories and poems)
1966   *Third Girl*
1967   *Endless Night*
1968   *By the Pricking of My Thumbs*
1969   *Hallowe'en Party*
1970   *Passenger to Frankfurt*
1971   *Nemesis*

1971   *Fiddler's Five* (play; 1972 renamed *Fiddler's Three*)
1972   *Elephants Can Remember*
1973   *Postern of Fate*
1973   *Poems*
1974   *Poirot's Early Cases* (*Hercule Poirot's Early Cases*)
1975   *Curtain: Poirot's Last Case*
1976   *Sleeping Murder*
1977   *An Autobiography*
1979   *Miss Marple's Final Cases*
1992   *The Problem at Pollensa Bay* (collected stories)
1997   *While the Light Lasts* (collected stories)

There are other collected volumes of the same short stories, put together in different editions – for example, for the American market.

All quotations used in this book have been taken from the following editions:

The Agatha Christie Collection
Published by Agatha Christie Ltd/Planet Three Publishing Network Ltd 2003

Poems
Published by Collins 1973

Mary Westmacott novels
Published by St. Martin's Minotaur (US) 2001

Endnotes

At the time of writing, most of the sources for this book were stored at Greenway House in Devon. They did not in any way constitute an 'archive': indeed, much of the charm of what I found at the house was its disorganised nature, the fact that any drawer or suitcase might yield treasure. Many of the writings, cuttings etc. I have used are mere scraps of paper: their meaning is clear, but they cannot be fully annotated.

Also, much of the correspondence kept at the house is undated. Agatha almost never wrote the year on her letters, and sometimes wrote no date at all (although this could usually be worked out from the content: reference to an event or a book she was working on, sometimes from the name of a horse she had backed). So, again, not all correspondence is annotated.

Abbreviations: 'AC' for Agatha Christie; 'MM' for Max Mallowan; 'CM' for Clara Miller

The contemporary value of the sums of money mentioned in this book can be gauged from the following:

In 1890, the year of Agatha's birth, £1 = £63.38 as at January 2007

In 1901, the year of her father's death, £1 = £60.87

In 1914, at the outbreak of the First World War, £1 = £52.33

In 1926, the year of the disappearance, £1 = £32.41

In 1930, the year of her second marriage, £1 = £35.37

In 1938, when she bought Greenway House, £1 = £35.73

In 1945, at the end of the Second World War, £1 = £27.47

In 1952, the opening year of *The Mousetrap*, £1 = £20.23

In 1955, when Agatha Christie Ltd was formed, £1 = £17.56

In 1964, the year of Agatha's £100,000-plus tax assessment, £1 = £14.26

In 1970, the year of Agatha's eightieth birthday celebrations, £1 = £10.88

In 1976, the year of her death, £1 = £5.06

The Villa at Torquay

1   From *The Mirror Crack'd from Side to Side*
2   From *Passenger to Frankfurt*
3   In the poem 'The Road of Dreams'
4   Letter from MM to AC, 6/8/1930
5   From *An Autobiography*
6   In 1989 the sixty 'belts', or tapes, on which Agatha had recorded *Postern of Fate* were sold at Sotheby's to a French collector for £7,480. This was contrary to the wishes of her daughter, Rosalind, who said: 'If this had to be made public I would rather it had been made when she was younger'. The tapes had fallen into the hands of the anonymous seller on the death of Agatha's typist, Mrs Jolly, for whose use the recordings had been made
7   Letter from Adelaide Ross to AC, 15/3/1966
8   Letter from AC to Bruce Way, who had contacted her to say 'I believe we are third cousins!', 15/6/1968
9   Letter from AC to MM, 23/7/1944
10   Interview with the *Sunday Telegraph*, 10/5/1964
11   From a story called 'Mrs Jordan's Ghost', written under the pseudonym 'Callis Miller'
12   Letter from AC to Enid Duncan (who was compiling a catalogue of Baird's works), 21/2/1967
13   Letter from Fred Lock to AC, 26/11/1943
14   As an old lady Agatha wrote a letter of praise to Lionel Jeffreys,

director of the 1970 film adaptation of Nesbit's *The Railway Children*. She gave a love of Nesbit to the 'railway-minded' killer in her detective novel, *The ABC Murders*

15 From *A Caribbean Mystery*

16 From the essay entitled 'The Guilty Vicarage'

17 The 1901 census shows the household to consist, at that time, of Frederick, Clara, Margaret and Agatha Miller, Jane Rowe ('Cook'), Marie Sijé (then employed as Agatha's French-speaking companion), Elizabeth Williams ('Parlourmaid') and Louise Baxter ('Housemaid'). The name 'Janet Rowe' was, incidentally, used for the nanny in *Crooked House*

18 From *An Autobiography*, and referred to again in *Postern of Fate*

19 From *After the Funeral*

20 From a letter sent in 1968 to Francis Wyndham, then editor of the *Sunday Times* magazine. Agatha quotes her grandmother, then goes on: 'I bet there *was* something wrong! And I bet that, deep down, people knew it all right'

21 From *Giant's Bread*

22 From *An Autobiography*

23 A further answer, to the question of whether scientific progress demanded the participation of women, was: 'I should say it could get on quite well without it'

24 In fact Scot was Monty's dog; he was then at Harrow. Scot was the painter Baird's first commission for the Millers, in 1893. He was run over at the age of fifteen and buried in the Dogs' Cemetery by Monty

25 Letter from Frederick Miller to CM, 9/5/1901

26 Letter from Frederick Miller to CM, 24/10/1901

27 From *An Autobiography*

28 In conversation with the author, 2003

29 From *Unfinished Portrait*

30 From *An Autobiography*

The Young Miss Miller

1 Agatha's brother Monty was named after this family friend

2 From *Sparkling Cyanide*

3 Letter from AC to CM, 9/5/1922

4 From *An Autobiography*

5 Letter from MM to AC, 15/6/1942

6   Letter from AC to MM, 5/11/1930

7   From *An Autobiography*

8   From Mary Westmacott's *The Burden*, when the young girl Laura is left alone at home with the servants

9   *The House of Beauty* was first published in 1926 (as *The House of Dreams*), in *Sovereign* magazine

10   In conversation with the author, 2004

11   From *An Autobiography*

12   From *Murder is Easy*

13   From *Taken at the Flood*

14   In *Agatha Christie and the Eleven Missing Days* by Jared Cade (Peter Owen, 1998)

15   Adelaide Ross to AC, 15/3/1966

16   Completed in 1848, this was described as the 'finest crescent of houses in the West of England'

17   From an interview with Francis Wyndham in the *Sunday Times*, 27/2/1966

18   From *An Autobiography*

19   Rosalind Hicks, in conversation with the author, 2004

20   This phrase was not forgotten: John Gabriel, the central male character in *The Rose and the Yew Tree*, is pitied for his common legs

21   From *An Autobiography*

22   'The Call of Wings' was first published in 1933 in *The Hound of Death*

23   Janet Morgan's biography (*Agatha Christie*, Collins, 1984), makes interesting mention of the way Agatha referred to the end of her music career. In successive drafts of her autobiography she increasingly downplayed the genuine hopes she had cherished: '"faint possibility" in the first draft . . . becomes "illusion" in the second and "dream" in the last'

24   Writing about Wagner's *Tristan and Isolde* in the *Independent* in 2006, the playwright Howard Brenton described how the 'music swirls round and round in a vortex of such power that you almost see the sound'

25   From 'A Masque from Italy', first published in 1924 in *The Road of Dreams*

26   The name of this house, owned by Sir Walter and Lady Barttelot, was used for the setting of *Dumb Witness* and featured in its original title, *Murder at Littlegreen House* (retained for the US edition)

27   From *Unfinished Portrait*

28   From *Sad Cypress*

29   From *An Autobiography*

30   In an interview with Marcelle Bernstein in the *Observer*, 14/12/1969

31   From a letter to Lord Louis Mountbatten, 2/12/1969. Agatha had been looking for an old letter sent by Mountbatten, regarding his suggestion of the original idea for *Roger Ackroyd*, and during her search had found eight of her old dance cards: 'It was sad to find I could not now remember any of the names on it.' She also, as she told him, found Margaret Miller's sealskin coat containing two £5 notes and 'six needlebooks labelled, "For the servants next Christmas" (you see where I get data for Miss Marple's life) . . .'

32   From the 1964 interview with the *Sunday Telegraph*

33   From *Triangle at Rhodes*

34   From *An Autobiography*

35   From *A Caribbean Mystery*

36   From *An Autobiography*

The Husband

1   From *A Daughter's a Daughter*

2   From *4.50 to Paddington*

3   From *Dumb Witness*

4   One of Agatha's favourite writers, May Sinclair (1863–1946) wrote about the occult but was also a considerable intellectual figure of the Edwardian era, moving in literary circles with Henry James, Ford Madox Ford, T. S. Eliot and Rebecca West. She wrote 'social problem' novels and pioneered the idea of the 'stream of consciousness' narrative. Ironically, in view of Agatha's own attitudes, she was a vociferous campaigner for women's suffrage and equal educational opportunities, and was latterly taken up by the feminist movement

5   Published in *The Thirteen Problems*

6   From *Death on the Nile*

7   From *Sad Cypress*

8   The 1901 census shows Ellen Christie, aged thirty-seven, living in part of 43 Upper Belgrave Road, Bristol with seven-year-old Campbell

9   Miss Marple's mother was also named Clara

10   In *The Thirteen Problems*

11   To Francis Wyndham in the *Sunday Times*

12   From *An Autobiography*
13   In her autobiography Agatha wrote that she saw the influence of *The Plumed Serpent, Sons and Lovers* and *The White Peacock* – 'great favourites of mine about then' – upon her story 'The House of Beauty'
14   To Francis Wyndham in the *Sunday Times*
15   Pearl Craigie (1867–1906) wrote – as Agatha had tried at first to do – under a male pseudonym (John Oliver Hobbes). Her early works were society novels but, after the breakdown of her marriage, she turned to the Catholic church and a far more serious style
16   Eden Philpotts to AC, 6/2/1909
17   From *Endless Night*
18   From Tennyson's *Idylls of the King*
19   From *Idylls of the King*
20   From *The Burden*, which contains a version of the incident in which Archie arrived unannounced at Ashfield
21   From *A Murder is Announced*
22   AC to MM, 21/5/1930
23   From *The Rose and the Yew Tree*
24   Archie Christie to AC, 4/4/1917
25   From *Unfinished Portrait*
26   Ibid
27   Ibid
28   To Gillian Franks, in one of several newspaper interviews that Agatha gave in September 1970, at the time of her eightieth birthday
29   In the interview given to the Imperial War Museum, accession number 493, recorded 16/10/1974
30   Ibid
31   Ibid
32   Archie Christie to AC, 26/11/1916
33   From *The Seven Dials Mystery*
34   From *The Secret of Chimneys*
35   From *White Heat – the New Warfare* by John Terraine (Sidgwick & Jackson, 1982)
36   Dr Haydock, who looks after Miss Marple and appears in several books, is one of Agatha's most likeable portraits. He is humorous, compassionate, broad-minded and sceptical about 'new-fangled' ideas: the kind of person she most liked. Dr Lord in *Sad Cypress* is also an attractive personality, as is Dr Stillingfleet in *Third Girl*, and Dr Christow in *The Hollow* is impressive if flawed. But Dr Bauerstein in

Styles is sinister and irritating; Dr Nicholson in *Why Didn't They Ask Evans?* is a drug addict; Dr Thomas in *Murder is Easy* and Dr Donaldson in *Dumb Witness* are cold fish. Furthermore, four of Agatha's doctors (five, if one counts Dr Armstrong in *And Then There Were None*) are murderers

37   From *Taken at the Flood*

38   With Lord Snowdon. After Agatha's death this inverview became the subject of controversy when the BBC asked for a copy for its sound archives. Rosalind Hicks (Agatha's daughter) rejected the request on the grounds that the interview had been taped 'illegally' by Lord Snowdon, who was supposed only to be taking photographs: 'it was not authorised as you know and my mother throughout her life always refused to give interviews in this way'. The tape was indeed suppressed, although an abridged version of the interview appeared in *Australian Woman's Weekly.* 'I don't think the remarks after lunch of an old lady – she was over eighty at the time, and didn't know she was giving an interview even – should be a great benefit to generations in the future . . .'. Rosalind was right, in principle, although in fact the full-length tape portrays Agatha in a charming and sympathetic light

39   In fact Eden Philpotts, in a letter to AC dated 4/10/1955, wrote 'I always set Poirot above Sherlock Holmes for the reason that he is a living man, as interesting in himself as his adventures. One develops a personal regard – almost an affection – for him . . .'

40   Sister of Hilaire Belloc, her most famous work was *The Lodger*, which was filmed by Hitchcock

41   From the 1969 *Observer* interview

42   From *The Hollow*

43   From *Endless Night*

The Child

1   Agatha herself was not precise about how many publishing houses rejected *Styles*: sometimes she said five, sometimes six. John Lane's nephew, Allen, later started Penguin Books, and in 1935 Agatha was one of the first authors to offer him her books. He became a good friend. In 1955, on the *Close Up* programme broadcast on the Light Programme, Allen Lane said that *Styles* was 'by way of being a new departure for us – for the Bodley Head was renowned for encouraging the poets of the 'nineties, and had been called "a nest of

singing birds" . . . So the appearance of a new woman writer of detective fiction *was* unexpected'

2   According to Jared Cade's book *Agatha Christie and the Eleven Missing Days*, 'Agatha was so impoverished that one of her greatest pleasures when visiting Nan was to be invited to examine the contents of her affluent friend's wardrobe'. As the sole source for Mr Cade's book is Nan's daughter Judith (and her husband Graham), this may be true; although Judith, born in 1916, would have needed a highly acute childhood memory to be sure about it. As usual with this book, the story about Agatha going through Nan's clothes is a) without external corroboration and b) presented as gospel truth by the author

3   Her only subsequent literary reference to St John's Wood was in *The Body in the Library*, in which the local squire Colonel Bantry is suspected of having had an affair with the sexy blonde dumped dead in his home. A village gossip, who has seen him get into a London taxi, offers this evidence of his transgressive behaviour: 'I distinctly heard him tell the driver to go to – *where do you think?*' 'An address in *St John's Wood!* . . . 'That, I consider, *proves* it'

4   From *An Autobiography*

5   From *Unfinished Portrait*

6   Ibid

7   In her autobiography Agatha wrote that in 1919 'I had £100 a year which I still received under my grandfather's will', although six years earlier the money had been used 'to support mother'. This apparent contradiction is not explained in the book, whose factual content is not entirely reliable. It would seem that Agatha regained control of her £100 when Archie returned from the war and the couple needed a home of their own. Madge – or her husband James – continued to give money to Clara, who also received an additional £300 or so a year after the death of Margaret Miller

8   From *An Autobiography*

9   Ibid

10   In her autobiography Agatha wrote of 'the night when we knew Rosalind would be born'; although of course she could not have known such a thing for certain

11   In a piece published in the *Spectator* in 1970, in memory of Allen Lane of Penguin Press

12   Ibid

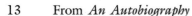

13   From *An Autobiography*

14   In the book the baby, which has kicked actively in the womb, is called Judy 'as being the next thing to Punch'. It was also the name by which Nan Pollock's daughter was usually known

15   From *A Daughter's a Daughter*

16   From *The Thirteen Problems*

17   From *Endless Night*

18   From the poem 'Progression'

19   From *An Autobiography*

20   George Joseph Smith, known as the Brides in the Bath Murderer, killed three wives for their life insurance between 1912 and 1914, and was hanged in 1915

21   The stories appeared in the *Sketch* from March 1923 onwards and were later published in book form. *Poirot Investigates*, a collection of eleven stories, appeared in Britain in 1924, and an extended version of fourteen stories was published in America in 1925. *Poirot's Early Cases* was published in 1974; among other stories it again contained the first twelve written for the *Sketch*. One of these, 'The Disappearance of Mr Davenheim', was the unlikely vehicle for Poirot's first-ever television appearance when it was shown in America, not very successfully, in 1962. Much later, between 1990 and 1993, all the short stories would be broadcast in the ITV *Poirot* series starring David Suchet

22   Very much like the Great Exhibition of 1851, this was a showcase for products from Britain and its then Dominions

23   From *The Man in the Brown Suit*

24   From 'Progression'

25   From the poem 'Love Passes'

26   From *The Man in the Brown Suit*

27   AC to CM, 3/5/1922

28   AC to CM, 9/5/1922

29   The Rand Rebellion, caused by the attempts to replace white workers in the gold mines with cheaper black labour

30   Francis Bates was the model for Sir Eustace Pedler's secretary, Guy Padgett, in *The Man in the Brown Suit*. Agatha appeared to be creating a stereotype by giving Padgett a saturnine, sinister air, which she then typically subverted: Padgett's dark secret turns out to be a wife and four children

31   AC to CM, 21/2/1922

32   AC to CM, 3/5/1922
33   AC to CM, 6/2/1922
34   AC to CM, 3/4/1922
35   AC to CM, 21/2/1922
36   AC to CM, 19/10/1922
37   As described by his son, also called Archie, in conversation with the author, 2006
38   AC to CM, 1/5/1922
39   Guilford was an effervescent correspondent; in one of his letters to Rosalind he wrote 'I had forgotten, and am appalled all over again to remember, that you like cricket'. After Agatha's death Rosalind wrote, in reply to his letter of condolence, 'you were always one of her favourites'
40   From 'Progression'
41   Ibid

The Secret Adversary

1   By Diana Gunn, daughter of Archie's friends Sam and Madge James, in conversation with the author, 2006
2   From the poem 'Love Passes'
3   Agatha had written a long story called 'Vision' in around 1908–9, which she attempted to foist on to the Bodley Head as the fifth and last book of her contract. Of course they refused it. Agatha wrote to them: 'I really do not see why you should have thought that this was not submitted as one of the works provided for in the main agreement. Whether it would have been advisable to publish it or not is another matter . . .' She did this not in the belief that the Bodley Head would accept 'Vision', but to force them to accept that her short stories, *Poirot Investigates*, constituted one of the five books. 'I certainly do not feel inclined to sign the agreement relating to the short stories, in which you have stipulated that these are not to count as a book under the terms of the main agreement, without getting the point about "Vision" cleared up first'
4   Agatha had been approached by the BBC to give a talk on the Third Programme explaining why she was 'violently allergic' to the organisation, as the *Observer* put it in a brief 1948 profile. 'A most sporting offer!' she replied. She denied that she was anti-BBC: 'but I am awfully allergic to its remuneration!'

5   A short story published in *The Listerdale Mystery*

6   Her son-in-law Anthony Hicks, in conversation with the author, 2004

7   From the 1974 interview with Lord Snowdon

8   Jared Cade, in *Agatha Christie and the Eleven Missing Days* took a sensationalist view. According to his sources, Judith and Graham Gardner, Archie 'had begun to resent the attention [Agatha] was starting to receive'. There may have been some truth in this but Cade presents it as unarguable fact

9   A letter sent to the *Sketch* from Brook House, Park Lane, in March 1924 has Lord Mountbatten presenting his compliments and offering the idea that, in an epistolary detective novel, the 'writer of the chief letters in the book' should be the criminal. In essence this was very much like *The Man in the Brown Suit*, although it was taken further in the extended scenario that Lord Mountbatten also offered (which included a scene in which Poirot was suspected of the murder). Agatha replied that 'the idea was most ingenious' and she intended to use it. In 1969 the two exchanged letters again, and Agatha wrote politely, if inaccurately: 'Thank you for presenting me with a first class idea – no-one else ever has'

10   From *A Pocket Full of Rye*

11   From *Unfinished Portrait*

12   A letter of complaint was written by a reader to *The Times;* the *News Chronicle* inexplicably described the book as 'tasteless', the Detection Club committee proposed a motion that Agatha should be expelled as she had broken the 'rules': only a vote by Dorothy L. Sayers saved her, although it is hard to believe that she would have much cared either way. Although Agatha became honorary president of the Detection Club she was a lone wolf when it came to her writing. Swearing to abide by the rules of detective fiction with one hand on Eric the Skull – part of the Club's initiation ritual – was not really her style

13   AC to CM, sent from Carezza al Lago in Italy, no date

14   Subsequently published in *The Listerdale Mystery* and filmed as *Love from a Stranger* in 1937. The film starred Ann Harding and Basil Rathbone. Joan Hickson, later the BBC's peerless Miss Marple, took a minor role; she also appeared in *Murder, She Said*, the 1961 adaptation of *4.50 from Paddington*, in which Miss Marple was played by Margaret Rutherford

15   From *The Burden*

16   According to Jared Cade, it had been Agatha's whim to call her
      secretary 'Carlotta', 'because she thought it sounded more exotic,
      although it was apparent that Charlotte did not much care for this'.
      There is no evidence to support this assertion. More likely the name
      was Rosalind's invention

17   In conversation with the author, 2006

18   In Jared Cade's *Agatha Christie and the Eleven Missing Days*

19   CM to AC, sent from Ashfield, no date

20   From *Unfinished Portrait*

21   CM to AC, sent from Abney, no date

22   AC to MM, 5/11/1930

23   From 'Progression'

24   From *An Autobiography*

25   In conversation with the author, 2003

26   Nancy Neele was never secretary to Major Belcher, although she did
      know him. In the film *Agatha* starring Vanessa Redgrave – a feeling
      but fanciful account of Agatha's disappearance – Nancy is portrayed
      as Archie's secretary, an inaccuracy that is sometimes cited as truth.
      In fact Nancy worked at the Imperial Continental Gas Association
      in the City

27   From *An Autobiography*

28   In conversation with the author

29   In conversation with the author

30   This version of events is described in Jared Cade's *Agatha Christie
      and the Eleven Missing Days*

31   From *Unfinished Portrait*

32   Diana Gunn, in conversation with the author

33   Archie Christie to AC, no date

34   From *The Rose and the Yew Tree*

35   Anthony Hicks in conversation with the author, 2004

36   From 'Progression'

37   From Jared Cade's *Agatha Christie and the Eleven Missing Days*

38   Archie Christie to AC, sent from RFC Netheravon, no date

The Quarry

1   From the fragment of short story about the young widow

2   Quotations from, respectively: *Sad Cypress, Death on the Nile, Five
     Little Pigs* and the short story 'The Edge'

3   In May 1930 Agatha wrote to Max Mallowan about the publication
       of her collection, *The Mysterious Mr. Quin*: 'Two of the stories in
       Mr Quin I consider good – "Harlequin's Lane" and "The Man from
       the Sea" . . .'

4   From Tennyson's *The Idylls of the King*

5   This was the title given to the serialised version of the book

6   The poison used by Dr Crippen to murder his wife

7   Edith Thompson's much younger lover, Frederick Bywaters,
       murdered her husband in a *crime passionel*; both were hanged as it
       was said that Edith had incited the murder. In fact she almost certainly
       knew nothing about it, but had been condemned as immoral because
       of her love affair

8   Throughout, this newspaper was very much like a modern-day tabloid:
       it was sensational, sceptical and highly readable. Yet very much later
       Rosalind received a letter from Trevor Allen, who had covered the
       story for the *Gazette* and was now writing his autobiography, asking
       for her 'true explanation of the disappearance'. She replied with the
       'official' version, which Allen then used, telling Rosalind 'I regard
       this as the complete and final explanation'

9   In 1960 Agatha received a letter from an old friend of James Watts,
       who wrote that back in 1926 he had 'got a long letter about you
       from him cursing the beastly press reporters who lay siege to the
       place'

10   In an article published in the *Sunday Chronicle*, 11/8/1929, on the
       subject of the Croydon murder case in which three members of the
       same family were poisoned

11   *New Statesman* 30/1/1976

12   An adaptation of *Agatha* by Kathleen Tynan (Weidenfeld & Nicolson,
       1979)

13   Rosalind brought a lawsuit in 1978 (a suit was also brought in the
       name of Agatha's estate) but a federal judge refused to block distri-
       bution of the film. In 1977 Rosalind also wrote to *The Times*: 'I
       would like to take this opportunity of saying that this film is being
       made entirely without consultation with any of my parents' family,
       is altogether against our wishes and is likely to cause us great distress.'
       The identification of her parents was 'particularly objectionable and
       morally beneath contempt'. Referring to the film's producer, David
       (now Lord) Puttnam, she wrote: 'Let Mr Puttnam have his fairy-
       tale, if he must, but please do not let my family be brought into it.'

Puttnam replied to Rosalind personally: 'It is of course *not* our intention for the film to cause unhappiness to anybody.'

But family friends were appalled by the prospect and rallied round Rosalind with (albeit useless) support. Richard (now Lord) Attenborough also wrote to Rosalind in reply to her request for advice. 'I fear, from all I can gather, that there is little one can do about it.'

Of Kathleen Tynan's *Agatha*, an American reviewer wrote: 'Christie would have hated this book'. Nevertheless an interview with Mrs Tynan did show her to have had some understanding of her subject, although her idiom was not exactly Agatha's: 'She was just going through a terrific growth period as a woman. The way she went about it may not have met the Victorian standards that she grew up with, and she always seemed bothered by that . . .'

A final note: the part of Agatha was played, exquisitely, by Vanessa Redgrave, who donated her £40,000 fee from the film to the Workers' Revolutionary Party. Her then partner Timothy Dalton (also excellent) played Archie, although when asked if he was similarly intending to donate his fee he replied: 'Am I hell'

14   The *Westminster Gazette* reported that Agatha could drive to London in fifty-five minutes: from Sunningdale to the centre is about twenty-five miles

15   Mr Pettelson's daughter also wrote to Rosalind in November 1977, explaining the circumstances in which Agatha and Mr Pettelson had met at Harrogate: 'your dear mother offered to accompany him on the piano . . . There was a particular song your mother enjoyed playing, entitled "Angels Guard Thee" (*Berceuse de Jocelyn*) which my father always sang so beautifully. This particular sheet of music was chosen and signed by your mother – "Tressa Neele" [sic]'

16   By her daughter, in conversation with the author, 2006

17   Berkshire reported extra costs of £6 or so, which Archie presumably thought had been reasonably incurred: he paid them

18   This statement was made in Gwen Robyns's *The Mystery of Agatha Christie* (Doubleday, 1978)

19   *The Times* 16/2/1928

20   From Agatha's poem 'There Where My Lover Lies'

21   All personal quotations are from conversations with the author

The Second Husband

1   From *Memories of Men and Women* (Eyre Methuen, 1980)
2   Diana Gunn, in conversation with the author, 2006
3   In conversation with the author, 2006
4   Diana Gunn
5   In conversation with the author, 2004
6   From *Memories of Men and Women*
7   'It was my idea to meet him,' says Mathew Prichard, but Archie died just before the proposed meeting
8   In conversation with the author, 2004
9   Letter from Rosalind to AC, sent from Caledonia school, no date
10   Rosalind to AC, 7/6/1931
11   Rosalind to AC, 14/6/1931
12   'I have always hated *The Mystery of the Blue Train*,' she wrote in her autobiography
13   This was wildly overdone in the 2005 ITV adaptation of the book, which made Poirot sick with unrequited love and entirely missed the delicate point of his relationship with Katherine
14   From *An Autobiography*
15   In *Memories of Men and Women*
16   Although the film is a triumph, it is hard to imagine how anyone came up with the idea of casting big, manly Albert Finney as Poirot in *Murder on the Orient Express*. In Rosalind's view 'he looked stuffed'. Similarly David Suchet, a gifted Shakespearean actor, whose mincing walk and beachball stomach have dominated the long-running *Poirot* series on ITV. Closest to the spirit of Poirot was, perhaps, the portrayal by Peter Ustinov in *Death on the Nile* (his subsequent Christie films were far less good). Ustinov was physically wrong – made few attempts not to be, bar sticking on a small moustache – but he infused the part with his own sharp and benign intelligence. He did not act, he just *was*, his scenes with Mia Farrow as Jacqueline de Bellefort are extremely touching
17   Agatha later explained to a reader that the name 'Marple' had come while she was staying with Madge at Abney 'and we went together to a sale at Marple Hall'. The house, she wrote, 'was a beautiful old manor, belonging to the Bradshaws descended from Judge Bradshaw who sentenced Charles I. I bought two Jacobean oak chairs which I still have . . .'
18   In conversation with the author, 2005

19   In a letter to AC, 18/6/1943, her friend Robert Graves also claimed to have admired the book. But he took Agatha to task over the plot; while noting that she had used his name for her policeman. His very funny letter is not unlike a John Sutherland literary mystery (Sutherland did in fact write one of these essays on *Curtain: Poirot's Last Case*). 'Elsie too was incriminated', he wrote. 'I think that Inspector Graves let the family down by not putting the bracelets on her too for failing to report the presence of Agnes' body in the cupboard when she returned the fishing rods there. No, Agatha, the boys *didn't* keep their fishing rods in the nursery . . .'

20   Joyce marries Miss Marple's novelist nephew, Raymond West, and thereafter becomes 'Joan'. This kind of sloppy editing plagued Agatha's books

21   In a 1970 letter to Yasuo Suto, who was writing a book on Miss Marple. 'If you know "the career of Miss Marple" from childhood upwards, you know more than I do!' wrote Agatha

22   Henrietta McCall, author of *The Life of Max Mallowan* (British Museum Press, 2001); in conversation with the author, 2006

23   In conversation with the author, 2006

24   *Mallowan's Memoirs* (Collins, 1977), dedicated 'To Rosalind With Love'

25   John Mallowan, in conversation with the author, 2005

26   Letter from AC to MM, no date

27   From *Mallowan's Memoirs*

28   Dr Julian Reade, in conversation with the author, 2006

29   AC to MM, sent from Ashfield, no date

30   AC to MM, sent from Ashfield, May 1930

31   Ibid

32   As compared with Dorothy L. Sayers, whose wedding night scene in *Busman's Honeymoon* between Lord Peter Wimsey and Harriet Vane ('before I've done I mean to be king and emperor') was once described by Ruth Rendell as the most embarrassing passage in literature

33   Letter from MM to AC, 14/5/1930

34   AC to MM, sent from Ashfield, no date

35   Ibid

36   AC to MM, 21/5/1930

37   Jared Cade claimed in *Agatha and the Eleven Missing Days* that Max

was never invited to spend Christmas at Abney Hall, although there is no corroborative evidence for this

38   AC to MM, sent from Ashfield, no date

39   AC to MM, sent from the Broadford Hotel, Skye, no date

40   AC to MM, sent from Ashfield, no date

41   Ibid

42   In conversation with the author, 2006

43   AC to MM, dated 'Wed. 10am'

44   MM to AC, 29/10/1930

45   AC to MM, no date

46   Ibid

47   This referred to a collaborative BBC radio play, the second of its kind that Agatha had worked on at the request of Dorothy Sayers (with whom she had an arm's-length friendship: no two women could have been less alike but they respected each other). The first play was broadcast in six parts in summer 1930. The second, *The Scoop*, went out in 1931 and was something of a nightmare for all concerned, not least the BBC itself. Agatha had to write and personally broadcast two instalments, quite a lot of work for just fifty guineas; consequently she treated the whole enterprise in slightly cavalier fashion, asking if she could record her episodes in Plymouth rather than London, then disappearing with Rosalind to Switzerland for a holiday. 'Will you explain to Mrs Mallowan, please,' wrote the producer J. R. Ackerley to Charlotte Fisher, 'the extreme difficulties her being unavailable has involved us in.' Later he said of Agatha that she was 'surprisingly good looking and extremely tiresome', which would not have bothered her one whit. The chief pleasure for her was the knowledge that Max was listening to her broadcast: 'my EMINENT ange . . . wish you could work in a cryptic message into the story!'

48   The *Chimneys* play in fact received its British premiere in 2006

49   AC to MM, 23/10/1930

50   AC to MM, 13/10/1931

51   Agatha once said to Rowse, after attending one of his lusty Elizabethan lectures, 'I hope it won't start up Max again'; a remark that Rowse, not an expert in heterosexual relationships, took deadly seriously. 'I wonder if that wasn't an element in the failure with the dashing, perhaps demanding, army officer?' he wrote. In fact Agatha found Archie deeply attractive throughout their marriage; the waning of sexual desire was on the other side

52   AC to MM, 23/10/1931

53   Anthony Hicks, in conversation with the author

54   From the poem 'A Choice'

War

1   In *Memories of Men and Women*

2   From *The Hollow*

3   Letter from MM to AC, 8/11/1930

4   Letter from AC to MM, 24/12/1944

5   *The Diaries of A. L. Rowse*, edited by Richard Ollard (Allen Lane, 2003)

6   AC to MM, 27/10/1942

7   Underneath the floor of the boathouse there is a dark and silent plunge pool

8   Max was knighted in June 1968 for services to archaeology; Agatha was made a Dame in the 1971 New Year's Honours List. The painter Oscar Kokoschka, who had done a superb portrait of Agatha for her eightieth birthday (as rugged and vital as an Amyas Crale), wrote to congratulate her and warned: 'I hope you are not forced to kneel down . . . Do not get a cold in a too light gala dress, please!'

9   The BSA was founded in 1932 as a memorial to Gertrude Bell, with the aim of promoting and supporting 'research relating to the archaeology of Iraq and surrounding countries'. A fellow archaeologist said that Agatha contributed heavily to a fund within the School. 'I'm sure not how much she actually put in . . .'

10   From the address given by Seton Lloyd at Max's memorial service, held at St James's, Piccadilly, 29/11/1978

11   In conversation with the author, 2006

12   Shown by the British Museum in its 2001 exhibition 'Agatha Christie and Archaeology'

13   AC to MM, 'Whit Sunday' 1944

14   In *Come, Tell Me How You Live*, Agatha Christie Mallowan (Collins, 1946)

15   'She will have to be changed into an American, preferably with what we call a "Cape Cod" background', wrote Ober to Cork about this proposed series. Unsurprisingly, Agatha did not agree to it; although later the actress Helen Hayes did create a perfectly acceptable Miss Marple of this type

16   Of which Edmund Cork wrote to Agatha: 'I'm afraid I don't like this book quite as much as some of the others'; her casual reply was 'I agree with you about it – not one of my best'

17   In this book Poirot is asked to investigate a murder that took place sixteen years previously; that is to say, in 1926. This has been viewed as significant, but in fact the book was written in 1941, and its events correspond only loosely with those of Agatha's own life

18   Letter from MM to Rosalind, 3/7/1940

19   One of Max's arguments was that his wife had written an anti-Nazi book; that is to say, *N or M?*

20   At the end of 1943 Max had been promoted to colonel, Archie Christie's rank. Perhaps with this dimly in mind Max wrote: 'You never thought that Mr Puper would one day for a time become a Colonel did you?'

21   MM to AC, 26/4/1943

22   This famous block, which was awarded second prize for Ugliest Building in *Horizon* magazine, had also been home to Nicholas Montserrat and Henry Moore; later members of the Isobar included Barbara Hepworth. It was sold in 1968 for £7,000 to the *New Statesman*

23   AC to MM, 27/10/1942

24   'How is James?' Max wrote in 1945. 'Has he succumbed to the Fishers and how are they, not married and if not why not?' Max did not especially like Carlo and Mary, whom he perhaps associated with Agatha's former life. The answer to his question was that 'Char did have someone during the war', according to her niece, although for whatever reason this did not lead to marriage; Mary Fisher's fiancé was killed

25   In an undated letter to Jeremy Pritchard, son of the original owner, who was collecting reminiscences from residents. A cousin of the family was Beryl, later married to the Mallowans' friend Robert Graves; possibly this is what directed Agatha to Lawn Road in the first place

26   AC to MM, 31/8/1942

27   MM to AC, 10/12/1942

28   Perceived by Max as the model for Mrs Dane Calthrop, the vicar's wife in *The Moving Finger*

29   The character is used in *Appointment with Death*, when a parallel is drawn between Ophelia and the mentally unstable Ginevra Boynton

30   AC to MM, 23/8/1942

31 AC to MM, 29/11/1942

32 Musings on the play also appeared in a much earlier book, *Why Didn't They Ask Evans?* "'You know, I've always thought", said Frankie, suddenly digressing wildly from the matter in hand, "that Lady Macbeth incited Macbeth to do all those murders simply and solely because she was so frightfully bored with life – and incidentally with Macbeth'"

33 AC to MM, 27/10/1942

34 MM to AC, 27/6/1943

35 AC to MM, 4/7/1944

36 AC to MM, 14/4/1943

37 MM to AC, 12/1/1943

38 '. . . The Assyrian craftsman's savage hands deline
    The tortures of the dying and record
    The suffering cries that echo through the ages' are the last lines of a sonnet written by the twenty-three-year-old Max

39 MM to AC, 22/12/1943

40 A.P. was Rosalind's nickname – 'Auntie Punkie' – later adopted by Agatha and Max

41 AC to MM, 1/7/1944

42 AC to MM, 26/8/1943

43 AC to MM, 27/3/1943

44 MM to AC, 13/8/1943

45 Stephen Glanville to AC, 9/4/1943

46 Stephen Glanville to AC, 11/7/1943

47 Stephen Glanville to AC, 18/11/1943

48 AC to MM, 17/11/1943

49 AC to MM, 9/1/1944

50 AC to MM, 2/8/1944

51 AC to MM, 19/5/1944

52 The words of Dr Glyn Daniel, who also knew Max and Agatha. In his autobiography he recalls asking Max what he had made of Tom Driberg, his contemporary at Lancing: 'Seemed all right to me, but I had no idea then of his specialised proclivities'

53 Rosalind to AC, 7/2/1931

54 AC to Rosalind, sent from the British Museum Foundation in Syria, no date

55 These cards, with the cartoon 'Bonzo' dog on the front, feature as a clue in *N or M?*

56 Rosalind to AC, 27/1/1936

57   Rosalind to AC, 24/4/1936

58   Rosalind to Charlotte Fisher, no date

59   Rosalind to AC, 16/5/1936

60   Agatha wrote to Rosalind that she had said to another mother '"I think we will be at Mrs Lambert Simnel's lunch at Claridges" and *she* said "Of course!" So we are all liars together!'

61   AC to Rosalind, 30/1/1937

62   AC to MM, 8/8/1943

63   AC to MM, 20/9/1943

64   MM to Rosalind, 7/12/1941

65   MM to Rosalind, no date

66   MM to Rosalind, 17/6/1943

67   MM to Rosalind, 15/10/1943

68   AC to MM, 30/9/1943

69   AC to MM, 12/10/1943

70   Dr Harold Davis was chief pharmacist at UCH and later published an article on Agatha's time there. Few people knew who she was, he wrote. 'She was a wonderful, cheerful and industrious colleague'

71   MM to AC, 5/3/1944

72   This name reappeared in *At Bertram's Hotel*

73   AC to MM, 25/5/1944

74   MM to AC, 16/1/1944

75   For example by John Mallowan, in conversation with the author

76   MM to AC, 27/9/1942

77   Edmund Cork to Harold Ober, 19/12/1940

78   The official rate of exchange was four dollars and three cents to the pound

79   Cork to Ober, 3/1/1941

80   Ibid

81   AC to MM, 11/9/1944

82   AC to MM, 13/10/1944

83   AC to MM, 2/11/1944

84   AC to MM, 16/12/1944

85   Agatha did something very unusual in this adaptation: she changed the solution. It made sense in dramatic terms but the original ending is better, being far less 'obviously' satisfying. The ending of *Ten Little Niggers* was also changed, in order to leave two people on stage rather than a mass of corpses, but the actual solution remained the same. A new version, produced in 2006, restored the original death

count and much of the original book dialogue; nevertheless it managed to be atrociously bad, proving that a knowing and self-conscious 'authenticity' is not the way to keep Christie alive

86   This play found it hard to get a London theatre. The reviews for *Appointment with Death* (which nonetheless did good business) 'left a prejudice against Christie plays', as Cork rather tactlessly told Agatha. Also the Ministry of Labour objected to the presence of a maid in the play

87   From *The Thirteen Problems*

88   So irritated was Agatha by William Collins's attitude that she asked Cork to place *The Rose and the Yew Tree* elsewhere; Heinemann stated that 'Billy is crackers' and snapped up the book for publication

89   Clement Attlee himself spoke charmingly of Agatha: 'Fifty books! Many of them have beguiled and made agreeable my leisure'

English Murder

1   A 1965 film was made starring Shirley Eaton, Dennis Price and the pop star Fabian; a 1974 version starred Oliver Reed and, as the judge, Richard Attenborough, a friend of Agatha who had starred with his wife Sheila Sim in the first cast of *The Mousetrap*. A more eccentric piece of casting had Charles Aznavour in the role of first victim

2   Campbell Christie also wrote the scripts to the films *Jassy* and (adapted from the play that he wrote with his wife) *Carrington VC*. In June 1963 his *Times* obituary reported that he had been 'found dead in the gas-filled kitchen of his home at West Byfleet, Sussex'. The obituary said 'Christie in social life could pack a punch, and he packed it in wit'

3   She had been expecting around £5,000. 'I am rather looking forward to breaking this to Rosalind,' Cork wrote to Agatha, when the news of the deal came through

4   'I would be ecstatic to be working on a Christie again,' Wilder later wrote to Agatha. 'How about a great big $8 million all-conclusive mystery to end all mysteries? Got anything up your sleeve?'

5   She moved out of Lawn Road in 1947 and for a short time used Cresswell Place before letting it (a tenant named 'Mr Portner' was intensely troublesome in the early 1950s). Campden Street had been sold and, thanks to the bombs, Sheffield Terrace was no more

6   This brilliant title, taken from the 'play within a play' in *Hamlet*,

was the idea of Agatha's son-in-law Anthony Hicks

7 From *Hallowe'en Party*

8 *Sunday Express*, 20/11/1935

9 From *Mrs McGinty's Dead*

10 These exquisite toy dogs were bred by Rosalind and eventually taken up as Agatha's favoured breed. The graves of her two, Treacle and Bingo, are in the garden at Winterbrook. In *A Murder is Announced* she has a character say of them 'such graceful little things. I do like a dog with *legs* . . .'

11 Agatha became very friendly with Allen Lane, nephew of her first publisher, John Lane, and he and his wife Lettice spent frequent weekends with the Mallowans. The Lanes also visited the site at Nimrud that Max excavated after the war; by way of thanks to Agatha for her early support of Penguin Books, Allen made a financial contribution to the dig

12 The *Close Up* was broadcast on the Light Programme, 13/2/1955

13 In conversation with the author, 2004

14 'Candidly, we don't feel that the Mary Westmacott is up to standard', wrote the American publishers Rinehart when turning down *A Daughter's a Daughter*; of *The Burden* Rinehart wrote that 'when Agatha Christie becomes Mary Westmacott she is not at all successful at characterisation'. This despite the fact that Rinehart had snapped up the earlier Westmacotts

15 To Gillian Franks in 1970

16 Or *Remembered Death*, as it was originally called; the title was considered inappropriate so soon after the war, but retained for the US edition

17 These were used in, respectively, 'The Thumb Mark of St Peter' (a short story in *The Thirteen Problems*); *The Pale Horse*; and *Ordeal by Innocence*

18 Agatha wanted this because she had received several letters from readers about the plot of *Sad Cypress*, saying that in law an illegitimate child would not be the automatic heir of a sole parent who died intestate. In fact this *was* the law according to the 1926 Act. Another letter about *Sad Cypress* came from a reader who objected that when Nurse Hopkins poisoned Mary Gerrard with the tea, she had no means of knowing that Elinor would not also drink it. This was a very good point; the excellent 2003 ITV adaptation of the book inserted a line for Elinor to say that she never drank tea

19 Bigbury-on-Sea is linked across the water to Burgh Island in South

Devon, still home to a smart Art Deco hotel (built 1932) at which Agatha stayed, and where she set *Evil Under the Sun* and *And Then There Were None*

20   Agatha also used her beloved Tennyson for the titles of *The Hollow* and *The Mirror Crack'd from Side to Side*; in *A Pocket Full of Rye* the children of the family are called Lancelot, Percival and Elaine

21   'Dorcas' became Brenda; 'Emma' became Josephine

22   It was on a Nile cruise in 1933, with Max and Rosalind, that Agatha saw a family resembling the Boyntons in *Appointment with Death*

23   The point was made by Bevis Hillier in his 1999 *Spectator* review of Charles Osborne's *The Life and Crimes of Agatha Christie*

24   Sayers wrote a religious play, *The Man Born to Be King*, and had almost completed her majestic translation of *The Divine Comedy* when she died in 1957

25   First published in *Tribune* in 1946

26   In *Famous Trials I* (Penguin, 1941)

27   In 'The Lernean Hydra'

28   Letter from AC to Edmund Cork, 31/12/1966

29   According to an essay entitled 'Dame Agatha's Poisonous Pharmacopoeia', written by two doctors, John and Peter Gwilt, and – on the whole – praising her understanding of toxicology

30   'Surely it is unnecessarily cruel to set forth Miss Tierney's problems and sorrows in such a manner', an American woman wrote in 1964, referring to the fact that the actress Gene Tierney had had a child affected by rubella. Cork replied that Agatha had not known about this

31   In conversation with the author, 2005

32   But Alan Coren, writing in *Punch*, saw the inherent absurdity: 'Next week,' he wrote, 'the Non-Gentile of Malta'

33   In a letter to George Harmon Coke, 27/6/1940. Julian Symons has similarly made reference to the frequent 'deplorably loose ends' in Christie, and one of the worst examples appears in *And Then There Were None*. After the discovery of Judge Wargrave's 'dead body', the reader is presumably supposed to believe that any of the four people left on the island – Vera Claythorne, Dr Armstrong, Lombard and Blore – might be guilty. In fact circumstances have clearly exonerated Vera: she could not have been killing the judge if at the moment of the murder she was screaming in her bedroom

34   Chabrol would have made a fascinating job of *Towards Zero*: his

magnificent *Le Boucher* has a serial killer as its central character and *La Cérémonie* is an adaptation of Ruth Rendell's *A Judgement in Stone*

35 AC to Rosalind, no date

36 In conversation with the author

37 Quoted respectively from *Dead Man's Folly, Appointment with Death, The Labours of Hercules, Murder is Easy, Five Little Pigs, The Thirteen Problems, Endless Night, A Pocket Full of Rye, And Then There Were None* and *Death on the Nile*

38 This point was made by Janet Morgan in her biography

39 John Sparrow to AC, 12/1/1969

40 Sidney Smith to AC, 3/6/1943

41 The contemporary French intellectual, Michel Houellebecq, is also a fan: his book *Platform* contains an adulatory passage about *The Hollow*. Agatha Christie, he wrote, understood 'the sin of despair'

42 Robert Speaight to AC, 21/9/1970

43 Broadcast in the ITV *Poirot* series in 2003

44 Geraldine McEwan plays the part in the ITV series *Marple*, first broadcast in 2005

45 This marvellous series was broadcast by the BBC between 1984 and 1992

The Late Years

1 John Mallowan, in conversation with the author, 2006

2 From *The Burden*

3 Ibid

4 Letter from Archie Christie to Rosalind, 24/10/1958

5 In conversation with the author

6 Agatha dedicated one book to Max, early in their marriage: *Murder on the Orient Express*, part of whose inspiration had come from a calamitous journey taken in 1931 from Nineveh to London. In Stamboul she had boarded the Orient Express, which was interminably delayed; an American lady (who evolved into the book's Mrs Hubbard) lamented how 'in the States they'd have motored some automobiles along right away – why, they'd have brought aeroplanes . . .'

7 Letter from MM to Edmund Cork, 24/4/60

8   Letter from Ivan von Auw at the Harold Ober agency to Cork, 9/4/1965

9   On *In Town Tonight*, a brief interview broadcast on the BBC Home Service, 12/5/1951

10 MM to AC, 11/4/1943

11 MM to AC, 21/5/1944

12 As described by his friend Glyn Daniel. In his autobiography Daniel also described being offered a job by Allen Lane, that of 'archaeological adviser' at Penguin; according to Daniel the job had been Max Mallowan's, but he was sacked as he 'would *only* plan books on Near Eastern archaeology . . . my dealings with Max were a little strained for several years'

13 In conversation with the author, 2006

14 Cork to Ober, 6/2/1953

15 Cork to AC, 5/8/1953

16 Agatha speaking on *In Town Tonight*

17 In 'Agatha Christie, Nimrud and Baghdad', from *Agatha Christie and Archaeology*, a collection of essays edited by Charlotte Trümpler, published by British Museum Press to coincide with its 2001 exhibition

18 Letter from AC to Rosalind, 1957

19 Joan Oates, in conversation with the author

20 Joan Oates, in conversation with the author

21 AC to Rosalind, sent from the Zia Hotel, date incomplete

22 This play was written for Margaret Lockwood, whose agent had approached Agatha via Peter Saunders; in a charming gesture Agatha included a part for Lockwood's 14 year old daughter Julia. The play – a lightweight thing but not without wit; almost a screwball comedy – was filmed in 1960

23 AC to Rosalind, sent from the British School of Archaeology, date incomplete

24 AC to Rosalind, sent from the BSA, date incomplete

25 From *Appointment with Death*

26 Rosalind to AC, sent from Pwllywrach, date incomplete

27 Cork to Rosalind, 6/5/1952

28 AC to Rosalind, 3/4/1952

29 Cork to AC, 22/5/1952

30 Agatha loved horse racing, as did Max, and in later life her dislike of television was tempered by the fact that she could watch the racing

on it. Her letters to Anthony Hicks, also a racing fan, are full of references to bets that had gone down – 'yes a bad blow on the horses' – although she did have the odd success (a letter from Edmund Cork congratulated her on backing My Love to win the 1948 Derby; he had placed the bet for her). She was also prevailed upon to present the 'Mousetrap Trophy' at Exeter races. Her books contain the occasional, wondrously normal reference to racing, which in the mid-twentieth century was very much a part of English daily life. In *The ABC Murders* the fourth murder is scheduled to take place at Doncaster on a certain Wednesday in September; the unworldly policeman in charge thinks that forewarned is forearmed and the killer will be picked up. 'Man alive', he is told, 'don't you realise that on *next Wednesday the St Leger is being run at Doncaster*?' In *4.50 from Paddington* an alibi is broken by a taxi driver, who 'identified the day because a horse called Crawler had won the 2.30 and he'd had a tidy bit on'. 'Thank God for racing!' says the policeman in charge

31   This story later became *Dead Man's Folly*, but for some reason in its original form it did not sell. 'The Bishop of Exeter's lawyers are being horrid about "Greenshaw's Folly"', wrote Cork to Obers in 1956. 'They say they find it difficult to believe that Mrs Mallowan would have presented the church with a story that would not sell!' The irony was that when the story was lengthened into *Dead Man's Folly* it was willingly bought: then cut.

32   AC to Cork, 19/2/1956

33   AC to Cork, no date

34   Cork to AC, 10/2/1956

35   AC to Cork, 19/2/1956

36   AC to the Hickses, 20/2/1956

37   Cork to AC, 10/3/1956

38   AC to Cork, 17/3/1956

39   In conversation with the author, 2005

40   AC to Cork, 20/1/1960

41   AC to Cork, 17/9/1961

42   This film starred Francesca Annis (as the invented character 'Sheila Upward') who would later play Lady Frances Derwent in the television adaptation of *Why Didn't They Ask Evans?*, one of the first of the Christie films to capitalise on the upper-class nostalgia boom of the 1980s; she also played Tuppence Beresford in the series *Partners in Crime*

43 A truly bizarre cast for this film included Anita Ekberg as 'Amanda Beatrice Cross', Robert Morley as Hastings and, in a small role, Austin Trevor, who had played Poirot in a 1934 film of *Lord Edgware Dies*

44 AC to Cork, 17/9/1961

45 AC to Lawrence Bachmann, 24/7/1963

46 Bachmann to AC, 7/4/1964. 'A typical report on the proposed new incarnation of Poirot was this in the *Daily Mail* 5/3/1964, which quoted Zero Mostel thus: "I don't know about the accent, but I'll certainly give him an eye for the girls. He solves his cases – but there are usually eight corpses strewn about before the end, so he obviously isn't so bright".'

47 In *Memories of Men and Women*

48 Cork to AC, 9/4/1965

49 Agatha Christie Limited, of which Mathew Prichard is managing director, is now owned by Chorion PLC

50 In April 1977 it was reported that the Authors' Division of Booker McConnell had increased its post-tax profits by more than a third to £487,000, 'most of it attributable to Dame Agatha', as *The Times* wrote

51 Mathew Prichard, in conversation with the author, 2006

52 Rosalind to Cork, 2/6/1956

53 Rosalind to Cork, 14/1/1957

54 Rosalind to Cork, 5/12/1958

55 Cork to Rosalind, 27/4/1962

56 Rosalind to Cork, 14/6/1962

57 Her distress was made plain in several newspaper articles; also in a letter to the crime writer Margaret Yorke, who had expressed her sympathy with Rosalind and spoken out in Agatha's defence. 'Naturally the programme was very unpleasant and hurtful for her family. It *is* unfair to make programmes like that about people who are dead and can't answer for themselves . . . I was disappointed that there wasn't more support for her in the press'

58 Rosalind to Cork, 29/3/1965

59 Rosalind to Margaret Yorke, 1992

60 AC to Rosalind, 5/4/1955

61 AC to Rosalind, sent from Swan Court, no date

62 In conversation with the author, 2003

63 In conversation with the author, 2006

64   In conversation with the author, 2006

65   In conversation with the author, 2006

66   Joan Oates, in conversation with the author

67   Ibid

68   In *The Life of Max Mallowan*

69   Joan Oates, in conversation with the author

70   In conversation with the author

71   From *Agatha Christie and the Eleven Missing Days*

72   Ibid

73   Pictured on the front of the original edition of Evelyn Waugh's *Edmund Campion*; Campion had set up his illegal printing press at Stonor in the 16th century

74   After Agatha's death this car had been sold to Max, for a nominal fee, by Agatha Christie Limited

75   D. in conversation with the author, 2006

76   Ibid

77   Ibid

78   Ibid

79   Rachel Maxwell-Hyslop, in conversation with the author

80   D. in conversation with the author

81   AC to Rosalind, sent from Winterbrook, date incomplete

82   MM to AC, 9/9/1936

God's Mark

1   Letter from Cork to Rosalind, 24/3/1960

2   AC to Cork, 9/4/1958

3   In *The Guardian*, 9/10/1987

4   Written in 1937 although not produced in Agatha's lifetime, the play was sent to John Gielgud as a putative producer. 'I think introspective characters like Akhnaton are inclined to be swallowed up in big productions,' he wrote. 'I also feel there is not enough humour, particularly after the First Act.' When the play was staged in a London fringe theatre in 1980, it was drastically cut: 'It's a bold experiment and one well worth seeing,' said *The Guardian*.

In 1973 the play was published, according to Agatha's wishes (and on the back of the Tutankhamun exhibition at the British Museum). Edmund Cork had read it the year before and wrote to the Harold Ober agency: 'We are tremendously impressed with it, and so is everyone who has read it.' Dorothy Olding at Obers 'thought Agatha's play very interesting'. In his memoirs Max Mallowan called it 'Agatha's most beautiful and profound play'.

5 Mathew Prichard to Cork, 15/11/1961
6 AC to Cork, 2/1/1963
7 Dorothy Olding's reaction, on reading in the newspapers that Agatha was to adapt *Bleak House* for the screen, was: 'What gives? Agatha bored these days?'
8 Dorothy Olding to Cork, 30/6/1970
9 Stella Kirwan to Cork, 19/12/1962
10 Cork to Dorothy Olding, 18/8/1966
11 In conversation with the author
12 John Mallowan, in conversation with the author
13 In her 1970 interview with Gillian Franks
14 From *Nemesis*
15 Despite the little jibes he made against her in his wartime letters – he also called her a 'martyr' in a letter to Rosalind – Max attended Charlotte's funeral
16 Cork to the Harold Ober agency, 21/6/1971
17 A. L. Rowse, in *Memories of Men and Women*
18 Released in 1970, the film starred Hywel Bennett, Hayley Mills and – as the girl in the scene to which Agatha objected – Britt Ekland
19 Dorothy Olding to Cork, 27/7/1973
20 The other book that Agatha wrote as her 'insurance policy' during the war, *Sleeping Murder*, was published after her death in 1976
21 In the book *Where Was Rebecca Shot?* (Phoenix 1998), which also contains a response to the essay from Ann Hart, author of a 'biography' of Poirot. She wrote that *Curtain* 'has an air of senility about it'; not true, although her suggestion that Anthony Hicks might have helped excise any 1940 references from the manuscript is an intriguing one
22 AC to MM, sent from Ashfield, no date
23 MM to AC, 24/2/1943
24 In a letter to the author, 2006
25 In conversation with the author, 2006
26 In conversation with the author, 2006
27 Letter from Adelaide Ross to AC, 1/3/1966
28 Letter from Clara Bowring to AC, 14/9/1970
29 AC to Judith Gardner, 4/12/1959

30   The Queen sent a telegram to Max Mallowan after Agatha's death. 'Please be assured', he replied, 'that you had in us two grateful and loving subjects'
31   Letter from Peter Saunders to Rosalind, 7/11/1974
32   Letter from AC to Dorothy Claybourne, 21/10/1970
33   From *Nemesis*

Index

Note: 'AC' denotes Agatha Christie. Subheadings are in chronological order. Subscript numbers appended to page numbers indicate endnotes. Asterisks appended to page numbers indicate an attribution in the endnotes.

any northerners to seek sanctuary in the south. It became a genteel place inhabited by the moderately well-off looking for somewhere greener to live.

The railways changed all that. The abundance of open space in the south meant that the area was ripe for development. Cheap housing was built south of the Thames for railway workers, and the population increased from under 3,000 in 1811, to 70,000 by 1900.

It was around this time that the psychological divide really established itself. Because south London was seen as a working-class area, northerners started to look down on it. The north-south snobbery has remained ever since.

But south Londoners are fiercely defensive about their patch. Indeed, some celebrities prefer to live there, rather than in some of the more fashionable and wealthy areas in the north. Among them are quite a few comedians, including Jenny Eclair, winner of this year's Perrier award for comedy. Eclair prefers the south, not only because it is more affordable, but also because of its untamed wildness and wackier street culture.

These southern celebrities are in the minority, though. Most live in the north in areas such as Primrose Hill (actors and writers), nearby Chalk Farm (budding pop stars), Hampstead (older stars with money), Kensington (younger stars with money), and Islington (the rest). Some of them seem to live in the north only because they can afford to do so. In their hearts they belong to the south.

The fact that half a million more people live in the north suggests that they can't all be wrong. So what is it exactly that south Londoners are always banging on about? What is so great about a place that has only two squares on a Monopoly board? True, property prices are far lower than in the north, and there are more parks and green spaces there, but what else?

Time Out recently compared the two sides of the river in everything from art to sport. The north got good marks for its music scene, bars, cafés and shops. The south, on the other hand, scored highly for avantgarde arts facilities like galleries, cinemas and theatres, as well as for clubs, restaurants and parks. But these southern venues do have to be sought out. The charms of the area are not always immediately apparent.

I once asked a southerner what made her so passionate about the place. After thinking about it carefully for two days, she suggested the following: parks and green spaces, Richmond, Wimbledon Lawn Tennis Club and the Oval Cricket Ground. Of course, we got into the inevitable north-south argument when I kidding, southerners!) ♦

pointed out that the north had Lords Cricket Ground and Wembley Stadium.

I had to admit defeat over Richmond, though, which is a lovely area, one which somehow I have never really thought of as being south of the river. It is probably the only southern location in which I would consider living.

Then again, I'm just one of those snooty northerners, so don't take my word for it. Go and see the south for yourself.

Visit the derelict Battersea power station, the "picturesque" South Bank complex; the main road through New Cross Gate and the Bullring in Waterloo, and tell me I'm wrong. (Just

Headline is explained in Language Live!

mutual ['mjuːtʃuəl] — gegenseitig
animosity — *Feindseligkeit*
to suck — *(ugs.) ätzend, mies sein*
hustle and bustle ['hʌsl] ['bʌsl] — *Geschäftigkeit*
accommodation — *Unterkunft; hier: Wohnung*
to be short-lived [lɪvd] — *von kurzer Dauer sein*
black spot — *hier: Niemandsland*
to be jammed solid — *völlig verstopft, total blockiert sein*
to found — *gründen*
to site sth. — *etw. ansiedeln*

AD (Anno Domini) — *n. Chr.*
to snub — *links liegen lassen*
plague [pleɪg] — *Pest*
sanctuary ['sæŋktʃuəri] — *Zuflucht(sort)*
genteel — *vornehm, fein*
well-off — *Gutsituierte(r)*
abundance — *Fülle*
divide — *Wasserscheide; hier: Grenze*
fiercely — *äußerst*
patch — *Flecken; hier: Gegend*
celebrity — *Prominente(r)*
comedian — *Komiker(in)*
award — *Auszeichnung, Preis*
wacky — *(ugs.) skurril*
budding — *angehend*

to bang on about sth. — *(ugs.) sich über etw. auslassen*
square — *hier: Feld*
board — *Spielbrett*
to score — *punkten*
venue ['venjuː] — *(Veranstaltungs)Ort*
apparent — *offensichtlich*
passionate ['pæʃnət] — *begeistert*
inevitable [ɪn'evɪtəbl] — *unvermeidlich*
location — *Ort*
snooty — *(ugs.) hochnäsig*
derelict ['derəlɪkt] — *verlassen*
power station — *Kraftwerk*
picturesque — *malerisch*
just kidding — *(ugs.) ich mache nur Spaß*

to me when I was there.

Interviewer: In what way?

Scott: Well, they kept greeting me by my name all the time. I still don't know how they knew what I'm called, but they all kept saying to me *Ruth Scott* on the street and in the shops.

Interviewer: And what do you know about the Austrian food?

Scott: They eat Viennese Schnitzel and apple strudel every day, and on special occasions they might get sausages and Sauerkraut, if they are really lucky.

Interviewer: And do you know anything about Austrian culture?

they go out on a Sunday picking edelweiss on the mountains and do a bit of yodelling while they are at it.

Interviewer: Ah, so yodelling is a typical Austrian pastime, isn't it?

Scott: Yeah, they are always doing it, when they are not climbing mountains or skiing that is.

Interviewer: Oh, yes, skiing, the national sport!

Scott: Mmmm, looks a bit dangerous, if you ask me. I always thought the Austrians must be really healthy, because they've got

A British view of Austria

Mandy Dunn tries to pinpoint some of the prejudices the >British have about the Austrians.

Interviewer: Excuse me, madam; I'm doing some research on behalf of the Austrian Tourist Board. Think about Austria and what springs to mind?

Ruth Scott: Austria? That is where they wear those fuunny leather trousers and green hats with feathers in them, isn't it?

Interviewer: Well,...

Scott: No, it's true. I've such rosy cheeks, but I've heard, it's all that *hunter's tea* they get through in the ski-hut. Though quite why a cup of tea should have that effect, I don't know, I really don't know. They drink a litre of schnapps for their breakfast, you know.

Interviewer: For their breakfast?

Scott: Yeah, that's why they can't speak German properly. I'd studied German five years before I went to Austria and I couldn't understand a bloody word they were saying to me. I reckon, they were all drunk. They spoke really slowly and

Scott: The *Sound of Music* was the best thing to come out of Austria. What a classic movie!

Interviewer: Well, thank you very much for your help.

A tale of two cities

One of London's best-kept secrets is that it is not one city but two — north London and south London, or, as they are usually called, "north of the river" and "south of the river".

Like the north-south divide in Britain as a whole, the two sides of the river have completely separate identities and a <u>mutual</u> <u>animosity</u>: northerners hate southerners, and southerners hate northerners.

A recent issue of the London magazine *Time Out* illustrated this with two different covers. Readers could buy a copy either with the message "North London <u>Sucks</u>" or with "South London Sucks".

The River Thames forms a natural barrier between the two sides. It is also a great excuse for n o r t h

Die Themse teilt London nicht nur auf der Landkarte, sondern auch in den Köpfen der Bewohner. KATHARINE CRACKNELL zeigt Ihnen die zwei Seiten Londons.

London's weekly guide

Time O...

Ritzy reborn
Inside the first arthouse multiplex
Emma Thompson
Beyond her Ken in 'Carrington'
Liv Tyler
Aerosmith daughter does Bertolucci
+ Win a Paris trip

SOUTH LONDON SUCKS

Which side are you on? North v South, and how to make the best of both worlds

Londoners not to visit their sister city — most don't really know what there is south of the river, anyway.

Meanwhile, south Londoners can claim to have discovered an urban paradise away from the <u>hustle and bustle</u> of the north where

they work, and away from north Londoners, too.

It is rare for people to change sides. If you start out as a north Londoner, you generally remain one. Moving south is such a great psychological step that few manage it. The property boom of the eighties did encourage some younger

people to head south in search of cheaper <u>accommodation</u> in places like Clapham and Battersea, but that was <u>short-lived</u>.

Whatever your viewpoint on the matter, south Lon-

don is disadvantaged. It is a transport <u>black spot</u>, served by only

10 per cent of the Underground network and with just 29 out of a total of 257 stations. The relatively few Thames bridges there are always seem to be <u>jammed solid</u>. And as any south Londoner will tell you, at certain times of the day there is an unwritten rule among taxi drivers that they won't go south of the river.

This northern dominance can be traced back to Roman times when London — or Londinium, as it was then known — was <u>founded</u>.

...t was the R... who chose to <u>site</u> thei... ...tal on the north bank ... River Thames in A... They built a walled ... the north bank and ... ply left those living s... the river to get or... defending themselves...

When William the ... queror arrived in th... century, he too <u>snubb</u>... south. This trend cor... for several hundred ... with south London ... specialize in enterta... and red-light districts ... 17th century, thoug... <u>plague</u> and the Great ... London did enc...

Acknowledgements

This book could not have written without the infinitely generous support of Mathew Prichard, Agatha's grandson. He has given every possible assistance, and my gratitude is boundless. I also met Agatha's daughter, Rosalind Hicks, on several occasions before she died. I talked to her and her husband, Anthony, at Greenway House; I shall always remember those meetings with great pleasure.

I met Sue Dawson and Sheila Alexander on my subsequent visits to Greenway, and they could not have been kinder or more helpful.

I was deeply appreciative of Janet Morgan's willingness to talk to me. I had much enjoyed her biography when it was published, and frankly admit that it was a wonderful source book. I also loved our stimulating and thought-provoking chats. Henrietta McCall, the biographer of Max Mallowan, was extremely charming and generous towards me.

Further thanks go to Mr and Mrs Archibald Christie; John Mallowan; Dr Joan Oates; the Reverend and Mrs Christopher Turner; Baroness James; Professor Harry Smith; Rachel Maxwell-Hyslop; Dr Julian Reade; Diana Gunn; Julia Camoys Stonor; Anne Sykes; Diana Howland; Lady Saunders; Brian Stone; Charles Vance; John Curran; Tony Medawar; Margaret Moore; John Neate; the owners of Winterbrook House, who took the time to show me round their home and garden; Tessa Milne and her colleagues in the Books and Manuscripts department at Sotheby's, who most kindly accommodated me while I read much of Agatha's correspondence; Dr Jessica Gardner at Exeter

University, always so friendly and helpful; the Bodleian Library, which tracked down the relevant Bradshaw Railway Guides; Meg Rich at Princeton University; Els Boonen at the BBC Written Archives Centre at Caversham; Jonathan Harrison at St John's College, Cambridge; Bridget Gillies at UEA; the Public Records Office at Kew; the Newspaper Library; the London Library; the Surrey History Centre; the Surrey Constabulary; Torquay Library; and the writer Margaret Yorke, who was a wonderful friend to this book.

Finally I thank Val Hudson and Jo Roberts-Miller at Headline; David Godwin; my friend Dena Arstall, with whom I had some terrific talks about Agatha; my mother, as always; and my late father, who loved Agatha Christie, and who would have enjoyed this book.